KT-520-411

WITHDRAWN FROM
THE LIBRARY
UNIVERSITY OF
WINCHESTER

REFERENCE

KA 0318049 2

FOURTH EDITION

MOTOR LEARNING AND PERFORMANCE

A Situation-Based Learning Approach

UNIVERSITY OF WINCHESTER
LIBRARY

HUMAN KINETICS ONLINE STUDY GUIDE

How to access the supplemental online study guide

We are pleased to provide access to an online study guide that supplements your textbook, *Motor Learning and Performance, Fourth Edition*. This study guide offers an interactive learning experience that will help you understand the research and practice of motor performance in today's society. We are certain you will enjoy this unique online learning experience.

Accessing the online study guide is easy! Simply follow these steps:

1. Using your web browser, go to the **Motor Learning and Performance** product Web site at **www.HumanKinetics.com/MotorLearningandPerformance**.
2. Click on the **View Student Resources** button on the right side of the home page.
3. Click on the please register now link. You will create your personal profile and password at this time.
4. Write your e-mail and password down for future reference. Keep it in a safe place.
5. Once you are registered, enter the key code exactly as it is printed at the right, including all hyphens. Click **Submit**
6. Once the key code has been submitted, you will see a welcome screen. Click the **Continue** button to open your online study guide.
7. After you enter the key code the first time, you will not need to use it again to access the study guide. In the future, simply log in using your e-mail and the password you created.

For technical support, send an e-mail to:

support@hkusa.com . . . . U.S. and international customers
info@hkcanada.com . . . . Canadian customers
academic@hkeurope.com . . . . European customers
keycodesupport@hkaustralia.com . . . . Australian customers

HUMAN KINETICS
The Information Leader in Physical Activity

Product: Motor Learning and Performance, Fourth Edition online study guide

Key code: SCHMIDT-4QFC78ZN-073606964X

This unique code allows you access to the online study guide

Access is provided if you have purchased a new book.
Once submitted, the code may not be entered for any other user.

FOURTH EDITION

MOTOR LEARNING AND PERFORMANCE

A Situation-Based Learning Approach

Richard A. Schmidt, PhD

President, Human Performance Research
and Professor Emeritus, Department of Psychology
University of California at Los Angeles

Craig A. Wrisberg, PhD

Professor of Sport Psychology, University of Tennessee at Knoxville

Human Kinetics

UNIVERSITY OF WINCHESTER
LIBRARY

Library of Congress Cataloging-in-Publication Data

Schmidt, Richard A., 1941-
Motor learning and performance : a situation-based learning approach / Richard A. Schmidt, Craig A. Wrisberg. -- 4th ed.
p. ; cm.
Includes bibliographical references and index.
ISBN-13: 978-0-7360-6964-9 (hard cover)
ISBN-10: 0-7360-6964-X (hard cover)
1. Motor learning--Textbooks. I. Wrisberg, Craig A. II. Title.
[DNLM: 1. Learning. 2. Motor Activity. 3. Kinesthesis. 4. Psychomotor Performance. BF 295 S353m 2008]
BF 295.S249 2008
152.3'34--dc22

2007037391

ISBN-10: 0-7360-6964-X
ISBN-13: 978-0-7360-6964-9

Copyright © 2008, 2004, 2000 by Richard A. Schmidt and Craig A. Wrisberg
Copyright © 1991 by Richard A. Schmidt

All rights reserved. Except for use in a review, the reproduction or utilization of this work in any form or by any electronic, mechanical, or other means, now known or hereafter invented, including xerography, photocopying, and recording, and in any information storage and retrieval system, is forbidden without the written permission of the publisher.

Notice: Permission to reproduce the following material is granted to instructors and agencies who have purchased *Motor Learning and Performance, Fourth Edition:* pp. 145, 326, 327. The reproduction of other parts of this book is expressly forbidden by the above copyright notice. Persons or agencies who have not purchased *Motor Learning and Performance, Fourth Edition,* may not reproduce any material.

Permission notices for material reprinted in this book from other sources can be found on pages xix-xx.

The Web addresses cited in this text were current as of August 2007, unless otherwise noted.

Acquisitions Editor: Judy Patterson Wright, PhD; **Developmental Editor:** Kathleen Bernard; **Assistant Editor:** Jillian Evans; **Copyeditor:** Julie Anderson; **Proofreader:** Joanna Hatzopoulos Portman; **Indexer:** Susan Danzi Hernandez; **Permission Manager:** Dalene Reeder; **Graphic Designer:** Fred Starbird; **Graphic Artist:** Yvonne Griffith; **Cover Designer:** Keith Blomberg; **Photographer (cover):** Al Fuchs/NewSport/Corbis; **Photographer (interior):** see pages xix-xx for a full listing; **Photo Asset Manager:** Laura Fitch; **Photo Office Assistant:** Jason Allen; **Art Manager:** Kelly Hendren; **Associate Art Manager:** Alan L. Wilborn; **Illustrator:** Keri Evans; **Printer:** Edwards Brothers

Printed in the United States of America

10 9 8 7 6 5 4

Human Kinetics
Web site: www.HumanKinetics.com

United States: Human Kinetics
P.O. Box 5076
Champaign, IL 61825-5076
800-747-4457
e-mail: humank@hkusa.com

Canada: Human Kinetics
475 Devonshire Road, Unit 100
Windsor, ON N8Y 2L5
800-465-7301 (in Canada only)
e-mail: info@hkcanada.com

Europe: Human Kinetics
107 Bradford Road
Stanningley
Leeds LS28 6AT, United Kingdom
+44 (0)113 255 5665
e-mail: hk@hkeurope.com

Australia: Human Kinetics
57A Price Avenue
Lower Mitcham, South Australia 5062
08 8372 0999
e-mail: info@hkaustralia.com

New Zealand: Human Kinetics
Division of Sports Distributors NZ Ltd.
P.O. Box 300 226 Albany
North Shore City, Auckland
0064 9 448 1207
e-mail: info@humankinetics.co.nz

UNIVERSITY OF WINCHESTER
03180492 | 152.334 SCH

To the memory of Virginia S. Schmidt and Allen W. Schmidt, as a small thanks for all the skills they taught me

Richard A. Schmidt

To Madelyn G. Wrisberg and Arthur P. Wrisberg for their unfailing love and encouragement throughout my life

Craig A. Wrisberg

Contents

Preface

Movement, moving, physical activity—regardless of what it's called—is a fundamental component of the human experience that most of us take for granted. Walking, eating, driving a car, riding a bike, and brushing teeth are among the more routine movement activities of everyday life. Most of us picked these up by trial and error. Other movements are more complex and challenging and take us considerably longer to learn. Consider, for example, the actions of dentists and surgeons, pilots and sculptors, athletes and performing artists (e.g., ballet dancers and musicians). Many of their movements require years of practice, often under the watchful eyes of teachers, coaches, or other types of movement practitioners.

Our purpose in writing this book is to help you learn more about the fundamental processes underlying the learning and performance of all kinds of movements. You'll discover how humans learn skilled actions and how the principles of motor (movement) performance and learning can be useful in teaching, coaching, rehabilitation, and the design of performer-friendly equipment and work environments (a field known as ergonomics, or human factors engineering). We designed this book so that even if you have little or no prior knowledge of physiology, psychology, statistical methods, or other basic sciences, you can understand the material. It is intended to be an introductory text for undergraduate students in physical education, exercise and sport science, kinesiology, biomechanics, ergonomics, psychology, physical and occupational therapy, and premedicine.

MISSION, METHOD, AND CONCEPTUAL MODEL

In this fourth edition we continue to combine a conceptual model of motor performance with a situation-based learning approach. Our intention is to provide you with a model you can use when attempting to identify effective responses to a wide range of practical issues in the performance and learning of motor skills. You will also find a variety of exercises and activities that should help you apply the concepts and principles you learn to real-world situations. As you respond to these questions and exercises, you will learn how to ask the kinds of questions that are relevant to the discovery of effective solutions. These questions include the following: Who is the person doing the learning? What is the movement or action the person is trying to perform? Where and under what conditions does this person need to be able to perform the movement? You will also come to realize that, although a lot of scientific information exists in the literature on motor performance and learning, the facts you might need for the perfect solution are not always available. In such cases, you must be able to support your decisions based on the information that *is* available and recognize the possible limitations of your solution.

ORGANIZATION

Before beginning your journey, we thought you'd like to see the "road map" we will be using to help you reach your destination. In part I (chapters 1 and 2), you'll find background information about the field of motor behavior, along with definitions of some of the foundational terms we use throughout the book. Chapter 1 contains a general overview of the text and its organization, along with an explanation of the key features that recur.

In part II (chapters 2 through 6) we begin to build the conceptual model of motor performance that, as you will see, occurs in stages over the course of several chapters. We start with a simple information-processing model and gradually add specific elements to it. Chapter 2 contains a general discussion of the information-processing approach and some factors that influence how people (a) identify important stimuli in the environment, (b) select the most appropriate action in response, and (c) produce that action. In chapter 3 we explore the role of feedback in controlling movements, and in chapter 4 we explain the concept of the motor program and its role in the control of rapid actions. Chapter 5 deals with some of the important principles of motor control and accuracy. Chapter 6 introduces you to the concept of motor abilities—the genetic "equipment" people bring with them to performance and learning situations—and the importance of this concept to movement practitioners, whether they are teachers, coaches, therapists, or human factors engineers. By the time you finish part II, you

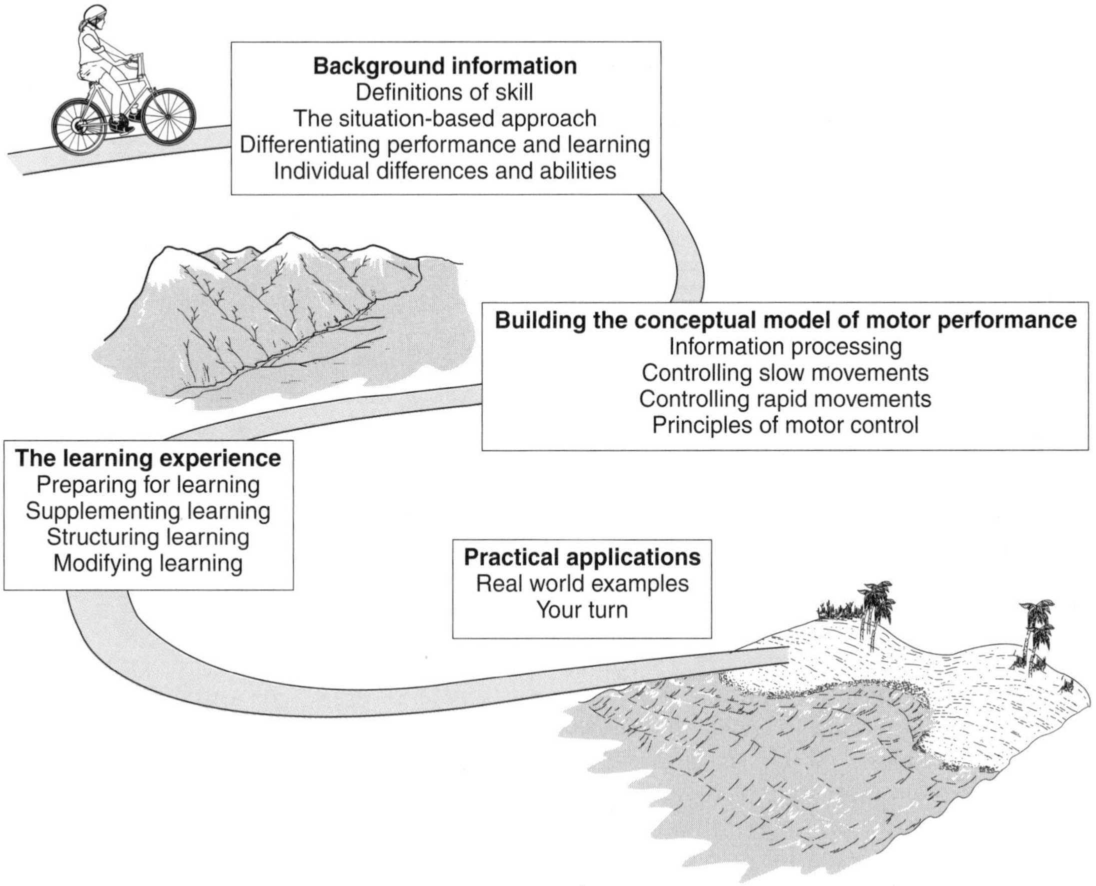

A road map for your journey through this book.

should have a reasonably coherent view of how the human motor system functions and be able to explain the key principles of skilled performance.

Part III (chapters 7 through 10) provides some of the evidence that underlies the learning of motor skills, and demonstrates some ways of applying the conceptual model to the teaching and learning of skilled movements. In chapter 7 we provide a framework to help you define people's learning experiences. In the next three chapters we explain how movement professionals can prepare for (chapter 8), structure (chapter 9), and provide feedback during (chapter 10) a learning experience.

In part IV (chapters 11 and 12) we offer some examples of ways professional practitioners might combine the conceptual model and a situation-based learning approach to assist learners. In chapter 11 we present four case studies to illustrate this approach, and in chapter 12 we give you the opportunity to use the approach yourself in defining an instructional experience of your own choosing.

We have emphasized the topics from the vast motor behavior literature that we feel have the best potential for use in real-world learning and performance situations. In deciding what information to present, we considered both theoretical ideas and empirical data, including competing viewpoints and seemingly contradictory research findings. We do not, however, interrupt the flow of the book with extensive justifications, rationale, and discussions of critical evidence for each of our points. Rather, we attempt to provide a simple, straightforward, and readable text that describes what we know about human motor performance and learning. Nevertheless, we have taken care to assure that every concept and principle presented in this book is defensible, or at least not contradicted, by the available research literature.

Continuing Features

After evaluating the feedback from users of the first three editions, we have decided to again integrate the following elements in this fourth edition of *Motor Learning and Performance*:

1. Chapter Objectives
2. Preview
3. Overview
4. Research Highlights
5. Running Glossary
6. Conceptual Model of Motor Performance
7. Chapter Summaries
8. Student Exercises
9. A full and useful Index

At the beginning of each chapter, we present a list of *Chapter Objectives* containing the most important outcomes readers should expect to achieve by the end of the chapter. Next we provide a *Preview* that introduces the chapter's topic using a real-life scenario and motor-skill example. Then we offer an *Overview* consisting of a brief summary of the purpose of the chapter and the contents to be covered.

Within the chapters, we include *Research Highlights* (in the maroon shading) that contain more detailed descriptions of important experiments and concepts. A *Running Glossary* in the margins of the page provides instant definitions of terms whenever they are introduced. For easy reference, definitions are sometimes repeated in later chapters where concepts reappear in the context of other discussions. Highlight boxes amplify particularly important or interesting topics and issues, and are organized so that they do not interrupt the flow of the main chapter materials. Some highlight boxes challenge you to identify important factors you think might contribute to the solution of motor performance and learning issues. As you'll soon find out, most answers require some qualification, depending upon the person, the task, and the context of the performance or learning situation. In addition, you'll discover that, rather than there being a single "right" answer, there may be several plausible answers, with the better ones based on more of the available scientific evidence or a greater number of relevant factors. From time to time within a chapter, you'll notice interesting facts and quotes that provide supplemental information and enliven particular topics. We set each of these elements apart in the book's design and give them individual titles.

The *Conceptual Model of Motor Performance* remains a signature item in the book. It is a defensible, coherent, personal viewpoint of how skills are performed and learned that Dick Schmidt developed over 30 years of basic research and consulting experience. The model, graphically shown in figures throughout most of the book, begins with a simple view of the performer as an information processor; gradually builds in detail; and concludes with a larger, integrated framework that conceptualizes how human motor performance "happens."

At the close of each chapter we offer a *Summary* to help you recall important concepts covered in the chapter. Then we conclude with several kinds of questions and exercises that you can use to test your ability to apply the concepts you have learned to real-world situations.

Finally, you will find an *Index* at the back of the book that gives you quick access to topics, terms, and names from the various chapters.

New in This Edition

In this edition we have added over 100 new references, many of which contain studies published since the previous edition of the book appeared. A number of these references illustrate how the concepts and principles presented in the book can be applied to the teaching and learning of everyday motor skills. We have also revised and expanded the exercises at the end of each chapter to make them more "student friendly." In chapter 11, we have included examples of some ways practitioners might assess the progress of learners using both outcome and process measures that are relevant to learners' goals. In addition, we have included a new example of one former student's approach to the assignment outlined in chapter 12. Finally, you will find many new figures and photos, along with an updated design, that make the book even more visually appealing and engaging than the previous editions.

FINAL COMMENTS

The previous editions of this book generated considerable interest among a wide variety of people. Of the many e-mails we received were those from readers who were movement practitioners of one sort or another. One person, a professional golfer, regularly corresponded with us about a number of concepts from the book that he wanted to add to his workshops for teaching professionals. One firearms training instructor requested feedback about some of the concepts from the book that he was attempting to apply in the classes he taught for a municipal police department. Also, we provided assistance to professionals who were writing books about golf instruction, race-car driving, and rock climbing.

We also received correspondence from several professors and students. A college professor teaching her first course in motor learning sought our assistance after several of the student athletes in her class remarked that some of the things their coaches were asking them to do did not seem to be based on scientific evidence. The result was a stimulating discussion of the importance of the principles on which practitioners base their instructional decisions. One graduate student sought our help in identifying additional articles from the research literature that dealt with the major theories of motor control. Other students contacted us with specific questions about something they had read in one or more of the chapters.

These experiences make us feel more strongly than ever that fundamental concepts from the literature in motor learning and performance are relevant to the life and work of many different kinds of people. As *you* read through this book, we encourage you to ponder the possible relevance those concepts might have for you and your professional future. We hope that when you finish the book you will understand many of the fundamental principles of motor performance and learning, you will be familiar with the supporting literature or research results for each, and you will be able to apply the principles to a variety of real-world situations. Once you acquire this knowledge, achieve a solid grasp of the conceptual model of motor performance, and develop some situation-based working strategies, you should be able to apply this information to a number of performance and learning scenarios you might confront and assist others who want to learn or relearn their own motor skills.

Acknowledgments

We would like to express our sincere thanks to a number of people who contributed to this edition of the book. Acquisitions editor Judy Wright, developmental editor Kathleen Bernard, and assistant editor Jillian Evans provided assistance in helping us move this fourth edition through the publishing process. In particular, we recognize Lisa McClary's work in putting together the online study guide that accompanies this fourth edition. We also appreciate all of the other Human Kinetics staff who contributed to this book and to the other ancillaries—the instructor guide, the presentation package, and the test package.

As in previous editions, we acknowledge the individuals who provided us with valuable insights and examples from their professional experiences, which we highlight in chapter 11. They include Dave Parrington, diving coach at the University of Tennessee; Nancy Fell and Lisa Kenyon, professor of physical therapy at the University of Tennessee at Chattanooga and practicing pediatric physical therapist, respectively; and Jerry Harnish, fire chief for the Knoxville Rural Metro Fire Department. Others who offered helpful suggestions for organizing several chapters or furnished various types of technical assistance include Jeff Fairbrother, Greg Young, and Howie Zelaznik. We also thank Nick Pons, a graduate of the exercise science program at the University of Tennessee and former student in one of Craig Wrisberg's human motor behavior classes, for granting us permission to use an adaptation of his outline for the assignment discussed in chapter 12. Finally, we express our sincere appreciation to Gwen B. Gordon and Sue R. Wrisberg for their patience and encouragement throughout the revision process. We appreciate their support more than they will ever know.

Credits

Tables

Table 6.2: Adapted with permission from *Research Quarterly for Exercise and Sport*, Vol. 28, pg. 510, Copyright 1967 by the American Alliance for Health, Physical Education, Recreation and Dance, 1900 Association Drive, Reston, VA 20191.

Table 7.4: Adapted, by permission, from D.V. Knudson and C.S. Morrison, 1997, *Qualitative analysis of human movement* (Champaign, IL: Human Kinetics), 155.

Figures

Figure on p. 31: Adapted from C.W. Scripture, 1905, *The new psychology* (New York: Scott).

Figures 2.3a and b: Adapted from R.S. Woodworth, 1938, *Experimental psychology* (New York: Holt). Data obtained by J. Merkel, 1885, "Die zeithlichen verhaltnisse der willenstatigkeit," *Philosophische Studien* 2: 73-127.

Figure 2.13: *Journal of Motor Behavior* 33, 1, 107, March 2001. Reprinted with permission of the Helen Dwight Reid Education Foundation. Published by Heldref Publication, 1319 Eighteenth St., NW, Washington, DC 20036-1802. Copyright © 2001.

Figure 2.14: *Journal of Motor Behavior* 33, 1, 107, March 2001. Reprinted with permission of the Helen Dwight Reid Education Foundation. Published by Heldref Publication, 1319 Eighteenth St., NW, Washington, DC 20036-1802. Copyright © 2001.

Figure 2.15: Reprinted, by permission, from P.B. Bender, 1987, "Extended practice and patterns of bimanual interference," Doctorial dissertation, University of Southern California.

Figure 3.7: Adapted with permission from *Research Quarterly for Exercise and Sport*, Vol. 31, pg. 226, Copyright 1960 by the American Alliance for Health, Physical Education, Recreation and Dance, 1900 Association Drive, Reston, VA 20191.

Figure 3.8: Reprinted, by permission, from D.J. Dewhurst, © 1967 IEEE, "Neuromuscular control system," *IEEE Transactions on Biomedical-Engineering* 14: 170.

Figure 4.4: Reprinted with permission from *Research Quarterly for Exercise and Sport*, Vol. 24, pgs. 22-32, Copyright 1953 by the American Alliance for Health, Physical Education, Recreation and Dance, 1900 Association Drive, Reston, VA 20191.

Figure 4.5: Adapted, by permission, from A. Polit and E. Bizzi, 1979, "Characteristics of motor programs underlying arm movements in monkeys," *Journal of Neurophysiology* 42: 184.

Figure 4.9: Adapted, by permission, from T.R. Armstrong, 1970, *Training for the production of memorized movement patterns: Technical report no. 26* (Ann Arbor, MI: University of Michigan, Human Performance Center), 35.

Figure 4.10: Adapted from J.M. Hollerback, 1978, "A study of human motor control through analysis and synthesis of handwriting." Doctoral dissertation, Massachusetts Institute of Technology.

Figure 4.12: Reprinted, by permission, from M.H. Raibert, 1977, *Motor control and learning by the state-space model: Technical report* no. *A1-TR-439* (Cambridge, MA: Artificial Intelligence Laboratory, Massachusetts Institute of Technology), 50.

Figure 5.1: Reprinted, by permission, from R. Schmidt, 1988, *Motor control and learning: A behavioral emphasis*, 2nd ed. (Champaign, IL: Human Kinetics), 244.

Figure 5.2: *Journal of Motor Behavior*, 13: 38, 1981. Reprinted with permission of Helen Dwight Reid Educational Foundation. Published by Heldref Publication, 1319 Eighteenth St. NW, Washington, DC 20036-1802. Copyright ©1981.

Figure 5.3: *Journal of Motor Behavior*, 13: 42, 1981. Reprinted with permission of Helen Dwight Reid Educational Foundation. Published by Heldref Publication, 1319 Eighteenth St. NW, Washington, DC 20036-1802. Copyright ©1981.

Figure 5.5: Adapted from P.M. Fitts, 1954, "The information capacity of the human motor system in controlling the amplitude of movement," *Journal of Experimental Psychology* 47: 381-391.

Figure 5.7: Adapted, by permission, from R. Schmidt et al., 1979, "Motor output variability: A theory for the accuracy of rapid motor acts," *Psychological Review* 86: 415-451.

Figure 5.8: Adapted, by permission, from R. Schmidt et al., 1979, "Motor output variability: A theory for the accuracy of rapid motor acts," *Psychological Review* 86: 415-451.

Figure 5.11: Adapted, by permission, from R. Schmidt et al., 1979, "Motor output variability: A theory for the accuracy of rapid motor acts," *Psychological Review* 86: 415-451.

Figure 5.13: Adapted, by permission, from R. Schmidt and D. Sherwood, 1982, "An inverted-U relation between spatial error and force requirements in rapid limb movement: Further evidence for the impulse variability model," *Journal of Experimental Psychology: Human Perception and Performance* 86: 167.

Figure 6.3: Adapted from E.A. Fleishman, 1964, *The structure and measurement of physical fitness* (Upper Saddle River, NJ: Prentice-Hall).

Figure 6.7: Adapted, by permission, from E.A. Fleishman and R.W. Stephenson, 1970, *Development of a taxonomy of human performance: A review of the third year's progress* (Tech. Rep, No. 726-TPR3). (Silver Spring, MD: American Institutes for Research).

Figure 7.3: *Journal of Motor Behavior*, 24, 269, 1992. Reprinted with permission of Helen Dwight Reid Educational Foundation. Published by Heldref Publication, 1319 Eighteenth St. NW, Washington, DC 20036-1802. Copyright ©1992.

Figure 8.4: Reprinted with permission from *Research Quarterly for Exercise and Sport*, Vol. 70, No. 3, pgs. 265-273, Copyright 1999 by the American Alliance for Health, Physical Education, Recreation and Dance, 1900 Association Drive, Reston, VA 20191.

Figure 9.2: Reprinted, by permission, from J.B. Shea and R.L. Morgan, 1979, "Contextual interference effects on the acquisition, retention, and transfer of motor skill," *Journal of Experimental Psychology: Human Learning and Memory* 5: 183.

Figure 10.6: Adapted with permission from *Research Quarterly for Exercise and Sport*, Vol. 68, pgs. 269-279, Copyright 1997 by the American Alliance for Health, Physical Education, Recreation and Dance, 1900 Association Drive, Reston, VA 20191.

Figure 10.7: Adapted with permission from *Research Quarterly for Exercise and Sport*, Vol. 68, pgs. 269-279, Copyright 1997 by the American Alliance for Health, Physical Education, Recreation and Dance, 1900 Association Drive, Reston, VA 20191.

Figure 10.10: Reprinted, by permission, from J.J. Lavery, 1962, "Retention of simple motor skills as a function of type of knowledge of results," *Canadian Journal of Psychology* 16: 305.

Figure 10.11: This article was published in *Human Movement Science*, Vol 9, R. Schmidt, C.A. Lange, and D.E. Young, "Optimizing summary knowledge of results for skill learning," pgs. 325-348, Copyright Elsevier, 1990.

Photos

Photos on p. 5, 7, 11, 24, 26, 37, 62, 68, 96, 106, 110, 124, 155, 160, 166 (bottom), 170, 174, 175, 177, 190, 199 (right), 212, 220, 221, 232, 236, 241, 254, 266, 270, 272, 284, 291, 299, 309, 322, 329, 335, 350, 353, 359, 360: © Human Kinetics

Photos on p. 2, 146: © Getty Images

Photos on p. 6, 10, 15, 20, 36, 49, 116, 132, 143, 188, 195, 245: © Photodisc

Photo on p. 65: Photo courtesy of Alejandro Bugacov

Photos on p. 81, 179: © 1998 Eyewire, Inc.

Photo on p. 104: © StockByte

Photo on p. 135: © Ted Spiegel/Corbis

Photo on p. 156 (left): © ALLEN FREDRICKSON/Reuters/Corbis

Photo on p. 156 (right): © CHARLES W LUZIER/Reuters/Corbis

Photos on p. 162, 265: © Kelly Huff

Photo on p. 166 (top): © Brent Smith/Reuters/Corbis

Photo on p. 171 (left): © David Papazian/Corbis

Photo on p. 171 (right): © Allen Russell/Index Stock/Corbis

Photo on p. 199 (left): © Eyewire, Inc.

Photo on p. 218: © Eyewire/Photodisc/Getty Images

Photo on p. 282: © Keith Brofsky/Getty Images

Photo on p. 300: Photo courtesy of David F. Job

Photo on p. 337: © Tom Stewart/CORBIS

Photo on p. 341: © Carl D. Walsh/Aurora Photos

PART ONE

INTRODUCTION TO MOTOR PERFORMANCE AND LEARNING

chapter 1

Getting Started

▷ Chapter Outline

▷ Chapter Objectives

When you have completed this chapter, you should be able to

- understand the definition of skill,
- explain the relationship between motor performance and motor learning,
- discuss the situation-based approach to motor performance and learning, and
- understand the organization and design of this book.

PREVIEW

Mark Zupan (see facing photo) brought quadriplegic rugby to the attention of millions of moviegoers in the film *Murderball.* In this sport, two teams in specially designed chairs attempt to advance the ball and score goals. Zupan, a former college soccer player who switched sports after breaking his neck in a truck accident, is a two-time quad rugby national champion, the 2004 quad rugby player of the year, and a Paralympic bronze medalist. Although Mark Zupan's experience is considerably more dramatic than that of most of us, it illustrates the capacity humans have for skill learning under even the most adverse conditions. In many cases, the skills we have learned during the course of our lives are functional, such as the one a paper carrier uses when tossing newspapers from a moving bicycle onto a narrow sidewalk or porch (some with more accuracy than others) or the one a motorist uses when driving along a busy street filled with pedestrians and other vehicles. Other skills present different types of challenges, such as when a child attempts her first somersault or soccer kick or a senior citizen finds that what was once a simple task of walking is no longer possible without a cane or a walker. Then there are the skills of more advanced performers, such as gymnasts, musicians, tennis players, and rock climbers, who seek to challenge themselves and their environments to the fullest extent. How we learn and perform motor skills in a variety of situations and how we might help others learn the skills they need are the primary emphases of this book.

OVERVIEW

Whether we think much about it or not, we spend a good deal of each day performing essential movement skills. Without the capacity for skilled performance, we couldn't type a term paper or an e-mail, couldn't drive a car, or couldn't hit a tennis backhand. When you add to these tasks the abundance and variety of other skilled movements we can perform, you realize that it is important for any student of exercise science, human factors (or ergonomics), kinesiology, physical and occupational therapy, the performing arts, physical education, and perhaps coaching to know the concepts and principles of motor learning and performance.

Human skills take many forms, of course, from those that emphasize the control and coordination of large muscle groups in relatively forceful activities (e.g., soccer or tumbling) to those that require the precise tuning of the smallest muscle groups (e.g., picking a banjo or repairing a watch). In this book we focus on the full range of skilled behavior. The reason for this is that many movements share the same features, regardless of whether people perform them in competitive sports, physical rehabilitation, the military or industry, or a common, everyday situation.

We are all born with some fundamental skills and need only a little maturation and experience to produce them in nearly complete form. Examples of these are walking and running, chewing, balancing, and withdrawing a finger from a hot stove. However, to achieve proficiency in other skills, such as doing a back flip, keyboarding, or paddling a white-water canoe, we need considerably more practice. We often need the assistance of an instructor or coach as well.

motor skill—A skill for which the primary determinant of success is the quality of the movement that the performer produces.

We begin this chapter by discussing a number of concepts that are essential to understanding motor performance and learning. The first is the concept of **motor skill**, which can be classified in various ways and characterized by several key features. Next, there is the relationship between motor performance and motor learning. Then we introduce the situation-based approach to motor performance and learning that we emphasize throughout the remainder of the book. We conclude the chapter by describing the logic behind our organization of the text as a whole and the design of individual chapters.

MOTOR SKILL: WHAT IS IT?

There are at least two ways to conceptualize the term *motor skill.* First, you might think of a motor skill as a task, such as spiking a volleyball, playing billiards, or carving a turkey. Viewed this way, motor skills should be distinguishable along a number of dimensions or on the basis of a variety of prominent characteristics. The second way you could conceptualize motor skill is in terms of the proficiency a person demonstrates when performing a movement, such as that of Michael Jordan shooting a basketball. In the following sections, we examine each of these conceptualizations of motor skill in more detail.

Task Perspective: Skill Classification

As just mentioned, we can view motor skill as an act or task. Because each task has unique characteristics, we should be able to identify some of the more prominent characteristics that distinguish one skill from another. Three characteristics that

Franklin M. Henry, Father of Motor Skills Research

Before World War II and during the 1950s and 1960s, researchers devoted considerable effort to studying performance of military tasks such as piloting an aircraft. Before that time, most experimental psychologists had conducted little research on gross motor skills, such as those produced by performers in sport and other movement contexts (e.g., dance and music).

A notable exception was the work of Franklin M. Henry at the University of California at Berkeley. Henry, a PhD trained in experimental psychology but working in the department of physical education, introduced a new tradition of laboratory experimentation in the field of motor skills. He primarily studied gross motor skills, many of which involved actions of the entire body, that were more representative of the kinds of tasks seen on the playing fields and in gymnasia. Faithful to his training in experimental psychology, Henry used laboratory-type tasks—many of which he designed and constructed in his workshop—that enabled him to conduct rigorous investigations of skill performance. During his career, Henry examined a number of important research topics, such as the underlying basis for differences among individuals in performance and the role of motor programs in the control of rapid movements. We review some of Henry's ideas in greater detail in chapters 2 and 5.

Many of Henry's students (including Dick Schmidt) eventually began their own research programs and mentored other students (including Craig Wrisberg). By the 1970s and 1980s, Henry's direct and indirect influence on the fields of physical education and kinesiology was widespread, earning him the title Father of Motor Skills Research.

movement scientists have used to classify skills are the way the task is organized, the relative importance of motor and cognitive elements, and the level of environmental predictability during performance. As with almost every other branch of science, we divide things into different classes because the classes are thought to be fundamentally different from each other. In our present case, different classifications of tasks suggest that the tasks are performed fundamentally differently, and/or that they are learned with fundamentally different principles or methods. We'll return to this theme many times throughout the book.

Throwing and catching a softball are examples of a discrete skill.

Skills Classified by Task Organization

One system for classifying skills concerns the way the movement is organized. At one end of this classification

Shifting gears in a stick-shift car involves a series of discrete actions and is classified as a serial skill.

system is the **discrete skill**, which is characterized by a defined beginning and end and is often very brief in duration. Discrete skills are tasks such as throwing and kicking a ball, firing a rifle, or casting a fishing lure. Discrete skills are prominent in many sports and games, especially those involving the distinct acts of hitting, kicking, jumping, throwing, and catching.

Sometimes discrete skills are strung together to form more complicated actions. These skill sequences are classified as **serial skills**, suggesting that the order of the elements is in some sense crucial to successful performance. Shifting the gears of a manual transmission car or truck would be considered a serial skill, because it includes three, four, or sometimes five discrete elements (gearshift, clutch, and accelerator actions) connected in a particular sequence. Other examples of serial skills are some gymnastics routines and the act of maneuvering around a sequence of gates in a downhill ski race. Serial skills differ from discrete skills in that they usually require a somewhat longer time to produce, yet each element in the sequence retains a discrete beginning and end. During the learning of serial skills, beginners initially focus on each element separately. Later on, after considerable practice, they are able to combine the elements to form a unified sequence. Accomplished performers are able to control the entire action almost as if it were a single, discrete movement (e.g., the smooth, rapid way a race-car driver shifts gears).

A final category of task organization involves movements with no definable beginning or end. These skills, referred to as **continuous skills**, are repetitive or rhythmic, often lasting many minutes. Examples of continuous skills are swimming, running, skating, and cycling. For these types of skills, either the performer or some environmental barrier or marker (e.g., a pool wall or a finish line) determines the beginning and ending points of the movement. Still another form of continuous skill is the tracking task, which requires performers to maintain contact with a target. Steering a car along a narrow and winding country road is a good example, because drivers need to move the steering wheel to keep the car in the correct lane. In table 1.1, we provide a capsule summary of the distinguishing characteristics of discrete, serial, and continuous skills.

discrete skill—
A skill or task that is organized in such a way that the action is usually brief and has a well-defined beginning and end.

serial skill—
A type of skill organization that is characterized by several discrete actions connected together in a sequence, often with the order of the actions being crucial to performance success.

continuous skill—
A skill organized in such a way that the action unfolds without a recognizable beginning and end in an ongoing and often repetitive fashion.

Table 1.1 Discrete–Serial–Continuous Skill Dimension

Discrete skills	Serial skills	Continuous skills
Distinct beginning and end	Discrete actions linked together	No distinct beginning or end
Throwing a dart	Hammering a nail	Rope skipping
Snapping the fingers	Taping an ankle	Rowing
Sit-to-stand transfer	Brushing teeth	In-line skating

Swimming has repetitive movements with no discernible beginning and end and thus is a continuous skill.

Skills Classified by the Relative Importance of Motor and Cognitive Elements

A second type of classification system emphasizes the relative importance of motor and cognitive elements during task performance. A skill for which the primary determinant of movement success is the quality of the movement itself rather than the perceptual or decision-making aspects of the task is classified as a motor skill. For example, the primary challenge of a high jumper in track is to produce a movement that maximizes vertical height. The jumper can easily see the bar and doesn't have any other decisions to make.

On the other hand, with a **cognitive skill** performance success depends more on the strategy dictating the movement than on the production of the movement itself. For example, in the game of chess it matters little whether a player moves the pieces quickly or smoothly; the player's challenge is to decide which piece to move and where to move it.

cognitive skill—A skill for which the primary determinant of success is the quality of the performer's decisions regarding what to do.

In short, then, a cognitive skill mainly emphasizes knowing what to do, whereas a motor skill mainly emphasizes doing it effectively. Notice we have inserted the word *mainly* in the previous sentence. This is because purely motor skills and purely cognitive skills actually lie at the opposite ends of a continuum, with most skills lying somewhere in between (see the line and arrows representing this continuum at the top of table 1.2). Thus, a more effective way of classifying skills with the motor–cognitive system is to consider the *degree* to which cognitive elements (i.e., knowing what to do) and motor elements (i.e., knowing how to do it) contribute to successful goal achievement.

For example, a patient beginning physical therapy after knee surgery may need to think about what to do when walking (e.g., heel strike, balanced posture) because she can no longer produce the movement automatically. After considerable treatment, however, the patient may be able to make her movements without doing much thinking. In a similar vein, a college student learning a new movement activity (e.g., three-ball juggling) initially may spend a great deal of time deciding what to do, whereas after many practice sessions the student is able to perform the movement without much thought. Rarely, however, do either cognitive or motor elements become entirely unimportant to performance. Even

Table 1.2 Motor–Cognitive Skill Dimension

Motor skills ←		→ Cognitive skills
Decision making minimized	**Some decision making**	**Decision making maximized**
Motor control maximized	**Some motor control**	**Motor control minimized**
High jumping	Playing quarterback	Playing poker
Weightlifting	Driving a race car	Cooking a meal
Changing a flat tire	Walking in a busy airport terminal	Coaching a sport

Table 1.3 Open–Closed Skill Dimension

Closed skills ←		→ Open skills
Predictable environment	**Semipredictable environment**	**Unpredictable environment**
Performing in gymnastics	Walking a tightrope	Playing soccer
Typing	Steering a car	Wrestling
Cutting vegetables	Crossing the street	Catching a butterfly

highly skilled athletes must think about what they need to do, such as the split-second tactical decisions that sailors in the America's Cup yacht race must make.

Skills Classified by Level of Environmental Predictability

open skill—A skill performed in an environment that is unpredictable or in motion and that requires performers to adapt their movements in response to dynamic properties of the environment.

closed skill—A skill performed in an environment that is predictable or stationary and that allows performers to plan their movements in advance.

capabilities—Characteristics of individuals that are subject to change as a result of practice and that underlie the performance of various tasks.

A third way to classify motor skills is to consider the extent to which the environment is stable and predictable during performance. Skills performed in an environment that is variable and unpredictable are classified as **open skills**. Examples are driving in traffic and engaging an opponent in wrestling. Athletes performing in sports such as wrestling can have difficulties effectively predicting their opponents' movements (and hence the best way to respond). Skills performed in an environment that is stable and predictable are classified as **closed skills**. Examples are performing a balance beam routine in gymnastics and driving down a vacant country road. As is the case for the motor–cognitive skill classification system, purely open and purely closed skill designations actually lie at the end points of a continuum (as shown by the line and arrows at the top of table 1.3), with the level of environmental predictability found in most situations being somewhere between high and low.

The open- and closed-skill classification system emphasizes the predictability of environmental demands placed on the performer. For skills that lie closer to the closed end of the continuum (e.g., golf, bowling, knitting a sweater), the environment is stable and waiting to be acted upon. In situations such as this, performers can evaluate the environment in advance, organize their movements without feeling rushed, and carry out the action without any need for sudden adjustments. However, for skills that are closer to the open end of the continuum (e.g., hitting ground strokes in tennis, fielding a ground ball in baseball or softball, shooting the rapids in white-water canoeing), performers must be able to "read" the environment to adjust their movements, often in a short amount of time. In table 1.3 we provide some examples of skills varying in environmental demand from predictable to unpredictable.

Each of these classification systems addresses a particular dimension of motor skills. However, they should be considered together when you are attempting to determine the demands of a particular skill or evaluating the **capabilities** of a person performing the skill. A good example of this approach to skill classification is shown in table 1.4.

Gentile's Two-Dimensional Classification System for Physical Therapy Settings

In an attempt to provide physical therapists with a tool for evaluating patients' motor skills and for determining appropriate treatment activities, Gentile (1987) developed a two-dimensional classification system that considers both the requirements of the action and the demands of the environment. The possible requirements of the action consist of body transport and object manipulation. Environmental demands include the degree to which the environment is stationary or in motion (shown as "regulatory variability" in table 1.4) and the extent to which the environment changes from one performance attempt to the next (shown as "context variability" in the table). Regulatory variability for closed skills (e.g., hitting a stationary golf ball, knitting a scarf) generally is minimal, whereas that for open skills (e.g., hitting a moving baseball, white-water canoeing) is considerable. However, in both cases the context might change from one attempt to the next (e.g., hitting a golf ball off the tee vs. hitting it out of the rough).

We present a simplified version of Gentile's system in table 1.4. The two components of each dimension (shown at the top and left sides of the table) are combined in various ways to form 16 task categories. As you can see, task complexity increases as you move from the top left side to the bottom right side of the table. A task classified in the top left box would be one for which no movement, or only a simple one, is required. There is no regulatory variability and the context remains the same from one attempt to the next. An example might be requiring a patient to maintain an erect posture or, while in an erect posture, to lift the right arm to shoulder level. The patient always performs the task in the same closed environment, such as the therapist's office. A task classified in the lower right box would be one that requires the patient to manipulate some object while transporting the body and responding to a regulatory stimulus that is in motion and is different from one attempt to the next. An example might be tossing and catching a beanbag with a partner while walking. On each occasion, the partner would toss the beanbag in a different way (e.g., one time with a higher trajectory, the next time with a slower speed). Although Gentile designed her classification system for use by physical therapists, her notion of combining several classification systems to achieve a more thorough description of task demands can be used by movement practitioners in other settings as well (e.g., sport, performing arts, industry, the military).

Performance Proficiency Perspective: Characteristics of Skill Performance

You can also view the concept of motor skill in terms of the features that distinguish higher-skilled performers from lower-skilled ones. Although there are many features of skilled performance we might consider, several of the earliest were proposed by the psychologist E.R. Guthrie (1952). According to Guthrie, skill proficiency "consists in the ability to bring about some end result with maximum certainty and minimum outlay of energy, or of time and energy" (p. 136).

When we talk about *skilled* movements, we are talking about movements performed with a desired environmental goal in mind, such as holding a handstand in gymnastics or eating a meal using a prosthetic hand. Movements having no particular environmental goal, such as idly tapping one's fingers, are not considered to be skilled under this system. Performers who are more proficient in movements designed to achieve a particular goal usually demonstrate one or more of the qualities Guthrie mentioned

Table 1.4 Extension of Gentile's Two-Dimensional Classification System

		Action requirements			
		Neither body transport nor object manipulation	**Object manipulation only**	**Body transport only**	**Both body transport and object manipulation**
Environmental demands	**Neither regulatory variability nor context variability**	Maintaining standing balance	Playing the flute	Walking on a city sidewalk	Walking on a city sidewalk while pulling a wagon
	Context variability only	Using sign language	Chopping wood	Ten-pin bowling	Twirling streamers in rhythmic gymnastics
	Regulatory variability only	Standing on a moving escalator	Standing in place while dribbling a basketball	Walking on a moving escalator	Dribbling a soccer ball while in motion without a defender
	Both regulatory variability and context variability	Balancing on alternate feet while on a moving escalator	Playing a video game (with joystick)	Line dancing	Dribbling a soccer ball against a defender

in his definition: maximum certainty, minimum energy expenditure, and minimum movement time.

Maximum Certainty of Goal Achievement

One quality of skill proficiency is movement certainty. To be skilled implies that a person is able to meet the performance goal, or end result, with maximum certainty. For example, anyone might throw a dart into the bull's-eye of a target on one occasion. But this action, by itself, does not ensure that the person is a skilled darts player. For most people, such an outcome would be the result of one lucky throw in the midst of hundreds of others that are not so lucky. Only those performers who show that they can achieve the goal with a high degree of certainty, on demand, without luck playing a very large role, can be considered skilled. This is one reason why people admire champion athletes who always seem to perform at the same high level regardless of the situation, and can do so on demand.

Minimum Energy Expenditure

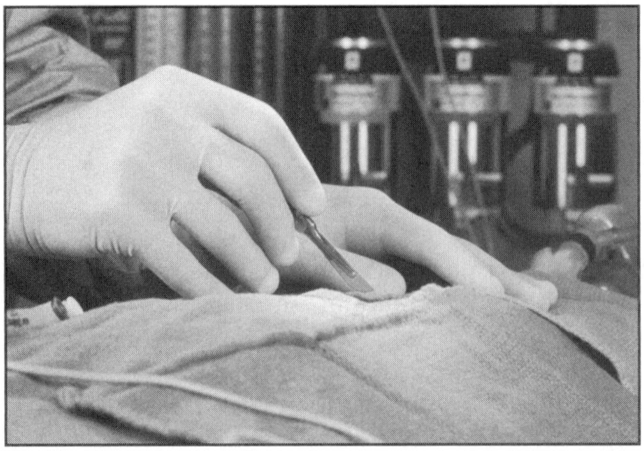

The skilled performance of surgery requires maximum certainty of movement.

A second quality of skill proficiency is the minimization, and occasionally conservation, of energy required for performance. For some performers, minimizing energy expenditure is clearly not a problem. In the case of the pool player, for example, the goal is to produce a smooth and coordinated movement that sends the cue ball to the desired target. Energy levels are not an issue even if the game lasts for hours. However, in other skills performers need to minimize their energy expenditure by reducing or eliminating unwanted or unnecessary movement. Examples are the skilled marathon runner who holds an efficient pace, or the skilled wrestler who saves strength for the last few minutes of a match. The minimum-energy notion also implies that skilled performers are able to organize their actions in a way that reduces the mental demands of the task. Performers who are able to produce their movements automatically can direct their thoughts to other features of the activity, such as the strategy of a NASCAR driver or the creative expression of a ballet dancer. Minimizing energy expenditure is also an important goal for individuals at the lower end of the skill spectrum, including those with disabling conditions such as multiple sclerosis. Finally, viewed from an ecological or evolutionary perspective, minimizing energy has a survival benefit, favoring those individuals who have learned to perform their activities with minimum energy.

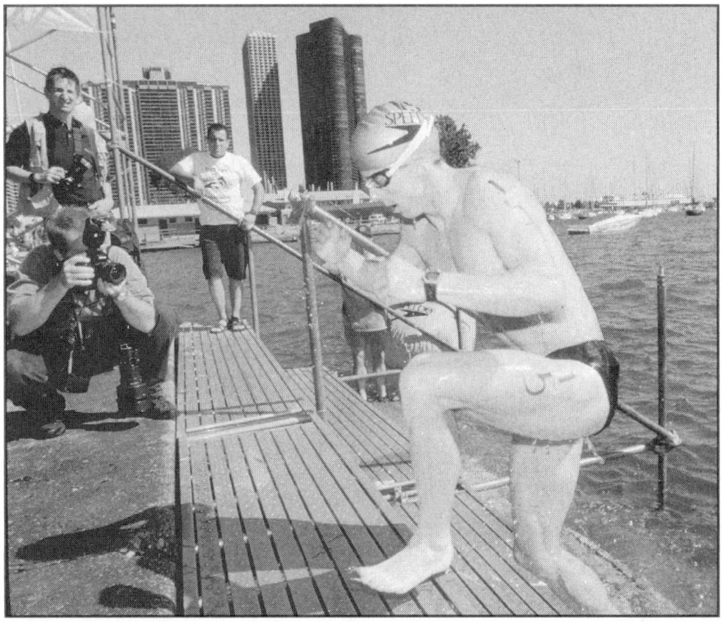

A skilled triathlete exemplifies all three characteristics of skill proficiency proposed by Guthrie (1952): achieving a desired result with maximum certainty, managing energy efficiently, and minimizing movement time.

Minimum Movement Time

A third quality of skill proficiency is achieving the goal in the shortest time possible. Many sport performers, such as sprinters in track, swimming, and cycling, know that to achieve their primary goal they must minimize their movement time. Piece workers in a factory can earn more pay if they are able to increase the number of units they assemble in less time. Minimizing time, however, can be a problem in some situations: for example, the running back in football who runs too fast for his blockers to adequately clear the way and the bricklayer who moves too quickly and lays a crooked line. This idea that performing too quickly leads to sloppy performance, or errors, is a well-known property of human performance; obviously, the solution is to slow down. Humans seem to have the capability to swap speed for accuracy, depending on the task requirements. We discuss this idea more formally under the label of speed–accuracy trade-off in chapter 5. Although it's important to consider these three qualities of movement proficiency when examining people's skill levels, it's also important to remember that, depending on the performer, the task, and the environment, various combinations of these qualities will be necessary for goal achievement.

THE CHICKEN AND THE EGG: MOTOR PERFORMANCE AND MOTOR LEARNING

As we mentioned earlier, the concepts of motor performance and motor learning are two of the prominent themes of this book. In many ways, these concepts are difficult to distinguish—in the same way that it's difficult to answer the question "Which came first, the chicken or the egg?" Each time a person attempts a motor skill, he produces some level of performance. If that performance is typical of what the person does most of the time (uninfluenced by temporary factors such as fatigue, anxiety, and boredom), it should indicate something about the person's level of learning.

There are, however, some fundamental differences between the concepts of motor performance and motor learning. **Motor performance** is always observable and is influenced by many factors (e.g., motivation, attentional focus, fatigue, physical fitness). **Motor learning**, on the other hand, is an *internal process or state* that reflects a person's current capability for producing a particular movement.

The best way for practitioners to assess motor learning is to observe people's motor performance, noting the changes that occur systematically with additional practice. Remember, though, that as in the game of darts, almost anyone can be lucky and hit a

motor performance—The observable production of a voluntary action, or a motor skill. The level of a person's performance is susceptible to fluctuations in temporary factors such as motivation, arousal, fatigue, and physical condition.

motor learning—The changes, associated with practice or experience, in internal processes that determine a person's capability for producing a motor skill.

It Depends . . .

Can You Distinguish the Skill Levels of Performers?

To test your ability to distinguish people's skill levels, spend some time watching people performing various tasks. You could do this while you're watching TV or during a live performance. The only stipulation is that the activity you observe must require the characteristics of a skilled movement that we mentioned earlier in the chapter (i.e., a movement designed to achieve a particular goal). The following list contains some possibilities, but feel free to come up with some of your own. The more interesting the skill, the more fun it will be to test your diagnostic ability.

- In-line skating
- Billiards
- Bowling
- NASCAR racing
- Ballet dancing
- Line dancing
- Playing a guitar
- Punting a football
- Heading a soccer ball
- Freestyle swimming

After observing several people's performances, rate their proficiency on several characteristics on a scale of 1 to 3, where 1 = *low,* 2 = *moderate,* and 3 = *high.* In addition to looking for the movement proficiency characteristics that Guthrie (1952) proposed, come up with some of your own. For example, you might include the characteristics of smoothness and accuracy when evaluating billiards players or characteristics such as timing and rhythm when evaluating line dancers.

bull's-eye once in a while, so this kind of performance should not be taken as evidence of learning. Instead, if a person's level of performance proficiency is relatively stable over a number of observations and under various conditions, the teacher or coach can assume that the performance accurately reflects the person's level of learning. However, even though a person has learned a task (internally), various factors can still impair a particular performance (e.g., fatigue). That's why it's a good idea to observe performance on several occasions before inferring anything about a person's learning.

implicit learning—Improvements that occur in a person's capability for correct responding as a result of repeated performance attempts and without the person's awareness of what caused the improvements (or that the improvements even occurred).

Two phenomena that illustrate the intimate connection between motor performance and motor learning are the notion of learning stages and the concept of **implicit learning**. We discuss each of these phenomena in the following sections.

Stages of Performance and Learning

A number of researchers have attempted to define the general performance characteristics of individuals at various points in the skill-learning process. In table 1.5 we present several of these theoretical depictions. The table offers a concise overview of people's activities during the early and later stages of learning, along with some of the observable motor performance characteristics of individuals in each stage.

In all cases, early learning is characterized by attempts to generate an idea of the movement (Gentile, 1972) or understand the basic pattern of coordination (Newell, 1985). To do this, learners must engage in considerable problem solving, involving both cognitive (Fitts & Posner, 1967) and verbal (Adams, 1971) activity. Performance during the early stage is characterized by considerable inaccuracy, slowness, inconsistency, and stiff-looking movements. Learners lack confidence and are therefore hesitant and indecisive in their actions. Even when beginners do something correctly, they are not sure how they did it.

After some period of practice, learners reach the stage where their performance becomes more accurate and consistent. Here they have a pretty good idea of the general movement pattern and can begin refining, modifying, and adapting the plan to meet particular environmental demands. As we have said earlier, many people (e.g., Gentile, 1972) contend that the nature and conditions of practice that will lead to the strongest learning will differ for various kinds of tasks. For example, for an open skill such as steering a car in traffic, it would be beneficial to practice in many traffic situations. This practice variation would not be so important in a closed skill for which the environment was always constant on every trial (e.g., springboard diving). As we emphasize later, the practitioner needs to tailor the nature of practice to fit the type of skill being learned.

Only after considerable practice do people sometimes reach the final stage of learning where their performance is virtually automatic. For psychologists and movement scientists, the term automatic means performing without attention, where the person makes the actions more or less unconsciously. Fitts and Posner (1967) called this

It Depends . . .

How Would You Estimate a Person's Stage of Learning?

Movement practitioners must estimate an individual's level of learning by observing various aspects of the individual's performance. To illustrate the difficulty associated with this task, we suggest that you spend some time at a local recreational area and observe the performance of a particular individual (without the person knowing, of course). As you watch this person perform, what aspects would you look for that might tell you something about her level of learning? List and describe each aspect as clearly as possible.

Table 1.5 Theoretical Depictions of the Stages of Motor Learning and Associated Motor Performance Characteristics

Reference	Early stage of learning ⟶	Later stage of learning
Fitts and Posner (1967)	Cognitive (trial and error), associative (homing in)	Autonomous (free and easy)
Adams (1971)	Verbal motor (more talk)	Motor (more action)
Gentile (1972)	Getting the idea of the movement	Fixation and diversification (closed or open skill)
Newell (1985)	Coordination (acquire the pattern)	Control (adapt the pattern as needed)
	Associated Motor Performance Characteristics	
Early learning ⟶		**Later learning**
Stiff-looking	More relaxed	Automatic
Inaccurate	More accurate	Accurate
Inconsistent	More consistent	Consistent
Slow, halting	More fluid	Fluid
Timid	More confident	Confident
Indecisive	More decisive	Certain
Rigid	More adaptable	Adaptable
Inefficient	More efficient	Efficient
Many errors	Fewer errors	Performer recognizes errors

UNIVERSITY OF WINCHESTER
LIBRARY

Learning About Learning From Watching Children

It is great fun to watch a group of children at play. It also teaches us something about the way people learn skills. At first a child observes a playmate or an adult doing something—such as swinging on a swing, sliding down a slide, or throwing and catching a ball. The child then attempts her own imitation of the task. If she has some degree of success or finds the movement challenging or enjoyable—or if she hears praise from a parent or friend—she may continue to engage in the task. The child may even achieve some degree of success at something simple (e.g., sliding down the slide feet first) and choose to repeat that action for several attempts. Once she feels reasonably confident, the child may attempt another, more difficult variation of the movement (e.g., sliding down the slide head first) or may decide to do something altogether different (e.g., swinging on the swings).

Skill learning seems to generally progress from the foundational to the sophisticated (Haywood, 1993). As individuals achieve one level of skill, they move to the next. If the task is throwing a ball, the child may throw and chase the ball many times before he has achieved sufficient skill to begin throwing to a partner. Catching comes even later because it involves the additional skills of visual tracking, anticipation, accurate hand placement, and timed grasping. If a skilled adult is throwing to a child, the latter may benefit from seeing and attempting to catch a ball that is coming at nearly the same speed and trajectory each time. In any case, considerable experience of throwing and catching in a variety of situations over a long period will be required before the child is able to pick up any type of ball and play a successful game of throw and catch with someone else.

Although adults bring a greater amount of experience to learning situations than do children, their performance progresses in much the same way: Starting with the basic skills, they gradually incorporate the more advanced details that allow them to execute their movements with greater accuracy, consistency, and diversity. In part III of this book we discuss some of the ways that movement practitioners can complement people's natural skill progression by presenting instructions and demonstrations, structuring practice sessions, and providing feedback.

automated movements—Movements performed with little attention to or conscious awareness of skill execution; a characteristic of advanced learners.

stage the autonomous stage, whereas Adams (1971) labeled it the motor stage, suggesting that performers place a proportionately greater emphasis on producing the action (i.e., motor elements) than on thinking about the verbal or cognitive elements. The skill proficiency of performers in this stage would be characterized by the qualities mentioned by Guthrie (1952) in his definition of skill. In addition to producing **automated movements**, these advanced learners are able to detect and correct errors in their performance, if and when errors do occur.

Although it's sometimes difficult to determine exactly which stage a learner might be in, you should be able to make reasonable inferences by checking the person's level of proficiency on some of the performance characteristics shown in table 1.5.

Implicit Learning

Another phenomenon that illustrates the close relationship between motor performance and motor learning is the concept of implicit learning. When people decide they want to learn a motor task and begin practicing it, the resulting performance becomes a vehicle for determining the appropriate pattern of movement, refining it as needed, and making it more controllable. As practice continues, learners begin to notice explicit (i.e., obvious) changes in a number of the characteristics shown in table 1.5.

However, there are also times when learners experience performance improvements about which they are unaware. A good example is where children who are just learning to speak learn the rules (grammar) of their language (implicitly) but without ever studying these rules directly (explicitly). Also, research evidence suggests that systematic practice can increase a person's level of motor learning, even when the person is oblivious to what may have caused the improvements. For example, in several studies, participants' learning of a repeated segment of a tracking task was found to be superior to their learning of other segments that were constantly changing (Magill, Schoenfelder-Zohdi, & Hall, cited in Magill, 1998b; Pew, 1974; Wulf & Schmidt, 1997), although the participants never reported that they noticed the repeated segment. More recent studies examining the learning of golf putting (Maxwell, Masters, Kerr, & Weedon, 2001) and of balancing while standing on a movable platform (Shea, Wulf, Whitacre, & Park, 2001) further suggest that learners perform and retain task components of which they are unaware more completely than components they notice; also, the greater the proportion of implicit components, the more skill learners demonstrated on the task and the more effectively they attended to additional environmental demands. Results such as these underscore the likelihood that every time individuals engage in motor performance, some type of motor learning is going on. The challenge for practitioners, therefore, is to design practice experiences that allow the learner to perfect the desired action—whether it be explicit learning or implicit learning. To meet this challenge, practitioners need to ask the right questions and then devise answers that allow them to help learners achieve their goals. In the next section, we discuss the situation-based approach to motor performance and learning, which emphasizes the factors that practitioners need to consider when providing instructional assistance.

Children at play exemplify some of the ways humans perform and learn motor skills.

SITUATION-BASED APPROACH TO MOTOR PERFORMANCE AND LEARNING

In 1981 the prominent educator Arthur Combs contended, "Tomorrow's citizens must be problem solvers, persons able to make good choices, to create solutions on the spot" (1981, p. 369). We believe that this viewpoint is more relevant today than it was then,

Choking in Stressful Situations: Shift From Implicit to Explicit Control Processes?

One explanation for the classic "choking" (see Beilock & Carr, 2004; Wulf, 2007) response sometimes seen in athletes performing under pressure (e.g., the professional golfer who misses a short putt) is a shift in motor control from implicit to explicit processes (Gladwell, 2000). Neuropsychologists believe that implicit processes partially reside in a region of the brain called the basal ganglia. Among other things, this region is responsible for producing appropriate movement force and timing. As performers achieve higher levels of skill, it is likely that implicit processes assume a greater degree of control until eventually people are able to produce actions with little or no conscious awareness about what their limbs are doing. Under stress, however, skilled performers can sometimes "regress" to become more aware of their movements, relegating control to more conscious, explicit processes housed in the cerebral cortex. When performers do this, their movements become more mechanical, awkward, and slow-looking compared with the more smooth, fluid, and effortless-looking actions of automatic performance. Such shifts can occur for skilled participants in nonsport activities, such as the concert pianist or brain surgeon who begins to focus on the movements of his hands rather than on the desired outcome (i.e., beautiful music and precise incisions). We talk more about this type of control in chapter 2.

The Amazing Motor System

Several clinical studies of individuals who have suffered permanent memory deficits following brain surgery suggest that the motor system is capable of organizing movements even when individuals cannot remember having performed them before. In one longitudinal study conducted by Milner, Corkin, and Teuber (1968), an adult male patient was reportedly able to learn and continue to produce a number of motor skills even though he could not remember the previous performance occasions. This individual was eventually employed in a rehabilitation center where he performed a variety of tasks, including one that involved mounting cigarette lighters on cardboard frames, for which he achieved a high degree of skill. In another case study (Gardner, 1975), a patient with severe amnesiac symptoms was found to be able to learn and recall piano melodies even though he couldn't remember any of the teaching sessions. Studies such as these seem to indicate that our motor system is able to organize an effective response with little more information than the movement goal and the environmental constraints.

situation-based approach— An approach to understanding motor performance and learning that emphasizes the situation (or context) in which performance and learning take place.

and that is why, in this book, we encourage a problem-solving approach strongly based on the situation (or context) under which motor performance and learning take place (i.e., a **situation-based approach**). In the following section we discuss some ways you can accomplish this task by asking the right questions.

Asking the Right Questions

To be an effective learner or movement practitioner, you must be able to ask the right questions. Put more simply, you need to obtain as much information as you can about three aspects of the performance or learning situation: person, task, and environment (see figure 1.1). Who is the person (e.g., child, athlete, therapy patient, senior citizen)? What is the task (e.g., catching a ball, driving in complex traffic, using a wheelchair, playing croquet)? Where is the person performing or learning the task (e.g., a playground during a noon recess, a piano recital or dance concert, a golf course, a basketball court in front of thousands of spectators)?

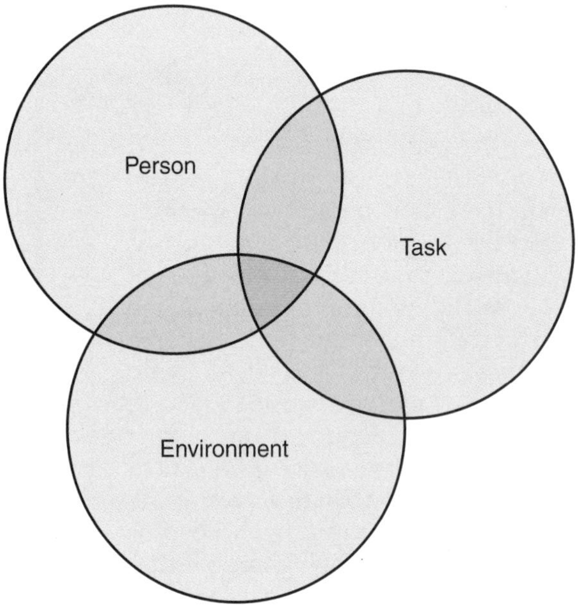

Figure 1.1 Effective movement practitioners consider the basic characteristics of the person, the task, and the environment before providing instructional assistance.

Who? The Person

The most important component of any motor performance situation is the person performing the skill. Every person possesses a unique set of innate abilities, a particular maturational level, previous movement experiences, a sociocultural background, a level of motivation, an emotional makeup, and in some cases a handicapping condition. All of these characteristics can influence the level of performance proficiency the person is capable of achieving. If he or she possesses the essential perceptual–motor abilities (a concept we discuss in more detail in chapter 6), has achieved a satisfactory level of maturation, has had previous movement experiences and a sociocultural background that are advantageous for performance, is motivated to excel, and is capable of maintaining an optimal emotional level, then he or she should be able to achieve a higher level of performance than someone not possessing one or more of these characteristics. Therefore, the nature of practice needs to be tailored to the individual doing the learning.

Some Thoughts on the Process of Skill Learning

Researchers spend considerable time contemplating the process of skill learning and the challenges facing practitioners trying to provide the best instructional assistance possible. Each of the following quotes addresses an important issue we deal with in this book.

The first concerns the definition of skill learning, a concept we discuss in this chapter. The second addresses several factors that influence people's information processing, which is the basis of the conceptual model of motor performance we begin developing in chapter 2. The third focuses on the importance of creating effective practice environments, a topic we treat extensively in part III of the book. For now, just read each quote and contemplate its importance to your own skill learning and to that of others you may eventually have the opportunity to assist.

> "Learning is not simply about behavior change that is persistent; instead, and in addition, it is about adaptive change or behavioral change in relation to the task goal." (Liu, Mayer-Kress, & Newell, 2004)

> "The overall efficiency of processing information is dependent on functional task difficulty, which is determined by the ability of the performer, the complexity of the task, and the conditions of practice." (Guadagnoli & Lee, 2004)

> "When practice time is limited, it is of primary importance that the available opportunities are used as effectively as possible." (Lee & Wishart, 2005)

What? The Task

The nature of the task is a second situational component you need to consider. Specifically, you'll want to find out as much as you can about the demands of the task. Some tasks contain sensory–perceptual demands, such as detecting the speed and direction of an approaching ball or analyzing the pattern of motion of opposing players. A second category of task demands deals with the decisions performers must make about what to do and how to perform the task. Finally, we consider the demands of skill execution itself, which tests the performer's capability of producing the correct movement pattern. For some tasks, one of these demands will be the principal determinant of performance success. For others, a sequence of effective perception, decision making, and action planning must be achieved for success to occur, and subpar performance can be attributable to a breakdown in any of these processes. For example, a successful tennis shot would depend on an accurate reading of the environment, a smart decision, and skillful planning, whereas an unsuccessful shot may be the result of deficiencies in one or more of these processes. A useful way to begin this process is to consider the task to be learned as belonging to one of the classifications discussed earlier in this chapter.

Where? The Environment

A third situational component is the performance environment. The following are questions you might want to ask: Where will the person practice the task? Where does the person want to be able to perform the task? Will performance be in the presence of spectators or alone in a workshop? Will the person be able to take all the time he or she needs to produce the desired movement (e.g., a golf shot) or must the person be able to perform the task in a brief interval of time (e.g., an emergency braking maneuver in a car)? An important aspect of the situation-based approach to motor performance and learning is the emphasis placed on practicing the desired movement in an environment that is similar to the one in which the person needs to eventually be able to perform the task. Later in this book we refer to this type of environment as the "target context,"

A Closer Look at the Components of Movement

If we take a closer look at the movements we produce, we see that several possible components are involved. First, there is the postural component, which supports most of our actions—for instance, the arms and trunk of an archer provide a stable platform that promotes accurate shooting. Physical therapists, particularly those who specialize in pediatrics and neurology, are very aware of the essential nature of postural components for motor control. For these specialists, the head, neck, and trunk are the starting points and building blocks of most therapeutic treatments. A second component of movements is the locomotor component, which we use to transport our bodies to locations where we perform other skills, such as when a waiter carries a tray of food from the kitchen to the table in a restaurant. Finally, our movements sometimes contain a manipulation component, which we couple and coordinate with postural and locomotor components or which is occasionally the major focus of a skill, such as the finger and wrist movements of a neurosurgeon. Classification systems such as the ones presented in tables 1.1, 1.2, 1.3, and 1.4 can be useful for determining the relative importance of movement components in the performance of skills.

It Depends . . .

Can You Identify the Elements of Motor Tasks?

Three elements that are important to the performance of many motor tasks are sensory or perceptual elements, decision-making elements, and motor-control elements. Can you think of an example of each type of element for one of the following tasks?

A goalie in a soccer game

A jockey in a horse race

A violinist in a concert performance

List and describe each element as clearly as possible.

meaning the setting where the person must eventually perform the task (e.g., a basketball player must be able to perform the jump shot in a gymnasium in the presence of spectators, whereas a woodworker will likely operate a lathe in the privacy of his own shop).

Throughout this book, we will challenge you to consider the person, task, and environment when deciding how to approach performance and learning situations. In each chapter you'll find several highlight boxes with headings that pose a particular question. The better you're able to answer these questions, the more effective you'll be in maximizing a person's motor performance and learning. In the next section, we discuss the ways that we are going to help you understand the concepts of motor performance and learning and use the situation-based approach.

Developing Your Understanding of Motor Performance and Learning

Because motor skills make up such a large part of our lives, scientists and educators have been trying for years to understand the basis of skilled performance and the factors that influence skill learning. The results of research studies offer important information for educators and movement practitioners in a variety of fields. For those in exercise science, kinesiology, physical education, and physical medicine and rehabilitation, the results suggest ways of designing skill instruction that lead to movement success for persons in a variety of situations. For coaches, the findings offer information about ways to structure practice sessions that produce more consistent skill execution and give athletes an advantage in competitive situations. For human-factors and ergonomics personnel, the information suggests principles of skills training that can help people learn how to operate machines and other types of equipment effectively and safely. For physical, speech, and occupational therapists, the results provide ideas for helping people relearn movements they have lost or that have been compromised as a result of injury, stroke, or birth defects. In light of recent initiatives in health-care reform, it would appear that a knowledge of motor performance and learning principles is more important than ever for therapists who must provide effective treatment in a shorter time, with fewer patient visits, and at a lower cost.

Although all of these settings are different and the physical capabilities of learners vary widely, there are principles that lead to successful performance in nearly every situation. Thus, we need to identify those principles to give performers and learners the best opportunity of achieving success. In this book we discuss the principles of motor performance and motor learning that have emerged from the results of scientific studies. In many cases, however, these principles will need to be modified slightly when we consider the specifics of the person, task, and environment.

In parts II and III of this book, we present the important principles of motor performance and motor learning, respectively. Even though we have talked in this chapter about how these two phenomena are highly related, we temporarily treat them separately in those two parts of the book to help you comprehend the principles of each more clearly.

What's It Like to Be a Movement Practitioner?

One way to appreciate the demands of a professional occupation is to ask the opinion of people who are working in the profession. To help you understand the challenges that face movement practitioners, we suggest that you interview a person who provides instructional or therapeutic assistance on a regular basis (e.g., a physical education teacher, a youth sport coach, a physical therapist, an occupational therapist, a dance or music teacher). Ask the person each of the following questions:

- What do you like most about teaching skills to people?
- What do you like least about teaching skills to people?
- What is the easiest part of your job?
- What is the toughest part of your job?
- What is the biggest challenge you face when you are trying to help a person improve his or her skill?

Summarize the person's comments and then discuss your own thoughts.

You might wonder why we have chosen to address the concept of motor performance before turning our attention to the concept of motor learning (perhaps you're thinking that a person has to learn a skill before she or he can be expected to perform it). The reason is that much of the research work on human motor learning has been discussed using concepts and terminology that have been developed during the study of human performance. The performance research gives us concepts and a vocabulary with which we examine the (largely separate) issues for motor learning. In addition, the literature on motor performance allows us to construct a conceptual **model** of motor performance that illustrates how the perceptual–motor system works, how individuals interact with their environment during skilled movement, and how additional factors (such as task complexity, types of feedback, practice structure, and the presence of others) influence people's skill learning. This model will be especially useful as we consider the questions about learning, how to practice, and what happens to performance when people learn.

In summary, then, we focus on two separate but related themes in parts II and III of the book. In part II we discuss the components and principles of motor performance. These include the nature of information processing (chapter 2), the ways in which people use sensory information to control their movements (chapter 3), the role of motor programs in movement production (chapter 4), the determinants of accuracy in rapid movements (chapter 5), and the role of **individual differences** (i.e., differences among individuals) in determining performance (chapter 6).

model—
A tentative description (or an analogy) of a system that captures many of its known properties; models typically facilitate understanding of systems and promote practical applications.

individual differences—
Stable, enduring differences among individuals' performances, often attributable to differences in their abilities.

In part III we turn our attention to issues related to the learning of motor skills. Here you'll discover some of the principles of effective skill practice and instruction. In chapter 7 we discuss the concept of the learning experience and describe methods practitioners might use to evaluate the progress of learners. In the remainder of part III, we discuss the principles and techniques practitioners should consider when supplementing the learning experience (chapter 8), structuring the learning experience (chapter 9), and providing feedback during the learning experience (chapter 10). As we progress through parts II and III we also build a conceptual model of motor performance to help you understand the interrelationships of the various mechanisms and principles of performance and learning.

Building a Conceptual Model of Motor Performance

To understand the process of motor performance and learning, you need to have a relatively consistent overall viewpoint, a big picture, a conceptual model. During some of your earlier educational experiences you were likely introduced to various types of models. In chemistry, for example, you may have used video software to build models in an attempt to approximate the structure of atoms and molecules.

The model of motor performance we begin constructing in part II of this book is an information-flow model, which presumes that people use information of various kinds to perform and learn skills. We begin constructing the model by talking about how sensory information enters the system through receptors (chapter 2). In subsequent chapters we explain how performers process, transform, and store this information and how they use it to make decisions and plan their actions. Next, we discuss several features of movement execution, such as the process of movement initiation and the activities that occur while the action is unfolding (e.g., the control of muscular contractions and the detection and correction of errors). Finally, we discuss the idea of individual differences, where one can think of differences among individuals in the ways that information is processed. By the end of part II, you should understand the components of the conceptual model and be able to identify the components that are most essential for the production of various types of movements in various situations. In part III we discuss various dimensions of

Consider the Source

Throughout this book we present concepts and principles that have emerged from research in motor performance and learning. To test your comprehension of this information, we pose a number of questions for you to contemplate and answer. Whenever possible you should provide supporting literature for your answers. That way you will demonstrate that your answers are not your best guess but rather that they have a strong basis in the scientific literature. Studies that have examined a particular research problem directly, such as those published in scientific journals, are referred to as primary sources. Examples from this chapter are the studies we referenced in the section on implicit learning (e.g., Maxwell et al., 2001). Less impressive is literature that represents others' interpretations of primary sources. These secondary sources include textbooks like this one. You should cite primary sources to support your answers if at all possible. However, if you choose to use the textbook to support your answers, be sure to cite it (i.e., Schmidt & Wrisberg, 2008) in your answer.

The conceptual model of motor performance attempts to account for how people learn and perform such complex skills as in-line skating.

motor learning and focus on those components of the model that are modifiable with practice—thus contributing to skill acquisition.

Applying the Situation-Based Approach to Skills Instruction

In part IV we illustrate how movement practitioners can use the conceptual model of motor performance and the important principles of performance and learning to devise a working strategy for providing instructional assistance. In chapter 11 we discuss the components of the working strategy and then demonstrate how practitioners in four settings (teaching, coaching, rehabilitation, and firefighter training) might use the strategy to diagnose, design, structure, and evaluate people's learning experiences. In chapter 12 we provide you with the opportunity to demonstrate your own (newly acquired) capability to use the working strategy to create a learning experience for a person, task, and situation of your choosing.

By that time you should comprehend the important principles of motor performance and learning, understand the conceptual model of motor performance, and be able to use a situation-based approach to help people achieve their movement goals. We hope you enjoy your experience.

SUMMARY

Motor skills are an important and often fascinating aspect of our lives. What we know about skills has come from a number of scientific disciplines, and the results of this research are useful to practitioners in a variety of settings, such as teaching, coaching, rehabilitation, and industrial or technical environments.

A skill may be viewed from a task perspective and classified according to dimensions such as

- the organization of the task,
- the relative importance of motor and cognitive elements, and
- the level of environmental predictability.

Skill can also be conceptualized as the level of proficiency demonstrated by a performer. Qualities associated with higher levels of performance proficiency are

- maximum certainty of goal achievement,
- minimum energy expenditure, and
- minimum movement time.

The concepts of motor performance and motor learning are difficult to distinguish. This is because repetitions of motor performance are required for people to achieve higher levels of motor learning, and an individual's level of learning can be estimated only by observing the person's motor performance. Motor learning is an internal process or state, the level of which reflects a person's capability for producing a movement at any particular point in time. However, motor performance is susceptible to fluctuations in temporary factors such as fatigue, boredom, anxiety, and motivation, which, if not considered, can lead to errors in our assessments of the level of learning. Also, performance repetitions sometimes produce implicit learning that is beyond the learner's awareness. In addition, different performance characteristics are evident at different stages of learning.

A situation-based approach to performance and learning presumes that three situational factors contribute to successful movement production. These are the person, the task, and the environment. To provide the most effective instructional assistance, practitioners usually ask questions, the answers to which will provide them with as much information about these three factors as possible.

FROM PRINCIPLES TO PRACTICE

Check your comprehension of the concepts and terms discussed in this chapter by responding to each of the exercises in the following sections. The first section contains several exercises designed to test your working knowledge of key terms. The second poses a variety of problems designed to check your understanding of key concepts. In the third you are challenged to apply your knowledge by discussing a defensible solution for two scenarios.

Know Your Key Terms

Matching: Motor Skill Task Classification

Match the following skill classifications with their respective categories or definitions by placing the most appropriate letter on each of the blanks.

Skill Classifications—Terms

a. closed skill
b. cognitive skill
c. continuous skill
d. discrete skill
e. open skill
f. serial skill
g. motor skill

Skill Classifications—Category or Definition

_____1. Action that is usually brief and has a well-defined beginning and end

_____2. Several distinct actions connected together in a sequence, often with the order of the actions being crucial to performance success

_____3. Action that unfolds without a recognizable beginning and end in an ongoing and often repetitive fashion

_____4. Skill for which the primary determinant of success is the quality of the movement

_____5. Skill for which the primary determinant of success is the quality of the performer's decisions regarding what to do

_____6. Skill performed in an environment that is unpredictable or in motion and that requires people to adapt their movements in response to dynamic properties of the environment

_____7. Skill performed in an environment that is predictable or stationary and that allows people to plan their movements in advance

Consider: Aspects of Skill Proficiency

For each of the following tasks, indicate which of the three aspects of skill proficiency would most distinguish the performance of beginning and advanced participants.

1. Putting a golf ball ______________________________
2. Walking with crutches ______________________________
3. Driving a car ______________________________
4. Beating an egg ______________________________

Fill in the Blank: The Chicken and the Egg

Complete the following sentences:

______________________________is observable movement behavior that is sometimes susceptible to temporary factors, such as ________________ and ________________. A person's level of ____________ ________________ can be estimated only by observing the person's ________________________.

Check Your Understanding

1. Discuss the concept of motor skill from a task-classification perspective and from a performance-proficiency perspective, and then explain how a person who is coaching a youth soccer team might apply each perspective when teaching skills to kids.
2. Explain the concepts of motor performance and motor learning, and discuss two movement characteristics a physical therapist might look for to determine if a stroke patient is learning how to walk with a cane.
3. Explain why a situation-based approach to motor performance and learning is an effective strategy for movement practitioners.

Apply Your Knowledge

Exercise 1

The situation-based approach to motor performance and learning is based on the premise that effective instruction depends on a practitioner's ability to ask the right questions. A practitioner—whether a teacher, a coach, or a physical therapist—should consider three questions before attempting to assist a person performing or learning a skill:

Who is the learner?

What is the skill?

Where will performance take place?

For this exercise, describe a hypothetical learner or performer, a particular motor skill (task) with which you are familiar (emphasizing the primary demands of the skill), and a possible setting in which the person would be expected to perform the skill. After you complete this task, discuss how a teacher or coach might use each piece of information in providing instructional assistance. Provide a rationale for your answer and include at least one supporting reference.

Exercise 2

In this chapter you learned that three characteristics of skill proficiency are maximum certainty of goal achievement, minimum energy expenditure, and minimum movement time (Guthrie, 1952). You also learned that the relative importance of these characteristics sometimes differs for various tasks (e.g., minimum movement time is probably more important for hitting a baseball than for walking with crutches). Think about your own movement experiences and discuss how you would go about evaluating the characteristic that you believe is the best indicator of a person's proficiency for one of the skills you have learned (e.g., playing a musical instrument, shooting a basketball, snow skiing, ballet dancing). Finally, use Gentile's (1987) two-dimensional system (table 1.4) to classify the skill or task. Provide rationale for your answers and furnish at least one supporting reference in addition to those cited.

chapter 2

Processing Information and Making Decisions

Chapter Outline

Chapter Objectives

When you have completed this chapter, you should be able to

- understand the nature of at least three information-processing stages,
- be familiar with the concept of reaction time and the factors that affect it,
- identify the primary information-processing demands of various tasks,
- understand how arousal and attention influence performance, and
- appreciate how three discrete components of human memory affect people's motor performance.

PREVIEW

A basketball player is dribbling down the court and spots an open teammate breaking for the basket. He immediately attempts a long pass but an opposing player intercepts it. Why didn't the player accomplish his intended goal? Did he throw an inaccurate pass? Did he not see the defender? Did the excitement of the situation affect his decision? What other options did the player have in this situation? Was the choice he made the best one for that situation?

OVERVIEW

Skilled performers are adept at analyzing environmental information, making good decisions, and producing effective movements. In this chapter we describe some of the principles of information processing that are most relevant to skilled performance. We begin by introducing a simple model of motor performance, based on an information-processing perspective, which we will continue to construct throughout much of the remainder of the book. We then focus on the decision-making component of the model and discuss ways that performers code, store, and use information to make decisions. Finally, we discuss several themes dealing with the processing of information: reaction time and the factors that affect it, information processing under different time constraints, the concepts of arousal and attention as they relate to information processing, and the role of memory in motor performance.

Experienced performers are more adept than beginners at perceiving and acting upon relevant environmental information.

In this chapter, we begin to address the processes or "software" that people use when they attempt to produce skilled movements. Readers who hope to one day assist people with physical or mental disabilities will find that impairments in one or more of these processes can cause many of the performance problems these individuals encounter. As we mentioned previously, highly skilled performers are adept at deciding what to do (and what not to do) in particular situations, even when they have very little time to do so. The most elegant soccer pass is usually the result of a quick and accurate decision by the passer, which comprises but one aspect of the player's skill in this activity.

INFORMATION-PROCESSING APPROACH

Some psychologists explain motor skill learning with a model that portrays the performer as a processor of information, similar in many ways to how a computer operates. In this model, the person begins to deal with available information from the environment (input), continues to process it using a variety of operations, and eventually produces a response (output). In figure 2.1 we depict this process with a simple flowchart. Some psychologists hold that the performer receives input passively, whereas others contend that the person selects information from the environment actively. The truth probably lies somewhere between these two views.

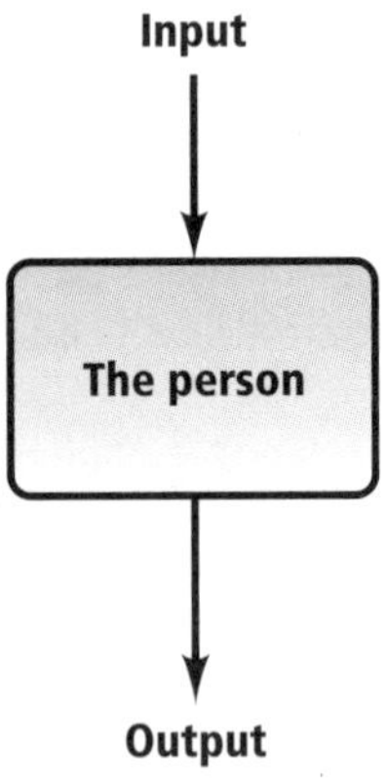

Figure 2.1 The simplest model of the information-processing approach to motor performance.

Sources of Input

In information-processing studies, **input** is usually represented by a stimulus that the experimenter presents to the research participant (e.g., illuminating a light or presenting some sort of sound signal). In these types of situations, participants need only see or hear the stimulus to begin processing a response to it. Simple input occasionally occurs in real-world environments (e.g., the firing of the starter's gun in track or swimming or the illumination of a warning lamp on an instrument panel).

input—
The information that people receive for processing.

What is Relevant?

Research by Williams and Davids (1998) illustrates nicely how more experienced and less experienced people pick up different aspects of the same environmental information. In this study, one group of soccer players possessed more than 13 years of playing experience, whereas another had approximately 4 years of experience. All players viewed films showing "life-sized" sequences of soccer plays projected on a 3.0- × 3.5-m screen. Each play ended with a pass by a member of the opposing team. Players were told to imagine themselves as a covering defender or "sweeper" whose task it was to stop the advance of the approaching opponents. Some scenes involved one offensive player and one defensive player; others consisted of three offensive and three defensive players. Players were told to step on footpads (which were located in the floor to their left, right, front, and back) to indicate when and how they would attempt to intercept the opponent's pass. The experimenters also obtained data about eye movements, as well as concurrent verbal reports, from the players to determine the location of their visual attention during both types of sequences.

The more experienced participants' foot responses were initiated more rapidly than those of their less experienced counterparts. Also, the eye-movement and verbal-report data suggested that the types of information extracted were different for the two groups. In the one-on-one situation, the more experienced participants fixated longer on the opponent's hip, whereas less experienced players spent more time watching the opponent's feet and the ball. The more experienced players also alternated their fixations more often between the opponent's hip and lower leg than did their less experienced counterparts. In the three-on-three scenario, the more experienced players allocated less attention to the opponent with the ball than did participants who were less experienced. More experienced players also reported shifts in their visual focus a greater percentage of the time (71%, compared with 58% for less experienced players), despite the fact that fixations to the left and right of the opponent with the ball were not different for the two groups. This suggests that, as compared with less experienced players, the more experienced ones made greater use of vision to monitor the activities of the two offensive opponents who were not in possession of the ball.

These findings imply that more experienced performers use their organization of task-specific knowledge to extract information that contributes the most to a quick and accurate response for each type of situation. In contrast, less experienced performers tend to fixate longer on the more obvious aspects of environmental information (e.g., the feet of the opponent with the ball), irrespective of situational circumstances.

However, input more often exists in the midst of a multitude of other environmental stimuli (e.g., a moving pedestrian in the midst of other components of city traffic). In these situations, the input must be selected for processing.

Although most psychologists agree that the search process is an active one, they offer different explanations as to how performers select environmental information. For example, Gibson (1966, 1979) contended that we perceive important information directly through our sensory systems (e.g., our direction relative to another person or the time before an oncoming vehicle could strike us); with increasing experience we become even more adept at perceiving and acting on this information. Critics of this view (e.g., Williams, Davids, Burwitz, & Williams, 1992) contend that additional factors—such as our memory of previous events or practice at some activity—need to be considered to understand how we deal with information (see the research highlight on this page).

Three Information-Processing Stages

stages of processing—Several distinguishable operations (stimulus identification, response selection, and response programming) that people perform on information between input and output; frequently examined by scientists in reaction-time experiments.

stimulus-identification stage—The first stage of information processing; during this stage, the input is detected and identified.

A major goal of psychologists interested in the control of motor skills is to understand the specific nature of the processes in the box labeled "The person" in figure 2.1. For the most part, psychologists have assumed that there are several discrete **stages of processing** through which information passes on its way from input to output. For our purposes, we focus on three of these stages (you can find a summary of the characteristics of each stage later in this chapter in table 2.2):

- Stimulus identification
- Response selection
- Response programming

When using a stages-of-processing analysis of performance, some psychologists assume that environmental information (i.e., input) entering the system is initially processed in the first stage, called stimulus identification. When the processing that occurs there is completed, the result of this processing passes on to the second stage, called response selection, for further processing. When that processing is finished, the result passes on to the third stage, called response programming, for more processing, and so on, until an action (i.e., output) is produced. In the following sections we discuss briefly the rationale for a stages-of-processing analysis and the kinds of operations that occur during each of the stages.

It Depends . . .

Where Should Performers' Attention Be Focused?

The particular information that performers attend to often depends on the situation. Which sources of information (e.g., the ball, teammates, opponents, the coach, the crowd, bodily sensations) might have occupied the attention of the basketball player in this chapter's opening preview scenario? What if the score had been close? What if the scenario had occurred during the first minute of the game? What if the crowd had been noisy? What if the player was fatigued? What would you say if the task were driving in traffic rather than passing a basketball?

Stimulus Identification (Stage 1)

During this first stage, the performer's task is to identify incoming information, referred to as the *stimulus.* Thus, in the **stimulus-identification stage**, performers analyze the content of environmental information using a variety of sensory systems, such as vision, audition, touch, kinesthesis, and smell. In addition, they assemble the components of this information. For example, a person might assemble a combination of edges and colors to form a visual representation of a moving object, such as a ball or an approaching vehicle. The individual might also detect patterns of the object's movement, such as whether it is moving at all, the direction and speed it is moving, and so on. Such patterns become important sources of information if the desired response is to catch the ball or to avoid the vehicle. When processing is completed in this stage, the performer has presumably achieved some representation of the important environmental information, which then passes on to the next stage—response selection—for further processing.

response-selection stage—The second stage of information processing; during this stage, it is decided which, if any, response should be made.

Response Selection (Stage 2)

Using the information coming from the stimulus-identification stage, the person must now decide how to respond to it in the **response-selection stage**. For example, a soccer goalie might decide to catch or trap the approaching ball or let it go to a teammate, and the pedestrian might decide to dodge the approaching car or quickly cross the

It Depends . . .

What Information Influences Performers' Decisions?

The basketball player in the preview scenario decided to pass the ball to his teammate, who was moving toward the basket. What other choices might the player have made? What if the teammate was a poor ball handler? What if the teammate was shorter than the defender? What if the defender had intercepted several earlier passes? What if the score was tied and there were 20 s left in the game?

street before it arrives. Thus, in this stage a translation of sorts occurs between the sensory input the performer has identified (e.g., the characteristics of the approaching ball or car) and one of the several possible options for a response (e.g., catch the ball, cross in front of the car).

Response Programming (Stage 3)

Once the performer has, in the response-selection stage, chosen a particular action—and before the action can begin—he or she must prepare an action. This is thought to occur in a third stage called the **response-programming stage**. In this stage, various processes are thought to occur, such as retrieving the motor program for action (which we discuss in detail in chapter 4), preparing the musculature for the upcoming commands to contract, orienting the sensory system in the appropriate way (e.g., looking at a particular part of the environment), and readying the postural system for the dynamics of the action that will be produced. When the action has been readied for action, it is initiated, resulting in the start of movement output that can be seen by observers and recorded by experimenters.

It Depends . . .

What Are the Controllable Components of Performers' Movements?

What was the basketball player in the preview controlling once he committed to throwing the ball to his teammate? Could he change the ball's direction, path, and force as he was throwing it? To avoid repeating the mistake he made, what other factors might the player consider when confronted with a similar situation?

Output

The end result of the activity of all three information-processing stages is termed the **output.** It could be the bat swing of a baseball, softball, or cricket player; the steering adjustments of a cyclist, pilot, sailor, or NASCAR driver; the timed movements of a dancer or a musician; or the sit-to-stand movement of a nursing-home resident. Note, however, that the output a person produces might not achieve the desired goal of the movement. The batter's swing might result in a hit or a miss; the cyclist's adjustment may result in successful navigation or a painful fall; the dancer's movement may be in or out of rhythm with a partner; and the elderly person's sit-to-stand attempt may produce vertical standing, a stumble, or a return to the sitting position. The

response-programming stage— The third stage of information processing; during this stage, the motor system is organized to produce the desired movement.

output— The motor behavior or action produced as a result of information processing.

actual control of the output, including modifications and corrections for any errors, is thought of as separate from the stages or processing by which the person detected the stimulus, chose the action, and organized and initiated it; we deal with many of these latter processes in chapters 3 and 4.

It Depends . . .

Why Might Performance Fail?

How might you explain the result of the basketball player's efforts in the preview? Did he fail to identify correctly the position or movement speed of the defender? Would a decision to throw a bounce pass have been more effective? Did he need to use more force to complete the pass accurately? Can you think of other explanations for the result? Which of your explanations concern the player's perception of the environment? Which deal with the player's decision? Which focus on the player's planning of his movement?

Beginning of a Conceptual Model

In figure 2.2 we add the stages of processing to the simple model shown in figure 2.1. This addition forms the first component of the conceptual model of motor performance on which we expand throughout the text. Less technical terms for depicting what goes on in each of these stages are shown in parentheses (i.e., perception, decision, and action planning). Using these stages we might describe the sequence mentioned in the basketball scenario at the beginning of the chapter in the following way: First, the player detected a teammate breaking for the basket (stimulus identification); second, the player decided to throw a quick pass (response selection); and third, the player planned the details of the pass and initiated it (response programming).

Although these stages are all located within the person's perceptual–motor system, they are not readily visible. Therefore, scientists have used several laboratory methods in an attempt to discover and monitor what is going on in the stages and how long performers require to process information in each stage. Most of this research has examined performers' reaction times to determine the speed of information processing.

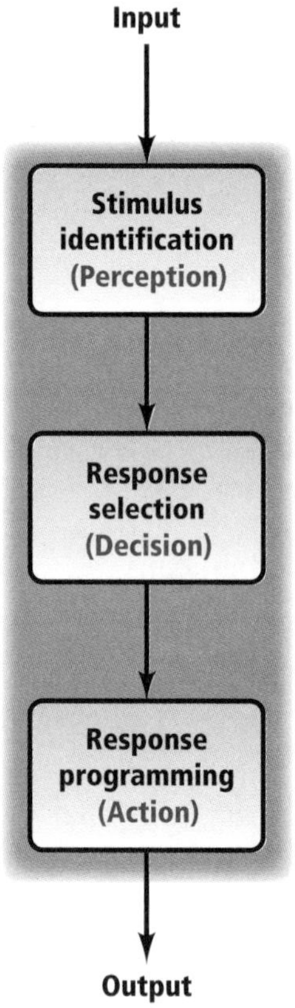

Figure 2.2 An expanded information-processing model showing the stimulus identification (perceiving), response selection (deciding), and response programming (action planning) stages.

It Depends . . .

What Would Cause Errors in Each Stage of Processing?

Errors can occur in any of the stages of processing we have just discussed. Which stages of processing might contribute to each of the following performance problems?

- A beginning dance student who is unable to walk to the beat of the music
- A beginning basketball player who is unable to make more than two baskets within 30 s during a continuous shooting drill
- A child who is unable to catch a ball
- An octogenarian who is unable to operate a TV remote control

REACTION TIME AND DECISION MAKING

reaction time (RT)—The interval of time that elapses from the sudden presentation of a stimulus to the beginning of a person's response.

Reaction time (abbreviated RT) is a good indicator of the speed and effectiveness of a person's decision making. It is also a component of some real-world tasks, such as the sprinter's start in the 100 m dash or the driver's braking action in a car in response to a red light. In the drawing from an old photograph of a foot race shown on this page, we see by the position of the smoke that the starter has already fired the gun (which represents the stimulus). Yet the runners all remain on the starting line and seem to be only just beginning to move. This picture depicts the RT delay that occurs between stimulus presentation and response initiation. Performers who are able to minimize such delays have a significant advantage in events like the 100 m dash.

Reaction time (RT) in a foot race: The starter's gun has fired, yet the athletes are only now getting off their marks after an RT delay. (Adapted from Scripture, 1905.)

In addition to reflecting processing delays in events such as the sprint start in track, RT can also tell us something about the time it takes people to make decisions and initiate actions. In many rapid skills, success depends on how fast the performer can detect some feature of the environment, such as an opponent's movement; decide what to do; and then initiate an effective countermove. Reaction time figures prominently in the performance of many open skills, including a variety of sports (e.g., boxing, driving a race car) as well as everyday activities (e.g., swatting a fly, braking a car, or catching a can of beans that suddenly falls from a kitchen cabinet). Because RT is a fundamental component of a number of skills requiring quick and effective decision making, it shouldn't surprise us that many researchers have used this measure to represent the speed of information processing.

RT has important theoretical meaning as well. Because it begins when a stimulus is presented and ends when a movement is initiated, RT is a potential measure of the total duration of the three stages of processing seen in figure 2.2. If we assume that these stages are sequential and do not overlap, then any factor that lengthens the duration of one or more of the stages will lengthen the total RT. Using this logic, some scientists use RT to estimate the speed of processing that takes place in each stage and to determine how and where various factors affect information processing. In the following section, we discuss how changes in RT can tell us something about the factors influencing a performer's decision making.

Factors Influencing Reaction Time and Decision Making

Many factors can influence the speed of a person's decision making, ranging from the nature of stimulus information to the type of movement being performed. In this section, we consider some of these factors.

Number of Stimulus-Response Alternatives

choice RT—
The interval of time that elapses between the presentation of one of several possible stimuli and the beginning of one of several possible responses.

foreperiod—
The interval of time between the presentation of a warning signal and the presentation of a stimulus.

Dick Schmidt's racquetball opponent has a number of good serves that all begin the same way (i.e., a simple bounce of the ball), but each ends with the ball moving at a different speed and trajectory, and Dick is often frozen for a moment, trying to decide where the ball is going and how to best respond to it. Why? One of the most important factors influencing RT and decision making is the number of possible stimuli to choose from at a given time—each of which leads to a distinct action. In the laboratory, scientists generally produce this situation by presenting a participant with one of several possible stimuli, such as different-colored lights, and requiring the person to choose one of several possible responses, such as pressing buttons with different fingers, depending on the stimulus presented. Situations such as this illustrate the phenomenon of **choice RT**, where the performer must first identify the stimulus and then choose the appropriate response. In choice RT experiments, each trial begins with a warning signal (e.g., the sound of a buzzer or tone), followed by an interval of time of unpredictable length (e.g., 2, 3, or 4 s), termed the **foreperiod**. Once the stimulus is presented (e.g., one of the lights is illuminated), the performer detects it, decides which button to press, organizes the response to press the button, and then presses the button. Thus, RT is a measure of the time required for the participant to complete all of these three substages—detection, decision, and response organization—with the RT ending when the performer initiates the action; note that the time involved in making the movement is not included in RT.

Hick's Law

More than a century ago, Merkel (1885, cited by Woodworth, 1938) conducted choice-RT experiments on himself involving 10 possible stimulus-response combinations. The stimuli were the Arabic numerals 1 through 5 and the Roman numerals I through V. Each stimulus was paired with one response key; for example, the numerals 1 to 5 were paired with the five digits of the right hand, and the numerals I to V were paired with the five left-hand digits. If the possible stimuli on a set of trials were the numerals 2, 3, and V (a three-choice case), Merkel responded with either the right index finger, right middle finger, or left thumb, depending on which one of the three stimuli was presented. Merkel varied the number of possible stimulus-response pairs during different sets of trials. The maroon line in figure 2.3*a* shows the results of his experiment, where choice RT is plotted as a function of the number of stimulus-response alternatives. You can see that as the number of pairs increased from one choice (simple RT), there was a sharp increase in RT, with these increases becoming smaller as the number of pairs increased, particularly beyond seven pairs.

Much later Hick (1952) and then Hyman (1953) discovered that the relationship between choice RT and the logarithm of the number of stimulus-response pairs is linear. In figure 2.3*b,* we have plotted the data from figure 2.3*a* as a function of the logarithm of the number of alternatives. This relationship has since become known as Hick's law; it has been shown to hold for a wide variety of situations using various types of participants, stimuli, and movements. Hick's law is one of the most important laws of human performance. The relationship implies that choice RT increases by a constant amount every time the number of stimulus-response alternatives is doubled (e.g., from 2 to 4 or from 16 to 32). This led to an important interpretation of Hick's law: Choice RT is linearly related to the amount of information that must be processed during the decision stage (i.e., when a performer is deciding what to do).

The shortest RT is generally found when there is only one stimulus and one response; this is referred to as **simple RT**. However, as the number of possible stimulus-response (S-R) combinations increases, the time it takes a person to respond to any one of them (i.e., choice RT) generally increases.

We discuss this famous relationship between the number of S-R alternatives and choice RT—known as **Hick's law**—in more detail in the research highlight on page 32. As you can see in figure 2.3*a*, RT increases substantially as the number of alternatives increases from one to two. An RT of about 190 ms with one S-R pair (simple RT) increases to more than 300 ms for two choices—a 58% increase in the time required to process the stimulus information and initiate a response! As the number of choices increases further, RT continues to increase, but the changes become progressively smaller (e.g., the increase in RT from 9 to 10 S-R choices might be as little as 20 ms, representing a percentage increase of only 2% or 3%).

RT delays can be of critical importance for individuals performing rapid open skills, such as blocking a punch in judo, digging a spike in volleyball, or swerving to avoid a squirrel that suddenly darts in front of your car. In baseball, the entire duration of a pitch might be only 4/10 s, or 400 ms, and the swing itself could take around 120 ms to execute. So if a batter takes an extra 100 ms to detect the speed and trajectory of the pitch, this would leave very little time for successful contact.

Because information-processing delays can sometimes be quite long, an important strategy for open-skill performers is to find ways of decreasing the number of S-R choices they have to deal with while increasing the number of S-R choices for their opponents. In softball, for example, a batter might decrease the number of S-R choices she has to process by detecting something in the pitcher's mannerisms that indicates the type of pitch the pitcher is going to throw (e.g., arm in one position means a fastball and arm in another position means a curveball). On the other hand, a pitcher might increase the number of S-R choices for the batter by increasing the number of different pitches she throws. As a general rule, then, open-skill performers try to find ways to decrease the number of choices they have to make so that their information-processing delay is as short as possible.

simple RT—
The interval of time that elapses between the presentation of one possible stimulus and the beginning of its associated response.

Hick's law—
Law describing the stable relationship that exists between the number of stimulus-response alternatives and choice reaction time; specifically, as the logarithm of the number of stimulus-response pairs increases, choice reaction time increases linearly.

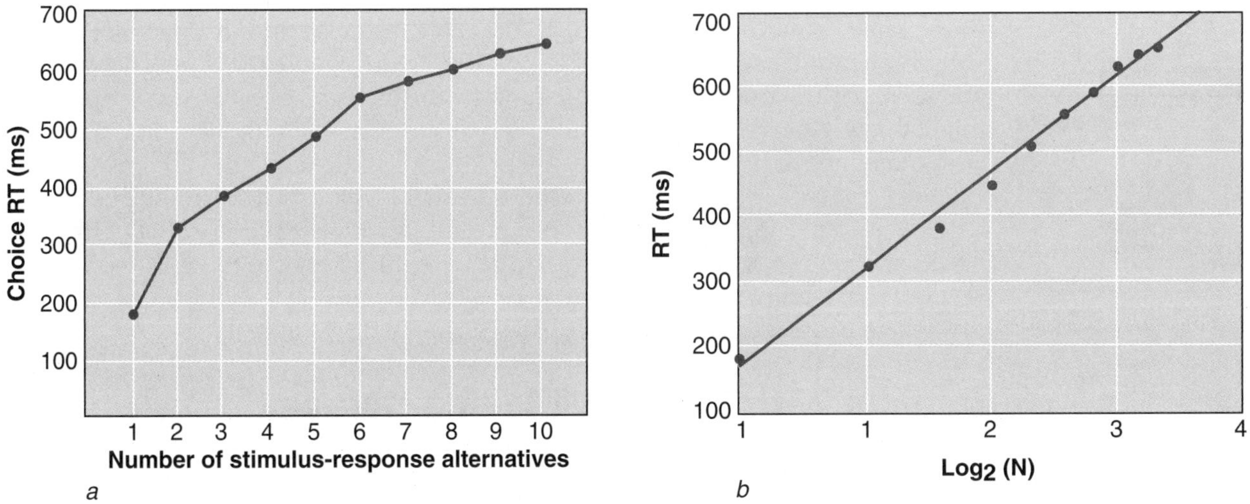

Figure 2.3 *(a)* The relationship between choice reaction time and the number of stimulus-response alternatives and *(b)* the linear relationship between choice reaction time and the $\log_2$ of the number of stimulus-response alternatives, which is the relationship known as Hick's law. (Adapted from Woodworth, 1938; data obtained by Merkel in 1885.)

Stimulus-Response Compatibility

stimulus-response (S-R) compatibility—The degree to which the relationship between a stimulus and an associated response is natural.

An important determinant of choice RT is **stimulus-response (S-R) compatibility**, usually defined as the "naturalness" of the connection between the stimulus and the associated response. For example, using the right hand rather than the left to respond to a stimulus to move right is more compatible because both the stimulus and the hand are moving in the same direction (to the right).

In the example shown in figure 2.4, the S-R pairs on the left (*a*) are more compatible than those on the right (*b*) because the location of the stimulus light and responding hand is the same (i.e., left with left and right with right). Research has clearly shown that for a given number of S-R choices, RT is faster the more compatible the S-R pairs. This faster choice RT presumably results from a more rapid information processing in the response-selection stage attributable to a more natural linkage between stimulus and response. The general rules regarding the relationship between the number of possible S-R pairs and choice RT (i.e., Hick's law) still apply here. However, the *amount* of increase in choice RT as the number of S-R choices increases is less when the pairs are compatible than when they are not.

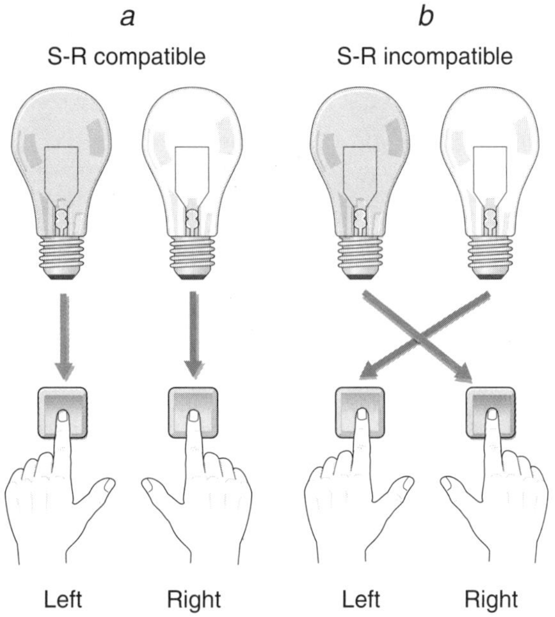

Figure 2.4 Stimulus-response compatibility. The relationship between stimulus and response is more natural, or compatible, in the situation on the left *(a)* than on the right *(b)*.

Practice

A highly practiced performer can overcome many things, including the disadvantage of more S-R choices and low S-R compatibility. The skilled sailboat racer almost instantly moves the tiller to the right as soon as it's obvious that the boat must be turned to the left. Research has shown that both the amount of practice and the nature of practice can affect choice RT. With extreme amounts of practice, high-level performers can produce reactions that approach automatic processing (see the section on automaticity later in this chapter); not only are these reactions very fast, but they are slowed down little, if at all, as the number of S-R choices increases.

In addition, practicing the same S-R combinations, that is, the same stimulus always leading to the same response, speeds up choice RT. We see this phenomenon quite often in sports like boxing where the experienced fighter knows which responses are most appropriate for the various punches an opponent might throw. Practice also makes a difference in everyday tasks like driving a car, where after thousands of hours of practice, the link between the red light and brake press is extremely natural and almost automatic. Research on experts in a variety of domains ranging from playing chess to playing a musical instrument suggests that performers need many years of systematic practice to achieve this level of automaticity (Ericsson, 1996). Thus, it is not unreasonable to presume that similar levels of practice are necessary when it comes to learning skills requiring rapid decision making.

Dealing With Decision-Making Delays

As we mentioned previously, a common way people cope with long decision-making delays is to anticipate the stimulus. Often, a highly skilled performer is able to determine what is going to happen and when it is going to happen *before* it happens. For example, the defensive lineman in football who detects something in an opponent's mannerisms that indicates a running play is about to occur reacts quickly and stops the play for a big loss. One reason the lineman is able to do this is because he can select and organize his response (using the second and third processing stages) *before* the ball is snapped.

The Eyes Have It

Defensive players in American football often look for regularities in the behaviors of their opponents in order to anticipate the upcoming play. Recently, a linebacker at the University of Tennessee said that his secret for making tackles for lost yardage was watching the eyes of his opponents. "Some offensive linemen look in the direction that the play is going," he said. "By watching their eyes, I'm able to anticipate the play and be ready for it." This is consistent with other laboratory findings showing that advance information is used to speed RT (e.g., Rosenbaum, 1980). Recent brain-wave research has also shown that advanced baseball batters recognize types of pitches faster than do intermediate-level batters (Radlo, Janelle, Barba, & Frehlich, 2001). It is likely that the more skilled batters' processing speed is a result of their extensive experience in watching and responding to different pitches, which improves their anticipation.

Experienced Athletes Can Detect Regularities in Their Opponents' Movements

Recent research by Ward, Williams, and Bennett (2002) suggests that experienced tennis players are able to speed up their preparation for an upcoming shot by watching their opponents' movements. In this study, experienced and inexperienced players observed a video of a life-sized model hitting forehand and backhand shots toward four locations on the court (left, right, center forecourt, center backcourt). The order of presentation of the various shots was randomized. On each trial, the participants' task was to move as quickly as possible in the direction they thought the shot was headed. Footpads were used to determine participants' RT (i.e., the time between when the visual sequence began and when a response was initiated). Experienced players had significantly faster decision times (i.e., RT) than their inexperienced counterparts. In addition, eye-movement recordings revealed that experienced players focused on different sources of movement information (i.e., head, shoulders, trunk, and hips of the model) than inexperienced players (i.e., racket, ball, and contact point). The findings suggest that experienced players focus on the movements of opposing players in order to anticipate the direction of their shots.

Because of their anticipation capabilities, skilled performers seem to behave almost as if they had all the time in the world; they do not appear rushed, in the manner of those who must react to an unanticipated event. Experiments have also shown that even beginning-level performers who are given advance information, or precues, about characteristics of an upcoming stimulus can reduce their choice RT. Researchers assume that this is the case because performers are able to organize their movements in advance by completing response-selection or response-programming activities *before* the stimulus is presented (Rosenbaum, 1980).

Types of Anticipation

Anticipation can be of two general types. First, it can involve a prediction about *what* will happen in the environment, such as the driver of a car who anticipates that another

UNIVERSITY OF WINCHESTER
LIBRARY

It Depends . . .

How Do Couples Avoid Collisions on a Crowded Dance Floor?

When swing dancers move around a crowded dance floor, how does the lead dancer help his partner avoid collisions with other couples? What types of information would the pair need to address in order to adjust their moves quickly? What types of dance situations might require effective anticipation? How might the pair prepare for these situations?

driver will turn in front of her. This type of anticipation is referred to as **spatial (or event) anticipation.** Predicting what will happen in the environment allows the driver to organize her movements in advance, so that if the event she is anticipating does occur, she is able to initiate the appropriate response more quickly (i.e., in a time far shorter than the usual RT). Also, in driving, the red signal light invariably follows the amber (which invariably follows the green), providing a strong basis for anticipating that one will have to apply the brakes in the near future. Research (Williams, Ward, Smeeton, & Allen, 2004) has revealed that beginning tennis players can improve their anticipation skills by watching and responding actively to an opponent's serve. Compared with control participants given technical instruction only, players in this study who were instructed to view the opponent's serve, or view and estimate the location of the serves, reduced their reaction times and increased their decision-making accuracy (i.e., determining whether the ball was coming to their left or right). These results suggest that with practice, learners were able to improve their event anticipation.

spatial (or event) anticipation—Predicting what is going to happen before the signal is presented.

temporal anticipation—Predicting when a signal to respond is going to happen or predicting the time-course of a sequence of events.

The other type of anticipation involves predicting *when* an environmental event will occur, such as anticipating the moment that the official will fire the starting gun in a swimming race or the moment a dropped object will hit the floor. This type of anticipation is known as **temporal anticipation.** Although it is always advantageous to know when some event will occur, it is probably even more important to anticipate what will happen so that the appropriate movements can be prepared in advance.

The quarterback and center respond simultaneously to the same signal.

Benefits of Anticipation

Either spatial or temporal anticipation can provide a strong advantage when performing many types of skills. However, if the person can correctly anticipate in both ways, the advantage becomes even greater. For example, in music, the orchestra leader often starts the music with a verbal 1-2-3-4 to set the timing and rhythm, and the orchestra members know that they are to begin playing on the next 1. Thus, the musicians can anticipate what is to be done (spatial anticipation) as well as when it is to be done (temporal anticipation), and this allows the group to begin playing at the same time in a coordinated fashion. This allows the orchestra to begin playing elegantly as a unit without rushing to do so.

The speed-up under conditions where the performer has both temporal and spatial anticipation is massive. Indeed, if you were to measure the reaction time from the presentation of the start signal (e.g., the second count of 1 in the previous orchestra example), you would find that the interval from the signal to the initiation of the performers' actions would be close to zero milliseconds, or it might even be slightly negative (where a performer moved a few milliseconds before the count of 1). This has also been found in the laboratory (Quesada & Schmidt, 1970). This should remind us that given the formal definition of RT as the interval from the presentation of a stimulus until the start of the response, reaction time does not really apply for the orchestra members in this situation, because the stimulus is anticipated and reaction processes occur in advance.

Costs of Anticipation

Although there are several advantages to anticipation, there are costs as well. One disadvantage occurs when the anticipated signal, for some reason, does not occur at all, such as in a sprint start when the starter decides to withhold the start signal. In this case, the anticipated response might be triggered anyway, resulting in a false start.

Here's another example. Suppose that while a driver is waiting to turn left at a busy intersection, the signal light turns yellow. This might cause the driver to initiate his left turn in front of an approaching driver, anticipating that the other driver will stop. However, if the approaching driver sees the yellow light and decides to enter the intersection while the light is yellow, a collision is likely. Clearly, anticipating correctly can result in benefits, but anticipating incorrectly can be clumsy, costly, and sometimes even disastrous.

We have discussed the notion that anticipating allows various information-processing activities to take place in advance of stimulus presentation. Suppose, though, that a person has gone through these preparatory processes, but then the events in the environment change, indicating that the prepared movement will be incorrect. First the person must inhibit, or "unprepare," the movement, which takes time, of course. Estimates from studies indicate that even very simple actions require somewhere around 40 ms to be stopped (Schmidt & Gordon, 1977). Then the person must organize and initiate the correct movement, requiring the additional activity of one or more information-processing stages. By the time she does all of this, the opportunity for advantage has usually passed.

The situation becomes even worse if the person begins the incorrect movement and it is headed in the wrong direction. In that case she would have to reverse the momentum of her body, which would also take time. For example, a squash player might anticipate that her opponent is going to hit to the left side of the court, and so she begins to move in that direction as the shot is made. Should the shot actually go to the right side of the court, it would be virtually impossible for the anticipating player to reverse direction and reach, much less return, the shot.

Correctly anticipating the actions of an opponent can benefit performance, but incorrectly anticipating can be costly.

Strategies for Preventing Anticipation

The potential gains and losses associated with correct and incorrect anticipations give rise to important strategic elements in many rapid sport activities. For example, athletes who want to discourage their opponents from anticipating try to produce movements that are unpredictable with respect to both spatial and temporal components. Once the opponent realizes that the costs of anticipating outweigh the benefits, he is forced to switch to a strategy that requires waiting for the movement to occur and using the slower stages of information processing to prepare a response. In the laboratory, we often attempt to prevent research participants from anticipating by using so-called catch trials, where the stimulus does not occur; if the participant does not respond, we can be reasonably sure that he or she is waiting for the stimulus and not anticipating it.

This can also be used in real-world situations. One way of preventing opponents from anticipating is randomization—keeping one's movements unpredictable so that the opponent is prevented from anticipating them. Another strategy is to lure the opponent into an anticipation that can then be used against her. A netball player who moves as if she is going to pass the ball in one direction might tempt her opponent to anticipate the pass and try to intercept it. However, if the anticipated pass turns out to be a fake followed by an actual pass in another direction, the opponent's attempt would be foiled. Conversely, while driving in traffic we want to act predictably, allowing other drivers to predict our actions so that they can make appropriate decisions. In driving, being unpredictable is asking for trouble, because other drivers might falsely anticipate what you are going to do, resulting in a collision.

Types of anticipation

- Spatial or event anticipation
- Temporal anticipation

Factors influencing reaction time and decision making

- Number of stimulus–response alternatives
- Practice
- Stimulus–response compatibility

Advantages and disadvantages

- If correct, response is faster
- If incorrect, response is slower, in error, or both

Figure 2.5 Factors influencing reaction time and decision making.

In figure 2.5, we summarize the factors influencing reaction time and decision making and indicate the advantages and disadvantages of spatial (or event) anticipation.

Information Processing Under Various Time Constraints

Up to now we have discussed information processing as it occurs under speeded conditions. However, many types of tasks take place in situations where time constraints are minimal or nonexistent. For example, the golfer has virtually unlimited time to examine the lie of the ball, the course conditions, and relevant environmental information (stimulus identification) before deciding which club to use and where to hit the ball (response selection). Once these tasks have been completed, the golfer's challenge is to prepare the desired swing (response programming). Here again, however, the golfer has practically all the time he needs to complete that task. Thus, when estimating the information-processing demands of various tasks, keep in mind the amount of time available to complete the processing.

It's also important to identify the more essential processing stages for tasks. In table 2.1, we present three tasks and situations varying in both the amount of time performers have to complete information processing and the stage of processing that is most essential to performance success.

Table 2.1 The Primary Information-Processing Demands of Three Different Tasks

		Primary information processing demand		
Task	Time available	Stimulus identification	Response selection	Response programming
Blocking a punch	100 ms	X		
Fielding a bunt	2-3 s		X	
Performing surgery	30-60 min			X

As you can imagine, blocking a punch thrown by an opponent in taekwondo must be completed in a very short time. The greatest processing challenge is in the stimulus identification stage, where the performer must identify correctly where the punch is coming from and where it is headed. Once that information is perceived, the performer must make a decision and prepare an appropriate response.

In the baseball example, the pitcher fielding a bunt has only a second or so to decide what to do. Stimulus-identification demands are relatively minor because the ball is coming directly toward him. However, the pitcher could make various decisions depending on the game situation (e.g., the score), so response-selection demands are quite high. Once the pitcher selects the response, all he needs to do is prepare the throwing action.

In the final example, the surgeon performing a complex operation has considerable time to prepare for each incision. She has minimal stimulus-identification and response-selection demands because the environment remains constant and fixed and the surgical procedure is one she has selected in advance. Her greatest demand is preparing each movement competently to enhance the prospects of a successful procedure.

Finally, although the primary information-processing demands of the tasks shown in table 2.1 occur in just one of the stages, there are many tasks for which processing demands exist in various combinations of the stages depending on the situation. For example, an aircraft pilot may face various levels of stimulus-identification, response-selection, and response-programming demands depending on the specific procedure he is attempting (taking off vs. landing).

INFORMATION PROCESSING UNDER CONDITIONS OF HIGH AND LOW AROUSAL AND ANXIETY

Arousal and anxiety are common aspects of many performance situations. **Arousal** refers to the level of activation or excitement of a person's central nervous system, whereas **anxiety** deals more with the way the person interprets a particular situation and the resulting emotions associated with that interpretation. If the person believes that the demands of the situation exceed her capability for meeting them, then she will probably perceive that situation to be threatening and experience more anxiety, particularly if she perceives the outcome to be important. Arousal levels can fluctuate for many reasons that have nothing to do with perceptions of threat (e.g., moving from a sitting to a standing position, attending a friend's wedding, seeing a beautiful sunset). However, changes in anxiety levels are always accompanied by changes in arousal (i.e., increased anxiety brings an increase in arousal).

arousal—
The level of activation of the central nervous system; varies from extremely low levels during sleep to extremely high levels during intense physical and/or mental activity.

anxiety—
A person's uneasiness or distress about future uncertainties; a perception of threat to the self (often characterized by elevated arousal levels).

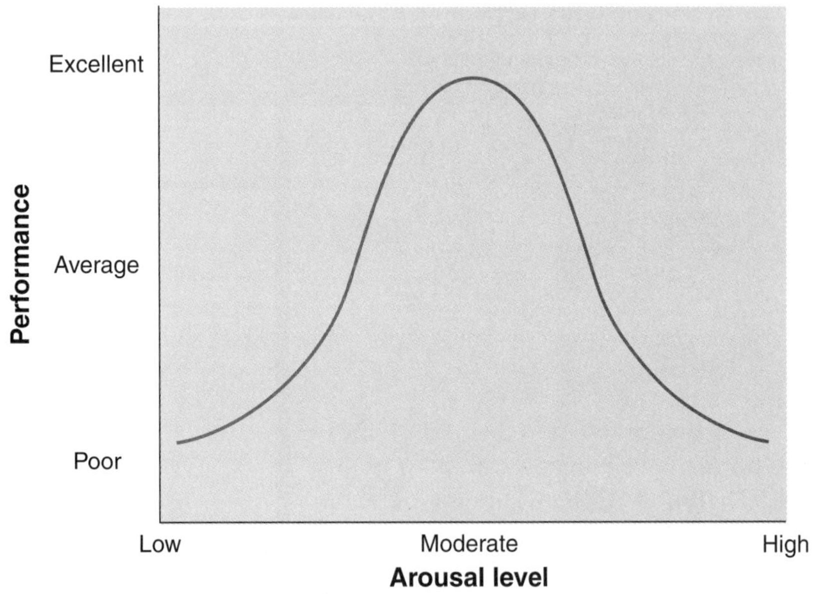

Figure 2.6 The inverted-U principle. Increased arousal improves performance only to a point, after which further increases in arousal degrade performance.

Both of these phenomena are a routine part of many everyday life events (e.g., taking exams, giving a speech, interviewing for a job) and most competitive athletic contests, where the pressure to win and the threat of losing are important sources of emotional arousal and anxiety for participants. The level of arousal imposed by a situation is an important determinant of performance, particularly if the performance depends on fast and accurate decision making. In this section we examine some of the effects of various levels of arousal and stress on information-processing activities and suggest some ways that performance can be enhanced under these conditions.

Inverted-U Principle

People's arousal (i.e., the level of excitement or activation generated in the central nervous system) can vary from low levels associated with almost sleeplike states to high levels associated with states of agitation and extreme alertness. Patients with damage to the reticular formation in the brain stem often experience difficulties associated with unpredictable shifts in arousal levels. The influence of arousal level on performance has been studied for many years, with the weight of the evidence supporting the **inverted-U principle**. This principle (illustrated by the shape of the curve in figure 2.6) states that increases in arousal (assuming that arousal is initially at a low level) are accompanied by increases in performance, but only to a point, with performance usually peaking at some intermediate level of arousal. If arousal continues to increase beyond that level, performance begins to be degraded.

inverted-U principle—Describes the relationship between arousal level and performance; as arousal level increases, performance improves—but only to a point. If arousal continues to increase, performance begins to be degraded.

trait anxiety—A person's general disposition to perceive situations as threatening.

The inverted-U principle might seem surprising to many people involved with sport and coaching who generally assume that the higher the athlete's level of arousal (or motivation), the more effective that athlete's performance will be. Some coaches use pep talks to raise their team's arousal level before competitions, and we often hear sportscasters argue that a team's performance was poor because the players were not "fired up" (i.e., aroused) for the game. Yet, this general view is contradicted by considerable experimental evidence showing that, depending on the task and other factors, performance is degraded when arousal levels are extremely high.

Perhaps the best way to determine the optimal level of arousal for task performance is to consider again the three factors we talked about in chapter 1. There, we emphasized the role of the person, the task, and the environment (Wrisberg, 1994). First there is the person. Simply put, people differ with respect to their normal range of arousal and the extent to which they perceive situations to be threatening (referred to as **trait anxiety**). Low-trait-anxious people rarely find situations threatening, whereas high-trait-anxious people perceive some level of threat in most situations. Not surprisingly, high-trait-anxious people tend to be more susceptible to further increases in arousal than those who are low-trait-anxious. Moreover, recent theoretical discussions and experimental testing suggest that different people perform best at different levels of arousal; also, the range of arousal associated with an individual's maximum performance differs from person to person. These depictions of arousal, which have been variously described as the **individual zone of optimal functioning** (Hanin, 1980) and the **individual affect-related performance zone** (Edmonds, Mann, Tenenbaum, & Janelle, 2006), can be added to the list of individual-difference factors (i.e., differences among individuals) we discuss in chapter 6 (see table 6.1). Therefore, it appears that the goal of each individual should be to achieve his or her own zone of optimal arousal to enhance the prospects of performance success.

Second, there is the nature of the task. If the task requires fine muscular control (as in archery or brain surgery) or contains important decision-making components (as in playing goalie in ice hockey or in piloting an airplane), then a lower level of arousal is probably needed for maximum performance (Weinberg & Hunt, 1976). On the other hand, skills that are dominated by large muscle actions, with little or no fine motor control required (such as powerlifting or lumberjacking), or that have a low level of cognitive complexity (such as sprinting in track or swimming) are performed more successfully at relatively higher levels of arousal. Figure 2.7 presents arousal–performance curves that consider the possible influence of task requirements. We show in this figure three tasks that differ with respect to type of motor control (fine, moderate, gross) and level of cognitive complexity (complex, moderate, simple). As you can see, a task like piano playing that requires a great degree of fine motor (i.e., small muscle) control and more complex cognitive demands is generally performed more effectively when the arousal level of the participant is lower (as in the curve on the left). However, as control of the task becomes more gross motor in

zone of optimal functioning—
The range of arousal levels associated with a person's maximum performance.

individual affect-related performance zone—
The emotional reaction of individual performers in various competitive situations.

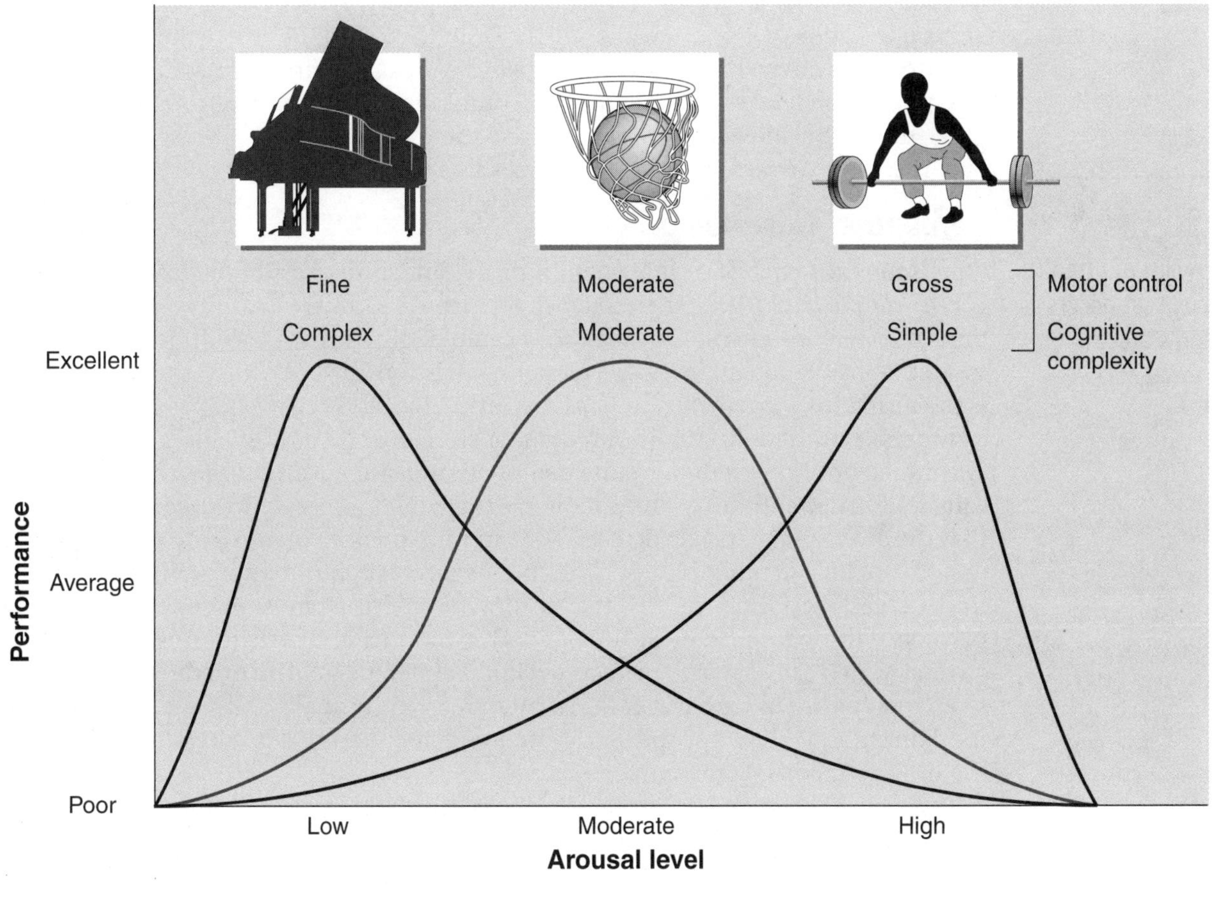

Figure 2.7 The inverted-U principle for various tasks. Optimal arousal level is higher for simpler tasks with more gross motor control.

nature (i.e., larger muscles) and cognitive complexity is moderate to simple (e.g., shooting a basketball, lifting a heavy weight), the optimal level of arousal required for successful performance generally becomes higher (as in the curves at the center and right of the figure).

Finally, there is the environment or, perhaps more accurately, the person's perception of the environment. As mentioned earlier, anxiety levels increase when a person perceives a situation to be threatening. In this case, if the person perceives that environmental demands exceed his capability to meet those demands, he will experience increased anxiety and an accompanying increase in arousal level. Conversely, if the person perceives that he is easily capable of meeting the challenge, his anxiety (and arousal) level will be lower.

Only when practitioners consider all three of these factors (person, task, environment) can they assist people in achieving the level of arousal that is optimal for task performance. The relationship between arousal and performance and the factors that influence this relationship have received considerable attention from researchers as well as practitioners in applied sport psychology. Their goal is to assist athletes in preparing for high-level performance by teaching them ways to adjust their arousal levels optimally to meet task requirements (Landers & Arent, 2006; Orlick, 1986, 2000). As a result, various arousal-adjustment techniques have been developed and are being practiced by many top athletes.

Information Processing Under High Arousal

During a 50 m sprint in his first big meet, a high school swimmer with a very high arousal level does a flip turn while still 3 m (10 ft) short of the end of the pool, leaving him treading water while the other competitors make the turn and finish the race. This swimmer's high level of arousal probably contributed to his faulty performance. Among other things, heightened arousal can affect the way performers process information. In this section we discuss some of the ways this happens.

Perceptual Narrowing

perceptual narrowing—The narrowing of attentional focus that occurs as a person's arousal level increases.

One important change in information processing under conditions of high arousal is **perceptual narrowing**, the tendency for people to miss certain types of information in the environment. Consider, for example, the stressful task of deep-sea diving to accomplish ship repairs (e.g., Weltman & Egstrom, 1966). When the novice diver is practicing his movements on land, his arousal level is relatively low and he is able to process a number of stimuli simultaneously. However, if he attempts his dives in a swimming pool or, even more threatening, the ocean, his arousal increases dramatically and his attention becomes more narrowly and intensely focused. The result is that the diver systematically detects fewer stimuli, missing many in the periphery; the majority of his attention is directed to those sources of information that are most pertinent to task performance (e.g., the location of objects he must manipulate or diving partners with whom he must interact). This narrowing of attention with increased arousal, which can also occur when a person is under the influence of drugs or suffering sleep loss (police officers under threat often refer to "tunnel vision"), is an important mechanism that allows people to devote more attention to stimulus sources that are the most immediately relevant.

Perceptual narrowing has its drawbacks, particularly under conditions of very high arousal. According to Easterbrook (1959), high arousal can produce an extreme narrowing of visual attention and a fixed gaze that causes performers to miss relevant stimuli (we discuss this phenomenon in more detail in the next section). However, more recent research indicates that high arousal can induce distractions as well. In one study (Janelle, Singer, & Williams, 1999), the performance of drivers was found to be impaired when they were anxious. Specific effects included a shift of attention from central (i.e., the road) to peripheral (e.g., surrounding objects and events) locations, more erratic eye movements, and slower RT. Regardless of the specific mechanisms for impaired performance under conditions of high arousal, it appears that performers who must continually monitor central and peripheral cues need to be aware of the influence of increased arousal on perceptual processes and take appropriate measures to reduce the prospects of impaired performance.

Cue-Utilization Hypothesis

Easterbrook's (1959) cue-utilization hypothesis helps explain the common performance decrements that occur under conditions of low and high arousal. When arousal level is low, the perceptual field is relatively wide and the person has access to a large number of cues. However, because only a few of these cues are relevant to the task at hand, the performer may detect some irrelevant cues and miss some of the relevant ones, resulting in suboptimal performance. As the performer's arousal level rises, though, attentional focus narrows onto the most relevant cues as more and more of the competing irrelevant cues are excluded. Therefore, proficiency improves because the performer is now mainly responding to relevant cues. However, with further increases in arousal and perceptual narrowing, the performer begins to miss important relevant cues, particularly those that are unexpected or in the periphery, so performance suffers. According to the cue-utilization hypothesis, an optimal level of arousal is one that produces an attentional focus narrow enough to exclude many irrelevant cues yet broad enough to pick up the most important and relevant ones.

cue-utilization hypothesis—An explanation for performance decrements under conditions of low and high arousal; perceptual narrowing under high arousal causes relevant cues in the periphery to be missed.

At the highest levels of arousal, we find a state of hypervigilance that is commonly referred to as "panic." When inexperienced drivers lose control of their vehicles on an icy road, they often panic, applying the brakes and freezing at the wheel, even when they know this is the wrong thing to do. They freeze because their decision-making ability is severely limited by an extreme perceptual narrowing and several other factors. Such a condition also degrades the physical control of movements, causing actions that are normally performed in a smooth and flowing manner under more relaxed circumstances to be stiff and halting (Weinberg & Hunt, 1976). Although hypervigilant states are relatively rare, it is not uncommon to see them in youth sports (for coaches as well as athletes!), particularly during important and close competitions. Regrettably, the winner of such contests is usually the athlete or team that doesn't perform poorly rather than the one that performs better.

Techniques for Managing Arousal Levels

Williams and Harris (2006) provided a comprehensive discussion of the two major categories of relaxation and energizing techniques that people can use to regulate their arousal levels. The first category includes so-called muscle-to-mind skills, which focus on the bodily aspects of arousal and in so doing clear the mind as well. Most notable of these are breathing exercises and progressive relaxation techniques. The latter involve a brief initial contraction of selected muscles (to illustrate what muscle tension feels like) followed by relaxation. After some practice, people can delete the contraction phase to achieve adjustments more quickly. The second category of arousal-regulation techniques includes mind-to-muscle skills, which induce relaxation or activation of the body by means of cognitive activity. The most often used skills in this category are meditation and visualization. Meditation is primarily used as a relaxation technique and involves easy breathing and a passive focus of attention on something that is relaxing, such as the words *calm* or *warm*. Visualization is used to decrease or increase arousal by creating a mental picture of either a relaxing or an energizing scene, such as lying on the beach or running from an angry bull. In chapter 8 we discuss some other ways movement practitioners can assist individuals in managing their arousal level.

muscle-to-mind skills—Techniques for regulating arousal that use somatic activity (e.g., rhythmic breathing, muscle relaxation) to relax or energize the mind.

mind-to-muscle skills—Techniques for regulating arousal that use cognitive activity (e.g., meditation, visualization) to relax or energize the muscles.

attention—
A limited mental resource, or a capacity to process information.

ATTENTIONAL CAPACITY: A LIMITATION TO INFORMATION PROCESSING

A very old and enduring idea in psychology is that people have a limited capacity to process information from the environment or to attend to more than one or two things at a time. In this section we discuss how the concept of **attention** is related to information-processing capabilities and can limit motor performance.

A performer in a spelling bee is about to spell an important word, when a baby crying in the crowd of spectators suddenly distracts him. The sound is distracting because it enters the speller's attentional space, which can handle only a limited amount of information. The baby's crying has barged in and begins to interfere with other information that is more relevant to the task of spelling the required word. Because attentional space is limited in capacity, the crying may even replace some of the relevant information temporarily. Unable to rectify the situation, the speller attempts the word anyway, misspells it, and is eliminated from the competition.

Not only is attentional capacity limited, but it also seems to be sequential in nature in that we usually focus first on one thing, then on another; and only with great difficulty (if at all) on two things at the same time. We all know what it's like to be accused of not paying attention to someone who is trying to talk to us while we are attending to something else. Sometimes factory workers attend to external sensory events (a colleague's voice), sometimes they focus on internal mental operations (the next action they will make), and sometimes they pay attention to internal sensory information (the feel their own movements). It is very difficult for most people to try to process more than one of these sources of information at a time (e.g., driving a car while talking on a cell phone).

Figure 2.8 shows how the fixed amount (or capacity) of attentional space (illustrated by the large circles) might be devoted to the performance of a primary task and a secondary task. When the primary task is relatively simple (see figure 2.8*a)*, it requires less attention than when it is more complex (see figure 2.8*b)*, leaving more attention for performance of the secondary task.

limited attentional capacity—
The notion that attention is limited to at most a few activities at any one time.

This notion of **limited attentional capacity** is very important to our understanding of high-level skilled performance. At the moment of skill execution there is usually an abundance of available information that could occupy performers' attention and be processed. Some of the information is relevant to performance, and some of it is not (the sound of the baby's crying). The performer's challenge is to manage the attentional space by making the right kinds of decisions about which information will be attended. Performers must also be able to *shift* attention skillfully among pertinent information in the environment, decisions about future actions, feedback from ongoing movements, and many other things.

Managing the Challenges of Information Processing

In this section we examine some ways individuals are able to process information more effectively despite their inherently limited attentional capacity. To understand the challenge they face, we need to review again the stages of information processing shown in figure 2.2 and consider possible sources of competition for available attentional resources. However, the existing research suggests that performers are sometimes able to meet this challenge in interesting ways. As you will see in the following sections, the ways they do this differ in the various stages of processing.

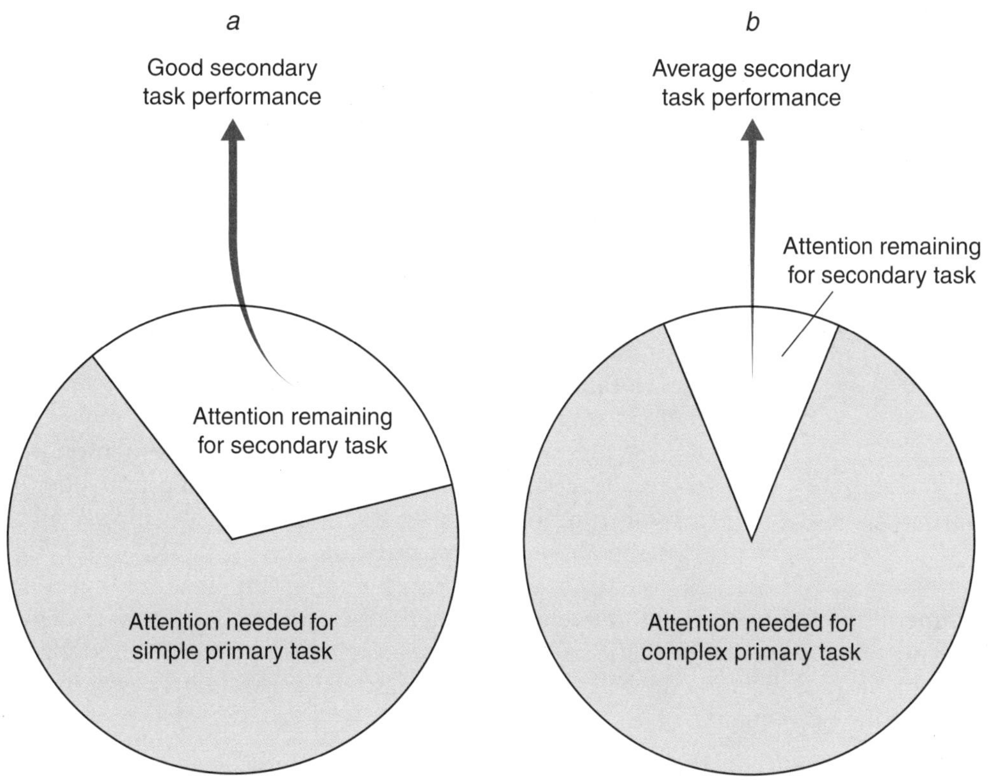

Figure 2.8 The available attention remaining for a secondary task is greater when the primary task is simple *(a)* than when it is complex *(b)*.

parallel processing—A type of information processing that allows people to handle two or more streams of information at the same time; usually occurs during the stimulus-identification stage.

Stroop effect—Competition between the response to color word (e.g., maroon) and the ink color in which it is presented; this effect shows that two stimuli (word form and word color) can be processed simultaneously, probably in the stimulus-identification stage (Stroop, 1935).

Stimulus Identification: Information Processing in Parallel

Quite a bit of research evidence suggests that several streams of information can be processed at the same time in the stimulus-identification stage without competing for available space. This type of processing is referred to as **parallel processing** because various types of information are processed simultaneously, in parallel. For example, the color and shape of objects in a visual display can be processed at the same time. Support for this notion has chiefly come from laboratory studies using an interesting test called the Stroop task (Stroop, 1935). Participants are presented with a series of visual stimuli printed in colored ink (e.g., maroon or black) on a white background. The stimuli consist of either irrelevant geometric forms or words that are the names of colors (see figure 2.9). Participants are told that as soon as the stimulus appears, they must identify the *ink color* as quickly as possible and ignore the *form* of the stimulus. In the example shown in figure 2.9, participants would press one key if the color were maroon and another if it were black. These studies consistently show that RT is longer when the stimuli are in the form of names of colors (as on the right side of figure 2.9) than when they are in the form of irrelevant objects or symbols (as on the left side). These results, referred to as the **Stroop effect**, suggest that two stimuli—the ink color in which the word is printed (e.g., black, maroon) and the name of the word (e.g., MAROON)—are processed together (i.e., in parallel) during the stimulus-identification stage. Because the RT is longer for the color names than for irrelevant forms, it is assumed that the

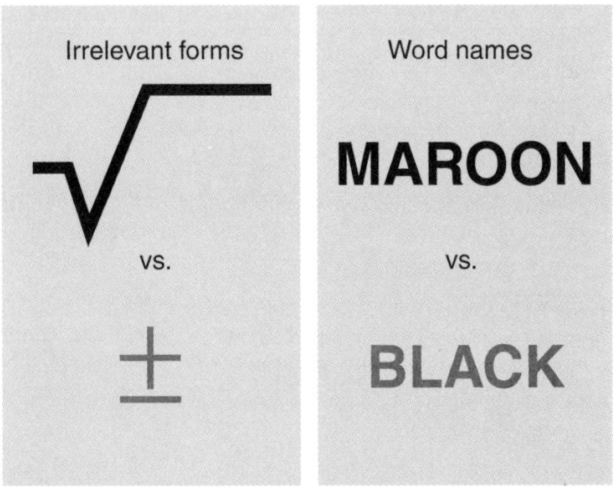

Figure 2.9 The Stroop effect. When ink color and form of stimulus conflict, reaction time to name the ink color is slowed.

competition for attentional resources occurs later, during the response-selection stage when individuals must decide which key to press—the one corresponding to the ink color or to the word. The idea is that when the word *maroon* is printed in black ink, two associated responses compete, and extra time is required to resolve the conflict.

Similar findings have been reported in studies showing that separate auditory messages delivered to the two ears can be processed together, even though one message is usually ignored intentionally. The standard view, then, is that sensory information can be processed in parallel during the stimulus-identification stage. Therefore, the attention required for the performance of two separate, but simultaneous, movement tasks is presumed to act in one of the later information-processing stages. For example, the soccer goalie may identify several stimuli simultaneously (e.g., the voices of spectators; thoughts about the game situation; and the sight of teammates, opponents, and an approaching shot) but does not experience competition for attention until he selects a response (e.g., to catch the ball, to deflect the ball over the goal, to head the ball toward a teammate) or produces simultaneous movements (e.g., heading the ball toward a teammate while avoiding a collision with an onrushing opponent).

Response Selection: Controlled and Automatic Processing

Competition between tasks is never more obvious than when a person tries to perform two actions requiring different mental operations simultaneously, such as dribbling a soccer ball while answering a coach's question or steering a car and talking on the cell phone. Some researchers believe that processing activities such as these take place during the response-selection stage via the competition among several choices. This type of processing is slow; attention demanding; sequential, occurring before or after other processing tasks; and voluntary, easily halted or avoided altogether. As a result,

Walking and Talking Can Be Dangerous

Recent research suggests that walking and talking on a cell phone can be dangerous (Hatfield & Murphy, 2007). In that study, the behaviors of more than 500 pedestrians were observed as they crossed a street. Pedestrians who were talking on a cell phone moved more slowly and were less likely to wait for cars to stop or even look at traffic before setting out compared with those who were not using a cell phone. These findings suggest that talking on a cell phone is a form of cognitive distraction that can put pedestrians at risk. These phenomena have also been demonstrated recently in studies about cell phones and driving (see Strayer, Drews, & Johnston, 2003). It is not simply the button-pressing that is distracting; the conversation itself is distracting—especially when you consider that button-pressing is brief and conversation may be lengthy. This casts doubts about the effectiveness of the recent bans on handheld cell phones (but not hands-free phones) while driving in various U.S. states; because it is not only the action of the hands that is distracting, these bans might not have very much effect on driver safety.

it is often referred to as **controlled processing**. Controlled processing is relatively effortful because it involves several separate information-processing activities. This is particularly so for tasks that are poorly learned or completely new to performers. Having to deal with two tasks at the same time, both of which require controlled processing, can create an information overload and disrupt a person's performance at one or the other (or both) of the tasks.

controlled processing— A type of information processing that is slow, sequential, attention demanding, and voluntary; it is more prevalent during the early stages of learning.

In contrast to this tedious form of controlled processing, another, very different, kind of processing is seen in the performance of highly practiced people. When asked to describe his thought process during gymnastics competition, Peter Vidmar, a 1984 Olympic silver medalist, said that he paid attention only to the first move (trick) in his routine; the remainder of the elements occurred almost automatically. Because the remaining elements required only minor adjustments while being run off, Vidmar was able to use his attentional resources to focus on the higher-order aspects of his routine, such as style and form. Clearly, his approach to this complex gymnastics routine is fundamentally different from the type of controlled processing mentioned previously. In contrast to controlled processing, **automatic processing** is fast; does not demand attention, in that there is very little interference or competition for attention among tasks; occurs in parallel, with several tasks performed simultaneously; and is involuntary, often unavoidable.

automatic processing— A type of information processing that is fast, parallel, not attention demanding, and often involuntary; it is more prevalent in the later stages of learning.

Highly automatic processing is thought to be the result of an enormous amount of practice. Your capability to recognize collections of letters quickly, as in the words you are reading in this sentence, has come from years of practice, as did Vidmar's capability to produce his entire gymnastics routine by focusing only on the first move. Thus, the effectiveness of automatic processing has strong implications for everyday tasks (like reading) as well as for the high-level performance of motor skills like operating an earth-moving machine and performing a complex gymnastics routine.

Although we have given the impression that these two kinds of information-processing activities are clear and distinct, many scientists believe that they simply represent the polar ends of a continuum. If so, then with more practice a task becomes increasingly automatic for the performer, meaning that the performance is somewhat less like purely controlled processing and more like purely automatic processing.

Production Units

One explanation for automatic processing is that with practice, a person develops a series of small, specialized **production units** to handle particular information-processing subtasks. Thus, when a specific stimulus is encountered, a production unit is activated to generate the appropriate output. For example, after much practice, high-level volleyball players, using automatic processing, are able to recognize their opponents' movement patterns that signal the direction and type of an upcoming shot, such as a spike to the left side of the court (e.g., see Allard & Burnett, 1985). The production units operate on these patterns and produce an immediate, automatic, internal decision to execute a blocking movement to the left. Once this decision is activated, the response (i.e., the block) is prepared in the response-programming stage.

production units— Units, developed with practice, that allow skilled performers to handle certain information-processing tasks automatically (i.e., without attention).

Costs Versus Benefits of Automaticity

Automaticity allows people to process information in parallel, quickly, and without competition from other information. But what if the volleyball opponents in the previous example produced movement patterns that usually accompany a spike to the left—and then executed a play that went to the right? On this occasion, the defender's automatic processing of the pattern would lead to a quick decision and response (i.e., a block), but it would fail to achieve the desired goal because the actual spike was hit to the right.

Clearly, then, automatic processing has its drawbacks as well as its benefits. Although very fast processing is advantageous for people performing in environments that are stable and predictable, it can lead to inappropriate responses and errors in environments (or against opponents) that produce different, unexpected actions at the last moment. Thus, automatic movements would appear to be relatively more effective for closed skills than for open skills.

Practicing for Automaticity

How do people develop the capability to process information automatically? Practice, and lots of it, is a very important ingredient, so we should not expect automatic processing to come quickly. Practicing for automaticity is generally more effective under conditions involving **consistent stimulus-response mapping**, that is, where the stimulus pattern always calls for the same response. For example, a red signal light always prompts a braking response. This type of mapping is different from a **varied stimulus-response mapping** condition, where a particular stimulus calls for different responses in different situations. For example, when a driver on a residential street sees a car backing from a driveway, it is not clear which of several responses should be made, and the proper one will depend on the situation. To develop automaticity in responding in situations with varied mapping, performers would need extensive practice in a wide variety of situations.

consistent stimulus-response mapping—A performance condition for which a given stimulus pattern always requires the same response.

varied stimulus-response mapping—A performance condition for which a given stimulus pattern requires different responses in different situations.

Response Programming: Sequential Movement Organization

A fencer moves the foil toward her opponent's shoulder but then quickly alters the direction of the movement and contacts the opponent's waist instead. The opponent's response is delayed because of the fencer's first move (i.e., the fake toward the shoulder), and she loses the point. This example suggests that some sort of competition for attention can occur in the response-selection (or perhaps the response-programming) stages (Pashler, 1993, 1994). Much of the support for this notion comes from laboratory research using a **double-stimulation paradigm**. In these experiments, participants are required to respond (usually by lifting their index fingers off buttons) to each of two stimuli presented very close together in time (usually no more than a few tenths of a second apart). This situation is in many ways analogous to the problem by the opponent in the previous scenario, who responded to the first move (the fake) and then had to adjust to the second move (the thrust).

double-stimulation paradigm—A research design requiring separate reactions to two different stimuli presented together closely in time.

Double-Stimulation Paradigm: Psychological Refractory Period

In a typical double-stimulation study, participants are asked to respond to a tone (stimulus 1) by lifting the right index finger from a key and respond to a light (stimulus 2) by lifting the left index finger. The separation between the onsets of the tone and the light, called the **interstimulus interval (ISI)**, might range from zero seconds (for simultaneous presentation) to a few hundred milliseconds (a few tenths of a second), and this is usually unpredictable for the performer. Regardless of the length of the ISI, participants are instructed to respond to both stimuli as quickly as possible. In these studies, psychologists are usually interested in the RT to the second stimulus (RT2) for different lengths of ISI.

interstimulus interval (ISI)—The length of time separating the onsets of two stimuli in a double-stimulation paradigm.

The general findings from this research are depicted in figure 2.10, where RT2 (i.e., RT to the second stimulus) is shown for different lengths of ISI. The black horizontal line (control RT2) represents the RT of participants to the second stimulus when it is not preceded by the first stimulus. When both stimuli are presented, the longest RT2 occurs when the interval between the two is about 50 to 60 ms in length; when this happens, RT2 can be more than twice as long as the control RT2. As the ISI increases, RT2 decreases, but it still is longer than the control RT2 even when the ISI reaches 200 ms or more. These results clearly show that the processing of a second stimulus is seriously delayed when it occurs soon after a first stimulus.

This delay in responding to the second of two closely spaced stimuli is known as the psychological refractory period (PRP). Apparently, in situations where two stimuli are presented unexpectedly closely together in time, the system takes in the first stimulus and begins to select and then to generate a response to it. Then, when the second stimulus is presented, the system is already processing the first stimulus, and interference with the second stimulus-response pair occurs. The current understanding is that there is a temporary bottleneck in the response-selection or response-programming stage, or both (Pashler, 1993, 1994), because in these stages only one action can be selected (response selection) or organized and initiated (response programming) at a time, as diagrammed in figure 2.11. Any other action (such as the organization and initiation of a response to the second stimulus) must wait until the preparation of the first response is completed. This delay is longest when the ISI is very short (approximately 50-60 ms) because at this point the response-selection stage has just begun to select a response to the first stimulus; this selection must run its course before a second response can be selected. As the ISI increases, more preparation of the first response has been completed by the time stimulus 2 arrives, so there is less delay in preparing the second response.

psychological refractory period (PRP)— The delay in a person's reaction time to the second of two closely spaced stimuli compared with the person's reaction time to the second stimulus presented by itself.

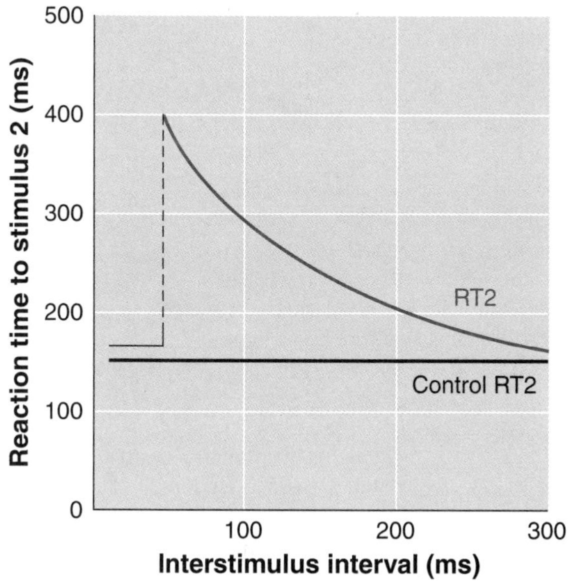

Figure 2.10 The psychological refractory period effect. Reaction time to the second of two closely spaced stimuli (RT2) is delayed, depending on the interstimulus interval.

One more phenomenon is of interest here. When the ISI is extremely short, say, less than 40 ms, the system responds in a very different way, producing both responses at the same time, as if the two stimuli were one. This grouping of responses presumably occurs because both stimuli are detected as a single event that produces the organization and initiation of a single, more complicated response of both limbs at the same time.

The Fake in Sports: Capitalizing on the PRP

Earlier in this chapter we talked about strategies for minimizing opponents' anticipation in open skills. For example, basketball players often fake a shot shortly before actually shooting the ball. Overly enthusiastic defensive players will often try to block the first shot (i.e., the fake), putting themselves out of position to stop the actual shot that follows.

The phenomenon of the PRP offers a good explanation for why a fake followed soon after by an actual movement is such a successful strategy. In the basketball example, the player with the ball plans a single, relatively complex action that involves making a shooting movement (the fake) followed closely by the actual movement (i.e., the shot). The performer organizes this sequence as a single unit, as he would any other movement in the response-programming stage.

A faked movement followed closely in time by an actual movement can lure an opponent into an incorrect anticipation.

However, the defender assumes that the first part of the sequence, the fake, is in fact the shot. The fake, then, is analogous to the first stimulus in a double-stimulation paradigm that triggers the first response (i.e., in this case the attempted block). As the defensive player is executing this response, the second stimulus (i.e., the shot) occurs—and he is unable to adjust in time to stop it.

Some important principles of faking in sports have emerged from research examining the PRP. First, for the fake to be effective, it must look realistic and be perceived as the expected movement (e.g., the shot), so that the opposing player responds to it. Second, the single action sequence that contains both the fake and the shot must be planned and executed in such a way as to separate the first movement (fake) and the second (shot) by a sufficient amount of time (i.e., ISI) to delay the defender's response to the shot. The available research data indicate that this time is somewhere around 50 to 60 ms (see again figure 2.11). If the ISI is shorter than that, the defensive player

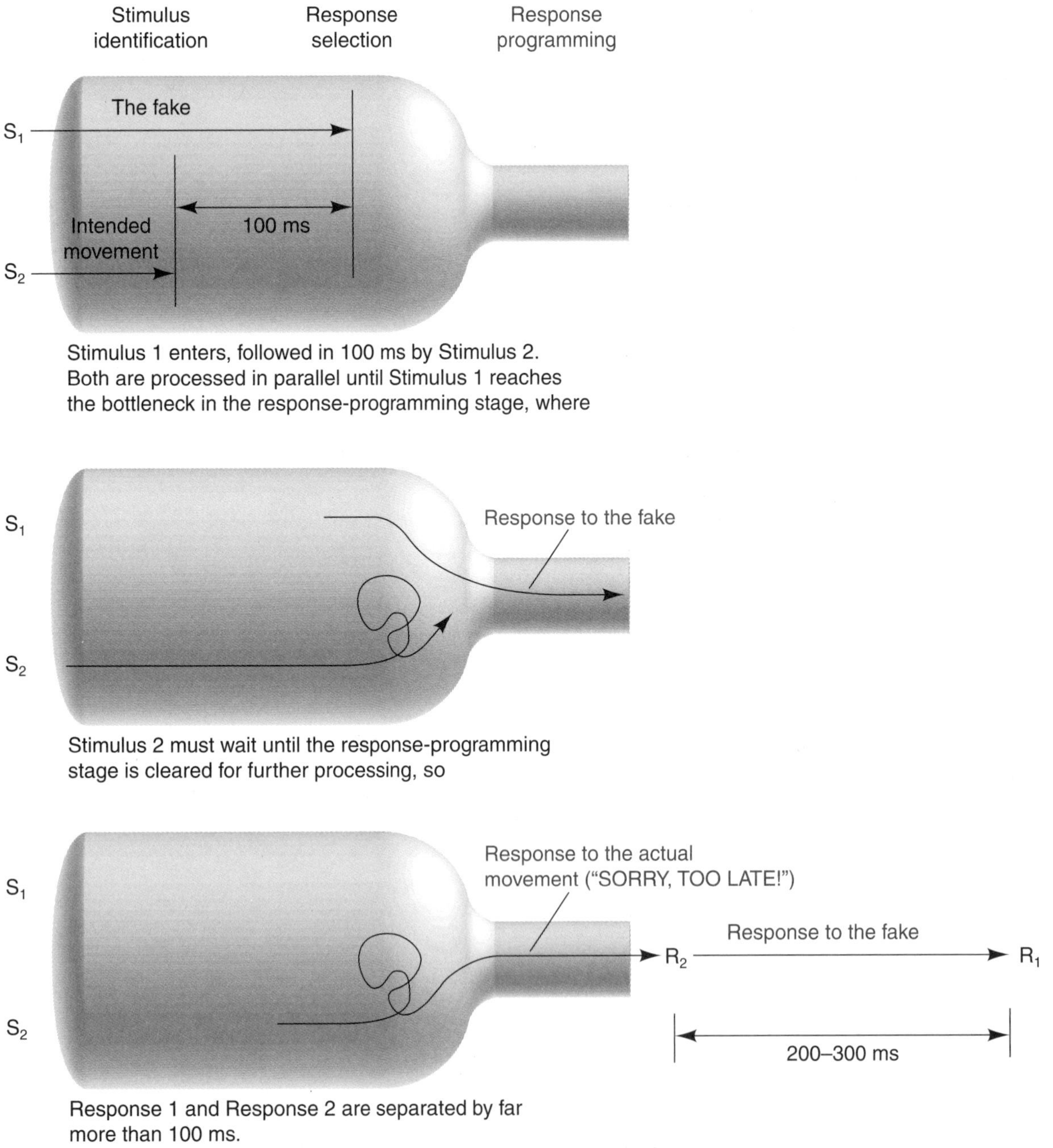
Stimulus identification
Response selection
Response programming
The fake
S1
Intended movement
100 ms
S2
Stimulus 1 enters, followed in 100 ms by Stimulus 2. Both are processed in parallel until Stimulus 1 reaches the bottleneck in the response-programming stage, where
S1
Response to the fake
S2
Stimulus 2 must wait until the response-programming stage is cleared for further processing, so
S1
Response to the actual movement ("SORRY, TOO LATE!")
Response to the fake
R2
R1
S2
200–300 ms
Response 1 and Response 2 are separated by far more than 100 ms.

Figure 2.11 An information-processing bottleneck in the response-programming stage.

can ignore the fake and respond quickly to the fake–shot combination. If the ISI is longer than that, the defender has time to complete the response to the fake and then respond quickly to the shot as if the latter were a single stimulus.

Movement-Output Chunking

The PRP effect is also important for understanding how we produce a sequence of movements. Because separate actions, each triggered by a separate stimulus, cannot be produced very closely to each other in time, the movement-control system must produce bursts or chunks of activity that occupy several hundred milliseconds each. Researchers have estimated that these chunks can be separated in time by no less than about 200 ms (Kahneman, 1973). Thus, it is likely that when we need to string numerous chunks together (sometimes referred to as **movement-output chunking**), as in steering a car, the system produces the chunks at a maximum rate of about three per second. Researchers think that these movement chunks are organized in the response-programming stage and then run off so as to appear to be a single action (see chapter 4), as shown in figure 2.12.

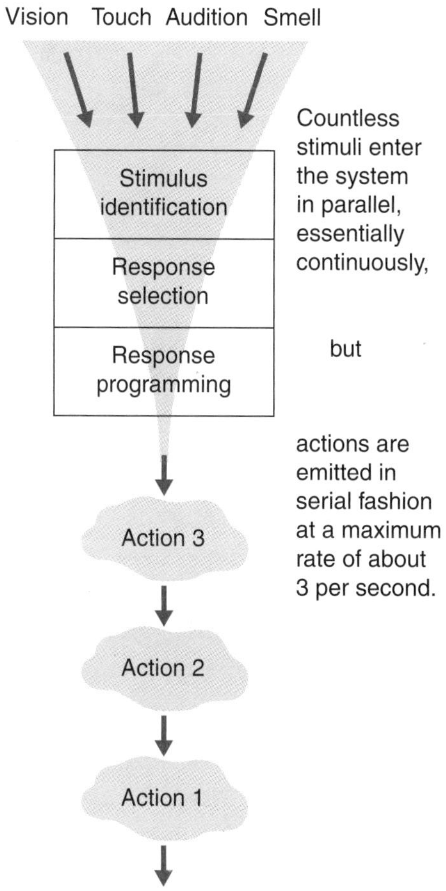

Figure 2.12 Information from sensory stimuli is provided continuously, but responses are generated in units, or chunks (see "actions").

The clear difficulty associated with producing two actions at nearly the same time might seem to be a serious limitation to motor control. From an ecological viewpoint, however, this mode of control is quite reasonable (Gibson, 1979; Neumann, 1987). Presumably, the movement apparatus is organized to produce actions that are effective in meeting environmental demands; an example might be the person raising her hand in response to seeing an oncoming rock to prevent being hit in the face by it. Now, if some almost simultaneous second stimulus (a sound) should lead to an eye movement to detect its source, the original response would have to be aborted in favor of the second. If this were to happen, the person would be struck by the rock. Rather than allow this kind of thing to happen, the system seems to protect the first action from other competing actions for a few hundred milliseconds, allowing an action that was deemed important enough to be chosen to run its course in an uninterrupted way so that the desired goal is actually achieved. Viewed in this way, refractoriness is not a limitation at all; rather, it is a mechanism that contributes to survival.

movement-output chunking— The act of organizing and producing several movements as a single unit; a common feature of skilled performance.

Producing Different Movements at the Same Time

You have undoubtedly tried to rub your belly and pat your head at the same time, and, if you are like most people, you have experienced difficulty coordinating the two hands. It's as if they refuse to do two different things. As a result, both end up doing the same thing (patting or rubbing). This activity illustrates how some pairs of movements are difficult to coordinate. At the same time, we know that other pairs are easy to produce simultaneously (as when we play "chopsticks" on a piano). Simultaneous two-hand movements also tell us about some of the principles underlying coordination of the limbs in general.

Role of Timing and Rhythm

An interesting aspect of many types of bimanual (both hands) movements is that the hands often seem to be linked to each other. For example, it is easy for us to make simultaneous movements of the hands when the patterns are the same for both hands and

UNIVERSITY OF WINCHESTER LIBRARY

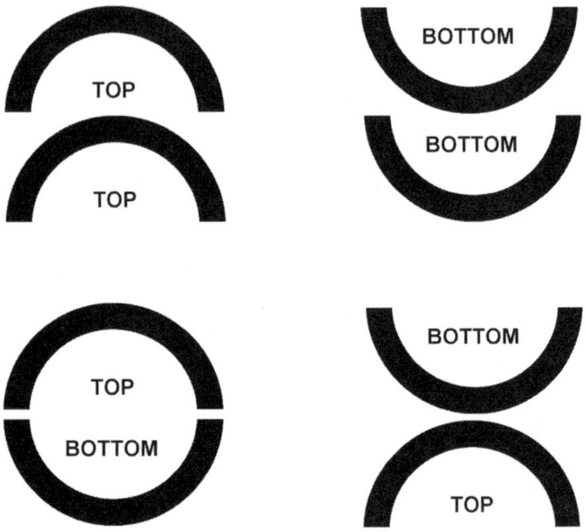

Figure 2.13 Static representation of the templates shown for the four bimanual tasks. (Reprinted from Franz et al., 2001.)

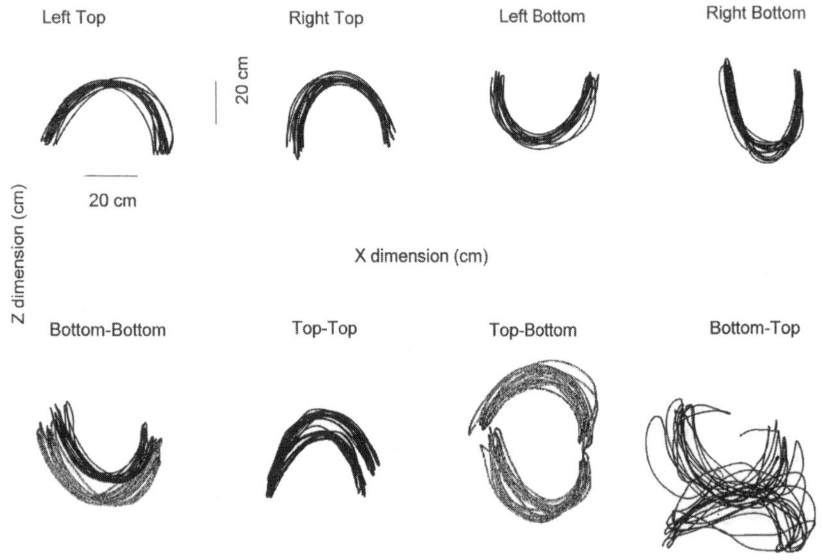

Figure 2.14 Typical x–z displacement paths for the middle 16 s of a trial for one participant in all conditions. The top row depicts unimanual conditions, and the bottom row depicts each hand in bimanual conditions. Note the less coherent spatial pattern in the bottom–top conditions. That result was typical for all participants. (Reprinted from Franz et al., 2001.)

even easier when the patterns are mirror images of each other. You can experience this phenomenon by scribbling with both hands on a large sheet of paper or a blackboard. If you try this exercise, you'll see that it is extremely easy to make the same pattern (or, even easier, a mirror image of it) with the left and right hands. Research that has involved more sophisticated analysis of bimanual movements has shown that these actions possess a common time structure, in that the muscular forces that produce the various submovements do so at the same time (and rhythm) in the two hands. The spatial structure of these movements is not so strongly constrained, however, as you can demonstrate for yourself by attempting to scribble in large strokes with the left hand and in small strokes with the right. Notice that although this spatial discrepancy is not difficult to achieve, the time structure to produce the movements remains virtually the same for both hands. Analyses of these types of situations have led researchers to conclude that, especially for relatively unpracticed bimanual movements, the system prefers to operate in a fashion that allows the two hands to produce a single temporal (i.e., timing) structure or rhythm.

Put another way, it is particularly difficult to produce bimanual movements in which the two hands are moving in different rhythms (see figures 2.13 and 2.14). To experience this, try tapping a constant rhythm with your left hand while tapping as quickly as possible with your right. Researchers have shown that it is also difficult for people to attend to an externally produced rhythm (e.g., by listening to a metronome) while attempting to tap a different rhythm of their own (Klapp et al., 1985). All of this suggests that the system prefers to produce simultaneous movements that have a common underlying rhythm. So what does this tell us about the way bimanual control works best? One explanation is the two movements are combined or "chunked" as if they were one rather than two.

Output Chunking

It appears that the motor system can organize only one action at a time during the response-selection or response-programming stage. The word *action* in the previous sentence requires some elaboration. When we snap our fingers, quite a few fingers and joints comprise the hand move. Of course, we do not mean to say that each of these finger and joint movements is a single action. Rather, the collection of finger movements, with its specific temporal organization and coordination that together make up the finger snap, is what we mean by an action. Only one such finger-snap action can be selected and initiated at a time.

In the case of bimanual control, however, the focus is on the production of the movement after it has been organized and initiated. Fundamental here are the notions (which we develop further in chapter 6) that a single action has a specific timing structure (or rhythm), that only one rhythm can be produced at any one time, and that this rhythm provides a basis for the timing of the action regardless of which limbs produce it (e.g., right and left hands, right and left feet). In light of these notions, an attempt to pat your head and rub your belly simultaneously is frustrating because it requires the system to produce different rhythms at the same time. A similar problem has been shown in experiments where people try to produce the Greek letter gamma (γ) and the letter V simultaneously (see figure 2.15) or when they attempt to produce different tapping rhythms at the same time. However, when the hands are linked together and controlled by the same timing structure, as in two-handed scribbling, two-hand movement production is easy.

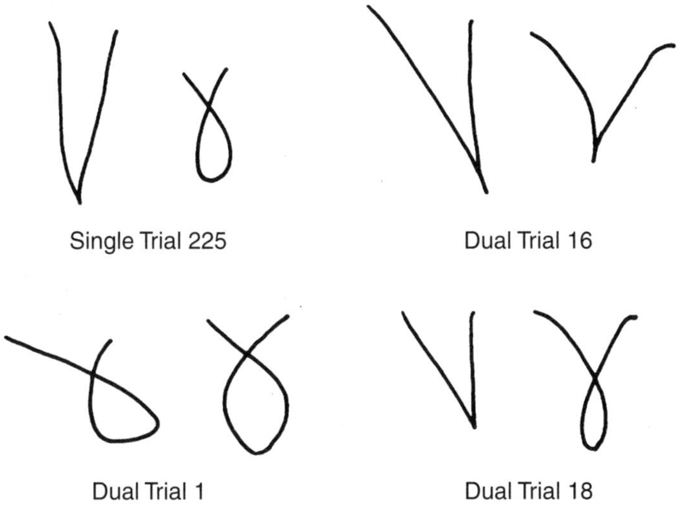

Figure 2.15 The gamma–V experiment. Results of attempts to draw gammas and Vs either separately (single trial) or together (dual trials) after various amounts of practice. (Reprinted from Bender, 1987.)

But how do we explain the effective bimanual control of athletes, musicians, and industrial workers, who perform tasks involving independent and distinct movements of the two limbs? For example, it is hard to see much in common in the movements of the two hands while the performer is making a tennis serve, playing the violin, or operating a forklift. There are a number of ways to think of this.

One possibility is that performers learn to control their hands separately with practice, so that one hand produces a relatively well-learned pattern automatically while the other operates under a type of controlled processing. Another likely possibility, particularly for very highly practiced skills, is that the system develops a more sophisticated representation that enables the control of both hands at the same time (Schmidt, Heuer, Ghodsian, & Young, 1998). How people develop this type of higher-order coordination, and the types of factors that influence it, are among the most puzzling problems for movement scientists. Table 2.2 summarizes the characteristics of the response-programming stage and the two stages we discussed previously.

Presumably, perception, decision making, and action planning require people to use some type of information they have acquired and retained from previous experiences. In the next section we discuss the general concept of memory and how performers use this system before and during information processing and motor performance.

Table 2.2 Characteristics of the Sequential Stages of Information Processing

Characteristic	Stimulus-identification stage	Response-selection stage	Response-programming stage
Function of stage	Detect, identify signal	Select response	Organize, initiate action
Effect of number of stimulus-response alternatives	Minor	Large	None
Type of processing	Parallel	Parallel and sequential	Sequential
Attention required	No	Sometimes	Yes

THREE MEMORY SYSTEMS

memory—
The persistence of the capacity for knowledge or action; comprised of three components: short-term sensory store, short-term memory, and long-term memory.

short-term sensory store (STSS)—
The most peripheral memory system, which holds incoming information by modality (auditory, visual) until the person identifies it; believed to be almost unlimited in capacity but extremely brief in duration.

short-term memory (STM)—
The memory system that allows people to retrieve, rehearse, process, and transfer information from STSS; believed to be limited in capacity and brief in duration.

An important process associated with the production of effective movements is **memory**, which is usually viewed as the persistence of acquired knowledge or capability for action. Movement scientists might say that practice at some task has resulted in the storage of some capability for the action in memory. The common view is that at least three distinct memory systems can be identified, each of which is involved in some fashion in processing information that results in movement production: short-term sensory store, short-term memory, and long-term memory (see figure 2.16).

Short-Term Sensory Store

The most peripheral, or sensory, component of memory is the **short-term sensory store (STSS)**. As we discussed earlier, numerous segments or streams of information are processed simultaneously and in parallel during the stimulus-identification stage. Initially stimuli enter the system and are briefly held in different STSSs according to their sensory modality (auditory, visual, kinesthetic, tactile). Each stream is held for only a few hundred milliseconds before being replaced by the next stream. Scientists believe that STSS storage occurs before the performer's conscious involvement with the information and therefore entails very little attentional processing.

Short-Term Memory

Although a considerable amount of information passes through a person's STSS, relatively little reaches a conscious level. Rather, a selective-attention mechanism selects some of the information in STSS for further processing (see figure 2.16) in **short-term memory (STM)**, with the remainder being lost or replaced by the next stream. Researchers think that the decision regarding which information in STSS is selected for further processing in STM depends on its relevance, or pertinence, to the present task. For example, when someone says your name unexpectedly at a crowded party (a relevant auditory stimulus), your attention is immediately directed to that source of information and you select it for further processing into STM, perhaps rejecting the information spoken to you by your date. It follows, then, that the overwhelming majority of information entering STSS at any moment never reaches the level of STM where it can be attended to and processed further. Thus, a challenging and often difficult part of the skill-production process involves learning which sources of environmental or kinesthetic information are most relevant for goal achievement at different points in time.

People use a mechanism called selective attention to determine which sources of information to include in the short-term memory (STM). STM is thought to be a kind of temporary workspace (termed *working memory* by some authors) where relevant information is processed by controlled information-processing activities. If STM can be likened to consciousness (which is reasonable), its "holding space" is limited to only a small number of items. Experiments have suggested that, for a wide range of forms of information, STM capacity is at most only about 7 ± 2 items or "chunks" (Miller, 1956). Depending on the type of stimulus, the information is transformed into one of several more abstract codes (e.g., words, phrases, sounds, images). For example, one's (well-learned) telephone number is not represented as 10 separate numerals but rather as a single element with 10 numerals in it—your phone number.

People can hold information in STM only as long as they direct attention to it, such as by recycling, rehearsing, repeating the information over and over, or associating it with other items. If they direct their attention elsewhere, they forget some of the contents, with complete forgetting occurring in perhaps 30 s. A classic illustration of

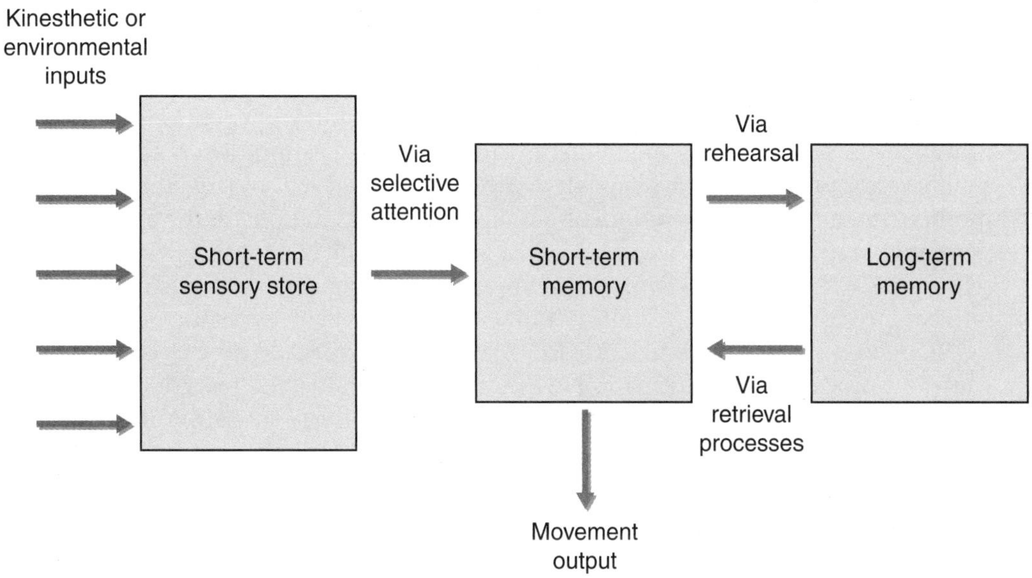

Figure 2.16 Three discrete components of human memory.

this phenomenon is the person who looks up a phone number, then fumbles for a credit card or activates a cell phone, and in only a few seconds forgets the number. In the realm of motor skills, an example of the rapid forgetting of unrehearsed movements in STM might be a physical-therapy patient who has one of his limbs guided to a particular position only to forget it the location when instructed to reproduce the movement a few minutes later.

Because of both the limited capacity and brief duration of items in STM, performers must learn how to use this workspace effectively and efficiently, selecting only those pieces of information that are most relevant for immediate performance situations. For example, the baseball pitcher needs to remember the pitch count, the score, the game situation, and relevant characteristics of the batter when determining the next pitch. Research has shown that the act of retrieving information from long-term memory (discussed next) for use in STM (see again figure 2.16) is an important aspect of skill learning. In chapter 9, we discuss some ways of structuring the practice of tasks that require learners to rehearse the STM retrieval process. For now, you need remember only that STM is the memory component people use when preparing for and performing skills.

Long-Term Memory

The third component of memory is **long-term memory** (LTM), considered to be the storage space for experiences people accumulate over the course of their lives. Experiments have shown that LTM is essentially unlimited in both capacity and the length of time information is preserved. We can all think of skills we learned long ago and have not forgotten, even if we haven't practiced them for many years (e.g., riding a bicycle and roller-skating). Probably the only reason we cannot remember someone's name or an old telephone number is because we cannot find it in LTM (psychologists would say that you could not retrieve it from LTM), and not because it is no longer stored there. The way people code information for storage is thought to be very abstract, with elaborate connections to other stored information, and in many possible forms (e.g., images, thoughts, feelings, and representations of actions).

long-term memory (LTM)—The memory system that holds information and life experiences; believed to be vast in capacity and unlimited in duration.

Information in LTM arrives there as a result of controlled and generally effortful processing (involving things such as rehearsal and the connecting of new information to previously learned information), which is considered as taking place in STM. For example, learning your new cell phone number takes effortful, repetitious, conscious processing in STM before it is permanently stored in LTM. Learning a new action such as a tennis serve presumably involves retrieving other learned actions (e.g., throwing) and modifying them in STM for production. Only after many attempts at the action does a permanent representation become formed in LTM. As the learner practices retrieving, rehearsing, refining, and storing this representation, it is easier and easier for her to retrieve the representation from LTM and use it (in STM) whenever she needs it.

When we say that someone has learned something, we really mean that she has in some way processed the information in STM and transferred it to LTM. For many motor skills, particularly continuous ones such as riding a bicycle or swimming, research evidence and common experience tell us that retention (i.e., the effective retrieval of information from LTM and effective use of this information via STM) is almost perfect for years—even decades—without intervening practice. However, we do seem to forget some discrete motor skills somewhat more easily, such as gymnastics stunts, but scientists are not quite sure why.

Choking Under Pressure

People who participate in or observe competitive sports on a regular basis are well aware of the phenomenon that occurs when athletes perform more poorly than expected. They refer to this phenomenon as "choking under pressure" because it usually occurs during situations when the performer is trying his or her hardest to achieve success. Recent research (see Beilock [2006] for a review) suggests that choking can occur for at least two different reasons. Each of these has its basis in a concept we have discussed in this chapter. The first deals with the *type of processing* the performer uses, controlled vs. automatic. For skilled athletes, automatic processing usually produces their best performance. However, in high-pressure situations these athletes are sometimes guilty of "thinking too much" and trying to control their movements in a conscious fashion (i.e., using controlled processing). A recent study revealed that when national level trampolinists attempted to use controlled processing they were unable to produce a move they had previously automated. The researchers labeled this condition the "lost-move syndrome." The second reason athletes choke is because they have too many procedural things to remember and, under pressure, don't have enough *short-term memory capacity* to do so. An example might be a football quarterback who fails to remember that a particular opposing team changes its pass defense in crucial situations. As game pressure increases, the quarterback devotes less attention to that piece of information because he is attending to other pieces (e.g., which receiver to throw to, which pass rusher to be aware of, how many seconds remain on the play clock, how many time-outs are left, etc.). Since the capacity of short-term memory is small and since attention narrows under pressure, an important piece of information like the opponent's sudden shift in defense might not be processed. As a result, the quarterback fails to recognize the change and his pass is intercepted. In the following day's newspaper, the sportswriters conclude that the quarterback "choked."

Although we don't include the three memory components discussed in this section in the conceptual model we begin building in the next chapter, they are an important aspect of most types of information processing (Anshel, 1990). Recent studies have demonstrated that the memory strategies of advanced and beginning performers differ markedly for activities as varied as jazz dancing (Poon & Rodgers, 2000) and rock climbing (Boschker, Bakker, & Michaels, 2002). Compared with beginning performers, experts organize information more efficiently and are able to detect the functional relationship between what to do and how to do it more effectively.

SUMMARY

A prominent view of the way people perform and learn motor skills is by processing information, with signals received by the various sense organs (input), processed through various stages, and produced as movements (output). There are three main information-processing stages:

- Stimulus identification (detecting and perceiving), which detects the nature of environmental information
- Response selection (deciding), which decides on the action that should be made
- Response programming (action planning), which organizes the system for a response

Reaction time is an important measure of information-processing speed. Its duration is affected by the number of stimulus-response alternatives (described by Hick's law), by the naturalness of the relationship between the stimuli and their associated movements (stimulus-response compatibility), and by the predictability of the upcoming events. Arousal and anxiety generally show an inverted-U relationship with performance. Increases in arousal enhance performance, but only to a point; further increases beyond this optimal arousal level diminish performance.

Attention, the general capacity to process information, is a limiting factor in many performance situations. The delay in a person's response to the second of two closely spaced stimuli (known as the psychological refractory period, or PRP) suggests that the motor system can organize and initiate only one action at a time, with a functional maximal rate of about three actions per second. There is potential for massive competition in the control of two-handed movements, unless people produce them using a common timing structure or rhythm.

Finally, there appear to be at least three memory systems that preserve information across time:

- Short-term sensory store, with a large capacity for information but an extremely brief holding duration of only a few hundred milliseconds
- Short-term memory, with a small capacity and a holding duration of about 30 s
- Long-term memory, with a capacity and holding duration that is virtually unlimited

FROM PRINCIPLES TO PRACTICE

Check your comprehension of the concepts and terms discussed in this chapter by responding to each of the exercises in the following sections. The first section contains several exercises designed to test your working knowledge of key terms. The second section poses a variety of problems designed to check your understanding of key concepts. In the third section you are challenged to apply your knowledge by discussing a defensible solution for two scenarios.

Know Your Key Terms

Matching: Reaction Time and Anticipation

Match the following terms with their respective categories or definitions by placing the most appropriate letter on each of the blanks below.

Reaction Time and Anticipation—Terms

a. temporal anticipation
b. foreperiod
c. S-R compatibility
d. choice RT
e. spatial (or event) anticipation
f. consistent S-R mapping
g. psychological refractory period (PRP)

Reaction Time and Anticipation—Category or Definition

_____1. The delay in a person's reaction to the second of two closely spaced stimuli

_____2. The capacity of a person to predict what is going to happen in a performance situation

_____3. The degree to which the relationship between a stimulus and its required response is natural

_____4. The interval between a warning signal and an unanticipated stimulus

_____5. The capacity of a person to predict when an event is going to happen

_____6. For example, the task of a defender during a three-on-one fast break in basketball

_____7. Illustrated by the fact that a warning signal at a railroad crossing usually prompts drivers to apply their brakes

Consider: Optimizing Arousal for Effective Performance

For each of the following scenarios, indicate how the performer's arousal level might shift (i.e., increase or decrease) and how this shift might influence performance (i.e., improve or diminish it). Provide rationale for your answers.

1. An average-skilled industrial machine operator with a moderate level of trait anxiety is working quite effectively. His supervisor then arrives and begins watching him work.
2. A young driver-education student with a high level of trait anxiety is attempting a complex parking maneuver and is making numerous errors. Her instructor suggests that she select one component of the maneuver and practice it by itself.
3. A powerlifter with a low level of trait anxiety is attempting to exceed his previous maximum weight in the clean and jerk. Another lifter enters the room and begins to verbally taunt him.
4. A moderately trait-anxious person is playing golf with three of her friends. They decide that the player with the most putts on the first nine holes will buy lunch for the others. She finishes with the lowest number of putts. After lunch, the friends agree to play the back nine holes with no challenges.

Fill in the Blank: Two-Hand Coordination

Complete the following sentences:

An interesting aspect of many types of ___________ movements is that the hands seem to be ___________ to each other. Research and our own experience suggest that the motor system prefers to produce simultaneous two-hand movements that have a common underlying _________________. A classic example of the difficulty people have in attempting to produce two different actions simultaneously is _________________ the head and _________________ belly.

Check Your Understanding

1. Describe the information-processing activities that might occur in the stimulus-identification, response-selection, and response-programming stages for a soccer goalie.
2. What might be a positive consequence of a correct anticipation by a pedestrian crossing a busy street? What might be a negative consequence of an incorrect anticipation?
3. Use the cue-utilization hypothesis to explain how the performance of a person playing a fast-action video game might deteriorate as his or her arousal increases from a low to a high level.
4. Describe an activity in which you participate regularly and then indicate the level of arousal (low, medium, or high) you believe accompanies your best performance of that activity. Under what circumstances would you be concerned about being underaroused when performing the activity? Overaroused?
5. When you participate in the activity you discussed in the preceding question, what things do you attend to when your performance is good? When your performance is not good? How do your answers relate to the notion of a limited attentional capacity?
6. What limitations prevent you from producing two different hand movements simultaneously, or at least make it very difficult for you to do so? What types of simultaneous hand movements do you find easy to perform? Why do you think that is? What types of simultaneous hand movements do you find difficult to perform? Why?

Apply Your Knowledge

Exercise 1

While watching a neighbor tossing a beach ball to her younger brother, you notice that the boy is becoming frustrated because he is unable to catch it. From an information-processing perspective, the boy's difficulty may result from inadequate stimulus identification, inappropriate response selection, incorrect response programming, or perhaps some combination of the three. Explain how his older sister might determine which stage of processing is causing the boy the most difficulty. Suggest one thing the sister could do to simplify the stimulus-identification process for her brother. Then do the same for response selection and response programming. Please provide rationale for your suggestions and furnish two supporting references.

Exercise 2

An important aspect of skilled performance is the interaction between short-term memory (STM) and long-term memory (LTM). STM is the memory component that deals with the rehearsal, labeling, storing, and retrieving of immediate information, and LTM is the component that serves as the large-capacity holding space for information that has been previously rehearsed and labeled. When people are preparing for performance, they retrieve information from LTM temporarily, and then move it to STM, where they can use it to organize the required actions. Describe a specific performance situation (e.g., dancing or playing a musical instrument in front of an audience, snow skiing on an icy slope, playing wheelchair basketball) and explain what pieces of information a person might retrieve from LTM to prepare for effective skill execution. Remember that the person can probably maintain no more than about seven (+/– 2) items in STM at a time. Provide a rationale for your answer and furnish two supporting references.

PART TWO

PRINCIPLES OF HUMAN SKILLED PERFORMANCE

chapter 3

Sensory Contributions to Skilled Performance

▷ Chapter Outline

▷ Chapter Objectives

When you have completed this chapter, you should be able to

- explain the contributions and limitations of a closed-loop model of movement control,
- understand the various ways that sensory information is used in movement control,
- discuss the various roles of vision in movement control, and
- understand how sensory contributions to movements are part of a conceptual model of motor performance.

PREVIEW

A rugby player watches the ball leave her teammate's hand. With but a few tenths of a second of viewing time, the player realizes she must turn her back on the ball and cut sharply to her left to catch it. She predicts the ball's flight correctly, visually focuses on it, and times the ball's arrival into her hands. After a few steps, the player is tackled from behind, senses the ball slipping away, and compensates by grasping it with both hands, all the while maintaining her balance.

OVERVIEW

Skilled performers seem able to receive and process vast amounts of sensory information quickly and accurately and make effective adjustments when needed. How does just a brief glimpse of the ball tell the rugby player where to run to catch the pass? How does she know when the ball will arrive? How does she obtain and process all this information?

What Would It Be Like If We Couldn't Feel Our Bodies?

Clinical accounts of patients with distorted or nonexistent proprioception suggest that those sensory systems are much more important than most of us realize. In one case study, a 27-year-old woman who was given an antibiotic before surgery suffered a complication in which she lost all awareness of her proprioceptive feedback. By the day of her surgery, "standing was impossible—unless she looked down at her feet. She could hold nothing in her hands, and they 'wandered' unless she kept an eye on them. When she reached out for something, or tried to feed herself, her hands would miss, or overshoot wildly, as if some essential control of coordination was gone. She could scarcely even sit up—her body "gave way." Her face was oddly expressionless and slack, her jaw fell open, even her vocal posture was gone. "Something awful's happened," she mouthed, in a ghostly flat voice. "I can't feel my body. I feel weird—disembodied'" (Sacks, 1985, p. 45).

In this chapter we focus on some of the many processes that allow performers to detect patterns of information in the environment and then use this information to determine their future actions. More specifically, we discuss the ways people use sensory information to plan their actions, correct their movement errors, and regulate their performance. First, we describe how the neuromuscular system uses sensory information in general, and then we expand our conceptual model of motor performance to incorporate some of these elements. We then focus on the visual system in particular and discuss some principles of visual control of movements. We conclude the chapter by adding these visual components to the conceptual model of motor performance.

Successful performance often depends on how effectively participants detect, perceive, and use relevant sensory information. It could be a rugby player who detects the pattern of an opponent's actions or a truck driver who senses the movements of his vehicle on a slippery road. Many coaches devote considerable practice time to activities designed to improve the speed and accuracy with which their athletes detect and process relevant sensory information. In another vein, therapists frequently work with people who have impaired functioning of one or more sensory systems. These helping professionals must understand the ways that people process sensory information in order to provide their patients with the most appropriate guidance and compensatory activities.

exteroception—Sensory information that comes primarily from sources outside a person's body, primarily vision and smell.

proprioception—Sensory information that comes primarily from sources in the muscles and joints and from bodily movements.

interoception—Sensory information arising from within the body, such as hunger and thirst.

SOURCES OF SENSORY INFORMATION

Information that performers might use to produce skilled movements arises from several basic sources, but much of it comes from the external environment. This source of information is typically referred to as **exteroception**, with the prefix *extero* indicating that the information arises from outside the body; classically, this consists primarily of vision, audition (hearing), and olfaction (smell). The second basic source of sensory information comes from within the body, largely from the muscles and joints, and is generally termed **proprioception**, with the prefix *proprio* meaning that the information comes from inside. Finally, **interoception** concerns functions that are wholly within the body, such as hunger and thirst, and is not particularly important for skilled performance.

Exteroceptive Information

Chief among the sources of exteroceptive information is, of course, vision. At the most fundamental level, the things we see help to define the physical structure of our environment, such as the edge of a stairway or the presence of an object blocking our path. In this context, vision allows us to anticipate upcoming events. Vision also affords us information about the movement of objects, such as the flight path and speed of an approaching ball, a subway train, or an angry dog. Another function of vision is to help us detect the spatial and temporal aspects of our own movements in our environment, such as swinging a bat, stepping onto a train, or leaping over a fence. Later in this chapter we discuss in more detail the visual system and the ways we use vision to control our movements.

The second major source of exteroceptive information is audition, or hearing. Although audition is not as obvious a component of motor performance as vision, there are many activities for which audition is an important source of sensory information. For example, in sailing, skilled performers use the sound of the hull of the boat moving through the water to estimate boat speed, and the carpenter uses the sound of his saw blade cutting wood to control the pressure he applies. Audition is also an important source of sensory information for people with visual impairments.

Skilled sailors can tell how fast a boat is moving by listening to the sound of the hull moving through the water.

Proprioceptive or Kinesthetic Information

More relevant for motor control is proprioception. Examples of proprioceptive information are the positions of our joints, the forces produced in our muscles, and the orientation of our bodies in space (e.g., the feeling of being upside down). Another type of information coming from the body's movements is termed **kinesthesis**, where the prefix *kines* means "movement" and the suffix *thesis* means "the sense of." Kinesthesis is the sense or awareness we have of the movements of our joints and the tension in our muscles during motor activity. The distinction between proprioception and kinesthesis has blurred over the years, and the terms are used almost synonymously today. Proprioception is particularly important for performers in sports such as gymnastics (i.e., for balance) and springboard diving (i.e., for orienting the body). In therapeutic settings, kinesthesis is essential for patients who are attempting to hold or alter their posture.

Several important receptors provide the neuromuscular system with information about kinesthesis. The **vestibular apparatus** in the inner ear detects movements of the head and is sensitive to its orientation with respect to gravity. Not surprisingly, the information provided by these structures is important for posture and balance (see figure 3.1).

kinesthesis—Sensory information coming from the motor system that signals contractions and limb movements; similar to proprioception.

vestibular apparatus—Proprioceptive sense organs located in the inner ear that provide information about posture, balance, and movements of the head.

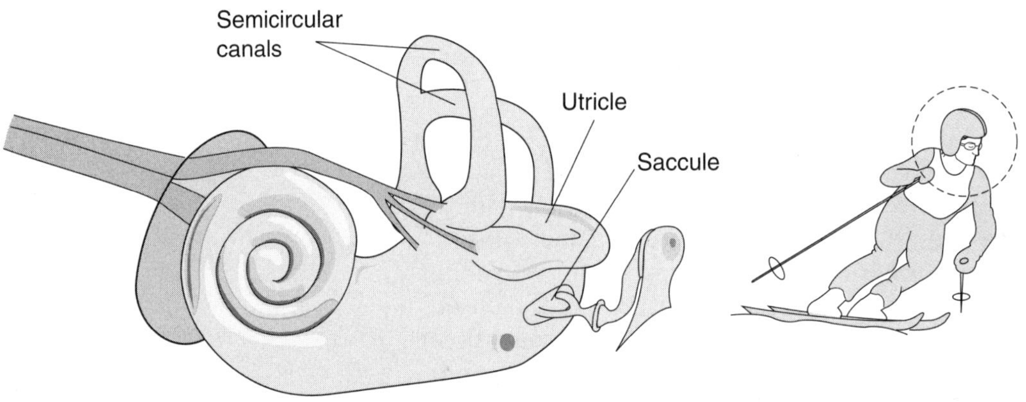

Figure 3.1 The vestibular apparatus in the inner ear provides important information for posture and balance.

muscle spindles—Sensory receptors located in the muscles that provide the nervous system with information about changes in muscle length.

Golgi tendon organs—Proprioceptive sense organs located at the junction of muscles and tendons that signal information about force in the muscles.

cutaneous receptors—Proprioceptive sense organs located in most skin areas that signal information about pressure, temperature, and touch.

Other receptors provide information about the limbs. Those located in the joints and in the surrounding joint capsules signal joint position, especially at the extremes of the limb's range of motion. Embedded within the belly of skeletal muscle are receptors called **muscle spindles**, which shorten when the muscle shortens (i.e., contracts) and provide information about the rate of shortening as well as the changing position of the joints (see figure 3.2). Located near the junction between the muscle and the tendon are receptors known as **Golgi tendon organs**, which signal the level of force in the various parts of the muscle (see figure 3.3). Finally, receptors are found in most skin areas that are responsible for providing haptic (meaning "sensations from the skin") information. Referred to as **cutaneous receptors**, they include several kinds of specialized detectors of pressure, temperature, and touch (see figure 3.4).

Each of these receptors provides more than one type of sensory information. For example, muscle spindles inform performers about their joint position, muscle velocity, muscle tension, and limb orientation with respect to gravity. Therefore, unlike vision and audition, which are unitary senses, kinesthesis involves a complex combination of inputs from various receptors that must be integrated by the central nervous system.

Because of the multiple, complex receptors involved in kinesthesis, our perception of movement can be affected by the way we produce our movements. For example, our perception (or kinesthetic "feel") of a normal, active pattern of movement, such as a kick, is different from our perception of a passive, guided action, such as when a therapist manipulates a patient's limb. Similarly, a patient's perception of the feel associated with standing up from a seated position can be distorted if a therapist assists the patient manually. Many guidance techniques used by practitioners in teaching motor skills can also present kinesthetic sensations that are different from the ones associated with active movement (e.g., when the golf instructor moves the learner's limbs through the desired range of motion). Guidance or manual manipulation techniques are commonly used in therapy settings as well as in certain types of sport-skill situations (e.g., when a therapist guides a patient's lower extremity in gait or when a swimming teacher moves the student's arms through the correct movement pattern for the breaststroke). The problem with these techniques, of course, is that they create a feeling or sensation that is different from the one the learner experiences when performing the movement in an unassisted fashion.

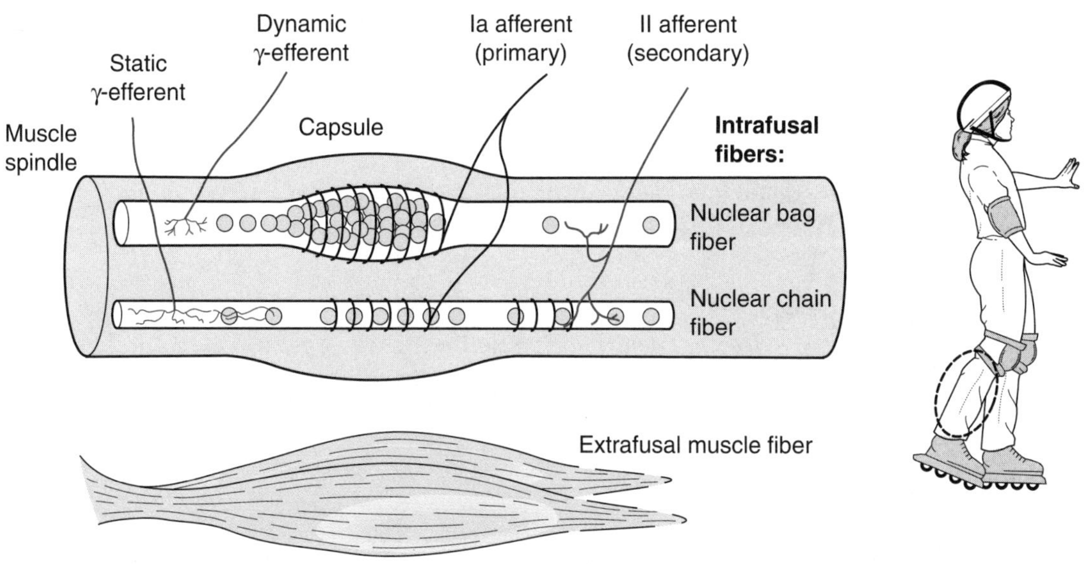

Figure 3.2 Muscle spindles provide important information about limb position and movement.

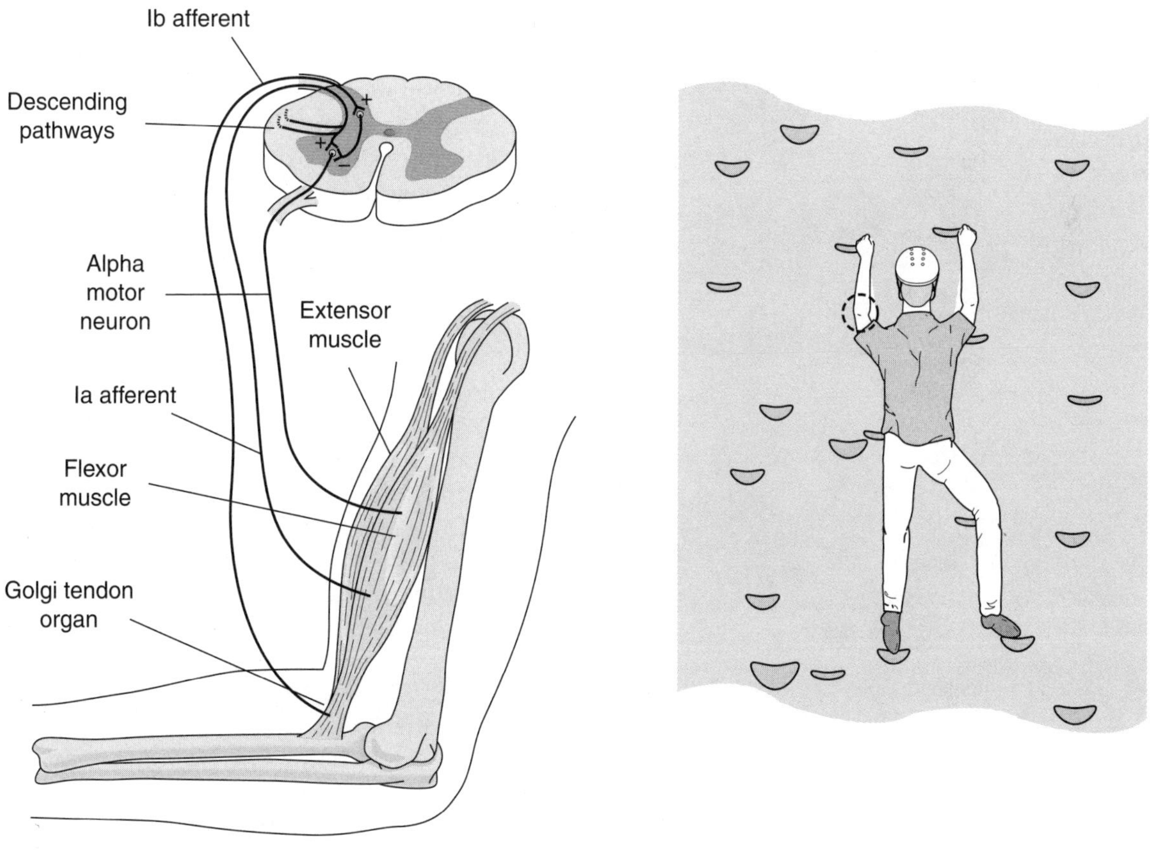

Figure 3.3 Golgi tendon organs provide important information about muscle tension.

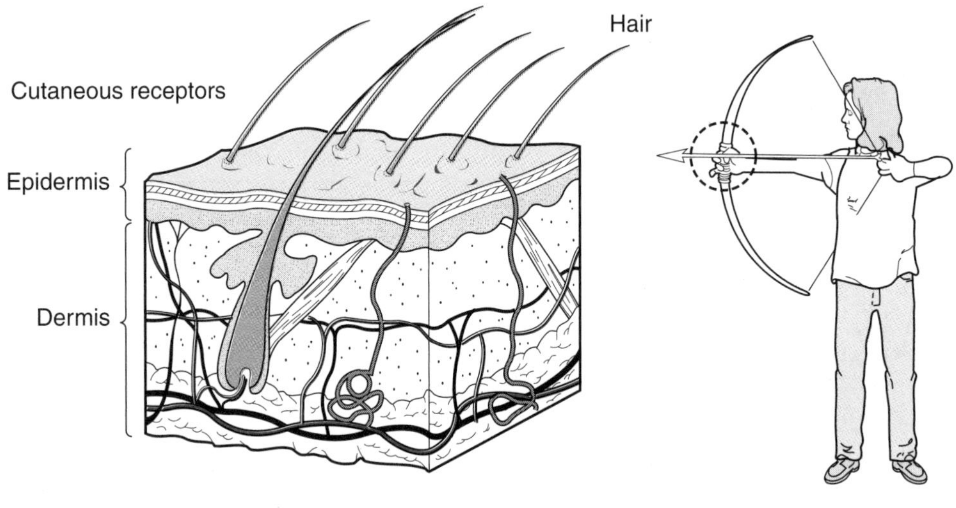

Figure 3.4 Cutaneous receptors provide important information about pressure and touch.

Guidance procedures should direct learners' attention to the feel associated with correct performance.

Although practitioners sometimes find such techniques necessary during the beginning stages of learning (e.g., for defining the boundaries of the correct movement pattern or for safety), they must take care not to overuse them. To do so may distort the learner's sense of the feel associated with active movement.

human factors—A field of study concerned with the interaction of human characteristics and the design of machines or instruments used by people (e.g., tools, vehicles).

One field that has used alterations in kinesthesis in positive ways is **human factors** engineering, where modifications in control mechanisms enhance the operation of various types of equipment and industrial machinery. For example, adding spring resistance to a car's steering system improves the operator's feel of steering movements, making the vehicle easier to control. In a similar fashion, designing aircraft instrument knobs that differ in shape (and "feel") improves the pilot's recognition of the appropriate control device for a particular task. Clearly, many sources of sensory information are available for movement control. In the next sections, we focus on ways the central nervous system uses this information in producing skilled movements.

CLOSED-LOOP CONTROL SYSTEMS

One way to conceptualize how we use sensory information in the control of movements is to consider the way common physical systems use environmental information in everyday situations. Take, for example, the heating and cooling system in most homes. When the system is in operation, its goal is to maintain a desired room tem-

It Depends . . .

Can You Identify the Relevant Sensory Information for Various Tasks?

What types of sensory information did the rugby player in the preview use when she attempted to catch and hold onto the ball? What types of sensory information do you use when riding a bicycle? What would you do if you couldn't see? Couldn't hear? Couldn't feel your legs? What type of information would you first notice if you attempted to ride a friend's bicycle?

perature. The mechanisms needed to achieve this goal are a **comparator**, an **executive**, an **effector**, and **feedback** (see figure 3.5). The comparator, which in this example is the thermostat, senses the difference between the desired room temperature and the actual room temperature (feedback). If it detects no difference (i.e., zero error), it takes no action. However, if the comparator detects a difference—for example, the actual room temperature is higher than the desired temperature—it relays an error signal ("too warm") to the executive, which is the command or control center of the system. When the executive receives this signal, it issues a command to the effector mechanism responsible for carrying out the action, which in this example is the cooling system. The resulting action (air conditioning) continues until the desired temperature is once again achieved. At that point, the feedback from the room's actual temperature is evaluated in the comparator, which senses zero error, and this information is sent to the executive, which forwards the command to the effector to turn off. This process continues indefinitely as the system attempts to maintain the temperature near the desired state.

Systems such as these are called closed-loop systems because the desired state and output are dictated by the executive, carried out by the effector, and then routed back to the comparator in the form of sensory information, or **feedback**. This feedback loop (a closed loop) provides the system with the necessary information for maintaining the desired state.

People use **closed-loop control** processes for certain types of human performance, such as driving a car. Drivers use visual information about the position of the car on the road to obtain feedback about differences between the actual position of the car and the desired position. If such differences occur, the driver senses them as errors. If a correction is necessary, the driver determines the hand and arm movements needed to bring the vehicle into the desired position. The nervous system sends commands to the muscles to execute those movements, and the muscles perform them until the vehicle is once again in the desired position. As you can see in this example, the feedback that the driver uses to maintain the desired position comes from sensory information that is both exteroceptive (e.g., vision of the car and the road) and proprioceptive or kinesthetic (e.g., the feel of the steering wheel and movement of the hands and arms). Presumably, each type of information is compared with its desired state (in the comparator), and any errors are relayed to the executive as input for correction (see figures 3.5 and 3.6). Once the system arrives at a solution, it relays the necessary adjustment to the effectors (hands and arms) for execution.

comparator—The error-detection mechanism contained in closed-loop control systems; compares feedback of the desired state to feedback of the actual state.

executive—One of the components of a closed-loop control system; determines the actions necessary to maintain the desired goal state.

effector—The component of a control system that carries out the desired action; for example, the arm is usually the effector that carries out the action of throwing a ball.

feedback—Information produced from the various sensors as a consequence of moving; sometimes called response-produced feedback.

closed-loop control—A type of control that involves the use of feedback and the activity of error detection and correction processes to maintain the desired state; used by people to control slow, deliberate movements.

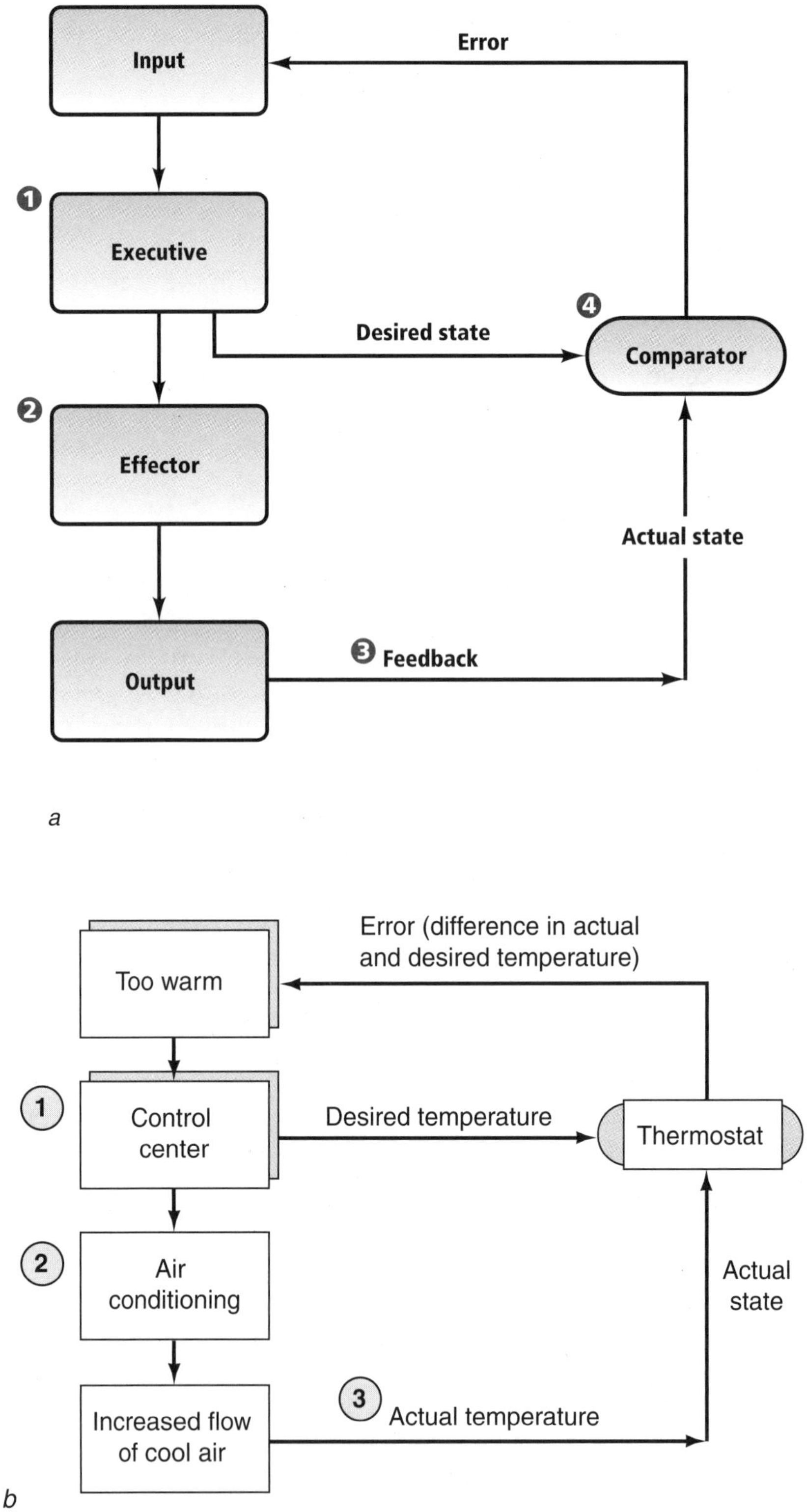

Figure 3.5 A closed-loop control system (*a*) and a practical example (*b*).

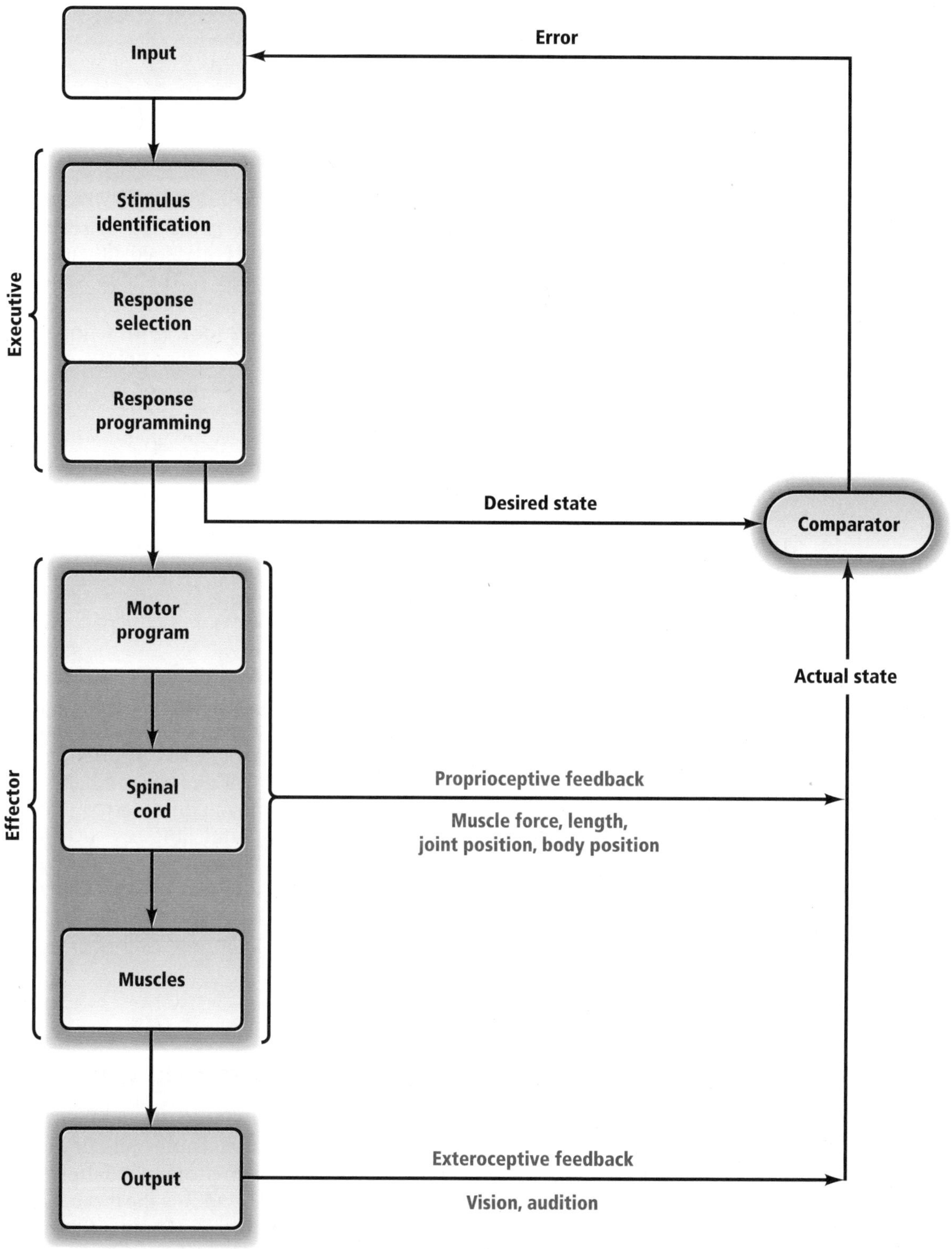

Figure 3.6 An expanded conceptual model of motor performance. The elements of the closed-loop control system are integrated with the stages of processing.

Error Detection and Tickling Yourself

You may wonder why figure 3.6 has a comparator in it. There are many reasons why such a comparator is needed in these kinds of models of human performance. It is obvious that we can detect errors in our own performances—often before the golf ball has finished flying or the basketball reaches the hoop and sometimes before we see any ball movement at all. We seem to know when an action is going to be in error because it just didn't feel right. This capability to evaluate our own performances is called **error detection.**

error detection—
The capability of individuals to evaluate their own performance.

feedforward—
Information about the intended action or a copy of the expected feedback generated before the action begins.

To detect our own errors, we need to have two sources of information in short-term memory as the movement unfolds: a representation of the sensory qualities of the actual action and a representation of the sensory qualities of the intended action. Furthermore, these two sources must represent different states, because if they didn't, we could not detect a mismatch between them and would always conclude that the action was correct. The state representing the actual action is feedback, or sensory information from the movement itself. The state representing the intended action is **feedforward,** or a copy of the expected feedback.

This brings us to the question of why we can't tickle ourselves, when others can tickle us. Blakemore, Wolpert, and Frith (2000) discussed this interesting phenomenon. The idea is that when we try to tickle ourselves by scratching the bottom of our own foot with a fingertip, the preparation for the finger movement generates the sensory feedback we expect to get from our foot along with the commands to move our finger. Then, when our finger touches our foot, we receive the feedback we already expected; thus, the actual information and intended sensory information are practically the same. No tickling. However, when someone else tickles our foot, there are no expected sensory consequences (because we don't know exactly when or how the person is going to do it or how it will feel), so the same feedback from the foot produces a very different sensation—tickling.

These ideas of feedback and feedforward help us understand many kinds of phenomena in movement control and human behavior, including eye movements, error corrections, and even mental illnesses such as schizophrenia (Blakemore et al., 2000). For our purposes here, they help us understand how we can obtain error information from our movements to improve our skills.

Closed-Loop Control Within the Conceptual Model

model—
A tentative description (or an analogy) of a system that captures many of its known properties; models facilitate understanding of systems and promote practical applications.

In the previous chapter, we introduced a conceptual **model** of motor performance that illustrates how people process information in three stages—stimulus identification, response selection, and response programming—to convert environmental input into response output (see figure 2.2). Now we expand the model by adding the mechanisms of closed-loop control shown in figure 3.5. This expanded model (figure 3.6) should help you understand the processes involved in controlling relatively slow movements (e.g., a patient's positioning of a limb in physical therapy) as well as more rapid ones (e.g., a golfer's swing). For slow movements, performers can make compensations during the action; for more rapid ones, they must wait until after the movement is completed to correct their errors.

Components of the closed-loop control system are highlighted in figure 3.6. When input arrives it is processed, and a desired state is determined that defines the sensory qualities (i.e., the look, sound, and feel) of the intended movement. The desired state

Four Components of Closed-Loop Control Systems

1. Executive—makes decisions about the desired state or corrective actions needed
2. Effector—carries out those directions
3. Feedback—provides information about the actual state of the system
4. Comparator, or error detection mechanism—compares expected feedback from the desired state to exteroceptive and proprioceptive feedback from the actual state and relays any difference (i.e., error) to the executive as input

represents the feedback the person should obtain if he performs the movement correctly and achieves the desired environmental goal, and a copy of this desired state is forwarded to the comparator. Commands for achieving the desired goal state are sent from the executive to an effector mechanism that consists of several components. First, there is what movement scientists call the motor program, which produces movement commands. These commands are relayed to the lower centers in the nervous system located in the spinal cord. The result is a contraction of muscles and movement of joints. Feedback of the actual state arising from this movement (e.g., a golf shot) is compared (in the comparator, of course) with the expected sensory feedback of the desired state. Any difference between actual sensory feedback and expected sensory feedback is registered as an error. Should this occur, the error message is transmitted from the comparator to the executive as input. Thus, one can conceptualize the closed-loop system as sensing and attempting to minimize error.

When people move, various forms of proprioceptive and exteroceptive feedback information are generated. Proprioceptive feedback comes from forces produced in the contracting muscles, from pressures exerted by objects in contact with the skin (e.g., the feel of the arms against shirtsleeves or the feel of the feet inside shoes), and from the joints signaling changes in body position. Exteroceptive information comes from the environment and is sensed by the receptors for vision, audition, and sometimes even olfaction (i.e., smell), generating still more feedback (e.g., the flight path of the ball, the sound of the club making contact with the ball, and the smell of the grass and dirt that are displaced by the shot).

As seen in figure 3.6, the stages of processing are an essential feature of closed-loop control. Every time an error signal goes to the executive for correction it must pass through the stages, and as we discussed in the previous chapter, this type of **controlled processing** requires attention and takes time. The processing of feedback can be even more challenging for inexperienced or disabled people. Fortunately, closed-loop control involving the stages of processing is not the only way people use feedback to regulate their movements; later in this chapter we discuss various lower-level reflexlike loops, which make their own closed-loop contributions to movement control.

controlled processing—A type of information processing that is slow, sequential, attention demanding, and voluntary; more prevalent during the early stages of learning.

Conceptual Model and Continuous, Long-Duration Skills

The closed-loop model depicted in figure 3.6 is useful for understanding how the nervous system maintains a particular state of motor performance. For example, maintaining posture in the standing position is a natural behavior that requires some form of continuous closed-loop control. Closed-loop control is also used for various learned postures, such as the one skilled gymnasts use when executing a handstand on the still rings. Most movement skills involving the use of various limbs require an accurate, stable posture as a platform. Without this base, people would be far less proficient at skills such as throwing darts or casting a fishing lure. In these types of tasks, the comparator evaluates the similarity or difference between the expected feedback of the desired limb positions and body orientation and the actual, movement-produced feedback of the actual limb positions and body orientation. Should errors be detected, they are transmitted to the executive for appropriate corrections. For posture, not all of these corrections are mediated by the stages of processing shown in figure 3.6; some are reflexive in nature and do not require attention. We discuss some of these processes later on in the chapter.

Other tasks, of course, require actual movements; some of these (such as the ones used in swimming) may continue for an indefinite period. For instance, continuous **tracking** skills require the performer to operate a control device to follow some continuously changing target. A common example is driving an automobile, where the driver operates a steering wheel to keep the vehicle positioned properly on the road. Control movements are made whenever the driver detects an error in the car's position relative to the road. Another way performers use feedback to control an ongoing movement is evident in the experience of a distance runner competing in a 10K race. The runner compares exteroceptive and kinesthetic feedback from her actual pace to an internal reference of the desired pace to make the necessary corrections for maintaining her pace. There are also tasks for which the reference of correctness changes over time or during the course of action, as in a slow karate movement that can be considered as a series of individual positions, each with its own reference of correctness. These tasks and countless other examples of dynamic movements illustrate the importance of closed-loop control during much of a person's daily behavior.

tracking—A class of tasks in which a moving track must be followed, typically by movements of a manual control.

Closed-loop models, such as the one shown in figure 3.6, are the most effective means for understanding how people control continuous, long-duration skills. They are also useful for certain types of performance applications. For example, human factors engineers have used the components of closed-loop models in designing and constructing a variety of electromechanical devices. These nonliving (often robotlike) machines are able to mimic some aspects of actual human behavior (e.g., polishing pianos) rather well (Amato, 1989). Despite their potential for application, however, closed-loop control models are not without their limitations. We discuss some of these in the next section.

See If You Can Do It

Models are intended to help us understand the way a phenomenon might operate. In figure 3.6 we present a conceptual model of motor performance. You can test the usefulness of this model by attempting to describe how you think each of the various components of the model might operate for a person who is attempting to pour a glass of wine.

Limitations of Closed-Loop Control

The expanded conceptual model shown in figure 3.6 contains a closed-loop control system that includes the three stages of information processing. The biggest disadvantage of the closed-loop system is that it makes control very slow, particularly in the response-selection and response-programming stages. As described in the following sections, a chief limitation of closed-loop control is time. Controlling movements continuously by comparing the actual and expected feedback takes time, and many tasks don't afford performers that kind of time.

Rapid Tracking Behavior

One important generalization you should remember from chapter 2 is that the stages of processing, particularly response selection and response programming, require considerable time and attention. Hence, closed-loop control systems that include these stages operate quite slowly as well. Recall that the stages of processing are critical components in reaction-time situations, where a stimulus or input requires the activity of various processing stages leading to a person's response or output (see figure 2.2). In the closed-loop control model, an error signal operates in much the same way as a stimulus or input—it is processed in the executive (containing the stages) and it leads to a response (i.e., a correction in the movement). Numerous studies of tracking performance suggest that corrections occur at a maximum rate that is relatively slow—about three per second.

In the conceptual model, corrections occur a few hundred milliseconds after an errant action is produced. The error signal is processed in the stimulus-identification stage, a movement correction is chosen in the response-selection stage, and modifications to the movement are organized and initiated in the response-programming stage. Once the correction is initiated, the movement continues in its corrected form until the next segment of error information is processed. This type of closed-loop control is adequate as long as only two or three changes in the movement are required per second. However, if corrections must be made at a faster rate than this, performance is poor. This explains why baseball or cricket players find it difficult to catch a rapidly moving ball that is bouncing over a rough surface—the changes in direction of the ball occur too quickly, leaving the performer with little time to make adequate adjustments in the fielding movement.

Discrete Tasks of Brief Duration

Closed-loop control is also inadequate for performing skills that are brief in duration (e.g., the hitting, throwing, kicking, and striking tasks that are so common in many sports). When hitting a pitched baseball, for example, the batter first evaluates the environmental situation, particularly the path and speed of the approaching ball. He then selects a movement that is designed to achieve the goal (i.e., solid bat–ball contact, aimed in the proper direction). Using the stages of processing, the system selects a program and organizes it for initiation. Once the program is activated, effector processes carry out the movement pretty much as planned. As long as the environment (i.e., the pattern of ball flight and the pitch speed) remains as it was when the movement was organized, the response should be effective in achieving the goal.

But what if something in the environment suddenly changes? For example, what if the ball curves unexpectedly during its flight? Now the batter would need to alter the path of the swing or perhaps stop it altogether. A review of the conceptual model (see figure 3.6) allows us to estimate how much time it would take the batter to process this change and amend the ongoing swing. If such information had to pass through the stages of processing, it would take several hundred milliseconds before even the first modification in the movement could be made.

It Depends . . .

What Makes Closed-Loop Control Difficult?

People typically use closed-loop control for continuous tracking tasks such as driving a car. However, closed-loop control is not always effective for this task. What are some driving situations that make this type of control more difficult? Why is it important for a driver to slow down if the road is icy or if there is heavy fog? What if a squirrel suddenly crosses the road? Why might the driver be unable to avoid hitting the squirrel? What key factor determines the effectiveness of closed-loop control in situations like these?

And while processing of the change was occurring, the movement would continue to proceed as originally planned. If too much of the swing transpired before a correction could be made, successful contact with the ball would be unlikely.

Because closed-loop control is simply too slow to allow corrections during very rapid actions, performers must initiate a fully planned movement to achieve the goal.

Slater-Hammel's Experiment

Arthur Slater-Hammel (1960) conducted an experiment in which participants were asked to hold down a reaction key with a finger while watching the sweep hand of a timer that made one revolution per second. When participants lifted the finger, it caused the sweep hand to stop immediately. The participants' task was to watch the hand make one complete revolution (1 s) and then lift the finger from the key in such a way as to stop the sweep hand at the 800 ms position—that is, 800 ms after the sweep hand passed the zero position. With a little practice, these people learned to anticipate this action and lift their fingers in time to achieve the goal. Once they had attained a good level of proficiency, participants performed additional trials on the task. On a few of these trials, the experimenter stopped the sweep hand at various locations before it reached the 800 ms position. Participants were told that whenever this happened they were to keep their finger on the key—that is, to inhibit the finger-lift response. To determine how difficult it was for participants to inhibit the finger-lift response, Slater-Hammel plotted the probability of their lifting the finger at the different points at which the sweep hand was stopped.

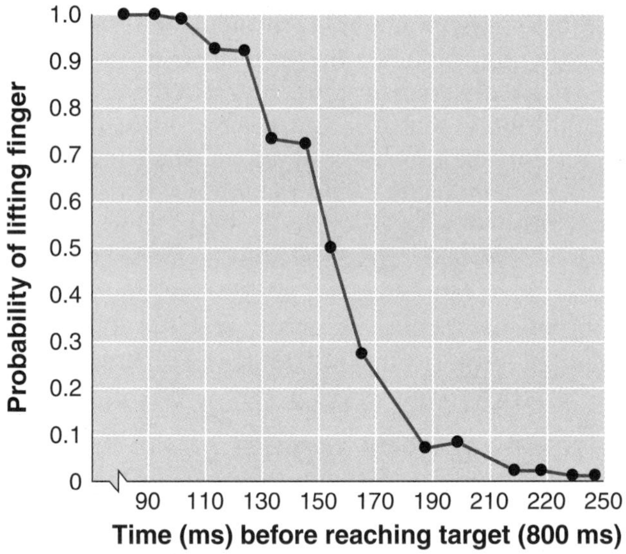

Figure 3.7 The probability of lifting the finger though the clock hand had stopped, plotted as a function of the interval of time before the 800 ms position. (Adapted from Slater-Hammel, 1960.)

His results are shown in figure 3.7. When the length of time before the 800 ms position was relatively long (greater than 210 ms), the probability that participants would lift their finger was practically zero; that is, they had no difficulty inhibiting the movement. However, as the length of time decreased (i.e., the sweep hand stopped nearer to the 800 ms position), the probability of their lifting their finger increased, to the point that, if the clock hand was stopped at 700 ms (i.e., leaving 100 ms to abort the response), the participants were almost never able to inhibit the movement. If the clock hand was stopped between 150 and 170 ms before the 800 ms position, participants were able to inhibit the movement successfully only about half the time. The most likely interpretation of Slater-Hammel's results is that the performers issued an internal "go" signal between 150 and 170 ms before the sweep hand arrived at the 800 ms position. This go signal triggered the finger-lift action and the movement occurred, even though later visual information (i.e., the stopping of the sweep hand) indicated that they should not make the movement.

Undoubtedly, you have experienced occasions where you initiated a movement and then wished you could stop it—like the times you realized that you did not have your keys just before slamming shut the locked door of your car or house. Perhaps you have tossed a tennis ball to your friend just as she looked away, hitting her in the back of the head. You found that you couldn't stop the toss once you had started it. We recall a compelling example from American football on TV. The quarterback was back to pass and a member of the opposing team knocked the ball away from behind, while the quarterback's arm was moving backward in preparation for the throw. The ball was now on the ground. In a perfect world, what would the quarterback now do? Of course, he would reach down and pick up the ball. But what did he do? He completed the throw, rotating his hips and moving his arm and hand forward just as if the ball were still there. And he even made the wrist rotation at the end of the throw to impart spin to the ball—all without the ball! In the preceding situations you may have thought that you planned the movement, then something happened that made you want to stop it, and then—seemingly a long time later—the movement occurred automatically, almost as if someone else were controlling it. Our view is that the someone or something controlling the movement after the internal go signal is given is a motor program. We discuss this concept in more detail in the next chapter.

Therefore, the general rule is that the first few hundred milliseconds of a brief rapid movement transpire more or less without modification. As you will see later in this chapter, though, sensory information plays a more important and effective role as the duration (i.e., time) of the movement increases (i.e., the action slows down in time).

More than any other observation, the sluggishness of closed-loop, feedback-based control has led scientists to propose that the production of most rapid movements depends on some form of advanced planning and movement preparation. In this view, moment-to-moment control is dictated by a preorganized plan, usually called the motor program, and is not dependent on the relatively slow stages of information processing used during closed-loop control. (However, feedback can sometimes act reflexively to modify movements far more quickly than indicated here. We discuss this aspect of feedback-based control in the next section, and we explain the concept of motor program control in more detail in chapter 4.)

Finally, scientists assume that performers initiate rapid actions in an all-or-none fashion, in much the same way that a trigger on a rifle, when pulled, causes a bullet to fire without the possibility of modification. Once some critical point, or threshold, is reached in the system, an internal "go" signal is delivered and the movement is initiated. Any signal given after the go signal has been executed is ignored by the system for a few hundred ms, and the movement proceeds without interruption. This is the kind of process discussed in chapter 2 and illustrated in fig. 2.11 (see page 50). Scientists believe that this internal signal occurs during the response-programming stage, as suggested by the results of an experiment by Slater-Hammel (1960), which we discuss in the research highlight and display in figure 3.7.

REFLEXIVE MODULATIONS IN MOVEMENT SKILLS

To this point, we have considered only one kind of closed-loop control process: the consciously controlled adjustment of performers' actions based on sensory information. However, other kinds of movement corrections of which we are not aware take

reflexes—
Stereotyped, involuntary, automatic, and usually rapid responses to stimuli.

electromyography (EMG)—
A method for recording the electrical activity in a muscle or group of muscles.

place when we perform skills. Relatively low-level processes lying in the spinal cord and brainstem mediate these modifications, which often involve little or no conscious control. They are termed **reflexes** because they mainly occur in a stereotyped, involuntary, and usually rapid fashion. In this section, we discuss how these adjustments operate and the circumstances under which lower-level reflex processes can contribute to motor control.

Types of Compensations

Imagine that you are a participant in a simple experiment. While in a standing position, you attempt to hold one of your elbows at a right angle with the palm of your hand facing up to support a moderate load, such as a book. You have a measuring stick in front of you to indicate the height of the book, and you are instructed to keep the book at a particular target height. While you are doing this, an experimenter is monitoring the electrical activity in your biceps muscle using **electromyography (EMG).** Suddenly, without warning, the experimenter adds another book to the one you are holding. Your hand immediately begins to drop, but after a brief delay you compensate for the added load by bringing your hand back up to the target position. The moment-to-moment position of your limb would look something like the dark line shown in the bottom half of figure 3.8.

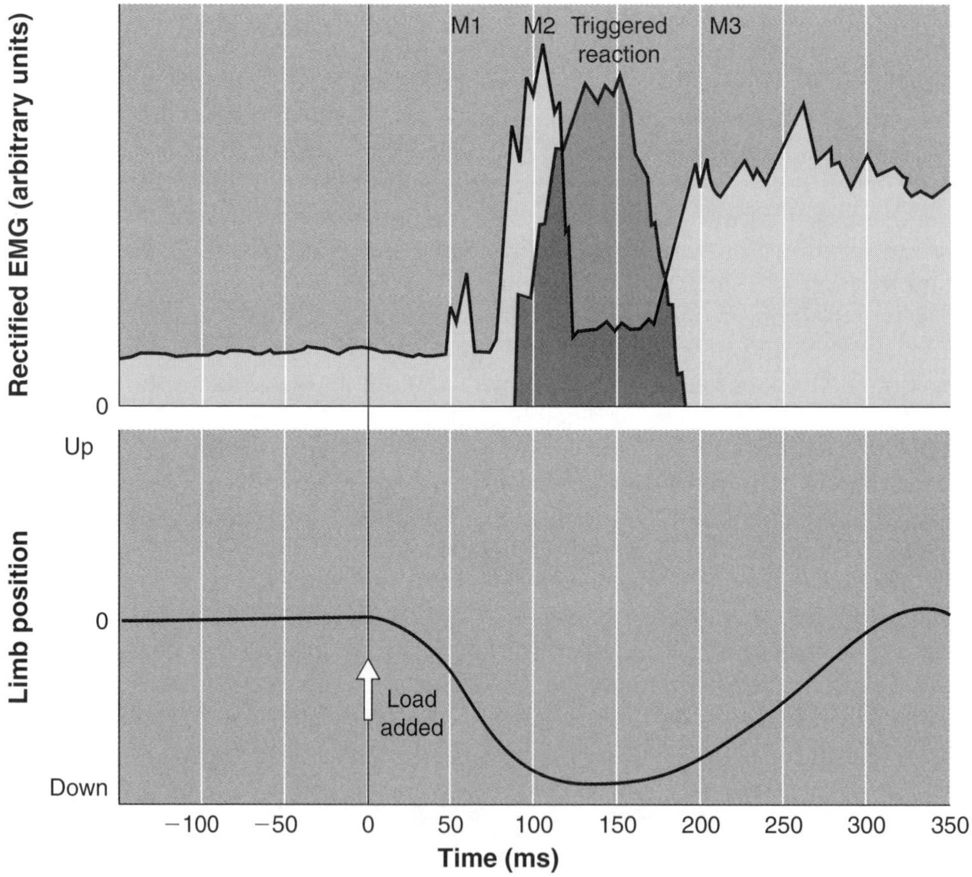

Figure 3.8 Electromyographic (EMG) responses to stretch of the biceps muscle and change in arm position when a load is suddenly applied. (Reprinted, by permission, from D.J. Dewhurst, © 1967 IEEE, "Neuromuscular control system," *IEEE Transactions on Biomedical-Engineering* 14: 170.)

What processes contribute to these compensations? A record of the EMG might look like the one shown in the top of figure 3.8. The gray shaded portion at the left of the figure represents the amount of EMG activity necessary for the biceps to hold the limb at the target position initially. After the experimenter adds the second book (i.e., where it says "load added" in the bottom half of the figure), several modifications to this level of activity occur, which are the motor system's compensations for the added load. These modifications involve the following:

1. M1 response, with a latency of 30 to 50 ms
2. M2 response, with a latency of 50 to 80 ms
3. Reaction-time response (M3), with a latency of 120 to 180 ms

Here, "latency" is the time from the added load until the start of the modified EMG. A fourth modification known as the triggered reaction, with a latency of 80 to 120 ms, is also shown in this figure (see maroon shaded area), although we will wait to discuss this process until later. The triggered reaction can activate several muscles simultaneously, producing a relatively fast, coordinated, although nonconscious correction designed to promote goal achievement (we discuss the triggered reaction in more detail later).

M1 Response

The first reflexive modification is a burst of EMG activity that occurs about 30 to 50 ms after the load is added. This activity is brief, not resulting in very much added contraction in the muscle; the limb is still moving downward even after this response occurs (see bottom half of figure 3.8). Sometimes called the monosynaptic stretch reflex, the **M1 response** is one of the most rapid reflexes underlying limb control. It is prompted when a load is added unexpectedly by the stretching of the muscle spindles that lie in the stretched muscle. The spindles relay sensory information to the spinal cord, where a single connection (or synapse) is made. Then the information is routed directly back to the same muscle that was stretched, causing an increased contraction (seen in figure 3.8 as the small EMG burst labeled M1). The latency, or time of the start of this correction, is very short because it involves only one synapse (hence the term *monosynaptic)* and the signal has a relatively short distance to travel.

M1 response— The monosynaptic stretch reflex, with a latency of 30 to 50 ms.

The M1 reflex is thought to be responsible for modifications in muscle contraction caused by small stretches, such as those that occur during postural sways or when our limbs are subjected to unanticipated outside forces, such as when we step on a moving sidewalk (see figure 3.9*a*). These reflex processes are nonconscious and are therefore not affected by factors such as the number of possible stimulus-response alternatives—as described by **Hick's law,** discussed in chapter 2. Thousands of these modifications can occur simultaneously to control functions such as limb position and posture. Because they occur at the same time, in parallel, nonconsciously, and presumably without interfering with each other, these compensations do not require our attention and thus are automatic.

Hick's law— Law describing the stable relationship that exists between the number of stimulus-response alternatives and choice reaction time; specifically, as the logarithm of the number of stimulus-response pairs increases, choice reaction time increases linearly.

M2 Response

About 50 to 80 ms after the experimenter adds the load, there is a second burst of EMG activity (see figure 3.8). Sometimes called the functional stretch reflex, long-loop reflex, or M2 reflex, the **M2 response** generates a higher-amplitude burst of EMG than does the M1 reflex. In addition, this response has a longer duration, and it contributes a greater adjustment to the movement than does the M1 reflex. Like the M1 response, the M2 response arises from activity in the muscle spindles and travels to the spinal cord. However, the impulses continue up the cord to higher centers in the brain (i.e., the motor cortex, the cerebellum, or both), where they are processed and more synapses are

M2 response— The polysynaptic, functional stretch reflex, with a latency of 50 to 80 ms; sometimes called the *long-loop reflex.*

Figure 3.9 Practical examples of involuntary and voluntary responses.

involved. Motor impulses are then sent back down the cord to activate muscles (which in our example control the elbow). The longer distance traveled and the additional synapses at the higher brain levels account for some of the added latency, or time lag, before the M2 response occurs.

The M2 response, in combination with the M1 response, is responsible for the well-known knee-jerk reflex we have all experienced at the doctor's office. We sit on an examination table, with our lower leg hanging down. The doctor taps our patellar tendon, located at the base of the kneecap. This causes the quadriceps muscle on the front of our thigh to stretch, initiating a reflex response that contracts the quadriceps and produces an involuntary extension of the knee, raising the lower leg.

What are some of the characteristics of the M2 response? Like the M1 response, it is not affected by the number of stimulus-response alternatives and thus does not conform to Hick's law. In addition, the M2 response is more flexible than the M1 response, allowing for the involvement of a few additional sources of sensory information during the response. This response is also sensitive to instructions. In our example, if the experimenter had instructed you to let go when the added weight was applied (rather than to resist), the M2 response would have been largely abolished and your limb would have settled into a new position. At the same time, the M1 response would have occurred unmodified by the instruction and thus would have played a small role in determining the new position.

M2 Response: Combining Voluntary and Involuntary Motor Control

The M2 response is an interesting one because it is influenced by instructions (and therefore is, in this sense, voluntary) yet has reflexive properties as well (and therefore is involuntary). One way to conceptualize this combination of voluntary and involuntary motor control is to think about the way a home security system works. To set it, the homeowner enables the system by turning a key when she leaves in the morning; this is clearly the voluntary part. Does this ring the alarm? No. So what causes the alarm to ring? When a burglar tries to force open the window or door, this provides a stimulus to the alarm system. That's what triggers the ring. In this sense the ring is reflexive (triggered instantly by the stimulus) but it is modified by a voluntary event (the homeowner's decision to enable the system). If the homeowner decides she doesn't want the alarm to work on Friday (because a friend will be stopping by to pick up a package inside the unlocked kitchen door), she doesn't make the voluntary decision to enable the system that day, and the alarm doesn't sound when the friend enters the house.

triggered reaction—A relatively complex, coordinated reaction to a particular stimulus, with a latency of 80 to 120 ms; it is flexible yet faster than the M3 response.

We can adjust the size or amplitude of the M2 response voluntarily for a given input to generate a powerful response when the goal is to hold the joint as firmly as possible, to produce no response if the goal is to release under the increased load, or to produce some degree of rigidness in between. This capability for variation is fortunate because it allows us to prepare our limbs to conform to different environmental demands. In skiing, for example, the performer wants her knees to be supple and to yield to sudden bumps (see figure 3.9*b*), yet in other situations (e.g., wrestling) an athlete might want his muscles to resist when his opponent applies a sudden force to them.

In some ways, the M2 response is a unique kind of response. It is too fast to be called a voluntary response, which, as we learned in the previous section, would require 150 to 200 ms to be initiated. Yet it can be modified voluntarily through conscious processes, such as our perception of sensory information (perhaps the nearby moguls in downhill skiing) and the instruction to "yield to sudden bumps."

A skier can voluntarily adjust the amplitude of the M2 response to match environmental demands, making the knees supple and yielding to sudden bumps.

Triggered Reactions

A third type of response (see figure 3.8) has a somewhat longer latency than the M2 response. Referred to as the **triggered reaction,** this response is also too fast to be a voluntary reaction, having a latency of 80 to 120 ms, but it is too slow to be an M2 (or M1) response. The triggered reaction can affect

UNIVERSITY OF WINCHESTER
LIBRARY

musculature that is quite far from the actual stimulation site, it generates coordinated reactions, and it is thought to be sensitive to the number of stimulus alternatives in the same way as the conventional reaction-time response. Apparently, the triggered reaction can also be learned and can become a more or less automatic response (similar to the kind we discussed in chapter 2).

People experience triggered reactions in a number of everyday situations, such as when someone lifts a wineglass and it begins to slip, its red contents perhaps threatening a white carpet. These tiny slips generate vibrations that are detected by cutaneous receptors in the fingertips. The vibrations trigger several very fast compensations to stop the slip. First, an increase in grip force is produced in the muscles of the forearm, which causes our hand to squeeze the glass somewhat tighter. There is also a decrease in force in the biceps muscle, slowing the upward acceleration of the lift and reducing the tendency of the glass to slip. These reactions, sometimes termed the wineglass effect (Johansson & Westling, 1984), are coordinated beautifully, being triggered as a single, unitary compensation for the slip. They are faster than a typical reaction time, with latencies of about 80 ms, and the compensations appear to be nonconscious in that they are made even before we are aware that the glass is slipping. Another example of the triggered reaction is found in the sport of wrestling. When a wrestler wraps his arm around an opponent's waist and the opponent attempts to escape the hold, the escape action is detected by cutaneous receptors in the forearm of the wrestler applying the hold. The resulting combination of rapid compensations in the arm and elsewhere allows the wrestler to maintain the hold (see figure 3.9*c*).

M3 response— The voluntary reaction-time response, with a latency of 120 to 180 ms.

Voluntary Reaction-Time Response (M3 Response)

A final type of response that occurs when the experimenter increases the load unexpectedly is the voluntary reaction, sometimes called the **M3 response.** Seen as the fourth burst of EMG activity in figure 3.8, it is powerful and sustained, bringing the limb back to the desired position and holding it there. The latency of the M3 response is about 120 to 180 ms, depending on the task and circumstances, and it can affect all of the muscles of the body, not just those that are being stretched. The M3 response is the most flexible of all the responses discussed here, being modified by a host of factors, such as instructions and the performer's anticipation of sensory information. Of course, the delay in the M3 response makes it sensitive to the number of stimulus-response alternatives, following Hick's law. However, voluntary reactions require the stages of information processing, discussed in chapter 2 and illustrated in figure 3.6, meaning that adjustments occur in a sequential fashion and require the person's attention (see figure 3.9*d*).

Table 3.1 Characteristics of Classes of Muscular Responses to Perturbations During Movement

Response type	Latency, ms	Flexibility or adaptability	Role of instructions	Effect of number of choices
M1 response	30-50	Almost none	None	None
M2 response	50-80	Low	Some	Possible
Triggered reaction	80-120	Moderate	Large	Moderate
Reaction-time response	120-180	Very high	Very large	Large

Coordinating Compensations for Unexpected Loads

The four kinds of compensations we have discussed, along with their major characteristics, are summarized in table 3.1. An important feature to note is that as the latency of the response increases (i.e., it takes more time to initiate), the response becomes systematically less rigid, or increasingly flexible. At one extreme is the M1 response, which is practically insensitive to environmental demands but is very fast. At the other extreme is the M3 or reaction-time response, which is extremely sensitive to environmental demands but is comparatively slow. The other two types of responses fall between these extremes. The four types of responses illustrate a trade-off between the flexibility and the speed of reactions. If more flexibility is called for, more sources of sensory information must be taken into account before the action is defined. This means that more information-processing activities must occur, requiring more time.

It Depends . . .

How Do Reflex Responses Contribute to Motor Control?

Let's say you decide to go mountain biking on an unfamiliar trail. During your ride, it is likely that all the responses shown in table 3.1 will occur at one time or another. Which response would occur if you suddenly hit a bump? If a rabbit darted in front of you? If the brakes failed? If you hit some loose dirt and felt the bicycle sliding out from under you? What factors seem to govern the functioning of each of these responses? What might you do to diminish the activity of M1 responses, M2 responses, and triggered reactions during your ride?

Reflex Responses in the Conceptual Model

Now we can integrate two of these reflexive modifications in movement control into the conceptual model shown in figure 3.6. Figure 3.10 contains the same diagram as presented earlier but with the addition of the M1 and M2 responses. The M1 feedback loop (thin maroon line) carries feedback about muscle length (stretch), and perhaps muscle tension, to the spinal cord, which relays modifications directly to the muscles. This loop is fast, is relatively inflexible, and includes the lowest level of feedback-based corrections in movement control, having minimal contact with any of the higher brain centers.

The M2 feedback loop (thick line) is the long-loop or functional stretch reflex. Here information about muscle force and length as well as joint position and body position is fed back to somewhat higher centers in the brain concerned with planning and initiating the action. Once this feedback arrives, programming processes modify movement commands slightly and send this information back to the spinal cord and muscle levels. This loop is longer and slower than that for the M1 response, but it has more flexibility because it involves higher control centers.

Final Common Path

The final common path (Sherrington, 1906) is an important idea for motor control. Contributions to movement control arise from at least three sources, as illustrated in figure 3.10. First is the original set of movement commands coming from the motor program down the spinal cord to the muscles. Added to this is the contribution of the M1 response, sensitive to muscle force and length. Finally, there is the M2 response, sensitive to limb position and movement as well as to muscle force and length. Therefore, the final common path (or ultimate contribution) of the central nervous system to muscle action is the sum of all these separate flows of information, each having a different latency and a different type and amount of influence.

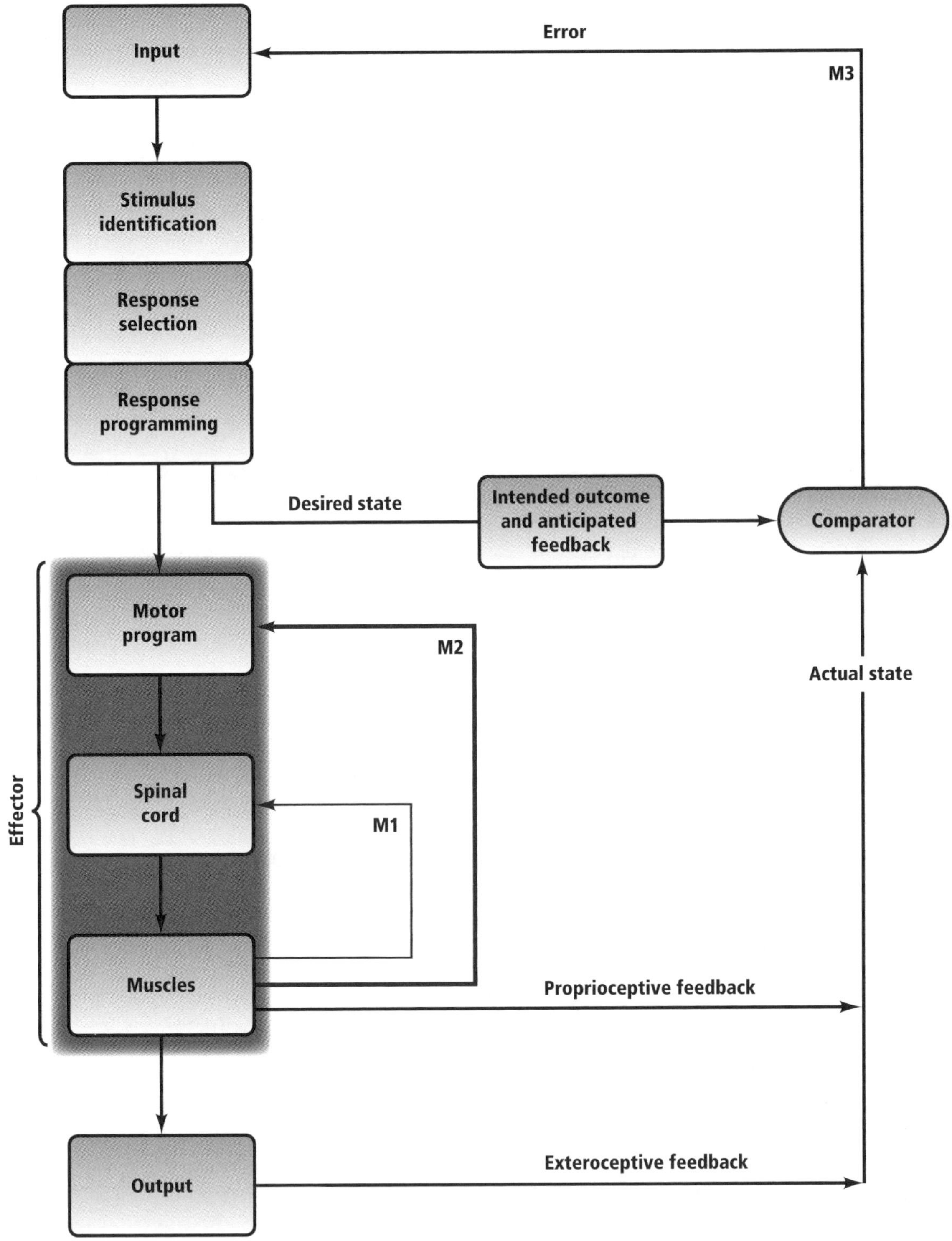

Figure 3.10 The conceptual model of motor performance expanded further, here by the addition of M1 and M2 feedback loops, shown by the thin and thick maroon lines, respectively.

Loops Within Loops

The notion of embedded feedback loops emphasizes that certain closed loops operate totally within other closed loops. For example, the M1 response shown in figure 3.10 operates between the muscles and the spinal cord, exerting its influence on the control of muscle length (or limb position) when the performer experiences an unexpected variation in load. This loop does not have access to higher-order information about the goals of the task but rather is restricted to the relatively dumb task of holding muscle length constant. Thus, the position of the elbow joint will be controlled for a while by the M1 response even though environmental circumstances might have changed such that a new elbow position would be better. The M2 response operates between the muscles and the motor program, initiating subtle adjustments as needed in the intended program. As with the M1 response, the M2 response is insensitive to the status of goal achievement (e.g., whether the driver is steering correctly or whether the basketball is going into the basket), but these responses faithfully attempt to hold muscle force and length constant and carry out the planned movement, respectively. Any information about goal achievement or lack of such is processed as an M3 response in the outer loop (shown on the right side of figure 3.10), which includes feedback from the environment (e.g., vision), the activity of the comparator, and, if there is an error signal indicating a failure of goal achievement, the information-processing stages to select a totally new action.

Role of Movement Time

movement time (MT)—The interval of time that elapses from the beginning to the end of a movement.

The relative roles of these responses depend on the duration of the movement the person is trying to produce, as shown in figure 3.11. The quickest of movements (e.g., a boxing punch) has a **movement time** (MT) of only 40 ms or so (see figure 3.11*a*). For these brief movements, the M3 response (outer feedback loop) and the M2 response (with a latency of 50-80 ms; shown as the thick maroon line in the inner loop) are incapable of completing their processing activities in time to modify the action once it is initiated. Even the M1 response (with a latency of 30-50 ms; shown as the thin maroon line) has only enough time to begin influencing the muscles near the end of the movement.

Movements that take longer to be completed, such as a stroke of the racket in racquetball lasting 100 ms or so, are more likely to be influenced by the M1 response. As shown in figure 3.11*b*, in 100 ms of activity the M1 feedback loop has the potential of reaching the level of the muscles, thereby influencing the movement and the environmental outcome. However, in that time activity in the M2 loop has not yet reached the muscles and is therefore capable of little influence. The outer, voluntary feedback loop (M3 response) can have no influence; the information has barely left the comparator (as indicated by the thick maroon line) and has not yet reached the executive.

Movements that take longer than 100 ms (e.g., the tennis ground stroke lasting about 200 ms) allow both the M1 and M2 responses sufficient time to contribute to all levels of the action, from the level of the motor program (for the M2 response) to that of the output or environmental results (see figure 3.11*c*). Still, information in the outer, voluntary feedback loop has just barely reached the stages of processing, so the information remains essentially incapable of influencing the action.

Only when the duration of the movement is about 300 ms or longer is there potential for the outer loop to be involved in amending the movement. A tennis serve takes about 300 ms to complete (see figure 3.11*d*; note how all loops reach all the way to the results or output of the action). Thus, for movements that take longer than 300 ms, closed-loop control is possible at several levels at the same time.

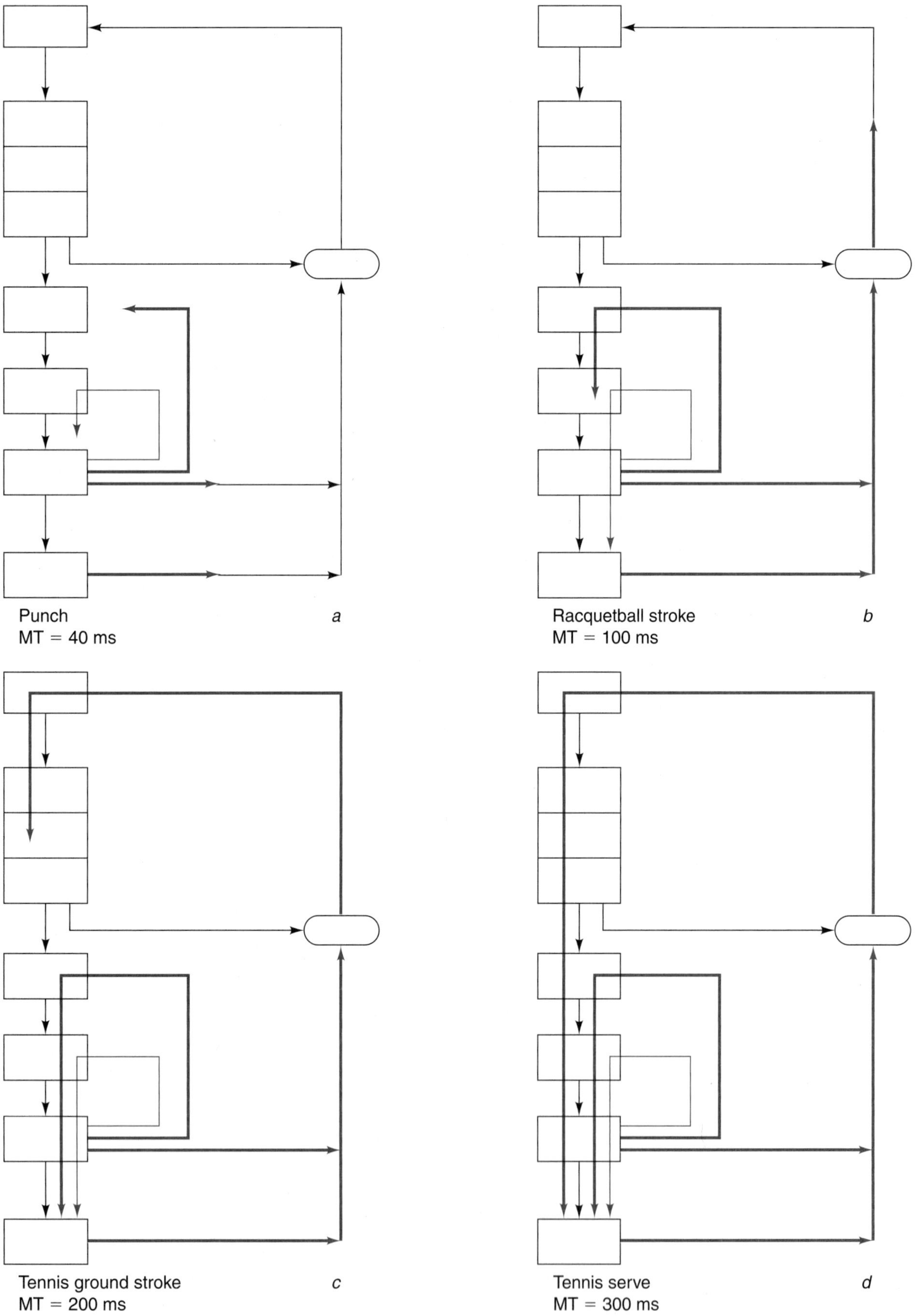

Figure 3.11 The progress of the various feedback loops after movements of various durations. The lowest-level reflex activities are completed first, and the highest-level responses are completed last.

As movement time increases (i.e., the movement becomes longer in time), there is greater potential for more feedback loops to contribute to the originally intended action. Given this observation, it should not surprise us that movement time is one of the most important variables influencing the way we control our movements. Specifically, movement time dictates the kinds of feedback-based corrections that are possible and the relative contribution of various types of modifications (i.e., M1, M2, and M3 responses) to the original movement commands.

Walking on Ice

A person walking along a sidewalk in winter might benefit from the activity of several of the responses shown in table 3.1. If the person suddenly stepped on a dangerous patch of ice, she might have time to use the voluntary reaction response (M3) to regain balance. However, if she began to fall, the M1 response would initiate a righting reflex in the trunk and legs, while the M2 response would either contribute to the righting reflex or produce a letting-go response, depending on the preference of the person. In the latter case, the lack of resistance might result in a more controlled fall.

The Problem of Controlled Processing

In many cases the performer can choose the type of motor control to use. If a movement is rather brief in duration, such as a component of a dance routine, the dancer can plan the action so that only the fast, automatic processes are necessary once the movement is initiated. On the other hand, the dancer could choose to preprogram only a small portion of the action and modify the rest as needed by using the outer, voluntary feedback loop using controlled processing, as shown in figure 3.11*d*. Although this style of control would seem to ensure great accuracy at the end of the action, it can cause problems during the movement. Teachers often see examples of this when they tell learners to concentrate on a particular part of the action or to focus on a particular source of movement feedback (e.g., the feel of the position of the feet). With such instructions, individuals attempt to control their movements in a more conscious, effortful fashion, with their decisions about the action being handled in a slow, attention-demanding way (i.e., with controlled processing). In such instances, performance is usually hesitant and choppy. Interestingly, the general notion that paying attention to one's actions can actually impair performance has been around for years and was known in the psychology literature as the Bliss–Boder hypothesis (Bliss, 1892-1893, Boder, 1935; see also Wulf, 2007). Gallwey's popular book *The Inner Game of Tennis* (1974) encourages performers to allow their movements to flow or to be run off without conscious intervention using what we have called

It Depends . . .

How Does "Paralysis By Analysis" Influence Movement Control?

Preplanned movement control relies on little, if any, of the slow, jerky, attention-demanding processes associated with outer feedback-loop operations (see figure 3.10). In fact, a performer's over-reliance on these types of conscious processes often results in a form of movement control that some have termed "paralysis by analysis." Perhaps that's why many recent studies have demonstrated that focusing attention on the intended outcome of a movement produces superior performance and learning compared with focusing on the mechanics of the action (e.g., Wulf, McConnel, Gärtner, & Schwarz, 2002; Wulf, Mercer, McNevin, & Guadagnoli, 2004). You can experience this phenomenon by attempting a skill familiar to you (e.g., playing a musical instrument, performing a dance, throwing an object at a target) under two sets of conditions. First, try to perform the skill by focusing only on the goal of the task (e.g., playing the song, staying in rhythm with the music, hitting the center of the target). After you do this, try to perform the skill by focusing on the movements themselves (e.g., the movements of the hands, the positioning of the feet, the mechanics of the throwing motion). Which set of conditions produces the better performance? Now, using the conceptual model shown in figure 3.10, explain what is happening under each set of performance conditions.

automatic processing. Gallwey contended that people perform best when they simply let the motor system control the action, rather than when they attempt to intervene using controlled processing. By preprogramming their movements, performers relegate control to the faster, inner feedback loops (see figure 3.11, *a-c*). Also, by attending to the movement itself, the person is not able to attend to and process information from the environment, which could be of use in the near future.

The slowness of conscious control and controlled processing also suggests that many actions are not preceded by much if any systematic conscious activity. Consider, for example, the reaction-time movements we discussed in chapter 2. It is likely that participants in reaction-time experiments become conscious of their movements only *after* they are completed rather than before they are initiated. Certainly, it is reasonable to presume that some form of conscious activity precedes the execution of many closed skills, particularly when there is adequate time for planning (e.g., sawing a board, performing a gymnastics routine). However, as we indicated in the previous section, the conscious control of movements once they are initiated becomes very difficult unless there is adequate time to process feedback and make the necessary adjustments. As Wegner (2002) suggested, "Consciousness and action seem to play a cat-and-mouse game over time. Although we may be conscious of whole vistas of action before the doings get underway, it is as though the conscious mind then slips out of touch" (p. 59). Given that there may be very little opportunity for the conscious control of movements, performers must provide the system with as much advance information as possible so that what is witnessed (at the conscious level) and adjusted (at the reflexive level) is an outcome that is as close to the intended one as possible.

Feedback Processing in Ice Hockey

Applied research in ice hockey has demonstrated that players who are more skilled at skating can devote their attention to processing additional sources of feedback information. Leavitt (1979) examined the skating time (time to skate a given distance) of six groups of ice hockey players, differing in age (6-19 years old) and experience level (less than 1 year to more than 15 years), under several skating conditions. In the simplest condition, participants skated as fast as they could for a distance of 50 ft (15.2 m). In another condition, they skated as fast as possible while attempting to control a puck with their hockey stick (referred to as "stick handling"). Not surprisingly, the older, more experienced players had shorter skating times than the younger, less experienced players in both conditions. Of interest, however, was the additional finding that skating times for the two oldest and most experienced groups were virtually the same in both the skating-only and the skating-plus-stick-handling conditions, while for the younger and less experienced players, the additional stick-handling task resulted in a greater slowing of skating speed. Because the task of skating is probably not as automated for younger, less experienced players as it is for their older, more experienced counterparts, it is likely that younger players have to rely on slower feedback-based control for the skating component of stick handling. In subsequent experiments, Leavitt found that beginning players who used larger pucks and ice hockey sticks with larger blades both skated and stick-handled faster than beginners who used smaller (regulation) pucks and junior ice hockey sticks with smaller blades. This is probably because larger pucks and sticks are easier to control and require less feedback processing.

Let It Flow

When asked to describe the characteristics of their best performances, athletes usually mention the sensation of being on "automatic pilot." Conscious control of the movement seems to be next to nonexistent. In some cases, the performer's primary focus is on "letting the movement happen" or on a particular performance goal. In other situations, the performer's focus is on some source of environmental information that gets her into flow. Orlick and Partington (1986) provided these examples, based on interviews they conducted with Canadian Olympic athletes:

- Rhythmic gymnast: "I'll just say, 'Okay, now, you've got to do it, that's all there is to it. Go out, start it,' and from then on it's great (let it happen)." (p. 60)
- Alpine skier: "I like to put it (the performance goal) in a positive way, 'Stay on line and go with the flow.'" (p. 66)
- Pairs kayak athlete: "I used to look out over my partner's paddle when I was in the back of the boat because I found that was the easiest way to keep in stroke with her. I could see a 'big look' by looking beyond her paddle (external environmental information). When I did that, I would feel myself move into 'sync' with her." (p. 75)

Mind Games

Sometimes competitive athletes use psychological tactics designed to make their opponents think about the control of their movements. For example, a tennis player might casually ask her opponent, "What are you doing differently with your serve today? You seem to be hitting it really well!" If the opponent begins to think about the things she might be doing differently, resulting in a shift to a more conscious form of movement control, she will likely begin hitting her serves less effectively.

ROLE OF TWO VISUAL SYSTEMS IN MOVEMENT CONTROL

To this point, we have treated all sources of sensory information as if they operated in essentially the same way during skilled action. In reality, one sensory system—vision—tends to dominate the others. Therefore, it deserves special mention for its unique role in movement control.

Over the past 30 years or so, it has become increasingly clear to scientists that two essentially separate visual systems underlie human behavior. Visual information is delivered from the retina of the eye along two separate pathways to two places in the brain, and there is good evidence that these two pathways are used differently in the control of behavior (Trevarthen, 1968). More precisely, the two systems (see table 3.2) are

- focal vision, specialized for object identification, and
- ambient vision, specialized for movement control.

Focal Vision for Object Identification

focal vision—The visual system people use primarily to identify objects; it uses the center of the visual field, leads to conscious visual perception, and is degraded in dim lighting.

Focal vision is the system that is the most familiar to us as a result of personal experience. This system is specialized for the conscious identification of objects that lie primarily in the center of our visual field. Its major function seems to be providing answers to the general question "What is it?" In fact, you are using this system right now to identify images such as the words on this page. Focal vision contributes to our conscious

Table 3.2 Comparison of the Two Visual Systems

Feature	Focal vision	Ambient vision
Visual field location	Central only	Central and peripheral
Awareness	Conscious	Nonconscious
Effect of low illumination	Degradation	Very little
General question resolved	What is it?	Where is it?

perception of the objects to which we attend visually, leading to identification and perhaps action. Focal vision is severely degraded by dim lighting conditions, as we know from trying to read or to find a lost coin in the grass without adequate light.

Ambient Vision for Movement Control

ambient vision—The visual system that allows people to detect the orientation of their body in the environment; it is nonconscious, takes in all of the visual field, and is used for action and movement control.

A second, less obvious visual system is **ambient vision.** Distinct from focal vision, ambient vision involves both central and peripheral portions of the visual field. Furthermore, it is not seriously degraded in dim lighting conditions. Ambient vision allows us to walk on uneven terrain in near darkness; we have no trouble making our way without tripping, even though the light is far too dim for reading a book.

Scientists believe that the ambient system is specialized for action and movement control. It detects the positions of objects in the environment as well as their movement. Ambient vision also provides us with information about our own movements in relation to other objects. Thus, we use ambient vision to answer questions such as "Where is it?" or "Where am I in relation to it?" Our ambient system contributes to the fine control of movements without our being aware of it, which may be why we have so much difficulty appreciating its value. In table 3.2, we summarize the essential features of focal and ambient vision.

VISUAL CONTROL OF MOTOR PERFORMANCE

How do we use visual information for movement control? What factors determine its effectiveness? In the following section we discuss the separate roles of the focal and ambient visual systems in motor performance.

Focal Vision and the Orienting of Attention

Although we use focal vision primarily for object identification, it is wrong to conclude that this system has no role in movement control. Focal vision has access to consciousness, so visual information handled by this system is processed through the information-processing stages (discussed in chapter 2). The processing of this type of visual information leads to action in much the same way as the processing of any other information. In the conceptual model shown in figure 3.6, vision is represented as another source of exteroceptive information obtained from the environment. Therefore, the only way individuals can use focal vision for movement control is to process it through the stages. In one sense, focal vision is the lens we use to direct our attention to relevant environmental information. We focus visually on a narrow cylindrical object with a fine point on one end, identify it as a pencil, and organize an action to pick it up. The baseball batter focuses on the pitcher's hand containing the baseball because that is the source of information that is most relevant for effective hitting. Failing to focus on relevant environmental information can lead to performance errors, such as when the batter cannot determine the details of a pitch. Clearly, then, focal vision contributes to motor performance by helping us orient our attention to certain types of environmental information that are essential for our success.

Before realizing that there could be an ambient system for movement control, scientists also believed that a conscious focal system was the only way visual information could influence action. According to this outmoded view, a baseball batter watching a pitch approaching the plate would be able to use only the relatively slow information-processing stages to detect the ball's flight pattern and initiate changes in the swing. This idea was supported by numerous experiments revealing that it takes about 200 ms (or approximately the duration of visual reaction time) for someone to use visual information for movement control (Keele & Posner, 1968) and that the visual control of action is particularly slow and cumbersome. However, recent information about the ambient visual system, together with the discovery of optical-flow processes in vision, has changed our understanding of the ways people use visual information to control their movements markedly.

Focal Vision and the Quiet Eye Phenomenon

An important challenge for scientists is determining how performers use vision to control their movements. Research by Vickers (1996) suggests that an important difference in the visual control of expert and nonexpert performers is a preexecution period of visual fixation Vickers called the "quiet eye." The four characteristics of quiet eye are a directing of attention to a critical location or target in the performance environment, an onset that occurs prior to the intended movement, a duration that is longer for elite performers than for those of lesser skill levels, and of course a high level of stability. Recent research examining the quiet eye phenomenon has substantiated Vickers' predictions and shown that preperformance visual fixations are fewer and longer but cease earlier (as the movement is being executed) for highly skilled than for lesser skilled performers in closed skills such as basketball shooting (Oudejans, Koedijker, Bleijendaal, & Bakker, 2005; Vickers, 1997), billiards (Williams, Singer, & Frehlich, 2002), and small-bore rifle shooting (Janelle et al., 2000), as well as in open skills such as goaltending in ice hockey (Panchuk & Vickers, 2006) and defensive tactics (Martell & Vickers, 2004). In the study by Janelle and colleagues (2000), participants attempted 40 rounds of target shooting on a simulator. In addition to recording shot accuracy and duration of aiming, the researchers obtained eye-movement and brain-wave data that allowed them to estimate visual gaze behavior of the shooters. Performance accuracy was significantly higher and the visual fixation period preceding shot execution longer for experts than for nonexperts. Brain-wave results also indicated superior engagement of visuospatial resources by experts compared with nonexperts. The results of all these studies suggest that superior performance in some closed- and open-skill situations is attributable in part to the performer's capability of achieving a fixation of the eye (i.e., quiet eye) prior to movement execution.

optical flow—The movement (or continuous flow) of patterns of light rays from the environment over a person's retina, allowing the person to detect motion, position, and timing.

Ambient Vision and Movement Control

The late James J. Gibson (1966) prompted scientists to begin searching for aspects of visual information that performers process for movement control. A fundamental concept that stimulated their search was a phenomenon called **optical flow**.

Optical Flow

When you look into a lighted, textured environment, each visible feature reflects rays of light that enter your eye at particular angles (see figure 3.12). Imagine that objects A and B in this environment each reflect light rays into your eye, which is located at position 1a or 1b (only one eye is shown at each position for simplification). As you (and thus your eye) begin to move toward position 2a or 2b, the angles at which the light from the object enters your eye change predictably over time. These changes are continuous and can be thought of as a flow of light patterns across the retina. This pattern of optical flow provides an observer with the following kinds of information about his or her movement:

- Stability and balance
- Velocity of the movement through the environment
- Direction of the movement relative to the position of fixed objects in the environment

Bridgeman, Kirch, and Sperling's Experiment

Bridgeman, Kirch, and Sperling (1981) provided some of the strongest evidence for the existence of an ambient system for movement control. In their experiment, participants sat in a darkened room in front of a screen. Projected on the screen was a rectangle (like a picture frame) with a spot of light located inside of it. Unbeknownst to the participants, the frame was moved back and forth a few degrees while the dot remained in a fixed position. Under these conditions, participants experienced the illusion of the dot moving back and forth within the (fixed) frame, rather than the frame moving back and forth as it actually was. This phenomenon suggests that the focal visual system (the one with access to consciousness) can be deceived: In this study it caused the participants to think they were seeing the dot move, when actually it remained stationary.

Next, Bridgeman and his colleagues attempted to manipulate the ambient system. In a second condition, participants were instructed that, if the frame and dot were suddenly turned off, leaving the room in total darkness, they should immediately point to the position they last remembered seeing the dot. If the focal system was used to control the hand, and if participants' conscious perception was that the dot was moving back and forth, then the pointing movements should have varied from right to left in coordination with the perceived movements of the dot. Bridgeman and his colleagues found that when the lights were turned off, participants pointed to where the dot actually was located, not to where they perceived it to be. That is, the ambient system was not deceived by the movements of the frame. The investigators interpreted this to mean that people use their nonconscious ambient vision in movement control, at least in tasks like this. This investigation provides support for the existence of two separate visual systems: the focal system and the ambient system. The focal system, which is conscious, is used to identify objects in the center of the visual field (e.g., the dot) and is biased by the movement of surrounding objects (e.g., the frame). The ambient system, which is nonconscious, is used for movement control and is not biased by the movement of surrounding objects.

- Movement of environmental objects relative to the observer
- Time until contact between the observer and an object in the environment

Assume that you were moving directly toward object A, as in figure 3.12*a*. You would sense forward motion (from position 1a to position 2a) by an increase in the angle between the light rays entering your eye coming from the two edges of object A. (Also, the rays of light from object B would sweep across your retina.) If you were moving backward, these changes would be reversed, indicating opposite motion in the environment. You would sense the speed of movement by the rate of change of the angles of the light entering your eye from the sides of objects A and B, with faster movement producing more rapid changes in these angles.

In addition to providing information about the backward–forward dimension, optical flow provides information about subtle differences in the direction of travel. In figure 3.12*a*, the observer is moving directly toward object A, so the angles of the light from the object as they enter the eye form meaningful patterns. In general, a person perceives that he is moving directly toward or away from an object when the angles of light entering his eye from both sides of the object change in opposite directions at the same rate. The combined angle becomes bigger if he is moving toward the object, and it becomes smaller if he is backing away from the object. However, if the observer is moving so that the object is passing on his right side (see figure 3.12*b*), then the angles of light from both sides of the object entering the eye change in the same direction, with the one entering the eye from the right side of the object changing more quickly than the one entering from the left.

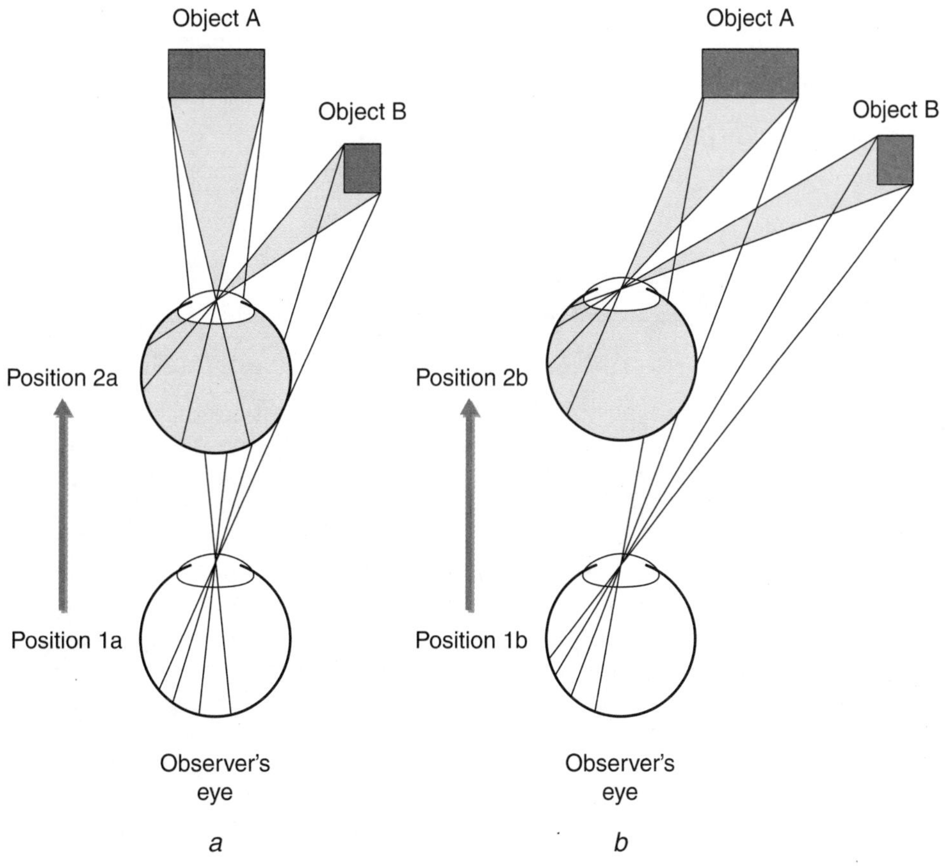

Figure 3.12 Optical-flow information specifies the direction and speed of an observer's eye moving forward through an environment containing objects A and B (*a*) or moving past the objects located on the person's right side (*b*).

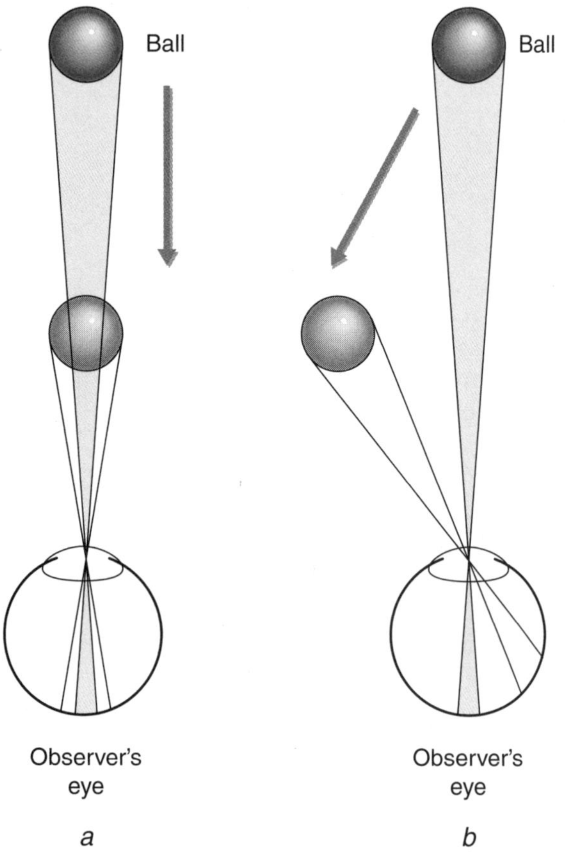

Figure 3.13 Optical flow provides information about an approaching ball's speed and direction when it is traveling directly toward the eye (*a*) and at an angle that takes it to the left of the eye (*b*) of a fixed observer.

Presumably, a hiker knows how to walk through a forest or a rugby player knows how to avoid a tackler by processing information about the relative rates of change in the visual angles of light from the respective objects in those two environments. The term **visual proprioception**, suggested by D.N. Lee (1980), describes the type of sensory information that arises when vision, usually considered strictly a form of exteroceptive information, provides performers with information about proprioception, the movement of their bodies in space.

Visual proprioception may also occur in situations where an object, such as a ball, moves toward a motionless observer. In figure 3.13*a*, the angles of the light rays entering the eye from the edges of the ball change at the same rate from each side of the ball, indicating that the ball is coming directly toward the eye. In figure 3.13*b*, the ball is not moving directly toward the observer, so the angles of light entering the eye from both sides of the ball are all changing in the same direction, but those entering from the left side of the ball are changing at a faster rate than those entering from the right side. This information indicates that the ball is moving toward the observer's left side, possibly serving as input to the person's motor system to move the arm to the left to catch the ball.

A special case of visual proprioception is the involuntary avoidance response. We've all had this experience: An object suddenly hurtles directly toward our eyes. Our response is a nearly automatic blink of the eyes coupled with a jerk of the head to avoid being struck. Visual scientists refer to this as *looming*. Even a newborn baby shows this response when someone suddenly moves a hand directly toward the infant's face, even if the baby has never experienced being struck in

visual proprioception—Sensory information provided by the visual system about proprioceptive aspects of a person's movements.

How Do Fielders Intercept a Ball in Flight?

Research examining the eye and body movements of fielders attempting to catch a fly ball illustrates the interaction between vision and proprioception (i.e., visual proprioception) during movement control (McLeod & Dienes, 1996). In this study, skilled ballplayers (one from soccer and five from cricket) attempted to catch a ball projected toward them by a machine at an upward angle of 45°. The speed of projection was randomly varied to create situations where participants had to run forward to catch balls landing in front of them and run backward to catch balls landing over their heads. Using video analysis, the researchers calculated the position and velocity of participants' movements and the angle of their visual gaze. Fielders ran to the point where the ball was going to land but were always moving as they caught the ball. In addition, the gaze data indicated that fielders attempted to run at a speed that preserved a visual angle greater than 0° and less than 90°. When they were successful at doing so they caught the ball successfully; when they weren't, they didn't. These findings suggest that skilled fielders adopt a gaze angle that allows them to process ambient information most efficiently and then use visual proprioception to ensure arrival at the interception point at the moment of ball landing.

the face before. This suggests that the looming response is essentially inherited, rather than learned through experience. People probably have an innate capability of detecting particular patterns of optical flow that specify an impending threat; fortunately, our nervous system generates an effective avoidance response to these patterns.

tau—
An optical variable proportional to time until contact, defined as the size of the retinal image divided by the rate of change of the image.

Time-to-Contact Information

The pattern of optical flow produced by an approaching object, such as a ball, indicates something about the time remaining until the object reaches the plane of the observer's eye (Lee & Young, 1985). The retinal image of an approaching object expands as the object approaches. The faster an object is approaching, the larger the rate of expansion of its image on the retina of the eye. The optical variable **tau** is determined from this rate of expansion and is proportional to the time remaining until contact; mathematically, tau is equal to the size of the retinal image at some moment divided by the rate of change of the image size at that moment. Presumably, tau is computed by the central nervous system on the basis of optical-flow information. Tau is important for people (or animals) who perform interceptive actions (e.g., catching a ball) or coincident-timing tasks such as striking or catching a ball or preparing the body for vertical entry into the water at the proper moment of a springboard dive. Tau may be critical in other situations as well, such as when a bicyclist attempts to avoid a suddenly approaching car on the street.

Balance

Early scientific viewpoints emphasized the role of the proprioceptors in detecting postural sway and loss of stability. For example, when a person's body sways forward, the ankle joint is moved and the associated musculature is stretched, producing signals from the joint receptors and muscle spindles that indicate the body is moving. Also, vestibular receptors in the inner ear are sensitive to movements of the head, providing information about body sway.

More recently, however, research has indicated that the role of vision in balance may be far greater than previously believed. You can demonstrate this for yourself by looking straight ahead at an object on the wall but paying attention to an object on your right. Without shifting your direction of gaze, move your head forward and backward a few inches and pay attention to the changes in visual information. You will probably notice that the objects in your peripheral visual field seem to move and that this motion is dependent on the pattern of your head movement.

Lee and Aronson (1974) demonstrated that balance is strongly affected by the visual information presented to observers. In their experiment, the participant stood in a special room surrounded by suspended walls that did not quite touch the floor. The walls could be moved, to influence the participant's optical-flow information, while the floor remained fixed. Moving the walls slightly away from the participant caused his body to sway slightly forward, and moving the walls closer caused a backward sway. With a toddler, an away movement of the walls caused the child to stumble forward, and a toward movement of the walls caused a rather ungraceful plop into a sitting position. Moving the walls toward or away from the observer generated optical-flow information that was interpreted by the motor system that his or her head was moving in a direction opposite that of the walls. To the motor system, this means being out of balance and the sensation of falling in the direction opposite that of wall movement. The result was an automatic postural compensation in the same direction as wall movement. Such visually based compensations are far faster (with latencies of about 100 ms) than those requiring voluntary feedback processing by the focal visual system (Nashner & Berthoz, 1978). Experiments such as these suggest that optical-flow information and the ambient visual system are critically involved in the control of normal balancing activities.

UNIVERSITY OF WINCHESTER
LIBRARY

Some athletes use ambient vision and visual proprioception to coordinate their actions with environmental events.

This notion has strong implications for learned postures as well. When a gymnast is performing a handstand on the still rings, where it is important to remain as motionless as possible, the gymnast's visual system can signal very small changes in posture, providing a basis for tiny corrections in body position to hold the posture steady. Thus, it is probably important to train performers of tasks like this to fix their gaze on a particular spot on the mat below them so that they can see the changes in visual information more easily.

Keep Your Eye on the Ball!

It sometimes seems strange to hear a coach remind a golfer to keep his eye on the ball during the swing. This reminder makes more sense for baseball, cricket, and softball batters because by watching the approaching ball they are better able to detect information about its flight characteristics. But a golf ball is certainly not going anywhere until after it is hit, so why should keeping one's eye on it help the golfer's swing?

The role of optical-flow variables in balance can help us speculate about the answer to this question. It is probably important to hold the head in a constant position over the ball during a golf swing. Very small changes in head position during the swing are signaled by optical-flow information, just as they are during other movements requiring good balance. Small movements of the golfer's head backward during the backswing are detected rapidly, and small changes in muscle activities are generated to compensate for these unintentional movements, thus holding the head in a steady position via closed-loop processes and ambient vision. The resulting adjustments are nonconscious and are very fast—far faster than those produced by the focal visual system (which are accomplished in the outer feedback loop shown in figure 3.10).

How Do Somersaulters Land on Their Feet?

Research by Lee, Young, and Rewt (1992) suggests that vision is important for landing a successful somersault. In this study, two proficient trampolinists attempted four sets of 10 single forward somersaults. They kept their eyes open during the first and third sets and closed them between takeoff and landing during the second and fourth sets. Motor control was more precise when the trampolinists' eyes were kept open than when they were closed during the somersaulting action. More specifically, participants demonstrated greater consistency of body orientation during their approach to landing, greater consistency of vertical body angle at the moment of landing, and fewer falls when they kept their eyes open throughout the somersault than when they didn't. These findings suggest that somersaulters require optical information to land reliably without losing their balance; vestibular and other nonvisual information is not sufficient. It appears that somersaulters use visual information to control vertical angle at landing, time to landing, or both.

Where Do Successful Baseball Batters Direct Their Eyes?

Research has shown that high-performance baseball hitters do not watch the ball all the way to the bat (Hubbard & Seng, 1954). More recently, scientists have also discovered that skilled batters tend to fix their gaze on the small area of the pitcher's forearm prior to ball release (Kato & Fukuda, 2002). It is likely that these batters fixate on a point (i.e., the pitcher's forearm) that allows them to see the ball as it leaves the pitcher's hand and then use their ambient vision to judge the speed and trajectory of its flight. By keeping their head relatively still (rather than turning it to watch the ball all the way to the bat), batters enjoy the additional benefit of a more consistent optical-flow pattern.

Vision in the Conceptual Model

We can now add these principles of visual information processing for movement control to our conceptual model, as shown in figure 3.14. Note that visual feedback from the focal system and the ambient system travels along different loops. Information from the focal system is carried in the outer feedback loop (thin maroon line) to the comparator; the processing of this information is conscious, slow, and attention demanding, so it is conceptualized as being carried in the loop that passes through the stages of information processing. Information from focal vision can affect the control of a movement but only after a relatively long delay, although experienced performers likely process this form of visual information more effectively and efficiently than do inexperienced performers. The loop for focal vision is, however, very flexible.

Visual feedback from the ambient system (shown by a thick maroon line) goes directly to the motor-program level for more immediate adjustments in the intended movement. Because ambient information is handled in a nonconscious, relatively fast, and inflexible manner, it is routed to relatively low levels of the central nervous system, considerably downstream from the higher processes that select and initiate movements but upstream from the muscles and the spinal cord. Thus, ambient vision seems to operate at an intermediate level in the system, making minor adjustments in already programmed actions, such as compensations for head movements in the golf swing and alterations in posture to maintain balance on the still rings. The final common path to the muscles is based primarily on the originally planned action—but notice that these commands can be supplemented by at least four feedback loops (M1 response, M2 response, ambient vision, and the outer loop carrying information from focal vision, exteroception, and proprioception) that signal various features of the movement, the environment, or both.

You Don't Suppose . . . ?

In 1998, an Australian sport fashion designer discovered that his golf game improved when he began wearing a wide-brim hat with a length of heavy wire wrapped around the rim ("Heavy Hat Credited With Best Golfing," 1998). The man decided to attach the wire after playing a particularly frustrating round of golf in a strong wind that kept blowing his hat off. "Before I knew it," he said, "my game started to get better in quantum leaps and I realized it could only be the hat." How might the heavier hat have helped the man's golf swing? How would you interpret the effect using the conceptual model in figure 3.14?

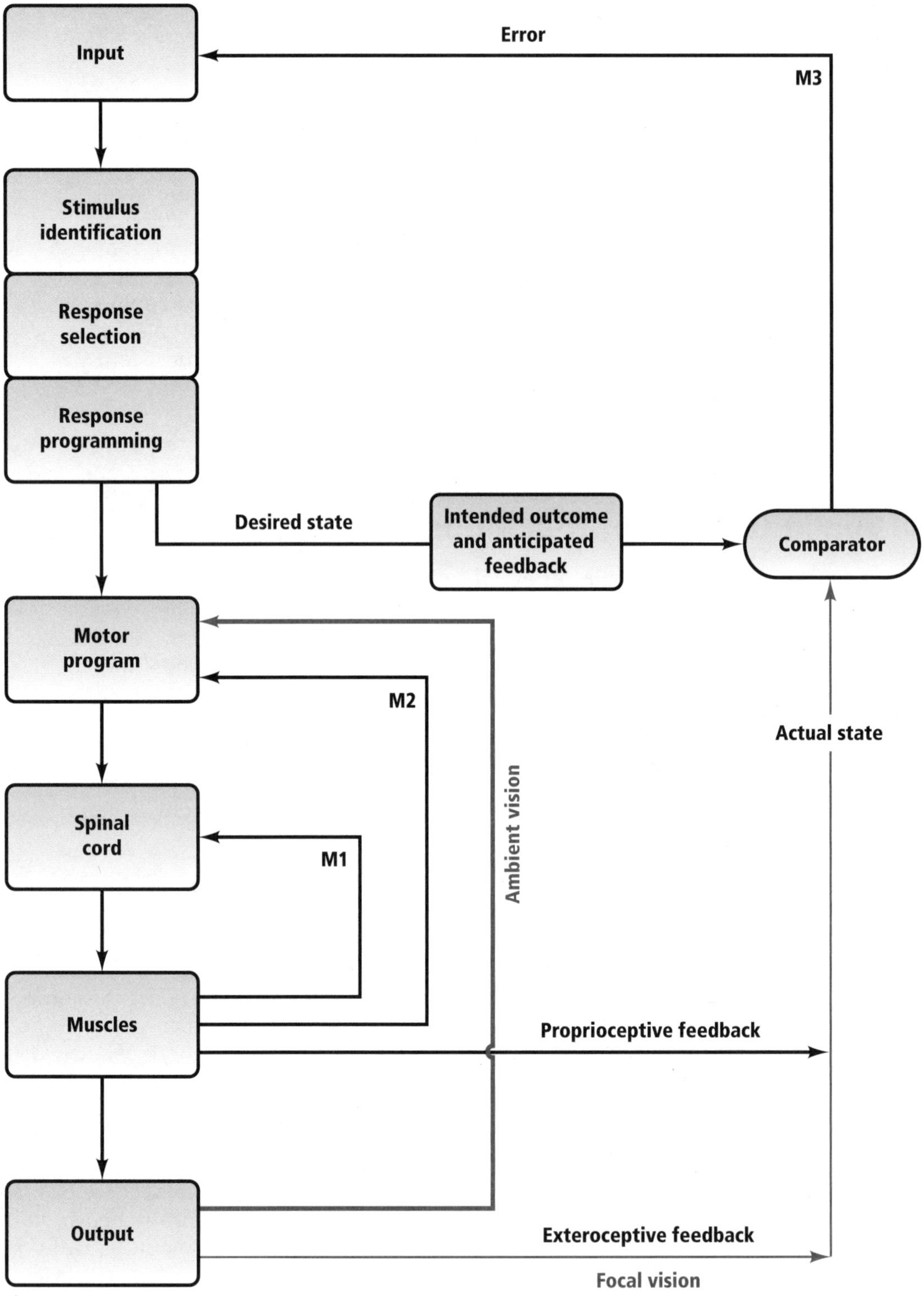

Figure 3.14 The expanded conceptual model of motor performance, here including the pathways for focal and ambient vision, shown in maroon.

Visual Dominance and Visual Capture

Although vision can exert a powerful influence on movement control, its impact is not always positive. As a result, the motor system often selects other modes of control. For example, consider that the race-car driver or pilot monitors engine performance by the sounds of the engine—instead of by the visual information provided by cockpit gauges. More often, however, performers opt to use vision, because it is the most dominant sensory system (visual dominance) and has the power to capture their attention unavoidably (visual capture).

visual dominance—The tendency for visual information to dominate information from the other senses during the process of perception.

visual capture—The tendency for visual information to attract a person's attention more easily than other forms of information.

In situations where visual information is very important to task performance (e.g., threading a needle), relying on vision is not a problem. However, in other situations a person's over-reliance on vision may cause an ineffective performance. Take, for example, the sport of sailboat racing, in which a sailor has rich visual information about the aerodynamic shapes of the sails and the way the wind is flowing over them. Although this plentiful visual information can yield a good performance, a sailor who focuses exclusively on visual information would miss other sources of information, such as the sounds the boat makes as it goes through the water, the action and position of the hull sensed by the seat of the pants, and the feel of the forces exerted on the tiller. Such sources provide additional useful information about speed. For this reason, some Olympic-level sailors use blindfolds during training in an attempt to diminish their reliance on vision. Being deprived of vision for long periods presumably heightens the sailors' sensitivity to less dominant sources of sensory information, such as sound and feel.

Looking again at the conceptual model in figure 3.14, we see that focal visual information takes longer to process in the voluntary feedback loop (M3) than does kinesthetic information in the M2 loop. If the performer uses focal vision in a conscious information-processing mode (i.e., the outer loop), processing is slow and attention demanding. On the other hand, if the person uses kinesthetic information, routed

It Depends . . .

What Sources of Sensory Information Are Important for Controlling Open and Closed Skills?

Two issues that confront people when they attempt to perform skilled movements are the goal of the movement and the most appropriate focus for achieving the goal. Whether the goal is to perform a gymnastics activity or to play the piano, the performer needs to decide on what sources of information to focus. Briefly describe the goal of an *open skill* and a *closed skill* with which you are familiar and indicate the types of exteroceptive information and proprioceptive information that might be important for goal achievement. How might performers of each skill use focal vision and ambient vision?

open skill—A skill performed in an environment that is unpredictable or in motion and that requires performers to adapt their movements in response to dynamic properties of the environment.

closed skill—A skill performed in an environment that is predictable or stationary and that allows performers to plan their movements in advance.

through the M2 loop, the corrective response is speeded noticeably. The relative slowness of visual information processing has been demonstrated in experiments on fencers (Jordan, 1972), where the presence of additional visual information actually slowed performers' responses by shifting their attention away from more relevant kinesthetic information.

In the same general way, performers who are instructed to concentrate on certain visual events often perform more poorly as a result. Such a shift to conscious processes shifts visual control from the relatively fast ambient system to the slower focal system (see figure 3.14). Thus, when baseball coaches instruct batters to watch the ball and then swing when the time feels right, the coaches may be offering greater assistance than if they tell batters to swing when the ball looks like it is about halfway to home plate. The feels-right instruction encourages the use of the batter's ambient visual system and time-to-contact information that is more reliably derived from optical flow (McLeod, McLaughlin, & Nimmo-Smith, 1985). The point-in-space instruction encourages the use of the batter's focal visual system and conscious control, resulting in poorer, rather than better, performance.

This is another example of the Bliss–Boder hypothesis mentioned earlier—performance is sometimes impaired by instructions that encourage performers to engage in conscious activities demanding attention and controlled processing. This is particularly so for high-level performers who have developed many elegant, nonconscious processes for detecting and processing visual and kinesthetic information, along with very fast and effective processes for making corrections based on this information. If these performers are forced out of these nonconscious modes of processing (by coaches' instructions, thoughts about not making mistakes, or whatever) and into the more conscious, controlled information-processing activities, their performance usually suffers. See Wulf (2007) for more information.

SUMMARY

The effectiveness with which people process various forms of sensory information often determines the level of their overall performance. Sensory signals from the environment are usually termed exteroceptive information, whereas those from within the body are referred to as proprioceptive information. For human performance, it is useful to think of these signals operating within a closed-loop control system that contains an executive for decision making, an effector (i.e., muscles, joints) for carrying out the actions, feedback about the state of the environment, and a comparator for contrasting the actual state with the desired state. In general, human closed-loop control systems that involve the three stages of processing have the following characteristics:

- They use many sources of sensory information.
- They operate relatively slowly, allowing only about three compensations per second because of limitations in processing speed.
- They are flexible and adaptable and thus are effective in controlling slow, continuous actions, such as various types of tracking movements (e.g., steering a car).

FROM PRINCIPLES TO PRACTICE

Check your comprehension of the concepts and terms discussed in this chapter by responding to each of the exercises in the following sections. The first section contains several exercises designed to test your working knowledge of key terms. The second section poses a variety of problems designed to check your understanding of key concepts. In the third section you are challenged to apply your knowledge by discussing a defensible solution for two scenarios.

Know Your Key Terms

Matching: Sources of Sensory Information

Match the following terms with their respective categories or definitions by placing the most appropriate letter on each of the blanks below.

Sources of Sensory Information—Terms

a. cutaneous receptors
b. kinesthesis
c. muscle spindles
d. vestibular apparatus
e. proprioception
f. Golgi tendon organs
g. exteroception

Sources of Sensory Information—Category or Definition

_____ 1. Any sensory information arising from within the body

_____ 2. Provides information about posture and balance

_____ 3. Any sensory information arising from the body's movements

_____ 4. Provides information about pressure, temperature, and touch

_____ 5. Receptors that stretch when muscle contracts and provide information about the speed of contraction and limb position

_____ 6. Any sensory information arising from outside the body

_____ 7. Provides information about the level of force in various parts of a muscle

Consider: Using Sensory Information for Movement Control

For each of the following scenarios indicate how the performer might use exteroceptive and proprioceptive information to control the movement. Provide rationale for your answers.

1. A potter shaping a ceramic bowl
2. A person walking up a flight of stairs in the dark
3. A gardener pushing a wheelbarrow through a vegetable patch
4. A person paddling a kayak

Fill in the Blank: Using Vision for Movement Control

Complete the following sentences:

Performers use __________________________ vision to identify objects in the center of their visual field and __________________________ vision to detect the orientation of their body in the environment. __________________________ refers to the movement of light patterns over the retina that allows people to perceive __________________, __________________, and __________________. __________________________ is a type of sensory information arising from the visual system that also provides performers with information about their movements.

Check Your Understanding

1. What are the four essential components of any closed-loop control system? Describe how each of the components might function for a child who is using a crayon to color a figure in a coloring book.
2. Explain how movement time influences the type of control a person can use in performing a task. Discuss why it is problematic for a woodworker to sand surfaces or drill holes rapidly.
3. People are often told to pay attention to what they are doing. Under what conditions might paying attention to movements hinder the performance of a concert pianist? Why does this happen?
4. Describe how optical-flow information informs a badminton player about the time of arrival of a shuttlecock that is moving directly toward him. Does this process depend on either the size of the shuttle or the distance it must travel?
5. Define and describe the four principal responses involved in producing compensations for unexpected disturbances in a person's movement. How might each function for someone who stubs her toe while walking along a sidewalk?

Apply Your Knowledge

Exercise 1

A middle-aged man wants to learn how to dribble a basketball. He is visually impaired, having lost most of the sight in both eyes as a result of a work-related accident. Using figure 3.14, see if you can explain how the man would have to control the movement. Then describe how you might assist this person in achieving his goal. In particular, discuss some things you might do to encourage the man's use of other forms of sensory information (besides vision). Provide rationale for your suggestions and include two supporting references.

Exercise 2

A person is training to operate a remote robot for handling radioactive materials (e.g., picking up and moving objects from one location to another) in an enclosed, lead-lined chamber. The controller's task is to manipulate the robot's movements using a remote-control device. A camera mounted in the room provides visual feedback of the robot's movements and displays this information on a video monitor. Discuss the type of control the operator must use to accomplish this task and explain how this type of control is similar to and different from the type of control a person would use to handle the materials directly (i.e., without using the robot). Describe how the available sensory information would be different in the two situations. Provide rationale for your answers and furnish two supporting references.

chapter 4

Movement Production and Motor Programs

▷ Chapter Outline

▷ Chapter Objectives

When you have completed this chapter, you should be able to

- understand the concept of open-loop control for movement;
- describe the rationale for and characteristics of motor programs;
- understand how people might use generalized motor programs to produce various versions of a particular type of movement (e.g., long, medium, and short hops), including versions they have never attempted previously (e.g., a new hopscotch sequence); and
- apply the principles of motor programming to practical performance situations.

PREVIEW

During a high-hurdles race in track and field, runners produce a number of separate actions almost simultaneously. At each hurdle, they stretch forward with one leg (let's say it's the left) to clear the hurdle; bring the right arm forward, almost touching the toes; move the left arm backward with the elbow flexed; bring the right leg to the side with the knee sharply flexed to clear the hurdle; and then bring the left leg down sharply to the ground to initiate the next step. Runners execute this combination of clearly identifiable movements in an instant, with correct sequencing and a level of coordination that

Performers must learn how to manage the possible combinations of their muscle and joint activity (i.e., degrees of freedom) to produce each action in the most effective way.

gives the impression of a single, fluid action. How do these people—and other types of skilled performers—produce so many movements so quickly? How do they control the individual components and combine them to form a whole movement?

OVERVIEW

In the last chapter we talked about the role of closed-loop processes in movement control. We learned that some forms of closed-loop control take too long for corrections to be made in the movement before it is completed. Clearly, performers are able to control rapid acts of a discrete or serial nature, but it is unlikely that they use closed-loop processes to do so.

In this chapter we examine the idea of open-loop control and introduce the concept of the motor program, structures thought to be responsible for the control of many kinds of rapid acts. We then discuss how motor programs might be used in conjunction with various reflex pathways (mentioned in the previous chapter) to give a more complete picture of central and peripheral contributions to movement control. Finally, we describe the concept of the generalized motor program which, because of its flexibility, may be the sort of mechanism that allows people to produce slight variations of particular types of movements (e.g., hopping, but with different distances and speeds and using either leg).

Functional Electrical Stimulation: An Example of Open-Loop Control

Many rehabilitation settings use functional electrical stimulation (FES), an open-loop control system. In FES systems, therapists program patterns of electrical stimulation that produce particular movements, such as the dorsiflexion of a patient's ankle (i.e., toe up) on the swing leg that allows the foot to clear obstacles, such as a step or a curb. Once the necessary open-loop programs have been developed, the patient may activate them by operating a hand switch that controls a small computer worn on the belt (Hausdorff & Durfee, 1991). When the desired movement is required, the patient presses the hand switch and the computer triggers the programmed pattern of stimulation. The movement is then carried out without modification. Various types of FES systems are particularly useful for patients with various paralyzing injuries (hemiplegia, paraplegia, and quadriplegia). Recently, researchers at the Rehabilitation Institute of Chicago developed a more advanced open-loop control system that has allowed a woman who lost her left arm in a motorbike accident to control her bionic arm by simply thinking about performing a movement ("Woman Is Fitted With 'Bionic' Arm," 2006). Among other things, the woman is able to fold clothes, eat a banana, and wash dishes with her new arm. The same researchers are trying to find a way to transmit signals from the fingers on the prosthetic device to the brain so that the woman will be able to feel pressure, heat or cold, and even a sharp edge.

MOTOR PROGRAM CONCEPT

For many actions, particularly those that are brief in duration and are produced in stable and predictable environments (e.g., dropping a load of dirt from a front-end loader into a dump truck, slamming a door, serving a volleyball), people usually plan the movement in advance and then trigger it into action. Once underway, the movement runs its course without much modification. There is very little conscious control once the movement begins; rather, the action just seems to take care of itself. In this respect, we are fortunate. The possible combinations of muscle and joint activity that our bodies are capable of producing are so large in number that it would be virtually impossible for us to regulate them consciously when executing rapid, skilled actions. All of the independent components of a control system and the number of ways each component can function are sometimes referred to as the system's **degrees of freedom**. The challenge for performers is learning how to manage the available degrees of freedom so that they produce the desired action in the most effective way.

How performers are able to do this is one of the fundamental questions for students of motor behavior because it deals with how biological systems of all kinds control actions. To address this issue we need to have some idea of how the central nervous system is functionally organized, both before and during action, and how this organization contributes to the control of the preplanned movement. In chapter 3, we considered the ways sensory information might contribute to or modify movement production. However, we did not examine in much detail *what* this sensory information is modifying. Most likely, sensory information modifies a set of prestructured movement commands, referred to by some theorists as the **motor program**, which defines and shapes the action being produced. To understand the concept of the motor program, which is the central theme of this chapter, we need to first examine the notion of **open-loop control**.

degrees of freedom—The components of a control system that can vary independently and that are controlled to produce effective action.

motor program—A set of motor commands that is prestructured at the executive level and that defines the essential details of a skilled action; analogous to a central pattern generator.

open-loop control—A type of control that involves the use of centrally determined, prestructured commands sent to the effector system and executed without feedback; used by individuals to control rapid, discrete movements.

closed-loop control—A type of control that involves the use of feedback and the activity of error detection and correction processes to maintain a desired state; used by people to control slow, deliberate movements.

feedback—Information produced from the various sensors as a consequence of moving; sometimes called *response-produced feedback.*

comparator—The error-detection mechanism contained in closed-loop control systems; compares feedback of the desired state to feedback of the actual state.

Open-Loop Control

Figure 4.1 shows a diagram of a typical open-loop control system. It consists of essentially two parts: an executive and an effector. Figure 3.5 showed that these two components are also contained in the **closed-loop control** system. Missing from the open-loop control system, however, are the **feedback** loop and the **comparator**, which represent actual and desired states that together determine errors. The system shown in figure 4.1 begins with input being delivered to the executive or control center. This input is then processed, and a decision is made about the action to be taken. The plan for producing this action is then sent to the effector, which carries it out. Major modifications to the action are not made once the movement is initiated. When the action is completed, the open-loop system's work is finished. However, without feedback, the system is unaware of whether the action achieved the environmental goal.

This kind of control is used in a variety of real-world systems. For example, the open-loop mechanism that regulates traffic flow at many intersections often operates by illuminating a repetitive sequence of green, yellow, and red lights. If an accident should occur at the intersection, the system continues to activate the light sequence as if nothing had happened. Thus, one characteristic of an open-loop control system is that it is effective as long as the circumstances surrounding the action are unchanged. However, a less attractive characteristic is that it is inflexible in the face of unexpected changes.

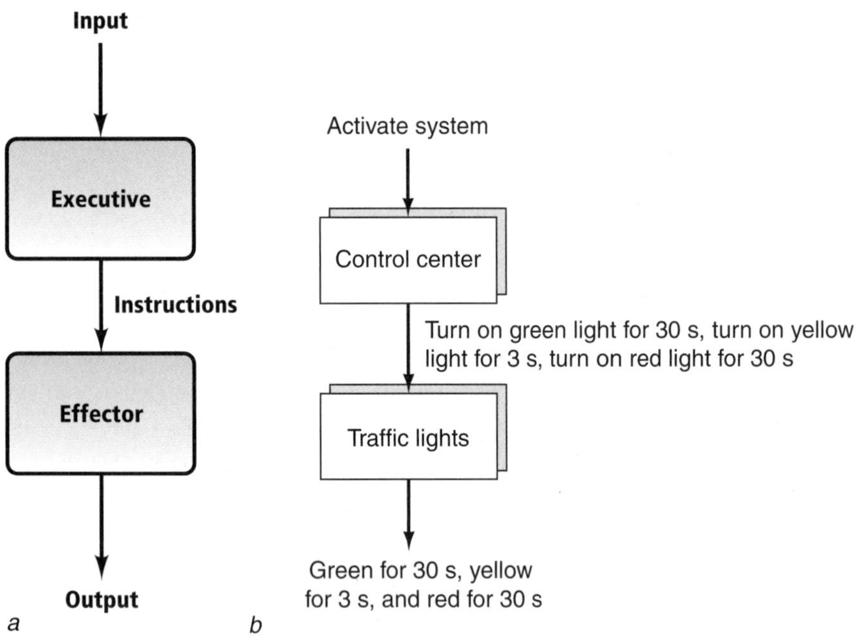

Figure 4.1 An open-loop control system (*a*) and a practical example (*b*).

Another example of an open-loop control system is a simple computer program, which some scientists have used as a model for the idea of the motor program. Put simply, computer programs are sets of instructions that tell the computer the functions it needs to perform and the order in which to perform them. In some cases, the computer program also specifies the timing of the operations (i.e., when and for how long to perform the various functions). Although many computer programs are sensitive to feedback (i.e., errors), the classical open-loop computer program is not. In such cases, the computer faithfully follows the instructions contained in the program without any regard for whether they are correct or whether the results achieve the programmer's intended goals.

Generally, then, we can characterize a purely open-loop control system as follows:

- Preplanned instructions specify the functions to be performed, as well as their sequencing and timing.
- Once the program is initiated, the system carries out the instructions faithfully without major modification.
- There is virtually no capability for detecting or correcting errors (other than the minor reflexive compensations discussed in the previous chapter) because feedback is not used extensively.

Motor Program as an Open-Loop Control System

In a sense, many of our movement behaviors—especially those actions that are quick and forceful, such as kicking and throwing—are controlled in an open-loop fashion and carried out without much feedback involvement. When performing these tasks we usually do not have time to process information about movement errors and must therefore plan the action properly before we initiate it. This is quite different from the type of control we discussed in the previous chapter, in which feedback processes could be used to modify slower movements while they are in progress.

Open-loop control seems especially effective in environmental situations that are predictable and stable, where the need for modification of the action is minimal. The psychologist William James (1890) popularized the general idea of program control more than 100 years ago, and it remains one of the most important contributions to our understanding of movement control. Figure 4.2 illustrates how program control might work by combining the basic open-loop system shown in figure 4.1 with some of the processes we discussed in earlier chapters.

Consider a task such as hitting a pitched baseball. In the executive (upper portion of figure 4.2), the stages of information processing (see chapter 2) are activated to evaluate the environment (stimulus identification); to decide whether to swing (response selection); and, if a swing is chosen, to organize and initiate the motor program for doing so (response programming).

Control is then passed on to the effector for movement execution (lower portion of figure 4.2). Here the motor program acts on the spinal cord and then the muscles, where the planned sequence of contractions takes place. If the resulting action (i.e., the bat swing) produces the intended outcome (i.e., contact with the ball), a change in the environment occurs (i.e., the path of the ball changes), but information from the environment at this point arrives too late for the system to do anything with it.

In this type of open-loop control system, the motor program determines which muscles to contract, as well as the order and timing of their contraction. The stages of processing are used to develop the program by determining the action to be initiated and, to some extent, the eventual form of the movement (e.g., the speed and trajectory of the swing). Movement execution in these rapid actions, however, is carried out in the absence of direct conscious control.

Initially a program might be capable of controlling only a short string of actions. With practice, however, the program can become more elaborate, controlling longer and longer sequences and perhaps even modulating various reflexive activities that support the overall movement goal. Once learned, the program is conceptualized as being stored in **long-term memory (LTM)** and retrieved when needed for use in **short-term memory (STM)** to prepare (during the response-programming stage) future movements for execution (see figure 2.16). One major advantage of motor-program control is that far less attention is needed for movement production. You have already learned that movement organization and movement initiation cause a bottleneck in the response-selection and response-programming stages of movement production (review figures 2.11 and 2.12 in chapter 2). With motor-program control, entire sequences of action can be produced without the need for additional organization. The more sophisticated the motor program, the longer it can run and the larger the chunk of skilled behavior it can control. When this happens, the response-programming stage is involved less frequently, and more attentional resources (see figure 2.8)

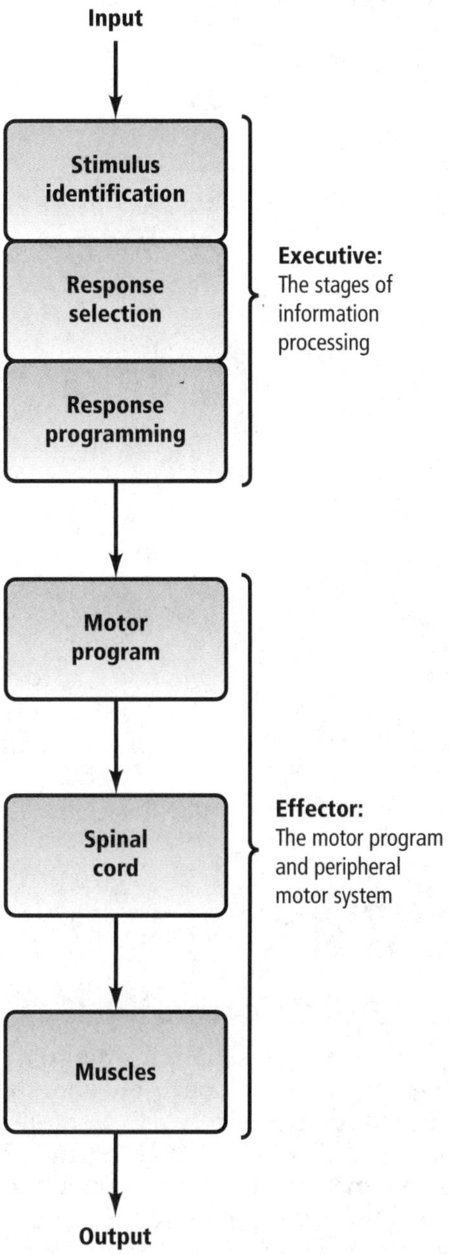

Figure 4.2 An expanded open-loop control system for motor performance. The executive contains the stages of information processing, which determine what to do; the effector carries out the chosen movement.

long-term memory (LTM)—The memory system that holds information and life experiences; believed to be vast in capacity and unlimited in duration.

short-term memory (STM)—The memory system that allows people to retrieve, rehearse, process, and transfer information from STSS; believed to be limited in capacity and brief in duration.

In quick, forceful actions, such as a bat swing, movements are largely controlled in an open-loop fashion, without much feedback involvement.

are thus available for other higher-order activities, such as monitoring movement form or style in gymnastics or dance, developing strategic plans in tennis, or paying attention to hazards when operating earth-moving equipment.

OPEN-LOOP CONTROL WITHIN THE CONCEPTUAL MODEL

How does the concept of open-loop control and the motor program fit into our conceptual model of motor performance? Figure 4.3 shows the conceptual model from figure 3.14, only now the shaded portions represent the open-loop control components shown in figure 4.2. The shaded portions illustrate how the control of rapid, programmed movements would take place. The feedback loops (i.e., the unshaded portion on the right side of the figure) remain available for the control of slower movements and for the various types of closed-loop corrections we discussed in chapter 3.

This more complete version of the conceptual model has the potential to operate in either of two basic ways, depending on the nature of the task. If the movement to be produced were of long duration, control would be dominated by the operation of feedback processes. If the movement were of a very short duration, control would be governed primarily by the operation of open-loop processes. However, most types of motor behavior represent a complex blend of *both* open- and closed-loop control operations. For example, a NASCAR driver must use open-loop control to operate the steering wheel, the clutch, and the accelerator pedal and use closed-loop control to process the visual and tactile feedback necessary for maintaining the best position possible on the track, avoiding collisions with other cars, and determining when to brake, accelerate, and adjust the steering. In complex tasks like these, it is not uncommon for both forms of control to be at work simultaneously or intermittently.

It Depends . . .

How Are Rapid Skills Controlled?

How fast can you spin a yo-yo? How do you think the spinning action is initiated—open or closed loop? How does the type of control change when you perform "walk the dog" or allow the yo-yo to remain in a spinning mode at the end of the string? How would your movements be different in those two situations? Which situations would require greater use of closed-loop control processes? Why?

With very fast actions, the notion of motor programs offers a useful set of ideas and vocabulary for discussing how the motor system might be organized functionally; that is, if a movement appears to be organized in advance, is triggered more or less as a whole, and is carried out without much modification by sensory feedback, it is reasonable to call it a programmed action. This type of language describes a style of motor control that involves central movement organization, where movement details are determined by the central nervous system and then sent to the muscles. This style of control contrasts sharply with that involving ongoing modification of a movement using peripheral feedback processes. As we mentioned previously, however, both forms

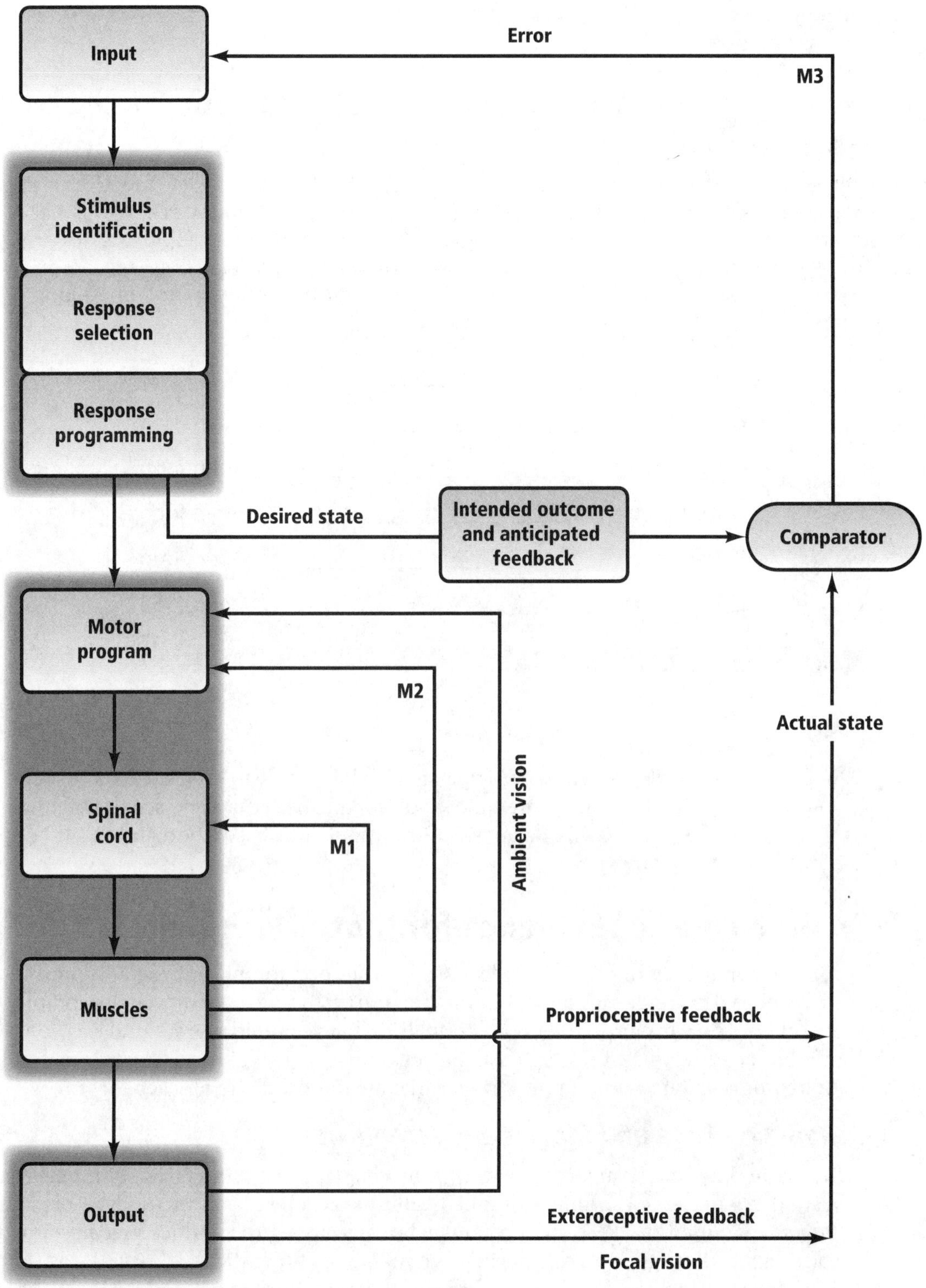

Figure 4.3 The conceptual model of motor performance, with the open-loop components highlighted.

It Depends . . .

Can You Estimate the Relative Contributions of Closed-Loop and Open-Loop Control?

Fishing is a popular recreational activity for many people. Have you ever thought about how the various movements involved in this task might be controlled? Using the following continuum as a guide, mark an X along the line to indicate the extent to which you think closed-loop and open-loop processes are controlling each of the movements. For example, if you put an X on the line halfway between *closed-loop* and *open-loop,* you would be indicating that the fisher is using both closed-loop and open-loop processes to the same extent to control that particular movement.

Baiting the hook	Closed-loop ________________________	Open-loop
Casting the line	Closed-loop ________________________	Open-loop
Reeling in the line	Closed-loop ________________________	Open-loop
Netting the fish	Closed-loop ________________________	Open-loop
Taking fish from net	Closed-loop ________________________	Open-loop
Throwing fish back	Closed-loop ________________________	Open-loop

electromyography (EMG)—A method for recording the electrical activity in a muscle or group of muscles.

reaction time (RT)—The interval of time that elapses from the sudden presentation of a stimulus to the beginning of a person's response.

of control are possible and may even operate simultaneously to varying extents depending on the nature of the task, the time involved, and other factors (see the highlight titled "Can You Estimate the Relative Contributions of Closed-Loop and Open-Loop Control?" for examples).

Three Lines of Evidence for Motor Programs

Three separate lines of research evidence suggest support for motor-program control of fast actions. This evidence includes studies examining the effects of movement complexity on reaction time, experiments on animals that have undergone surgical excision of feedback pathways, and research using **electromyography (EMG)** to analyze patterns of neuromuscular activity in movements that are unexpectedly blocked.

Reaction Time and Movement Complexity

Reaction time (RT), you may remember from chapter 2, is the interval of time between a suddenly presented stimulus and the beginning of a response. In 1960, Henry and Rogers examined the RT of participants who were trying to produce predetermined movements that varied in complexity (see the research highlight on page 113). They found that RT increased as the complexity of the movement to be produced increased. Since that time, several features of movements that make them more complex have been shown to lengthen RT:

- RT increases when additional elements are added to a movement. For example, the act of pressing and releasing a telegraph key requires a longer RT than simply pressing and holding the same key, because the former has more elements involved (press–release vs. press, respectively; see Klapp, 1996).

- RT increases when movements involve the coordination of a greater number of limbs. For example, a one-hand blocking movement in judo or boxing would likely be produced in a shorter RT than a more complicated two-hand movement (see Sternberg, Monsell, Knoll, & Wright, 1978).
- RT increases when the duration of the movement becomes longer. For example, a bat swing that lasts 100 ms would have a shorter RT than one lasting 300 ms (see Klapp, 1996; Sternberg et al., 1978).

Henry and Rogers' Experiment

One of Franklin Henry's many important contributions to the field of motor behavior was a study that he and Donald Rogers conducted in 1960. The experiment was actually quite simple, as are many important scientific investigations. Participants were instructed to respond as quickly as possible to a stimulus (a gong sound) by making one of three kinds of movements (see figure 4.4). However, because only one of the movements was tested during each set of trials, the study actually consisted of three simple-RT sessions. The three movements, designed to differ in complexity, were (a) a simple finger lift from a reaction key (RK); (b) a simple finger lift plus a rapid hand movement that involved reaching forward and grasping a tennis ball suspended on a string; and (c) a simple finger lift plus a rapid sequence of hand movements that involved striking a suspended ball, reversing direction, touching a "dummy" button (DB), reversing direction again, and striking a second suspended ball.

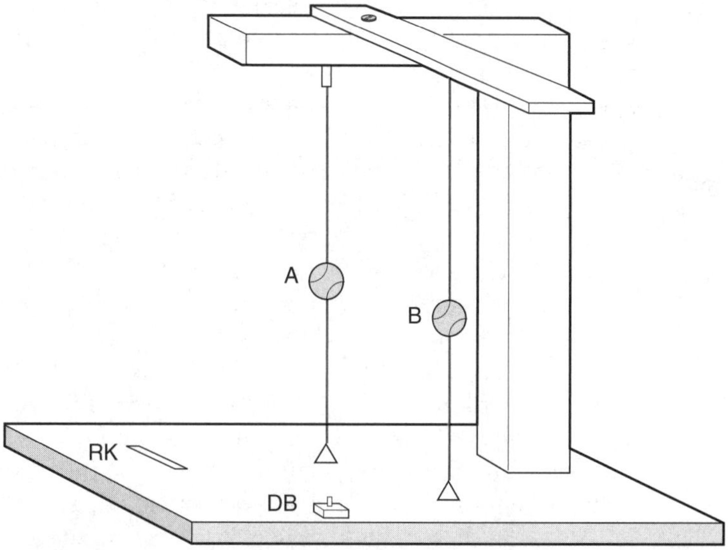

Figure 4.4 Apparatus used by Henry and Rogers (1960) to examine differences in RT for movements varying in complexity. (Reprinted from Henry & Rogers, 1960.)

For each of these movement conditions, Henry and Rogers measured RT, that is, the interval of time between the gong and the start of the finger lift. RT increased as movement complexity increased. The finger-lift movement (movement a) had an RT of 150 ms, the reaching and grasping movement (movement b) had an RT of 195 ms, and the movement with two reversals in direction (movement c) had an RT of 208 ms.

For each trial of this experiment, stimulus-identification and response-selection demands were presumably held constant; that is, for a given set of trials there was only one stimulus and only one response. The only demand that varied from one series of trials to the next was response programming, and that depended on the complexity of the action. Henry and Rogers interpreted these findings to mean that it required more time to program the movement as it increased in complexity. This notion has had a profound effect on our understanding of movement-organization phenomena and has led to many additional studies of these processes. Most important, these data support the idea that people organize movements in advance, which is consistent with the motor program concept.

The interpretation of these findings is that when actions are more complex (in any of the previously mentioned ways), RT is longer because more time is required to organize the system for movement initiation. This pre-movement organization process occurs in the response-programming stage. If a motor program is being used to govern the movement, the more complex the movement is, the longer it takes to organize the program to produce the action. This longer programming time is presumably reflected in the slower RT found for more complex actions.

Deafferentation Experiments

deafferentation—A surgical procedure in which an afferent pathway (i.e., one that carries sensory information *toward* the central nervous system) is cut, preventing nerve impulses from the periphery from reaching the spinal cord.

In chapter 3 we mentioned that sensory information from the joints and muscles is carried to the dorsal (back) side of the spinal cord, where it enters distinct bundles called dorsal roots. A surgical technique termed **deafferentation** involves severing one or more of the dorsal-root bundles at the points where they enter the cord. Once this operation is performed, the central nervous system no longer can receive sensory information from a particular portion of the periphery, such as an entire limb or even several limbs.

A number of researchers have used the deafferentation procedure to examine the motor-control characteristics of experimental animals. The question of interest is what types of movements are possible when animals are deprived of sensory feedback from their limbs. Polit and Bizzi (1978) found that monkeys that had previously learned to point at specific lights arranged in a semicircle could still do so after the forelimb was deafferented (see figure 4.5). In other studies, films taken of monkeys with deafferented upper limbs show that they are still able to climb around, playfully chase each other, and groom and feed themselves. In fact, it is often very difficult for the average viewer to recognize that these animals have a total loss of sensory information from their upper limbs (Taub, 1976; Taub & Berman, 1968). The monkeys do demonstrate some difficulty in fine motor control, however, such as in picking up a pea or manipulating small objects with their fingers. But on the whole, they show remarkably little impairment in most of their movement activities.

Studies of this kind illustrate clearly that sensory information from the moving limb is not essential for movement production; in fact, many movements can be produced easily without such sensory information. This evidence suggests that explanations of movement control that presume a need for sensory information from the responding limb should be viewed with caution. Because feedback-based notions of motor control cannot account for the monkeys' movement capabilities when feedback is eliminated, many scientists have argued that movement must be organized centrally, perhaps with motor programs, and carried out in an open-loop fashion.

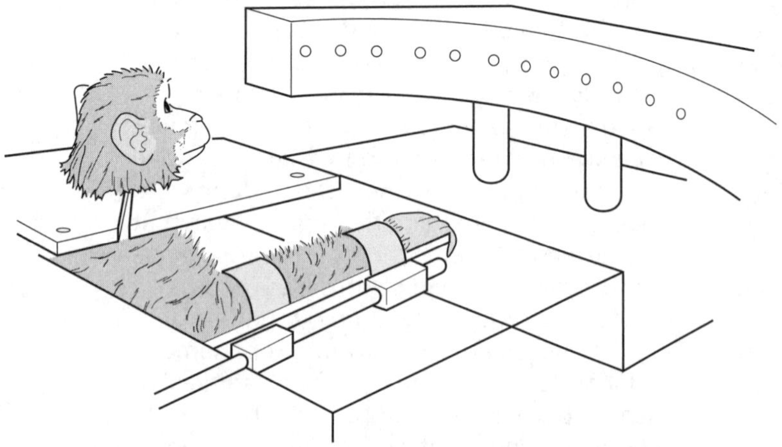

Figure 4.5 Monkey in the experiment by Polit and Bizzi (1978). During testing, the room was darkened and the animal was unable to see its forelimb. (Adapted from Polit & Bizzi, 1979.)

This thinking is similar to several ideas we presented in chapter 3, specifically those dealing with the fact that some actions are performed too rapidly for feedback to be used to control them. Very quick movements are completed before performers can use any emerging feedback to alter the action (see figure 3.11). Thus, if the movement is fast enough, a mechanism such as a motor program would have to be used to control the entire action, with the movement being carried out as though the performer were deprived of feedback.

Effects of Mechanically Blocking a Limb

A third line of evidence supporting motor program control comes from experiments in which people are instructed to make a quick limb action (e.g., move a lever to a target position as rapidly as possible). On most trials, participants begin and complete the movement with little difficulty. However, on a few trials, without the participant being able to anticipate it, the experimenter inserts a mechanical block that prevents participants from moving the lever at all. Figure 4.6 shows the pattern of muscle activity in the unblocked and blocked conditions (Wadman, Denier van der Gon, Geuze, & Mol, 1979). In the normal, unblocked condition (black lines), there is first a burst of activity in the agonist (triceps) muscle; then the triceps turns off and the antagonist (biceps) muscle is activated to decelerate the limb. Finally, the agonist turns on again to stabilize the movement near the target.

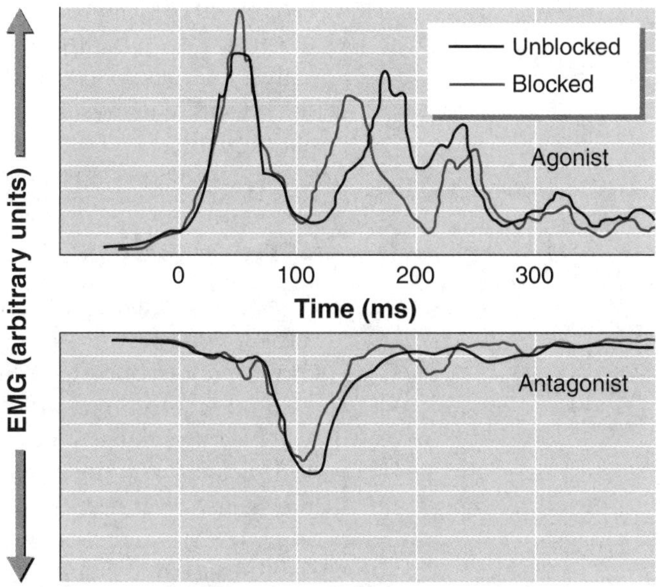

Figure 4.6 Agonist (triceps) and antagonist (biceps) electromyographic (EMG) activity in a rapid elbow-extension movement. The maroon traces are from a movement that was mechanically blocked at the outset.

The EMG pattern for trials in which the movement is unexpectedly prevented (maroon lines) appears virtually identical to that for the unblocked movement, especially for the first 100 ms. Only after that is there a modification of the blocked pattern, undoubtedly caused by some of the reflex activities (e.g., stretch reflexes) we discussed in chapter 3. The most important finding is that the burst of antagonist (biceps) muscle activity occurs at the same time in the blocked condition as in the unblocked condition. Why is the biceps muscle (which acts as the brakes in this action) activated if the limb does not move from the starting location? The answer is that the braking action was specified in the program, which was run off even though the limb was blocked from moving.

Although feedback from the blocked limb must be disrupted massively, the EMG pattern is essentially the same as that for the unblocked movement, particularly during the first 100 ms or so. Data such as these contradict the idea that feedback from the moving limb (during the action) acts as a signal (a trigger) to activate the antagonist muscle at the proper time. The feedback from the limb and the dynamics of the limb are disrupted massively when the movement is blocked (imagine the feeling of participants when they try to move and can't!), which argues against the idea that the timing of the EMG is determined by those dynamics (see Schmidt, 2003, for more on this). Rather, these findings suggest that agonist and antagonist EMG activities are planned in advance and the pattern is produced unmodified by sensory information for at least 100 ms, or until the first reflexive responses are activated.

How and When Do Programs Contribute to Actions?

In the case of rapid movements, open-loop control allows the motor system to organize an entire action ahead of time. For this to occur, the programming process would need to include the following specifications:

- The particular muscles used to produce the action
- The order in which these muscles would be activated
- The relative forces of the various muscle contractions
- The relative timing and sequencing of these contractions
- The duration of the respective contractions

Proponents of the motor program notion assume that a fast movement is organized in advance by a program that sets up some kind of neural mechanism, or network, containing time and event information—a movement script, if you will—specifying certain essential details of the movement as it unfolds over time. Some scientists even speak of performers "running" a motor program, which is clearly analogous to running a computer program.

Postural Adjustments Before Action

Imagine that you are a participant in an experiment in which you are instructed to stand with your arms at your sides holding a brick in your right hand. Then, on command, you are to raise your right arm, elbow straight, as quickly as possible until the brick is at shoulder level in front of you. After the command, where do you think the first detectable muscular activity associated with this movement would occur? Most people would guess the shoulder muscles, but in fact those muscles are activated relatively late in the sequence of events. Actually, the first muscles to contract, some 80 ms before noticeable EMG activity occurs in the shoulders, are those in the lower back and legs (Belen'kii, Gurfinkel, & Pal'tsev, 1967).

This order of muscular activity may sound strange, but it is really quite smart for the motor system to operate this way. Because the shoulder muscles are mechanically linked to the rest of the body (e.g., the back and arms), their contraction affects posture. If no preparatory compensations in posture are made before the arm is raised, the movement would alter the configuration of your limbs, and shift the center of gravity forward, causing a slight loss of balance. The motor system takes care of this potential problem by programming the appropriate postural modifications first, rather than requiring the body to make the necessary corrections after the arm begins to move.

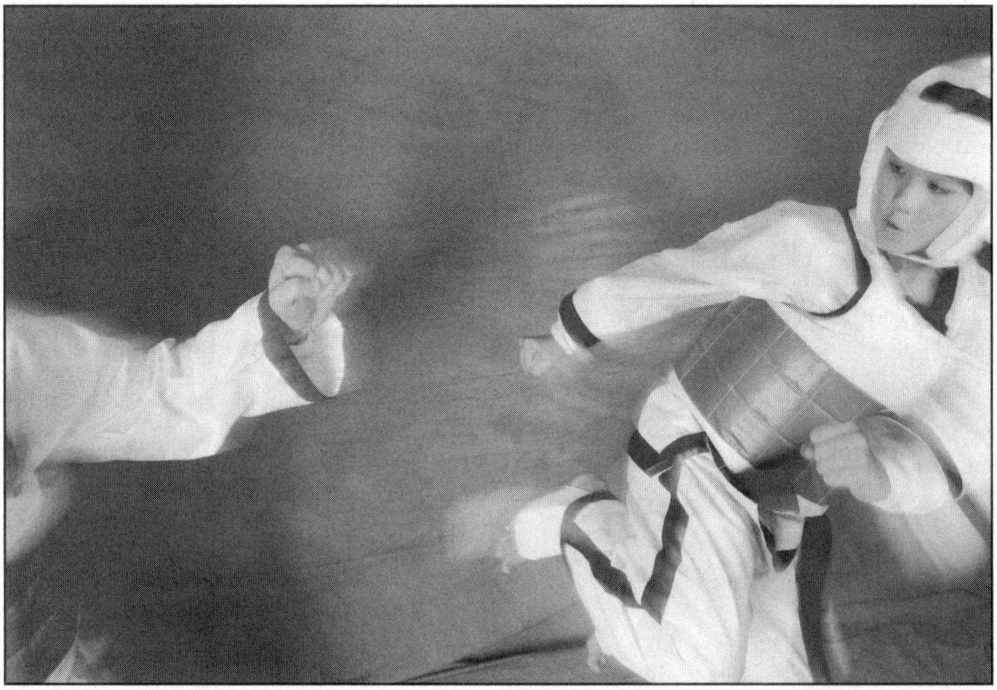

A one-hand blocking movement in judo or boxing is produced with a shorter RT than is a more complicated two-hand movement.

There is good evidence that these types of preparatory postural adjustments are really just a part of the motor program for arm movements (W.A. Lee, 1980). Thus, we should think of arm movement and postural control not as separate events but simply as parts of an integrated action that includes raising the arm while maintaining balance. Interestingly, these preparatory postural adjustments vanish from the EMG record when people lean against some type of support before performing the arm movement. The system apparently realizes that advance preparation of posture is not needed for that type of situation.

Central Pattern Generator

The idea of the motor program is similar to the concept of the **central pattern generator (CPG)**, which purports to explain certain features of repetitive actions, such as locomotion in animals, swimming in fish, chewing in hamsters, and slithering in snakes (Grillner, 1975). For these species, some genetically defined (inherited) central organization is established in the brain stem or the spinal cord. When the CPG's action is initiated by a triggering stimulus (via what is sometimes called a command neuron) in the brain, the CPG sends rhythmic, oscillating instructions to the musculature. These signals define a sequence of alternating and repetitive activities (e.g., right–left–right–left limb movements) such as those that occur during normal locomotion. Studies with nonhuman species indicate that the commands are forwarded even when sensory nerves are cut (deafferented), suggesting that this type of organization originates in the central nervous system.

central pattern generator (CPG)—A centrally located control mechanism that produces mainly genetically defined, repetitive actions, such as locomotion or chewing; analogous to a motor program.

Figure 4.7 shows an example of a simple network that could account for the alternating flexor–extensor pattern found in locomotion. Here, the input signal activates neuron 1, which activates neuron 2, as well as the flexor muscles. Neuron 2 activates neuron 3, which activates neuron 4, as well as the extensor muscles. Neuron 4 activates neuron 1 again, and the process continues to repeat. This, of course, is far too simple to account for all of the events in locomotion, but it shows how a collection of single neurons might be connected to each other in the spinal cord to produce an alternating pattern of motion once the action is activated.

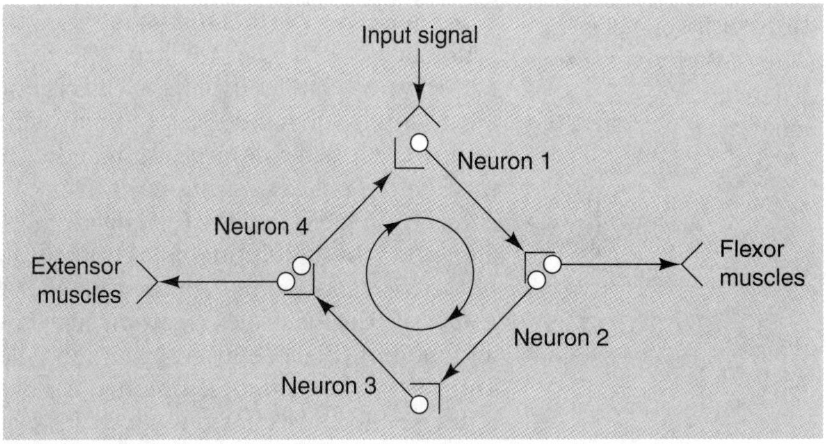

Figure 4.7 A simple network of neurons that could result in alternating flexor and extensor muscle movement in activities such as locomotion. Such a network could form the basis of central pattern generators (CPGs).

Although the notion of the CPG is almost identical to that of the motor program, there is an important difference. The CPG relates more to genetically defined activities, such as locomotion, chewing, and breathing, whereas the motor program is thought to be developed over practice and used to control learned activities such as kicking, typing, playing guitar, and skating.

Integration of Central Organization and Feedback Control

Although it is clear that the central organization of movements is a major source of motor control, it is also obvious that sensory information (including response-produced feedback) modifies these commands in several important ways (see figure 4.3). Thus, the question becomes how and under what conditions the central commands from programs and CPGs interact with peripheral sensory information to define the overall movement pattern.

We have already discussed various classes of reflexive activities that are capable of modifying originally programmed output (see figure 3.10). In addition to these feedback loops, another category of reflexive modulations has a very different effect on movement behavior. In examining the control of locomotion in cats, experimenters have applied a light tactile stimulus to the top of the animal's foot while it is walking on a treadmill. This stimulus has been found to have different effects on the movement at different locations in the step cycle. If the stimulus is applied at the moment the cat is placing its foot on the treadmill surface, the stimulated leg extends slightly, as if it is preparing to carry more load on that foot. This response has a latency of about 30 to 50 ms and is clearly nonconscious and automatic. However, if the same stimulus is applied when the cat is just lifting its foot from the treadmill surface in preparation for the swing phase, the response is very different. The hip and knee flex upward, raising the foot so that it travels above its usual trajectory, as if the leg is being raised above some object that is blocking it.

reflex-reversal phenomenon—A special case of reflex activity involving different responses to the same tactile stimulus when it is presented in different phases of the movement.

This leg reflex, causing either an extension or a flexion depending on where in the step cycle the stimulus is applied, has been called the **reflex-reversal phenomenon** (Forssberg, Grillner, & Rossignol, 1975). Most significantly, it challenges the usual conceptualization of a reflex, which is defined as an automatic, stereotyped response to a given stimulus. In the case of the reflex-reversal phenomenon, the same stimulus generates different responses at different times in the step cycle.

Scientists believe that this variation in response occurs because of an ongoing interaction between the CPG for locomotion and peripheral feedback carried along sensory pathways. As just discussed, the CPG is responsible for many of the major events that occur during locomotion and other rhythmic activities, such as the sequencing and timing of muscle contractions. In addition, CPGs are now thought to be involved in modulating reflexes during repetitive action, producing the reflex reversal phenomenon. The logic is that the CPG determines whether and when certain reflex pathways are to be activated during the action, as diagrammed in figure 4.8. During the swing phase of locomotion when the cat's foot is being lifted from the ground (see figure 4.8*a*), the CPG activates (maroon line) the flexion reflex (i.e., by closing the circuit) and inhibits (black line) the extension reflex (i.e., by opening or breaking the circuit). Thus, if a tactile stimulus occurs during the swing phase, it is routed to the flexion reflex, not to the extension reflex. However, if the stimulus occurs during the stance phase, when the foot is being placed on the ground (see figure 4.8*b*), it is routed to the extension reflex (maroon line) and not to the flexion reflex (black line). This process is repeated as long as the step cycle continues. If no tactile stimulus occurs at any time during locomotion, there is no reflex activity at all, and the CPG produces the action without modification.

We are only beginning to understand these complex reflex responses, but they undoubtedly play an important role in providing flexibility to motor control. The organization of the cat's reflexes probably has an important survival role. Receiving a tactile stimulus on the top of the foot while it is swinging forward might mean that the foot has struck some sort of object (e.g., a protruding tree root). The flexion reflex would cause the foot to be lifted quickly to keep the cat from tripping. However, receiving the same stimulus during the beginning of the stance phase would cause an extension of this weight-bearing leg because, at that moment, the opposite leg would be doing the swinging; indeed, if the flexion response would occur at this point, the cat would fall down.

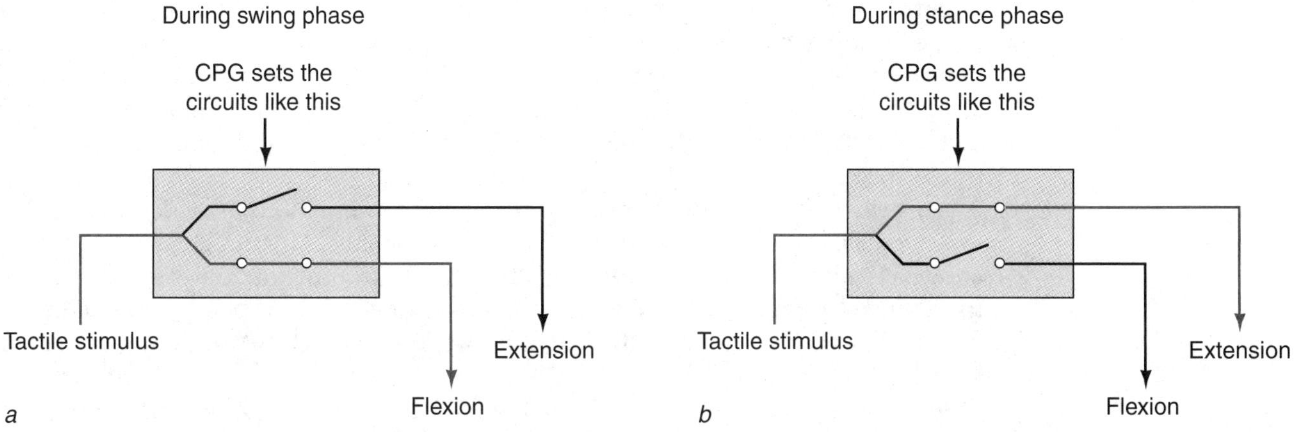

Figure 4.8 In addition to controlling the leg motion during locomotion, the central pattern generator (CPG) can inhibit or enable flexion and extension reflexes, depending on the phase of the step cycle.

These responses can be thought of as temporary reflexes in that they exist only to modify individual segments of a particular action under certain sets of conditions. Such responses ensure that the goal is achieved even when a disturbance is encountered. It is likely that similar reflex responses operate during human locomotion when, for example, we stub our toe while walking along a sidewalk and immediately elevate that foot to avoid falling. Analogous findings have also been reported in studies exploring the control of speech, where small, unexpected tugs on the lip musculature during the production of a sound cause rapid, reflexive modulations that allow the particular sound to be produced even though the lip is perturbed (Abbs, Gracco, & Cole, 1984; Kelso, Tuller, Vatikoitis-Bateson, & Fowler, 1984).

Motor Programs and the Conceptual Model

Motor programs are an important component of the conceptual model seen in figure 4.3. They operate within the motor system, sometimes in conjunction with feedback, to produce flexible skilled actions. For the most part, it is assumed that the open-loop part of these actions occurs first and provides the organization, or pattern, for the movement, which later may be modified by feedback processes, if necessary. For example, when catching a ball the fielder might program the positioning of the hand but then use feedback from the moving limb as well as the approaching ball to determine when to begin the grasping action. Research (Cole, 2004) suggests that feedback processes may also be an important prerequisite for movement planning. In that study, three individuals who had various forms of sensory impairment (acute elimination of position sense below the neck, acute meningitis, prolonged immobilization following a broken heel) reported that they not only had trouble producing goal-directed movements but also had difficulty focusing attention on the planning of the movements. As one participant put it, "It was as though I had forgotten what to do (in order to move)" (p. 243).

Regardless of how movements are planned, it is assumed that the primary function of motor programs is to assist performers in regulating the many degrees of freedom in their movements. Earlier in this chapter we defined degrees of freedom as "the components of a control system that can vary independently and that are controlled to produce effective action." To experience this concept for yourself, consider some of the ways you might choose to move the muscles and joints in just your index finger. If you lock or freeze the top two joints, you can move the straightened finger in a forward–backward or a left–right direction, or you can rotate it clockwise or counterclockwise in a circle. This example illustrates just a few of the available degrees of freedom for moving just one appendage. For other examples, see "Freeing and Freezing Degrees of Freedom" on this page.

A big challenge for performers is identifying the combinations of degrees of freedom that produce the most effective and efficient movements. Muscles and joints that are allowed to move during an action (e.g., the ones controlling the straightened finger in the previous example) are said to be free to vary, whereas those being prevented from moving (e.g., the ones controlling the top two segments of the index finger) are the ones said to be frozen.

Another factor that appears to influence the way people program their movements is the anticipated final position of the limb or appendage. In a study by Rosenbaum (1989), participants performed a task in which they reached forward to grasp a control handle and then rotated it to different locations along a 360° target surface. During the course of the experiment, participants rotated the handle under a variety of conditions that involved combinations of starting location and target location. The way people oriented their hand before grasping the handle at the starting location depended on the terminal location or target to which they would be moving, even with the same starting position. In some cases the hand was oriented at the start in a way that appeared quite awkward and contorted but that later appeared natural when the hand moved to the target position. One interpretation of these results is that the system programmed the orientation of the hand at the starting location in a (sometimes uncomfortable) way

It Depends . . .

Freeing and Freezing Degrees of Freedom

To demonstrate the concepts of freeing and freezing degrees of freedom to control movements, stand next to your chair and put an object on the seat (e.g., a coin, a pen, a book). Your movement goal is to pick up the object with your left hand and place it in your right hand. Attempt to perform this movement in three distinct ways. On the first attempt, keep your wrists and elbows locked. On the second attempt, bend your wrists and elbows but keep all of your fingers, except for the thumb, locked and straight. On the third attempt, pick up the object any way you like and then indicate which joints you allowed to move freely and which ones you froze.

Now rank order each of the following movements with respect to the degree to which the joints and muscles in the wrists, hands, and fingers are free to move. Assign a 1 to the movement that allows the most freedom for the joints to move and a 4 to the one that allows the least freedom (i.e., freezes joint movement in more ways).

_______ Playing the piano

_______ Sculpting with clay

_______ Chopping wood with an axe

_______ Shooting a basketball free throw

For each of these tasks, explain why it is important for the performer to free (or freeze) the degrees of freedom in the wrist, hand, or fingers.

to ensure that it would always be oriented in the same (and more comfortable) way when it reached the target location.

In summary, then, the major roles of motor programs are to

- define and issue commands to the muscles needed to produce the goal movement, including when and how forcefully the muscles are to contract;
- coordinate the many degrees of freedom needed to produce an effective and efficient action;
- specify and initiate any preliminary postural adjustments needed to support the upcoming action; and
- modulate the many reflex pathways needed to ensure goal achievement.

Bernstein's Dynamical Perspective

A principal rival to the notion of motor-program control is the dynamical perspective initially proposed by the Russian physiologist N.I. Bernstein (Bernstein, 1967; Kelso, 1995). Advocates of this view argue that the motor program concept places undue emphasis on the organization, control, and representation of every action in the central nervous system and ignores many of the dynamic features of movements, such as the springlike properties of contracting muscles and the preferred frequencies of oscillation of limb segments.

According to the dynamical perspective, regularities of movement patterns are not represented in motor programs but rather emerge naturally (i.e., physically) as the result of complex interactions among numerous connected elements. The idea of dynamical systems is analogous to theoretical propositions explaining the organization and structure of many complex physical systems that function in the absence of a central program or set of commands. Examples of such spontaneous organization include the sudden transformation of still water to rolling patterns as it begins to boil and the ordering of water molecules into crystals when the temperature drops to freezing. Proponents of the dynamical-systems viewpoint argue that, just as it would make little sense to postulate a central program for governing the patterns that emerge in boiling and freezing water, it is incorrect to think that motor programs are needed to control complex patterns of human movement. That said, a dynamical perspective cannot account for the invariance in the EMG patterns when the limb is blocked, and some kind of open-loop, programmed control seems needed (see figure 4.6).

Supporting evidence for the dynamical perspective for motor control comes mainly from ongoing continuous tasks and rhythmic activities, whereas evidence for motor

Experience Open- and Closed-Loop Control

You can experience a combination of open-loop and closed-loop control by performing the skill of bounce and catch. Stand in an upright position and bounce a tennis ball on the ground in front of you. As the ball rises from the ground, catch it. Repeat the task several times, bouncing the ball to a different height and catching it at the apex each time. Which aspects of this simple task are you controlling in an open-loop fashion? What are they? Which aspects are you controlling in a closed-loop fashion? What are they? How and when are you using sensory information?

Motor Programs, Along With Feedback, Manage the Degrees of Freedom in Movement Control

Motor programs operate within the motor system, sometimes in conjunction with feedback, to manage the degrees of freedom of movements and produce flexible skilled actions. In a study by Steenbergen, Marteniuk, and Kalbfleisch (1995), seven right-handed individuals were seated and performed a task in which they reached forward a distance of 30 cm, grasped a foam cup, moved it 20 cm, and placed it in the center of a plate. During half of the movement attempts, the cup was empty; during the other half, it was filled with cold coffee. Participants performed half of the movements with their right hand (involving a leftward movement of the cup) and the other half with their left hand (involving a rightward movement of the cup).The reaching and transporting phases of the participants' movements were slower when the cup was full than when it was empty, and when the task was performed with the left (nonpreferred) hand than when it was performed with the right. During these slower movements, participants reduced the angular motion of their elbow and shoulder joints and increased the motion of their trunk. One interpretation of these results is that under the full-cup condition, the motor system froze selected joints (in this case the elbow and shoulder) to reduce the frequency of feedback-based corrections needed to move the cup full of liquid. It is also possible that the system allowed more freedom for the trunk because the muscles that control the low spine are inherently more stable than those that control the elbow and shoulder, are less susceptible to outside disturbances, or can be controlled with smaller amplitude corrections.

dynamical perspective— An explanation for how people control coordinated movements that emphasizes the interaction of dynamic properties of the neuromuscular system and physical properties of environmental information.

Self-Organization in Dynamic Systems

One of the tenets of the *dynamical perspective* is self-organization, meaning that the human motor system is capable of adjusting itself spontaneously from one state to another under certain conditions. This concept was quite clearly illustrated in a study by Kelso and Schöner (1988). To experience the self-organization phenomenon for yourself, try the following task. Begin by placing your hands palm down on a flat surface in front of you (e.g., a desktop). Now begin tapping your two index fingers in an alternating fashion at a slow, steady pace. As you continue to do this, gradually increase the pace until you are moving your fingers at a maximum rate of speed. What happens? If you move fast enough, the motor system reorganizes the action, causing your fingers to tap at the same time (in phase) rather than alternately (out of phase). We are only beginning to understand the implications of such self-organizing properties (see Kelso, 1995), but the research to date has uncovered some interesting features of coordination.

programming comes primarily from brief, rapid, and discrete actions. The evidence for the dynamical perspective includes research showing that the exact dynamics of patterns of limb action during gait or locomotion are achieved by basic demands for stability (Hoyt & Taylor, 1981) and by the simple mechanical properties of the muscles in combination with gravitational forces (McMahon, 1984). Findings such as these suggest that an extensive motor program is not needed to govern the control of at least these aspects of repetitive actions.

The debate of these issues continues in a healthy scientific fashion (T.D. Lee, 1998; Newell, 2003; Schmidt, 2003; Sherwood & Lee, 2003; Sternad, 1998; Walter, 1998). However, it is likely that the best explanation for movement control lies in some combination of the various viewpoints (Colley & Beech, 1988) and that the most appropriate one for any particular movement depends on several situational factors, including the nature of the action itself, the environmental goal, and the skill level of the performer. Nevertheless, we believe that the motor-program notion continues to be a useful way of integrating many types of research findings into a unified structure (see again some of these lines of evidence cited earlier in this chapter). However, as we indicate in the next section, the motor-program notion as described so far here is too simple to explain some of the more sophisticated aspects of ongoing motor control.

GENERALIZED MOTOR PROGRAMS

Although the simple motor-program notion is useful for understanding the functional organization of certain kinds of actions, it fails to explain how people are able to produce novel movements and to create flexible movement patterns. We turn to these issues next.

How Is a Novel Movement Produced?

Frequently we see a champion tennis player demonstrate an amazing capability to produce actions that appear completely novel (i.e., new and different). The player may be out of position and yet is able to return her opponent's shot with a shot of her own that looks extremely unorthodox and almost certainly has not been practiced previously. If we consider the immense number of possible combinations of ball-flight characteristics (i.e., speed, angle, trajectory, spin, unpredictable bounces), changes in court position of the two opponents, and so on, it is likely that each shot each player hits is essentially novel, in that it has never been performed in exactly that way before. Despite all this, advanced players execute their movements with great style and grace, as if they are producing well-practiced actions.

Observations such as these raise problems for the simple **motor-program notion**. According to the simple view, each variation of the same general movement, such as the tennis swing, needs its own program because differences in ball-flight characteristics, positioning of the opponent, and so on require a particular, distinct set of instructions to the muscles, which are stored in LTM. Because there appears to be an unlimited number of variations (e.g., in speed, size, forcefulness) of most movements, performers would need to have countless numbers of motor programs in LTM to produce all of these variations. As you may have probably surmised by now, the number of variations possible in tennis, not to mention those in all other motor activities, creates the dilemma of an enormous number of programs being deposited in LTM, a problem that Dick Schmidt termed the **storage problem** (Schmidt, 1975; Schmidt & Lee, 2005).

In addition to the storage problem, the simple motor-program notion must also deal with the **novelty problem**. Before discussing this problem further, we would like you to try the following activity: From a standing position, jump up and rotate your body one fourth of a turn to the left and, while still in the air, touch the top of your head with your right hand and your left hip with your left hand. Were you able to do it? Although we doubt that you have ever attempted this movement before, our guess is that you were able to perform it rather effectively on the first or second try. Where did the specific program for this action come from? It could not have been learned and placed in LTM, unless you had practiced the movement before today. And it is

motor-program notion— An explanation for how people control coordinated movements that emphasizes the role of prestructured motor commands organized at the executive level.

storage problem— A deficiency of the simple motor-program notion, which presumes the need for a vast memory capacity to store separate programs for controlling the nearly infinite number of movements people are able to produce.

novelty problem— A deficiency of the simple motor-program notion, which presumes that people are unable to produce novel (i.e., new) movements or unpracticed variations of learned movements because they have not developed specific motor programs for producing them.

It is likely that most of the shots that experienced tennis players produce are never executed in exactly the same way.

not likely that the program was genetically wired in, because such a movement would seem to have little biological significance, unlike the movements that people need for locomotion or chewing. Clearly, the simple motor-program notion is at a loss to explain the performance of such novel actions as this.

generalized motor program—A motor program that defines a pattern of movement rather than a specific movement; this flexibility allows performers to adapt the generalized program to produce variations of the pattern that meet various environmental demands.

How Can Motor Program Output Be Modified?

In response to the storage and novelty problems inherent in the simple motor program notion, scientists began looking for alternative ways of understanding program control. One result was a characterization called the **generalized motor program** (Schmidt 1975). Unlike its simpler predecessor, the generalized motor program is presumed to contain a stored movement pattern that can be modified slightly when it is executed, allowing performers to adjust the movement to meet various environmental demands (see Shea & Wulf, 2005, for a more recent discussion of the generalized-motor-program concept).

About 75 years ago, the British psychologist Sir Fredrick Bartlett (1932) wrote this about his tennis stroke: "When I make the stroke, I do not . . . produce something absolutely new, and I never repeat something old" (p. 202).

The first part of Bartlett's statement suggests that a movement is never totally new. This was based on his own observation that all of his ground strokes resembled each other because they possessed his own style of hitting a tennis ball (don't we all have our own individual and unique style of moving?). Button, MacLeod, Sanders, and Coleman (2003) found systematic differences among players' basketball shooting patterns, with each having his own signature pattern. The second part of Bartlett's statement conveys the idea discussed in the previous section, that every movement is also novel in that it has never been performed exactly the same way at any other time before. Although that also makes sense in general terms, what might be some of the features that performers can change when they produce the same type of movement in different ways?

Movement Time

When we play throw and catch with a friend, sometimes we throw the ball faster and other times we throw it slower. That we are able to change the time or speed of our throwing movement without altering the fundamental pattern suggests that movement speed is one adjustable feature of generalized motor programs. Earlier research by Armstrong (1970) suggested that movement time is a likely candidate as well. He asked participants to move a control stick in a left–right–left–right–left pattern, controlling the movement at the elbow joint. The solid black line in figure 4.9 illustrates the goal movement pattern that these participants were trying to produce. As you can see, the pattern required them to move the stick to the left for the first 0.75 s, then back to the right until 1.95 s, then back to the left until 2.90 s, then back to the right until 3.59 s, and finally back to the left to stop at the original position in a total time of 4 s.

Not surprisingly, participants were often unable to produce their movements in exactly 4 s. An example of one such pattern is shown in figure 4.9 (maroon line). As you can see, the first reversal movement occurred slightly sooner than that of the goal pattern (i.e., at about 0.66 s, compared with 0.75 s) and resulted in subsequent reversals that occurred increasingly early. However, we can see that the participant's pattern was similar to the goal pattern even though it was produced too quickly (i.e., completed in closer to 3 s than to 4 s).

Another way to think of this relationship is to imagine the participant's pattern in figure 4.9 being drawn on an rubber sheet that could be stretched to make the final peak (maroon line) line up with the final peak of the goal pattern (black line). If we did this we would see that all of the other peaks in the participant's pattern would tend to be lined up with their respective peaks in the goal pattern. Armstrong's findings suggest that the performer changed the movement time of the action while still preserving the **fundamental timing structure.** In both actions, the goal pattern consists of an underlying timing and sequence of events that can be run off at different speeds.

fundamental timing structure— The sequencing and timing (or rhythm) of a movement that define the underlying pattern.

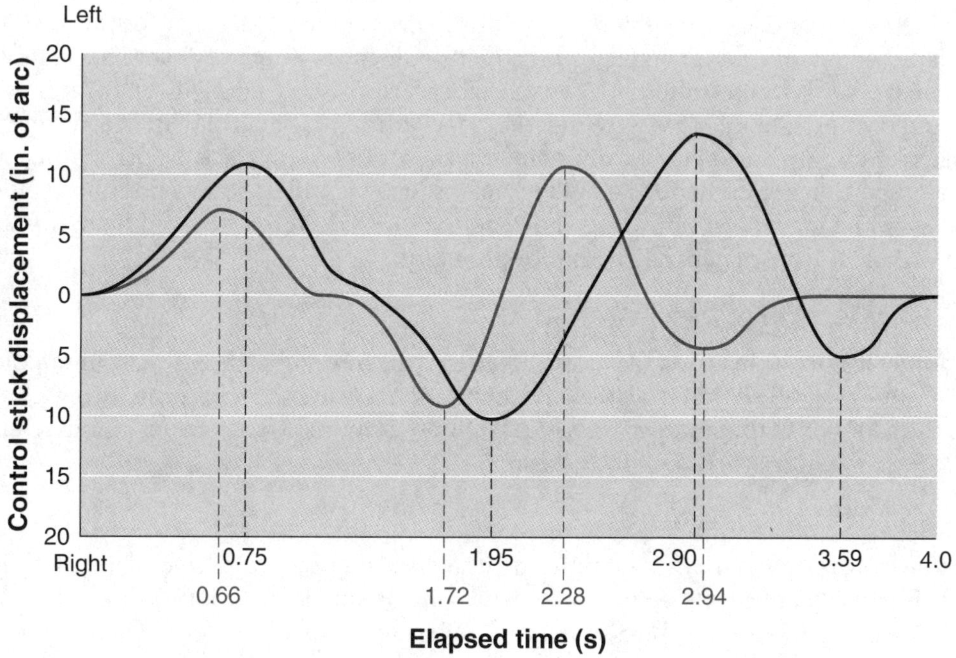

Figure 4.9 The position–time record of performance in an arm movement task. The black line is the goal movement, whereas a movement that is uniformly too rapid is shown by the maroon line. (Adapted from Armstrong, 1970.)

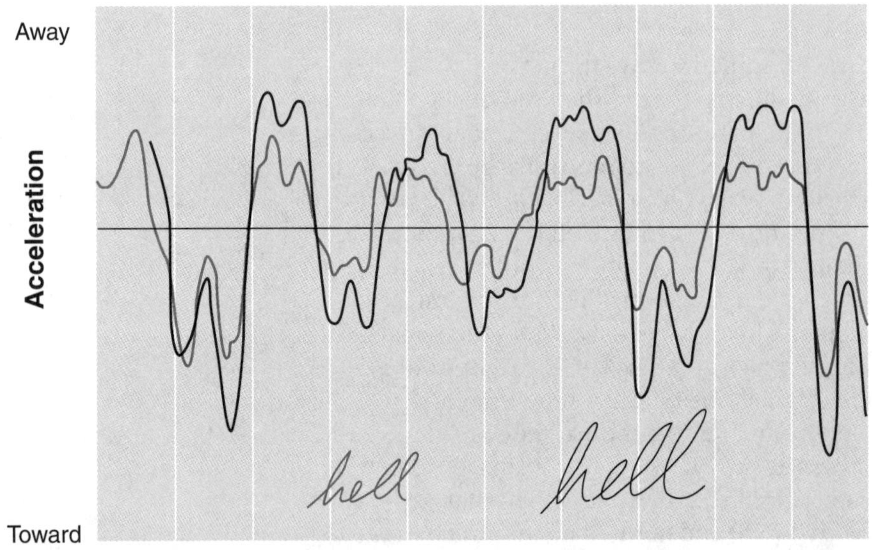

Figure 4.10 Similar patterns of acceleration produced during the writing of the word *hell*, even though one example has twice the amplitude of the other. (Adapted from Hollerback, 1978.)

Movement Amplitude

The amplitude of movements appears to be another feature people can change when they perform the same action in slightly different ways. For example, you can write your signature in quarter-inch (0.6 cm)–high letters on a bank check or in six-inch (15 cm)–high letters on a blackboard. In both cases, the signature is clearly that of the same person (Merton, 1972).

Hollerbach (1978) studied this phenomenon more formally by asking people to write the word *hell* in different-sized letters. He then measured the acceleration patterns (i.e., the forces, or changes in speed) of their finger movements. Patterns for two different-sized versions of one participant's performance are shown in figure 4.10; when the trace moves upward, the movement is accelerating away from the body, and the downward movement of the trace indicates that the movement is accelerating toward the body. Not surprisingly, when participants wrote the word in larger letters (black line), the overall magnitude of the acceleration trace was larger than when they wrote it in smaller letters (maroon line). Of greater interest, though, is the obvious fact that the *patterns* of acceleration over time for both versions are almost identical, varying from each other only in amplitude.

People can easily vary the amplitude of their movements (just as they can the time)—by increasing or decreasing the accelerations (forces) they produce uniformly—while still preserving the fundamental timing structure. Such variations appear to be possible for many kinds of movements. However, other factors, such as gravity, may limit this generalization. Surely, if we were to write on a vertical blackboard with a lead weight fastened to our wrist, simply scaling the forces would not produce proper writing, as the up portions of the actions would be against gravity and the down portions would be aided by gravity. Nevertheless, movement amplitude is another candidate for an adjustable feature of generalized motor programs.

Movement Direction

Another feature of an action that is easily varied is the movement direction. For example, I can throw a ball so that it strikes a target high on a wall or low, or I can throw a ball to the south or to the southeast. Changes in these simple surface features would retain the fundamental structure of the action.

Limb and Muscles Used

A third way people can vary their movements while still preserving the fundamental pattern is by using different **effector** systems (e.g., limb or muscle) to produce the movement. In the example about signatures, writing on a blackboard involves very different muscles and joints than writing on a bank check. In blackboard-writing our fingers are mainly fixed, and we perform the task using muscles that control the elbow and shoulder. In check-writing, our elbow and shoulder are mainly fixed, and we perform the movement

effector— The component of a control system that carries out the desired action; for example, the arm is usually the effector that carries out the action of throwing a ball.

by using muscles that control the fingers. Nevertheless, the pattern of our signature remains essentially the same. This indicates that we can produce the same movement pattern even when we use different muscles and effectors (see figure 4.11).

Figure 4.11 Generalized motor programs can be used to produce the same movement pattern with different effector systems (e.g., arms, legs).

Raibert (1977) studied the phenomenon of limb flexibility by attempting to write a sentence using different effectors. Raibert wrote the famous palindromic sentence (i.e., one that reads the same both forward and backward) "Able was I ere I saw Elba" using (A) his right (dominant) hand, (B) his right arm with the wrist immobilized, (C) his left hand, (D) his teeth, and (E) his foot with the pen taped to it. The resulting sentences (shown in figure 4.12) revealed an amazingly similar writing style even though they were written with different limbs and muscles (including those in the head and neck!). Once again, the fundamental timing structure of the movement appears to have been preserved under these varied performance conditions—in this case by a person using different effector systems to produce the goal movement.

surface features—The easily changeable components of a movement, such as movement time or amplitude; that are modified as a result of changing parameters.

A particularly useful analogy or model of the motor program is the old phonograph record. These records defined the sounds that would occur along with the order, the duration and timing (rhythm), and the relative intensities of the sounds. Unlike the phonograph record, however, the motor program would not specify every aspect of the movement, in that reflexive activities are possible, increasingly so as the movement time increases. Nevertheless, the motor program and the phonograph record operate conceptually in more or less the same way. In the next chapter we discuss the analogy between the two in more detail.

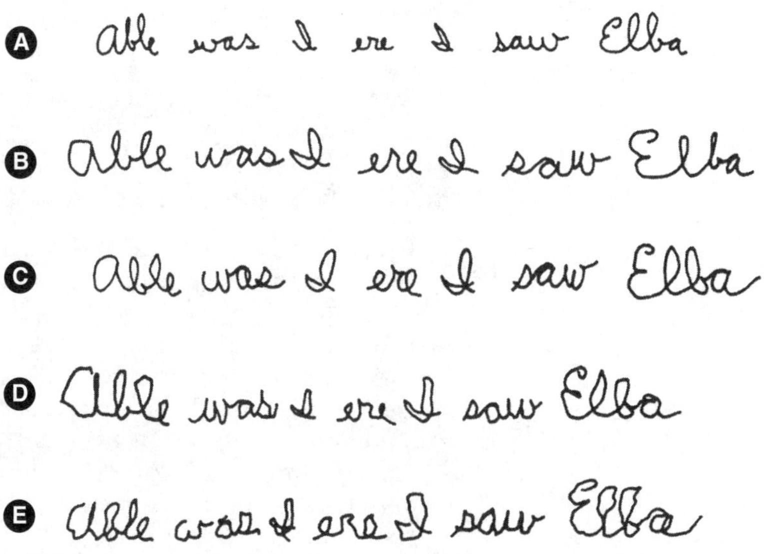

Figure 4.12 Similarities in writing with different effector systems. Line A was written by the right (dominant) hand, line B with the wrist immobilized, line C with the left hand, line D with pen gripped in the teeth, and line E with pen taped to the foot. (Reprinted, by permission, from M.H. Raibert, 1977, *Motor control and learning by the state-space model: Technical report no. A1-TR-439* (Cambridge, MA: Artificial Intelligence Laboratory, Massachusetts Institute of Technology)).

Identifying Movement Parameters

The generalized-motor-program concept presumes that characteristics such as movement time, movement amplitude, and the limb or muscles to be used in producing the action are relatively superficial features of the fundamental movement pattern. These superficial or **surface features** are generated by variable inputs to the generalized motor program (which scientists refer to as

parameters—The variable inputs to a generalized motor program, such as speed or amplitude of the movement, which result in different surface features.

parameters). Put more simply, surface features are modifiable components of the generalized motor program. Thus, when performers are faced with a particular situation requiring the use of a generalized program (say, throwing a ball), they adjust several parameters of the program to achieve the environmental goal, all while using the same, fundamental movement pattern.

Let's assume that a softball pitcher receives and interprets sensory information (stimulus-identification stage) and then selects (response-selection stage) a generalized motor program for throwing. This program would likely be organized in STM, having been previously retrieved from LTM for use in the practice or game. Once the pitcher selects the throwing program, she prepares it for initiation (in the response-programming stage).

The pitcher determines how she wants to modify the program for this particular occasion. Using environmental information available immediately before the action, the pitcher determines the most appropriate pitch to make (e.g., a very fast pitch). Once she does this, the pitcher estimates the specific parameters necessary for successful execution of the pitch. In this case, the pitcher would likely select a relatively short movement time and relatively short movement amplitude and perhaps a direction that has the ball come very close to the batter. We do not seem to be aware of these specific selections, however. Once the player has set these parameter values, she is ready to initiate and carry out the throwing movement.

By using generalized motor programs, performers are able to modify already-learned movement patterns to meet changing environmental demands. The more they practice the process of parameterization (e.g., shortening or lengthening the time or amplitude of a movement, selecting the appropriate limb to use), the better they become at deter-

It Depends . . .

How Would You Parameterize the Following Movements?

Notice how easily you are able to change movement time and movement amplitude when performing movements such as throwing, kicking, or scribbling. What happens to your movement time and movement amplitude when you want to throw or kick an object a short distance? A long distance?

Modifying Movements to Meet Situational Demands

Recent research has shown that skilled baseball players modify their overarm throwing patterns according to situational factors such as their fielding position at the time of the throw, the required distance of the throw, and the game situation (Barrett & Burton, 2002). In this study, the researchers videotaped the throwing motions of 100 NCAA Division I collegiate players during both active (i.e., to get someone "out") and inactive (i.e., noncrucial) game situations. Using Roberton's (1982) system for evaluating overarm throwing form, Barrett and Burton discovered that these highly skilled players used a variety of throwing forms and demonstrated the most advanced form only for certain circumstances (e.g., when a particularly strong and accurate throw had to be made). The researchers concluded that advanced players choose to produce a wider variety of throwing patterns than unskilled players because they have the strength, size, and skill to adjust the form of the motion and still achieve the desired goal.

mining the most appropriate parameters for various situations. This is an important process in learning, which we discuss in the second part of the book.

SUMMARY

When people want to produce rapid actions—that is, movements for which there is no time for the system to process feedback about errors and correct them—they must organize and produce the actions in an open-loop fashion (i.e., plan them in advance and execute them with minimal involvement of sensory information during the action). The motor program is the structure that presumably carries out this action. Several lines of experimental evidence suggest support for the notion of motor programs:

- Reaction time is longer for more complex movements than for simple movements.
- Animals that are deprived of sensory information using a surgical process of deafferentation are still capable of producing relatively effective movements.
- Muscular activity patterns (measured by EMG) during the first 100 ms of limb movement remain the same even when a person's limb is unexpectedly prevented from moving.

Although the motor program is responsible for determining the major events in the movement pattern, there is still considerable involvement of sensory and reflexive processes. These processes include premovement information (e.g., posture, body orientation), which performers use to prepare the movement, and various reflex mechanisms that are organized to generate rapid corrections that enable goal achievement in the face of changing environmental demands. Finally, the concept of the generalized motor program expands on the idea of the simple motor program by allowing the production of variations of a particular movement or class of actions (such as throwing) so that the action can meet slightly different environmental demands. The following features characterize generalized motor programs:

- They allow performers to modify their movements along several dimensions, such as movement time, movement amplitude, and the effector (e.g., arm, leg) needed to produce the action.
- They preserve the fundamental timing structure and spatial patterning of the movement under various kinds of superficial modifications (e.g., producing the movement at different speeds).

FROM PRINCIPLES TO PRACTICE

Check your comprehension of the concepts and terms discussed in this chapter by responding to each of the exercises in the following sections. The first section contains several exercises designed to test your working knowledge of key terms. The second section poses a variety of problems designed to check your understanding of key concepts. In the third section you are challenged to apply your knowledge by discussing a defensible solution for two scenarios.

Know Your Key Terms

Matching: Open-Loop Control

Match the following terms with their respective categories or definitions by placing the most appropriate letter on each of the blanks below.

Open-Loop Control—Terms

a. central pattern generator
b. generalized motor program
c. degrees of freedom
d. movement time
e. effector
f. surface feature
g. discrete skill

Open-Loop Control—Category or Definition

_____ 1. Component of a control system that carries out the desired action

_____ 2. An action that is usually brief in duration

_____ 3. Thought to control genetically defined, repetitive actions

_____ 4. Changeable component of a movement; also referred to as a parameter

_____ 5. Managed more effectively by skilled than unskilled performers

_____ 6. Factor that often dictates the type of control (i.e., closed-loop or open-loop) that is needed

_____ 7. Defines a flexible pattern of movement rather than a specific action

Consider: Some Advantages of Open-Loop Control

For each of the following skills, indicate one aspect of the task or environment the performer might be able to attend to once he or she is able to control the action in an open-loop fashion. Provide rationale for your answers.

1. Keyboarding ____________________
2. Dribbling a soccer ball ____________________
3. Dancing the waltz ____________________
4. In-line skating ____________________

Fill in the Blank: Generalized Motor Programs

Complete the following sentences:

A particular strength of generalized motor programs is that they allow performers to produce ____________ patterns of action. Three aspects of the generalized program that performers can adjust to meet changing environmental demands are ____________________, ____________________, and ____________________. However, regardless of the adjustments made, the fundamental ________________ structure of the movement remains essentially the same.

Check Your Understanding

1. What are the major components of an open-loop control system? How does this type of control system differ from the closed-loop system? Describe how each of the components of the open-loop system might function for a person who is tossing an empty soft-drink can into a recycling bin.

2. Why do we believe that motor programs exist? Discuss two of the three types of research evidence that suggest support for the motor-program notion. How does each type of evidence illustrate that performers plan their movements in advance?
3. How do performers produce novel movements? Are such movements really new? Provide an example of a novel movement that might be produced by a shuffleboard player, a professional golfer, an airplane pilot, or a wheelchair basketball player.
4. What is the generalized motor program? Indicate how this concept allows us to explain the way performers adjust their movements to meet different sets of environmental demands. Using the example you selected in the previous question, explain how the performer might use a generalized motor program to produce the novel movement.

Apply Your Knowledge

Exercise 1

A senior citizen has had one of her hands amputated as a result of a diabetic condition. Unfortunately, the hand that was removed is the one she has used predominantly for her entire life. The woman has been fitted for a prosthetic device and must now learn how to perform functional tasks (e.g., eating, brushing her teeth, combing her hair, making the bed) using this device as well as her nondominant hand. Assume that you have been asked to assist this woman. Discuss some of the motor-control challenges she will face as she attempts to adapt to her new situation. Discuss two functional activities she needs to relearn and explain how she might use closed-loop and open-loop control processes to achieve the goal of each task. Provide rationale for your answers and include two supporting references.

Exercise 2

A man wakes up, gets out of bed, and walks to the kitchen to fix breakfast. Starting with the task of getting out of bed and finishing with the task of putting the first bite of food in his mouth, describe four movements the man must control in a closed-loop or open-loop fashion, or both. Indicate which of the movements (or components of movements) would be controlled using open-loop processes and which would be controlled using closed-loop processes. For one of the movements primarily controlled in an open-loop fashion, describe one parameter of the generalized motor program the man would probably need to modify when performing the task. For one of the closed-loop-controlled movements, give an example of feedback the man might use to adjust the action. Provide rationale for your answers and furnish two supporting references.

UNIVERSITY OF WINCHESTER
LIBRARY

chapter 5

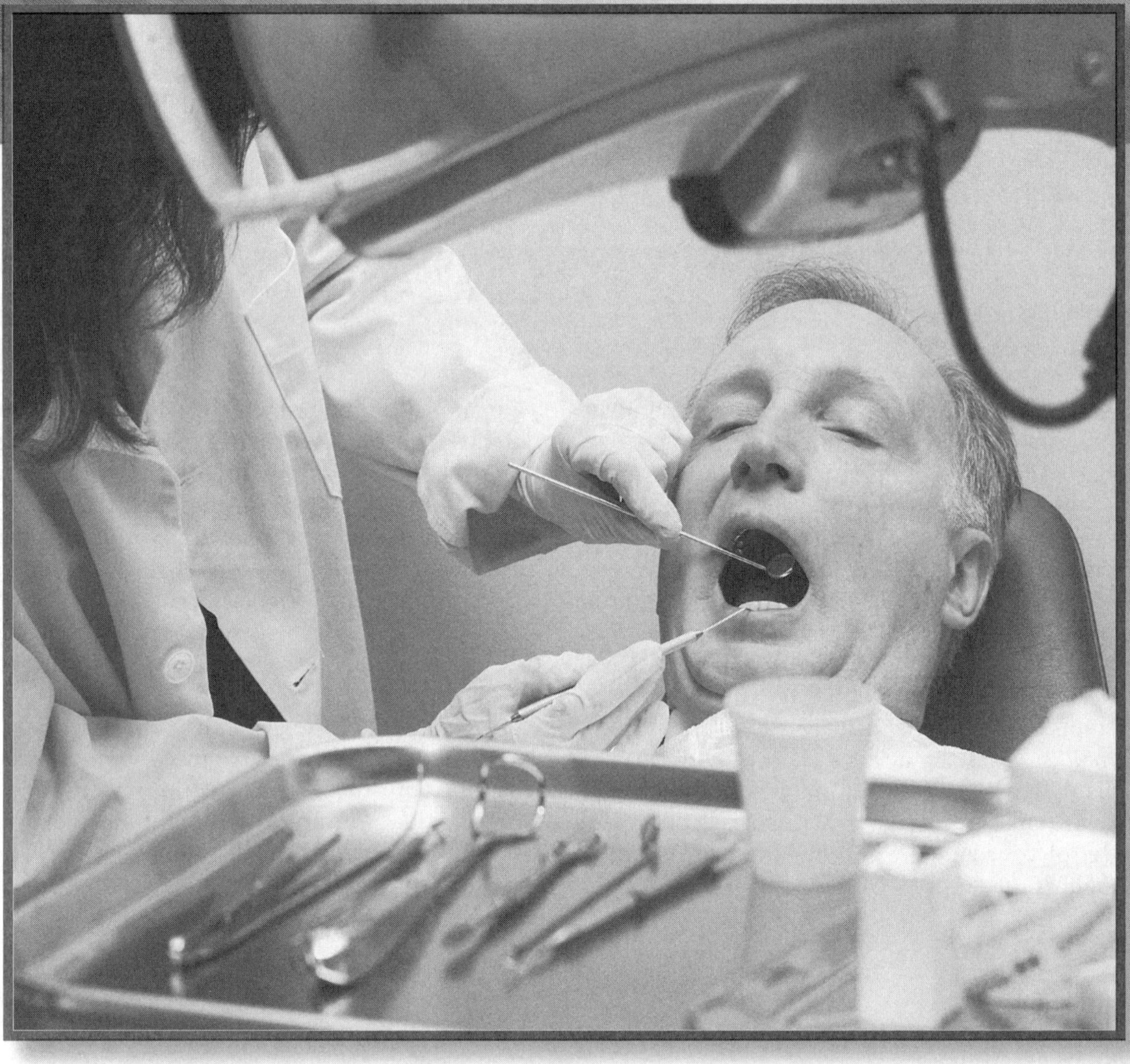

Principles of Motor Control and Movement Accuracy

▷ Chapter Outline

▷ Chapter Objectives

When you have completed this chapter, you should be able to

- understand the concept of invariance in motor control,
- explain how the speed and amplitude of a movement can influence movement accuracy,
- understand the fundamental causes of inaccuracy in quick movements, and
- apply the principles of rapid actions to real-world settings.

PREVIEW

It takes most dentists about 2 hr to complete a root-canal operation. They accept the fact that the job is a slow and tedious one, yet they realize that to be successful they must execute their movements precisely and accurately. This is but one example of the kinds of tasks people must perform slowly to achieve the desired outcome. Why is slower performance preferable for many tasks? Does speed of performance always have to be sacrificed for accuracy? Does haste always make waste?

OVERVIEW

In the previous chapter we discussed the concept of motor programs, focusing on the open-loop control of actions. An important aspect of our discussion dealt with how the surface features of fundamental movements may be altered, as when people throw snowballs at different speeds or jump over different-sized puddles. To tailor their movements to meet environmental demands in those types of control situations, performers adjust certain parameters (e.g., movement time and movement amplitude) of well-learned movement patterns (i.e., generalized motor programs for throwing or jumping).

In this chapter we continue our discussion of open-loop control and the concept of generalized motor programs. First, we show how each generalized program has its own characteristics and fundamental timing structure. Then we discuss some of the scientifically established principles of movement production—analogous to the simple laws of physics—that govern the relationships among movement speed, movement distance, and movement accuracy. Last we examine some of the underlying causes of errors in rapid movements and discuss several ways performers might maximize both the speed and the accuracy of their performance.

RELATIVE TIMING

invariant features—The characteristics of a movement that remain constant when the surface features of the movement change.

fundamental timing structure—The sequencing and timing (or rhythm) of a movement that defines the fundamental pattern.

relative timing—A measure of the temporal structure of a movement, in which the ratios among the durations of various movement features are used to define the temporal pattern.

In determining the way generalized motor programs are represented in long-term memory, scientists sought to know which features of movements remain the same, or are invariant, when people perform the movements with different surface features (amplitude or movement time). These **invariant features** remain constant even when a performer makes subtle adjustments in the movement to meet changing environmental demands. For example, a person may change the speed of raking leaves, but the fundamental raking pattern remains the same. Obviously, the invariant features of different classes of movements are different as well, which is why we are able to distinguish a leaf-raking motion from a dirt-shoveling motion.

In the 1970s, scientists began to search for the possible invariant features of generalized motor programs. Certain features of a movement pattern seem to remain the same regardless of the ways the movement might be adjusted to meet environmental demands. The most important feature they identified was the **fundamental timing structure** of the movement, which they called **relative timing.**

If you look back to figure 4.9, you will see Armstrong's (1970) data showing what happens to a movement when it is produced at various speeds. Perhaps you remember that there was something about the timing of that action that remained constant, even though the actual duration of the movement (i.e., total movement time) was different on different attempts. The question now is what feature remained invariant?

You can find the answer to this question in figure 4.9 by noticing that the timing of all parts of the movement changed *as a unit* (i.e., proportionately) when participants changed the duration of the whole movement. In other words, when participants sped up the whole movement, they uniformly sped up all of the parts as well, not just some of them. When this occurred, the ratio of the time of each part to the total time of the movement remained essentially the same. Put another way, the fundamental timing structure, or relative timing of the parts, remained *invariant* regardless of the overall movement time (see Gentner, 1987, or Schmidt, 1985, 1988a, for a more detailed discussion of this issue).

Relative timing, then, is a measure of the fundamental timing structure or rhythm of a movement pattern, and this rhythm remains the same even when people change

Invariance in the Relative Timing of Movement Sequences

Research by Summers (1975) clearly illustrates the persistent invariance of relative timing in the production of well-learned movements. Participants in this study first learned a key-press task that involved depressing each of nine keys for a designated length of time, determined by the illumination of a stimulus light corresponding to the key (e.g., key 5, 500 ms; key 9, 100 ms; key 1, 500 ms; key 7, 500 ms; key 4, 100 ms; key 2, 500 ms; key 6, 500 ms; key 8, 100 ms; key 3, 500 ms). Following several hundred practice attempts, participants were instructed to produce the sequence as rapidly as possible and to disregard the relative timing pattern they had learned. The interesting result was that, although these participants were able to produce the sequence in a faster overall time, they were unable to disregard the learned relative-timing pattern. In other words, their key presses looked like a speeded-up copy of the fundamental timing structure they had learned previously, much like the results Armstrong (1970) reported in his study shown in figure 4.9. More recently, Summers, Rosenbaum, Burns, and Ford (1993) observed a similar pattern of control in people's performance of tasks involving the simultaneous production of different tapping rhythms with opposite hands.

surface features— The easily changeable components of a movement, such as movement time or amplitude, that are modified as a result of changing parameters.

parameters— The variable inputs to a generalized motor program, such as speed or amplitude of the movement, which result in different surface features.

the flexible **surface features** (by changing the **parameters**) of the pattern (e.g., movement time). For example, the rhythm of a waltz fundamentally remains the same regardless of how fast the music is playing or how much of the floor the dancers are covering. This is because the relative timing of the various components of the waltz remains the same. Moreover, this pattern of relative timing is different from that of the fox trot, just as the rhythm of a skipping movement is different from that of a galloping movement. Thus the fundamental timing structure, or relative timing, of a movement pattern is the signature characteristic that helps us identify the movement and also differentiate it from other movements.

The waltz has a unique relative-timing pattern or rhythm that distinguishes it from other dance forms.

Comparing Movements as a Set of Ratios

A more precise way to look at relative timing is as a set of ratios that defines the temporal structure of the action. Consider, for example, two repetitions of a hypothetical throwing movement as illustrated in figure 5.1. The first repetition (movement 1) is performed in a shorter movement time (MT1) than the second repetition (movement 2 and MT2). We can calculate the set of ratios for these two movements by first measuring and recording the duration of muscular activity (measured by EMG) in three of the important muscles involved in the action and then dividing each by the total duration of the movement. The resulting set of ratios is one measure of the fundamental timing structure of the throwing movement. Although the actual movement times for each

UNIVERSITY OF WINCHESTER
LIBRARY

It Depends . . .

Relative Timing: Important Practical Implications

Relative timing is a measure of the fundamental timing structure or rhythm for a particular class of movements (e.g., throwing). It not only appears to be a signature characteristic of movements but is difficult to change once it is well learned. What implications does this permanence of a learned rhythm have for a basketball coach teaching a young player how to shoot a jump shot? For a physical therapist assisting an amputee who is learning to walk with a prosthetic device? For an elementary physical education instructor who is teaching children a country line dance? For someone trying to improve the readability of her signature?

component and the total movement are not shown in figure 5.1, can you guess how the set of ratios for movement 1 would compare with the set of ratios for movement 2?

When the set of ratios is basically the same for two repetitions of the same general movement, even when the movement is produced in different overall movement times, we say that the relative timing of the movement is invariant; beyond this, we can be reasonably assured that the same generalized motor program was used for both of the movements. According to the **generalized motor program** notion introduced in chapter 4, the fundamental timing structure of the two movements represented in figure 5.1 remains essentially the same because all parts of the action are either slowed down or sped up as a unit. Differences in the two

generalized motor program—
A motor program that defines a pattern of movement rather than a specific movement; this flexibility allows performers to adapt the generalized program to produce variations of the pattern that meet various environmental demands.

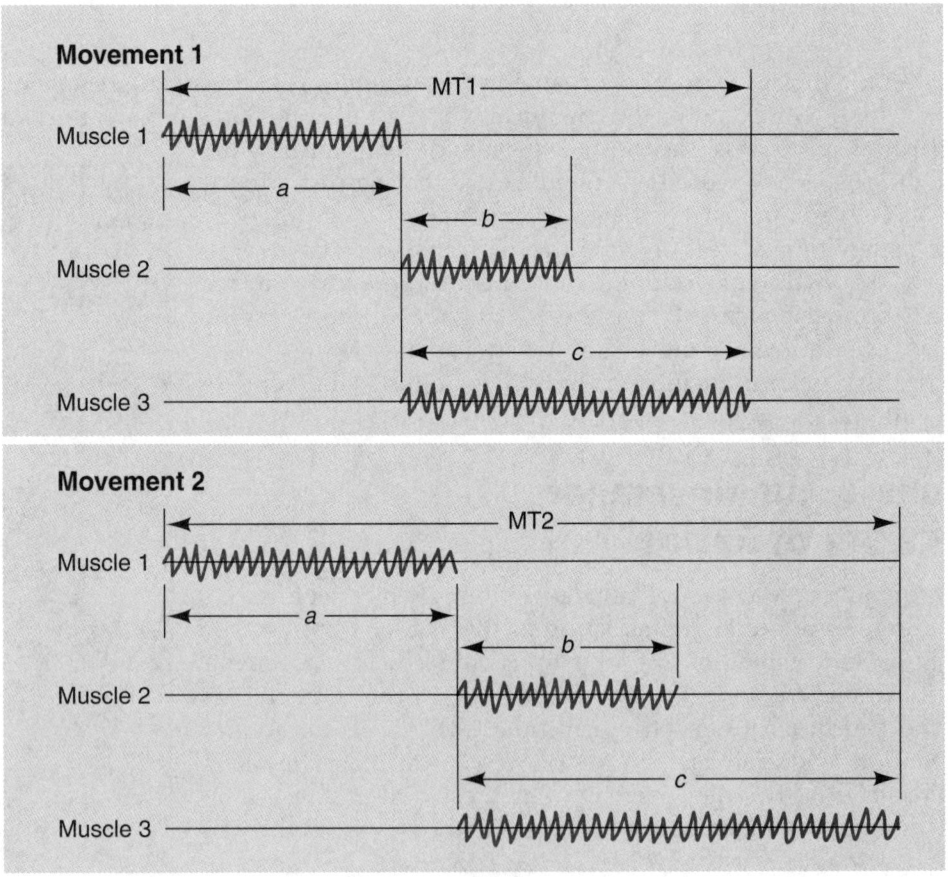

Figure 5.1 The duration of muscle activity (shown in a hypothetical electromyograph) for three important muscles involved in throwing is used to calculate the relative timing as a set of ratios for two movement repetitions. (Reprinted from Schmidt, 1988.)

repetitions are caused by differences in a surface feature or parameter (in this case, overall movement time).

One of the most important principles of movement control is that relative timing remains essentially the same (i.e., invariant) whenever performers change the

- speed of a rapid movement (e.g., a fast kick compared with a slow kick),
- size of the action (e.g., large handwriting compared with small handwriting),
- forces used to produce the action (e.g., throwing a tennis ball compared with throwing a basketball),
- trajectory of the movement (e.g., an overhead throw vs. a sidearm throw of a snowball), or
- the limb used for the action (e.g., your signature on a check [fingers] or on a blackboard [arm and shoulder]).

Another way to think of the relative timing of a movement pattern is as a kind of "fingerprint" that is unique to all movements within a particular class. Kicking actions have a common relative timing, but this would of course be different from the common relative timing pattern of a throwing action. Thus, when performers adjust some surface feature of the movement (e.g., force), the fundamental form and rhythm are preserved. Although some controversy exists about whether relative timing is *perfectly* invariant (see Gentner, 1987), there is little doubt that it is at least approximately invariant from one movement to the next within a given class—at least for rapid movements (Heuer, 1988).

It Depends . . .

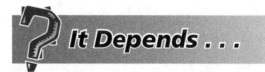

Can You Estimate the Relative Timing of a Familiar Movement?

Using the information shown in figure 5.1 as a model, diagram a set of ratios describing the relative timing of a movement with which you are familiar (except for walking or running). The movement must involve the activity of at least three muscle groups or limb segments (e.g., thigh, calf, foot; upper arm, lower arm, hand). Some possible candidates you might consider would be chopping wood, swinging a golf club, typing your name, and flipping and catching a pancake with a spatula.

Invariant Relative Timing in Throwing Movements

An activity such as throwing might be thought of as a class of movements containing numerous variations (e.g., overarm throws and sidearm throws; throwing objects that differ in size and weight; throwing objects different distances), but with one feature (relative timing) being invariant. The same generalized motor program, consisting of the same invariant relative timing structure, is thought to control all these throwing movements. The program requires that performers select parameters that adjust the flexible, surface features of the throws (movement time, movement amplitude, overall force), making it possible for performers to produce an essentially limitless variety of throws. Trained observers (e.g., coaches, movement therapists, physical education instructors) can detect the invariant relative timing of a person's throws (at least in general terms), see deficiencies in it, and differentiate that pattern from another pattern representing a different class of movements. For example, a Little League baseball coach can tell immediately when a young player shifts from a throw to a heave; usually this occurs when the player tries to throw the ball farther than he is capable of throwing it. Because the invariant relative-timing pattern for throwing is inadequate for achieving the desired goal (i.e., projecting the ball all the way to the target), the player shifts to another relative-timing pattern (i.e., one governing heaving movements) in an attempt to accomplish the goal. What evidence leads us to believe that performers change

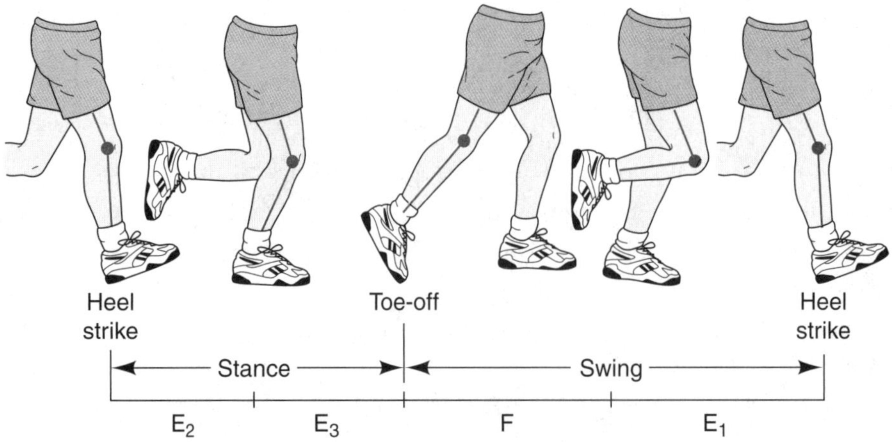

Figure 5.2 Dividing gait into phases (based on the Philippson step cycle). E_2 is the extension phase, E_3 is the propulsion phase, F is the flexion phase, and E_1 goes from the beginning of the knee extension to heel strike. (Reprinted from Shapiro et al., 1981.)

relative-timing patterns when changing from one class of movements to another? Some of the evidence comes from studies of running and walking, discussed next.

Invariant Relative Timing for Walking Versus Running

To determine the relative-timing characteristics of human locomotion, Shapiro and her colleagues (1981) filmed people walking and running on a treadmill at speeds ranging from 3 to 12 km/hr. For each speed, the researchers measured the duration of each of the four phases of the Philippson step cycle for the right leg (see figure 5.2). The intervals included the time between heel strike and maximum knee flexion (termed the *extension phase* and labeled E_2), between maximum knee flexion and toe-off (termed the *propulsion phase* and labeled E_3), between toe-off and the beginning of knee extension (termed the *flexion phase* and labeled F), and between the beginning of knee extension and heel strike (labeled E_1). Together, E_2 and E_3 made up the stance phase, whereas F and E_1 made up the swing phase of locomotion.

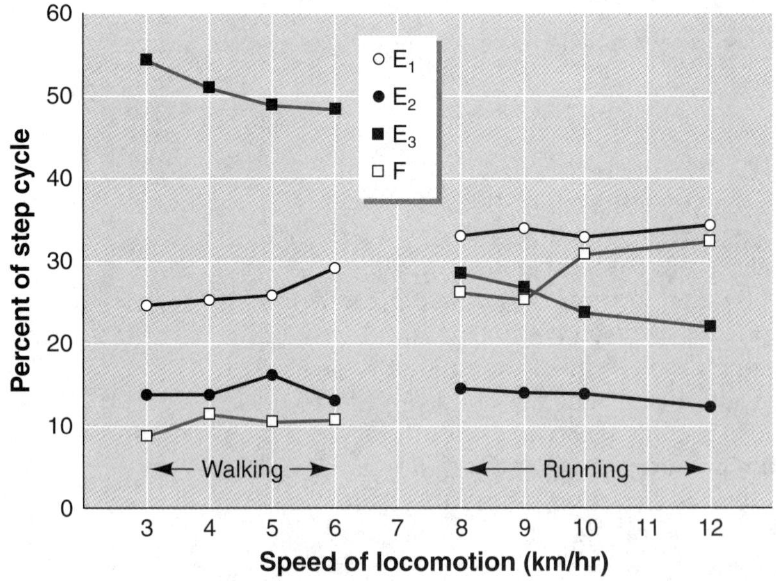

Figure 5.3 The step cycle in human gait, showing the proportion occupied by phases E_1, E_2, E_3, and F as the treadmill's speed is varied. Although the proportions differ for walking and running, they remain constant within each type of gait. (Reprinted from Shapiro et al., 1981.)

The data shown in figure 5.3 are the set of ratios defining the relative durations of the four phases of the step cycle: in other words, the duration of each phase divided by the duration of the total step cycle (vertical axis labeled percent of step cycle in the figure). When treadmill speed ranged from 3 to 6 km/hr (left side of figure), participants were walking. Notice that the relative-timing pattern of the four phases remained pretty much the same (as indicated by the relatively flat slopes of the lines) for all four walking speeds. Phase E_3 always lasted for about half of the step cycle, F and E_2 occupied around 10% each, and E_1 was about 28%. However, when treadmill speed was increased and ranged from 8 to 12 km/hr (right side of figure), all of the participants were running and, as you can see, the relative-timing pattern changed considerably. Now E_1 occupied the largest percentage of the step cycle (32%), closely followed by F (approximately 30%) and E_3 (approximately 28%). Only E_2 remained at a percentage similar to that for walking, but now this phase made up the smallest portion of the step cycle. As in the case of walking, changes in treadmill speed while participants were running (i.e., 8-12 km/hr range) produced very little change in the ratios.

One interpretation of the results shown in figure 5.3 is that performers use different generalized motor programs for walking and running, each with its own pattern of relative timing. When treadmill speed increased, performers continued to walk but needed to adjust the parameter of movement time (i.e., making movement time shorter) so they could walk faster. As we can see in the figure, the relative-timing pattern for walking remained roughly the same because the times for all four phases of the step cycle were decreased proportionally. It appears that at a treadmill speed of about 7 km/hr, however, participants shifted from a walking program to a running program characterized by a different pattern of relative timing. Another shift in the pattern would have occurred if participants had transitioned from running to sprinting (Hay, 1993). Evidence from earlier studies with cats suggests that other locomotion programs (and

Phonograph Record Analogy for Generalized Motor Programs

Our favorite analogy for generalized motor programs is that of the old standard phonograph record. In the "old days," large vinyl records used to be played on a device that contains a turntable and a needle, which sends signals from the record into an amplifier. The resulting output is then delivered to speakers. In this analogy, diagrammed in figure 5.4, the phonograph record is likened to the generalized motor program, and the speakers correspond to the muscles and limbs. The record has all of the features of the generalized motor program for a movement, such as information about the order of events (e.g., the trumpet comes before the drum, the right hand precedes the left), the fundamental timing structure of the events (i.e., the rhythm, or relative timing, of the sounds or of the movements), and the relative amplitudes of the output (e.g., the first drumbeat is twice as loud as the second; the hamstrings are contracted less forcefully early in the movement than they are later). This information is rigidly structured on the record and the generalized motor program in much the same way. And just as different records produce different types of music (rock, blues, classical, country, jazz, rap), so too do different generalized motor programs (throwing, jumping, shifting gears) produce different classes of movements. In both cases, though, each record or program contains a different pattern of stored information.

Notice again that the output of the record or the generalized motor program is not fixed: The speed of the music or the movement can be increased (by increasing the speed of the turntable or the rate of the commands sent to the muscles), yet the relative timing (rhythm) remains the same. Similarly, the amplitude of the output can be changed (by raising the volume or by increasing the force of muscle contraction). Even the effectors used can be changed (by switching the output from a set of speakers in the den to a second set located in the living room, or by producing a handball shot with either the left hand or the right).

It Depends . . .

Relative Timing for Movement Practitioners?

Physical therapists examine relative-timing patterns during gait analysis to assess improvements in patients' locomotion caused by developmental changes or therapeutic interventions (Ulrich, Ulrich, Coffer, & Cole, 1995). Can you think of other ways movement practitioners might use their knowledge of relative-timing patterns to assist performers and patients?

relative-timing patterns) may exist for trotting and galloping as well (Goslow, Reinking, & Stuart, 1973).

If you think of generalized motor programs in concrete terms such as phonograph records (see figure 5.4), it will help you to understand the generalized motor program concept rather easily. For example, when participants in the study by Shapiro and her colleagues transitioned from walking to running (see figure 5.3), their task became analogous to replacing a "walking record" on a phonograph with a "running record." Each time treadmill speed increased for one of the two movements (i.e., walking or running), performers had to adjust the movement time parameter in a manner similar to the way we could set the volume, speed, and speaker controls when playing the record. However, to change songs, say from "Happy Birthday" to "The Beer-Barrel Polka," a new relative-timing pattern (or record) would need to be activated, because there is no way that changing the scaling of one track could produce the sounds of the other track.

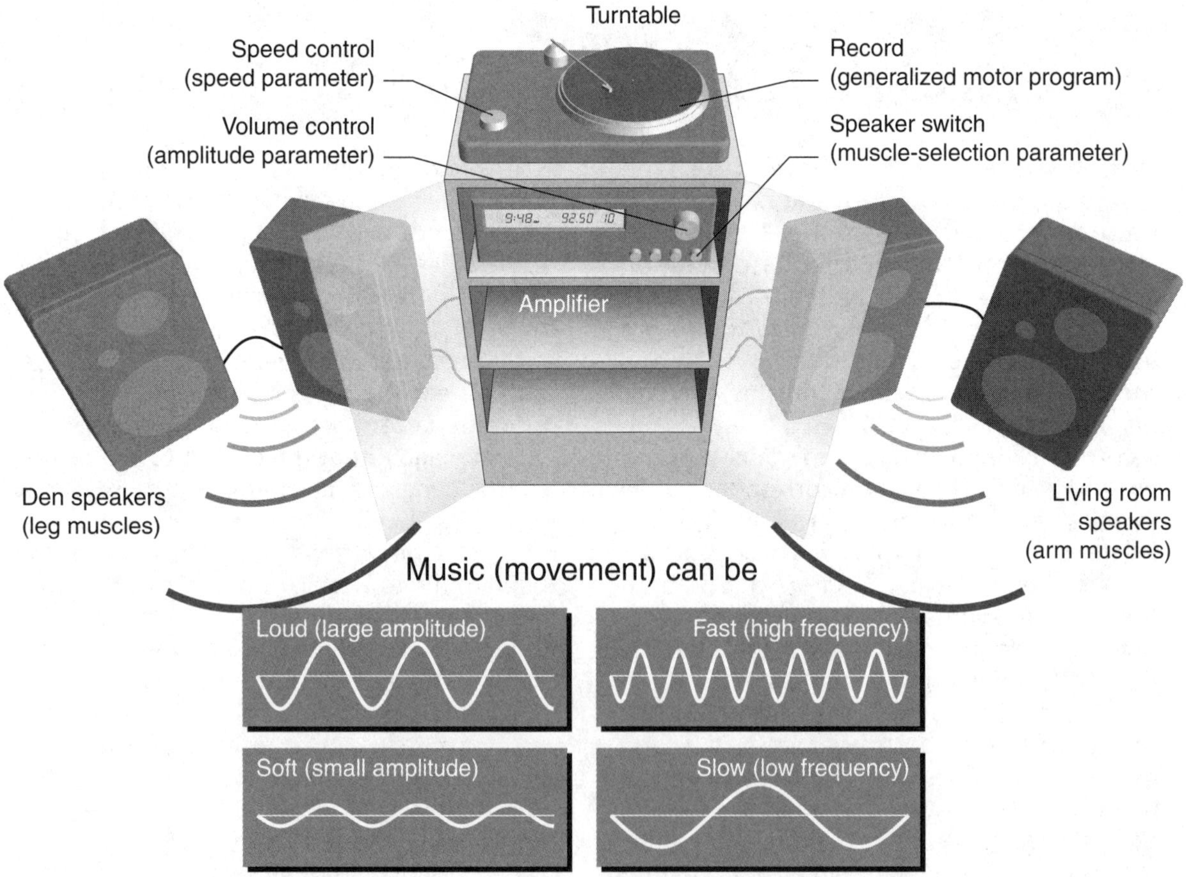

Figure 5.4 The phonograph record is like a generalized motor program. The record (program) has a fixed structure, which can be modified at output by the speed control (speed parameter), volume control (amplitude parameter), and speaker switch (muscle selection parameter).

DETERMINANTS OF ACCURACY IN RAPID MOVEMENTS

So far we have discussed ways that people can plan and control their movements by adjusting one or more parameters (e.g., more speed or greater amplitude) of the generalized motor program's output. Now we consider how adjusting these parameters affects the performer's achievement of an environmental goal.

In this section we present some of the laws or principles of simple movements. These principles include how the time required for a movement changes as the distance to be moved increases, and how the speed of a movement affects its accuracy. In many ways these principles are analogous to the simple laws of physics and mechanics that scientists use to describe the behavior of physical objects in the world. As such, these basic principles of simple movements form the foundation of much of our knowledge about voluntary actions.

Fitts' law—
The law of movement control for rapid aiming tasks, stating that movement time is linearly related to the index of movement difficulty (ID); ID is expressed mathematically as $\log_2(2A/W)$, where A = movement amplitude and W = target width.

speed–accuracy trade-off—
The tendency for individuals to substitute accuracy for speed, or vice versa, in their movements depending on task requirements.

Fitts' Law and the Speed-Accuracy Trade-Off

Perhaps the most fundamental principle of human movement is the one dealing with the relationship between the speed and accuracy of a movement. We all know that when we do things too quickly, we frequently tend to do them less effectively or accurately. The old English saying "Haste makes waste" suggests that people have been aware of this relationship for a long time. Woodworth (1899) studied the speed–accuracy phenomenon early in the history of motor skills research, showing that as performers increased the length and speed of line-drawing movements, their accuracy diminished. Then in 1954, psychologist Paul Fitts made a major contribution to our understanding of this relationship by describing for the first time a mathematical principle concerning movement speed and accuracy. This principle eventually came to be known as Fitts' law.

Fitts' law illustrates an important point about performance that requires fast and accurate movements—it forces people to make trade-offs between speed and accuracy. The task Fitts used to examine the speed–accuracy trade-off is illustrated in figure 5.5.

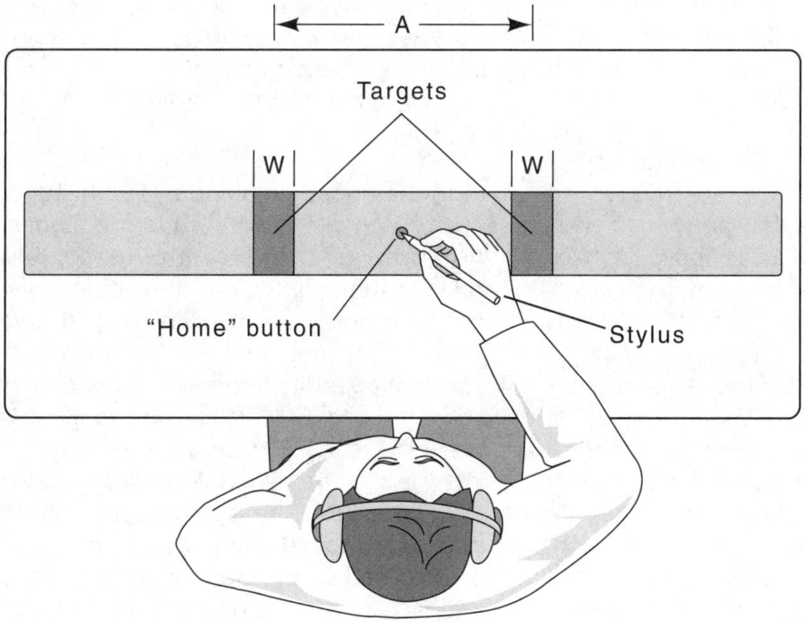

Figure 5.5 Fitts' tapping task. The participant taps as quickly as possible between two target plates of width W, which are separated by amplitude A. (Adapted from Fitts, 1954.)

Performance of this task involves tapping back and forth rapidly between two targets of width (W) separated by a given amplitude (A) for a fixed time (e.g., 30 s). When the accuracy requirements of Fitts' task are relaxed (i.e., by the use of wider targets, increasing W), performers' movement times are shorter than when accuracy requirements are more stringent (i.e., smaller W). Furthermore, as the amplitude (A) of the movement

Paul Fitts and Fitts' Law

In a landmark study, Fitts (1954) instructed participants to make movements between two target plates (see figure 5.5) using a handheld stylus. In this task, which has come to be called Fitts' tapping task, the width of the targets (W) and the distance or amplitude between them (A) can be varied to form various conditions of movement difficulty. In all cases, the performer's goal is to tap as quickly as possible back and forth between the targets while minimizing errors. A tap outside the target counts as an error (in Fitts' 1954 study, less than 5% of the participants' taps were errors). Fitts measured the number of taps that participants executed in a particular time—say, during a 20 s trial—and computed the average time taken per movement or, more simply, average movement time.

Fitts found, not surprisingly, that average movement time increased as the amplitude of the movement increased and as the width of the targets decreased. However, the major contribution of Fitts' study was the discovery that movement distance (amplitude, A), target width (required accuracy, W), and the resulting average movement time could be combined in a simple way that describes how these separate factors are related to each other. Specifically, Fitts found that average movement time (MT) was approximately constant whenever the ratio of the movement amplitude (A) to target width (W) was constant. That is, very long movements to wide targets required about the same average movement time as very short movements to narrow targets. In addition, Fitts found that MT increased as the ratio of 2A to W increased, by making either the amplitude longer or the target width smaller, or both. Fitts combined these various effects into a single equation that became known as Fitts' law: $MT = a + b [\log_2 (2A/W)]$.

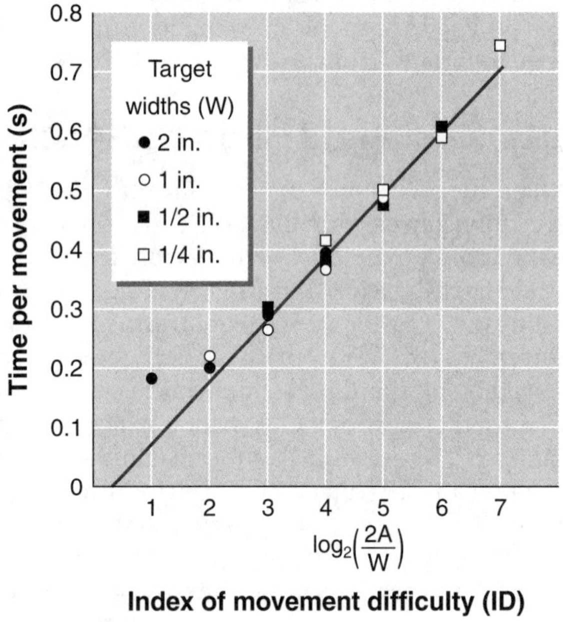

Figure 5.6 Fitts' law. The average time per movement is linearly related to the index of difficulty (ID). Target widths (W) are shown by the various symbols. For any given symbol, the movement distances (A) from left to right are 2, 4, 8, and 16 in., respectively.

In this equation, a and b are constants, and A and W refer to amplitude (i.e., movement distance) and target width, respectively. The relationships between movement distance (A), required accuracy (W), and average movement time (MT) for one of Fitts' data sets is plotted in figure 5.6. Fitts referred to the term $\log_2 (2A/W)$ as the index of movement difficulty (ID); so another way to state Fitts' law is that MT is linearly related to the ID. Put simply, the average time it takes a person to tap between two targets lengthens as the ratio of movement distance to target width increases (i.e., performers are required to move farther, hit smaller targets, or both).

is increased, movement time is also slowed, as you might imagine, because the hand must travel a longer distance.

The major contribution of Fitts' law, however, was that he combined the effects of different Ws and different As into the same expression. Fitts (1954) showed that the movement time was linearly related to the logarithm of the ratio of A and W, as described in the highlight box on page 142. Thus, either increasing the movement distance (increasing A) or decreasing the width of the targets (smaller W) increases movement time in a predictable way. Furthermore, an implication of Fitts' law is that the movement time will be the same for all reasonable combinations of A and W for which the ratio of A to W (i.e., A/W) is the same. That is, if I double the amplitude (A) and also double the target width (W), the ratio of A/W will not be changed and the movement time should be the same.

Fitts' task—An experimental task requiring performers to tap (using a stylus or other fine-pointed object) back and forth between two targets as rapidly and accurately as possible.

The general notion of a speed–accuracy trade-off—the tendency of people to substitute accuracy for speed, or vice versa, as well as the relationships among A, W, and movement time—has been verified in many settings and is a very general law of motor behavior. For example, it has been studied underwater as well as in the laboratory, for many classifications of people (children as well as older adults), and in movements using a number of effectors (fingers, hands, arms). Fitts' law even has relevance during the performance of more modern-day tasks, such as manipulating a mouse to move a cursor across a computer screen a distance of A to a target-button of width W (Jagacinski, Repperger, Moran, Ward, & Glass, 1980).

Even though the original statement of Fitts' law was based on reciprocal tapping movements, Fitts and Peterson (1964) later showed that it also holds for single movements of a distance A to a target of width W. Therefore, Fitts' law has application to a wide variety of movement situations. For example, it provides automakers with an estimate of how much increase in time would be expected for a driver to move the foot from the accelerator to the brake if a new design with wider pedal spacing was implemented. Of course, a benefit of such a law is that this increase can be estimated before the automaker actually builds the car.

In some skills, speed must be sacrificed for greater accuracy.

The continuous movements required in **Fitts' task**—either the continuous version or the discrete version—are almost certainly blends of programmed actions and feedback processing. In these situations, the performer programs an initial segment of each action that carries the limb in the direction of the target. At some point in that transport movement, however, the performer begins processing feedback (vision and perhaps proprioception) and makes the necessary corrections (if any are needed) to guide the limb to the target area. Thus, Fitts' law describes the effectiveness of combined

open-loop control—A type of control that involves the use of centrally determined, prestructured commands sent to the effector system and executed without feedback; used by individuals to control rapid, discrete movements.

closed-loop control—A type of control that involves the use of feedback and the activity of error detection and correction processes to maintain the desired state; used by people to control slow, deliberate movements.

motor program—A set of motor commands that is prestructured at the executive level and that defines the essential details of a skilled action; analogous to a central pattern generator.

open-loop and **closed-loop control** processes in producing fast and accurate actions. For such movements, all of the open-loop and closed-loop processes (see the conceptual model in figure 3.10) are potentially operating simultaneously. Also, note that the movement times in figure 5.6 range from about 200 ms to 1,000 ms, where feedback processes can be used, as discussed in chapter 4.

Participants who make errors too frequently in experiments using Fitts' task are instructed to slow down their movements so that they hit the target more frequently. It is reasonable to presume that slower aiming movements are more accurate, at least in part, because there is more time for the performer to detect errors and make corrections. In 1988, Meyer and colleagues introduced a more formal model of the processes involved when people trade off speed for accuracy. However, it is also possible that something about the accuracy of the initial (open-loop) part of the movement is also affected when the movement is speeded up. These two processes seem difficult to separate in Fitts' task. Recently, though, researchers have studied extremely quick actions—so quick that feedback-based corrections would seem unlikely—and have developed new insights about the determinants of the accuracy in the open-loop part of the action. We discuss these next.

Speed–Accuracy Trade-Offs in Very Rapid, Discrete Movements

Suppose that you have to make a very quick movement of your hand to a target, where *spatial accuracy* at the target is the major goal (i.e., it's essential that you hit the target). How does your accuracy change as your movement time or the distance you have to move changes? Scientists have examined this question by studying the performance of rapid, discrete aiming movements, where performers attempt to make a single movement with a handheld stylus from a starting position to a target. Research participants in these studies are instructed to produce the movement in a particular time, receiving feedback about the actual movement time after each attempt. The experimenter varies the instructed movement time and the movement distance systematically. One set of results from this paradigm is shown in figure 5.7, where accuracy is expressed as the amount of variability, or *inconsistency,* of the performer's movement end points at the target area. This measure of spatial variability might be likened to the spread of axe marks on a log a person is splitting.

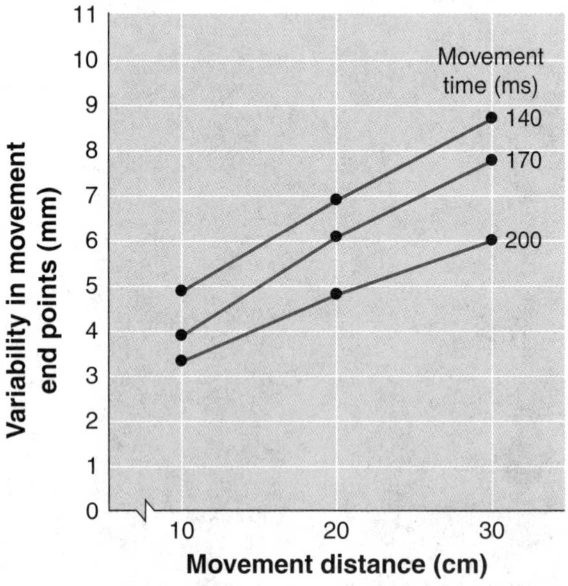

Figure 5.7 Variability (inconsistency) of movement end points in a rapid aiming task as a function of the movement time and distance. (Adapted from Schmidt et al., 1979.)

Notice that each of these movements is made very rapidly, each lasting 200 ms or less. After reading the previous sections, we would expect performers to control such movements by using open-loop processes or **motor programs.** Yet even with rapid movements such as these, where little or no feedback processing is possible, we see that increases in movement distance (from 10 to 20 to 30 cm) are accompanied by gradual increases in the spread or variability of the movement endpoints. Also, we see that a decrease in movement time (i.e., a speeding up of the movement) from 200 to 140 ms increases the spread as well. Aiming error (i.e., variability) is increased by both (a) increases in movement distance and (b) decreases in movement time.

These effects of movement distance and movement time on aiming accuracy suggest that open-loop processes, which performers use to produce the movement, are also subject to the speed–accuracy trade-off. In other words, when movement times are very short, decreases in accuracy are not simply attributable to the fact that there is less time for feedback to be processed and used; these effects occur even when movements are too brief for any feedback modulations to be made. Thus, it appears that decreases in movement time also affect the consistency of the processes that generate the initial parts of the action—that is, they affect the open-loop processes necessary to produce a quick movement.

We can combine into a single expression these separate effects of movement amplitude (A) and movement time (MT) on the accuracy of individual rapid-aiming movements, much the way that Fitts (1954) did for continuous alternate tapping task and the discrete-task case (Fitts & Peterson, 1964). In some of Dick Schmidt's research, he and his colleagues found that the amount of spatial movement error, or the variability of movement end points at the target (sometimes termed the **effective target width**, abbreviated W_e), is linearly related to the movement's average velocity—that is, to the ratio of movement amplitude to movement time, or A/MT (Schmidt et al., 1979). You can see this relationship in figure 5.8, where the variability of movement end points (W_e) is plotted against the average velocity of the movement (in centimeters per second, or cm/s)

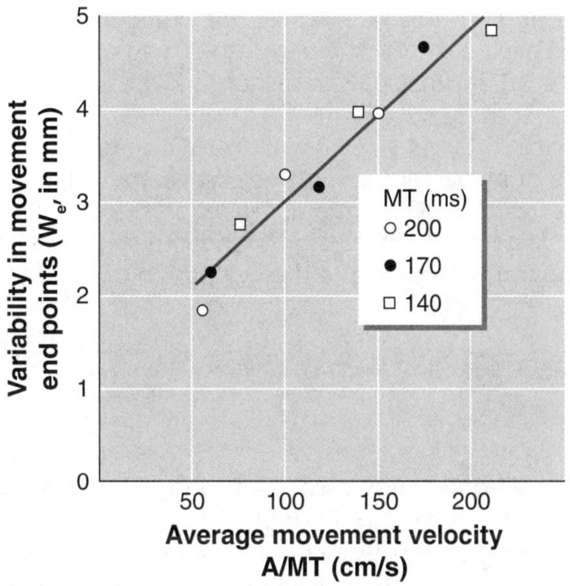

Figure 5.8 Variability of movement end points in an aiming task as a function of the average movement velocity (A/MT). (Adapted from Schmidt et al., 1979.)

effective target width— The amount of spread, or variability, of a person's movement end points about his or her own mean spatial position for repeated attempts of a rapid aiming task; abbreviated as W_e.

It Depends . . .

Which Affects Movement Speed the Most: Target Size or Movement Amplitude?

If you performed Fitts' task, which variable do you think would influence your average movement time the most: target size or movement amplitude? You can answer this question by photocopying the pairs of targets shown here and then tapping back and forth on each pair with a pencil or pen as quickly as possible for 20 s. Pairs a and b have the same amplitude (A, measured from the target center), but their target sizes (W) are different. Pairs a and c have the same target size but differ in movement amplitude. For each pair of targets, begin by resting the point of the pen or pencil in the center of one of the targets. Ask someone to time

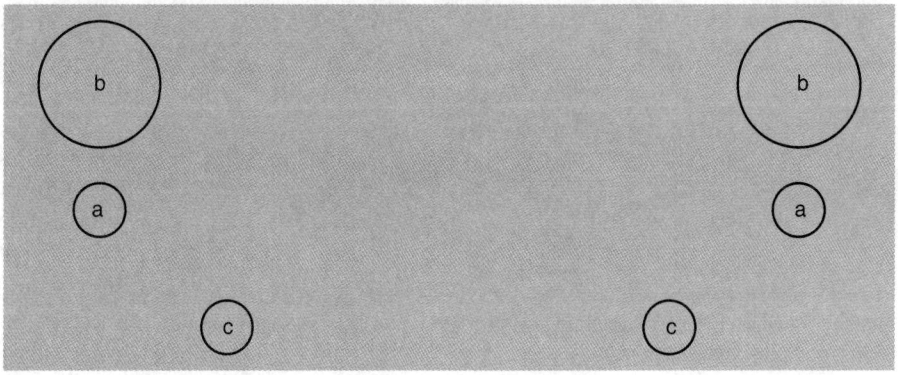

From R.A. Schmidt and C.A. Wrisberg, 2008, *Motor Learning and Performance,* 4th ed. (Champaign, IL: Human Kinetics).

(continued)

you for 20 s. After completing the three pairs, count the number of taps you made *inside the circles* for each condition. Now divide each of those numbers into 20 s to obtain your average MT. For example, if you count 37 taps, your average MT for that pair of targets is 20/37 = 0.54 s/tap. If you count 60 taps, your average MT is 20/60 = 0.33 s/tap.

To determine the influence of target size on average MT, compare your average MT for pairs a and b. To determine the influence of movement amplitude on average MT, compare your average MT for pairs a and c. Which factor, target size or movement amplitude, produced the biggest difference in average MT? Other applications of Fitts' law include the design of industrial workspaces, the organization of controls on the instrument panels of aircraft and cars, and the evaluation of head-controlled computer input devices (Radwin, Vanderheiden, & Lin, 1990).

linear speed–accuracy trade-off—The tendency for the spatial variability of movement end points (W_e) to increase as performers increase the velocity of rapid aiming movements.

for all of the movement times and movement distances shown in figure 5.7. As figure 5.8 shows, the spread of movement end points (i.e., spatial aiming error) increases as movement velocity increases. This principle is called the **linear speed–accuracy trade-off**, and it suggests that, for various combinations of movement amplitude (or distance) and movement time, the resulting average velocity (i.e., A/MT) is associated with a particular spread of movement end points (i.e., spatial aiming error). Thus, by decreasing the distance and increasing the time of aiming movements (i.e., moving a shorter distance or doing it slower), performers can trade off speed to maintain spatial accuracy.

Aiming variability and spatial accuracy are important facets of many sports (such as cricket) and other movement tasks.

Sources of Errors in Quick Movements

Why is it that even for quick aiming movements (when there is little time for performers to process feedback and make corrections), spatial errors are larger (i.e., accuracy around the target is reduced) when movement distance increases or movement time decreases? We might look for the answer by examining processes in the central nervous system that translate the motor program's output into body movements. We have already explained that motor programs are responsible for determining the ordering of muscle contractions and the amounts of force that are generated in the respective muscles. The location of this activity is indicated by the area shaded in maroon in the conceptual model found in figure 5.9.

What is it about the activity in this area that diminishes the accuracy of a person's rapid movements? Scientists have known for some time that even when attempting to produce the same force over and over, a performer exhibits considerable inconsistency in movement outcomes. Today scientists believe that the relatively "noisy" (i.e., inconsistent) processes

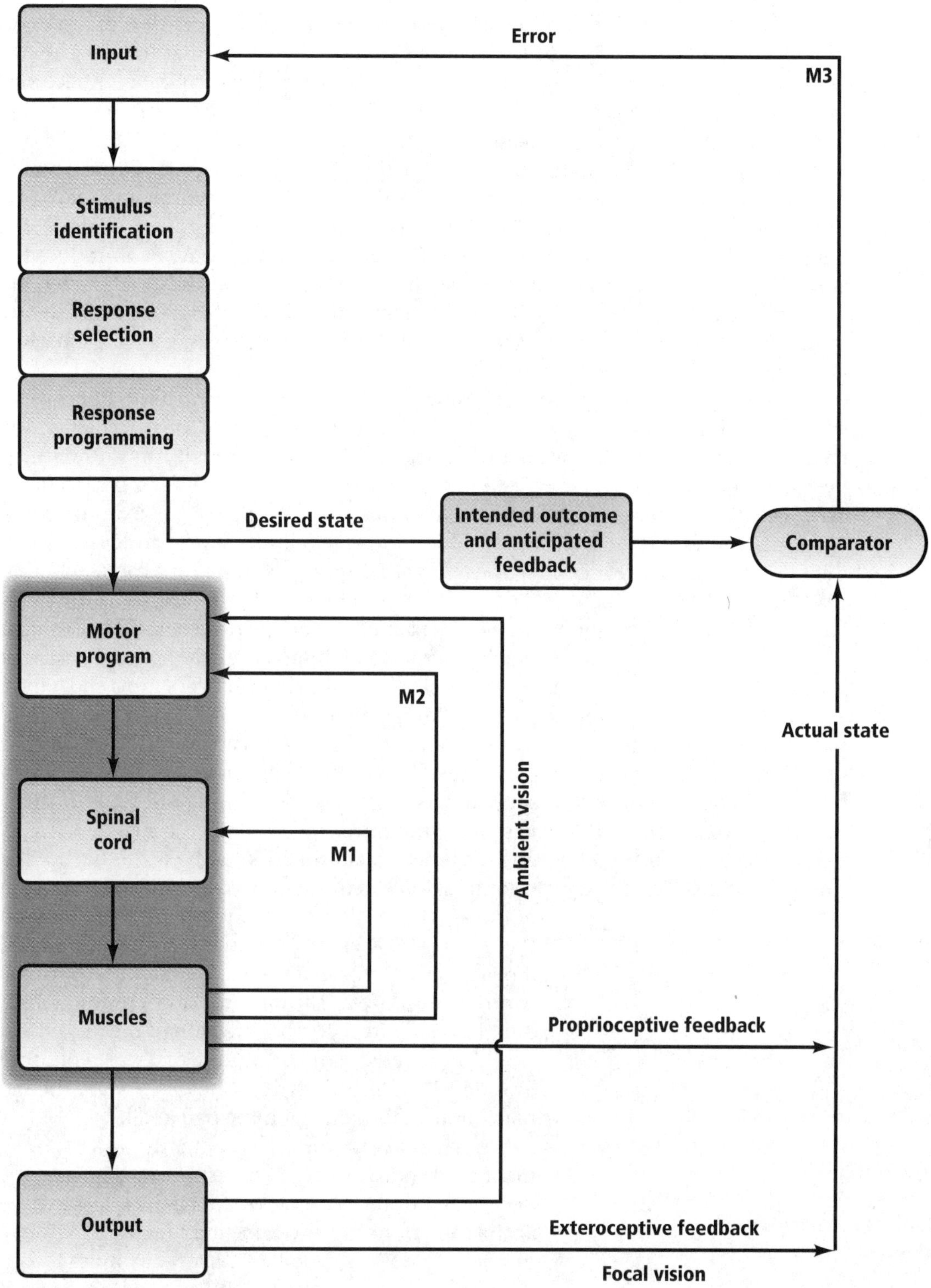

Figure 5.9 Conceptual model with the location of motor-program activity responsible for ordering muscle contractions highlighted.

M1 response—The monosynaptic stretch reflex, with a latency of 30 to 50 ms.

M2 response—The polysynaptic, functional stretch reflex, with a latency of 50 to 80 ms; sometimes called the *long-loop reflex.*

in the central nervous system cause this variability. These processes are responsible for converting nerve impulses into muscle contractions and for the exertion of forces on bones through tendons. In addition, various reflex activities, such as the **M1 and M2 responses** (see figure 5.9), may contribute their own variability to muscle contractions. Recently, Churchland, Afshar, and Shenoy (2006) have shown that there is variability in the movement-planning processes as well.

Of course, the presence of these processes in the system means that the forces actually produced during a contraction are not always the ones that the system intended. This phenomenon can be illustrated by returning to the phonograph record analogy (see figure 5.4 again). You can see that "noise" (i.e., inconsistency) could be introduced at several points in the system. For example, the electronics and wires lying between the turntable and the speakers might cause the sounds that the listener hears to be slightly different from the sounds that were originally recorded; and the speakers themselves (the muscles in this analogy) can add distortion.

To complicate matters, these noisy processes in the nervous system do not operate consistently but instead seem to change as the required amount of force or their timing changes. In other words, as the force of a muscle contraction increases, the noise created by these processes increases, which in turn increases force variability in contractions. This seems to be the case for forces up to about 70% of a person's maximum force. Beyond 70%, the noise level and resulting force variability appear to level off and then decrease slightly for contractions that are nearly maximal (Sherwood, Schmidt, & Walter, 1988).

How does this information help us understand the way error is generated in a routine movement? Consider an action such as striking a ball positioned on a tee situated at waist height. Using a bat, you try to make a horizontal swing with your arms and hands. To achieve this goal, many muscles would operate in the shoulders and the trunk to produce forces against the bones in the arms that direct the bat toward the ball. The direction of action of some of these muscles is in line with the intended movement, but the direction of action of many others is not, as shown in figure 5.10. In many actions, gravity is an additional contributing force. To complete the swinging action perfectly, the various muscles must contract in coordination with each other so that they each achieve just the right amount of force. If this happens, the final combination of forces (the resultant force, depicted by the maroon line in figure 5.10) should be in line with the intended movement. Of course, if there is an error in any of the contributing forces, say, an excessive contraction of muscle 1 in figure 5.10, the direction of the movement would be altered; some amount of error would be introduced; and, if the error is large enough, the bat may not make contact with the ball at all.

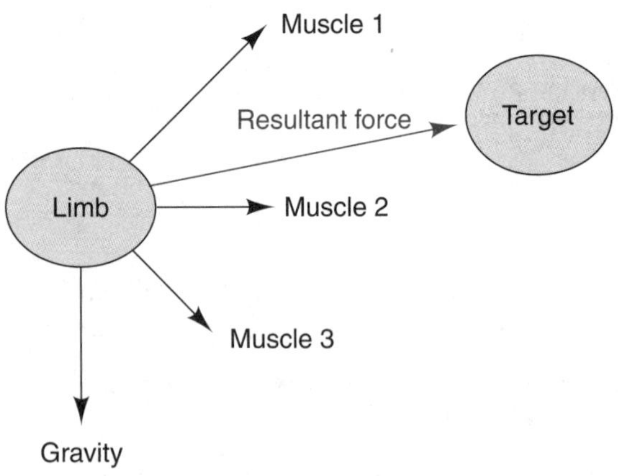

Figure 5.10 A limb being moved by three muscles and gravity toward a target. The eventual trajectory is a product of the many forces acting at a joint.

What would happen if you made a fast movement even more rapid? Of course, as movement time decreases (i.e., the action speeds up), the forces exerted against the bones of the arm must increase. As these forces increase (up to about 70% of maximum force), their noisiness increases as well. This adds some error to the muscle contraction, with each muscle responding slightly differently than specified in the motor program, with this error becoming larger as the movement speeds up. At some point, if the difference becomes too great, the bat will miss the ball.

Violations of the Speed–Accuracy Trade-Off

As common as the speed–accuracy trade-off phenomenon seems to be for many types of motor performances, there are situations when it does not appear to hold, or at least when the principles work somewhat differently. One of these situations involves the production of timing movements that are extremely rapid and forceful.

Timing Errors

We have already discussed situations in which the **spatial accuracy** of the movement is an important goal (sinking a putt in golf). However, many skills have **timing accuracy** as the goal (pressing a button in a computer game at the proper time). When timing accuracy is a goal, performers are required to produce movements in as close to a goal *time* as possible or to make some part of the movement occur close in time to some other event (e.g., a baseball batter attempting to hit a pitched ball as it passes the plate).

Still other skills have both timing goals and spatial goals, intermixed in complicated ways. For example, a batter must produce a swing that moves the bat through a spatial plane corresponding to the one occupied by the approaching ball. In addition, the batter must time the swing so that it arrives in the contact zone at the same

spatial accuracy—The type of accuracy required of aiming movements for which spatial position of the movement's end point is important to task performance.

timing accuracy—The type of accuracy required of rapid movements for which accuracy of the movement in time is important to task performance.

It Depends . . .

Achieving Spatial Accuracy in Single Rapid Aiming Movements

Research (e.g., Schmidt et al., 1979) suggests that we can produce single rapid aiming movements to a target more accurately if we move a shorter distance or move more slowly. See if you experience this phenomenon. From a starting point on a piece of paper, move your pen or pencil at near maximum speed to land on the target line, a target drawn perpendicular to the overall movement direction. Try to stop as closely as possible to target lines. Do this three times, with a separate piece of paper each time, with target lines drawn so that the movements from the starting point differ in distance (e.g., as in lines a, b, and c here). Perform at least five repetitions of each movement to determine the spatial variability (the spread) of movement end points for each movement distance. What is the effect of distance on variability?

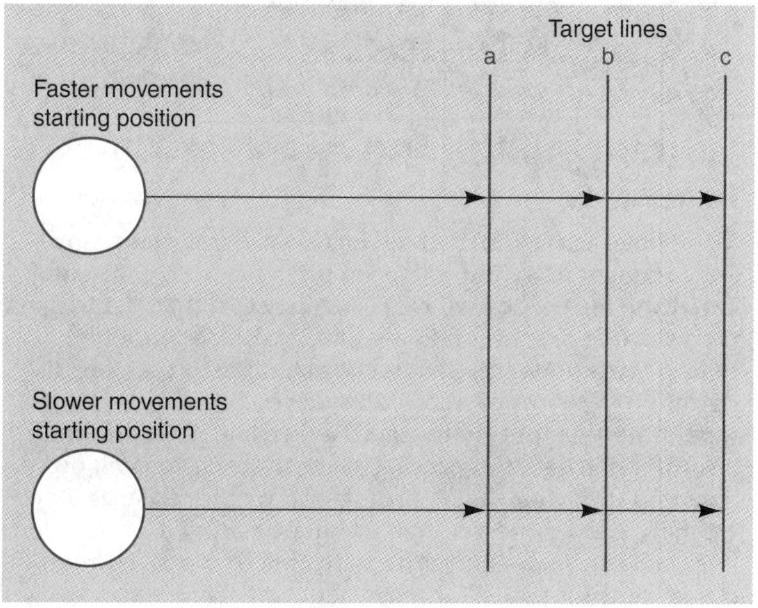

Now attempt the same rapid aiming movements at the different distances, but this time perform them at about three fourths of the speed you used before. Was the spatial variability of your movement end points influenced by decreases in movement distance? Was it influenced by increases in movement time (i.e., a slower movement)? If so in either case, how?

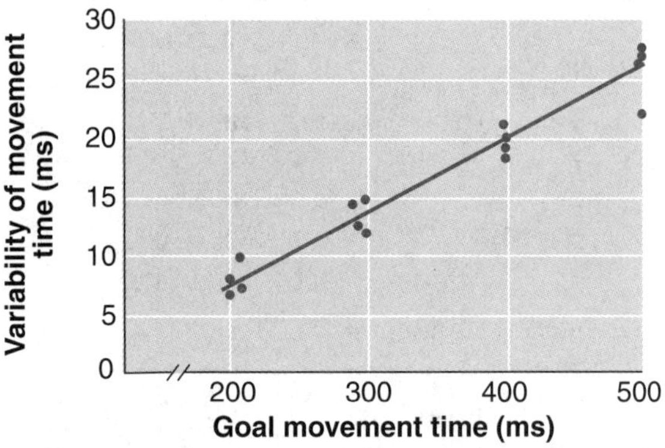

Figure 5.11 Variability of movement time as a function of the goal movement time. As goal movement time becomes longer (i.e., slower movement), the variability of movement time increases (i.e., movement time becomes less consistent). (Adapted from Schmidt et al., 1979.)

time as the ball. As long as the batter has some idea as to how long it takes to swing the bat (i.e., he can estimate his own movement time) and is able to produce that movement time consistently, he should be able to estimate when to begin the swing to ensure that the bat arrives in the contact zone at the same time as the ball.

In this section we address the timing component of rapid actions, focusing on the factors that affect timing accuracy. The timing component of rapid tasks can be isolated somewhat in the laboratory by requiring performers to produce a particular goal movement time as accurately as possible. Scientists have studied this type of timing accuracy by using tasks that require people to make movements of the finger, hand, or arm under different conditions of movement distance, movement time, and several other factors. The results of these studies indicate that skills requiring timing accuracy follow somewhat different principles than those requiring spatial accuracy (Schmidt et al., 1979).

Imagine you are a participant in one of those studies and are asked to produce a rapid movement of a given distance in different times (e.g., 300 ms vs. 150 ms). Would you expect that faster movements would have more timing error? You might, because you now know that faster aiming movements produce more spatial inconsistency, as illustrated in figures 5.7 and 5.8. But this is not what happens. In fact, decreasing the movement time (i.e., speeding up the movement) *decreases* timing error, making the movement *more* consistent in time rather than less. We see this effect in figure 5.11, where the timing of the movement is more consistent (i.e., lower variability of movement time) the shorter (i.e., faster) the goal movement time. This relationship is almost proportional; halving the goal movement time (within limits) reduces timing variability by almost half.

Researchers have also found that when movement distance increases but goal movement time stays the same, resulting in a faster movement, timing error hardly increases at all unless the distance is extremely short (Newell, Carlton, & Antoniou, 1980). Therefore, for skills in which the performer's goal is to produce a consistent movement time, timing is more accurate for shorter movement times than for longer ones, and movement distance has little influence. This effect is exactly the opposite of the one we find for rapid aiming skills in which spatial accuracy is the main goal, as can be seen if you compare figures 5.7 and 5.8 with figure 5.11 (see Schmidt et al., 1979).

It Depends . . .

Estimating the Durations of Time Intervals

If you have a stopwatch or a digital watch that has a stopwatch function, try the following timing task. Without looking at the face of the watch, click it twice so that it starts and then stops at exactly 2 s. Repeat this task nine more times, noting the amount of error you make on each trial (i.e., the deviation in tenths of a second from your goal of 2 s). Now repeat the task, but try to stop the watch at 4 s rather than 2 s. After a little bit of practice on both tasks, you will probably find that your timing error is about twice as large when estimating a 4 s interval than when estimating a 2 s interval. In a similar fashion, performers are able to produce faster movements (with shorter movement times) more accurately and consistently in time than slower movements (with longer movement times).

Producing a Very Forceful Movement

Consider a task in which the performer holds a pointer and makes a rapid, horizontal arm movement toward a stationary target, such as the task of batting in the child's game of tee

Targeting Movements: Fast or Accurate?

For some skills, performers must achieve both timing accuracy and spatial accuracy for effective performance. Research by Southard (1989) showed that in one such case, an emphasis on movement speed produced more desirable outcomes than an emphasis on accuracy. In this study, participants attempted to swing their arm to strike a small foam ball resting on a batting tee so that it traveled 5 m in the direction of a target 30 cm in diameter. One group was told to hit the ball as hard as possible, whereas a second group was told to hit the ball as accurately as possible (i.e., so that it landed more often in the target area). A third group was instructed to hit the ball as hard and as accurately as possible. The instruction to swing hard resulted in the development of a more effective swing pattern than did the instruction to strive for accuracy. In addition, although the instruction to hit the ball accurately produced slower swings than the instructions to swing hard, the slower swings were not more accurate. Thus, Southard concluded that sacrificing speed for accuracy is an unwise strategy for tasks like this because it impedes the development of a more effective movement pattern and it produces outcomes that are no more accurate than those achieved by moving faster. These results suggest that for discrete skills requiring both speed and spatial accuracy (e.g., a karate kick, a volleyball spike), performers may benefit more from an emphasis on speed than from an emphasis on accuracy.

ball, where the ball to be batted rests on a tee near waist level. In a study by Schmidt and Sherwood (1982), seated participants produced rapid, horizontal arm movements, attempting to strike a small (16 mm) stationary target suspended in front of them. Each attempt began with the arm extended to the right (elbow locked) at approximately shoulder height (see figure 5.12). When ready, the performer moved his arm forward about 90° and attempted to contact the target (with a follow-through allowed).

To determine the effects of increased force on spatial accuracy, Schmidt and Sherwood (1982) instructed participants to perform their movements with several different movement times. This would be like requiring baseball or cricket batters to swing the bat harder and harder, with minimum movement time being determined (in part) by each batter's own force capabilities. Speed–accuracy trade-off principles might lead us to believe that the movements with shorter goal movement times would be less spatially accurate. However, as you can see in figure 5.13, when the instructed (or goal) movement time became shorter (and a higher percentage of the participant's force capabilities was needed, labeled *% maximum torque),* spatial errors were generally greater, but only up to a point. However, if we look from right to left on the graph, it is clear that progressively shorter movement times produced a kind of inverted-V effect, with the shortest time (i.e., 80 ms) actually producing *less* spatial error than the next shorter time (i.e., 102 ms). This finding is contrary to the strict view of the speed–accuracy trade-off, in which faster movements are always less spatially accurate.

How can the fastest movement be more spatially accurate than a slightly slower one? Returning to figure 5.10, we are reminded that several muscles operate to determine the limb's trajectory in situations like this. We also know that when very large forces (i.e., greater than about 70% of maximum force) are increased further, force variability *decreases*. Therefore, the nearly maximal force used to produce the 80 ms movement in

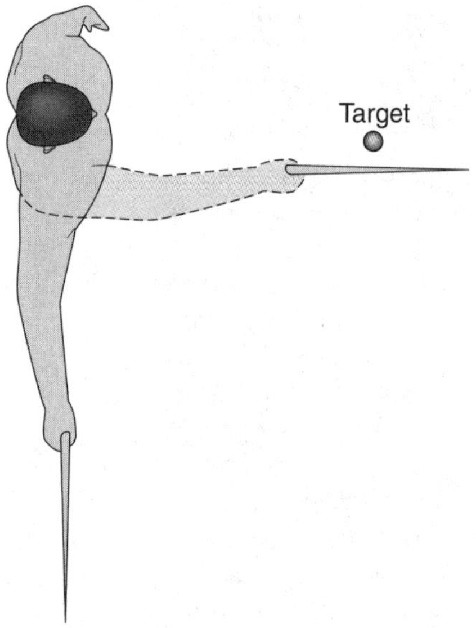

Figure 5.12 Imagine a performer holding a pointer and making a rapid, horizontal arm movement toward a stationary target.

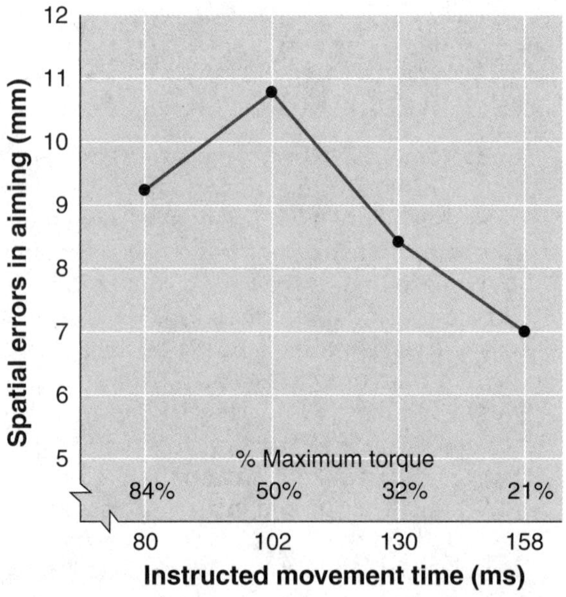

Figure 5.13 Spatial errors in aiming as a function of the instructed movement time. The estimated percentage of maximum torque (force) is indicated under the x-axis. (Adapted from Schmidt and Sherwood, 1982.)

figure 5.13 is probably within a range for which force production is more consistent than it is for forces needed to produce somewhat longer movement times. The lower variability of this very forceful action makes the trajectory quite consistent spatially. However, this effect is based on the results of a small number of studies using simple and linear arm movements. Therefore, we must use caution when attempting to generalize the effect to more complicated actions.

COMBINING THE PRINCIPLES: A BATTING EXAMPLE

coincidence anticipation—A type of task that requires performers to produce movements that coincide in time, space, or both with an external object or event (e.g., catching or hitting a moving ball); sometimes referred to as anticipation timing.

It may seem as though a dizzying number of sometimes contradictory principles are involved in rapid actions. To help clarify things, let's see how the various principles we have discussed in this chapter apply simultaneously in the performance of a common task requiring both speed and accuracy—hitting a pitched baseball. This skill is an example of a **coincidence-anticipation** task, and it requires several of the processes we have discussed. In addition to predicting the ball's spatial trajectory and arrival time, batters must be able to produce a quick movement that is both forceful and accurate.

Some facts about hitting a baseball are graphically summarized in figure 5.14. Pitchers in professional baseball can throw the ball at speeds exceeding 90 miles (144.8 km) per hour. In the example shown in figure 5.14, the pitch is moving at a speed of 89 miles (143.2 km) per hour. Because the distance between the pitcher and the batter is 60 ft 6 in. (about 18 m), we can estimate that the ball would travel from the pitcher's hand to the coincidence point (i.e., home plate) in about 460 ms (bold maroon line). A typical movement time of the swing for professional baseball batters is about 160 ms (Hubbard & Seng, 1954). We know from evidence presented in chapter 3 that the

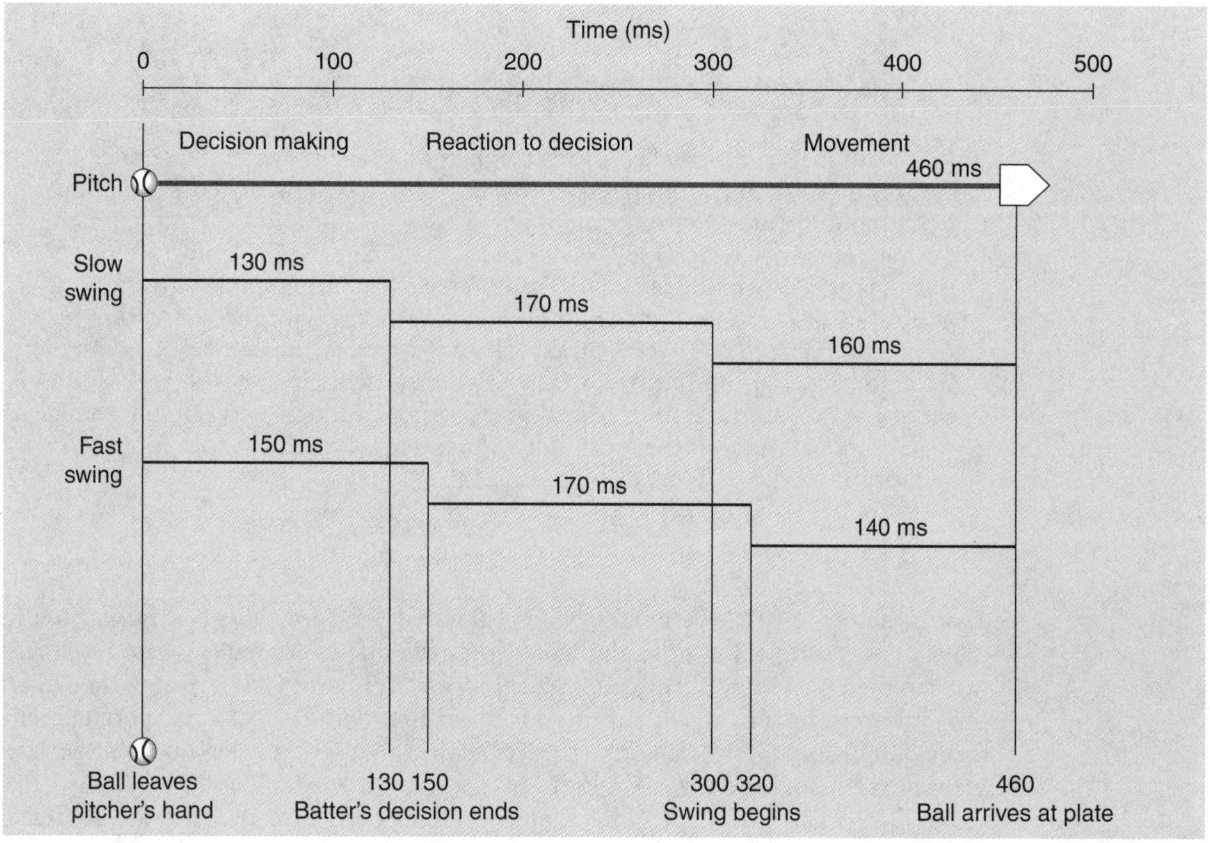

Figure 5.14 Time line showing the critical events in hitting a pitched baseball. The movement time is 160 ms for the slow swing, 140 ms for the fast swing.

Experienced Batters Use Vision to Control Movement Timing

An interesting study conducted in the early 1950s showed how skilled batters use vision in controlling their swing. In this research, Hubbard and Seng (1954) filmed the movements of batters from three Major League baseball teams. A mirror, positioned to the side of the batter, provided a simultaneous view of the pitcher, the flight of the ball, and the face and body movements of the batter. In general, batters tended to synchronize the beginning of the stride with the release of the pitch, finished the stride and began the swing progressively later for slower speed pitches than for faster speed pitches, and maintained the same swing speed or duration regardless of the speed of the pitch. There was no evidence that batters watched the ball up to the moment of contact (see also Bahill & LaRitz, 1984). Thus, it appears that these highly skilled performers used vision of the ball to control the timing of two aspects of their batting movements: the duration of the stride and the initiation of the swing.

internal signal to trigger a movement occurs about 170 ms before the action starts (Slater-Hammel, 1960; review the research highlight on page 76 and figure 3.7).

These facts suggest that batters must send the signal to trigger the bat swing at least 330 ms before the ball arrives at the plate, allowing them 170 ms for the swing to be triggered and another 160 ms to carry it out. Therefore, batters must make all decisions

Make Those Swings Fast and Forceful

Many American baseball players think that to improve their chances of contacting the ball, batters need to slow down their swings. Coaches sometimes even shout, "Just swing easy and try to meet the ball." However, research by Schmidt and Sherwood (1982) revealed that when performers produce timing movements with nearly maximal (84% of maximum) forces, they are almost as accurate spatially as when they produce movements with forces that are not even half as large (32% of maximum). These findings suggest that batters may be able to swing the bat much faster without sacrificing spatial accuracy or timing in hitting the ball. This notion is further supported by popular media reports indicating that the most feared hitters in baseball produce more *rapid* swings than other players (see figure 5.13).

about whether to swing before the ball has traveled barely one third of the way to the plate, or after only 130 ms of ball flight. Although batters may make minor modifications in their movements using the visual processes discussed in chapter 3, they must plan most of their actions in advance for the central nervous system to initiate them some 330 ms before the ball arrives (see research highlight, Experienced Batters Use Vision to Control Movement Timing).

We know that movement time is an important determinant of timing accuracy. So let's look at what would happen if a hypothetical batter shortened the time of his swing from 160 ms to 140 ms. To do this, he could shorten the length of the swing slightly, use a lighter bat, or change his batting style in various ways. By shortening his swing time, the batter would also alter the following performance components: the processing of visual information, the timing of the start of the swing, timing of the swing itself, spatial accuracy, and the force applied to the ball.

It Depends . . .

Can Performers Move Heavier Implements More Accurately Than Lighter Ones?

Research (Schmidt & Sherwood, 1982) suggests that performers attempting to strike an object as hard as possible with an implement (e.g., serving a tennis ball, splitting wood, driving steel spikes into railroad ties) might do so more accurately using a heavier implement (i.e., tennis racket, axe, sledgehammer) than a lighter one. Considering what you've read in this chapter, how would you explain this phenomenon? Can you think of a situation where this might not be the case? If so, what might be the reason?

Processing Visual Information

Figure 5.14 shows that when the batter shortens his movement time from 160 ms to 140 ms, he is able to wait longer before beginning his swing (i.e., for up to 320 ms compared with 300 ms). This extra 20 ms of visual information (from 130 ms to 150 ms, or about 3 ft [91 cm] of ball flight) gives the batter additional time to view the ball's speed and trajectory and to determine the time and place of contact (i.e., decision making). Therefore, his anticipation of when and where the ball is going to arrive should be more accurate. In summary, then, the batter can improve his visual information processing and anticipate

A batter selects movement time and prepares the swing to coincide with the ball's arrival.

flight characteristics of the ball more effectively by shortening the movement time of his swing (speeding up the swing).

Timing the Swing

By shortening his movement time, the batter would also be able to delay his decision about when to start the movement. In an experiment using a simulated batting task, Schmidt (1969) found that when participants shortened their movement time, their initiation time (i.e., the timing of the start of the movement) became more consistent. Therefore, by shortening his swing time, the batter in our hypothetical example would become more *consistent* in the time he starts his swing. This in turn would allow him to produce swings that arrive at the coincidence point more consistently, which should yield greater timing accuracy. And, because of our previous discussions (see also Schmidt, 1969), we know that the batter would be able to produce the swing itself more consistently in time by shortening his movement time (see figure 5.11).

Achieving Spatial Accuracy

It is reasonable to assume that a swing time of 140 ms would require a force of 70% or more of the batter's maximum force, and we know that force variability is lower for forces exceeding that percentage (see figure 5.13). Therefore, it appears that our hypothetical batter would improve the spatial consistency of his swings, promoting less variable bat trajectories, by shortening his movement time in a way that requires a near-maximal force.

Hitting the Ball Hard

By swinging faster, the batter—assuming he makes ball contact—would also able to impart more force to the ball, a critical factor in the game of baseball. He could increase

What Does Swinging a Weighted Bat Really Do for Batters?

For years it has been the practice of baseball batters to swing a weighted bat before taking their turn to hit. The thinking was that this type of warm-up activity would lighten the feel of the regular (i.e., unweighted) bat and improve the speed of the swing. Research examining the validity of this notion suggests that, although swinging a weighted bat may alter batters' perceptions of bat heaviness and swing speed, it does not influence actual swing speed (Otsuji, Abe, & Kinoshita, 2002). In this study, eight baseball and softball players attempted three sets of 15 bat swings during which they hit a ball suspended on a cord. Batters performed the first five swings and the last five swings in each set with a regular (nonweighted) bat and the middle five swings with a weighted bat. They were asked to estimate swing speed and bat weight (compared with the speed and weight they perceived during the first five unweighted swings) following the fifth weighted swing and after the first, third, and fifth unweighted swings. Actual swing speeds did not increase following swings with the weighted bat, but batters perceived their swings to be faster and their bats to feel lighter. For five of the eight participants, this illusion lasted for at least four unweighted swings. In another study (Southard & Groomer, 2003), the normal swing pattern of experienced batters was found to be altered and their swing speed slowed down for up to five swings following a warm-up with a weighted bat. The results of these studies suggest that batters would be better off taking warm-up swings with their normal (unweighted) bat than with one that is considerably heavier.

The swings of baseball's best hitters are produced at near maximal speeds.

the force of his swing by either swinging the same bat faster or swinging a heavier bat without slowing down his movement time. Either way, he should be able to hit the ball harder without diminishing spatial accuracy (Schmidt & Sherwood, 1982).

Nearly every factor associated with decreases in movement time appears to improve the batter's chances of hitting the ball solidly. Therefore, we should not be surprised when we see high-performance professional baseball players swinging the bat at near maximal speeds. Of course, such a strategy may not be as beneficial for inexperienced players or for children, particularly if it results in clumsy, uncoordinated, unstable movements.

SUMMARY

Invariance is an important concept in motor control. Invariant features of a movement pattern are those that remain essentially the same while other features are changing. One prominent source of invariance is relative timing or the fundamental timing structure of an action, estimated as a set of ratios among time intervals in the action. Patterns of relative timing

- are the basis for generalized motor programs that performers use to produce members of a class of movements (e.g., throwing);
- are different for different classes of movements (e.g., throwing vs. kicking);
- are the fundamental timing structure defining a class of movements; and
- remain invariant, even though movements within a class may be produced with different surface features.

Relatively rapid movements follow the speed–accuracy trade-off, where increasing the movement amplitude (A) and decreasing the target width (W) both slow the movement time. Furthermore, movement time increases linearly as the so-called index of difficulty [$ID = \log_2(2A/W)$] increases, which is known as Fitts' law. And, movement time is roughly constant whenever the ratio of A to W remains constant.

Rapid movements controlled by generalized programs also display a speed–accuracy trade-off. Research investigating the speed–accuracy trade-off in rapid skills suggests that

- unless movements are extremely rapid, increases in movement distance or decreases in movement time usually diminish spatial consistency;
- spatial errors are linearly related to the movement's average velocity, A/MT;
- these spatial errors are caused by relatively "noisy" low-level processes in the spinal cord, muscles, and planning operations, which produce contractions that are slightly different from those that were originally intended; and
- decreases in movement time usually increase the consistency of movement time or timing accuracy.

FROM PRINCIPLES TO PRACTICE

Check your comprehension of the concepts and terms discussed in this chapter by responding to each of the exercises in the following sections. The first section contains several exercises designed to test your working knowledge of key terms. The second section poses a variety of problems designed to check your understanding of key concepts. In the third section you are challenged to apply your knowledge by discussing a defensible solution for two scenarios.

Know Your Key Terms

Matching: Invariance and Flexibility

Match the following terms with their respective categories or definitions by placing the most appropriate letter on each of the blanks.

Invariance and Flexibility—Terms

a. generalized motor program
b. relative timing
c. parameter
d. phonograph record analogy
e. fundamental timing structure
f. invariant feature

Invariance and Flexibility—Category or Definition

_____ 1. Practical illustration of how output can be both invariant and flexible at the same time

_____ 2. Remains the same when performers adjust a particular movement

_____ 3. The sequencing and rhythm of a movement pattern

_____ 4. Changeable component of a movement; also referred to as a surface feature

_____ 5. The durations of various movement segments divided by the total movement time

_____ 6. Defines a flexible pattern of movement rather than a specific action

Consider: Speed and Accuracy

For each of the following skills, indicate how the proposed shift in task requirements might influence the speed or accuracy or both (i.e., increase, decrease, or no change) of the movement. Provide rationale for your answers.

Shift in Task Requirements—Requirement for Speed and Accuracy

1. From walking on a paved sidewalk to walking on a balance beam: ______________________________
2. From paddling a canoe through shallow rapids to paddling on a calm lake: ____________________ ______________________________
3. From throwing a ball a maximum distance to throwing a ball 25 m to a 100 cm diameter target: ______________________________
4. From breaking a thick board with a karate kick to breaking a thin board: ____________________ ______________________________

Fill in the Blank: Fitts' Law

Complete the following sentences:

Fitts' law illustrates an important point about performers when they are required to make movements that are both ________________ and ________________. To examine the ________________________ trade-off, Fitts devised a task that required participants to hold a __________________ and ________________ back and forth between two targets as ________________ and ________________ as possible. The two variables Fitts manipulated to make the task more or less difficult were________________ ________________ and ________________ __________________. Fitts found that for many combinations of these two variables, increases in movement difficulty were linearly related to increases in the _____________ ______________ _______________.

Check Your Understanding

1. Explain the concept of relative timing. How might practitioners use this concept to determine differences between classes of movements? How might the relative timing of dart throwing differ from that of putting the shot? (Hint: Think of the difference in terms of the relative speeds of the wrist, lower arm, and upper arm in the two movements.)
2. What do movement scientists mean when they say that relative timing is an invariant feature of the generalized motor program? What implications does this statement have for performers who practice their movements at different speeds (e.g., dancers, jugglers, rhythmic gymnasts, drummers)?
3. Under what conditions are performers' movements more spatially accurate when they're produced more rapidly? What implications might this have for an elementary physical education instructor who is teaching children how to throw or kick a ball toward a target?
4. Explain how an error in a lower level of the conceptual model of motor performance (e.g., the muscles) might cause a player throwing darts to miss the target area she is aiming for.

Apply Your Knowledge

Exercise 1

While sitting in a local park, you notice several children skipping and galloping. Explain the differences in the relative-timing patterns of those two movements in a way that someone unfamiliar with the concept of relative timing would understand. Provide rationale for your answer and furnish two supporting references.

Exercise 2

A baseball coach is having difficulty with one of his pitchers. The pitcher is able to achieve a fairly high velocity with his pitches, but his control is poor—in other words, he is unable to locate his pitches in the strike zone consistently. Assume that you have access to a radar gun and a video camcorder that allow you to determine the speed of the pitched ball, the speed (or movement time) of the pitcher's arm, the spatial location of the pitcher's release point (i.e., the location of the hand at the moment the ball is released), and the spatial location of the ball when it crosses home plate. Explain how you might determine the sources of the pitcher's control problems and then discuss possible remedies for each. Provide rationale for your solution and furnish two supporting references.

chapter 6

Individual Differences and Motor Abilities

Chapter Outline

Chapter Objectives

When you have completed this chapter, you should be able to

- understand the concept of individual differences,
- discuss the fundamental nature of motor abilities,
- discuss several things practitioners should remember about peoples' abilities,
- explain how a practitioner might use the concept of motor abilities to classify skills and perform task analyses, and
- discuss the difficulties inherent in predicting a person's future performance success based on assessments of that person's abilities.

PREVIEW

Have you ever noticed that some people seem to be good at something even when they've had no previous experience? Have you ever had a friend who decides to take up a sport you play because it's something the two of you could enjoy together, and then the first time you play each other she nearly beats you? Her proficiency seems to be the same as yours, and you have been practicing the sport seriously for several years. Over time you notice that your friend continues to improve whereas you seem stuck at your present skill level. Her skill in playing the sport is clearly different from yours, and you suspect that she will eventually be much better than you. Why? Could there be some important underlying differences between the two of you? Does her superior performance in this sport mean she is going to be better than you in other activities as well?

People come in all sizes and shapes and have a variety of abilities.

OVERVIEW

It's no secret that people differ in many ways. In some cases the differences are attributable to things over which people have little control, such as body size, sex, age, race, and cultural background. Sometimes these differences influence a person's motor performance and learning. In this chapter we examine some of the characteristics of people that can influence their performance and learning of motor skills. First, we discuss the concept of individual differences, focusing more specifically on the notion of abilities, which are largely inherited traits that underlie or support people's performances. Next we describe several theoretical notions about abilities and discuss the relative merits of each. Then we suggest several things to keep in mind when considering people's abilities, and we discuss some ways teachers, trainers, and therapists might use the notion of abilities to classify skills and perform task analyses. Last we discuss some of the difficulties people face when they try to predict a person's future level of skill in an activity based solely on estimates of the person's abilities.

CONCEPT OF INDIVIDUAL DIFFERENCES

Have you ever thought about all the factors that make people different from one another? If not, you might want to spend an afternoon at a shopping mall or other public gathering place and just watch people. You'll immediately notice that they come in all sizes, shapes, ages, genders, racial groups, and cultural backgrounds. Some may have handicapping conditions of a physical or mental nature. If you could talk with them you'd find that they have a variety of temperaments, social influences, and types of life experiences. In addition to having all of these kinds of differences, people have factors that can influence the quality of their motor performance. Table 6.1 lists a variety of factors on which people differ that have the potential to influence their performance.

When the first author of this book was a boy, he knew a guy by the name of Charlie Breck who used to infuriate him. It seemed as if Charlie could do every sport skill better than other kids. He could throw a baseball harder and hit it farther, dribble and shoot a basketball better, and run faster than everyone else his age. Charlie clearly had something the other kids didn't have, and he used it to become an outstanding athlete in several team sports during high school. However, there was one sport in which Dick Schmidt could outperform Charlie: gymnastics.

While Charlie struggled, Dick mastered the kip maneuver on the horizontal bar. Dick could also tumble Charlie into the mat. And there were other kids far better than either Charlie or Dick in activities such as archery, cross-country running, and swimming. It seemed as though each person had an inherited talent for performing some skills better than others. Scientists call these talents *abilities,* a major topic of this chapter.

Table 6.1 Individual-Difference Factors That Can Contribute to Differences in People's Motor Performance

Factor	Examples
Abilities	Finger dexterity, stamina, trunk strength
Attitudes	Open, closed, or neutral to new experiences
Body type	Stocky, tall, short, lean, muscular, round
Cultural background	Ethnicity, race, religion, socioeconomic status
Emotional makeup	Bored, excitable, fearful, joyful, risk-taker
Fitness level	Low, moderate, high
Learning style	Visual, verbal, kinesthetic
Maturational level	Immature, intermediate, mature
Motivational level	Low, moderate, high
Previous social experiences	One-on-one, small group, large group
Previous movement experiences	Recreational, instructional, competitive

Why do people excel in some activities and not in others? Are people born with special talents that make it easy for them to master certain skills and that make mastery difficult for other skills? Or can everyone achieve the same level of performance on any skill if they just practice it long enough? Can a person's innate abilities be observed and measured? If practitioners knew something about people's fundamental abilities, would they be able to provide more effective instruction?

Scientists who try to answer questions like these spend most of their time studying the phenomenon of **individual differences** in people's behavior. This **differential approach** to research focuses on factors that make people different from each other. This approach contrasts sharply with the **experimental approach**, which is the one that has been used in most studies cited so far in the text. With the experimental approach, researchers are interested in identifying the principles that influence *all* people in the *same* way (e.g., the more muscles are fatigued, the less weight that can be lifted). With the differential approach, however, the focus is on the factors or characteristics that make people different from each other—or, from the standpoint of this book, factors that make each person's performance unique. In addition to being affected by the amount of practice or experience, these differences in performance are also assumed to be attributable to differences in people's innate, stable, enduring abilities that are largely unmodified by practice and experience. These abilities are the main focus of the differential approach.

Most of the research on individual differences has focused on two issues. First, researchers have attempted to identify some of the underlying **abilities** that might contribute to differences in the performance of various people. Second, researchers have tried to determine whether accurate predictions can be made about a person's future performance on a particular skill, or in an occupation or sport, based on estimates of the person's abilities. We deal with both of these issues here.

individual differences—Stable, enduring differences among individuals' performances, often attributable to differences in their abilities.

experimental approach—A method scientists use to examine factors that influence the performance or behavior of people generally.

differential approach—A method scientists use to examine differences among people.

abilities—Stable, enduring traits that, for the most part, are genetically determined and that underlie a person's skill in a variety of tasks. People differ with respect to their patterns of strong and weak abilities, resulting in differences in their levels of skill.

ABILITIES AND INDIVIDUAL DIFFERENCES

The main reason motor performance researchers have been interested in studying people's abilities is to determine the impact of those abilities on the performance of various kinds of activities or skills. For the most part, scientists assume that abilities are genetically determined and fixed, which means they don't change much no matter how much practice or experience the person has. You might think of abilities as the hardware that individuals bring with them to a performance or learning situation.

Research suggests that many kinds of abilities exist throughout the human perceptual–motor system, such as visual acuity, body configuration (height and build), reaction time, manual dexterity, and kinesthetic sensitivity. Some abilities are important for accurate perception and decision making, others are helpful for organizing and planning movements, and still others contribute to producing movements and evaluating feedback.

Correlation: The Language of Individual Differences

To interpret the results of studies examining the relationship between abilities and motor performance, you need to understand the statistical method researchers use to measure this relationship: the correlation. This is a term people sometimes use in everyday conversations to describe the relationship between two things (e.g., "I don't see any correlation between your talk and your actions."), but scientists use the concept in a more precise way.

Researchers calculate correlations when they are interested in determining the strength of a relationship between the performances of a group of people on two tasks. To illustrate this concept, let's assume that you obtain scores for a large number of individuals (say 100 or more) on two different tasks (task X and task Y). Task X might be a task that measures their visual acuity, and task Y might be a task that measures their performance in catching a ball. If you plotted everyone's scores on the two tasks, you would create a display that looks something like the ones shown in figures 6.1 and 6.2. Each person's scores would be represented as a single dot on the graph. If the dots tended to lie close to a line drawn through the middle of them (referred to as the line of best fit), you would conclude that the participants' performance on task X was closely *related to* their performance on task Y. In figure 6.1, this relationship is positive. In other words, participants with higher scores on task X tended to be the same ones with higher scores on task Y. The plot in figure 6.2 shows a negative relationship: People with higher scores on task X were the ones with lower scores on task Y.

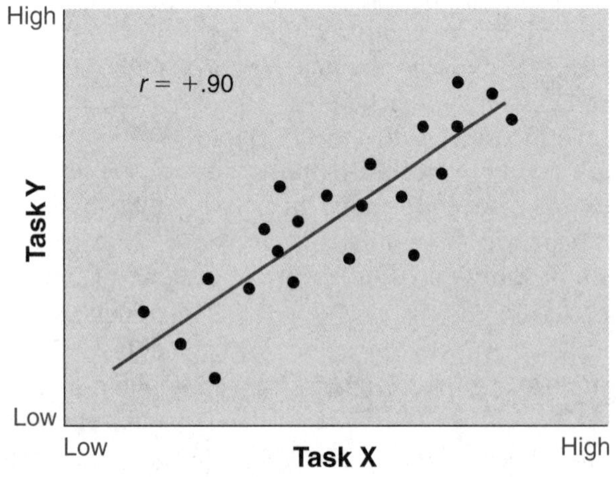

Figure 6.1 Showing a strong, positive relationship.

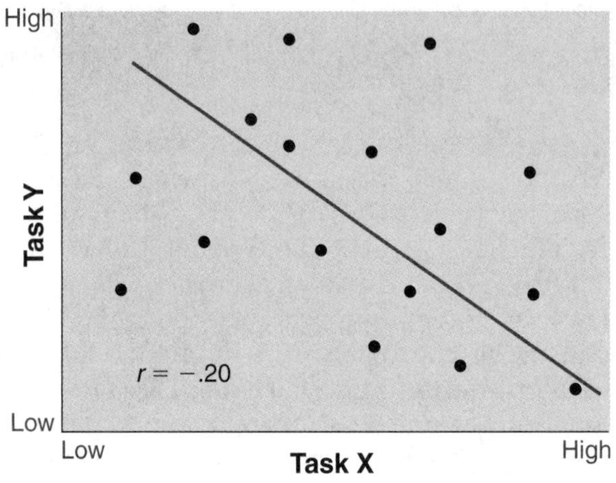

Figure 6.2 Showing a weak, negative relationship.

When researchers analyze such relationships, they obtain a statistic called the Pearson product-moment correlation coefficient (abbreviated *r*). The possible values of *r* are from −1.0 to +1.0. If in your hypothetical study you obtained an *r* with a positive sign, that would that mean higher scores on task X (i.e., visual acuity) were related to higher scores on task Y (i.e., ball-catching). If *r* had a negative sign, that would mean that higher scores on task X were related to lower scores on task Y. Remember, to interpret *r* you always need to look at both the size of *r* and the algebraic sign. If *r* is close to 1 and the sign is positive, the scores, if plotted on a graph, would look something like the ones in figure 6.1 (in this case, $r = +.90$). In figure 6.2 you see that the dots are relatively far away from the line and the slope is negative (in this case, $r = -.20$). A correlation close to zero would produce a graph with dots scattered in a shotgun pattern, in which case you would conclude there is no relationship between performance on tasks X and Y.

Another way to estimate how much there is in common between performances on two tasks is to square *r* and multiply the result by 100 to create a percentage. This value would tell you what percentage of the factors important to performance on task X are also important to performance on task Y. For example, if you calculated r^2 for the correlation of +.90 shown in figure 6.1, you would estimate that 81% ($.9 \times .9 = .81 \times 100$, or 81%) of the factors important to performance on task X (i.e., visual acuity) are also important to performance on task Y (i.e., ball catching). Scientists who study relationships assume that the percentage reflected by r^2 represents the relative contribution of an underlying ability, or a collection of abilities, to performance of the two tasks in question. For example, we might expect a larger r^2 between people's visual acuity and their ball-catching performance than between people's reaction time and their golf-putting performance.

So far, scientists have identified around 20 to 30 cognitive and motor abilities, and they anticipate discovering more in the future. They assume that all people possess some level of all of these abilities but that individuals differ with respect to the amount of each ability (or, as is sometimes said, the strength of each ability). For example, one person might have a very low level of kinesthetic sensitivity but a very high level of visual acuity, whereas another might have a low level of eye–hand coordination but a high level of static balance.

Researchers investigating individual differences assume that a particular combination of abilities is relevant to the performance of any given motor task. For example, the task of threading a needle probably requires a high level of near-visual acuity and arm–hand steadiness but not much lower-body strength. Powerlifting, on the other hand, requires a great deal of lower-body strength and dynamic balance but little near-visual acuity or arm–hand steadiness.

An important practical implication of the relationship between abilities and skill is that a person who possesses high levels of the abilities important to the performance of a particular task should, other things being equal, perform the task at a higher level of skill than another person who possesses lower levels of those abilities. This is probably one reason that Charlie Breck was better at hitting a baseball than Dick Schmidt, whereas Dick was better at tumbling than Charlie. A second practical implication of the ability–skill distinction is that a person possessing high levels of several abilities would be expected to excel at tasks requiring those abilities. For example, the abilities important for serving a tennis ball and serving a volleyball might be similar because those two tasks seem to have very similar requirements; they both involve tossing a ball with one hand and hitting it with the other so that the ball goes over the net and into the target area. If so, one would expect that people who demonstrate more skill in one of these activities would also demonstrate more skill in the other. Surprisingly, this relationship turns out not to be as simple as it appears, as we will see later on in the chapter.

Quarterback Peyton Manning's pattern recognition and passing skills probably result from a combination of inherited abilities and countless hours of practice.

Ability Versus Skill

We often hear people talk about ability and skill as if they were the same thing. Movement scientists, however, differentiate the concepts of ability and skill: They consider ability (or abilities) to be, for the most part, genetically determined and largely unchanged as a result of practice or experience, whereas they think of **skill** as something that people chiefly develop as a result of practice. Thus, the scientist would probably say that an expert performer has developed considerable skill for the various tasks and subtasks needed for superior performance. For example, a good motorcycle rider would have considerable knowledge of driving rules as well as high levels of skill in gear shifting, braking, and maneuvering.

As we mentioned earlier, abilities can be considered the basic genetic equipment with which people are born. A rough analogy would be the cards a person is dealt in a game of poker. The better the cards, the better the player's chances of winning. However, holding great cards doesn't necessarily guarantee success, unless the player who is holding them knows how to play them. That takes skill. Skill, then, reflects a person's proficiency in performing a particular task, such as playing a poker hand or playing the viola in an orchestra. Just about any expert performer we can think of not only appears to have high levels of the necessary abilities but also has spent countless hours practicing and perfecting her performance. In summary, then, the level of skill any person is ultimately able to achieve in a particular activity depends on the level of the person's abilities that are relevant to that activity *and* on the quantity and quality of the person's practice experiences.

skill—
The underlying potential for performance in a given task, which changes with practice, experience, and a host of situational and environmental factors.

The abilities that a musician needs are, in large measure, specific to the instrument played.

Abilities as Limiting Factors for Performance

An important idea is that a person's abilities influence the level of skill he is able to achieve on any particular task. Craig Wrisberg never had the potential to become a skilled gymnast, regardless of how much time he practiced gymnastics activities, because he was somewhat too big and lacked sufficient upper-body strength to match his size. People who are color-blind will never be very proficient at identifying wildflowers, people with low levels of finger dexterity will not feel comfortable playing the guitar, and someone with poor balancing abilities will probably not be a very effective tightrope walker. Unfortunately, even with extensive practice and quality coaching, some people will never achieve high levels of performance in a particular task because they lack "strength" in the fundamental abilities required for that task.

How Should Practitioners Conceptualize the Notion of Abilities?

Historically, several theoretical views of abilities have been proposed. In the next few sections we briefly discuss each of these.

Singular Global Ability

One of the earliest views was that a singular, global ability was the basis for all skill performance (McCloy, 1934). Perhaps not surprisingly, this concept of a general motor ability was popularized approximately the same time that theorists in the field of cognitive or intellectual functioning were proposing the existence of a general mental ability, known as intelligence and measured by the intelligence quotient, or IQ. Likewise, the notion of general motor educability was thought to be the unitary ability that allowed people to learn new skills (Brace, 1927).

At first glance, the concept of general motor ability appears to be reasonable. It is certainly consistent with our observation that some people—think of Charlie Breck, mentioned earlier—seem to be successful at performing most sport tasks, whereas others are unsuccessful at performing any of these activities. Doesn't it make sense to conclude that the all-around athlete must have a very high level of general motor ability, whereas people who can't do anything very well have little or no such ability? If the idea of a singular general motor ability is valid, then we should always expect a high correlation (r) between people's performance on any two motor tasks. Those people with high levels of general motor ability would be expected to perform well on any two tasks whereas those with low general motor ability would be expected to score poorly on those tasks. From this way of thinking, we should expect performance on any two tasks (A and B) to correlate strongly, because performance on both tasks is based on the level of each performer's general motor ability.

However, considerable research suggests that this is not the case. An excellent example is a study by Drowatzky and Zuccato (1967). These researchers examined participants' performance on six balance tasks; they found that the correlations among these tasks were quite low. As shown in table 6.2, the highest r between all of the possible pairs of tasks was only .31, suggesting a low relationship (9%) between participants' performances on the various tasks. These results, and many others like them, are particularly damaging to the notion of a general motor ability. Even more interesting is the observation that the tasks Drowatzky and Zuccato examined in their study all involved the act of balancing (albeit in different ways and contexts); the low correlations they found suggested that there isn't even a general ability for balance. Rather, it appears that different balance tasks require different abilities for controlling posture in different ways. In summary, then, the findings of this study as well as others like it (e.g., Fleishman & Parker, 1962; Lotter, 1960) offer no support for the notion that people possess a solitary, general motor ability.

It Depends . . .

Can You Tell Which Tasks Require Similar Abilities?

Look at the following pairs of tasks and rank pair each according to the number of underlying abilities you think they have in common. You should give a rank of 1 to those pairs sharing the greatest number of abilities, a rank of 2 to those sharing a moderate number, and a rank of 3 to those sharing very few abilities. Now look at figures 6.3 and 6.4 and see if you can identify one or two of the abilities shared by each pair of tasks.

Rank

____ Performing the overhead smash in badminton and tennis

____ Performing the breaststroke and the backstroke in swimming

____ Throwing a fastball and a curveball in baseball pitching

____ Playing the violin and playing the saxophone

____ Splitting wood with an axe and hammering boards onto a fence

____ Driving a car and flying a small airplane

____ Performing the back handspring and the iron cross in gymnastics

____ Performing the serve and the volley in tennis

____ Putting and driving a golf ball

____ Performing the spike and the jump serve in volleyball

Table 6.2 Correlations Among Six Tests of Static and Dynamic Balance

	Stork stand	Diver's stand	Stick stand	Sideward stand	Bass stand	Balance stand
Stork stand	—	.14	–.12	.26	.20	.03
Diver's stand		—	–.12	–.03	–.07	–.14
Stick stand			—	–.04	.22	–.19
Sideward stand				—	.31	.19
Bass stand					—	.18
Balance stand						—

Adapted from Drowatzky & Zuccato, 1967.

Perceptual-Motor Abilities

Multilimb coordination—Ability to coordinate the movement of a number of limbs simultaneously. A high level of this ability is probably important when serving a tennis ball or playing the piano.

Control precision—Ability to make highly controlled movement adjustments, particularly when large muscle groups are involved. An example is operating a bulldozer or other type of earth-moving equipment that requires careful positioning of the arms and feet.

Response orientation—Ability to make quick choices among numerous alternative movements, more or less as in choice reaction time. An example is the task of a goalie in hockey, where the type of shot on goal is often uncertain.

Reaction time—Ability to react quickly, important in tasks where there is a single stimulus and a single response and where speed of reaction is critical, as in simple reaction time. An example is the sprint start in a 100 m dash.

Rate control—Ability to produce continuous anticipatory movement adjustments in response to changes in the speed of a continuously moving target or object. Examples include the tasks of high-speed auto racing and white-water canoeing.

Manual dexterity—Ability to manipulate relatively large objects with the hands and arms. An example is package handling at the post office.

Finger dexterity—Ability to manipulate small objects. Examples include threading a needle and eating spaghetti with a fork and spoon.

Arm–hand steadiness—Ability to make precise arm and hand positioning movements where strength and speed is not required. A waiter who carries trays of food and dispenses the contents without incident has a high level of this ability.

Wrist–finger speed—Ability to rapidly move the wrist and fingers with little or no accuracy demands. An example is playing the bongo drums or keyboard entry tasks.

Aiming—A highly restricted type of ability that requires the production of accurate hand movements to targets under speeded conditions. An example is the task of hitting a target with a rapid throw of a dart.

Physical Proficiency Abilities

Explosive strength—Ability to expend a maximum of energy in one explosive act. Advantageous in activities requiring a person to project his or her body or some object as high or far as possible. Also important for mobilizing force against the ground. Examples of tasks requiring high levels of explosive strength include the shot put, javelin, long jump, high jump, and 100 m dash in track and field.

Static strength—Ability to exert force against a relatively heavy weight or some fairly immovable object. Tasks requiring high levels of static strength include near maximum leg and arm presses in weightlifting, as well as moving a piano.

Dynamic strength—Ability to repeatedly or continuously move or support the weight of the body. Examples include climbing a rope and performing on the still rings in gymnastics.

Trunk strength—Dynamic strength that is particular to the trunk and abdominal muscles. Tasks requiring high levels of trunk strength include leg lifts and performing on the pommel horse in gymnastics.

Extent flexibility—Ability to extend or stretch the body as far as possible in various directions. An example of a task requiring high levels of extent flexibility is yoga.

Dynamic flexibility—Ability to make repeated, rapid movements requiring muscle flexibility. Ballet dancers and gymnasts need high levels of dynamic flexibility.

Gross body equilibrium—Ability to maintain total body balance in the absence of vision. Circus performers who attempt to walk across a tightrope while blindfolded require high levels of this ability.

Balance with visual cues—Ability to maintain total body balance when visual cues are available. This ability is important for gymnasts who perform on the balance beam.

Speed of limb movement—Ability to move the arms or legs quickly, but without a reaction-time stimulus, to minimize movement time. Examples include throwing a fast pitch in baseball or cricket or rapidly moving the legs when tap dancing or clogging.

Gross body coordination—Ability to perform a number of complex movements simultaneously. Individuals needing high levels of this ability include ice hockey players who must skate and stick-handle at the same time or circus performers who try to juggle duckpins while riding a unicycle across a tightrope.

Stamina—Ability to exert the entire body for a prolonged period of time; a kind of cardiovascular endurance. Individuals requiring high levels of stamina include distance runners and cyclists.

Figure 6.3 Links between various motor abilities and selected movement skills. (Adapted from Fleishman, 1964.)

Movement rate—Similar to Fleishman's speed of limb movement, this ability applies more to situations in which a series of movements must be made at a maximum speed. Examples include typing or keyboarding.

Motor timing—Ability to perform tasks in which accurately timed movements are essential. Examples include most open sport skills as well as driving an automobile in traffic, stepping on a moving escalator, and playing drums in a band.

Perceptual timing—Ability to perform tasks in which accurate judgments about the time course of perceptual events are required. Examples include making judgments about the timing of a musical score by a ballet dancer or a vocalist, timing a partner's movements in pairs dancing or of a horse's movements in equestrian competition, or estimating the speed of a moving object such as a ball in tennis, cricket, or soccer.

Force control—Ability to perform tasks in which forces of varying degrees are needed to achieve the desired outcome. Examples include changing mood or emphasis when playing musical instruments such as the piano or violin and performing sport tasks such as billiards, figure skating, and floor exercise in gymnastics.

Figure 6.4 General coordination factors identified by Keele and his colleagues (1982, 1987).

How are the abilities required for the serve and the volley in tennis similar and different?

How are the abilities required for hammering boards onto a fence and chopping wood similar and different?

Many Specific Abilities

The most vocal opponent of the general-motor ability notion was the late Franklin Henry (see the research highlight on page 5 in chapter 1). In his **specificity hypothesis**, Henry proposed that all types of motor performance are based on a very large number—perhaps thousands—of specific abilities that are independent of each other (Henry, 1961, 1968). Henry also contended that a person's performance on any given task, such as fly-fishing, is based on a unique combination of abilities, with some being more important than others. Finally, the abilities needed for fly casting would be different from the abilities needed for nearly any other task unless that task was essentially identical to fly casting.

specificity hypothesis—A view proposed by Franklin Henry that a large number of distinct, specific, and independent motor abilities are the basis for each specific motor performance.

According to Henry's view, a champion tennis player would be someone who has inherited high levels of the unique combination of abilities that is important for playing tennis. However, that player might not possess the unique combination of abilities important for handling an all-terrain vehicle. According to Henry, the correlation between people's performance on any two tasks should be close to zero because each task would require a unique combination of abilities. Clearly, the correlations obtained in the studies mentioned in the previous section (see table 6.2) seem much more supportive of Henry's specificity view (e.g., Drowatzky & Zuccato, 1967; Fleishman & Parker, 1962) than they do of the notion of general motor ability.

Groupings of Abilities

Although the correlations obtained in most studies examining the relationship between abilities and performance have been relatively low, they have also not been zero (see again table 6.2). Such findings suggest that there must be at least *some* abilities that are important to the performance of almost all tasks. What might those abilities be?

Different Perceptual Abilities in Similar-Appearing Motor Tasks

Research by Beals, Mayyasi, Templeton, & Johnston (1971) suggests that selected perceptual abilities in motor performance may be quite task-specific. First, these researchers obtained the field goal and free throw shooting percentages of college basketball players, using game statistics for a single season. Then they tested each of the players to estimate levels of the following visual abilities: static visual acuity (the perception of fixed visual objects), dynamic visual acuity (the perception of moving visual objects), size constancy (the perception of objects of different sizes), and depth perception. Subsequent correlational analysis revealed that dynamic visual acuity was the only test that contributed significantly to field goal shooting performance ($r = .76$) and that static visual acuity was the only one that was significantly associated with free throw shooting accuracy ($r = .59$). Interestingly, some studies in ecological psychology (Gibson, 1966, 1979) emphasize that optical flow patterns are different depending on whether a performer or the environment (or both) is dynamic and moving (as in most field goal shots) or static and stationary (as in the free throw shot). These results also suggest that even within a single sensory modality (i.e., vision), different perceptual abilities may be required for the performance of similar-appearing motor tasks (i.e., field goal and free throw shooting).

One possible answer to this question surfaced during the 1950s and 1960s in a series of studies by Edwin Fleishman and his colleagues. These researchers examined the performance of a large number of young military personnel on a wide range of motor tasks (Fleishman, 1964, 1965; Fleishman & Bartlett, 1969). They then used a more complex correlation technique (called factor analysis) to identify some possible groupings of abilities that might be important to the performance of different tasks.

Fleishman's concept of abilities, like Henry's, is that abilities are independent of each other. However, he differed from Henry with respect to the total number of presumed abilities, the number of abilities involved in the performance of any given task, and the extent to which the same abilities are important to the performance of different tasks. In Fleishman's view, the total number of abilities and the number of abilities important in the performance of tasks are considerably smaller than those suggested by Henry. In addition, Fleishman contended that two tasks may require some of the same underlying abilities, particularly when the requirements of the tasks are similar. Thus, the abilities proposed by Fleishman are considerably more general in nature than those proposed by Henry but are nowhere near as general as in the notion of general motor ability.

Fleishman (1964) separated abilities into two fundamental categories, which he labeled perceptual–motor abilities and physical–proficiency abilities. We present samples of those abilities, along with examples of skills that might rely on each, in figure 6.3. Although you might find this list helpful for identifying human abilities generally, keep in mind that they were discovered in research studies examining the performance of young male participants on tasks requiring the manipulation of various types of apparatus with the hands or feet, mainly from a sitting position. Therefore, we can't

General Timing Ability May Not Exist

Research (Robertson et al., 1999; Spencer & Zelaznik, 2003) has indicated that timing processes may not be shared across a wide variety of motor tasks and that timing ability may be specific to the task in question. In several experiments, these researchers found low correlations between people's performance on tapping and drawing tasks. The researchers proposed that different types of timing processes exist for different types of tasks. For example, tapping tasks that require a general timekeeping ability (because performers must be able to estimate time intervals) rely on a timing process different from the one people need for the timing of movement production processes (e.g., drawing tasks). These researchers pointed out that the results of experiments supporting the notion of a general timing ability are based on people's performance of only one of these types of task (Franz, Zelaznik, & Smith, 1992; Ivry & Hazeltine, 1995; Keele & Ivry, 1987) but not both (see also Spencer, Zelaznik, Diedrichsen, & Ivry, 2003, for neurophysiological evidence). The results of these studies argue against both a strict version of the specificity hypothesis of motor abilities (Henry, 1968) and a strong model of a central common timing process for movement production (Ivry & Hazeltine, 1995). In fact, it is likely that timing ability has both a specific and a general component (Robertson, Lantero, & Zelaznik, 1997).

be sure about whether the same abilities would surface if other types of participants or tasks were examined.

More recent research by Keele and his colleagues (Keele & Hawkins, 1982; Keele, Ivry, & Pokorny, 1987; Keele, Pokorny, Corcos, & Ivry, 1985) suggests that there may also be several abilities related to the performance of timing- and force-control tasks (see figure 6.4). These abilities include a variety of general coordination factors such as movement rate (measured by repetitive tapping), motor timing (measured by timed tapping), perceptual timing (measured by a person's ability to judge the duration of time intervals between events), and force control (measured by button presses of various magnitudes with the finger and forearm).

An important outcome of Keele's work has been the discovery of relatively consistent levels of task performance within individuals (i.e., similar levels of timing performance by the same person when using the finger, thumb, wrist, forearm, and foot) but considerable differences in performance between individuals. These results suggest that some type of timekeeping ability may underlie the performance of a variety of timing tasks. This notion has received support from laboratory studies showing more consistent timing performance of professional pianists compared with nonpianists (Keele et al., 1985) and nonhandicapped children compared with children classified as "motorically clumsy" (Williams, Woollacott, & Ivry, 1992). However, more recent research suggests that even timekeeping ability might be specific to classes of timing tasks (see "General Timing Ability May Not Exist").

How Many Ability Groupings Might There Be?

Neither Fleishman, Keele, nor more recent researchers has examined the performance of movements involving total-body coordination, such as those found in many real-world skills (e.g., jumping, dancing, piano moving). Until researchers study these kinds of movements in a systematic fashion, we can only guess about how long the final list of ability groupings might be.

Performance Success Results From a Combination of Factors

Differences in people's performances at any given time are attributable only in part to differences in the strength of their motor abilities. Research by Deshaies, Pargman, and Thiffault (1979) illustrates this point. In this study, the authors attempted to determine the relative importance of 14 variables representing physiological–anthropometric, psychological, and motor-skill factors to the ice hockey performance of 116 Quebec Junior Major League players, ages 16 and 17 years. A combination (battery) of four variables (forward skating speed, achievement motivation, visual–perceptual speed, and anaerobic power) separated the higher-skilled players from the lower-skilled players. Using a similar approach, Landers, Boutcher, and Wang (1986) found that the variables of relative leg strength, reaction time, depth perception, body type, imagery usage, confidence, and a focus on past mistakes differentiated the shooting performance of above-average and average archers. The results of these studies suggest that various combinations of stable and changeable factors contribute to differences in people's performance for practically every type of motor skill.

It Depends . . .

What Would You Say to a Skill Instructor?

In some skill-learning situations, practitioners must assist a number of performers simultaneously. Given what you have learned so far about the nature of people's underlying abilities, what advice might you offer an instructor who has been hired to teach a group of people how to perform a welding task in an industrial setting? Assume that all the instructor knows is that some folks seem to have low levels of the abilities important to skilled performance, whereas others possess moderate or high levels.

Two people performing the same activity can have different patterns of abilities.

Abilities and Practical Application

What we know about the nature of motor abilities suggests several things that practitioners need to keep in mind when providing instructional assistance. First and foremost, we assume that all people possess the same abilities but that the patterns of people's strengths and weaknesses are different. Second, the pattern of each person's strengths and weaknesses will determine which kinds of tasks for which we would expect excellence or failure in that person's performance; remember that someone with weak color-vision abilities will probably not become a wildflower expert. Third, the pattern of each person's abilities is but one of many factors contributing to the individual's ultimate level of performance, with practice, experiences, opportunities, and a host of other factors also playing a role. In the following paragraphs, we discuss each of these points in more detail.

The early practice stage is not adequate as the basis for judging a person's potential.

Identifying Learners' Abilities

It would be fortunate if instructors could identify each learner's strong and weak abilities and then tailor instruction based on this information. Most good practitioners can do this to some extent. For example, a coach might realize that a very tall girl might be a good candidate for basketball or that a teenage boy who is quite big and strong might make a good defensive tackle. But the strengths of more subtle abilities necessary for, say, playing piano or driving a truck are far more difficult to identify. Even scientists are not very certain about what those abilities are, because identifying them often requires laborious and expensive data collection and analysis. And in some cases scientists are not quite sure how to measure these abilities. Finally, the advanced level of skill that an individual demonstrates on a particular task (e.g., machinery operation) might fool us into thinking that he had strong abilities relevant for that task when, in fact, the person may have simply devoted many years of practice to that activity.

It is also risky to assume that a person's abilities will be revealed when he or she has only begun to practice, because the collection of abilities important for performance is different during the early stage of performance than in the more advanced stage. We illustrate this phenomenon in the simple diagram shown in figure 6.5 (see Fleishman & Hempel, 1955, for the results of a study that demonstrated this point). For some arbitrary task, let's assume that the hypothetical subset of abilities that might be useful for performance is shown in the set of lower circles labeled A, B, C, . . ., H. These letters could correspond to some of the abilities shown earlier in this chapter in figures 6.3 and 6.4. In early practice, depicted as the beginner on the upper left, performance depends on abilities A, B, F, and C and not on abilities D, E, G, and H. With extensive practice and experience, however, the pattern of supporting abilities gradually changes. As shown on the upper right side of the figure (depicted as the expert), the important abilities for successful performance are now abilities A, B, D, and E. Notice that two of the abilities, A and B, are important for both beginning and expert performers. However, two other abilities, F and C, become less important with practice and are eventually replaced by abilities D and E, which were not important during the early stages of practice. Also, note that abilities G and H are not important for performance at any time in this task.

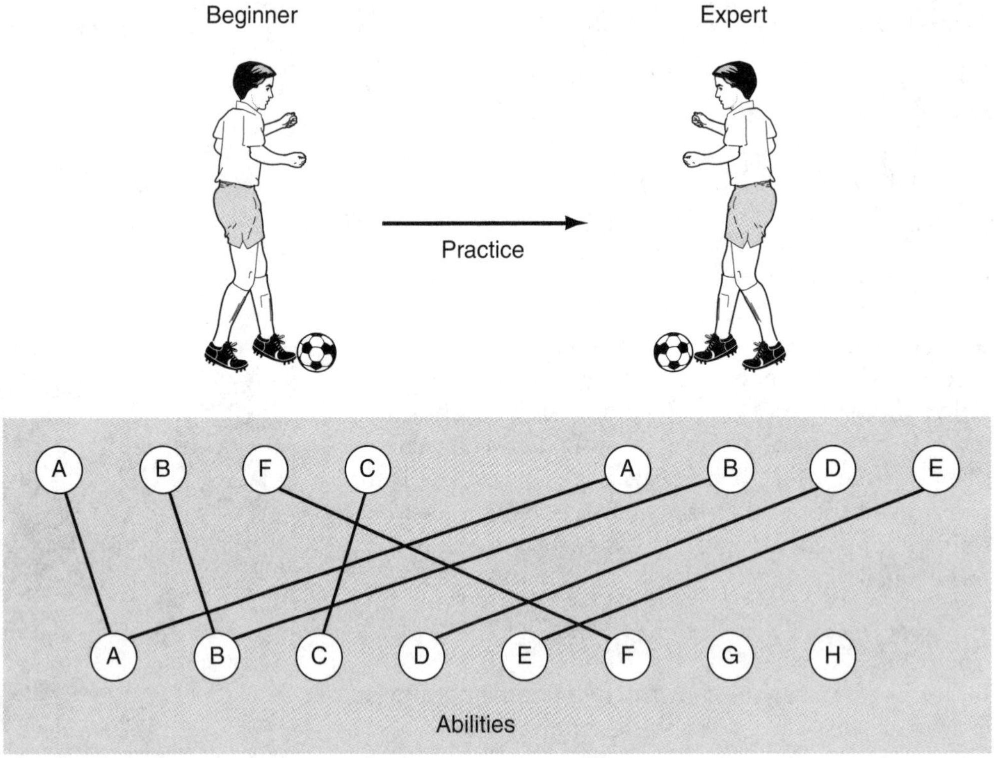

Figure 6.5 The pattern of abilities is important for successful performance changes as the learner progresses from beginning to expert levels.

Because people's abilities are by definition genetically defined and not modifiable by practice, we would expect that, other things being equal, people with high levels of abilities A, B, F, and C should perform better during the beginning stage of practice, whereas those with high levels of abilities A, B, D, and E would have the potential to be experts. Only those players with high levels of all of those abilities would be expected to perform at a high level during both the beginning and advanced stages of practice.

To put this issue in perspective, consider the common situation in youth sports in which many youngsters try out for a particular team or activity. After a relatively brief screening session of a few hours, the coach informs some of them that they have been selected for the team and others that they have not made it. The coach would be retaining those with high levels of abilities A, B, F, and C, which are the ones important for initial performance. The coach's decision might have a devastating effect on the children who are cut from the team, and it is possible that some of the players who are released could actually become the better performers if given sufficient practice. However, those with high levels of abilities D and E, but not F and C, would not be detected in this example.

A Particular Pattern of Stronger Abilities Will Facilitate Performance on Some Tasks More Than Others

Most individuals know which activities are better suited to their stronger abilities. They come to these conclusions as a result of experiences they have had with a variety of tasks, some of which they performed well (and sometimes quite easily) and others at which they struggled. Because everyone enjoys succeeding rather than failing, it shouldn't surprise us that people tend to repeat those activities that rely on their stronger

Differences in people's motor performance likely result from a combination of factors including abilities, motivation, mood, age, experience, and practice.

abilities. In this way, individuals self-select themselves into the appropriate activities. One has to be careful, though, as indicated in the previous section; just because an individual is having trouble during initial practice in an activity does not necessarily mean that the person could not become an excellent performer later on.

Personality, Mood, and Performance

In addition to motor abilities, other factors can contribute to differences in performance. One of these is a person's mood, viewed generally across various situations. In the 1970s, William Morgan of the University of Wisconsin used the Profile of Mood States inventory to assess the mental health of successful and unsuccessful candidates for the 1974 U.S. Olympic crew team and for the 1972 and 1976 U.S. Olympic wrestling teams. Morgan (1979) found that successful candidates (i.e., those who made the team) scored higher on vigor and lower on depression, anger, fatigue, and confusion than did their less successful counterparts.

Ability Is Only One Factor Contributing to Performance

In addition to people's stronger and weaker abilities, other factors can influence how well people perform motor skills, including the types and amount of previous movement experiences they have had, their body configuration, and a variety of other personal characteristics. Beginning at an early age, some people have more opportunities to participate in movement activities than have others. A child whose parents are particularly supportive of athletics or other performance activities will likely be exposed to a variety of valuable movement experiences and extensive rehearsal opportunities. As the child's skill level improves, she or he is likely to join groups of similarly skilled participants (e.g., sport teams, dance or musical groups), resulting in additional opportunities for even more advanced movement activities. Conversely, children who are not exposed to movement activities at an early age would not have a wealth of experience and would likely demonstrate lower skill, giving observers the false impression that they just don't have high levels of the necessary motor abilities.

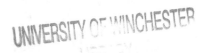

UNIVERSITY OF WINCHESTER

Helping Parents Help Their Children

Practitioners who understand the nature of motor abilities can assist parents in three important ways. First, they can encourage parents to provide their children with a broad range of movement experiences early in life. This allows children to discover those activities that are best suited to their stronger abilities. Second, practitioners can instruct parents to observe how well their child performs various activities. In this way parents may be able to identify the child's dominant pattern of underlying abilities and encourage the child to pursue activities that will produce the greatest success and enjoyment. Third, practitioners can caution parents that many factors (e.g., body size, achievement motivation, motor abilities) can influence the performance of individuals at various times and levels of maturation. Therefore, parents should not be surprised if their child performs some activities better (relative to his or her peers) at a younger age than at an older age and vice versa. It seems best to remain flexible and allow the child to pursue those activities the child enjoys performing the most—at any age.

Body configuration is another factor that can influence a person's performance. Bigger, stronger children who mature at an earlier age have an advantage over smaller, weaker kids when it comes to performing a number of physical skills required in playground sports (e.g., throwing, jumping, striking). As a result, observers might assume that the bigger, stronger children have a wider range of strong motor abilities than do kids who are smaller, weaker, or physically less mature. Body configuration can also affect the performance of adults in such activities as basketball, ballet, gymnastics, and springboard diving. Other factors that can contribute to individual differences in performance are personal characteristics such as achievement motivation, competitiveness, and willingness to take risks. Thus, some people may demonstrate high levels of performance on certain tasks because they possess high levels of some of these personal characteristics that are important for success.

How Abilities Contribute to the Performance of Skills: A Toolbox Analogy

A helpful analogy practitioners can use to conceptualize the role of abilities in motor performance is that of the toolbox. When a person is born, he or she inherits a "toolbox" containing stronger and weaker abilities. People use these abilities to perform the nearly infinite number of tasks they face during the course of their lives. Abilities are like the tools a builder uses to complete various tasks (e.g., installing a sink and faucet, framing a door or window, laying brick or stone). Each ability serves a particular purpose (e.g., coordinating several limbs at the same time or responding quickly to a single stimulus), in much the same way that each tool is designed to perform a specific function (e.g., cutting, striking, twisting, smoothing). Every skill or task (such as jumping over a fence or playing the trumpet) requires a certain set of abilities that are important to successful performance.

task analysis—A method of estimating the key components of motor tasks. Once the components are identified, the abilities that underlie performance can be estimated.

At the top of figure 6.6, we show some of the motor abilities from figure 6.3 (space does not permit a complete depiction of all the abilities). At the bottom of figure 6.6, we present a list of selected movement skills for which some of these abilities might be important. If we were to do a *task analysis* of each skill, we might estimate that a race-car driver requires a different pattern of underlying abilities than does a quarterback in American football. However, race-car driving and quarterbacking probably have at least one important ability in common (i.e., reaction time). Another aspect of the toolbox analogy is that the strengths or levels of people's abilities differ (e.g., some people inherit higher levels of movement–speed ability than do others), in much the same way that the quality of tools in a toolbox may vary (e.g., an industrial-grade power tool is of a higher quality than a home power tool). The pattern of an individual's stronger and weaker underlying abilities predisposes him or her to perform certain types of tasks more effectively. People who possess high levels of the abilities that are important for the performance of a particular task (e.g., reaction time, speed of limb movement, and manual dexterity for the race car driver) can be expected to perform better on that task than would individuals who possess lower levels of those abilities.

This figure illustrates three important points. The first is that different skills rely on different combinations of underlying abilities. The second is that different skills can sometimes use one or more of the same abilities. And the third is that people should perform better on tasks that depend on their stronger abilities than on tasks that depend on their weaker abilities.

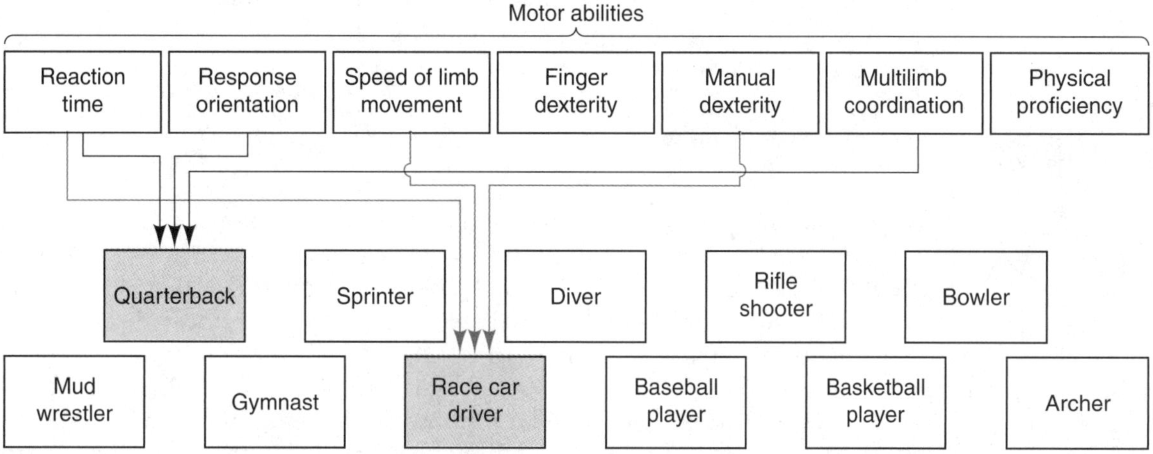

Figure 6.6 Links between various motor abilities and selected movement skills.

Task Analysis

In chapter 1 we discussed the concept of skill classification and presented several systems for classifying skills (e.g. discrete–serial–continuous, motor–cognitive, open–closed). In addition to classifying skills, practitioners can also prepare for instruction by analyzing the various components or demands of tasks and then considering the types of abilities that might be important to the performance of each. We present an example of the task analysis approach in the highlight box on page 180 titled "Sportprofessiograms." We also show how specific abilities might be important for the performance of an American football quarterback and a race-car driver in the highlight box titled "How Abilities Contribute to the Performance of Skills: A Toolbox Analogy" on this and the facing page. Note that in both of these examples, different abilities seem to contribute to different activities.

Highly skilled performers are not always aware of how they do what they do.

Sportprofessiograms

Sport psychologists in the former Soviet Union amassed large amounts of scientific data during the 1960s and 1970s from which they compiled lists of the most important physical characteristics and psychological traits of successful performers in various sports. For each sport, the psychologists combined the traits of the leading athletes, including psychological, physical, and emotional components. They also obtained input from coaches regarding the task requirements of various sports and activities. Each task analysis of this type resulted in a profile, called a sportprofessiogram, which sought to depict the ideal athlete for a particular sport (Rodionov, 1978). Thus, the sportprofessiogram estimated the basic abilities and personal characteristics supposedly needed to achieve success in important activities. Instruments like these are often used to select individuals for participation in various sports and to identify deficiencies in need of attention.

In addition, most teachers, coaches, and therapists can conduct a task analysis on an informal level by simply using their knowledge and experience to estimate the essential task components and the possible underlying abilities. If they do not have a sophisticated understanding of the task, practitioners can sometimes solicit the advice of people who do, such as expert performers.

However, some highly skilled performers may not be able to explain how they do what they do; remember our discussion of implicit learning in chapter 1, where we emphasized that some processes operating during skilled performance are nonconscious. Polanyi (1958) found that champion cyclists could not explain the fundamental principles of balancing on the bicycle. In addition, comments of expert performers are sometimes inconsistent with the findings from controlled experiments. For example, the great professional baseball player Ted Williams frequently claimed that he could see the seams of the ball rotating right up to the moment of bat–ball contact (Williams & Underwood, 1988). Scientific evidence concerning the length of time it takes to process visual information and the speed and accuracy of eye movements proves such an event virtually impossible.

There are more formal methods for conducting task analyses. Consider an activity such as soccer. Let's assume that we want to do a task analysis to determine the abilities that are important for performance success for beginners and for experts. Figure 6.7 is a flowchart that guides a practitioner through the process of estimating which abilities are required for some task. By starting at the top and answering each question about the skill, you are guided to an initial understanding of what abilities might be required. Try this for some skill with which you are familiar.

Predicting Performance Success

Another way practitioners have attempted to use the notion of motor abilities is to predict the future performance success of individuals based on estimates of their various abilities or characteristics. Predictions like this are in fact a part of many aspects of our lives. In a number of instances, batteries of tests have been developed with the intent of predicting future performance or outcomes in some way. For example, insurance companies attempt to predict the likelihood that we will have an automobile accident

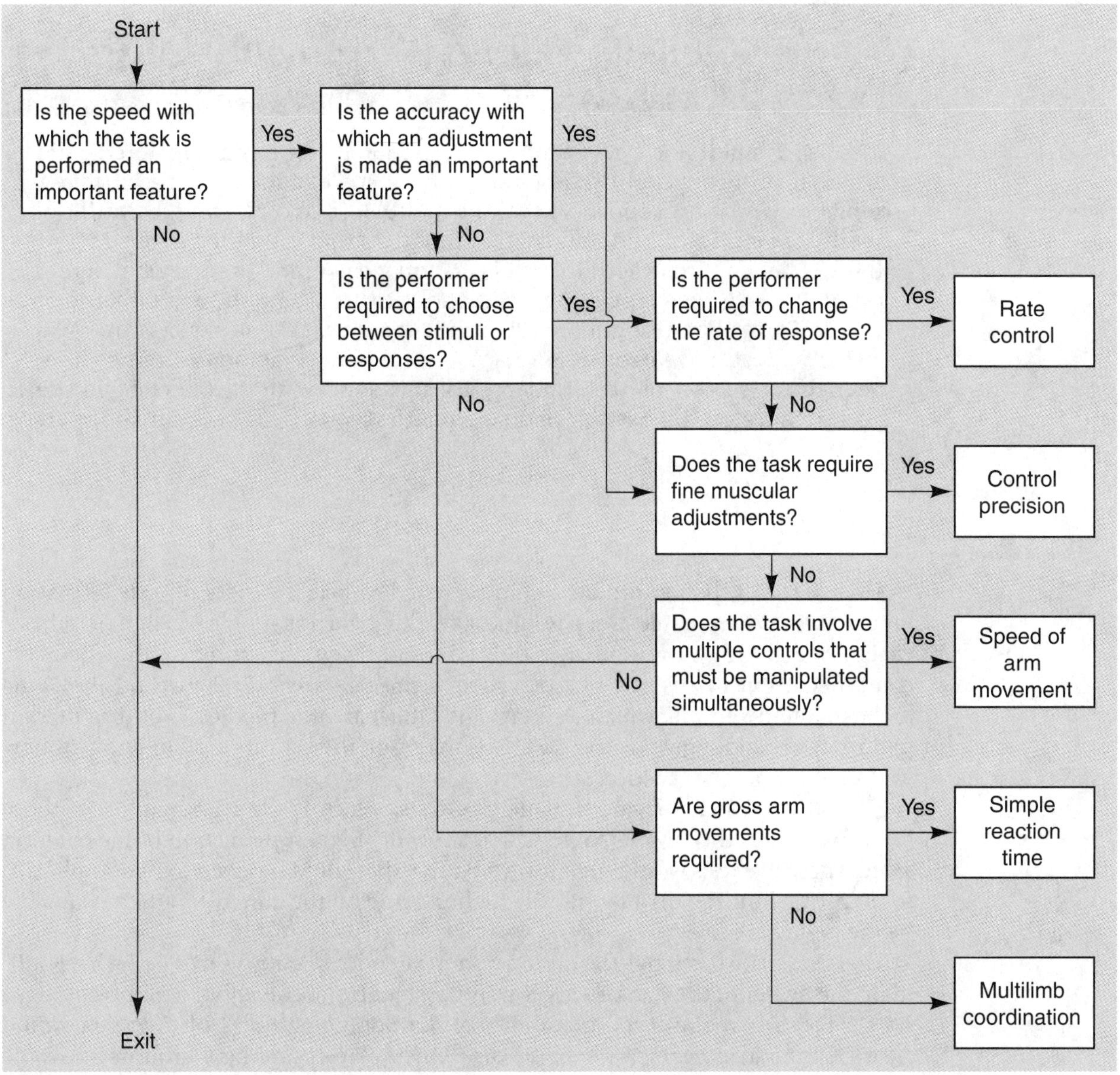

Figure 6.7 A flowchart for interviews with expert performers helps you map out a task analysis. (Adapted from Fleishman and Stephenson, 1970.)

based on a battery of information such as our age, sex, driving record, postal zip code, and type of car we drive. Those individuals with the characteristics indicating they are most likely to have an accident are charged higher rates. In industrial and business settings, a personnel director attempts to predict, using a variety of measures, which of several applicants for a job is going to be most successful after a year's training and experience.

How are these batteries developed? In most situations, the process is laborious and expensive. Typically, a group of 40 to 50 expert or experienced performers in some task—say, truck driving—are selected; they are then ranked from best to worst according to some criterion—such as the number of miles driven without causing an accident, the net revenue the driver generates per year, or any other skill indicator.

Predicting Future Performance Success is a Difficult Task

In 1974, Schmidt and Pew attempted to design a test battery for predicting whether a person had the abilities to be a successful dental technician—someone who makes appliances for the mouth (e.g., crowns, bridges, artificial teeth). Their final battery consisted of four tests that estimated about 25% of the abilities important for successful performance. Although somewhat higher estimates have been reported for test batteries predicting the performance of U.S. Air Force pilots (Fleishman, 1956) and American football players (McDavid, 1977), no tests have been able to account for more than half of the abilities needed for successful performance. Thus, it appears that predicting future performance on the basis of people's abilities alone is, at best, an imperfect science.

Then, each of the performers might be asked to take a variety of tests (say 50 in number). These tests could evaluate almost anything, such as simple reaction time, body weight, visual acuity, or number of older siblings. Then, the scores on these tests are combined using a statistical method called *multiple regression*. This method allows the researcher to determine which tests are, and which are not, predictors of the criterion performance, and it gives a set of weights that rank the various tests in terms of how well they predict the criterion score.

Then the researcher creates a battery of tests, selecting the combination of those few (say, five) of the 50 original tests that show the highest prediction of the criterion score. These five tests would then form a battery that could be given to new applicants for a driving job. The drivers with the highest score on the battery would presumably be the best candidates for hiring.

This kind of process could be done for sport situations. Many years ago, Ewing Kauffman, the owner of the Kansas City Royals baseball team, consulted with psychologist Edwin Fleishman about the possibility of developing batteries of tests that would allow Kauffman's organization to predict which players among a group of possible recruits would be most likely to succeed at the professional level. This project was never completed, to our knowledge, probably in part because this kind of research was very expensive and the potential benefits were not great enough.

Although developing such batteries might seem to be desirable, even the most successful of the prediction batteries developed for skills are not very good at predicting success. Probably the strongest efforts have been directed at predicting who would become the best U.S. Air Force pilots, and considerable effort and expense have been directed at this problem. Even so, the best of these batteries account for only about half of the information we need to know to make a perfect prediction (see Fleishman, 1972, for a review of this area).

As a result, we are not in a very strong position to be able to predict, with much certainty, which people are most likely to succeed at any given activity. The basic problems are that there are many abilities, many of these have not been discovered yet, and we don't know how to measure the existing ones very well. The laborious and expensive research simply has not been done in many areas (e.g., sport), and when it has been conducted (e.g., industrial settings), the results have been disappointing. In short, we simply don't understand the role of individual differences in human performance very well.

SUMMARY

People differ in numerous ways. Many of the factors that make people unique also contribute to differences in people's movement performance. For example, people differ with respect to the strength levels of various abilities, which are defined as stable, genetically determined traits. The concept of abilities is different from that of skill, which deals with the proficiency of a person's performance on a given task. Theoretical views about abilities include the general motor ability notion, the specificity of abilities hypothesis, and the notion of groupings of abilities. The last view appears to have the broadest scientific and anecdotal support and presumes that

- a number of independent, fundamental abilities exist, perhaps more than 50;
- different combinations of these abilities underlie the performance of different tasks;
- some abilities play a dominant role in a particular task performance, whereas others have a lesser role; and
- some abilities may be important for a number of tasks.

Practitioners can use the notion of abilities when preparing for instruction by first conducting a task analysis to determine the requirements of the task and then estimating the important abilities that are necessary to meet those requirements. Once this is done, learning experiences can be designed that allow individuals to capitalize on their stronger abilities and practice activities to compensate for their weaker abilities.

Except in the case of highly experienced performers, practitioners would be wise to avoid making predictions about a person's future success based on observations of that person's initial (relatively unskilled) performance at a task. This is because the patterns of abilities necessary for successful performance change with practice; therefore, performers who do well on a particular task early in practice may not be the ones who do well later on, and vice versa.

Finally, developing batteries of predictive tests is laborious and expensive, and this kind of research simply has not been conducted in many areas (e.g., sports). In a number of other areas, such as the military and industry, batteries have been developed with mixed success.

FROM PRINCIPLES TO PRACTICE

Check your comprehension of the concepts and terms discussed in this chapter by completing each of the exercises in the following sections. The first section contains several activities designed to test your working knowledge of key terms. The second section consists of a variety of exercises designed to check your understanding of key concepts. In the third section you are challenged to apply your knowledge by discussing a defensible solution for two situations.

Know Your Key Terms

Matching: Abilities and Capabilities

Match the following abilities and capabilities with their respective categories or definitions by placing the letters on the lines to the left of the numbers below.

Abilities and Capabilities—Terms

a. multilimb coordination

b. reaction time

c. finger dexterity

d. explosive strength

e. extent flexibility

f. perceptual timing

g. force control

Abilities and Capabilities—Category or Definition

_____1. Ability important for performing tasks requiring accurate judgments about the time course of external events

_____2. Ability to expend a maximum of energy in one brief and forceful act

_____3. Ability important for serving a tennis ball or playing the piano

_____4. The interval between an unanticipated stimulus and the beginning of a response

_____5. Ability important for performing tasks requiring the manipulation of small objects

_____6. Ability important for performing tasks requiring changes in the intensity of muscle contractions

_____7. Ability to stretch the body as far as possible in various directions

Consider: The Shifting Importance of Different Abilities

For each of the following tasks, select one ability from figure 6.3 or 6.4 that you think would be more important for performance success on the first day of practice and one ability that would be more important for performance success after several years of practice.

1. Hitting a golf ball at a driving range __________
(first day)
____
(after several years)

2. Performing a parallel bar routine __________
(first day)
____
(after several years)

3. Throwing the discus __________
(first day)
____
(after several years)

4. Playing the drums __________
(first day)
____
(after several years)

Fill in the Blank: Skill Classification and Task Analysis

Complete the following sentences:

Practitioners can classify __________ by analyzing the various __________ or __________ of the task and then considering the types of __________ that underlie performance. Different __________ rely on different combinations of underlying __________.

Check Your Understanding

1. Distinguish the concept of abilities from that of skill. Why is this distinction important for movement practitioners?
2. Explain the logic of statistical correlation in words that a friend or family member might understand. What are two important aspects of abilities that have been discovered by researchers who have used correlations to examine people's performance on two or more tasks?
3. How does Fleishman's concept of abilities differ from that of Henry? In what way does Fleishman's notion strike a balance between the general motor ability notion and Henry's concept of specificity?
4. What role do motor abilities play in an individual's performance?
5. How might practitioners determine which abilities are important for various types of tasks?
6. What factors should practitioners be aware of when trying to predict a person's future performance success?

Apply Your Knowledge

Exercise 1

Your neighbor has a teenage daughter who wants to learn how to drive a stick-shift (manual transmission) car. During an informal conversation he asks you for advice. The neighbor says he's afraid his daughter will have difficulty because she's not very "coordinated." You tell him you'll think about it and get back to him. Explain how you would determine the requirements for effective operation of a stick-shift car and the abilities necessary for successful driving performance. Provide a rationale for your decisions. Then discuss how you might determine the daughter's stronger and weaker abilities and explain the implications of each to her father. Include two supporting references with your answer. How would you explain to your neighbor that the notion of his daughter being "not very coordinated" is not particularly useful, and is not grounded scientifically?

Exercise 2

You are the volunteer coach of a soccer team made up of 5- and 6-year-old girls. You are committed to providing practice opportunities that will challenge your players, but you notice that some kids are having more difficulty than others. Explain how you would determine the task requirements for two different skills (e.g., receiving a pass and attempting a shot on goal) and list two or three abilities from figures 6.3 and 6.4 that might contribute to the successful performance of each. Then briefly discuss how you might provide your players with practice experiences that promote each person's skill development. Include rationale for your suggestions and provide two supporting references.

PART THREE

PRINCIPLES OF SKILL LEARNING

chapter 7

Preparing for the Learning Experience

▷ Chapter Outline

▷ Chapter Objectives

When you have completed this chapter, you should be able to

- discuss the concept of the learning experience,
- explain the role of the movement practitioner in defining learning experiences,
- describe several learner characteristics of which practitioners should be aware,
- explain how movement practitioners can evaluate the progress of learners, and
- assist someone in developing a blueprint for a motor learning experience.

PREVIEW

In Lewis Carroll's classic children's story *Alice in Wonderland* (1994 version), Alice and the Cheshire cat have the following verbal exchange:

Alice: Could you tell me which way I should go from here?

Cheshire cat: Well, that depends a good deal on where you want to go.

Alice: Oh, I don't much care where.

Cheshire cat: Then it doesn't matter which way you go.

Movement activities are an important aspect of people's lives.

OVERVIEW

In many ways, learners are like Alice and movement practitioners are like the Cheshire cat. For learning experiences to be rewarding and productive, learners must know where they want to go, and movement practitioners must be able to assist them in their efforts to get there. In chapters 2 through 6 we introduced and developed a conceptual model of motor performance. This model contains a variety of systems that underlie people's processing of information and their production of voluntary movements. By now you should understand the mechanisms of motor performance as well as some of the principles of motor control and movement accuracy. In chapters 7 through 10 we turn our attention to the process of motor skill learning and the factors that influence people's acquisition of skills. In chapter 7 we discuss the concept of the learning experience and some of the factors that movement practitioners consider when preparing to assist learners. Then, in the next three chapters, we discuss instructional techniques practitioners can use when assisting learners (chapter 8), ways practitioners can structure the practice of tasks during learning sessions (chapter 9), and some principles to remember when providing feedback for learners (chapter 10).

We conceptualize learning as it typically seems to occur, not as an event artificially produced in a laboratory but as an experience that takes place under everyday conditions, which are often messy. There is considerable scientific literature on the factors that influence people's motor learning, and much of it provides useful information for application. In part III we present the research that is most relevant for practitioners and learners in everyday situations.

In this chapter we begin our discussion of motor learning by presenting several concepts practitioners might consider when preparing to provide instructional assistance. These include goal setting, transfer of learning, learner characteristics, and the process of performance assessment.

DEFINING THE LEARNING EXPERIENCE

The capability to learn is essential to biological existence. It allows organisms to adapt to the particular features of their environment and to profit from their experiences. For humans, learning is crucial. Think of the difficulty individuals would have if they were forced to go through life equipped with only the **abilities** they inherited at birth. If that were the case, people would be relatively simple beings indeed, unable to walk, talk, write, or read, much less perform the complex movements involved in sports, the performing arts, or even everyday settings.

In many ways, human learning seems to occur almost continuously, as if everything we do generates knowledge or capabilities that affect how we do other things tomorrow and beyond. In chapter 1, **motor learning** was defined as the changes, associated with practice or experience, in internal processes that determine a person's capability for producing a motor skill. This definition of skill learning pertains to situations in which people attempt to improve their performance of a particular movement or action, and throughout part III we refer to those situations as **learning experiences** (or what some researchers term *deliberate practice*). We emphasize that learning experiences can take place in a variety of settings, involving either an individual learner or a group of learners. Most of the time, although certainly not always, an instructor, a therapist, or a coach is present to guide the learning experience and to assess the learner's progress.

One issue that practitioners usually consider before assisting any learner is the intended purpose of that person's learning experience. Practitioners must remember that the experience belongs to the learner. Every learner approaches a new skill-learning situation with some idea of what he or she wants to accomplish. The learning experience is an interaction between instructor and learner that should focus on the achievement of the learner's goals. Therefore, when preparing to assist learners, it is helpful for practitioners to know something about the concepts of goal setting and transfer of learning.

abilities—Stable, enduring traits that, for the most part, are genetically determined and that underlie a person's skill in a variety of tasks. People differ with respect to their patterns of strong and weak abilities, resulting in differences in their levels of skill.

motor learning—The changes, associated with practice or experience, in internal processes that determine a person's capability for producing a motor skill.

learning experiences—Situations in which people make deliberate attempts to improve their performance of a particular movement or action.

goal setting—The process of establishing targets for performance.

Goal Setting

As we suggested in the preview to this chapter, an important prerequisite for productive learning is a clear understanding of the learner's intended goal or destination. Where does the person want to go? What skills does the learner want to master? Under what conditions does the person want to be able to perform those skills? Effective movement practitioners are able to assist learners in achieving their goals, but to do this they must first know what the learners' goals are.

Some learners approach learning situations with their goals clearly in mind; others do not. For maximally effective practice, learners must set goals to identify the specific skills and behaviors that they want to achieve and to have a reference point for assessing progress. **Goal setting** has been used successfully in many environments, particularly in business and industry, and it has strong implications for skill learning in other instructional settings (Locke & Latham, 1985). Goal setting is a highly individual matter: One person's goals are likely to differ from those of another. When learners set goals, they are more committed to goal achievement, and they usually have a better understanding of the purpose of various learning activities (Tubbs, 1986).

Research indicates that goals that are challenging, attainable, realistic, and specific can improve people's performance (see Gould, 2006). This means that the most effective goals encourage improvement, are achievable given the conditions of learning (e.g., sufficient time, available equipment), are based on people's prior performances, and are measurable. When goals satisfy these criteria, they can increase the quality of people's learning experiences.

outcome goals—Targets for performance that focus on the end result of the activity.

performance goals—Targets for performance that focus on improving some aspect of performance.

process goals—Targets for performance that focus on the quality of movement production.

target skills—The skills a person wishes to be able to perform.

target behaviors—The actions people must be able to produce to perform target skills successfully in the target context.

target context—The environmental context in which people want to be able to perform a skill or skills.

Sometimes people set **outcome goals** that emphasize the results of performance and often involve comparisons with other people's performance (e.g., beating a friend in tennis, winning a conference championship, leading the league in field goal percentage). The problem with this kind of goal, however, is that it is an outcome over which people often have little control (e.g., a gymnast could perform her best ever and still finish third). Therefore, learners should set two other types of goals as well (Gould, 2006). **Performance goals** focus on a person's improvement relative to his or her own past performance (e.g., a basketball player's goal of increasing her free throw percentage from 70% to 75%). **Process goals** emphasize particular aspects of skill execution (e.g., pumping the arms while running the 100 m dash, leading with the healthy leg when walking up a flight of stairs with crutches, or scanning traffic efficiently when driving a truck).

A tennis player might set an outcome goal of winning two out of three sets in a tennis match, a performance goal of improving his first-serve percentage from 50% to 60%, and a process goal of focusing his eyes on the seams of the ball every time he serves. Other examples of outcome goals, performance goals, and process goals are shown in table 7.1.

As we have previously suggested, an important advantage of goal setting is that it allows people to identify the skills they want to develop during their learning experiences. For our purposes, we call these skills **target skills** because they are the actual tasks people need to acquire to achieve their goals (e.g., keeping a tennis ball in play or performing the proper steps in a dance routine). Target skills for a person who wants to be a successful tennis player might include hitting ground strokes that land within the boundaries and within 5 ft (1.5 m) of the opponent's baseline, hitting volleys that land beyond the opponent's service line, and hitting serves with a good pace that land within 1 ft (30 cm) of the opponent's service line.

Once movement practitioners identify the relevant target skills that need to be learned, they must determine the observable **target behaviors** associated with successful performance of those skills. For the tennis ground stroke, target behaviors might include a visual focus on the ball, early racket preparation, and a smooth follow-through after ball contact. During instruction, effective practitioners encourage learners to focus on one or more of these behaviors until each becomes a consistent characteristic of the player's performance.

Practitioners must also consider the **target context**, or the environment in which learners want to produce their target skills. The target context for a tennis player might be a highly competitive tournament; for a truck driver, it might be driving very late at night on open roads. The target context for a stroke patient learning to feed himself with his nonpreferred hand might be at home in the presence of concerned family

Table 7.1 Examples of Outcome Goals, Performance Goals, and Process Goals for Different Activities

Activity	Outcome goals	Performance goals	Process goals
Rifle shooting	Finish first in a local shooting competition	Improve bull's-eye percentage from 60% to 70%	Exhale slowly before each trigger squeeze
Waterskiing	Qualify for the regional championships	Increase average number of successful buoy passes from 4 to 5	Visually focus on outside of buoys
Volleyball	Win the conference title	Improve blocking percentage from 40% to 50%	Penetrate the plane of the net on each blocking attempt

CARS

You can easily remember four of the key elements of successful goal setting by remembering the acronym formed by the first letter of each word: CARS.

- **C**hallenging
- **A**ttainable
- **R**ealistic
- **S**pecific

Table 7.2 Examples of Target Skills, Target Behaviors, and Target Contexts for Activities

Activity	Target skills	Target behaviors	Target contexts
Playing the piano	Error-free performance	Proper hand and finger alignment	Regional piano competition
Basketball	Effective rebounding technique	Use of body to block out opponent on each shot	Junior varsity basketball game
Surfing	Riding a moderately difficult wave	Appropriate adjustments of body and feet	Local beach with friends

members. Some more examples of target skills, target behaviors, and target contexts are shown in table 7.2.

By encouraging learners to follow sound goal-setting principles, practitioners should be able to determine a person's intended destination. Then they can assist the learner in identifying the target skills and behaviors necessary for goal achievement.

It Depends . . .

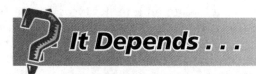

How Would You Apply the CARS Principle for Goal Setting?

Briefly describe a skill with which you are familiar (e.g., playing the guitar, operating a chain saw, hitting a racquetball forehand) and a person you know who might be interested in learning the skill. Then explain how you would use the CARS principle to help the person set three goals for learning the skill.

Transfer of Learning

Another concept for practitioners to consider when preparing to offer instructional assistance is **transfer of learning**. In experiments on transfer of learning, researchers attempt to determine the influence of prior experiences on people's performance (or learning) of a new task. Researchers do this by using an experimental design in which some participants practice an initial task before attempting a second task. A control group receives no experience on the initial task and attempts only the second task. When prior experience on the initial task is beneficial (compared with the control group) for second-task performance, positive transfer is presumed to have occurred. If the prior experience is detrimental or has no influence, negative transfer or no transfer, respectively, is assumed.

transfer of learning—The gain or the loss of a person's proficiency on one task as a result of previous practice or experience on another task.

Sometimes it can be difficult to see the real-world applications of transfer of learning. However, several aspects of transfer of learning are particularly relevant for practitioners. Perhaps the most important deals with the relationship between what a person learns during practice sessions and what that person can do when required to perform the skill

It Depends . . .

Can You Identify Similar and Different Target Skills?

For one of the following pairs, suggest one target skill that might be the same for each activity and one target skill that might be different: bowling and croquet, tennis and squash, snow skiing and waterskiing, cycling and canoeing, ballet dancing and ballroom dancing, surgery and dentistry, physical therapy and athletic training. Provide rationale for each of your choices.

Locus of Control and Goal Setting

One factor to keep in mind when deciding whether to give learners input during goal setting is locus of control. According to Rotter (1954), people with an internal locus of control perceive that they are in control of what happens, whereas those with an external locus of control perceive that some outside source (e.g., coach, teacher) is in control. Research suggests that, compared with performers with an external locus of control, those with an internal locus of control demonstrate more persistent practice behaviors when they have input in the goal-setting process than when they don't. Moreover, the opposite seems to be true for performers with an external locus of control. In a study of young female gymnasts, Lambert, Moore, and Dixon (1999) found that gymnasts with an internal locus of control spent more time on the beam when they were given the opportunity to set their own goals, whereas gymnasts with an external locus of control demonstrated more on-beam behavior when the coach set the goals.

generalization—A type of transfer of learning that occurs from one task or situation to another very similar task or situation; also referred to as near transfer.

near transfer—A type of transfer of learning that occurs from one task or situation to another very similar task or situation; also referred to as generalization.

in the target context. A second aspect of the transfer concept concerns the potential impact of foundational motor learning (e.g., so-called fundamental movement patterns) on the future performance or learning of other skills. Finally, there is the question of whether practicing simpler versions (or parts) of a task actually transfers positively to a person's subsequent performance or learning of the whole task. In the following paragraphs we discuss each of these practical applications of transfer of learning in more detail.

Perhaps the most frequent demonstration of transfer is **generalization**, sometimes referred to as **near transfer**. With respect to the design of learning experiences, generalization deals with the transfer of skilled performance from the instructional setting to a particular target context, such as an athletic contest, a piano recital, a construction site, or, for the therapy patient, the home. In some cases, this means that the performer adapts the target skill to meet the demands of another situation, such as when the basketball player puts more arc on the jump shot she has learned in order to clear the outstretched arms of a taller defender during a game. In other cases, near transfer means that the performer produces essentially the same movement he has been practicing all along but does so under a different set of environmental conditions, such as when the therapy patient with a prosthesis picks up objects in the home after learning how to pick up similar objects in a clinical setting.

Another way practitioners can apply the transfer notion is when helping learners develop more general capabilities for producing a wide variety of actions in the future, sometimes referred to as **far transfer**. Perhaps the best-known technique for developing far transfer is the movement-education approach that many elementary school teachers use. Instructors who use this method encourage children to attempt a variety of fundamental movement activities, such as throwing, jumping, running, and skating. According to movement-education advocates, children who learn these basic skills are better prepared to perform them in the context of future activities that involve these movements in some way. For example, throwing is an important foundational skill for baseball pitching and tennis serving (see Zebas & Johnson, 1989), jumping is essential for hurdling and playing basketball, running is needed for soccer and football, and skating is a prerequisite for ice hockey and ice dancing.

Still another application of transfer of learning concerns the simplification of skill practice—to make a difficult task easier to practice initially—and the subsequent transfer to whole-task performance. For example, relatively long-duration serial skills, such as certain gymnastics routines, might be broken down initially into shorter elements for practice. Before deciding to do this, practitioners should consider whether having a learner practice various parts of a task in isolation is going to be beneficial when it's time for the person to perform the whole task. We address the issue of part-whole practice in more detail in chapter 8.

Figure 7.1 Effective learning experiences encourage transfer of skill between the practice environment and the target context.

far transfer—A type of transfer of learning that occurs from one task or situation to another very different task or situation.

THE LEARNER

The central figure in every learning experience is the learner; to create the most effective learning experiences, movement practitioners must be aware of some of the important characteristics of learners. These characteristics include a person's motivation, abilities, past experiences, and present stage of learning.

Highly motivated people devote greater effort to the task.

UNIVERSITY OF WINCHESTER
LIBRARY

achievement motivation—The direction and intensity of a person's effort to reach a performance goal, either for personal mastery or for demonstrating superior competence compared with other performers.

Motivation

Anyone who has attempted to teach someone will testify that a key ingredient for productive learning is the learner's motivation (Deci & Ryan, 1985). Highly motivated people devote greater effort to the task, are more conscientious during practice sessions, and are willing to practice for longer periods. People who are not motivated to learn do not practice or, at best, make only half-hearted attempts.

The general context of motor learning is achievement-oriented. Therefore, it is reasonable to presume that the motivation of most learners is related to their perceptions of success in achieving their goals (i.e., **achievement motivation**). People can judge their success in one of two ways: with respect to improvements in their performance of the task itself (i.e., task-referenced judgments) or with respect to improvements in their performance as it compares with the performance of others (i.e., norm-referenced judgments). Learners who believe that they are competent or successful are more likely to remain motivated (Duda, 1993; Duda & Treasure, 2006; Nicholls, 1989).

People feel more highly motivated when they see the relevance of the learning activity to their lives. With the popularity of movies such as *Swing Kids* and *Saturday Night Fever*, certain dance forms became popular. Retro swing movements as seen in the Gap television commercials in the late 1990s led to increased interest in that type of dance instruction. The current popularity of Latin music and movies has enticed non-Latin dancers to learn how to perform not only the salsa and tango but other Latin dances as well. In such cases it is a pleasure for teachers to have interested dancers flock to class, eager to develop their skills and express their emotions.

Unfortunately, there are also instructional situations in which learners are not so enthusiastic. High school students who are required to take physical education classes may not see the personal relevance of the activities they are being asked to perform. Sometimes injured athletes or stroke patients are so discouraged about their physical condition that they have a difficult time mustering the energy to attend therapy sessions. To enhance the motivation of people like these, effective instructors or therapists attempt to find creative ways to forge a connection between the learner and the target skills. A major challenge for all movement practitioners is to design practices that motivate learners to continue to practice (Lee & Wishart, 2005). Fortunately, practitioners can use a variety of helpful techniques to achieve this objective (e.g., videos, group discussions, presentations by skilled performers, encouragement, and praise), some of which we describe in more detail in the next chapter.

One effective way practitioners can enhance learners' motivation is to involve them in goal setting. When doing this, successful practitioners remember that people are motivated by goals that are personally relevant and process-oriented. When learners are given the opportunity to select their own goals and then are encouraged to evaluate their success in reaching those goals, they are more likely to see themselves as competent performers. When people feel successful about their own goal achievement, they have the best chance to remain motivated to learn.

Past Experiences

Another way to look at transfer of learning is to consider the influence of people's previous movement experiences on their learning of a new target skill. If those experiences include the learning of tasks containing motor, perceptual, or conceptual elements similar to ones constituting the target skill, the practitioner can emphasize those similarities when providing instructional assistance (see Schmidt & Young, 1987). For example, people who want to learn in-line skating might be reminded of similar elements in other tasks they have already learned, such as ice-skating, roller-skating, or skateboarding.

Table 7.3 Examples of Similar Movement Elements, Perceptual Elements, and Conceptual Elements for Movement Activities

Activities	Movement elements	Perceptual elements	Conceptual elements
Tennis and badminton	Shoulder rotation prior to shot	Visual tracking of ball or shuttlecock	Variation of shot selection
Bowling and shuffleboard	Follow-through in direction of target	Accurate judgment of target location	Effective placement of object
Ice hockey and soccer	Maintaining balance while in motion and while manipulating an object	Accurate interpretation of opponents' movements	Maintaining proper spacing with teammates

The earliest discussions of transfer of learning dealt with the notion of identical elements between tasks (Thorndike, 1914). The essence of this notion is that tasks sharing a greater number of similar elements will transfer from one to the other (i.e., benefit each other) to a greater extent than tasks with little in common. When many similar elements are present, performers can capitalize on their previous task experiences when learning new skills. Recent research suggests that given sufficient practice, significant transfer of cognitive–perceptual skills and physiological adaptations can occur across certain ball sports (Baker, Côté, & Abernethy, 2003). Elements that might be identical, or at least very similar, between tasks are movement elements, perceptual elements, and conceptual or strategic elements. Examples of these categories of potentially similar elements for three pairs of movement activities are shown in table 7.3.

movement elements—Aspects of a task that deal with the fundamental patterns or actions associated with correct performance.

perceptual elements—Aspects of a task that deal with the environmental or movement information that leads to correct performance.

conceptual elements—Aspects of a task that deal with the rules, principles, guidelines, or strategies of performance.

Movement elements deal with the fundamental patterns of various actions. For example, throwing a baseball and casting a fishing lure seem to involve quite similar movement patterns. Therefore, practitioners could remind learners who have had previous experience throwing baseballs that the casting action is similar to throwing a baseball. People who have not had prior experience throwing might be encouraged to practice throwing to get a better feel for the movement pattern used in casting. The notion of fundamental, underlying movement patterns was an important part of our discussion of generalized motor programs in chapters 4 and 5.

Perceptual elements are task-related stimuli that people must be able to interpret to achieve successful performance. For example, racquetball, squash, paddleball, and handball require accurate perception of the speed and spatial trajectory of the ball as it rebounds off the walls and floor. Practitioners can promote transfer of learning either by calling learners' attention to previous experiences they have had with these tasks or by allowing learners to practice tasks containing similar perceptual elements.

Some motor tasks contain similar **conceptual elements**, such as strategies, rules, principles, or informal guidelines. Maintaining a narrow focus on the target is an important principle to remember when performing activities such as setting a diamond in jewelry, threading a needle, or suturing a wound. Some sports have similar rules (e.g., baseball and softball, gymnastics and diving, racquetball and paddleball); some have similar strategic elements (e.g., controlling or defending an area of the field, court, or ice in basketball, rugby, soccer, ice hockey, field hockey, and lacrosse). Learners who have had previous experience with tasks that have conceptual elements similar to those of the target skill can be reminded of those similarities to facilitate transfer. In figure 7.2 we depict some of the possible ways that transfer of learning might occur during skill learning and performance.

The transfer of similar elements is more pronounced when people are just beginning to learn a skill than after they have achieved a consistent level of proficiency. For example, a beginner practicing her tennis serve might benefit from additional

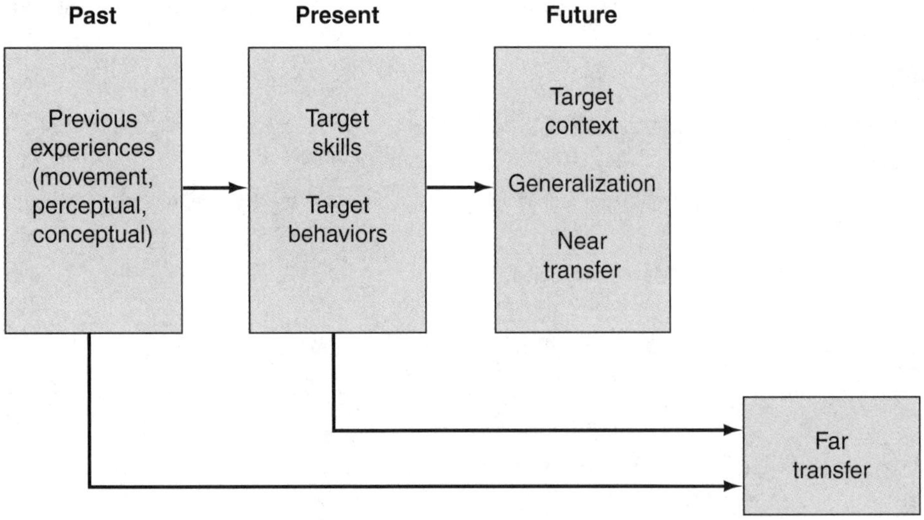

Figure 7.2 Possible ways that transfer of learning might occur.

specificity of learning— The notion that the best learning experiences are those that approximate most closely the movement components and environmental conditions of the target skill and target context.

experiences of overarm throwing, because the arm motion is similar to that needed for the serve. However, once the learner has acquired the basic serving motion, she would profit by spending more time hitting various types of serves than practicing her throwing. As skill levels improve, a greater proportion of a person's learning experience is best devoted to performance of the target skill in situations that resemble the target context (e.g., serving the tennis ball to an opponent in a gamelike situation). Indeed, the **specificity of learning** principle (Henry, 1968) holds that the best practice is that which approximates most closely the movements of the target skill and the environmental conditions of the target context. More recent movement scientists refer to this type of practice as transfer training (Christina & Alpenfels, 2002). Although there may be minor exceptions to the specificity of learning principle, it is for the most part a sound principle that can aid the design of instructional settings.

It is possible that a learner's previous experiences might transfer *negatively* to the performance or learning of a new skill. For example, previous experiences in racquetball or badminton could degrade a person's performance or learning of tennis skills. The assumption here is that the actions necessary for racquetball and badminton (i.e., flexible wrist) are just different enough from those needed for tennis (i.e., firm wrist) that if the learner has experienced the former actions to any great extent, her tennis skill might be susceptible to negative transfer.

Laboratory research suggests that negative transfer is virtually nonexistent in the realm of motor skills. Only during the very early stages of learning, when performance is dependent on conceptual elements (what to do, where to go) or when the level of a person's skill is more general in nature, might she or he be susceptible to the negative influence of prior learning. Even here, though, the evidence suggests that most transfer between motor skills is at least mildly positive. Moreover, practitioners can minimize potential problems by pointing out to learners those aspects of a new skill (e.g., swinging a tennis racket with a firm wrist) that are different from those of a previously learned one (e.g., swinging a badminton racket with a flexible wrist).

A child might be able to transfer previous jumping experience in learning other jumping skills.

It Depends . . .

Can You Identify the Similar Elements of Two Different Activities?

Try to identify one similar movement element, one similar perceptual element, and one similar conceptual element for any two of the following activities: archery, bowling, croquet, dentistry, engine repair, fencing, golf, horseback riding, ice-skating, jai alai, kickboxing, leaf raking, moon walking, nail filing, oboe playing, painting, quarterbacking, racquetball, sewing, tap dancing, urinalysis, vivisection, welding, xylophone playing, yo-yo playing, zoysia planting. Provide rationale for each of your choices.

Abilities

As we discussed in chapter 6, people inherit different levels of abilities that predispose them to the successful performance and learning of various tasks. For example, a person who inherits a high level of static balance (Fleishman, 1964) might be expected to have relatively more success, at least initially, in activities such as balance beam skills or handstands in gymnastics. There is little doubt that learners have an advantage if they have high levels of the abilities important to successful task performance. For those who don't, as well as for those whose abilities are impaired because of accident, illness, or genetic predisposition, one can make the performance goals less rigorous (see again the CARS goal-setting guidelines); in addition, more practice of the learning task may be necessary to ensure goal achievement.

Many people hold the common misconception that fundamental abilities can be improved by practicing various drills. Coaches sometimes use balancing drills in an attempt to increase athletes' general balancing ability or use eye-movement exercises to improve athletes' vision. The most popular drills seem to be the "quickening" exercises designed to improve athletes' quickness. If all of these activities accomplished what coaches think they do, it would be great news for the many athletes who would love to improve their balance, vision, or quickness. Unfortunately, evidence suggests that exercises such as these do little more than improve people's performance of the drills themselves.

stages of learning—Relatively distinct and sequential phases in the learning process; see verbal–cognitive stage, motor stage, and autonomous stage.

Stages of Learning

People also begin their learning experiences at various levels, or **stages of learning** (not to be confused with the stages of information processing discussed in chapter 2). As mentioned in chapter 1, a number of authors have discussed the concept of learning stages (Adams, 1971; Fitts & Posner, 1967; Gentile, 1972). Although authors propose different numbers of stages (either two or three) and call them by different names, the characteristics that authors assign to learners in the various stages are quite similar.

In this section, we discuss again the relatively distinct stages of the learning process in more detail and describe the distinguishing characteristics of learners in each. We say "relatively distinct" because there is some overlap between the stages, and learners occasionally demonstrate characteristics of different stages at different times. The three stages we discuss here are the verbal–cognitive stage, the motor stage, and the autonomous stage.

Verbal–Cognitive Stage

Learners in the verbal–cognitive stage are confronted with an entirely unfamiliar task. Their challenge, as Gentile (1972) suggested, is to get a general idea of the movement. For example, people trying to use a sailboard for the first time must learn how and where to stand, how to hold the sail, and how to balance. As they go through this stage, they might be fascinated (as Dick Schmidt was) simply by the many ways they can manage to fall off a sailboard!

As the label implies, learners in the verbal–cognitive stage spend a lot of time talking (verbal) to themselves about what they are trying to do and thinking (cognitive) about strategies that might work. Questions they tend to ask themselves deal with such issues as identifying the goal (i.e., What am I trying to accomplish?), deciding what to do or not do, figuring out how to perform the movement, perhaps determining when to perform it, and evaluating how well they did (i.e., What went wrong? Did I get that right?). Some learners engage in a great deal of self-talk during this stage, verbally guiding themselves through their actions. This activity demands a lot of attention and

Perceptual Learning and Conceptual Learning Often Accompany Motor Learning

During the early stage of skill learning, beginners sometimes need to experience the perceptual and conceptual elements of the skill as well as the general movement pattern. For example, a person learning to play racquetball might improve her perception of ball-flight characteristics by observing the way the ball moves within the confines of the court (e.g., rebound depending on speed, angle, and spin). Such perceptual learning would improve the learner's anticipation of the approaching ball and allow her to position herself in an optimal location for effective returns. A beginning tennis player may need to think about the racket as an extension of his arm before he is able to position himself for effective ground strokes. Once the player understands this concept, he will begin to allow for that extra length when setting up for his shots and, as a result, will make more frequent ball contact with the strings of the racket rather than with the shaft (Moen, 1989).

prevents learners from processing other information, such as appropriate strategies and the elements of proper form. Although verbal–cognitive activity can help learners grasp the general idea of the skill, this activity begins to drop out as learners become more experienced with the task. As might be expected, verbal and cognitive abilities dominate this initial stage of learning. Therefore, people who are good at figuring out what to do and how to go about doing it have a distinct advantage at this point.

Gains in performance proficiency in this stage tend to be rather large and to occur rapidly, indicating that people quickly discover and use more effective strategies for performance. However, teachers and therapists should expect the performance of beginners to also be halting, jerky, uncertain, and poorly timed to objects and events in the external environment.

Instructions, demonstrations, and other types of verbal and visual information (discussed in chapter 8) are particularly beneficial for learners in this stage. One goal of instruction is to help learners see how something they have learned or experienced in the past is similar in some way to the new skill they are trying to learn. Practitioners can capitalize on the concept of transfer by pointing out the similarity of elements in previously learned tasks and ones in the new task. In another vein, a demonstration or visual model can provide learners with a picture of the desired movement pattern, which they can then attempt to reproduce with their own actions.

Motor Stage

Eventually, learners progress to the motor stage. Having solved most of the strategic or cognitive challenges and having achieved a general idea of what the movement is, they now shift their focus to refining the skill by organizing more effective movement patterns (Nourrit, Delignières, Caillou, Deschamps, & Lauriot, 2003). For example, studying movement organization, Landers and colleagues (1995) found that systematic changes in brain-wave patterns accompanied skill improvements in participants' learning the sport of archery. Fitts and Posner (1967) called this stage the associative stage, and Gentile (1972) labeled it the fixation/diversification stage, suggesting that the learner's focus is on a variety of processes necessary for skill refinement. When Dick Schmidt reached this stage in his sailboarding experience, he displayed a much more consistent stance and control, his confidence improved, and he started to work on the finer details of the task.

closed skill—
A skill performed in an environment that is predictable or stationary and that allows performers to plan their movements in advance.

open skill—
A skill performed in an environment that is unpredictable or in motion and that requires performers to adapt their movements in response to dynamic properties of the environment.

A person's skill refinement is slightly different for quick movements than for slower ones. If the skill requires a rapid action (e.g., performing the tennis stroke, swinging a cricket bat, beating an egg, chopping vegetables), the learner begins to refine the motor program for accomplishing movement requirements. If the skill involves slower movements (e.g., balancing in gymnastics, steering a car, cross-country skiing, threading a needle), the learner becomes more adept at processing and using movement-produced feedback to control the action. Similarly, this refinement will be different for **closed skills** (e.g., golf, bowling, chopping wood) than for **open skills** (e.g., soccer, cricket, white-water rafting), which, as discussed before, depend on different processes. For example, if movements are performed in a predictable environment, learners can fixate on reproducing the same actions each time. However, if movements must be adapted to meet the demands of a changing environment, learners must find a way to diversify their actions in response to varied environmental conditions.

Several factors change markedly during the motor stage, most of which are associated with producing more effective movement patterns. Learners demonstrate more consistency as their strategies for skill refinement become more sophisticated and their movements become more grooved and stable. They are more efficient in producing their movements; at times they appear to be performing almost effortlessly. Self-talk is less frequent. As learners discover regularities in the environment (e.g., the speed of an approaching ball, the tendencies of an opponent to do certain things at certain times), their anticipation and timing develop, making their movements appear smoother and less rushed. In addition, performers begin to monitor their own feedback and become adept at detecting their own errors.

This stage generally lasts considerably longer than the verbal–cognitive stage, perhaps for several years, or even decades if the task is extremely complex. At the same time, instructional assistance and feedback become somewhat less important. When feedback is provided, it is best if it is precise and targets those aspects of the movement that the learner is attempting to refine, as well as providing some possible ways of attaining success.

Autonomous Stage

After extensive practice, some learners may enter the autonomous stage, where they are able to produce their actions almost automatically with little or no attention (see chapter 3). These highly skilled performers have developed capabilities to control action for increasingly long periods of time (e.g., in dance). As a result, they don't have to think about every component of the skill when they are performing. For example, an accomplished gymnast is able to run off several seconds of a high-bar routine or a skilled typist or concert pianist produces longer strings of words or notes. By programming longer sequences, highly skilled performers don't have to initiate the program so often, which consequently diminishes the demands on their attention (see chapter 2). Although our first author Dick Schmidt never quite entered the autonomous stage in sailboarding, he has seen other performers who have clearly reached this stage, displaying very skillful sail handling in high winds, with plenty of attention left over to contemplate strategies for a race or determine creative ways to surf large waves.

As the label implies, learners in the autonomous stage also demonstrate increased automaticity in their sensory analysis of environmental patterns. For example, highly skilled taxi drivers recognize subtle characteristics of traffic flow patterns, expert white-water rafters notice shifts in water currents and the presence of potential obstacles, and advanced open-skill sport performers (e.g., squash players) identify aspects of their opponents' movements that indicate the use of a particular strategy. This capability frees the best performers to engage in higher-order cognitive activities, such as split-second shifts in strategy during a basketball game or spontaneous adjustments in the form or style of a movement in dance or in figure skating.

During the autonomous stage, self-confidence increases, and the capability of detecting errors in one's movements becomes highly developed. Confident individuals engage in very little self-talk while performing. In fact, to prevent performance breakdowns, they need to avoid focusing on their movements (e.g., a concert violinist would likely falter if she began to analyze her finger and arm movements). More productive self-talk might, however, be devoted to higher-order aspects of the task (e.g., a figure skater might remind herself to add emphasis or expression during the performance of a jazz dance routine).

Performance improvements are more difficult to detect during this stage because performers are nearing the limits of their skill potential. However, the quality of their movements can be characterized by increased automaticity (or automatic processing), reduced physical and mental effort, and improved style and form. For example, the best bricklayer in the United States is determined by an annual contest that measures performance in terms of the time it takes to set up the mason's station, the number of bricks laid in one hour, and the number of voids in mortar joints ("Illinois Mason Wins," 2005). Because individuals have achieved high levels of skill does not mean that their learning in the autonomous stage is over. This fact was perhaps best illustrated in a classic industrial study conducted by Crossman (1959). In that study, the performance of production-line workers in a cigar factory was examined over a 7-year period; the time required for these workers to make each cigar continued to decrease even after approximately 10 million repetitions! Obviously, the task of the movement practitioner is much more subtle when he or she is working with performers in the autonomous stage of learning than when assisting individuals in the earlier stages.

It Depends . . .

How Might You Individualize Instruction for Three Different Learners?

Assume that three of your friends have asked you to teach them a skill with which you are familiar. The first person has considerable previous experience performing the skill, the second has a modest level of experience and can perform some of the basic actions, and the third has no experience with the skill at all. These individuals are obviously at different stages of learning. Explain two things you would do to create a beneficial learning experience for each person. Provide rationale for each of your suggestions.

ASSESSING PROGRESS

To determine the effectiveness of instruction and provide feedback, we must be able to assess learners' progress. Two important issues related to these assessments are the goals of the learner and the aspects of performance that best indicate skill level. Because much motor learning takes place with particular goals in mind, assessments of progress are made in a way that indicates something about the level of goal achievement. And because learning must be inferred from performance observations, practitioners must assess those aspects of performance that accurately reflect goal achievement. In the case of the stroke patient, the therapist may decide to simulate various environmental situations (e.g., the patient's home) and then assess the patient's **skill** in entering rooms, opening doors, moving on various types of surfaces (e.g., gravel, tile, hardwood floors, carpet, grass, asphalt pavement), and navigating around a variety of obstacles (e.g., chair, table, bed).

skill—
The underlying potential for performance in a given task, which changes with practice, experience, and a host of situational and environmental factors.

When assessing progress, effective movement practitioners ask, "How does the assessment I am about to conduct indicate the progress this person has (or has not) made toward achieving her or his intended goal?" To conduct effective assessments, practitioners must identify valid indicators of skill, obtain observable products of learning, and determine when and how often to assess progress.

Measuring Motor Learning

By far, the most common method for evaluating motor learning—both in the laboratory and in practice—is through the use of performance curves (sometimes called learning curves). An example from a study by Young and Schmidt (1992) is shown in figure 7.3. In this study, participants performed a computer-based laboratory task that simulated hitting a pitched ball. Each point in figure 7.3 represents the mean (i.e., average) score of a group of participants. Scores could have been plotted for each trial in a practice session or for groups of trials averaged together in blocks as was done in figure 7.3. Performance can be recorded for individual performers as well, showing the progress made over several weeks of practice.

These curves have been common in research studies since learning was first studied scientifically in the late 1800s. It has been tempting to regard the shape of these curves—steep at first and more gradual later—as a way to evaluate the learning that has occurred. Recently, though, it has become clear that these curves are not very effective for evaluating the amount of learning that takes place as a result of practice. These curves are not so much learning curves as they are performance curves, in that they simply plot a person's (or a group's) performance on each of a series of practice attempts. Of course, performance on a task is determined not only by the level of learning that has been achieved but also by any number of factors that influence performance only temporarily. So, the changes in performance we see may not necessarily tell us much about what the person has learned.

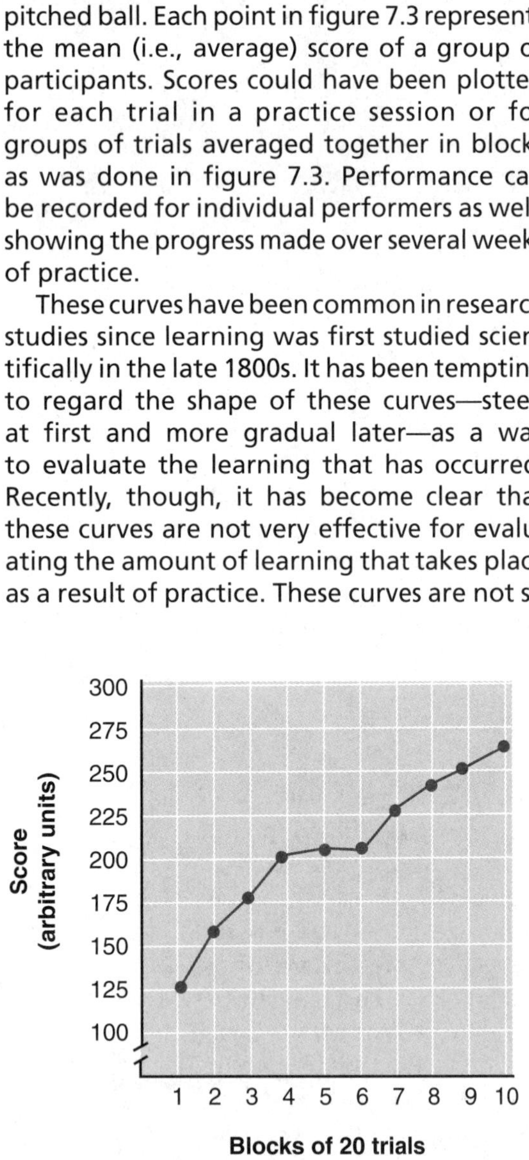

Figure 7.3 Performance curves depicting the average performance as a function of practice for a group of participants. (Reprinted from Young & Schmidt, 1992.)

Many factors during practice can influence performance temporarily. Fatigue associated with effortful practice or boredom from practicing too long can depress performance temporarily, resulting in lower scores that underestimate the level of learning. Giving motivational instructions or encouragement, allowing repeated attempts of the same action, or giving feedback about performance can elevate performance temporarily, resulting in higher scores that overestimate the level of learning. These factors alter the shapes or heights of the curves, or both, giving a false picture of the amount that the person has actually learned.

When scientists study learning, they are interested in the factors that produce relatively permanent gains in performance. We generally regard these gains as accurate reflections of what a performer has learned—not simply the temporary changes caused by motivation or fatigue that can be obliterated with rest or the passage of time. To determine actual learning, scientists use so-called transfer or retention designs. Here, performance is evaluated during an acquisition phase; then, usually on the day following the end of acquisition, learning is assessed with a delayed transfer or retention test that mimics the transfer context of interest. The idea is that the delay allows the temporary effects from the acquisition phase to dissipate, revealing only the level of (relatively permanent) learning that remains.

Let's say we want to compare two methods of practicing a skill to determine the effect of each on learning—some new method compared with an old method for learning a task involving hitting a target. Note in figure 7.4 that the new method results in more target hits during the practice phase (i.e., the first 10 blocks of trials) than does the old method. But is this because the new method is better for learning or because it has just influenced performance temporarily? We can determine the answer by examining performance on a retention test given on the next day under the same conditions for each group.

Three possible outcomes on this retention test are shown in the figure. The first shows that the performance of the two groups was almost the same as in acquisition; here, we conclude that the new method influenced learning and not just performance during practice. The second case shows that the new and old methods produced the same level of retention performance. Here, we conclude that the new method affected performance only temporarily, in that all of the advantage demonstrated during practice dissipated over rest; the new method had no advantage over the old method in terms of learning. Finally, the third case involves a blend, where some of the advantage was temporary and some was relatively permanent.

These results are typical of research studies examining the effects of different methods on the learning of two or more groups of performers. But the approach can be applied equally well to individual learners. Measures intended to reflect the relative amount a performer has learned (e.g., for grading purposes) are not very meaningful if they are taken during practice or when temporary factors are operating (e.g., fatigue) that might change the level of performance only temporarily. Rather, the best way to evaluate learning is to have performers practice on one day and then assess their performance on another day, preferably under conditions close to those for which the skill practice is actually intended (i.e., the target context).

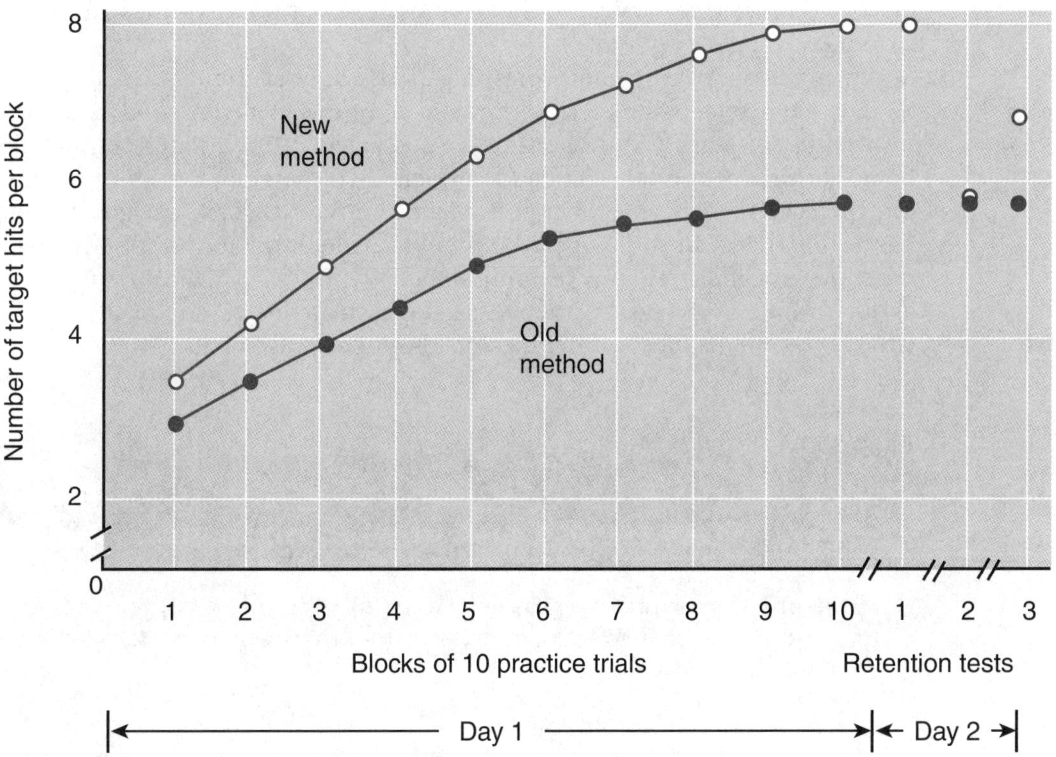

Figure 7.4 Retention tests showing several possible learning effects of initial practice.

Selecting Valid Indicators of Skill

Once the learner and the practitioner have clearly determined the goals of learning, they must then decide which aspects of performance or target behaviors to evaluate to determine the learner's progress. To be of any value, target behaviors must first be valid indicators of the desired action. A measure is valid if the score informs the practitioner about the aspect of performance that was intended. For example, valid measures of archery skill might be the distance of the arrows from the center of the target and the tightness of a grouping of arrows. A less valid measure might be how much time was required to shoot 10 arrows. Valid measures also reflect something about the learner's capability of producing the desired skill in a particular context. The target context for someone who is learning archery might be a particular competition, either simulated or real.

Practitioners who identify appropriate target behaviors and select valid measures of performance are in the best position to assess learners' progress. Practitioners can choose from two categories of performance measures: outcome measures and process measures.

outcome measures—Performance observations indicative of the end result of performance.

Outcome Measures

Outcome measures indicate something about the results of a person's movements (e.g., a 100 m dash time of 11 s or a year of taxi driving without an accident). Outcome measures might include measures of time (e.g., how long it takes to perform the movement), distance (e.g., how high or far the person moves), frequency (e.g., number of successful attempts), accuracy (e.g., how close to the center of the target an object lands), and consistency (e.g., the percentage of attempts that hit the target). In the example of a stroke patient, outcome measures might be the time it takes the person to move from her car to the front door of her house or the number of stops she makes to adjust her walker.

When assessing the outcomes of younger learners, practitioners may need to modify their scoring systems to detect performance improvements. A good example comes from a study (Bennett, Button, Kingsbury, & Davids, 1999) that examined the one-hand catching performance of children (ages 9-10 years). In this study, performance outcome was scored using a 5-point system: 5 = clean catch, 4 = juggle and catch, 3 = hand contact and drop, 2 = upper-body contact and drop, 1 = lower-body contact and drop, 0 = no contact. For any learning situation, effective practitioners think carefully about the outcome measures they select and evaluate them periodically to determine which ones are the most valid indicators of skill improvements.

Questions to Ask Before Attempting to Assess Learners' Progress

Assessing the progress of learners is not a simple task for movement practitioners. Before conducting a performance assessment, practitioners can consider the following questions:

- What are the learner's goals?
- What am I going to learn from this performance assessment?
- What is the learner going to learn from this assessment?
- How am I going to use the information I obtain from this assessment to assist the learner in achieving his or her goals?

The Woodchoppers' Contest

What are the characteristics of skilled performance? This is a question movement practitioners need to answer to assess learners' progress. An entertaining fable (Johnson, 1961) relates the story of a group of citizens in a small town in the great northern woods who came face to face with this question. It seems that a considerable debate existed among the townspeople as to which of two highly skilled individuals was the most skilled wood chopper in the land. To determine the true champion, the townspeople decided to hold a contest. The first test was of speed. Each contestant attempted to split 10 cords of wood in the shortest time possible. As it turned out, the two choppers struck their final blows at exactly the same moment. The second test was of accuracy. Contestants alternately tried their hand at splitting everything from straws to buckshot. Again, the result was a draw. Next, the choppers were tested for efficiency. Each was given all the wood he wanted and told "Chop till you drop!" As with the first two tests, the outcome was declared a tie. Just when it appeared there would be no winner, a bearded old sage stepped forward and suggested a final test. The sage correctly pointed out that in all of the previous tests, the woodchoppers had performed standard cutting tasks using their own axes. "Now," the sage said, "let's see how adaptable they are." So the combatants were required to chop wood of various lengths, under various conditions, using a variety of axes. Under these conditions, the contest was finally decided. One of the men chopped masterfully under all of the required conditions, whereas the other was able to do no better than would be expected of any ordinary woodchopper, allowing a winner to be declared. Therefore, the moral of the fable is that for some types of skilled performance, one defining characteristic is adaptability, or generalizability.

This point was recently illustrated in a real-world contest to determine the most skilled operator of a heavy construction machine, called the Toolcat 5600 ("Contractor Wins Toolcat Challenge Contest," 2005). Competitors attempted a variety of landscaping, construction, and farm tasks, including lifting objects, such as logs, rocks, and hay bales, and maneuvering in confined spaces. While contestants were attempting to complete the tasks, heavy rain soaked the course and mud became a factor. One of the entrants commented, "Competing in the rain really added to the list of experiences that a person would encounter if operating a Toolcat machine on a daily basis" (p. 1). As was the case for the mythical woodchoppers, the winner of the Toolcat contest needed to adapt his skill to meet the demands of more challenging environmental conditions.

Process Measures

Process measures indicate something about the quality of the actions themselves (i.e., the extent to which movements are performed correctly, accurately, and efficiently). In the laboratory or the therapy clinic, movement scientists or therapists can use sophisticated instrumentation, such as **electromyography (EMG)**, which measures patterns of muscle electrical activity, or **electroencephalography (EEG)**, which measures brain electrical activity. If adequate instrumentation is available, instructors or therapists can examine changes in a variety of movement characteristics as they occur with practice or with improvements in a performer's skill.

In most practical learning situations, sophisticated instruments are not available, however. Even if they are, the equipment may not be portable enough to allow assessments of movement quality in the target context (e.g., at home, at the mall, at a music recital, during a squash competition). Therefore, practitioners typically use less precise alternatives such as subjective ratings of movement form (e.g., a tennis instructor's rating of a learner's form during the serve).

process measures—
Performance observations that indicate something about the quality of movement production; they can involve the use of sophisticated instrumentation or the subjective evaluation of an expert.

electromyography (EMG)—
A method for recording the electrical activity in a muscle or group of muscles.

electroencephalography (EEG)—
A method for recording the electrical activity in various regions of the brain.

Skilled practitioners (e.g., instructors, therapists, coaches, or human factors engineers) who are able to observe learners' movements directly or on videotape can judge the quality of those movements. To ensure that the process measures they select are valid, effective practitioners first identify the components of the learners' movements that reflect the target behavior most accurately. See table 7.4 for an example of criteria a therapist might use to assess the quality of a person's gait (Knudson & Morrison, 1997). For a sport skill such as the volleyball spike, a coach might use the following form criteria to assess movement quality: a fast approach, a forceful arm swing at takeoff, rotation of the body away from the ball before contact, a forceful arm swing into the ball, a high contact point, wrist flexion during contact, and a two-foot landing (Wilkerson, 1988). Practitioners then need to discover the best means of observing those components (e.g., front view, side view, back view) and of scoring them (e.g., rating and summing individual movement components or assigning an overall form rating).

Table 7.4 Movement Criteria for Assessing Human Gait

Criterion	Cues to watch for
Minimal sway	Positions body over base of support
Arm opposition	Uses opposite arm or leg
Minimal rise	Makes smooth recovery, smooth push-off
Cushioning	Gives with the leg
Leg support	Pushes down and backward
Push-off	Presses with toes

Adapted from Knudson and Morrison, 1997.

Measuring Aiming Movements

Some motor tasks require performers to produce movements that project objects toward targets (e.g., archery, darts, fly-fishing, skeet shooting, tennis and volleyball serving). One way practitioners can evaluate learners' progress in these tasks is to examine the spatial accuracy of their attempts. The most common measures are arbitrary scores that indicate how far objects (e.g., arrows, darts) are from the center of the target; the closer to the center, the higher the point value. In addition to this global measure of accuracy, other methods are available to assess the pattern of learners' performance.

For tasks such as dart throwing, where a series of throws is attempted and then the score is calculated, practitioners can examine visually and perhaps record the spatial configuration of the darts. Figure 7.5 shows a spatial configuration of five darts that have landed above the target center. If there is time for more precise measurement, the practitioner could determine the exact extent of unidimensional (in this case above or below the target) directional bias and inconsistency of the spatial configuration of the darts. The practitioner might draw a horizontal line through the center of the target to distinguish attempts that land above the bull's-eye from attempts that land below the bull's-eye. For the example shown in figure 7.5, all darts are assigned a positive value because they all landed above the line. If any darts had landed below the line, they would have been assigned a negative value.

The practitioner would measure the distance of each point from the line and calculate the average **constant error (CE)** by adding the values and dividing the total by the number of darts thrown. In the figure 7.5 example, the CE value is +3 in. (7.6 cm; see the arithmetic for this example in table 7.5). This means that the thrower's configuration of darts has a positive (i.e., above the bull's-eye) directional bias of 3 in. (7.6 cm) on average. Other examples of CE might be a golf putter who, on average, misses 3 in. (7.6 cm) to the left of the hole. Average CE is the average location of the results of several movement attempts (e.g., three putts that stop an average of 2.8 in. [7.1 cm] to the left of the hole).

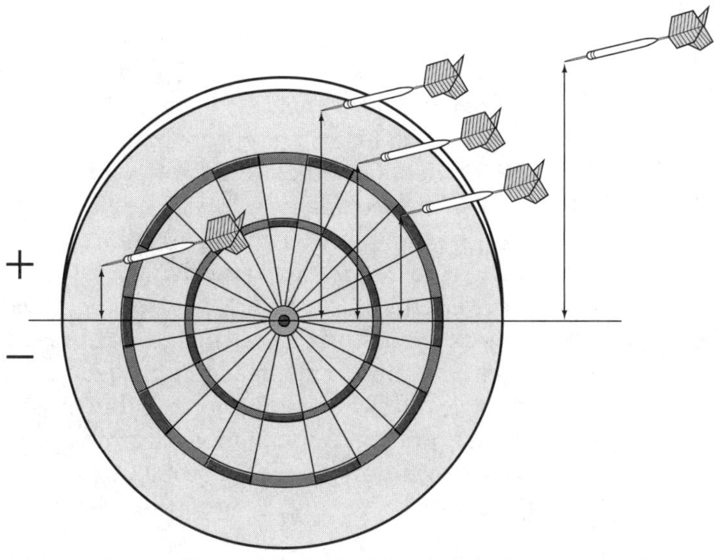

Figure 7.5 Error measures such as constant error and variable error can provide useful information about the direction and inconsistency of a learner's performance outcomes.

To determine the spread, or variability, of the grouping of darts, the practitioner would calculate **variable error (VE)** by (a) subtracting the average CE from each value, (b) squaring each difference, (c) adding the squared differences, (d) dividing that total by the number of attempts, and (e) taking the square root of that number. The result (i.e., VE) would be the standard deviation of the performer's throws (in this case approximately 1.4 in., or 3.6 cm) about her average CE (in this case 3 in., or 7.6 cm). Three golf putts with an average CE of 0 in. (0 cm) and a VE of 5 in. (12.7 cm) would be more variable than three golf putts with an average CE of +2.8 in. (7.1 cm) and a VE of 1 in. (2.5 cm); put another way, the higher the VE value, the less consistent the person's performance.

The practitioner might then use this information to instruct the learner to change her release point or perhaps apply less force when attempting her next series of dart throws. By keeping a record of periodic changes in the CE and VE of the learner's throws, the practitioner and the learner could determine what adjustments to make to most dramatically reduce bias (i.e., CE) and inconsistency (i.e., VE).

Table 7.5 Arithmetic Calculations of Average Constant Error (CE) and Variable Error (VE) for the Dart Throwing Example in Figure 7.5

Attempt	CE	VE
1	+5	$(+5) - (3) = 2^2 = 4$
2	+3	$(+3) - (3) = 0^2 +0$
3	+4	$(+4) - (3) = 1^2 =1$
4	+1	$(+1) - (3) = -2^2 = 4$
5	+2	$(+2) - (3) = -1^2 =1$
	Average CE = +15/5 = 3	$VE = \sqrt{10/5} = \sqrt{2} = 1.4$

constant error (CE)—The deviation, with respect to amount and direction, of the result of a performer's movement relative to some target value. Average constant error is the average value of several movement attempts.

variable error (VE)—The inconsistency of results of several movements with respect to a performer's average constant error for the movements.

stimulus-identification stage—The first stage of information processing; during this stage, the input is recognized and identified.

response-selection stage—The second stage of information processing; during this stage, it is decided which response, if any, should be made.

response-programming stage—The third stage of information processing; during this stage, the motor system is organized to produce the desired movement.

motor program—A set of motor commands that is prestructured at the executive level and that defines the essential details of a skilled action; analogous to a central pattern generator.

Some of the Observable Products of Learning

Learning can occur at all levels of the central nervous system, but the levels highlighted in figure 7.6 are probably the ones where the biggest changes take place. Some examples of improvements occurring in these areas are (a) the increased use of automatic processes in analyzing sensory patterns (**stimulus-identification stage**) that indicate the activity of external objects or events (e.g., the speed of an approaching object, the movements of other performers); (b) the improved selection (**response-selection stage**) and parameterization (**response-programming stage**) of movements (e.g., a shot on goal in ice hockey, driving a car in heavy traffic); and (c) the development of more effective **motor programs** for very rapid actions (e.g., a golf swing).

When practitioners see changes in observable performance characteristics, they can infer that improvements have occurred at one or more of these levels and, therefore, in the learner's performance capability or skill. A number of observable characteristics change over the course of motor learning (Magill, 1998a). In the following paragraphs, we briefly summarize each of these and suggest some ways practitioners might examine them when assessing the progress of learners.

Knowledge of Concepts

One characteristic of skilled performers is an understanding of the rules, strategies, and finer points of the activity. An advanced or expanded knowledge of these concepts allows accomplished performers to assess task demands, determine the most appropriate actions, and effectively analyze the results of their performance. Put simply, skilled learners have a more sophisticated conceptual understanding of what's going on and what needs to be done compared with beginners, who may be able to comprehend a number of isolated facts but are not able to integrate them in a meaningful way (Housner, 1981; McPherson, 1999; Ward & Williams, 2003). As learners' knowledge improves, the instructor should be able to detect more rapid and appropriate decision making. One way to measure this is by charting the types and number of correct decisions (e.g., a basketball player taking the shot when he is open) or response-selection errors (e.g., forcing the shot when not open) that learners make while performing in the target context.

Control and Coordination

The movements of skilled performers are characterized by a smoothness that suggests more efficient control and fluid coordination of joints and muscles. Research examining changes in control and coordination shows that performers' movements become less stiff with increased practice. In one study, Southard and Higgins (1987) examined changes in the coordination pattern of learners' backswings for the racquetball forehand shot. Initially, the pattern was characterized by similar limb velocities for the upper arm and forearm and by comparable joint angles at the elbow and wrist. After 10 days of practice, however, the pattern showed a higher limb velocity in the forearm than in the upper arm (indicating a more whiplike action) and an increase in the range of joint angles at both the elbow and wrist. As learners' control and coordination improve, instructors should notice an increase in the speed and smoothness of their movements. Many expert practitioners can assess these characteristics by using form ratings (Knudson & Morrison, 1997). In addition, an excellent reference for identifying the observable coordination patterns of classes of movements is Carr's (2004) *Sport Mechanics for Coaches, Second Edition*.

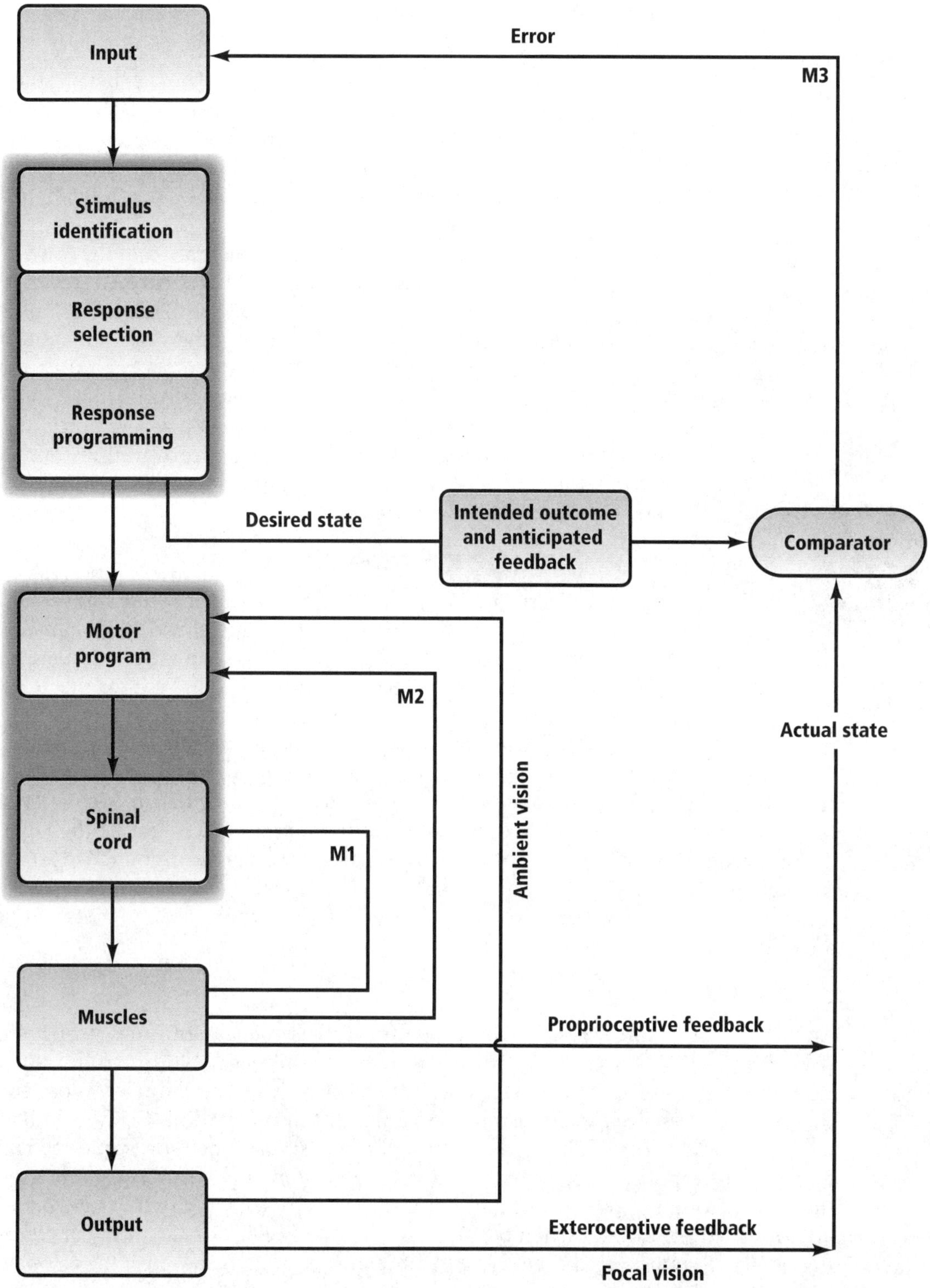

Figure 7.6 The conceptual model of motor performance, highlighting some of the major processes subject to alterations during practice.

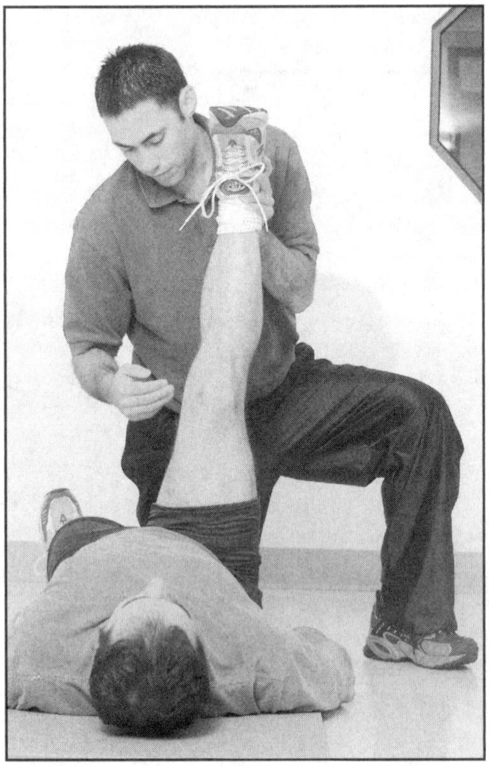

A therapist can measure a patient's range of motion and observe improvement in limb flexibility.

Muscles Used

Changes in the patterns of muscle activity also occur over practice. EMG studies have typically shown that, initially, learners demonstrate a pattern of muscular activity characterized by the simultaneous contraction of agonist muscles (i.e., those that produce the action) and antagonist muscles (i.e., those that oppose the action), sometimes referred to as co-contraction. This type of activity is somewhat analogous to driving a car with one foot on the brake and the other on the accelerator at the same time. With practice, however, the pattern shifts to one of sequential contraction (i.e., accelerating and then braking), with agonists and antagonists contracting only at the appropriate and necessary times (Moore & Marteniuk, 1986). Behaviorally, learners' movements appear more fluid over practice as the amount of co-contraction is diminished. Again, form ratings may be the best way for practitioners to assess the smoothness of muscle contractions.

Movement Efficiency

Not surprisingly, the energy costs of learners' movements diminish with practice (Gaina & Sparrow, 2006; Sparrow & Irizarry-Lopez, 1987) as control, coordination, and muscle activity patterns become more efficient. Perhaps this is one reason that accomplished individuals are able to perform effectively for extended periods of time (e.g., skilled bricklayers). Behaviorally, performers should appear progressively less fatigued during performance bouts or be able to sustain their movements for longer time periods. A possible outcome measure of efficiency might be the length of time people are able to continue performing a standard amount of activity. Practitioners might also ask individuals to rate their perceived exertion at the end of a learning session, particularly when task performance includes a significant endurance component.

Attention

An important characteristic of skilled performers is their attentional proficiency (Abernethy, 1993). Accomplished performers not only are able to sustain attention for longer periods but also are adept at identifying and attending to those cues that are most essential to successful performance (Shim, Carlton, & Kwon, 2006). Behavioral indicators of changed attentional processes include more rapid recognition of and response to complex patterns of environmental stimuli (e.g., different movements of an opponent, unfamiliar traffic patterns, playing with a new band), an unhurried appearance when performing open skills, and the capability of adjusting quickly to unexpected events (e.g., a tire blowout at high speed on the freeway). Practitioners might assess the progress of learners by measuring their reaction times in particular situations or by subjectively rating their overall recognition capability during a performance bout.

As performers improve their skills, the attention demands of their movements also diminish as control is shifted to more automatic processes. Such reductions are often evidenced by more free-flowing and fluid movements and by the capacity to do several things at once. Recent research on closed skills such as golf putting (Vickers, 1992), basketball free throw shooting (Vickers, 1997), and billiards (Williams, Singer, & Frehlich, 2002) indicates that preparatory visual fixations just before movement execution are longer for higher-skilled performers than for those possessing lower levels of skill. Thus, it appears that eye-movement recordings (e.g., duration and direction of visual focus) may be another effective means of assessing changes in performers' visual attention during skill learning.

As performers improve their skills, the attention demands of their movements diminish, and their capacity to do several things at the same time increases.

Error Detection and Correction

As learners become more proficient in producing their movements, they also become more adept at recognizing and correcting their own errors (Liu & Wrisberg, 1997). Errors may be attributable to faulty movement selection (e.g., a dancer confuses or transposes several parts of a sequence) or improper execution of the intended action (e.g., a diver fails to completely extend the arms before entry into the water). With practice, learners begin to pay more attention to relevant feedback information, both proprioceptive (e.g., joint position) and exteroceptive (e.g., vision and audition), which allows them to detect performance errors (e.g., the sight, sound, and feel of an errant shot in darts, tennis, or ice hockey). Behaviorally, people performing continuous skills (e.g., driving a car, in-line skating, skiing) should demonstrate the capacity to adjust their movements more effectively during the course of the action. Participants who perform discrete skills (e.g., kicking, throwing, striking) should be able to assess their mistakes accurately after the movement is completed and explain how they intend to correct the error on the next attempt.

Deciding When and How Often to Assess Progress

There are no simple, fixed rules for determining when and how often to assess the progress of learners. As we mentioned previously, the best evaluations are those conducted in contexts similar to the ones where the learned action must be produced eventually (e.g., at home for the patient, in a jam session for the musician, in a mixed-doubles match for the tennis player). Therefore, skilled practitioners attempt to simulate the target context as much as possible when assessing learners' progress. They are also aware of temporary factors (e.g., mood, fatigue, weather conditions) that might alter learners' performance and distort learning assessments, so they evaluate performance under

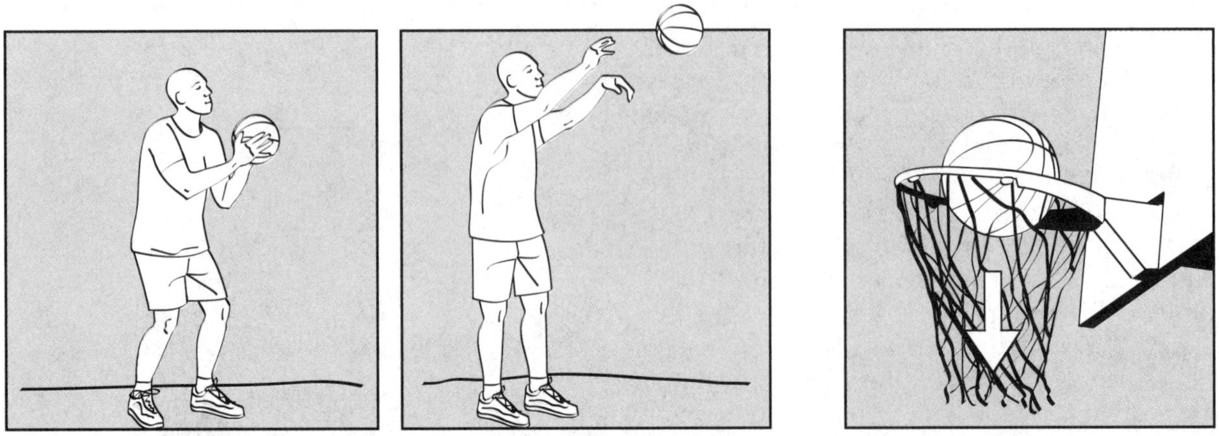

Figure 7.7 Effective practitioners obtain both process and outcome measures when assessing learners' progress.

conditions that minimize the influence of such factors. In all cases, the practitioner's goal is to evaluate performers under circumstances that allow the most valid assessments of skill.

To some extent, decisions about when and how often to assess a person's skill depend on the needs of the individual learner. Some learners may wish to have an initial assessment of their performance to determine which areas require particular attention and to serve as a reference point for subsequent evaluations. The best time for initial assessment is probably after the learner acquires the basic capability of producing the goal movement. After that, practitioners might conduct periodic evaluations using both process and outcome measures (see figure 7.7) to determine the effectiveness of instructional interventions and to provide learners with helpful information about their progress toward goal achievement.

SUMMARY

Learning experiences take many forms. Skilled movement practitioners are aware of a number of factors when attempting to design experiences that are beneficial for learners. Two concepts that are helpful when preparing for learning experiences are goal setting and transfer of learning. Once learners know which movements they want to be able to perform (target skills) and where they want to be able to perform them (target context), the process of goal setting can begin. Some of the key ingredients of effective goal setting are summarized as follows:

- Learners have input in the goal-setting process.
- Goals serve as road maps to successful performance of the target skills in the target contexts.
- Goals are challenging, attainable, realistic, and specific (CARS).
- Learners are encouraged to set performance goals (focused on self-referenced improvement) and process goals (focused on correct movement execution) in addition to outcome goals (focused on the achievement of some external standard of performance or favorable comparisons with other performers).

To enhance transfer of learning, practitioners might do the following things:

- Direct learners' attention to elements of previously learned tasks that may be similar to those of the target skill.
- Provide opportunities for learners to practice other tasks that contain elements that are similar to those of the target skill.
- Allow learners to practice the target skill in situations that are similar to the target context.

Learners differ with respect to their level of motivation, past experience, abilities, and stage of learning. Instructors can maximize each person's learning experience by

- designing experiences that are relevant to the needs and interests of the learner,
- designing experiences that allow the learner to achieve goals,
- encouraging the learner to focus on his or her own skill improvements rather than on the improvements of others, and
- considering the person's stage of learning when providing instructional assistance.

When assessing learners' progress, effective practitioners select measures that

- represent observable characteristics of the target skill,
- are valid indicators of goal achievement,
- reflect both outcome and process features of the target skill, and
- provide learners with meaningful feedback about their skill improvements and level of goal achievement.

FROM PRINCIPLES TO PRACTICE

Check your comprehension of the concepts and terms discussed in this chapter by completing each of the exercises in the following sections. The first section contains several activities designed to test your working knowledge of key terms. The second section consists of a variety of exercises designed to check your understanding of key concepts. In the third section you are challenged to apply your knowledge by discussing a defensible solution for two different situations.

Know Your Key Terms

Matching: Measuring Performance

Match the following terms with their respective categories or definitions by placing the most appropriate letter on each of the blanks below.

Measuring Performance—Terms

a. constant error
b. process measure
c. valid measure
d. variable error
e. outcome measure
f. movement efficiency
g. muscle activity

Measuring Performance—Category or Definition

_____ 1. Might be evaluated by obtaining ratings of perceived exertion following a performance bout

_____ 2. Used to evaluate the end result of a performance

_____ 3. Most accurately assessed with electromyography (EMG)

_____ 4. Used to determine the direction of a performer's outcome errors

_____ 5. Allows the practitioner to make an accurate inference about a learner's skill level

_____ 6. Used to evaluate the quality of movement production

_____ 7. Used to determine the inconsistency of a performer's outcome errors

Consider: Target Skills and Target Behaviors

For each of the following movement activities list a target skill and an appropriate target behavior. Provide rationales for your answers.

1. Ice hockey ______________________________

____

2. Volleyball ______________________________

____

3. Rugby ______________________________

____

4. Waterskiing ______________________________

____

Fill in the Blank: Stages of Learning

Complete the following sentences:

The stages of learning are ______________ ________ ________, because some overlap usually exists between them. In the ______________ stage, gains in performance tend to be somewhat large. According to Gentile (1972), the primary goal of learners in this stage is to get a __________ __________ of the movement. The motor stage of learning is primarily devoted to the task of __________ __________ and to meeting the particular demands of the performance environment. After extensive practice, some learners enter the __________ stage of learning, where they are able enjoy the advantage of diminished __________ __________ for movement production.

Check Your Understanding

1. What are four important goal-setting principles practitioners might keep in mind when assisting someone wanting to learn a particular skill? How might a practitioner apply each of the principles in assisting a person who wants to learn how to roller-skate?
2. Discuss the relationships among target skills, target behaviors, and target contexts. For one of the following activities, give an example of a target skill, a target behavior, and a target context: fly-fishing, billiards, using a prosthetic hand while eating a baked potato, piloting an airplane, shooting a basketball.
3. Sometimes people's past movement experiences can help them pick up a new skill more quickly. Select one of the following pairs of motor tasks and give an example of a motor element, a perceptual element, and a conceptual element that might be a feature of both tasks: white-water canoeing and snow skiing, operating an automobile and operating a speedboat, playing wheelchair basketball and playing wheelchair floor hockey.
4. When assessing learners' progress, practitioners may select both outcome and process measures that are valid indicators of performance. Give an example of a valid outcome measure and a valid process measure for one of the following activities: hang gliding, playing bocce, rappelling, operating a lathe, reading Braille, playing the flute, shuffling a deck of playing cards, hitting a tennis volley.

Apply Your Knowledge

Exercise 1

A friend of yours wants to learn how to perform a cartwheel. To assist your friend, see if you can estimate the relevance of each of the following aspects of the target skill: information-processing demands, target behaviors, target context, movement elements, perceptual elements, and conceptual elements. Once you have completed this task, see if you can come up with one outcome goal and one process goal that might satisfy the CARS criteria and benefit your friend. Finally, for each of those goals, suggest a valid outcome measure or process measure that your friend might obtain to determine her progress toward goal achievement. Provide a rationale for your recommendations and furnish two supporting references.

Exercise 2

A wheelchair patient, paralyzed from the waist down, wants to obtain his driver's license. He has purchased a car that has the necessary control devices for safe operation and has solicited your assistance in helping him achieve his outcome goal. You realize that successful outcomes are the product of effective performance. Indicate how you might discuss each of the following concepts with this person: information-processing demands, target behaviors, and target context. Suggest three target behaviors on which the person might focus during practice sessions, and for each, describe one process goal or one outcome goal that would indicate successful performance. For each goal, propose one process measure or outcome measure you might use to evaluate skill improvements. Provide a rationale for your answers and furnish two supporting references.

chapter 8

Supplementing the Learning Experience

▷ Chapter Outline

▷ Chapter Objectives

When you have completed this chapter, you should be able to

- discuss instructional techniques that movement practitioners can use to supplement people's learning experiences and assist them during practice sessions,
- explain the concepts of attentional control and arousal regulation and describe how practitioners might assist learners with each,
- discuss the value of balancing practice and rest periods during and between learning sessions,
- explain the function of instructions and demonstrations and discuss the principles to keep in mind when providing these forms of assistance,
- describe the advantages and disadvantages of guidance procedures, and
- discuss several techniques of physical practice and mental rehearsal that people might use during skill learning.

PREVIEW

A young boy asks a skilled performer to help him learn how to waterski. The skilled performer obviously knows how it feels to ski correctly, yet she also remembers how difficult it was to make early progress when she was learning to ski. She wants to help but isn't sure how. What instructions could she provide? Would it be best if she demonstrated the skill for him to observe? What other types of assistance could she provide? When would it be best to allow him to attempt the skill on his own?

Good two-way communication can reassure learners and open doors to helpful assistance.

OVERVIEW

The questions that the skilled waterskier is contemplating in the preview to this chapter are like those that many movement practitioners ask themselves when they are preparing for instruction. Most practitioners want to help learners without becoming a distraction themselves. Ideally, formal learning experiences are cooperative efforts between the practitioner and the learner. As we discussed in chapter 7, learners need to identify the skills they want to learn and the contexts in which they want to perform those skills before goal setting can begin and beneficial practice experiences can be designed.

Once the learners' goals have been set and the appropriate target skills have been identified, the practitioner can begin planning the learning experience and providing instructional assistance. In this chapter we examine a number of instructional techniques that practitioners might use to supplement people's learning experiences. First, we suggest several ways to create a learning atmosphere that is open and nonthreatening for learners. These include familiarizing learners with the instructional situation, opening communication, directing learners' attention to task-relevant information, creating optimal arousal levels, and balancing practice and rest. After that, we discuss some ways instructors can assist learners in achieving a general idea of the learning task. These include instructions, demonstrations, and guidance procedures. Finally, we describe several types of physical- and mental-rehearsal techniques available for practitioners to use during skill instruction.

PRELIMINARY CONSIDERATIONS

Before providing instructional assistance, practitioners need to consider several aspects of the learning situation. These include familiarizing learners with the practice environment, developing open communication, directing learners' attention to sources of important task-related information, and diminishing learners' anxiety. In addition, effective instructors consider how to balance practice and rest periods, particularly if fatigue might put learners at risk when they are practicing their skills.

Familiarizing Learners and Opening Communication

Effective public speakers use a simple sequence: They begin their presentations by outlining what they intend to say. After that, they say what they said they were going to say, and then they conclude by reiterating what they have just said. By preparing their audiences in this way, speakers increase listeners' receptivity to the information presented. In a similar vein, movement practitioners can increase the receptivity of skill learners by familiarizing them with the instructional process. Alerting learners to what they can expect during learning sessions can diminish their uncertainty and alleviate their concerns.

Let's face it. Most of us are apprehensive when we encounter unfamiliar situations. It's natural for us to ask, "What will this experience be like? Will I do okay? Will the teacher embarrass me if I make a mistake? Could I be injured?"

Instructional situations provide learners with many opportunities to experience success, and most folks are motivated when they achieve it. However, formal learning experiences can also be threatening if learners are afraid of the possible consequences of not doing well. As a result, many learners approach new learning situations with excess caution; they don't want to take risks that might lead to failure and embarrassment (Ames, 1992). By familiarizing learners with the practice environment and offering them support and encouragement, practitioners can make learners more willing to take the kinds of risks that can improve performance substantially.

Familiarization, in addition to alleviating learners' concerns and establishing a vocabulary for the words important for the skill, can establish a line of two-way communication between the practitioner and the learner. Learners who have questions or concerns can then feel freer to communicate them to the practitioner. This allows the practitioner to provide the best assistance possible and encourages the learner to take an active role in the learning process (Ainsworth & Fox, 1989).

Let's say that the advanced skier in this chapter's preview scenario decided to explain the main points of waterskiing and then demonstrate several components of the skill, so that the learner could get a mental picture of the actions he needed to produce. Given what we know about people's limited attentional capacity (chapter 2), it is likely that providing both verbal instructions and a visual demonstration might be more information than could be handled all at once. More is not necessarily better when providing instructions, and the learner might sometimes be the best person to determine how much information is too much. This is one reason why open two-way communication between the instructor and learner is important.

Learners may view instruction as threatening or as an opportunity for improvement.

attentional focus—The information at which the performer's attention, or consciousness, is directed.

external focus—A focus on information that is the consequence of the action being produced—e.g., the movement of the golf club, the flight of the ball, etc.

internal focus—A focus on information associated with the body's movement in producing the action—e.g., how much the elbow is bent, the timing of hip rotation, etc.

narrow focus—A focus on a narrow range of information sources at one time.

broad focus—A focus on a wide range of information sources at one time.

But there is more to it than this. In addition to the *amount* of instruction, one needs to consider to *what aspect* of the skill the instruction refers, and what such instructions do to adjust the learner's focus of attention. We treat these issues in the next few sections.

Directing Attention

Practitioners can assist learners in managing their **attentional focus** by directing it to the most relevant sources of task information. Nideffer (1995) and, more recently, Wulf (2007) have suggested some helpful guidelines for doing this.

Nideffer's view is that people have the capability of controlling two dimensions of attention (see figure 8.1)—the direction of the focus, and the breadth of the focus. With respect to direction of focus, it is useful to distinguish between an **external focus** (attending to the consequences of the action to be produced, such as the golf club or golf ball) and an **internal focus** (attending to the movements of the body that actually make the action). The second dimension concerns the width of the focus—a **narrow focus** would encompass a small range of informational sources, whereas a **broad focus** would be sensitive to a large number of cues at the same time. Although the directional dimension is more discrete (i.e., it's difficult for performers to focus both externally and internally at the same time), the width dimension seems to be more of a continuum (i.e., performers have a range of narrow-to-broad foci). It is debatable as to whether learners actually have much conscious control of their focus width, however.

In learning situations, practitioners can instruct individuals to direct their attention to any of a number of internal or external sources of information. A physical therapist might ask a patient to direct his attention to the feeling in his left knee (internal–narrow focus) as he attempts a leg-strengthening exercise, a yoga instructor might tell a beginning student to close her eyes and attend to the feel of her entire upper body (internal–broad focus), a roofing contractor might instruct a trainee to focus on the head of the nail he is hammering (external–narrow focus), and a rugby coach might encourage a player to focus on the movements of several opponents who are attempting to advance the ball (external–broad focus). To focus learners' attention on the intended effects of various actions, practitioners might use verbal cues such as "contact on shoelaces" for kicking a soccer ball, "smooth release" for tossing a package into the appropriate bin in a mail room, and "low to high" for imparting topspin when hitting a tennis ball (Parson, 1998).

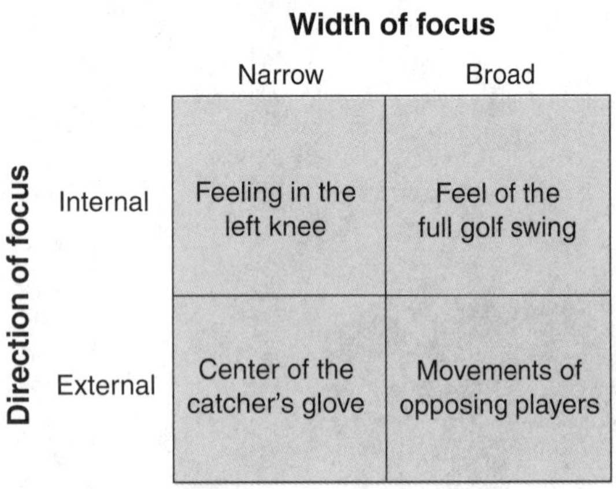

Width of focus
Narrow
Broad
Direction of focus
Internal
External
Feeling in the left knee
Feel of the full golf swing
Center of the catcher's glove
Movements of opposing players

Figure 8.1 Nideffer (1995) conceptualized two dimensions of attention: direction (internal and external) and width (narrow and broad).

By helping learners identify task-relevant cues and then encouraging them to direct their attention to the most appropriate cues or information at specific times, practitioners can promote the development of attentional control. With practice, then, learners should become more adept at managing their attention, which in turn should contribute to their goal achievement. But what is important for a focus of attention, and does this change with the learner's level of skill? Some research indicates that attentional focus is more important at some points of a movement than at others. For example, the horseshoe pitching movement requires more attention at the beginning of the action and just before the release of the shoe than it does during the ballistic phase between those two points (Prezuhy & Etnier, 2001; see Posner & Keele, 1968, for older research on this issue). Attentional control of other types of tasks is discussed next.

Systematic Routines Can Help Focus Performers' Attention

Recent research suggests that learning a systematic preperformance routine can improve performance accuracy. Harle and Vickers (2001) provided quiet eye (QE) training (discussed in chapter 3) for university women's basketball players and found that it improved free throw shooting performance from preseason to postseason compared with control players who received no training. QE is an objective measure of the location, onset, offset, and duration of a person's visual gaze recorded during the performance of a motor skill. In this study, the quiet eye protocol consisted of the following sequence of behaviors:

- Take stance, direct gaze to rim, repeat "nothing but net" three times while bouncing ball.
- Maintain QE for 1.5 s, fixating on one location (e.g., back rim), and say, "sight, focus."
- Shoot quickly using fluid action; release gaze once ball is released.

In addition to improving their accuracy (from 54% to 77%), players receiving QE training demonstrated a more economical preshot routine consisting of a longer duration of QE, a more stable QE on one location, a longer "prep-down phase" (i.e., from the beginning of downward movement of the last ball bounce until shot initiation), and a shorter shot movement time compared with control players. Research has also shown that beginners in the early stages of skill learning can be taught to use systematic routines that improve performance accuracy (Singer, Lidor, & Cauraugh, 1993). Therefore, practitioners working with performers at all levels might consider including such routines in the regular practice of motor skills.

The challenge for practitioners, of course, is to determine the optimal focus for each learner and task. Landin (1994) suggested that when good teachers provide instructional cues for **open skills**, they direct learners' attention to important environmental information (i.e., an external focus), which then triggers the necessary motor response (Hagemann, Strauss, & Cañal-Bruland, 2006). In some **closed skills**, though, where the environment is stable, predictable, or where movement form is essential (e.g., springboard diving, gymnastics), one might profit more from an internal focus on the movement itself.

open skill—
A skill performed in an environment that is unpredictable or in motion and that requires performers to adapt their movements in response to dynamic properties of the environment.

closed skill—
A skill performed in an environment that is predictable or stationary and that allows performers to plan their movements in advance.

Although it might be presumed that an internal focus is preferable for the learning of all closed skills, a growing body of evidence (see the research highlight "Learning Advantages of an External Focus of Attention") suggests that an external focus (e.g., a focus on the pendulum movement of the golf club, or the ball) may be more beneficial than a focus on the movement itself (i.e., on the mechanics of the arm swing). And, this seems to depend on the level of skill of the learner (see Wulf, 2007). Presumably, by focusing on the intended effects of the action, performers are less likely to inject slow and clumsy conscious processes into the action. As a consequence, learners are less likely to experience the "paralysis by analysis" that sometimes occurs when they focus on their own movements (Prinz, 1997). This proposal seems to be borne out in the findings of recent research showing that the simple instruction to increase the speed of a nondominant arm throwing movement (a novel task for the learners) enhanced the learning of the correct throwing pattern to a greater extent than more detailed instructions regarding proper throwing mechanics (Southard, 2006).

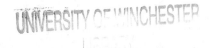

UNIVERSITY OF WINCHESTER
LIBRARY

anxiety—
A person's uneasiness or distress about future uncertainties; a perception of threat to the self (often characterized by elevated arousal levels).

arousal—
The level of activation of the central nervous system; varies from extremely low levels during sleep to extremely high levels during intense physical or mental activity.

In light of these results, some have suggested that an external focus may also improve the motor control of people with neuromotor deficits (Guadagnoli, McNevin, & Wulf, 2002). For example, encouraging older adults to focus on the intended outcome during a bout of postural activity (e.g., avoiding potholes while crossing a street) might encourage the use of automatic control processes (and reduce falls) more so than saying, "Watch your step."

Managing Arousal

As we mentioned earlier, learners often perceive formal instructional settings to be threatening. Research suggests that people's **anxiety** is particularly high when they believe that their performance is being evaluated (see Wrisberg, 1994). For people in the early stages of learning, elevated anxiety and **arousal** can contribute to a shift toward a more internal focus, and can interfere with movement production. Fortunately, practitioners can do a couple of things to help learners maintain arousal levels that are appropriate for performance.

Learning Advantages of an External Focus of Attention

Research examining the optimal attentional focus for skill learning suggests that people who are instructed to focus on the intended environmental effects of their actions (i.e., an external focus) perform and retain (i.e., learn) target skills more effectively than those who are told to focus on the movement itself (i.e., an internal focus). In one study, Wulf, Höß, and Prinz (1998) manipulated the attentional focus of participants learning a slalom ski maneuver on a ski simulator (see figure 8.4 on p. 235); they found that learners who were told to focus on an external cue (i.e., the wheels of the simulator) demonstrated greater learning than those who were instructed to focus on the forces exerted by their feet (i.e., an internal focus). This is interesting, as the feet and the wheels of the apparatus are very closely connected, so that movement of the foot has a more or less direct effect on the movement of the wheels. It is surprising that simple instructions to change the focus from the foot to the wheels would make such a large difference. In a subsequent experiment with beginning golfers (Wulf, Lauterbach, & Toole, 1999), those who were told to focus on the pendulum movement of the club and the weight of the club head (external focus) learned and retained the chip shot more effectively than learners who were instructed to focus on the swinging motion of their arms and the correct grip (internal focus).

Wulf's (2007) ideas are related to the concepts of automatic movements discussed in chapter 2. The idea is that instructions that direct the learner's focus toward the body's movements (e.g., "feel your elbow this time") cause the learner to shift toward more conscious control of the action, which leads to jerky, hesitant, and "unnatural" movements. On the other hand, a focus toward the environmental effect of the action ("Note the sound of the ball," "Note how far the ball goes") directs the focus away from the movement itself, preventing conscious processes from interfering with the action, and allowing the action to be controlled more automatically with motor programs and learned reflexive activities.

These principles seem to be dependent on the level of learning. In one study (Wulf, McNevin, Fuchs, Ritter, & Toole, 2000, experiment 2), beginning golfers who focused on the intended effects of the action (i.e., the movement of the club) produced higher performance and more learning than participants using an external focus directed to the ball's trajectory and the target. Wulf's (2007) concept is that, for rank beginners, a focus on the ball is not closely related enough to the body's movements to be of use for learning.

She and her colleagues (McNevin, Shea, & Wulf, 2003) also showed that increasing the "distance" from the body to the location of focus increases learning. Using the stabilometer task (see figure 8.2*a*), they found that having subjects focus attention on platform markers adjacent to the feet was more effective than an internal focus, but focusing attention on platform markers 10 in. (26 cm) away from the feet generated even more learning. See Wulf (2007) for a very readable discussion of these and many other findings.

First, the practitioner can emphasize **process goals** rather than **outcome goals** (Filby, Maynard, & Graydon, 1999). Process goals typically involve aspects of the action over which the learner has control (producing an effective pattern), whereas outcome goals are often beyond the learner's control (e.g., winning the match). Also, the practitioner can encourage the learner to set realistic goals, realizing that what is realistic for one learner may be unrealistic for another (McClements, 1982). Learners who believe that they are capable of meeting the demands of the task show increased commitment to learning the task (Williams & Harris, 2006). It is particularly important for beginners to focus on a single aspect of the task at a time (e.g., the pilot might focus on smooth steering in a forward direction). Once performers achieve a consistent level of success in performing that aspect, they can shift their attention to another skill component (e.g., smooth banking when turning the airplane).

process goals—Targets for performance that focus on the quality of movement production.

outcome goals—Targets for performance that focus on the end result of the activity.

massed practice—A practice schedule in which the amount of rest between practice attempts or between practice sessions is relatively shorter than the amount of time spent practicing.

distributed practice—A practice schedule in which the amount of rest between practice attempts or between practice sessions is relatively longer than the amount of time spent practicing.

Balancing Practice and Rest

The scheduling of practice is another concern that practitioners need to address when designing a program of instruction. Practice-scheduling decisions might include the number of days per week learners will practice, whether some days can be devoted to no practice at all, how long practices will be each day, and how much time learners will rest during practice periods. Many of these issues have been studied in laboratory settings, and the results suggest several interesting and useful applications.

When supervising the long-term practice of movement skills, as in coaching an athletic team or monitoring the recovery of a stroke patient, a basic question for instructors is how often per week learners are to practice. Frequently, there is a limit to the amount of time available for instruction. For example, coaches may be restricted by the rules of their sport to a certain number of hours of practice per week or the number of weeks of practice before the start of the competitive season, or therapists may be limited by the terms of a health insurance policy to a certain length of time for patient rehabilitation.

Historically, there has been much more research effort devoted to the study of performance–rest ratios within practice sessions than to the amount of time between sessions. Typically, researchers have described practice sessions as either massed or distributed, depending on the relative amounts of performance and rest that take place during practice. There is no fixed dividing line between massed and distributed practice, but **massed practice** usually means minimal rest between performance attempts, whereas **distributed practice** means more.

Researchers interested in the influence of massed and distributed practice schedules on skill learning have been so for a variety of reasons (see Lee & Genovese, 1988, for a review), but one reason has been to examine the effects of physical and mental fatigue (caused by practice itself) on learning processes. The influence of the various performance and rest schedules seems to be different for discrete and continuous tasks. For discrete skills such as shooting a basketball, slicing a piece of fruit, or fastening a button, reducing the rest time between practice attempts has little influence on performance or on learning, and in some cases less rest is even beneficial (Carron, 1967). These skills have very short movement times, so fatigue probably does not accumulate to a marked degree with massed practice.

For continuous skills such as handwriting, beating eggs, and in-line skating, fatigue-like states are more apt to build up within a performance bout, so decreasing the amount of rest between practice attempts might have a negative impact on performance, and perhaps on learning. The bulk of the laboratory research suggests support for this notion—less rest between performance bouts degrades performance and has a relatively permanent degrading influence on learning (i.e., measured by a retention test). What is interesting is how small these effects are, however, which forces us to the conclusion that fatigue might not always be a serious problem for learners.

blocked practice—A practice sequence in which individuals rehearse the same skill repeatedly.

This research suggests several practical applications. First, with discrete tasks, having minimal rest between practice attempts does not seem to diminish learning. Thus, for discrete actions with short movement times (throwing, striking, etc.), instructors could encourage learners to perform many repetitions, even without much rest. Be careful, though, as repetitions of a given task (what is called **blocked practice**) have been found to be ineffective for learning; see chapter 9. To avoid blocking practice, an aspiring cook might improve his slicing skill by increasing the number of repetitions, but doing so with a variety of vegetables and using various types of knives so that practice of a given action is not repetitious and blocked. In the next chapter, we discuss repetition and several ways practitioners might structure practice sessions to facilitate skill learning.

Shorter Practice Sessions Spread Out Are More Effective Than Longer Ones Bunched Together

Baddeley and Longman (1978) found that, for maximal learning resulting from a given amount of actual practice time, there is an upper limit to the amount of practice per day. In this study, postal trainees receiving 60 total hr of practice learned how to operate mail-sorting machines far more effectively when their practice sessions were shorter and more spread out (1 hr sessions once a day for 12 weeks) than when sessions were longer and bunched together (2 hr sessions twice a day for 3 weeks). It is possible that those trainees who practiced according to the more distributed format showed more learning because of the well-known beneficial effects of spaced practice, where the spacing refers to the time intervals between practice sessions rather to the rest between trials as in massed/distributed practice. According to Bjork (1994), because of forgetting between sessions, spaced practice requires learners to "struggle" somewhat more to achieve the correct solution than when they are permitted to practice with less spacing between sessions. Bjork termed such benefits of spacing "desirable difficulties." We explore the possible learning benefits of spaced practice in greater depth in the next chapter.

Another reason that shorter practice periods may be more effective is that they are less tiresome or boring for learners. Indeed, a challenge for practitioners designing longer practice sessions is to find ways to sustain learners' interest and attention (e.g., industrial trainers might rotate trainees among sessions of individual-skill rehearsal, small-group rehearsal, large-group rehearsal, and discussion). If the practitioner is successful in doing this, learners are usually able to practice for longer periods without diminishing the quality of their performance.

Determining Optimal Practice–Rest Ratios

In 1968, Graw conducted a study examining various combinations of practice- and rest-time on two balance tasks learned separately: the stabilometer balance board task and the Bachman ladder task (see figure 8.2*a* and 8.2*b*). For both tasks, the percentage of time actually spent in physical practice was 20%, 30%, 40%, 57%, or 77% of the total 30-min practice period. Graw then tested participants' learning by administering a retention test, which he gave on the second day. Notice that, as the percentage of practice time increases, the actual number of trials practicing the task increases as well. For the stabilometer task, the optimal condition for learning occurred when 57% of the time was spent practicing. For the Bachman ladder task, the 30% practice condition was most effective. These results showed that there was no single optimal practice–rest ratio for all tasks: The ladder task was learned most effectively when more time was spent resting, whereas the stabilometer task was learned best when more time was spent practicing.

Some task differences determine which schedule is most effective for learning. Energy cost, for example, is one important factor. The energy costs with the Bachman ladder task are relatively large (the learner must climb a free-standing ladder quickly, over and over, during the trial's duration), and energy costs increase as the performer improves and is able to climb higher and faster. In the stabilometer task, less energy is required for balancing (little movement occurs in the major muscle groups), because the optimal performance is no movement at all. These differences suggest that instructors would benefit from estimating the energy requirements of a task as a way to choose an optimal practice–rest ratio.

Second, for continuous tasks or for skills that contain an element of physical risk (e.g., rock-climbing activities or, for elders, certain balance tasks), fatigue can be a problem, generating a clumsy performance that could lead to reduced learning, not to mention a serious accident or fall. In these situations, instructors and therapists typically ensure that sufficient rest is provided between practice attempts.

What factors determine the performance–rest balance that is most effective for learning? One important factor is the energy requirements of the skill. Practitioners can make a rough estimation of the physical demands of skills to be sure that those requiring more

a

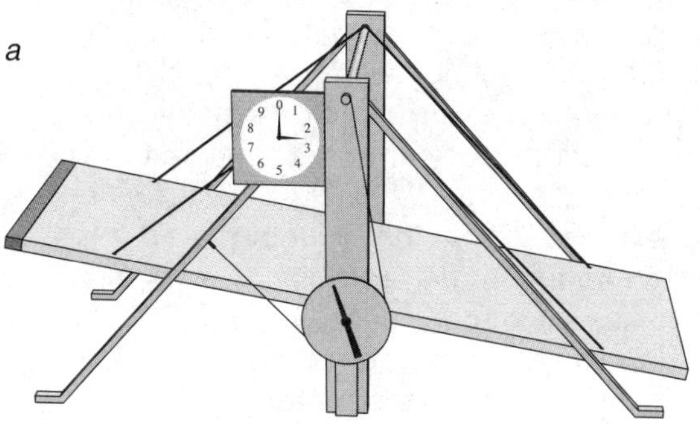

b

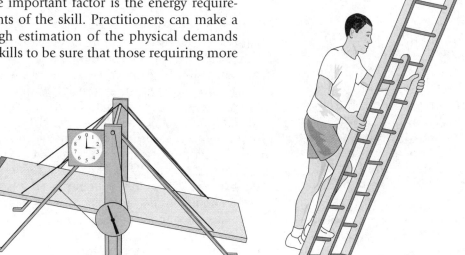

Figure 8.2 The stabilometer balance board *(a)* and the Bachman ladder task *(b)*.

energy are practiced with more rest between attempts (see Graw, 1968). Instructors might also consider the fitness levels of learners when teaching skills with high energy requirements that might place participants at risk during fatigued practice. For these types of skills, low-fit learners might benefit from longer rest periods between practice bouts.

SKILL PRESENTATION TECHNIQUES

When we discussed the stages of learning in the last chapter, we emphasized that the primary goal during the initial stage of learning is to acquire a general idea of the movement. A big challenge for practitioners, then, is to teach learners how to approximate what actions a task entails.

For the young boy in this chapter's preview scenario, the general idea of waterskiing would probably require some image of correct form, a sense of what needs to be done to produce this form, and an awareness of the pattern of sensory feedback that accompanies successful performance attempts. The instructor's job, then, would be to help the learner achieve these thoughts and images. In this section, we discuss a number of techniques that movement practitioners can use to introduce learners to the practice situation and help them acquire a general idea of the desired movements. We group these methods under the general headings of instructions, demonstrations, and guidance procedures.

Selecting Instructional Assistance

Instructional assistance is important for skill improvement in many tasks. However, not all assistance appears to be of equal value. In a study by Beek and van Santvoord (1992), young adult volunteers attempted to learn how to juggle three balls in a cascade, or figure-eight pattern. Before practice, all participants received the following sequence of instructions:

1. Take one ball and throw it from one hand to the other. Throw it from about waist height to a point level with the top of your head.
2. Hold one ball in each hand. Throw the right-hand ball in an arc toward your left hand. As it peaks, throw the second ball in an arc underneath it toward the right hand. Catch the first ball in your left hand and the second in your right.
3. Hold two balls in your right hand and one in your left. Throw the first ball in your right hand toward your left hand. As it peaks, throw the ball in the left hand toward the right. As the second ball peaks, throw the final ball from your right hand. Catch none of the balls.
4. Do as before but now catch the balls and throw them as the previously thrown ball peaks. Keep repeating the sequence, and you are juggling. (p. 88)

Participants practiced these tasks for three half-hour sessions on separate days and then were divided into two groups for a final seven sessions. Using high-speed video-camera and film motion-analyzer, the researchers found that greater skill was associated with the identification of fixed points in space for the ball's location. Once participants determined these points, their performance became more accurate, consistent, and flexible. These findings suggest that instructions (these offered information about spatial anchors in the environment—see how many of these you can find by looking again at the instructions) can be quite helpful initially for people learning skills.

Instructions

Instructions are a feature of nearly every formal teaching situation. Practitioners usually provide them in spoken (i.e., verbal) form, although they might be written, and the instructions typically contain general information about the fundamental aspects of the skill. Such aspects might include how to use the skill in particular situations (e.g., in a group activity, in sport competition, with a partner), where and how performers should attempt to move, how they should try to hold an apparatus or other implement (e.g., a ball, a walker, a welding torch), what cues are most important (e.g., the seams of the ball, the hand position or posture for someone learning to use a walker), and what results performers should try to achieve.

Practitioners can also use instructions to emphasize similarities between skills, a concept we discussed in chapter 7. A verbal cue or phrase, such as "Throw the racket head at the ball," is a useful instruction that alerts a person learning how to serve a tennis ball to the similarity between the arm action of the overarm throw and the arm action of the serve (Landin, 1994). In other activities it is helpful for instructors to use consistent labels for similar skills, for example, emphasizing that kips on the horizontal bar, rings, and mat are really the same movement (i.e., a forceful extension of the hip) and then referring to all these movements as kips, regardless of the gymnastics event learners are practicing. Many skills have similar mechanical principles that practitioners can emphasize in their instructions (e.g., shifting body momentum when throwing, keeping the head still when striking an object, or maintaining a wide base of support when balancing or lifting). Using these techniques, instructors can remind learners of previously experienced principles that the learners can then use to learn a new activity.

Instructions can also provide learners with information about the feelings they might experience when performing the skill (e.g., "You should feel a firm tug in your shoulders during this movement"). Instructions that contain information like this are likely to raise beginners' awareness, improve their skill, and boost their confidence. Simple, direct statements that start people on the right track can also serve them well in the long run. Clear instructions are an important part of skill learning.

Instructions can be ineffective, though. One problem with words is that sometimes they fail to describe the subtle aspects of movements. For example, try verbally explaining how to tie your shoelaces. Also, biomechanical or physical principles of movements, dealing with concepts such as the transfer of momentum and action-reaction, are sometimes difficult to communicate clearly in words. Verbal descriptions of concepts or principles such as these may be useful, but learners might not understand these concepts well enough to apply them when learning a new skill. And, even when learners do understand the concepts, there is no guarantee that they will be able to use the concepts effectively (Wulf & Weigelt, 1997).

Practitioners can also provide too much information in their instructions. When this happens, learners have trouble remembering everything they hear—particularly if some time elapses between when learners hear the instructions and when they try to carry them out. Recall from chapter 2 that our **short-term memory** (STM) for once-presented materials is limited in capacity to just a few items, that forgetting is rapid (occurring in about 30 s), and that information in STM is subject to interference from other input (e.g., other spoken words). Therefore, if instructions contain more than one or two key points, learners are likely to forget the instructions before they can attempt the skill.

short-term memory (STM)—The memory system that allows people to retrieve, rehearse, process, and transfer information from STSS; believed to be limited in capacity and brief in duration.

Another factor is that instructions can have the effect of directing the learner's focus of attention. If the instructions generate an internal focus (e.g., "Your elbow should be straight at the top of the swing"), this can have the inadvertent effect of encouraging the conscious control of actions. An external focus can also be generated by instructions (e.g., "Listen to the sound the club makes when it hits the ball"), so the nature of the instructions can determine the learner's attentional focus. (See the highlight box, "Learning advantages of an external focus of attention" earlier in this chapter.)

Regardless of the attentional focus the instructions generate, or what aspects of the skill are mentioned, the evidence strongly implies that practitioners do best by keeping their instructions brief and to the point, emphasizing no more than one or two major concepts at a time. To make instructions simpler, teachers and therapists might relate their instructions to things learners have previously experienced that they can readily transfer to the new skill. For example, a therapy patient who is trying to learn to lift his feet when walking on a thick carpet could be reminded of the kind of foot movements he used to use when walking through high grass. By spacing instructions throughout the first few minutes of practice—giving only the most fundamental information first and then adding finer details later—practitioners can help learners remember instructions. All of these considerations are particularly relevant for young and elderly learners, as well as for those who are cognitively challenged, because they have a more **limited attentional capacity** for processing information.

limited attentional capacity— The notion that attention is limited to at most a few activities at any one time.

Instructions Can Make a Difference for Parkinson's Patients

People with Parkinson's disease often demonstrate a gait pattern that is characterized by small, slow, shuffling steps with little or no arm swing. However, the findings of one research study suggest that this pattern can be normalized to some extent by instructions (Behrman, Teitelbaum, & Cauraugh, 1998). In this experiment, the gait patterns of eight Parkinson's patients were compared with those of age-matched controls before and after the presentation of five sets of instructions. The instructions pertained to taking large steps, walking fast, and walking while counting aloud. Patients given such instructions followed them and demonstrated immediate improvements in a series of walking behaviors relative to control participants who did not receive these instructions. Although the impact of instructions on walking performance is likely to depend on the stage of disease progression and the degree of patients' attention to the instructions, it appears that clearly worded instructions that describe intended effects of the action have the potential to enhance the gait pattern of Parkinson's patients.

Instructions Are Sometimes Difficult to Convey in Spoken Form

Try to describe the process of tying shoelaces, opening a combination lock, peeling an apple, or performing a cartwheel. Which instructions are easier to convey in spoken form? Which are more difficult? Why?

Demonstrations

Good companions to instructions are various forms of visual information, such as still pictures of proper actions; film clips or videos of successful performances; and demonstrations (sometimes referred to as **modeling**), usually provided by the instructor, the therapist, or some other skilled person. The familiar adage "A picture is worth a thousand words" seems to be particularly true when it comes to learning motor skills, because movement information can often be transmitted more easily by a visual demonstration than by a verbal description. The simple instruction, "Do this," followed by the instructor's demonstration, is a frequently used technique.

modeling—A practice procedure that involves the demonstration of a skill for the benefit of a person who is trying to learn the skill.

observational learning—The process by which learners acquire the capability for action by observing the performance of others.

Much of our movement learning comes from our attempts to reproduce actions we see in others; this is often called **observational learning**. How observational learning works prior to actual movement is a question that has stimulated considerable debate. Nevertheless, there is little doubt that a substantial amount of learning, particularly that which occurs early in practice, comes from studying and imitating the actions of others. Effective movement practitioners regularly capitalize on this phenomenon when providing instructional assistance.

The person who models a movement can be either an unskilled peer or a skilled teacher or therapist (McCullagh, 1986, 1987), as long as he or she is able to perform movements that contain some of the essential features of the skill (Shea, Wright, Wulf, & Whitacre, 2000). One feature provided by the model is the fundamental pattern of relative timing, which is an important invariant component of generalized motor programs (as we discussed in chapters 4 and 5). Studies indicate that

It Depends . . .

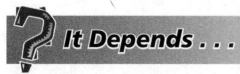

Can You Detect the Imitations of Children?

Observe the behavior of preschool children at a nearby playground or community park. What types of actions are the children imitating? What aspects of the children's imitations are similar to those of the people they are imitating? How relevant are the children's imitations to successful performance of the action?

It Depends . . .

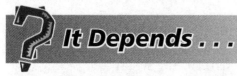

Can You Provide Clear Instructions?

A lot can be learned simply by experiencing a movement. However, to do this, learners sometimes need a few instructions that point them in the direction of goal achievement. What few basic instructions might you give someone who wants to experience what it's like to play a guitar? Shoot an arrow at a target? Hit a pitched ball with a bat? How would you know if your instructions were effective?

It Depends . . .

Can You Think of Some Transferable Concept to Include in Instruction?

Sometimes instructions can contain concepts that people have previously experienced, which they can then transfer to the learning of a new task (e.g., "Hit the handball just as if you were throwing it"). Can you think of some transferable concepts that a practitioner might use to assist a person learning to drive a car? Head a soccer ball? Throw a Frisbee? Do a front dive?

Parents model all sorts of behavior for their children, who may observe them to learn essential features of motor skills.

learners can detect relative-timing patterns by either observing (Blandin, Lhuisset, & Proteau, 1999; Horn, Williams, Scott, & Hodges, 2005) or listening to (Shea, Wulf, Park, & Gaunt, 2001) models of the correct relative-timing pattern. Auditory models, which could consist of either the sounds of the movement in isolation (e.g., CD or audiotape) or the sounds produced by a visualized model, might be particularly effective for the observational learning of rhythmic patterns in events such as the hurdles and triple jump in track and field as well as in most dance routines. Recent research has also shown that observation of a model can promote the development of error-detection and -correction capabilities about as well as actual physical rehearsal of the target skill does (Blandin & Proteau, 2000). Models give learners an image of the desired state and are therefore especially effective very early in practice. The strengths and weaknesses of guidance procedures are discussed in the next section.

Of course, demonstrations and modeling cannot be effective if observers are not paying attention or if they are unable to view the model from a perspective that is helpful. For example, a side view of a model demonstrating a dance step may not be as helpful as a front view or a rear view. Also, when you face your learners, the action you demonstrate is "backward" (a kind of mirror image) for the students; demonstrating with your back to a group of learners often makes more sense. Therefore, practitioners must gain learners' attention before presenting the model and be sure the model provides observers with the most beneficial view of the appropriate relative-timing pattern.

Instructional technology allows practitioners to provide models and demonstrations using video or computer simulations of the desired action (Seat & Wrisberg, 1996). Research suggests that such demonstrations can be quite helpful. Schoenfelder-Zohdi (1992) found that when people watched a video of a skilled model before beginning their own practice attempts on a ski simulator, they improved at a faster rate and demonstrated better coordination than learners who received only verbal instructions. Wrisberg and Pein (2002) reported similar results in a study examining the effects of video modeling during the learning of the badminton long service. Groups that

Delaying the Imitation of Modeled Actions Enhances Learning

Demonstrating the actions of a skilled model is a common technique that practitioners use to give learners an idea or representation of the movement they are attempting to produce. In a study by Weeks, Hall, and Anderson (1996), three groups of beginners attempted to reproduce the one-hand sign-language gestures of a skilled model who performed a series of letters from the American manual alphabet (see figure 8.3). During practice, one group imitated each of the model's actions as it was being demonstrated. A second group observed groupings of three actions and attempted to imitate them during a 10 s delay following the observation. A third group practiced a combination of imitations; participants imitated the model's actions in a concurrent manner during the first half of practice and in a delayed fashion (three actions at a time) during the second half. Retention was examined 5 min and then 48 hr after the conclusion of practice. Observational learning, as measured by performance on the 48 hr retention test, was enhanced when learners were instructed to *delay* their imitations, compared with performing them concurrently with the model. These findings suggest that observational learning conditions that increase learners' cognitive effort (providing *desirable difficulties;* see page 262 for further discussion of this concept) during practice enhances skill retention in the absence of the model. Fortunately, in most skill learning situations, modeling occurs in a delayed-imitation format (i.e., learners view the model first and then attempt to imitate the action after a brief delay), which increases cognitive effort. We discuss the concept of increased cognitive effort, and the structuring of the learning experience in greater detail in the next chapter.

viewed a model before every practice trial or only upon request demonstrated better form during acquisition and on a retention test (without the model) than a group that received only verbal instructions. Interestingly, the group that viewed the model only when they asked to see it requested the model on relatively few practice trials, most of which occurred at the beginning of the first day of acquisition. These findings suggest that a model is more useful to learners early in practice than later on, and that instructors might want to give learners the option of viewing the model once they have obtained a general idea of the target skill. Also, recent work on modeling by Clark and Ste-Marie (in press) has shown that learners viewing themselves in videos, with the videos edited to show only their best performances, is effective for children learning to swim. One effect these modeling techniques have is to generate considerable self-talk among the learners about ways to improve (Clark, Ste-Marie, & Martini, 2006).

As in the case of instructions, models and demonstrations can sometimes provide too much information for learners. Therefore, practitioners should use cueing techniques that direct the learner's attention to important aspects of the model's movements. For example, a golf instructor might say, "Watch how his hips lead the action of his arms" for beginning learners observing a golf swing, or a physical therapist might say, "Notice how far she moves the crutches on each step" for patients observing a particular phase of crutch walking. The kinds of movement cues that practitioners emphasize may depend on the performers' skill level, with higher-skilled performers having instructions that have an increasingly external focus. For example, the golf instructor might direct a beginner's attention to the basic relative-timing pattern of the swing but may point out some other aspect of the model's movements to a more advanced performer (e.g., how the ball sounded when it was struck, or in what direction it went).

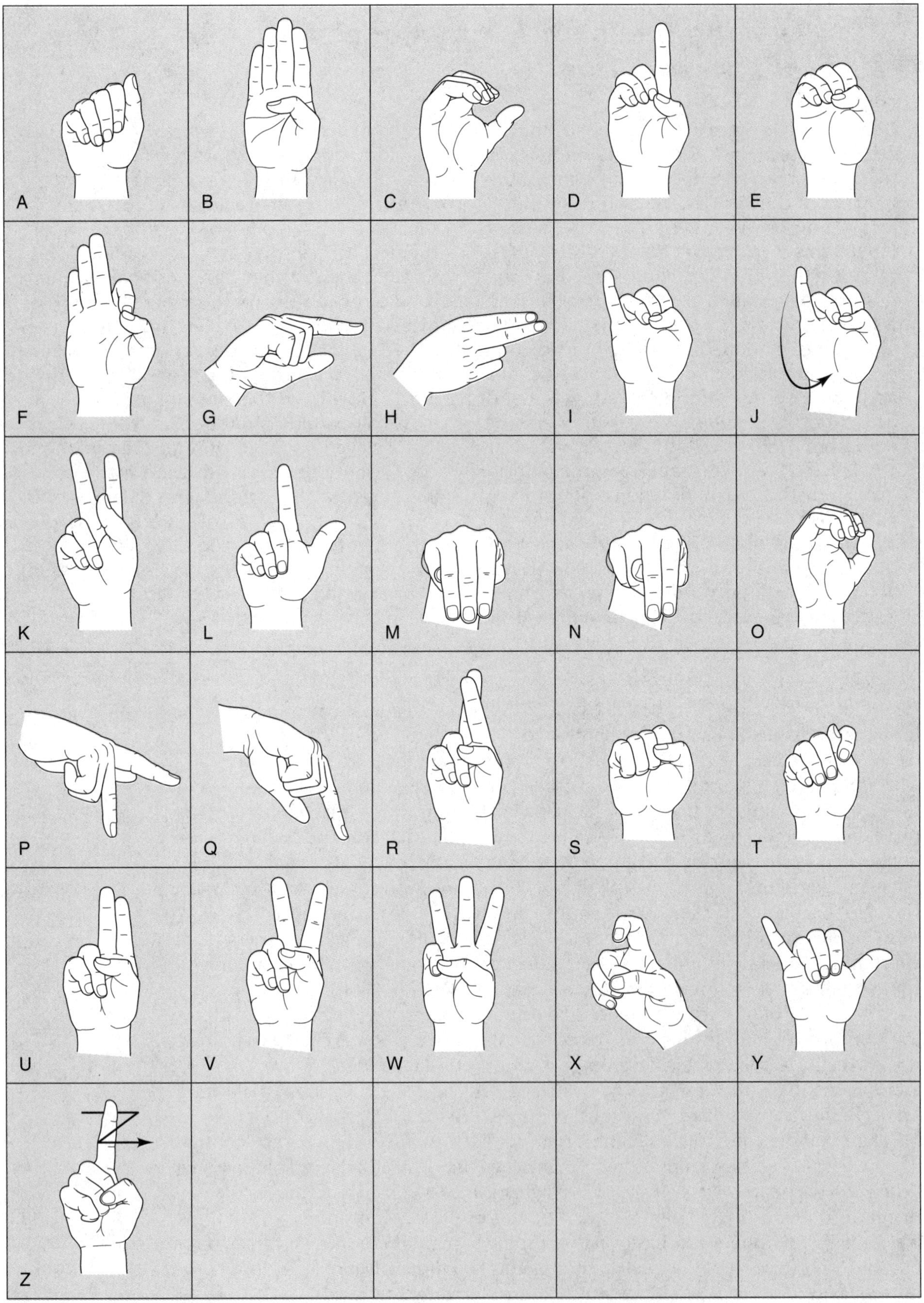

Figure 8.3 The American manual alphabet, which has been used to study the effects of delaying imitation.

Guidance Procedures

Movement professionals or practitioners often assist individuals in the early stages of physical rehearsal by guiding them through the movement pattern in various ways. **Guidance** methods vary widely in different settings. Some methods provide the learner with only slight assistance, such as when a therapist talks a patient through a rehabilitation movement, or a dance instructor offers occasional verbal reminders to help students remember a new step sequence. Other forms of guidance are far more intrusive. For example, a therapist might grasp a patient's hands to assist with walking and to minimize the chances of a serious fall. Many mechanical performance aids physically constrain learners' movement patterns, such as the training wheels parents sometimes attach to their children's bicycles when the children are learning how to ride. It never ceases to amaze us how many different guidance "gimmicks" are marketed in the golf-learning industry.

Physical guidance is designed to provide the learner with temporary assistance during the early stages of skill practice. The hope is that learning, as measured by the level of performance when the assistance is removed, will be enhanced as a result of the guided practice. Unfortunately, research suggests that physical guidance is not always effective for enhancing learning (see the research highlight "Physical Guidance Doesn't Always Promote Skill Learning" on page 237). Next we distinguish two different kinds of guidance—active and passive guidance.

guidance—
A procedure used to direct (either physically, verbally, and/or visually) learners through task performance in an effort to reduce errors or reduce fear.

active guidance—
A type of guidance procedure that involves active movement by the performer, which tends to preserve the relative-timing pattern and feel of the target skill.

passive guidance—
A type of guidance procedure that involves passive movement of the learner (e.g.,, the instructor moves the learner's limbs through the fundamental pattern), which can alter the nature and feel of the target skill.

Active Guidance

With **active guidance**, the practitioner manipulates the performance environment in a way that allows the learner to assume (active) control of the movement in an otherwise independent fashion. As a result, the learner gains a general idea of the requirements of the action and the resulting feedback that accompanies movement production. A good example of this type of guidance can be found in experiments where participants are given the opportunity to use ski poles while attempting to learn slalom-type movements on a ski simulator (see figure 8.4). The results of these studies indicate that this form of guidance can promote the development of the desired coordination pattern needed for unassisted (unguided) performance (Wulf, Shea, & Whitacre, 1998; Wulf & Toole, 1999). More importantly, the findings suggest that, rather than becoming dependent on the poles, learners used them to discover the correct relative-timing pattern and intrinsic feedback associated with unassisted movements.

Active guidance plays a prominent role, of course, in activities such as gymnastics, where falls can result in injuries. For many gymnastics activities, instructors use safety belts attached to adjacent support structures by ropes to catch learners if and when they slip or fall, reducing the chances of serious injury; unless a slip occurs, the belts provide almost no physical influence. If belts are not available, instructors or other students provide active guidance by offering the support of their hands and arms at critical points in the movement (e.g., "spotting" when the gymnast is first learning). Learners who are confident that they will not be injured can concentrate more effectively on the movement pattern, and how to produce it more smoothly and efficiently.

Figure 8.4 Schematic of experimental participant using ski poles during practice on a ski simulator apparatus. (Reprinted from Wulf & Toole, 1999.)

Passive Guidance

A second type of physical guidance relegates the learner to a much more passive role than with active guidance. Examples of **passive guidance** are sometimes seen in rehabilitation settings, such as when a physical therapist

Instructors can use active guidance to help learners achieve the feel of the target skill and minimize risk of injury.

places her hands on the hands of a stroke patient and manipulates the patient's hands to introduce a new wheelchair maneuver. There are several problems with passive guidance. First, it modifies the feel of the task, so that the movement is different when the learner then attempts it unassisted. In addition, decision-making processes may be different when learners are not required to control their movements as opposed to when they are moving for themselves. Finally, passive guidance can diminish learners' experience of performance errors and the opportunity to correct errors, either during the production of slower movements or on the following attempt for more rapid ones.

None of this would be a problem if passive guidance were always available during performance in the target context. However, for most skills, learners must at some time perform their movements in a situation that does not allow such assistance. The patient does not always have the therapist there to assist him in using his wheelchair. Passive guidance

Awareness Through Movement: The Feldenkrais Method

Many movement practitioners use a popular technique for enhancing movement awareness that was initially developed by Feldenkrais (1972). With this technique, the practitioner directs students' attention to movement-produced feedback by guiding the students (verbally or manually) through various movements (i.e., talking them through the movement or manually moving their limbs in various ways).

The primary objective of this form of training is to help the students become aware of the sensory information that accompanies movement and attune them to the feel of new possibilities for moving. Although some have suggested that this method has the potential to promote learners' discovery of more effective forms of movement control (Buchanan & Ulrich, 2001), scientific support for such a notion is currently lacking. Observed differences in the effectiveness of assistive and restrictive guidance procedures suggest that Feldenkrais procedures that use verbal guidance (and that allow the student to do the moving) may be more advantageous than those that rely on manual guidance (and that introduce sensations different from the ones accompanying unassisted actions).

might be useful initially when learners are developing their most basic ideas about the task, as this form of temporary assistance might help learners recognize basic features of the skill, give them a rough indication of what they should try to do, and start them on their way to making their first unassisted attempt. However, this assistance is best removed as quickly as possible, probably as soon as the learner or patient begins to demonstrate the capability of performing the task independently.

Physical Guidance Doesn't Always Promote Skill Learning

In a classic experiment by Annett (1959), participants tried to learn how to apply a particular amount of pressure to a hand-operated lever. During the practice phase, participants in one group received additional guidance in the form of a visual display that indicated the amount of pressure they were applying at all times. Participants in the other group did not receive this guidance but rather were told after each trial how well they did (i.e., how close they came to the desired amount of pressure). Not surprisingly, the guidance group performed more accurately during training because these participants always stopped at the correct force indicated by the display. However, when the visual guidance was removed in the retention test, this group performed very poorly compared with the no-guidance group, with some participants pressing so hard on the apparatus that they damaged it. Clearly, the participants who had practiced this task with the aid of visual guidance were unable to apply the correct amount of pressure to the lever when the guidance was taken away; for them, the guidance in practice became a kind of "crutch."

These results illustrate an important principle of guided practice. Guidance, almost by definition, is usually effective for performance when it is added to regular practice. The beginning golfer whose swing is aided by the instructor will produce a more correct looking action, make fewer errors, feel more confident, and so on. The real test of guidance effectiveness, though, is seen in the level of performance produced by learners when they are no longer given assistance (i.e., on a retention test in the target context), and here is where guidance procedures often fail. This phenomenon is related to the specificity-of-learning principle we discussed in chapter 7. If guided practice changes the task requirements markedly, then the task the person is practicing becomes different from the one the person must produce under unguided conditions.

It Depends . . .

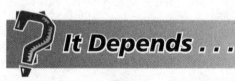

Can You Tell When Physical Guidance Is Helpful?

Sometimes movement practitioners attempt to assist a learner by moving the learner's limbs to simulate a particular action. With the cooperation of a partner, attempt each of the following movements with and without partner assistance: tossing a coin back and forth from one hand to the other, drawing a straight line on a piece of paper, and balancing on one foot with your eyes closed. What differences did you notice in the two conditions? Was the guidance helpful? If so, how?

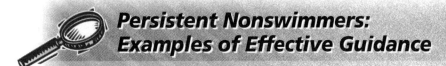

Persistent Nonswimmers: Examples of Effective Guidance

Years ago (in the 1960s) at the University of Illinois, Dick Schmidt was involved in teaching "persistent nonswimmers" how to swim. Initially, many of the students were so terrified of the water that they would not put their face below the surface. Dick and the other instructors used many strange and novel methods to deal with these unique learners.

After considerable time and effort, students worked up to floating on their backs and doing an elementary backstroke in the shallow end. They were eventually instructed to swim toward the (terrifying) deep water, but as they did the instructor walked alongside them on the pool deck holding a long wooden pole that touched the student's hip. If the student became alarmed, the pole was right there to grasp, but it did not interfere with or contribute to the actual swimming motion. Gradually, the pole was moved farther away but was still kept within easy reach. Later, it was held above the student's hip and lowered only if the student needed help. Eventually, the instructor simply walked alongside the swimming student with the pole held well away and then finally stopped providing any form of guidance at all. The elimination of students' fear by the presence of the pole, and the gradual removal of this form of guidance with additional practice, worked very well. In those days, more than 90% of the so-called persistent nonswimmers swam a mile nonstop for their final exam at the end of the semester and very proudly received a gold-embossed certificate. This guidance was effective because it did not interfere with or change the action and it greatly reduced the fear that was inhibiting individuals' learning.

FORMS OF PRACTICE

All learning requires some form of rehearsal, practice, or experience. The practice of motor skills can occur at many times and places, under a variety of conditions. Sometimes it happens almost unintentionally (e.g., when a child plays with toys or when a person uses a walker to aid locomotion). Sometimes it is highly purposeful. Other times rehearsal is highly guided and structured (e.g., when a musician rehearses with a conductor or a stroke patient practices with a therapist). Rehearsal can even occur in covert ways (e.g., when the learner thinks about future attempts).

In the remaining sections of this chapter, we examine some of the ways people might practice the movements they are trying to learn. First we describe various types of physical practice, and then we discuss the concept of mental rehearsal. When helping learners achieve their goals, practitioners must decide which forms of practice are the most effective at different times.

Physical Practice Techniques

Whoever coined the phrase "Practice makes perfect" knew that, if nothing else, skill improvement requires systematic physical repetition. However, we have learned that physical repetition alone does not guarantee improved skill, as this will depend on the nature and quality of the practice. Therefore, the old adage might be more accurately phrased "Effectively designed physical practice makes perfect." In this section, we discuss some of the techniques practitioners might use to facilitate learners' practice experiences. These techniques include simulator practice, part practice, slow-motion practice, and error-detection practice.

Simulator Practice

A **simulator** is a practice device that mimics certain features of a real-world task. Simulators are often elaborate, sophisticated, and expensive, such as the devices airline pilots use during flight training. But simulators need not be elaborate at all. Craig Wrisberg's dad had a small pressure-sensing platform in his office that he used whenever he wanted to practice his golf putting skills. When the ball landed on the pressure sensor (located under a simulated hole), it was projected back toward him. Simulators can be an important part of instructional programs, especially when the skill being learned is expensive or dangerous (e.g., when one is learning to fly a jet fighter), when the availability of facilities is limited (e.g., when there is only one putting green at a golf course), or when normal practice is not feasible (e.g., when it's raining).

simulator— A training device that mimics various features of a real-world task.

target skills— The skills a person wishes to be able to perform.

target context— The environmental context in which people want to be able to perform a skill or skills.

The goal of simulation is the transfer of learning from simulator practice to performance of the **target skill** in the **target context**. Because transfer between any two tasks increases as the similarity between the tasks increases (see chapter 7), simulator practice needs to be realistic; the simulated task should possess as many of the motor, perceptual, and conceptual elements of the target skill as possible. Not surprisingly, the creation of simulators can be very expensive, so before embarking on such a task manufacturers have to be reasonably sure that the simulator has the potential to produce considerable transfer.

A more practical concern has to do with the amount of transfer that is produced by the simulator in relation to the amount of time it takes to use it. If simulated practice results in better performance of the target skill in the target context than would be expected from the same amount of time practicing the target skill itself, then it makes sense to use the simulator. If this is not the case, learners would be better off spending the entire practice time on the target skill, if that is feasible. Usually, because the simulator is somewhat different from the target skill, an hour of practice "spent" on the simulator usually results in less than an hour of practice "saved" on the target skill, so other criteria besides time spent come into play.

Other relevant factors need to be considered before deciding to use a simulator. Other than the time spent or saved, the effectiveness of a simulator might also be judged according to the relative cost of simulator practice and target skill practice, the availability of resources and facilities, or learner safety. Compared with the cost of practicing in a flight simulator, practice in an actual jetliner would be staggering, not to mention the additional concerns it would create for the safety of the learners and equipment.

As in the case of guidance procedures, simulators can be helpful during the early stages of practice, when people are learning the rules, strategies, and other cognitive and decision-making aspects of the target skill. However, as soon as learners demonstrate more consistent patterns of movement control, they are less likely to benefit from simulator practice than from practicing the target skill, unless of course the two are nearly identical.

Above Real-Time Training

A simulation technique that has been used successfully to train airplane fighter pilots is called above real-time training (ARTT). This training requires trainees to perform standard tasks in a cockpit simulator, but each scenario takes place in a shorter time than would occur during an actual flight segment (e.g., a 5 min air-intercept task is completed in 2 or 3 min), and with less "down time" between critical events. Thus, learners must make their decisions, and generate their actions, more rapidly than they would under normal flight conditions. Pilots who experience this type of training report that ARTT promotes greater efficiency than conventional simulation, as well as making the training conditions less fatiguing and boring. The results of studies using ARTT also indicate that this simulator technique increases pilot performance and decreases training time (Miller, et al., 1997).

Part Practice

Some skills are very complex, involving the coordination of many limbs and/or many actions strung together sequentially to form a **serial skill**. Clearly, for skills such as these, learners would be overwhelmed if the initial physical rehearsal contained all aspects of the skill at once. Fortunately, in some cases, instructors can break tasks down into parts for rehearsal (Christina & Corcos, 1988). Once learners become proficient at **part practice**, they can begin rehearsing the target skill in its entirety, in essence "putting it back together."

The three types of part practice mentioned in the motor learning literature—**fractionization**, **segmentation** (or progressive part practice), and **simplification**—are all techniques that instructors can use to reduce the complexity of skill practice (Wightman & Lintern, 1985). For example, a swimmer practicing the leg kick by itself, using a kickboard, is experiencing fractionization. Someone practicing ten-pin bowling by first working on just the steps and then combining the steps and the ball movement is using segmentation. A child hitting a baseball off a tee-support is learning through simplification.

Important issues concerning part practice include how the subunits (i.e., the parts) of skills are created and how they are practiced for their maximum transfer to the whole skill. It is usually a simple matter to divide skills into parts, but how these parts are created is quite important. Gymnastics routines can be separated into several component stunts; the pole vault can be divided into run-up, pole-plant, and vault segments. Each of these subparts could be divided even further. But the primary issue practitioners face when considering the use of part practice is the level of contribution such practice will make to the learning of the whole target skill.

At first glance, the answers to these questions seem obvious. In some cases, practicing a part of the task in isolation or in a simplified way seems the same as practicing the whole target skill (e.g., beating an egg, chopping nuts, sifting flour, and then doing all three when preparing to bake a cake). When this is the case, transfer of part practice to whole-skill performance should be almost perfect. However, there are some situations in which part–whole transfer is far less than perfect, nonexistent, or occasionally negative (meaning that it is actually detrimental for the target skill).

The least likely candidates for effective part practice are rapid, discrete skills (e.g., a rapid bat swing) and skills requiring bimanual coordination (e.g., the toss and swing in the tennis serve). Research suggests that when such actions are broken down into arbitrary parts, the parts become so changed from the way they operate in the context of the whole skill that practicing them in isolation contributes little to whole-task performance (e.g., Lersten, 1968; Miller & Franz, 2005; Schmidt & Young, 1987; Wenderoth, Puttemans, Vangheluwe, & Swinnen, 2003). In a skill such as hitting a golf ball, for example, practicing the backswing separately from the forward swing changes the dynamics of the action at the top of the swing. Stopping the backswing at that point eliminates the active stretching of the muscles, which, by the action of their springlike properties, produce a downswing that is smooth and powerful. Therefore, the dynamics of the backswing when it is practiced in isolation are quite different from those of the same backswing performed in the context of the whole swing, and we would be surprised if practicing one such part would transfer to the whole.

As a result, the effectiveness of part practice usually depends on the nature of the target skill being learned. As suggested in the previous cake-baking example, part practice works best for long-duration serial skills, where the actions (or errors) involved in one part do not influence the actions involved in the next. For example, passing the baton is a component of relay races in track and field that is essentially independent of the running phases of the race. In tasks such as relay racing, learners can devote more time to the practice of troublesome parts (e.g., the baton pass) without having to practice the easier, time-consuming, or fatiguing elements (e.g., running) every time. That is, the

serial skill—A type of skill organization that is characterized by several discrete actions connected together in a sequence, often with the order of the actions being crucial to performance success.

part practice—Practice of a complex skill in a more simplified form; the three types of part practice are fractionization, segmentation, and simplification.

fractionization—A type of part practice in which one or more parts of a complex skill are practiced separately.

segmentation—A type of part practice in which one part of a target skill is practiced for a time, then a second part is added to the first part and the two are practiced together, and so on, until the entire target skill is practiced; also referred to as progressive-part practice.

simplification—A type of part practice in which the complexity of some aspect of the target skill is reduced (e.g., slow-motion practice or the use of an oversized ball for the tennis serve).

Part Practice Isn't Always Helpful

The therapeutic literature suggests that part practice does not always improve performance of the whole target skill. If the target skill is normal walking, for example, encouraging patients to practice stepping forward and back repeatedly with one foot in a rocking type of motion—essentially practicing a single step—is probably not very helpful. Separated from the typical gait of stepping forward and moving into the stance phase, repeated stepping forward and back changes the dynamics of the walking action. The natural walking pattern uses substantial momentum to facilitate forward movement, whereas the forward-and-back pattern of the part produces little momentum (i.e., hip and knee flexion with eccentric contraction of the hamstrings to hip and knee extension with concentric contraction of the hamstrings). Thus, the dynamics of the forward step during part practice differ markedly from those of the forward step produced in the context of normal locomotion.

component interaction— The extent to which actions involved in one part of a complex skill influence actions involved in other parts.

motor program— A set of motor commands that is prestructured at the executive level and that defines the essential details of a skilled action; analogous to a central pattern generator.

components of running and passing the baton do not interact. This absence of **component interaction** is an important determinant of the effectiveness of part practice.

In some serial skills, however, performance of one part of a task does influence performance of the next part—i.e., they interact. If the ski racer comes out of a turn too low and fast, this will affect his approach for the next turn. Small positioning errors in one move on the balance beam will determine how the gymnast performs the next move. Exactly where and how high you toss the tennis ball in a serve determines where and when you will hit it. If the relationship between two parts of a task is high, performers must be able to adjust a subsequent action if their performance of an earlier part is altered or ineffective.

Unfortunately, learners cannot practice adjustments between parts of the entire target skill when they are practicing parts in isolation. Therefore, mastery of individual parts of a serial skill does not guarantee effective performance of the whole skill, unless learners also practice making adjustments in some components based on the action of previous ones. Research suggests that patients with Parkinson's disease experience special difficulty in transitioning from one part of a sequence to the next (Weiss, Stelmach, & Hefter, 1997). Therefore, therapists might want to encourage simplified practice that includes transitioning from the end of one movement component to another. The relationship between the degree of interaction among the components of a task and the effectiveness of part practice is depicted in figure 8.5.

Instructors sometimes break practice into parts to help people learn complex skills such as pole vaulting, but the effectiveness of this method depends on the extent to which the components interact with each other.

You may recall from studying the **motor program** concept in chapters 4 and 5 that people control quick actions in an essentially open-loop fashion, with decisions about the action's structure being specified in advance. If only a part of a programmed action is practiced, particularly if

specificity of learning—
The notion that the best learning experiences are those that approximate most closely the movement components and environmental conditions of the target skill and target context.

generalized motor program—
A motor program that defines a pattern of movement rather than a specific movement; this flexibility allows performers to adapt the generalized program to produce variations of the pattern that meet various environmental demands.

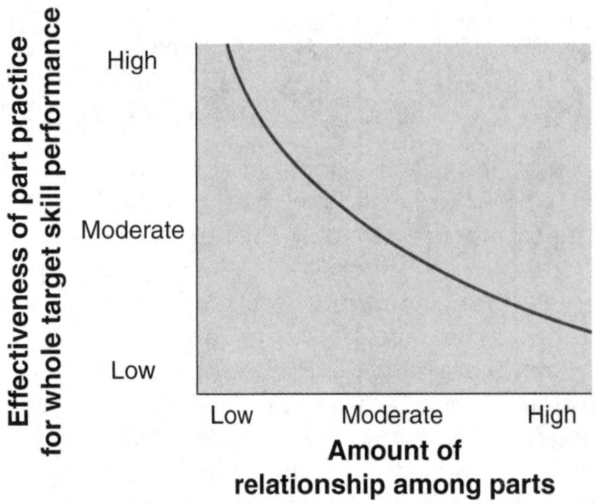

Figure 8.5 Part practice is more effective when the parts of a task are not highly related.

that part has different dynamics when performed in isolation than when it is performed as part of the whole task (e.g., the backswing in golf), performers must use different programs to produce the part in isolation versus the "same" part when it is included in the whole. Practicing this part-program contributes to the learning of the isolated part, but it does not contribute to the learning of the program needed to produce the whole movement.

Slow-Motion Practice

One method practitioners sometimes use to simplify the learner's practice of a target skill is slow-motion practice. A relevant question is whether the slow-motion version of the target skill is really the same (aside from speed) as the normal-speed version. Of course, the **specificity of learning** principle would argue that, if the slow-motion version would differ too much from the normal-speed version, perhaps using a different pattern, then it would not result in much transfer to the faster version of the task.

However, from the perspective of the **generalized motor program**, slow-motion practice may yield some benefit. One parameter of the generalized motor program is overall speed (chapter 4), which performers select depending on how slowly or quickly they decide to execute the movement pattern. If performers decide to slow a movement down slightly, the idea is that they use the same generalized motor program required to produce the movement at faster speeds, but perform it more slowly as a whole. Slow-motion practice of this type can be useful early in the learning process. By practicing a movement in slow motion, learners should be able to control it more effectively, thereby reducing errors in the fundamental pattern yet practicing the same relative-timing structure as the more rapid version.

Practitioners need to be careful, however, if slow-motion practice becomes too slow. When learners slow their movements down too much (e.g., a throwing motion that lasts for 5 s), they change the essential dynamics of the movement, perhaps controlling it with

? It Depends . . .

How Would You Structure Part Practice of the Freestyle Stroke in Swimming?

Assume a beginning swimmer is unafraid of the water and "drown-proofed" but is having difficulty practicing all of the parts of the freestyle stroke (i.e., arm movement, leg kick, breathing) at the same time. How might part practice of the freestyle stroke be structured? What parts of the skill might need to be practiced together? Why?

an entirely different program. Obviously, a slow-motion program of this type will not help performers much if the target context requires normal-speed movements. Recent research also suggests that bimanual movements (e.g., playing musical instruments) are best practiced at or near the speed they need to be performed in the target context rather than at slower speeds (Bogacz, 2005).

Not Too Slow

Some beginning learners produce their movements more slowly than normal in practice in an attempt to achieve more accuracy. Woods (1967) studied three groups of adolescent males with no previous tennis experience; they were taught to hit the tennis forehand ground stroke. The groups were instructed to emphasize either rapid ball velocity, ball placement accuracy, or both rapid velocity and placement accuracy. Halfway through the learning sessions, participants in the first two conditions were instructed to switch their emphasis (i.e., from rapid velocity to placement accuracy or from placement accuracy to rapid velocity). The group that switched to an emphasis on rapid ball velocity after initially emphasizing placement accuracy had the most difficulty. When these learners tried to hit the ball with greater velocity, their accuracy was poorer than that of participants in either of the other two groups. It is possible that, by emphasizing accuracy initially, these players developed closed-loop skills for arm guidance, and this closed-loop strategy was different from the open-loop strategy they needed to hit the ball with rapid velocity (see chapters 3, 4, and 5). Slow-motion practice is not always effective.

Practice for Error Detection

We tend to focus our attention on the *production* of skilled performance, and rightly so. But there is another, mainly neglected, aspect of learning that has a very important contribution—the learning to detect and correct one's own errors.

As people proceed through the stages of practice (see chapter 7), they become more adept at detecting errors in their own movements, almost as a natural consequence of becoming skilled. The capability to detect one's own errors is an important skill in and of itself, as it allows the learner to detect, and subsequently correct, errors that might occur when the teacher or coach is not available to give feedback and instruction. In this way, learners can learn on their own. If error-detection is important, how can we organize practice to maximize this form of learning?

Learning to detect errors is just like other types of learning: It takes practice. The golfer who wants to detect errors in her movements must become sensitive to the

It Depends . . .

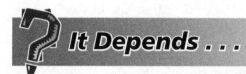

Can You Identify the Relevant Movement-Produced Feedback in Various Skills?

To which sources of movement-produced feedback might learners be instructed to attend when practicing (physically) the following tasks? How might this feedback assist them in learning to detect and correct their errors? Would the answer depend on whether the skill was performed in an open- versus closed-loop way? Why? Can you also identify one source of information that requires an internal focus of attention and one that requires an external focus of attention?

Throwing darts
Chopping wood
Eating spaghetti
Walking with a cane

wide range of information produced by the movements. Such information can be kinesthetic—feelings associated with the movements and forces in the muscles and joints, with ball contact, and with shifts in balance. Information can also be visual—seeing the movements of the limbs in relation to each other and to the environment. Information can sometimes be auditory—hearing the sound of the club against wind resistance and the click that accompanies ball contact (or the "whoosh" that you hear when the ball is missed). Other tasks produce additional sensations, but almost all are richly associated with various forms of movement-produced feedback that can inform learners about the quality of their actions.

For people to improve their error-detection capability they must become sensitive to the particular patterns of movement-produced feedback associated with various performance outcomes. This means that they must be able to associate the nature of the sensations that come from the action with the quality of the action in terms of the extent to which it has met its environmental goal. That is, the learner should be able to estimate the quality of the action he or she has just produced by evaluating the sensory consequences it produced.

Practitioners can also enhance the development of learners' error-detection capability by encouraging them to become sensitive to movement-produced feedback, and developing methods that foster this kind of learning. People usually don't monitor this type of feedback unless someone directs their attention to it or asks them to perform an act that is dependent on the feedback. One way instructors might do this is to ask learners to describe, or estimate, what they felt when they moved—before providing them with any additional feedback. Practitioners might ask learners to describe various aspects of their movements. For example, a physical therapist might ask a patient to describe the movement sensations (after the movement, of course) that accompany a successful sit-to-stand maneuver.

Another way to bring the learner in contact with response-produced feedback is to ask the performer, right after the movement, how effective the action was in terms of achieving the overall goal (without first allowing the performer to know his score). Presumably, this procedure requires the learner to recall how the action looked, felt, and sounded in order to provide an answer to the question about the objective score. Some examples: What was your race car's exit speed in that last corner? What was your timing error on that last attempt? Methods like this have been used in research for several decades (e.g., Schmidt & White, 1972).

Encouraging Learners to Evaluate Their Own Feedback

An excellent illustration of how practitioners might encourage learners to develop their own error-detection capabilities was obtained in a study examining coach–athlete communication (D'Arripe-Longueville, Saury, Fournier, & Durand, 2001). The following quote came from an interview with an archer who was commenting on the behavior of his coach after he completed a performance bout.

> "There, you see, first he (the coach) is asking me what I think about it. You go to him to get an answer and first he makes you talk. He's funny that way . . . when he knows all along what's wrong. He was right behind me! But it forces me to analyze better what I do, that's for sure, and to become aware of all this." (p. 292)

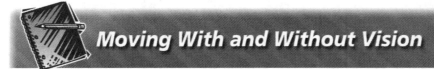

Moving With and Without Vision

One way to sharpen your experience of the feel of a movement is to perform it with your eyes closed. Obviously, this is not a good idea in all cases (e.g., driving a car), but for some skills performed open-loop it can be very illuminating.

Here's an experiment you can try: Stand about 10 ft from a temporary tape-mark on your carpet. Now in one motion, toss a coin so as to have it land exactly on the tape. Repeat this movement five times with your eyes open. Now do it five more times with your eyes closed, leaving them closed until well after the action. In the eyes-closed trials, after each attempt, guess how close you are to the target before opening your eyes. Without vision, you can't see the outcome directly, so you must use some other source of sensory information on which to base your guess. What feedback do you become aware of when you move with your eyes closed that you weren't aware of when you moved with your eyes open? How might the eyes-closed movement experience benefit your performance of the eyes-open movement?

What sources of sensory information are required for evaluating your own performance in skills like this?

Schmidt and White (1972) had learners perform a task requiring timing accuracy. After each trial, participants were asked what their error was (subjective error), and only then would the experimenter tell them their actual error (objective error). Across 170 trials of practice, participants improved their capability to detect their own error markedly. Presumably, the requirement to guess their own error made the participants sensitive to their own response-produced feedback (how the movement looked, felt, sounded), allowing them to learn the relationship between these sensations and their actual (objective) score.

Movement outcomes are often obvious—people can see whether the basketball went into the basket, how close the car is to the curb, or whether the paintbrush stroke covered the desired area of the canvas—shortly after the movement is produced. As a result, asking performers to detect obvious outcomes can be an essentially meaningless exercise. Therefore, in order to use this form of error-detection practice, practitioners must devise a way to prevent the learner from seeing (or otherwise receiving) the actual objective score, and then asking for the learner's own evaluation of the action. Videotaping a performance, then having the learner guess about errors in some aspect of it (subjective error), and then showing the learner the videotape (objective error) is one way that this could be done in real-world settings.

Once participants have increased their capability to detect their own errors, they can confront the problem of learning how to correct them. Once an error is detected, the therapy patient will be able to try various kinds of corrections, and eventually will learn that some types of adjustments to the error are more effective than others. Thus, instructors and therapists can help individuals develop both (a) the capability of detecting their own errors and (b) correcting them effectively. Armed with these capabilities, the patient can correct his or her own errors at home, and can even continue to learn, without the therapist being present.

mental practice—The practice of a motor skill in the absence of overt movement.

Mental Practice Techniques

Because people set aside time to practice their movements doesn't mean they have to spend all of that time moving (i.e., physically performing). Some of this time can be devoted to **mental practice**—that is, thinking about or mentally imaging certain aspects of the skills they are learning, without actually moving. Can mental practice actually contribute to the learning of *motor* skills? Early in motor skills research, scientists doubted that skill acquisition could actually be enhanced through mental practice. Their general understanding of practice and motor learning was that overt physical action, and the feedback that follows it, was essential for motor learning to take place. It was difficult to comprehend how any *motor* skill learning could occur if there were no actual movement, active practice, or movement-produced feedback.

The overwhelming evidence (e.g., Hird et al., 1991) and probably our own personal experience tell us that physical practice is superior to mental practice for learning movement skills. However, in some instances, mental practice has been shown to produce results similar to those found for physical practice (see Feltz & Landers, 1983, for a review of this research). Moreover, mental practice is almost always superior to no practice at all, which makes it an effective technique for athletes away from the practice facilities, for patients whose physical activity is restricted, or for people who sustain an injury that prevents them from performing a movement skill physically (Warner & McNeill, 1988).

During mental practice, learners might practice the procedural or symbolic aspects of the skill (e.g., the sequence of steps in a dance routine or the reminder to follow through when throwing a ball), or they might try to see and feel themselves actually performing the skill (e.g., throwing a dart that results in a bull's-eye), sometimes referred to as mental imagery. We discuss each of these types of mental practice in the following sections.

Mental Rehearsal in Therapy Settings

Mental rehearsal appears to be particularly useful in therapy settings with patients who are unable to engage in large amounts of physical practice because they lack endurance (e.g., patients with multiple sclerosis, cardiac disease, or myasthenia gravis). For example, Linden and colleagues (1989) found that mental rehearsal, compared with no rehearsal at all, improved the balancing capabilities of elderly women (ages 67-90) on a task that required walking while carrying an object in each hand.

Practicing Procedural or Symbolic Elements of Skills

Sackett (1934) formulated the earliest theory addressing the mental practice of motor skills. He proposed that the reason mental practice is beneficial is because it facilitates performers' understanding of the cognitive–symbolic elements of the skill. Examples of cognitive–symbolic elements are the sequence of steps involved in the assembly of a rifle, or the reminder that the stretch and reach are important parts of the arm movements used in many swimming strokes. These cognitive elements were originally thought to be important only during the very early stages of learning (i.e., the **verbal–cognitive stage**). However, when Feltz and Landers (1983) conducted an extensive review of the research literature, they found that mental practice was effective regardless of the skill level of participants. This makes sense, really, when we consider the kinds of mental activity that take place when people produce effective movements. Strategies, focus cues, and general instructional information fall under the category of cognitive–symbolic elements of skills, and are something performers and learners should be able to practice mentally at any stage of practice. The mental practice of cognitive, symbolic, or procedural elements of tasks requires no apparatus, can be done at virtually any time and place, and allows a large group of learners to engage in the activity at the same time.

verbal–cognitive stage—The initial stage of learning, in which verbal and cognitive processes dominate the learner's activity.

But that is not all there is to mental practice. First, there is considerable evidence that alternating or combining mental practice with physical practice is an effective strategy for improving movement performance (Etnier & Landers, 1996; Gabriele, Hall, & Lee, 1989; McBride & Rothstein, 1979; Rawlings, Rawlings, Chen, & Yilk, 1972). In fact, Rawlings et al. (1972) showed that mental practice was highly effective for a task (the rotary pursuit task, or pursuit rotor) in which it is difficult to detect any major cognitive or decision-making components. In this task, with a handheld stylus, the learner attempts to follow a target-dot on a rotating turntable-like structure. Here, the major concern does not seem to involve any cognitive or decision-making activities, but rather the coordination of smooth, accurate arm movements with the target movements. These kinds of findings change our view of mental practice from the earlier views, suggesting that many aspects of movement control—not just cognitive elements—can also be learned with such methods. The challenge for the instructor or therapist is to find ways to intertwine physical and mental practice to promote maximal performance gains.

mental imagery—A mental-practice technique in which people imagine themselves performing a motor skill from either a first-person or a third-person perspective.

Possible Effects of Mental Practice

Mental practice could have an effect at several places in the motor system, as indicated in the conceptual model shown in figure 8.6. More specifically, mental practice could

- activate the stages of processing dealing with the cognitive, symbolic, and decision-making aspects of the skill;
- assist the response-programming process, producing a clearer depiction of the desired state;
- evoke minute neuromuscular activity, far too small to produce action, in the spinal cord and muscles used during the actual movement; or
- help focus performers' attention on task-relevant cues, leading to more effective physical performance.

Mental Imagery

A second category of mental practice is often referred to as **mental imagery**. During mental-imagery sessions, performers try to see and feel themselves actually performing the skill. The earliest support for these sorts of activities came from Jacobson (1930). He observed that when people formed mental images of a movement, weak electrical activity (measured by EMG) occurred in the participating musculature, although

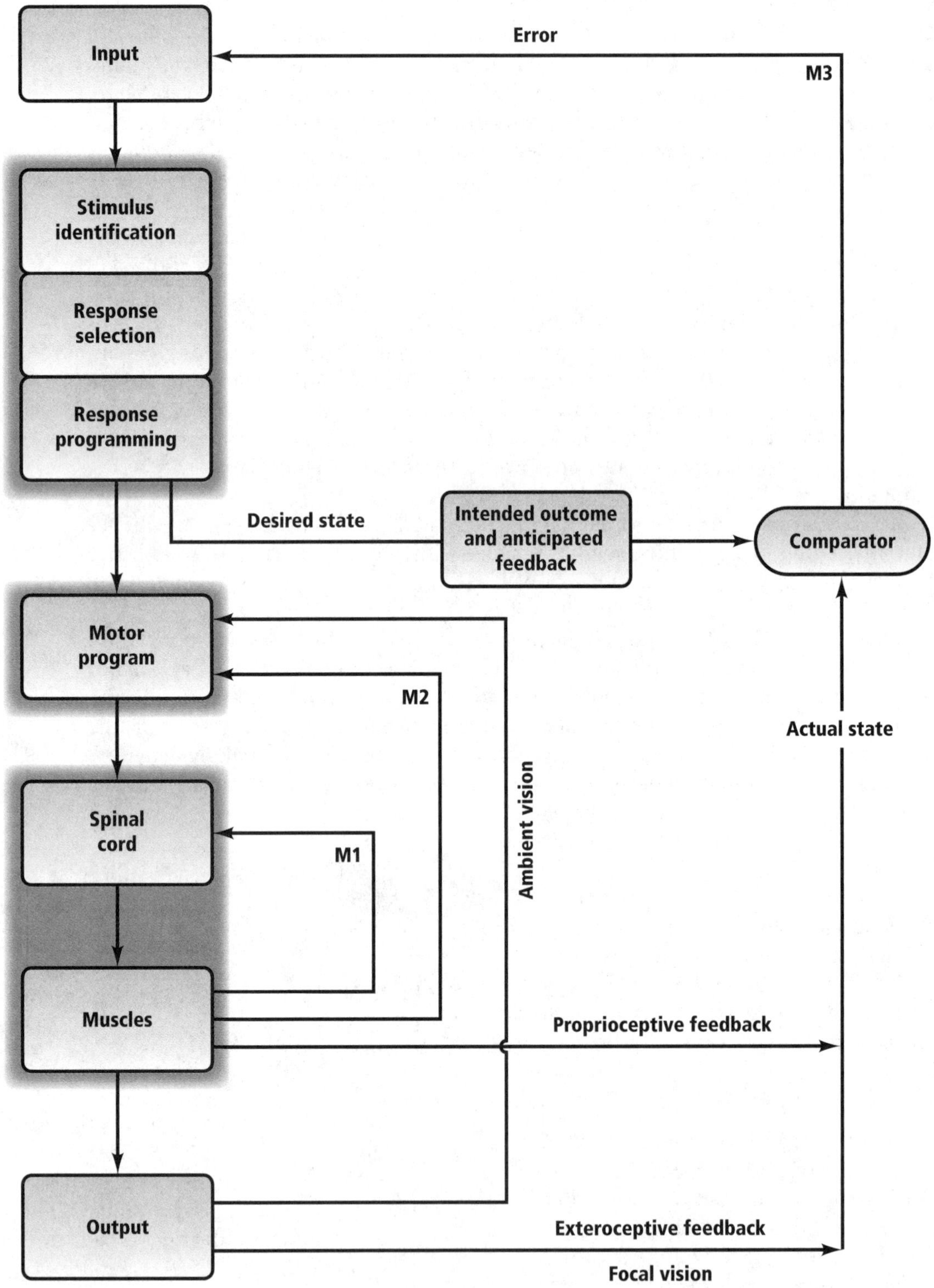

Figure 8.6 The conceptual model of motor performance, highlighting the major processes thought to be affected by mental practice.

the activity was far smaller in size than that necessary to produce the action. Thus, Jacobson proposed that when people imagine themselves moving, the central nervous system conveys a plan of action to the muscles—with the contractions being too small to produce actual movements—which provides a form of practice in the absence of actual bodily motion. Unfortunately, the similarity between EMG patterns of imaged movements and those of actual movements was less obvious, so this hypothesis for mental practice seems unlikely.

MacKay (1981) proposed another explanation for the benefits of imagery during motor skill learning, in which motor representations are primed for action during mental imagery. Recent research has demonstrated support for the priming notion by showing similar patterns of late EEG brain-wave activity for both real and imagined movements (Smith & Collins, 2004). This view has received considerable interest in the sport psychology literature, which shows that high-performance athletes, as well as beginners, seem to benefit from imagery (e.g., Gregg & Hall, 2006; Nordin, Cumming, Vincent, & McGrory, 2006). Moreover, research has shown that mental imagery enhances sport performance and learning (e.g., Kendall, Hrycaiko, Martin, & Kendall, 1990; Woolfolk, Parrish, & Murphy, 1985; Wrisberg & Anshel, 1989), reinforces thoughts and emotions critical to performance (e.g., Callow, Hardy, & Hall, 2001; Calmels, Berthoumieux, & d'Arripe-Longueville, 2004; Hale & Whitehouse, 1998), and is used more extensively and systematically by successful athletes than by less successful ones (Calmels, d'Arripe-Longueville, Fournier, & Soulard, 2003; Hall, Rodgers, & Barr, 1990; Salmon, Hall, & Haslam, 1994).

Practicing Mental Imagery

As with many new activities, learners need systematic instruction in the methods of mental imagery as well. It does not seem to be sufficient merely to suggest that learners go somewhere and imagine themselves performing. The most successful methods have learners move to a quiet, relaxing place where there will be no interruptions. Resting comfortably, they attempt to achieve a state of physical relaxation by closing their eyes and focusing simply on the breathing process, saying the word *relax* each time a breath is released. Once they are relaxed, learners might try to image a simple event in as vivid a form as possible, even in color and with all of the sounds and other sensations of the actual movement.

People can image movements from either an *internal perspective* (the way they experience the movement and the movement environment when they are physically performing the action) or from an *external perspective* (the way they experience the skill when they view a video replay of their performance). The perspective that works best appears to depend on the type of skill. For example, research suggests that an external perspective is more effective than an internal perspective for people who perform closed skills that are evaluated on form, such as gymnastics, figure skating, and karate (Hardy & Callow, 1999). A basketball player imaging the free throw shot (where form is not the major outcome) might benefit more from an internal perspective that connects the action to the desired outcome. The most effective imagery, regardless of perspective, simulates both the look and feel (and sometimes even the sounds and smells) of the actual movement (Hardy, 1997).

As an example, imagine yourself walking into your kitchen at home. You notice the surrounding sights, sounds, and smells; you feel yourself taking a lemon out of the refrigerator and slicing it in half, slowly squeezing the juice on the tongue. Once learners become comfortable with simple scenes, they can attempt to image simple movement skills. In such cases learners should try to allow the event to unfold in real time (e.g., walking from a street location to the door of their house or apartment). In addition to rehearsing sport or recreational skills physically, learners might begin imaging individual actions or sequences of activities as they become more and more a part of the skill. In all cases, the focus is on *successful* skill execution, avoiding images of failure (Cumming, Nordin, Horton, & Reynolds, 2006; Nordin & Cumming, 2005). For additional tips on maximizing mental imagery, see Orlick (1986, 2000).

Performed in this way, mental imagery can be a particularly effective method of skill practice (Calmels, Berthoumieux, & d'Arripe-Longueville, 2004). People can practice imagery at almost any time—between performance attempts, between days of physical rehearsal, while relaxing at home, or when lying in bed at night. As with any skill, the more frequently mental imagery is practiced the more effective it becomes. Therefore, to maximize its effectiveness, learners might set aside specific times in the day for systematic mental imagery. Typical sessions last no longer than 5 to 15 min, and emphasis should be given to quality rehearsal (i.e., creating vivid, lifelike images) rather than to quantity.

SUMMARY

Practitioners can use a variety of techniques to supplement people's learning experiences. Before providing instructional assistance, they can do the following:

- Familiarize learners with the learning situation to diminish their anxiety and allow them to focus more readily on the process of performance improvement.
- Open communication with learners to encourage them to express their preferences and provide information about the types of assistance they find most helpful.
- Assist learners in determining the most relevant attentional focus for various tasks and situations.
- Encourage learners to practice shifting their attention between an internal and an external focus.
- Instruct learners to focus on process goals rather than outcome goals.
- Help learners set realistic goals that are attainable in order to enhance motivation and effort in practice.
- Schedule shorter practice sessions that are more spread out in time rather than longer ones that are bunched together.
- Balance the amount of practice and rest within a rehearsal period according to the fitness level of learners and the energy requirements of the skill.

When presenting the target skill, good practitioners often do the following:

- Provide instructions that are brief and simple—emphasizing no more than one or two points at a time.
- Give instructions that emphasize concepts with which learners are familiar and that remind them of previous experiences that can be transferred to the learning of the target skill.

- Provide demonstrations that convey the essential features of the target skill.
- Direct beginners' attention to the key features of demonstrations.
- Use physical guidance procedures only to present learners with a basic idea of the target skill or to minimize the risk of injury.
- Eliminate physical guidance as soon as learners understand the basic movement pattern or are at minimal risk of injury.

Learners can engage in both physical and mental practice when developing their skills. Practitioners can encourage learners to combine both types of practice to obtain a deeper appreciation of the various dimensions of movement production. Practitioners might supplement the physical and mental practice of learners in these ways:

- By using simulators, but only when they convey the essential features of the target skill.
- By providing opportunity for part practice when the target skill is too complex to be practiced in its entirety, but not for rapid skills performed open-loop.
- By using slow-motion practice to increase learners' control and consistency of movement production, but without disrupting the movement pattern used in normal-speed action.
- By directing learners' attention to movement-produced feedback to encourage their development of error-detection capabilities.
- By encouraging learners to adopt an internal or external focus of attention that is consistent with the task and their level of skill.
- By asking learners to report their own performance errors as a way to develop error-detection capabilities.
- By teaching learners how to engage in effective mental practice and imagery.

FROM PRINCIPLES TO PRACTICE

Check your comprehension of the concepts and terms discussed in this chapter by responding to each of the exercises in the following sections. The first section contains several exercises designed to test your working knowledge of key terms. The second section poses a variety of problems designed to check your understanding of key concepts. In the third section you are challenged to apply your knowledge by discussing a defensible solution for two scenarios.

Know Your Key Terms

Matching: Forms of Rehearsal

Match the following terms with their respective categories or definitions by placing the most appropriate letter on each of the blanks below.

Forms of Rehearsal—Terms

a. error-detection practice
b. fractionization
c. simulation
d. mental imagery
e. segmentation
f. simplification
g. mental practice

Forms of Rehearsal—Category or Definition

_____ 1. For example, slow-motion practice

_____ 2. The gradual addition of parts of a complex skill; also known as progressive part practice

_____ 3. The practice of a single part of a complex skill

_____ 4. Helps learners remember the procedural aspects of a motor skill

_____ 5. Helps learners become more adept at interpreting the feedback that arises from their movements

_____ 6. For example, a springboard diver attempting to see and feel the dive before performing it

_____ 7. Essential when the target skill is expensive or dangerous (e.g., learning to fly a jetliner)

Consider: Target Skills and Target Behaviors

For the following movement progression, list the appropriate attentional focus for each phase using Nideffer's four categories of focus. Provide rationale for your answers.

Movement progression for heading a soccer ball	Appropriate attentional focus
1. Watching the approaching ball	__________________
2. Sensing the location of teammates and opponents	__________________
3. Deciding on the location where the header should go	__________________
4. Making ball contact with the forehead	__________________

Fill in the Blank: Creating an Effective Learning Environment

Complete the following sentences:

Before providing instructional assistance, practitioners should familiarize learners with the learning environment and encourage an open line of ________________ ________________ communication. Because the attentional capacity of people is limited, practitioners need to assist learners in identifying ________________ ________________ that are relevant for performance at different moments. Those who experience anxiety during performance or learning sessions should be encouraged to focus on ________________ goals rather than on ________________ goals. ________________ practice sessions are helpful for learners who are rehearsing discrete skills for which minimal rest has little or no influence on learning. However, ________________ practice sessions are sometimes necessary when fatigue leads to sloppy performance or places learners at risk of injury.

Check Your Understanding

1. Explain why it is important for practitioners to familiarize learners with the instructional situation, and then discuss how doing this might be helpful for a therapist working with an elderly nursing home resident who is trying to learn how to use a motorized bed.
2. Describe the process of two-way communication and explain how a coach might use it to provide more effective instruction for a collegiate gymnast who is trying to learn the elements of a balance beam routine.
3. Briefly describe Nideffer's four categories of attentional focus and indicate which category you think is most appropriate for performance of each of the following tasks: threading a needle, driving a car on a busy interstate, remembering a friend's phone number, and plotting a strategy for defeating a racquetball opponent.
4. List three features of effective instructions and illustrate how an adult might incorporate each feature into the instructions he or she gives to an 8-year-old child trying to learn how to do a headstand.
5. Explain the purpose of demonstrations during skill learning, and then discuss two features of a coin-flip motion that a person might point out to a friend before demonstrating the action.
6. Discuss the concept of part-practice and then describe how an instructor might use this type of practice in assisting a person who is learning how to drive a stick-shift car.
7. Describe the concept of error-detection practice and then explain how a practitioner might assist a dart thrower in developing the capability of detecting errors.
8. Explain the difference between mental practice of procedural elements and mental imagery. Give an example of how a person who is learning to perform ballroom dancing might use each of these types of mental practice.

Apply Your Knowledge

Exercise 1

A young soccer player is having difficulty learning how to head the ball. Her coach thinks that the player is just afraid of the ball, and that once she overcomes her fear she should be able to perform the skill with no problems. Discuss some things the coach might do to open communication with this player. Then suggest some steps the coach might take to create an instructional setting that encourages all of his players to provide him with information about their learning experiences. In what ways might such input enhance the effectiveness of the coach's instruction? Provide rationale for your answers and furnish two supporting references.

Exercise 2

A college student who is hearing-impaired wants to learn how to drive a car. A major challenge for the instructor is to find ways to provide this learner with focus cues he can use to develop his skills. First discuss how the instructor might establish communication with this special-needs student. Then give an example of a practice situation that might place a hearing-impaired learner at a disadvantage. Finally, explain how the instructor might adapt instructions, present demonstrations, provide physical guidance, or implement a combination of these to focus the learner's attention in this situation. Provide rationale for your suggestions and include two supporting references.

UNIVERSITY OF WINCHESTER
LIBRARY

chapter 9

Structuring the Learning Experience

▷ Chapter Outline

▷ Chapter Objectives

When you have completed this chapter, you should be able to

- discuss the concept of practice structure and explain its importance to goal achievement and the performance of target skills in the desired target contexts,
- describe the difference between blocked- and random-practice schedules for situations in which participants are attempting to learn several tasks,
- provide several explanations for the advantages of random-practice schedules in the learning of a number of tasks,
- describe the difference between constant- and varied-practice schedules for situations in which performers are attempting to learn how to adapt a particular movement to a variety of target contexts,
- contrast random- and varied-practice schedules and explain how practitioners might combine the two during motor skill learning, and
- discuss the difference between consistent and varied mapping and explain how practitioners might assist learners in automating their responses for each type of mapping situation.

PREVIEW

Two skills practitioners are puzzled and concerned. They have been supervising volleyball instruction for a group of preadolescents at a summer camp. For several weeks the campers have practiced a variety of skills in a series of 12 one-hour sessions. During each session, campers practice one skill for a while, then shift to a second skill and practice it, then move to a third skill, and so on. The instructors assume that by structuring practice in this way, they are encouraging full concentration on each skill and providing learners with sufficient repetitions to achieve a good level of mastery. When the campers practice this way, they seem to be increasingly proficient and perform most of the skills fairly well. However, each time they attempt to play an actual game of volleyball, they fail to demonstrate the level of skill they had previously demonstrated in practice.

The instructors wonder why this is happening. Are they failing to give the campers enough practice? Should they wait longer before introducing the campers to the game situation? Have they chosen the wrong type of practice schedule for the campers? How else might they structure skill rehearsal to improve the campers' transition from practice sessions to game conditions?

OVERVIEW

As we discussed in the previous chapter, the most important contributor to motor learning is proper physical rehearsal, or practice. Accomplished performers demonstrate extremely high skill levels because of the enormous amount of time and effort they devote to practicing. Kottke and colleagues (1978) estimated that a typical quarterback in American football throws 1.4 million passes, and a typical basketball player attempts a million shots, during their respective 15-year professional sport careers! Clearly, people who desire to be accomplished performers must spend vast amounts of time practicing their skills.

But the amount of time a person spends practicing is not the only concern here. Certainly, the *quality* of practice sessions is crucial as well. A person can exert considerable effort during many hours of ineffective practice, with little to show for it except boredom, frustration, or perhaps a type of skilled performance that is not appropriate for the target context. With this in mind, good instructors exercise diligence in organizing and structuring practice sessions that will be effective.

There are countless ways that physical practice might be organized, so instructors need to understand the pros and cons of all of these variations and the ways they can affect learning. Fortunately, the scientific literature contains many studies dealing with practice structure and its influence on performance and learning. In this chapter we turn to the structure of practice sessions, showing how people can practice two or more tasks together to facilitate learning and how practicing variations of a single task can increase performers' capability of adapting movements to meet the demands of new situations. We conclude the chapter by discussing ways practitioners might structure the practice of rapid, open skills that require performers to match their responses to environmental demands.

PRACTICING SEVERAL SKILLS

In many real-world settings, the instructor's goal is to teach several skills during a fixed time, often within a single practice session. For example, a tennis practice might involve the forehand and backhand ground strokes, the volley, and several types of serves, not to mention the numerous variations of spin or placement that players might practice.

Rehabilitation sessions that are designed to help stroke patients recover manual skills might include buttoning a shirt, tying shoelaces, opening a can of tuna, and threading a needle. One question confronting teachers and therapists is how to organize, or sequence, the practice of a number of skills within a session to maximize learning. Two variations of sequencing, or practice scheduling, have been shown to have powerful effects on learning: random practice and variable practice. We discuss both of these approaches to sequencing practice in this chapter.

blocked practice—A practice sequence in which individuals rehearse the same skill repeatedly.

random practice—A practice sequence in which individuals perform a number of skills in a (quasi-) random order, thus avoiding or minimizing consecutive repetitions of any single skill.

Blocked Practice and Random Practice

Suppose that a person wants to learn three skills that are reasonably different, such as three tennis strokes (e.g., forehand, backhand, volley) or three stroke rehabilitation activities (e.g., brushing teeth, pouring a glass of water, and buttoning a shirt). A common-sense approach to scheduling would be to devote a fixed block of time to practicing the first task before moving on to the next. Then the learner would devote a period of time to the second task before moving on to the third. This approach to scheduling, where a substantial portion of the learner's time is spent on one skill before practicing the next, is referred to as **blocked practice**. Blocked practice is typically seen during drills, with people attempting the same movement over and over (see figure 9.1*a*). This kind of practice seems to make sense in that it allows learners uninterrupted time to concentrate on performing one skill at a time, correcting, refining, and ingraining each skill before proceeding to the next.

Another approach to learning multiple skills consists of a greater variation of rehearsal within a single practice session. In **random practice**, for example, the rehearsal of the various skills is intermingled, or mixed, during the practice period (see figure 9.1*b*). Learners rotate continually among the tasks and, in the most extreme cases, they never perform the same skill twice in a row. In a similar way, practice repetitions that are increasingly separated (spaced) in time allow more time for intervening actions to occur, and this has a similar effect to randomizing practice among several tasks.

What are some effects of these two practice schedules (blocked and random) on learning? They may not be what you would expect. Numerous experiments have generated very surprising findings that seem to contradict standard views of practice. In 1979, Shea and Morgan conducted the first of these studies (see "Shea and Morgan's Experiment" on page 259) and found that, although superior performance during practice was associated with blocked practice, superior learning (as measured on a delayed test of retention) was found when practice occurred under random, rather than blocked, conditions. Their findings have been reproduced many times in other controlled laboratory experiments (Lee & Magill, 1983; Shea, Kohl, & Indermill, 1990; Tsutsui, Lee, & Hodges, 1998), in studies conducted in more everyday instructional settings (Boyce & Del Rey, 1990; Goode & Magill, 1986; Hall, Domingues, & Cavazos, 1994; Wrisberg & Liu, 1991), and in rehabilitation environments (Hanlon, 1996).

Why Random Practice Is So Effective for Learning

Most research has shown that when people practice a variety of skills randomly, their performance is less successful during practice than when they practice skills in a blocked sequence. However, when participants resume performance at a later time on a test of retention, those who originally practiced under random conditions demonstrate superior retention compared with those who originally practiced under blocked conditions. For example, Ste-Marie, Clark, Findlay, and Latimer (2004) found that elementary school students who practiced writing letters and symbols in a random format performed more poorly than students practicing in a blocked (i.e., repeated) format, but they demonstrated superior handwriting accuracy and speed during retention

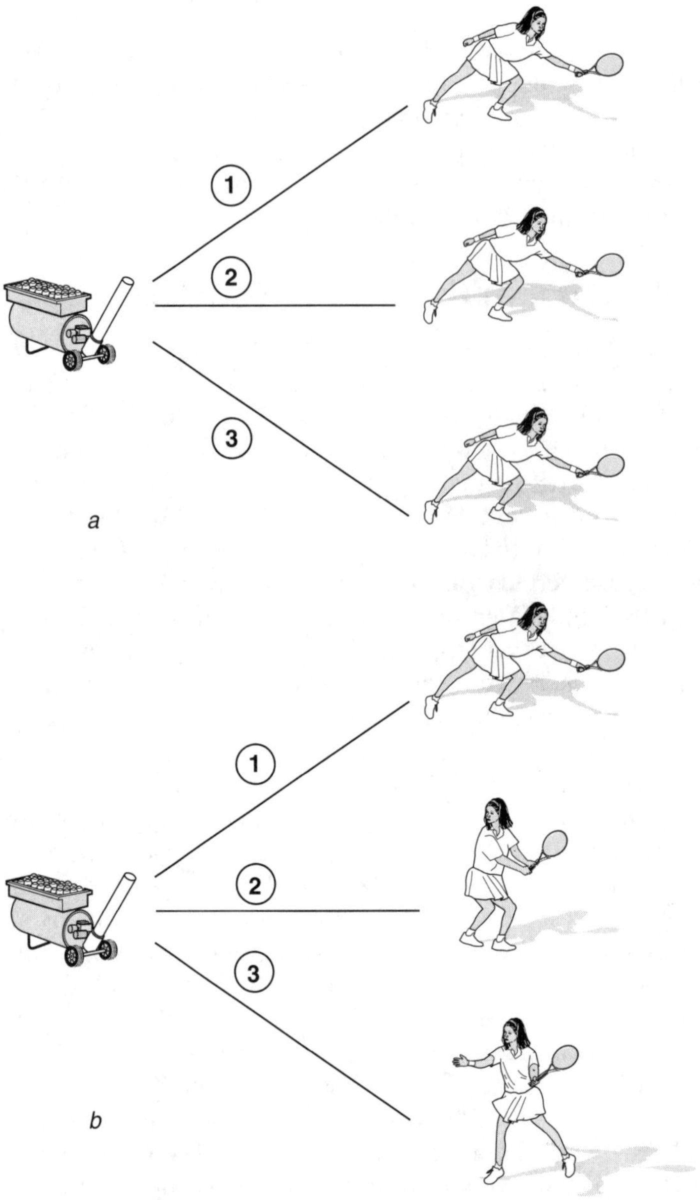

Figure 9.1 Blocked practice *(a)* enhances immediate performance, but random practice *(b)* produces superior learning.

contextual interference effect—A collection of findings showing that certain conditions that depress performance during practice produce more learning as measured on delayed tests of retention.

tests and superior performance in transfer to variations in the tasks (i.e., attaching the letters, as in forming the word *h-a-y*). This pattern of results, termed the **contextual interference effect**, challenges conventional wisdom—that those practice conditions that produce the most proficient performance in practice will be best for learning. Thus, in the results of contextual interference studies, we find one of those counterintuitive phenomena of human learning: Poorer initial performance (during practice sessions) leads to increased learning as measured on delayed tests of retention. It is an extremely general phenomenon, valid for both motor and verbal–cognitive skills, for learners at almost all levels of skill, and for learners of various ages (e.g., Schmidt & Bjork, 1992; Ste-Marie, Clark, Findlay, & Latimer, 2004).

Two interesting hypotheses have been proposed to explain why the contextual-interference effect occurs. One suggests that random practice makes practice more meaningful and distinctive, and the other suggests that random practice forces learners to relearn each of the repetitions. We explain these views next.

Elaboration: More Meaningful and Distinctive Learning

Shea and Zimny (1983) interpreted the beneficial effects of random practice in terms of an increased meaningfulness or distinctiveness of the movements, sometimes referred to as the **elaboration hypothesis.** They argued that when individuals shift from one skill to another during a random-practice session, they are forced to become aware of the distinctiveness among the skills, making each one more meaningful in their long-term memory. More meaningful or distinctive memories are presumably more durable and, therefore, more easily retrieved for use at a later time, resulting in more effective

elaboration hypothesis—The idea that random practice during practice causes people to elaborate or discover the distinctiveness among skills (whereas blocked practice does not), which is beneficial for performance in a retention test.

Shea and Morgan's Experiment

John Shea and Robyn Morgan (1979) conducted a groundbreaking experiment that revolutionized the way movement scientists think about the processes involved in skill learning. Following some of the original ideas of William Battig (1966), Shea and Morgan placed participants in two groups that practiced three different arm and hand movements (skills A, B, and C), the goal being to move as rapidly as possible on each attempt. During the practice phase, one group performed the three skills in a blocked order; that is, they completed all their attempts on skill A before moving to skill B and then completed all their attempts on skill B before moving to skill C. The other group practiced the three skills in a random order, with their attempts being randomly intermingled among the skills, with no skill being repeated on successive trials. Both groups performed all three skills the same number of times during the practice phase. You can see from figure 9.2 that, during the practice phase, the blocked group produced movements that were far faster (i.e., smaller mean movement times) than were those of the random group.

To determine how the two practice schedules influenced skill learning, Shea and Morgan required participants to perform the movements again on two other occasions in a retention test. The first occasion occurred just 10 min after participants completed their last attempt of the practice phase, and the second occasion took place 10 days later (see figure 9.2). During the retention phases, each group (those who had practiced under random conditions and those who had practiced under blocked conditions) was asked to perform the movements in both a blocked and a random format in different sets of trials. In the retention phase, there was a large advantage for the participants who had learned the task under random conditions. These effects were very large and dramatic when the retention test was administered under random conditions and were considerably smaller (but still present) when the retention test occurred under blocked conditions.

These results indicate that, although blocked practice may produce faster immediate *performance* (during practice), random practice produces better *learning.* Recall that learning is usually measured on tests of retention or transfer—which are not given during the practice (or acquisition) phase. Here, blocked (vs. random) practice facilitated performance temporarily while these conditions were operating in acquisition but had the opposite effect on learning as measured on the retention tests (see the review by Schmidt & Bjork, 1992, for more on this concept). Shea and Morgan's findings surprised scientists in the field who had previously assumed that consecutive repetitions of the same movement would produce more learning than nonconsecutive repetitions of several movements. Ever since the publication of this study, the challenge for researchers has been to understand how random-practice conditions, which produce poorer performance during practice, can actually lead to better long-term learning.

short-term memory (STM)—The memory system that allows people to retrieve, rehearse, process, and transfer information from STSS; believed to be limited in capacity and brief in duration.

long-term memory (LTM)—The memory system that holds information and life experiences; believed to be vast in capacity and unlimited in duration.

forgetting or spacing hypothesis—The hypothesis that random practice prevents the repetition of a given task on successive attempts, allowing short-term forgetting, which requires the learner to generate the solution on every trial (whereas blocked practice does not); the method of generating the solution is learned, which is effective on delayed tests of retention.

performance in retention tests (see again our discussion of **short-term memory** and **long-term memory** in chapter 2).

In a later study, Shea and Zimny (1983) interviewed participants at the conclusion of one of their contextual-interference experiments and found support for the elaboration hypothesis. Random-practice participants spoke of elaborate relationships they had noticed among the spatial patterns of the movements they were producing as well as between those movement patterns and the patterns of other objects and shapes with which they were familiar. For example, in postexperiment interviews, some random-practice participants said that they noticed that the pattern for movement A was essentially the same as that for movement C, except that the first part of the movement was reversed. One particular participant even observed that the pattern of one of the movements was similar in shape to a mirror image of the letter Z. Comments such as these suggest that participants in the random-practice condition derived greater meaningfulness and distinctiveness from the movements they were practicing than did participants in the blocked-practice condition. Those in the latter group talked of producing their movements more or less automatically, almost by rote. Apparently, the repetition of single movements during separate series of attempts did little to promote comparisons of the similarities and differences among the movements or between those movements and others with which participants were familiar.

Spacing of Movements: The Forgetting Hypothesis

Another explanation for the benefits of random practice is the **forgetting, or spacing, hypothesis**. According to this hypothesis, when learners shift from skill A to skill B during practice, they forget some aspects of what they did on skill A while they are figuring out what to do on skill B. Therefore, when it's time for them to attempt skill A again, they have to generate the action plan for that skill all over. For this reason, the forgetting hypothesis is sometimes referred to as the action-plan-reconstruction hypothesis (Lee & Magill, 1985). Because random-practice learners are continuously

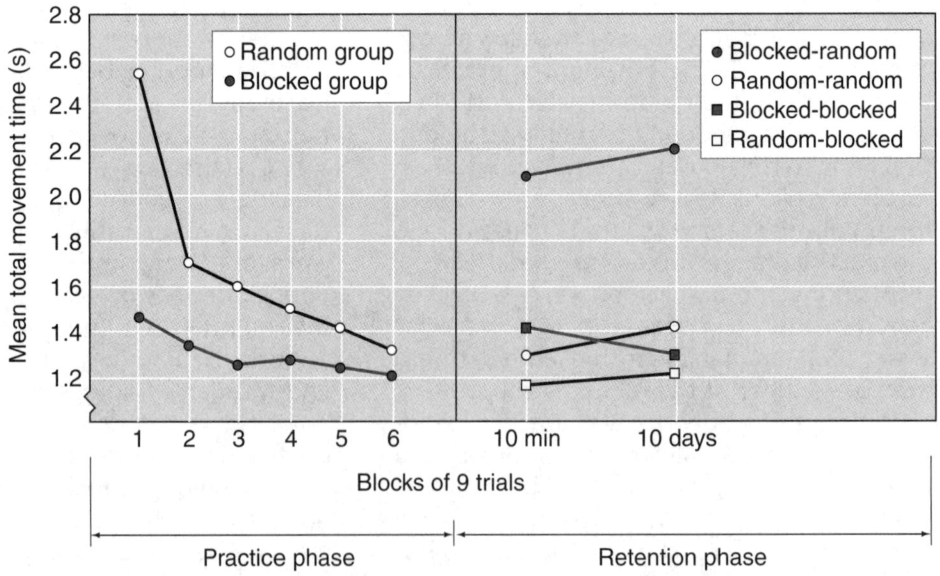

Figure 9.2 Performance on movement-speed tasks under random and blocked conditions. The relative amount that the groups learned is indicated by their retention performance at the right. (Reprinted from Shea & Morgan, 1979.)

being challenged to produce the appropriate plans for various movements, their performance during initial practice is relatively poor. However, they benefit from this more rigorous form of practice when they resume skill performance at a later time, presumably because they have had more practice at developing a memory representation for each skill. Recent research (Overduin, Richardson, Lane, Bizzi, & Press, 2006), along with older studies of verbal learning (Cuddy & Jacoby, 1982), show that, compared with repetitive practice, intermittent practice (i.e., more spacing or interfering activity between attempts) promotes the stabilization of motor memories.

In contrast to random-practice learners, blocked-practice learners can simply apply essentially the same plan they use on the first attempt of each skill for all subsequent attempts. Not surprisingly, their performance is quite good during practice sessions. Unfortunately, longer-term learning is not as good as with random practice, presumably because of the minimal experience these people have in generating different movement plans during their rehearsal of the skills. They have not been forced to generate new action plans, so they do not become very proficient at doing so in retention performance.

The act of generating skill solutions or action plans provides one way to understand how random practice (compared with blocked practice) actually enhances learning. This process is sometimes referred to as **retrieval practice**, because learners are required to practice the skill of retrieving the necessary performance information from LTM (Bjork, 1975, 1979; Landauer & Bjork, 1978). According to this hypothesis, the extensive retrieval practice that occurs during random practice leads to more effective performance in future situations requiring these retrieval operations.

retrieval practice—The act of generating a solution to a motor problem (e.g., retrieving a motor program and its parameters from long-term memory); facilitated by a random-practice schedule.

Mathematical Analogy to the Forgetting Explanation for the Contextual Interference Effect

Cuddy and Jacoby (1982) suggested a mathematics example of the difference between blocked practice and random practice that is analogous to the forgetting explanation for the contextual interference effect in motor learning. Suppose that you are a 10-year-old practicing to do long division in your head; the three problems you are asked to solve during practice are 21 ÷ 7, 18 ÷ 2, and 12 ÷ 4. If you are practicing under blocked conditions, the instructor might ask you for the answer to 21 ÷ 7 first, and you would struggle to come up with the answer—3. However, if the instructor next asks you to come up with the answer to 21 ÷ 7 again, you could simply remember the previous answer, 3, without going through the mental processing that you used to generate the solution the first time. This continued repetition of the same solution would continue to occur for as long as the instructor asked you to solve 21 ÷ 7. Your performance would be essentially perfect because you would have to do nothing more than repeat the same solution each time.

If you are practicing under random conditions, on the other hand, the instructor might ask you for the answer to 21 ÷ 7, the answer to 18 ÷ 2, and then the answer to 12 ÷ 4. After that the instructor might ask for the answer to 18 ÷ 2 or 21 ÷ 7 again, and by now you would probably have forgotten the answer you gave a little while earlier. Thus, you would be forced to come up with the solution each time. Improvements in your performance would come much more slowly and with considerably more difficulty than they would under blocked-practice conditions, but your long-term learning and retention would be enhanced because you would be forced to solve each of the problems more frequently. Finally, what is the meaning of Cuddy and Jacoby's (1982) title, "When forgetting helps memory"? Forgetting can't help memory, or can it? If so, how? If not, why not?

generalized motor program— A motor program that defines a pattern of movement rather than a specific movement; this flexibility allows performers to adapt the generalized program to produce variations of the pattern that meet various environmental demands.

parameters— The variable inputs to a generalized motor program, such as speed or amplitude of the movement, which result in different surface features.

parameterization— The act of assigning parameters to a generalized motor program (e.g., large force, left hand, short movement time) that allows the performer to achieve a particular movement goal.

desirable difficulties— Elements of practice that make effective performance more difficult to achieve during practice yet result in more effective learning later on.

transfer-appropriate processing— The learning of various information-processing activities, which are exercised in particular types of practice, that are appropriate for performance in retention or transfer situations.

How might we use the conceptual model of motor performance (see figure 9.3) to explain the way people retrieve task solutions or movement plans? Remember (from chapter 4) that when performers are to produce a rapid, goal-oriented movement, they must retrieve a desired state and a **generalized motor program** from long-term memory (during the response-selection stage). Once they have done this, they select **parameters** (during the response-programming stage) that dictate how the specific action should be executed (i.e., how rapidly, forcefully, for how long). The act of selecting the appropriate generalized program and determining the desired parameters can be thought of as a kind of solution to the motor problem facing the learner. During random practice, learners must retrieve a program and "parameterize" it before each movement, because they are producing different movements (requiring different motor programs and parameters) from one practice attempt to the next. During blocked practice, learners can use the same generalized motor program and parameters (almost without modification) for a series of movement attempts, thereby avoiding the effortful processes of retrieval and **parameterization**, which are important for learning.

By causing learners to retrieve and parameterize the generalized motor program before each movement, instructors introduce what Bjork (1994, 1999; Roediger & Karpicke, 2006) termed **desirable difficulties** into skill practice. Conventional wisdom suggests that practice should be made as easy and comfortable as possible for the learner so that errors are minimized. Bjork and others (e.g., Schmidt & Bjork, 1992) emphasized, however, that certain ways of making practice difficult for learners—ways that make learners struggle somewhat—are more beneficial in the long run. That is, even though (compared with other methods) these desirable difficulties might not lead to optimal performance during practice, they increase long-term learning as measured later on. Among other things, random practice seems to be one way of creating desirable difficulties. Another way is illustrated in the highlight titled "Adding Desirable Difficulties to the Practice of Stroke Patients." Keep your eyes open for further illustrations of this theme as you read the remainder of this chapter and chapter 10.

Finally, there are undoubtedly many ways that we can make practice difficult for learners, but we should not expect all of these to produce gains in learning as random practice does. The notion of desirable difficulties is that certain kinds of practice methods make practice difficult for the learner, they degrade the performance somewhat (compared with less difficult conditions), and some of these require learners to practice certain processes that are beneficial for performance in the target context. Sometimes, researchers refer to this kind of practice as involving **transfer-appropriate processing** (Bransford, Franks, Morris, & Stein, 1979), meaning that learners are practicing processes that are appropriate for (or useful for) performance in later transfer tests. Thus, we could say that random practice, as opposed to blocked practice, exercises processes (e.g., retrieval operations) that are appropriate for performance later on when those retrieval operations are needed for performance.

Practical Implications of Blocked and Random Practice

One of the most important implications of the research on blocked and random practice concerns the impact of movement repetitions on skill learning. How often have you heard people say that learners need to practice a task over and over until they get it right, as if a massive number of repetitions are somehow going to "stamp in" the correct movement to the learners' brains?

The concept of repetition is deeply rooted in many traditional training methods. Serious students of piano, violin, and dance are required to devote nearly countless hours of repetition to the fundamental movement patterns considered essential for effective performance. Athletes practice some of their movements hundreds of times,

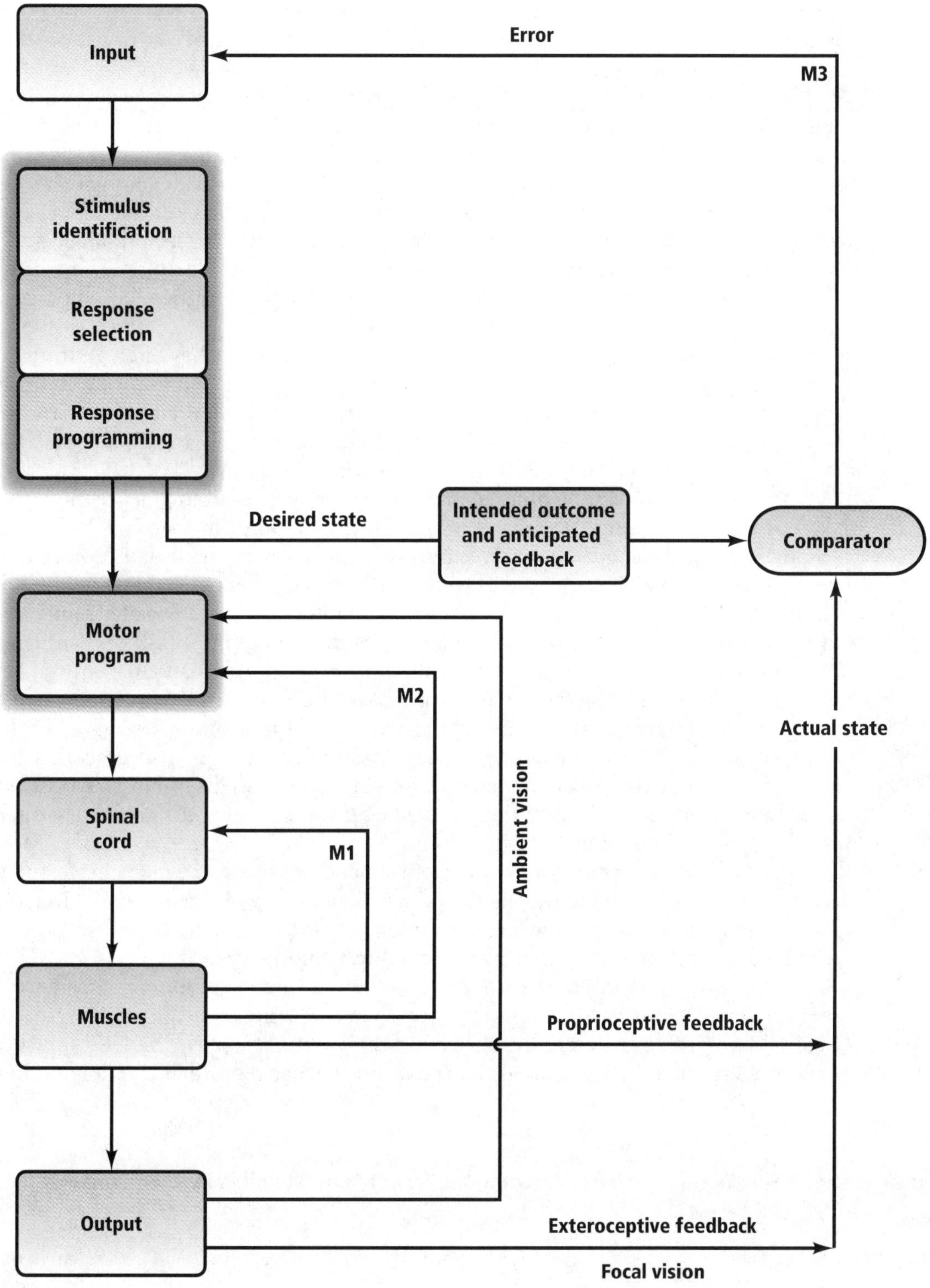

Figure 9.3 The conceptual model of motor performance, highlighting the processes where random practice effects are thought to occur.

often in a single practice session, in an attempt to perfect the correct action (e.g., free throw shots in basketball, serves in tennis, chip shots in golf). Therapy patients attempt the same actions over and over during rehabilitation sessions in an effort to recover the control of functional movements (e.g., feeding, locomotion, dressing). The main point is that many *repetitions* in practice are essential for highly skilled performance—but *repetitiveness* in practice is not effective.

The paradox of blocked-practice scheduling is that it produces effective performance during initial practice but does not promote lasting learning. Learners achieve good performance with blocked practice because they are able to fine-tune essentially the same movement parameters from one attempt to the next. Blocked practice may also invite the influence of minor, temporary factors that contribute to consistent performance (such as an optimal level of arousal and an appropriate focus of attention). The result is an artificially high level of performance that gives learners a false sense of accomplishment.

Many of our golfing friends tell us they can "do anything" during blocked practice at the driving range, implying that their skills have risen to some new level. However, when these folks take their skills back out onto the golf course, they often perform no better than they did before their driving range experience. In a similar way, patients may experience temporary performance improvements during therapy sessions but then become frustrated when the skills they thought were improving disappear in the target context—at home or in other everyday environments. Why?

target skills—The skills a person wishes to be able to perform.

target context—The environmental context in which people want to be able to perform a target skill or skills.

specificity of learning—The notion that the best learning experiences are those that approximate most closely the movement components and environmental conditions of the target skill and target context.

One answer is that during blocked practice, either people fail to practice the **target skill** or they practice the target skill in a context that is not the same as the **target context**. For example, during concerts, musicians and dancers are usually expected to perform movements that are in synchrony with those of other performers—while still maintaining their own degree of expressiveness—rather than repeat isolated sequences of fundamental movement patterns in an almost robotlike (rote) fashion. Similarly, during competition, athletes are often called on to produce a particular movement in any of a number of situations (e.g., one basketball free throw shot after regular play)—quite different from producing numerous repetitions of the movement in the same situation. The **specificity of learning** notion (see chapter 7) suggests that the most effective practice experiences are those that bring learners as close as possible to the conditions of the target skill and the target context. Such conditions are often absent in many blocked-practice situations.

Some tasks require people to produce movements in the target context in ways that are quite different from the way they produce them during blocked practice. In table 9.1, we summarize some of the features of skill performance in the target context that may be different from those that are present during blocked practice.

The fact that blocked practice does not include the almost random characteristics of many target skills is not the only factor operating here. Recall from the research highlight on page 259 that in the Shea and Morgan (1979) study, a random-practice condition during initial practice produced more effective performance at a later time

Table 9.1 Features of a Skill That Might Be Different in the Target Context and in Blocked Practice

Target context	Blocked practice
Preceded by regular varied conditions.	Not preceded by regular varied conditions.
Requires the generation of a solution on each attempt.	Requires the generation of a solution only on the first attempt.
Allows only one chance for success.	Allows many chances for success.
Same movement is not repeated on successive attempts	Same movement is repeated on successive attempts.
Corrections are not allowed on next attempt.	Corrections are allowed on next attempt.

Adding Desirable Difficulties to the Practice of Stroke Patients

Little research has been conducted to determine how practice structure affects stroke patients' learning, but a study by Hanlon (1996) suggests that adding desirable difficulties (Bjork, 1994, 1999; Schmidt & Bjork, 1992) to skill practice may improve patients' limb function. In Hanlon's study, 24 individuals with hemiparesis (semiparalysis to one limb) resulting from a cerebral stroke practiced a sequence of functional skills (opening a cupboard door, grasping a coffee cup by the handle, lifting the cup off the shelf, placing it on a counter, and releasing the grasp) under one of two practice conditions. Both experimental groups attempted the functional skill sequence 10 times daily until they achieved the desired level of performance (defined as three consecutive correct attempts). However, following each practice attempt, one group performed three additional tasks with the semiparalyzed limb (pointing, touching objects, touching spots on a flat surface) while the other group rested. A control group practiced neither the functional skills nor the additional tasks. All three groups were then given retention tests (involving five attempts on the functional skill sequence) 2 and 7 days after the practice phase. No difference was found between the two experimental groups in the number of attempts needed to achieve a predefined level of functional skill performance in practice. However, the experimental group, which performed the additional tasks during acquisition, produced significantly more successful completions of the functional skill sequence than the other two groups during both retention tests. These findings suggest that, for stroke patients relearning functional skills, a practice schedule that includes additional experiences with a number of unrelated motor tasks produces stronger retention than does practicing the skills alone. The additional tasks inserted between repetitions of the skills in practice may be another example of the desirable difficulties discussed in this chapter (see also Cuddy & Jacoby, 1982; Roediger & Karpicke, 2006).

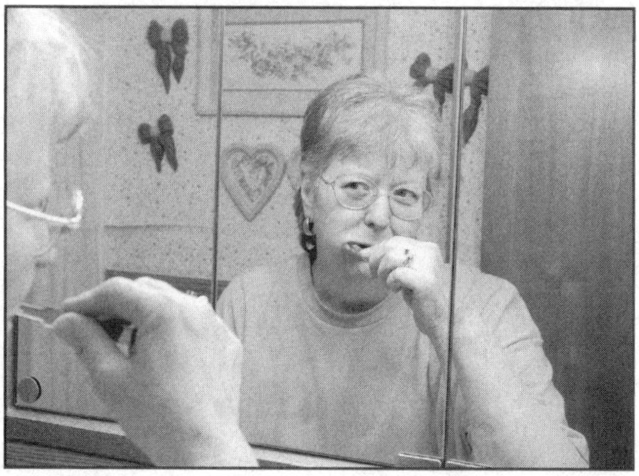

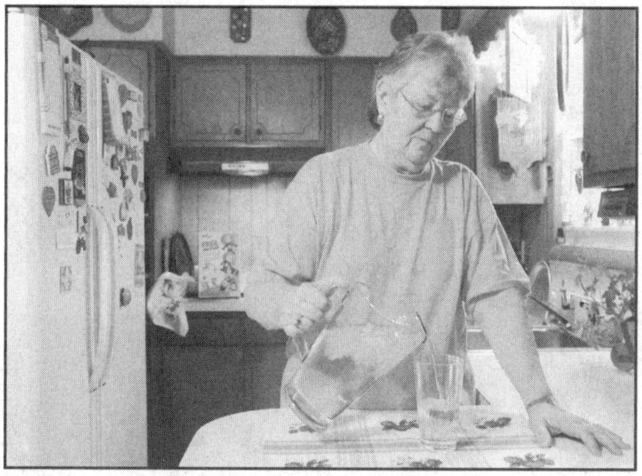

The random practice of various tasks may help stroke patients relearn functional skills.

Blocked Practice Is Not Effective for Some Target Skills

On the golf course (i.e., the target context for most golfers), a performer rarely hits the same shot twice in a row (unless the ball goes into the lake on the first shot!), and most shots are preceded by a long walk (or maybe a search for the ball). The target skill involves a series of decisions about where to hit the ball, which club to use, how to adjust the stance depending on the slope of the ground, and how far to take the backswing back. The target context (i.e., a round of golf on the golf course) requires a solution to a particular movement problem for each shot, not minor changes in a shot that has just been attempted a few seconds earlier, as might be done on a driving range. Furthermore, golfers (at least those who adhere to the rules of the game) get only one chance to make each shot, with no opportunity to modify that shot on the next attempt. In light of all this, blocked practice at the driving range does not simulate the target context of golf very well and is probably not the best way to practice the target skills of that sport.

Performance in some target contexts requires the random generation of several skills.

than did a blocked-practice condition, even when participants were instructed to perform the skill at a later time under blocked conditions (see right side of figure 9.2). These results suggest that, even when skills are performed in a blocked fashion in the target context (e.g., 100 repetitions of a rifle shot from a fixed distance, piecework on an assembly line, shoveling dirt), it is still slightly more effective for learners to have practiced those skills under random conditions.

It Depends . . .

Why Might a Football Team Practice Better Than It Plays?

Consider the following quote from Sam Wyche, former head coach of the Tampa Bay Buccaneers' professional football team:

> "I told our players I don't know what happens on Friday night and Saturday, because we see a whole different team on Sunday from what we see during the week. It's frustrating to me as a coach because I don't have an explanation. . . . I take the blame for it. For some reason, this team doesn't play as well as it practices." (*Los Angeles Times,* October 25, 1993)

Coach Wyche noticed a difference in his team's performance during practice versus in games. What are some of the things he might have been doing during practices that could have contributed to the problem?

How to Use Blocked and Random Practice During Instruction

For the first few practice attempts of a new skill, people in the **verbal–cognitive stage** of learning may benefit more from blocked-practice conditions than from random-practice conditions (Shea, Kohl, & Indermill, 1990), perhaps because they need a number of repetitions to produce the action at all. However, the research evidence suggests that as soon as learners acquire a rough approximation of the fundamental movement pattern, a shift away from blocked practice to a random schedule can be beneficial (see table 9.2 for a sample progression). For therapy patients, who almost always have some knowledge of and experience with the tasks they are practicing (e.g., buttoning a shirt, brushing teeth, pouring water), blocked practice may never be appropriate.

The research evidence suggests that by the time individuals reach the **motor stage** of learning, repetitious blocked practice is not very effective at all and in many cases could be avoided altogether. One way to do this is by practicing several skills, shifting continually from one to another. Springboard divers, for example, could practice a different dive on each successive attempt, rotating through the various dives in their routine. Athletes in team sports such as basketball, football, volleyball, and team handball could practice different skills or plays rather than the same ones over and over.

Surprisingly, research indicates that a random-practice structure is particularly effective when performers are practicing skills that are dissimilar (see Magill & Hall, 1990), so there seems to be no need to have practice variations that are similar at all. Thus, a therapy patient might benefit as much from the random practice of several everyday skills (e.g., brushing hair, tying a shoe, opening an aluminum can) as from the random practice of more similar skills (e.g., opening an envelope, unwrapping a package, peeling a banana). Learners may resist this type of practice because it doesn't allow them as much immediate success as they experience in a blocked-practice format. Moreover, right after practice, blocked-practice learners often are more confident that they will perform well later on than are their random-practice counterparts (Simon & Bjork, 2001); in fact, blocked-practice learners perform more poorly, contrary to learners' expectations. But, as Bjork and his associates pointed out, practice conditions (like those found within a blocked-practice session) that keep "multiple aspects of

verbal–cognitive stage—
The initial stage of learning, in which verbal and cognitive processes dominate the learner's activity.

motor stage—
The second stage of learning, in which motor programs are developed and the person's performance becomes increasingly consistent.

Blocked Practice May Sometimes Be Helpful During Initial Learning

How much the practice of variations of a skill is randomized during initial learning depends, among other things, on the age and skill level of learners. Learners who are younger and less skilled may need more opportunity to experience repetitions of one variation before practicing another (Wrisberg & Mead, 1983; but see Ste-Marie, Clark, Findlay, & Latimer, 2004, for research on small children). However, for older learners or for those who have achieved a higher level of skill, random practice of several variations may be more appropriate. In a study by Guadagnoli, Holcomb, and Weber (1999), college students classified as either novice or experienced in the sport of golf practiced 36 putts in either a blocked format (i.e., 12 consecutive putts to each of three targets) or a random format (i.e., 12 putts to each of the three targets but in a random order). On a retention test administered later, the novice golfers who had practiced in a blocked format performed better than those who had practiced in a random format. However, the reverse was true for experienced golfers (i.e., retention was higher for those who had practiced in a random format compared with a blocked format).

Research by Landin and Hebert (1997) suggests that moderately experienced performers may benefit from a combination of blocked and random practice. In this study, moderately skilled college students (with 2 years of competitive high school basketball experience but no intercollegiate experience) practiced the basketball set shot from six locations that varied in distance and angle to the basket. Practice conditions differed according to the number of repetitions attempted at one location before moving to the next (1, 3, or 6). Following initial practice, participants were tested to determine shooting accuracy under each of the following conditions: four attempts from each of the locations in a blocked format, four attempts from the same locations in a varied and repeating format (i.e., 1, 2, 3, 1, 2, 3), and 10 pairs of free throw shots with a brief rest after each pair. The performance of the group that had initially practiced three successive repetitions at each location was more accurate than that of the groups that practiced either one or six successive repetitions, suggesting an optimum number of blocked-practice trials for relatively low-skilled performers.

Despite these kinds of results, there is massive evidence for the benefits of random practice for both low-skilled performers (children; Ste-Marie, Clark, Findlay, & Latimer, 2004) and highly skilled performers (college baseball players; Hall, Domingues, & Cavazos, 1994). Clearly, much more research is needed to understand some of these apparent contradictions.

Table 9.2 Gradual Progression From Blocked to Random Practice for Volleyball Skills

Blocked	Spike, spike, spike, spike, spike, spike
	Block, block, block, block, block, block
	Pass, pass, pass, pass, pass, pass
Mixture of blocked and random	Spike, spike, block, block, pass, pass
	Block, block, spike, spike, pass, pass
	Spike, spike, pass, pass, block, block
Random	Spike, pass, block, pass, block, spike
	Pass, block, spike, block, pass, spike
	Block, pass, spike, pass, spike, block

Bernstein on the Process of Learning

The late Russian physiologist N.I. Bernstein (1967), known especially for his contributions to our understanding of the neurological basis of learning, said this about the learning process:

> "The process of practice towards the achievement of new motor habits essentially consists in the gradual success of a search for optimal motor solutions to the appropriate problems. Because of this, practice, when properly undertaken, does not consist in repeating the means of solution of a motor problem time after time, but in the process of solving this problem again and again." (p. 134)

the task environment fixed and predictable are conditions that, in effect, deny learners the opportunity to learn what they *don't* know" (Jacoby, Bjork, & Kelley, 1994, p. 72, italics added). One key to successful practice is allowing learners to experience the conditions they can expect to see in the target context—even when this means more frequent errors and slower performance improvements. Learners need to know that mistakes will occur, and perhaps more important, they need to find out what is causing the mistakes to occur so that they can reduce them in the future, or at least have some practice at correcting them.

Learners also need to be assured that although their performance during random practice may not be as effective as they would like it to be, their performance will be much better when they perform their skills in the target context. Lee and Wishart (2005) suggested that one way to solve the conundrum of lower confidence but higher performance for random-practice participants compared with blocked-practice participants is to make practices optimally challenging for learners. That is, depending on participants' skill levels, some repetition (i.e., occasional and small blocks of practice to enhance learners' confidence) might be interspersed within bouts of random practice.

Preparing Performers for the Target Context

Former Princeton University coach Pete Carril offered the following comment about the relationship between practice structure and the target context for the sport of basketball:

> "There is a whole bunch of dribbling drills, but my complaint about some of them is that they aren't connected to the actual skill and situation in a game. No drill is any good unless it's used in some form in the game." (Carril & White, 1997, p. 44)

VARIED PRACTICE: PRACTICING SEVERAL VERSIONS OF THE SAME SKILL

Sometimes people want to learn a single skill that they can perform in a variety of ways. For example, the skill of throwing involves a collection, or class, of movements that take various forms. If a performer's goal is to be skilled at throwing, she must develop the capability of throwing objects of various sizes, shapes, and weights over various distances, with parabolic and flat trajectories, quickly or slowly, to stationary and moving targets; there are of course many other possible variations.

People control different versions of the same class of movements by using a generalized motor program (see chapters 4 and 5). The generalized motor program is characterized by a number of fundamental **invariant features.** For example, the program for throwing might include the stepping action and hip rotation, the arm action, the wrist movement, and the follow-through. The way we can tell that a movement belongs to a particular class of actions (e.g., throwing) is that each time a performer produces the movement (e.g., throwing a baseball), we see the same invariant features that are observed in other versions of the movement (e.g., throwing a newspaper). In addition, the invariant features for a single class of movements (e.g., throwing) differ from the invariant features for other classes of movements (e.g., kicking, striking, hopping, catching).

invariant features— The characteristics of a movement that remain constant when the surface features of the movement change.

stimulus-identification stage— The first stage of information processing; during this stage, the input is recognized and identified.

Once people have learned the generalized motor program for a particular movement class, say, for throwing, they can use it in many situations. A helpful way of understanding how they might do this is illustrated in the conceptual model of motor performance (see figure 9.3 on page 267). Let's say that a performer needs to produce a particular tossing movement, such as tossing a damp, dirty sweatshirt into a laundry hamper. First, he would evaluate (in the **stimulus-identification stage**) the present environmental conditions (e.g., location of the hamper, weight of the sweatshirt, distance it must be

People probably control different versions of the same class of movements, such as throwing, by using a generalized motor program.

thrown, height of the ceiling, location of possible obstacles between the thrower and the hamper). Next, he would decide (in the **response-selection stage**) what kind of toss is needed (e.g., an underarm action with a particular trajectory). Finally, he would set the program parameters (in the **response-programming stage**) needed to produce the required movement (e.g., force, velocity, release point).

Hallmark of Effective Training

"The effectiveness of a training program should be measured not by the speed of acquisition of a task during training or by the level of performance reached at the end of the training, but rather by learners' performance in the post-training tasks and real-world settings that are the target of training." (Druckman & Bjork, 1991, p. 47)

An important challenge for movement practitioners is determining what type of practice structure to use to develop the capability to parameterize generalized motor programs. In the next section, we address two types of practice structure that scientists have examined in research studies. Then we discuss the relative merits of each type of structure in promoting generalized motor program development.

response-selection stage—The second stage of information processing; during this stage, it is decided which, if any, response should be made.

response-programming stage—The third stage of information processing; during this stage, the motor system is organized to produce the desired movement.

Constant Practice and Varied Practice

Determining the type of practice structure that develops the individual's capacity to produce a variety of actions from the same movement class is a fundamental issue for practitioners. Throwing is one example of such an action (e.g., throwing balls at various speeds to different locations, throwing darts to different areas of a target, throwing several types of objects into trash receptacles of various sizes, and using various throwing motions to cast fishing lures toward targets). One way for learners to practice such skills is to practice a single-movement version of the skill repeatedly (e.g., throw the same object the same distance to the same target). If there are no intervening attempts at other tasks, this form of practice structure is similar to the blocked practice discussed previously and is sometimes referred to as **constant practice**. However, if the goal of learning is to acquire a number of potential variations of the movement class, it would seem to make more sense to have learners attempt different versions of the action when they are practicing (e.g., throwing objects various distances to different targets). This type of rehearsal is referred to as **varied practice**.

constant practice—A practice sequence in which people rehearse only one variation of a given class of skills during a session.

varied practice—A practice sequence in which performers rehearse a number of variations of a given class of skills during a session; also referred to as variable practice.

A particular strength of varied practice is that it allows learners to develop competence in setting parameters for various dimensions of the action. An example of how this might work for the throwing action is illustrated in figure 9.4. On the horizontal axis are several possible distances a person might throw an object to a target during a practice session, with 40 m being the maximum distance. Regardless of which distance the person chooses, she would use the same generalized motor program. For any particular distance, the person would specify the parameters needed (e.g., force, velocity) to produce the desired throw. For a 10 m throw, the person would set the force parameter at a lower level (i.e., less force); for a 40 m throw, she would set the force at a higher level. A timing parameter

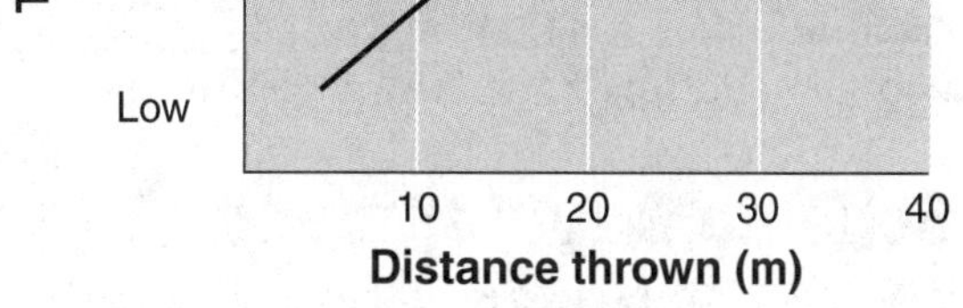

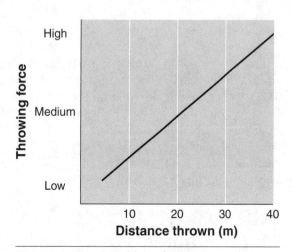

Figure 9.4 Hypothetical forces for throwing an object various distances. More force produces longer throws.

would have to be altered for these two throws as well, with the 40 m action being produced in less time that the 10 m action. If the performer sets these parameters at ineffective levels, her throws are going to be too long or too short. Skilled performers, in this sense, are those who choose parameters effectively, so that the action matches the task demands and leads to goal achievement (i.e., a successful throw).

This thinking implies that learners would profit from practicing a full range of variations of a given generalized motor program. Practicing at a full range of target behaviors means that therapy patients learning to feed themselves would be given practice with many types of foods and utensils, dental students learning to insert fillings in cavities would be given practice with various shapes of teeth and mouths, and hockey goalies would be given practice stopping many types of shots. This type of practice requires a wide range of target behaviors and is much more similar to the requirements of the target context than if the performer had practiced repeatedly with only one of the target possibilities. In each of these cases, the performer would be prepared more effectively for the next behavioral requirement—perhaps one that he or she had never experienced previously. This transfer to novel versions of the task is treated next.

When children engage in varied practice, they are able to develop a general capability for producing many versions of the movement governed by the same generalized motor program.

Assume you are teaching a child to throw a ball, and during practice sessions you instruct her to throw the ball three distances (e.g., 10, 20, and 40 m). You suspect that someday the child will need to be able to throw balls other distances and you want her to be able to do it successfully. Let's say that after the child has had considerable varied-practice experience, she is placed in a target context (e.g., playing catch with her brother at a family picnic) where she needs to produce a 30 m throw. In a sense, this might be considered a novel skill for her, because the child has never attempted throws of this particular distance before. At the same time, this skill should not be thought of as novel at all, because she has used this generalized motor program before, and has practiced throwing the ball several distances that are both less than and greater than 30 m.

Laboratory research (e.g., Carson & Wiegand, 1979; Kerr & Booth, 1978) and our own experience suggest that the child should have little difficulty producing the 30 m throw. However, in this case, the research and our experience would be in conflict with the notion of specificity of learning, which predicts that people perform best *exactly* what they practice. According to this view, the child should be able to perform throws accurately for the particular distances she has practiced (i.e., 10, 20, and 40 m), but she should not be able to produce the novel (i.e., 30 m) throwing distance very well. The fact that people are able to perform novel versions of a movement successfully, however, indicates that when they engage in varied practice, they acquire much more than the capability of producing those specific actions. Rather, what they develop is some generalizable capability of producing many variations within a class of actions—a capability that is not strongly tied to any particular version of the skill. What allows people to do this? One answer to this question is a schema.

schema—
A set of rules relating the various outcomes of a person's actions (e.g., short distance of a throw) to the parameters that the person sets to produce those outcomes (e.g., small amount of force).

Schema Development: Motor Programs and Parameters

When people practice a number of specific throwing distances, they learn something that allows them to generalize this experience to throwing other distances. One conceptualization that has been proposed to account for this phenomenon is the **schema**

Characteristics of a Generalized Motor Program for a Class of Movements

A class of movements consists of the following characteristics:

- Common sequencing among the elements of the action
- Common temporal, or rhythmic, organization (i.e., relative timing)
- Variable parameters or surface features (e.g., speed) that performers specify before each movement attempt, depending on goal requirements

(Schmidt, 1975). According to schema theory, when people practice a particular class of movements, they acquire a set of rules, called the schema, which they use to determine the **parameters** necessary for producing different versions of the action (e.g., throwing an object various distances) in the future. How would this work?

parameters—The variable inputs to a generalized motor program, such as speed or amplitude of the movement, which result in different surface features.

Figure 9.5 illustrates how someone might use the schema to determine the values for the parameter of force needed to produce throws of various distances. Suppose this person begins by generating a force with a value of A, which leads to a throw that travels a distance of 15 m. On the next attempt, he chooses a force value of B, which produces a throw of 36 m. This is followed by a force value of C, which results in a throw of 24 m, and so on. With each throw, the person begins to associate the specific force values he chooses with the actual distances the object travels. With practice, this process of association becomes the basis for the schema (i.e., set of rules) that governs a general relationship between force values and distances thrown. The diagonal line (the so-called line of best fit) in figure 9.5 that comes closest to passing through the black dots represents the schema. With each successive throw, the person updates the schema, so that by the time he has produced hundreds or thousands of throws, he has established a set of stable and strong rules relating force values to distances thrown.

How might the person use the schema once it is developed? Say he decides to throw a ball to a friend and estimates that the required distance is 40 m. Then he uses the schema (during the response-programming stage) to determine the force parameter necessary to propel the ball that distance. Referring again to figure 9.5, we see that theoretically, the person does this (follow the maroon line) by connecting the estimated distance (40 m) to the point on the diagonal line representing the schema that governs throwing force. He then connects this point to the force level (D) needed to produce a throw that will travel 40 m. He then "delivers" that parameter (i.e., D) to the generalized motor program, which specifies the amount of force required for the throw. Finally, he produces the throwing movement.

Using this process, the performer generates a throwing movement with a force parameter (as well as parameters for other dimensions of the throw, such as movement time and movement distance) based on his past experience with the program. Thus, we can understand how performers who experience varied practice of a skill are able to produce skill variations they have never specifically practiced before.

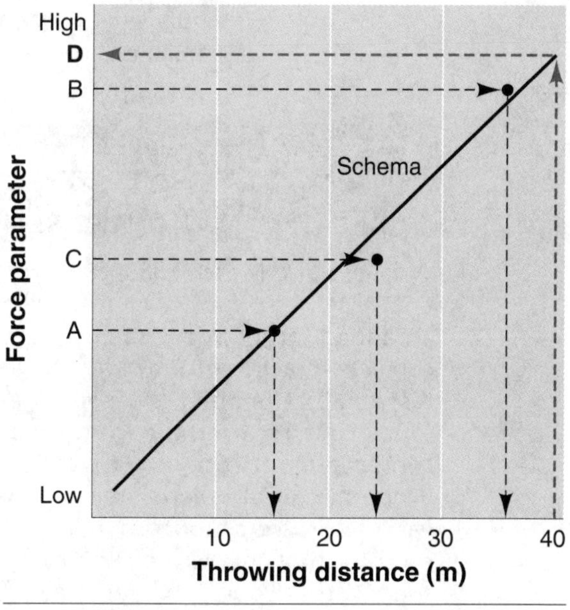

Figure 9.5 The schema relating the force parameter to throwing distance. To produce a throw of 40 m, the performer uses a schema to set the necessary force (with a value of D).

UNIVERSITY OF WINCHESTER

closed skill—A skill performed in an environment that is predictable or stationary and that allows performers to plan their movements in advance.

coincidence anticipation—A type of task that requires performers to produce movements that coincide in time, space, or both with an external object or event (e.g., catching or hitting a moving ball); sometimes referred to as anticipation timing.

open skill—A skill performed in an environment that is unpredictable or in motion and that requires performers to adapt their movements in response to dynamic properties of the environment.

Role of Varied Practice in Schema Development

Considerable research evidence suggests that varied practice plays a role in the development of schemas. In typical experiments examining this issue, two groups of participants are assigned to different sets of practice conditions. A constant-practice group is divided into subgroups, each of which attempts one of the predetermined versions of a single class of movements (e.g., throws of 20, 30, or 40 m). A varied-practice group performs all of the versions (e.g., 20, 30, *and* 40 m throws) for an equal number of throws. Thus, both groups perform the same total number of practice attempts, but varied-practice participants experience each of the versions for one third of their attempts whereas constant-practice practice participants experience only one version for all of their attempts (e.g., 20, 30, *or* 40 m throws).

The results of these studies show that the constant-practice group outperforms the varied-practice group during initial practice, when the groups are practicing one versus three different things. This is not surprising, in that each of the constant-practice participants is producing a single movement version and does it more effectively than the varied-practice participants, who are producing the three versions in an intermingled fashion. The results of studies with adults (Catalano & Kleiner, 1984) generally indicate that when both groups are later transferred to a novel version of the movement (e.g., 25 or 35 m throws), the group that practiced under varied conditions performs at least as well as, and frequently better than, the group that practiced under constant conditions—even though neither group had produced that particular variation before. Varied practice is producing generalizability to novel variations of the skill. The result is even stronger than this in studies with children. Kerr and Booth (1978) showed that for different tossing distances A, B, C, D, and E (all of which are **closed skills**), retention-test performance on distance C was more accurate for a group that practiced A, B, D, and E in a randomized order than it was for a group with the same number of practice trials at distance C alone!

One interpretation of these research findings is that people acquire movement schemas when they practice, and varied practice enhances the development of these schemas. Therefore, varied-practice learners perform new versions of the skill more effectively than do their constant-practice counterparts. Put another way, varied practice enhances the *flexibility*, adaptability, or generalizability of movement production, allowing people to apply what they have learned during varied practice to the performance of similar actions they have not specifically attempted before (e.g., Catalano & Kleiner, 1984).

Young Learners May Need to Mix Constant and Varied Practice of Open Skills

Wrisberg and Mead (1983) examined the learning of four groups of 6- to 8-year-old children on a *coincidence-anticipation* task, which involved watching a sequential light pattern and tapping a padded target at the same moment that the last bulb in the sequence was illuminated. Two constant-practice groups trained with a single-speed light pattern (for one group the speed was fast and for the other it was slow), and two varied-practice groups trained with four light speeds (one group received the speeds in random order, whereas the other group received a set of six consecutive repetitions with one speed before receiving a set of six repetitions with the next). When the groups were later switched to light speeds they had not previously experienced, the varied-practice group that had experienced six consecutive repetitions of each training speed during initial practice demonstrated the most accurate overall timing performance. These results suggest that young children may benefit from some repetition of a moving stimulus during the varied practice of an *open skill* (see also Pigott & Shapiro, 1984).

Keep Varied Practice Within the Boundaries of the Generalized Motor Program

When organizing varied practice, instructors and therapists need to be sure that the learners' movements do not exceed the boundaries of the generalized motor program they are using. For example, if a learner is practicing for throwing objects a variety of medium-range distances, it might not be a good idea for the learner to practice throwing either very short or very long distances. Throws of very long (or very short) distances may not use the same generalized motor program that is used for medium-distance throws because the very long or very short distances might exceed the boundaries of the medium-distance program. Therefore, to enhance transfer within the boundaries of the generalized motor program, learners will profit most from practicing movement variations within those boundaries.

It Depends . . .

How Might an Aspiring Postal Worker Practice the Required Skills?

A young person is thinking about applying for a job as a postal employee. The job requires workers to lift packages from a moving conveyer belt and toss them into bins situated in various locations around the conveyor. How might the person practice these skills so that she can improve her chances of being hired?

A possible contradiction to this idea was suggested in research by Keetch, Schmidt, Lee, and Young (2005). Their studies show that performers who practice single skills in *massive* amounts—in this case a free throw shot by experienced basketball players—develop a single, specific capability that is different from a more general capability of performing a class of basketball shots—in this case set shots from various positions and angles to the basket. Keetch and colleagues termed these single-capability skills **especial skills**, which stand out from adjacent actions. These especial skills are special versions of skills that, because of their role in a particular context (e.g., in a game), have received *massive* amounts of practice. As a result, probably only a few especial skills exist.

especial skill—A particular skill variation that receives massive amounts of practice; as a result it emerges as a highly specific skill for achieving a highly specific goal (e.g., the free throw shot in basketball).

RANDOM OR BLOCKED PRACTICE VERSUS VARIED OR CONSTANT PRACTICE

It may seem that the distinction between varied practice and constant practice is identical to that between random practice and blocked practice. However, there are some important differences, and the related mechanisms influencing the learning process in each case seem to be quite different as well (Wulf & Schmidt, 1988).

The random–blocked practice concept refers to those situations where learners practice several different skills involving various generalized motor programs (e.g., throwing, kicking, and catching). The major difference between random practice and blocked practice is the order in which people experience these different skills. In random practice, performers don't repeat a single skill on consecutive movement attempts. In blocked practice, they repeat one skill numerous times before switching to the practice of the next skill. The key factor here is that, usually, all of the skills require different generalized motor programs (e.g., kick, throw, catch).

The varied–constant practice concept involves the rehearsal of variations of the same generalized motor program (e.g., kicking) rather than the practice of just one of these variations. These multiple variations represent instances of some dimension of the program, such as force, speed, direction, or distance—but all using the same program. In varied-practice sessions, learners attempt a number of movement variations, while constant-practice learners rehearse a single variation. The key factor here is that, usually, all of the skills use the same generalized motor program (e.g., all involve throwing but at varied distances).

Both random practice and varied practice are beneficial to learners—but for different reasons. Random practice causes gains in learning attributable to the trial-to-trial forgetting of task solutions to the movement problems, to the development of more meaningful and distinctive representations of the skills in memory, or to both; it is probably related to the learning of the generalized motor program itself. On the other hand, varied practice produces gains in learning because it promotes the development of a set of rules for moving (i.e., the schema) that allows people to determine the parameters needed to produce appropriate skill variations (e.g., kicks of various speeds). It is likely that under the right conditions, both processes might act at the same time, as indicated next.

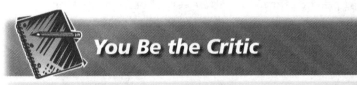

You Be the Critic

Dick Schmidt watched a session of baseball practice at the local high school. The coach had a learner standing to the right of the plate facing "backward" toward the backstop, bat in hand. The coach was kneeling on the left side of the plate. The coach would toss a baseball gently upward into the strike zone, and the learner would attempt to hit it into the backstop with a bat swing. After each swing, the coach would give feedback information about the batter's action. The coach had the batter perform about 20 such trials (all identical to each other), while five other learners waited their turn behind him. He then performed the same practice for each of the other five learners.

What seems effective about this method of practice? What aspects would you criticize? Knowing what you do about the organization of practice from this and earlier chapters, write down the strengths and weaknesses of this method. How could you make this practice more effective?

COMBINING RANDOM AND VARIED PRACTICE

The benefits of random practice over blocked practice and of varied practice over constant practice can be combined to produce further learning gains. For example, performers learning to throw a ball might be given 100 trials of varied practice using either of two practice structures—where the practice variations are presented in either a blocked or random order. With a blocked-practice order, people might perform 20 throws at a distance of 20 m, 20 throws at a distance of 30 m, and 20 throws at a distance of 40 m. With a random-practice order, on the other hand, they might perform one throw at a distance of 20 m, the next at 30 m, the next at 40 m, the next at 20 m, and so on, until a total of 20 throws at each distance are attempted. Research by Lee, Magill, and Weeks (1985) showed that the gains in learning attributable to varied practice compared with constant practice are far greater when people experience varied practice in a random order than when they practiced variations of the skill in a blocked order. Perhaps this is because learners who practice several movement variations in a random order are forced to generate a different parameter before each movement attempt, thus increasing their capability of setting parameters.

Random and varied practice can be merged even further. Suppose that performers are given a series of randomly ordered variations of a single class of movements, such as throwing. If these throwing variations are interspersed with the practice of a second class of movements, say, catching, the benefits are even larger (Lee, Wulf, & Schmidt, 1992). In situations like this, performers must generate not only different parameters on each attempt but also must retrieve a different motor program (throwing vs. catching) on each attempt. Presumably, these types of generation processes are extremely beneficial for learning, as we discussed earlier. With the proper combination of varied and random practice, performers can sometimes experience stronger gains in learning than if they attempted either mode of practice alone.

PRACTICING FOR CONSISTENT AND VARIED MAPPING

Some skills require performers to produce rapid responses to various sources of sensory information. Automobile drivers, for example, must move a foot quickly from accelerator to brake whenever they see brake lights immediately in front of them; no other response to that stimulus pattern is likely. For these kinds of skills, the same response is required each time the stimulus is presented. Other examples of consistent responding to the same stimulus might be hitting the backspace key on the computer when a typing error is made, or pushing the snooze button on an alarm clock when it sounds in the morning. This type of stimulus-response situation is referred to as **consistent mapping** in the motor skills literature, meaning that the mapping (or assignment) of a response to the stimulus is always the same.

consistent mapping—A performance situation for which a given stimulus pattern always requires the same response.

For such skills, high levels of practice produce profound gains in performance. In early practice with these tasks, the mapping between stimuli and responses is not well established, so the learners use the stages of processing (see figure 9.3), and the outer loop if the action is of long duration, to produce the action. Naturally, this process is slow, effortful, serial (in the case of several such actions), conscious, and attention demanding (in that it interferes with other processes in response selection and response programming). As we discussed in chapter 3, tasks produced this way require controlled processing.

This type of processing is in marked contrast to the kind of processing that occurs following considerable practice with these skills. After several hundred trials or so under consistent-mapping conditions, performers begin to produce what has been called automatic processing. Such processing, compared with controlled processing, is fast and effortless, is performed in parallel with other tasks (in that other tasks do not interfere with it), is nonconscious, and does not demand very much attention (see Shiffrin & Schneider, 1977, for early documentation of these kinds of effects). A high level of practice coupled with consistent-mapping conditions appears to build a kind of special-purpose information-processing "device" that functions very quickly, effortlessly, and automatically to produce a particular response every time its associated stimulus is encountered.

Speaking aloud the words you are reading right now is a good example of automaticity, where the translation from printed stimulus information to spoken word is fast, nearly nonattentive, and unavoidable (try reading the first word in the next sentence and *not* saying it to yourself). However, if you think back to when you were a third grader and were asked to read aloud in class, most likely you remember struggling through the passage. Certainly, no special-purpose device had yet been constructed, so you were forced to rely on controlled processing to perform this task.

The development of automaticity is much more difficult, if not impossible, for skills involving stimuli that are not consistently mapped to responses. In these situations, the mapping from stimulus to response varies from situation to situation—a configuration known in the motor performance literature as **varied mapping**. For many of these skills, the appropriate action depends on several other factors that must be considered at the same time. For example, if an alarm is heard in the school building, students may not know whether to evacuate the building, get under the desk, or call

varied mapping—A performance situation for which a given stimulus pattern requires different responses at different times or under different circumstances.

Training an American Football Player for Rapid Responding

Many American football coaches use films and game videos to familiarize their players with the tendencies and mannerisms of opposing teams. It is generally assumed that this type of training improves players' stimulus identification and response selection. In 1990, Christina, Barresi, and Shaffner used a modified video-training procedure to improve the response-selection accuracy of a defensive player on a college football team. Before training, the player's coaches observed that, during games, he responded quickly, but often incorrectly, to the opposing team's plays.

The training task that the researchers devised required the player to view a series of offensive plays that normally occurred in game situations, to focus on the movements of key players on the opposing team in each play, and to make a quick arm movement in the direction he should go if he were actually responding to the play. From the beginning to the end of the training, the player achieved a progressive increase in the percentage of correct responses (going from 25% to more than 95%) without slowing down his response times. Perhaps more significant, the player transferred his improved response-selection accuracy to actual game situations. These results suggest that a video-training procedure (a simulation in the sense discussed earlier) that incorporates both random practice and consistent mapping is a potentially effective supplement to normal physical rehearsal.

their parents on their cell phones. In baseball, a ground ball to third base may call for several different actions depending on the number of runners on base, the bases they occupy, and the number of outs. As you might imagine, in such situations, errors (sometimes very serious ones) are made when people are put under time pressure. Performers hope to speed up processing, making the actions not only faster but also more accurate at the same time, but you should not expect them to become automatic in the sense described earlier.

In team sports such as American football, coaches commonly show their players game films of opposing teams. By watching those films, players are able to identify distinguishing patterns that lead invariably to certain outcomes (e.g., a certain formation and initial movements by the opposing team always precede a running play to the right). If such consistencies can be identified (i.e., the mapping is consistent), players can be trained to recognize those stimuli automatically and produce the appropriate responses far more quickly than if such consistencies aren't detected, making controlled processing necessary. A possible problem is that if the opposing team subsequently changes its way of operating, so that the predictable stimuli precede something other than the expected outcome, response errors may occur because of incorrect anticipation (discussed in chapter 2); this would also force the responding team to abandon automatic responding and shift to slower, controlled processing. For situations that contain varied-mapping conditions, the practitioner needs to make it clear to performers that automatic responding is going to be difficult, if not impossible, to attain and that they should not be surprised or disappointed if they have to resort to slower, controlled-processing strategies.

SUMMARY

Movement practitioners can promote the learning of skills by choosing an appropriate practice structure. One type of practice that has been shown to be particularly effective is random practice. During random practice, learners attempt several skills in an intermingled order. Compared with blocked practice, in which learners perform a single skill numerous times before moving to another, random practice produces far greater learning (as measured on retention tests) and higher transfer, particularly when the target skill is also performed under random circumstances. Some of the key aspects of random practice are summarized as follows:

- Performance *during the early stage of skill practice* is usually more effective under blocked-practice conditions than under random-practice conditions.
- The learning benefits of random practice over blocked practice are evidenced by superior performance in either a random or blocked type of target context; but the benefit is especially strong in a target context that is randomly configured, as is the case in many games and other activities in life.

Varied practice is an effective practice structure for performers trying to learn how to produce variations of one particular task. Varied practice involves the practice of different versions of the same target skill, such as practicing throws of various distances. Compared with constant practice, in which learners practice a single version of the skill, varied practice facilitates retention, adaptability, and generalizability of movement performance, particularly when performers have to produce a specific variation they have not attempted previously. The benefits of varied practice are thought to result from the development of stronger schemas that define the relationship between the parameters of a generalized motor program and the desired movement outcome. Varied–constant practice may be distinguished from random–blocked practice in the following ways:

- Varied practice involves practice of a number of variations of a single class of actions; constant practice consists of only one of the variations.
- Random practice involves practice of several skills in a jumbled order; blocked practice involves repetitive practice of just one skill.
- Varied practice involves variations of a single class of movements (e.g., short, medium, and long kicks), whereas random practice involves non-repetitive practice of different classes of movements (e.g., throwing, kicking, catching).
- Varied practice enhances learning by facilitating the development of more effective schemas (i.e., sets of rules), which people use to govern the production of movement variations of a particular class of actions.
- Random practice enhances learning attributable to the trial-to-trial forgetting and recalling of movement plans, the development of more meaningful and distinctive memory representations of several tasks, or both.

When learning requires the matching of responses to environmental stimuli, the performance situation may consist of varied-mapping or consistent-mapping conditions. Varied-mapping conditions require performers to produce different responses to the same stimulus at different times, places, or situations, whereas consistent-mapping conditions require performers to invariably produce the same response to a given stimulus. Automatic responding is far more easily developed in consistent-mapping situations than in varied-mapping situations and in fact may not be possible at all for the latter.

FROM PRINCIPLES TO PRACTICE

Check your comprehension of the concepts and terms discussed in this chapter by responding to each of the exercises in the following sections. The first section contains several exercises designed to test your working knowledge of key terms. The second section poses a variety of problems designed to check your understanding of key concepts. In the third section, you are challenged to apply your knowledge by discussing a defensible solution for two scenarios.

Know Your Key Terms

Matching: The Practice Process

Match the following terms with their respective categories or definitions by placing the most appropriate letter on each of the blanks.

Forms of Practice and Outcomes—Terms

a. retrieval practice
b. schema
c. contextual interference
d. parameterization
e. generalized motor program
f. varied practice
g. random practice

Forms of Practice and Outcomes—Category or Definition

_____ 1. A set of rules relating movement outcomes to the parameters set by a performer

_____ 2. The practice of different versions of the same movement pattern

_____ 3. Allows performers to adapt their movements to meet varying environmental demands

_____ 4. Makes practice more difficult but enhances the learning of multiple skills

_____ 5. Occurs more frequently during random practice than during blocked practice

_____ 6. The process of selecting a specific parameter, such as force or movement time, to meet a particular environmental demand

_____ 7. Higher for random practice than for blocked practice

Consider: Structuring Practice

List a practice structure that would be appropriate for each of the following performers and skills. Provide rationales for your answers.

1. An intermediate tennis player who wants to improve the effectiveness of her serves
2. A child who is trying to learn a somersault
3. A collegiate volleyball player who wants to improve her blocking skills
4. A recovering stroke patient who wants to learn how to play shuffleboard, darts, and miniature golf

Fill in the Blank: Matching Responses to Environmental Stimuli

Complete the following sentences:

_____________________ skills are those that require performers to produce often rapid responses to changing environmental events. If performers know which responses are more effective for particular stimuli, they can speed up the _____________ of _______________ in the ___________________ ________________ and ___________________ ___________________ stages. An effective way for practitioners to increase learners' response speed is to provide them with ____________ mapping practice opportunities. The development of response speed is more difficult, however, for _________________ _________________ situations in which a given stimulus may require different responses at different times or in different situations.

Check Your Understanding

1. Explain what it means to say that, compared with blocked practice, random practice is detrimental to performance but beneficial to learning. Why is this an important concept for movement practitioners to communicate to learners?
2. Discuss the relative merits of varied practice and constant practice for people who are trying to learn a single task they must perform in a variety of ways. Describe how a practitioner might structure a practice session for a 10-year-old girl who wants to learn the jump shot in basketball.
3. Explain how a coach might combine random practice and varied practice when teaching a person to play soccer.
4. Discuss the difference between varied and consistent mapping of stimuli and responses. Which of these situations leads to automatic responding? Why?

Apply Your Knowledge

Exercise 1

An elementary school teacher is assigned to supervise physical education classes for all of the first-grade children at her school. She wants to provide them with practice involving a variety of fundamental motor skills (e.g., balancing, jumping, throwing, kicking, striking). In addition, the teacher wants to develop students' capability of performing the skills and of adjusting them to meet differing environmental demands. Suggest two or three examples of practice structures the teacher might use (you pick the skills) to achieve her goals. Please provide rationale for your recommendations and furnish two supporting references.

Exercise 2

A soccer coach wants his players to respond more quickly to various situations they confront during competition. Discuss how the coach might simulate several stimulus-response mapping conditions in soccer. For three of those situations, describe how the coach might structure practice in a way that would enhance the speed of players' responses to the stimulus and that would promote transfer of those responses to the target context (i.e., competitions). Please provide rationale for your answers and include two references from the literature on stimulus-response mapping.

chapter 10

Providing Feedback During the Learning Experience

Chapter Outline

Chapter Objectives

When you have completed this chapter, you should be able to

- discuss the difference between intrinsic and extrinsic feedback and give examples of each;
- explain the difference between knowledge of results and knowledge of performance and give examples of each;
- describe how instructional feedback can serve as a source of motivation, reinforcement, and error information;
- discuss the dependency-producing properties of instructional feedback;
- explain the principles involved in giving instructional feedback—that is, what type, how much, how precise, and how often; and
- apply the principles of feedback to a variety of real-world instructional settings.

PREVIEW

A physical therapist is frustrated and a bit bewildered. Her job is to oversee therapy for a number of stroke patients who are trying to recover the functioning of their limbs. The therapist wants to provide as much assistance as possible, but given her large patient-load, she is unable to provide a lot of feedback to any particular individual. As a result, patients must spend most of the time practicing on their own.

How and when can the physical therapist provide feedback for the patients? What kinds of information can be transmitted to them about their performance? What will happen if the therapist attempts to provide feedback about more than one aspect of patients' movements at a time? When she is assisting a particular patient, should she give feedback following every performance attempt or wait until the person makes several attempts before providing feedback?

OVERVIEW

In this chapter, we continue our discussion of the decisions practitioners must make to provide the most effective experience possible for learners. In chapter 8, we discussed some factors to consider when organizing the practice experiences of learners. In chapter 9, we focused on practice structure and examined the ways practitioners might structure a learning session. In chapter 10, we turn our attention to instructional feedback and explore its effect on learning.

First we classify the two major categories of feedback—intrinsic and extrinsic—and then we distinguish between two types of extrinsic feedback: knowledge of results and knowledge of performance. Next we examine the motivational, reinforcing, informational, and dependency-producing properties of extrinsic feedback. Finally, we address several questions effective practitioners consider when providing feedback for learners, such as what type of feedback to give, how much information to include in feedback, how precise to make feedback, and how often to provide feedback.

Sometimes people need feedback from outside sources to determine how well their skills are progressing.

CLASSIFYING FEEDBACK

The term *feedback* was originally popularized near the end of World War II, when scientists developed the concepts of the servomechanism and closed-loop control systems (e.g., Wiener, 1948). In the context of those discussions, feedback was characterized as sensory information that indicates something about the actual state of a person's movements (e.g., proprioceptive feedback informs performers about the "feel" of the action). We assumed that performers compare this actual feedback with the expected feedback of the desired, or goal, state to determine the amount of error in their movements. As long as an error exists, performers attempt to adjust the movement to reduce or eliminate the error—that is, the discrepancy between the actual state and desired state (see chapter 3). Although the error-reducing function of movement-produced feedback continues to be a prominent theme of motor control discussions, contemporary definitions characterize feedback more broadly as any kind of sensory information produced as a result of the movement.

One of the most important ways practitioners can influence the learning process is by providing performers with feedback about their actions. Some forms of feedback are a natural consequence of movements, such as when a person sees the plastic bottle he has thrown land in the recycling bin or when a carpenter feels the impact of the hammer coming solidly into contact with a nail. Feedback sometimes occurs in more artificial forms, such as when judges rate athletes' performances during figure skating, gymnastics, or springboard-diving competitions, or when a therapist evaluates the gait of a stroke patient who is trying to walk while using a cane.

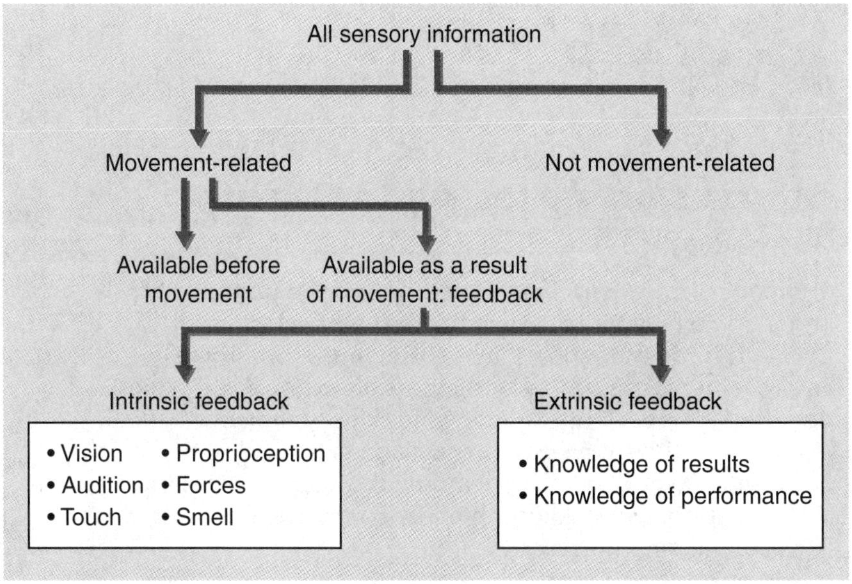

Figure 10.1 A classification system for sensory information.

One way we can categorize feedback is by classifying the various sources of sensory information that generated the feedback (see figure 10.1). In most performance situations, a great deal of sensory information is out there, but only some of it is relevant to the movement a performer is producing. When learning to drive a car, a teenager might notice several sources of unrelated sensory information, such as the color of the dashboard, the smell of the upholstery, or the sounds of music on the CD player. The driver, however, would also obtain sensory information that is important to driving, such as the feel of the steering wheel, the location of traffic signs, and the motion of vehicles detected in the rearview mirror. Of the sensory information that is relevant to performance, some is available before the driver initiates a particular movement (e.g., the speed and location of other vehicles), and some is available after the driver completes the movement (e.g., vision of the car centered in the proper lane). Information that is available before the driver produces the action is important for movement planning, and it affects the driver's anticipation, decision making, and parameter selection. However, information that arises as a result of the movement (and is *fed back* to the driver) is the kind that scientists usually refer to as feedback. This class of postmovement information may be divided into two main categories: intrinsic feedback and extrinsic feedback.

intrinsic feedback—Sensory information that occurs normally when performers produce movements; it can come from sources outside the body (exteroception) or inside the body (proprioception).

exteroception—Sensory information that comes primarily from sources outside a person's body, primarily vision, audition, and smell.

proprioception—Sensory information that comes primarily from sources in the muscles and joints and from bodily movements.

Intrinsic Feedback

Sometimes called inherent feedback, **intrinsic feedback** is the sensory information that arises as a natural consequence of producing a movement. As we discussed in chapter 3, intrinsic feedback can come from sources outside a person's body (**exteroception**) or from within the body (**proprioception**). Perhaps you remember that this type of feedback (which we initially referred to as movement-produced feedback) was an early addition to our conceptual model of motor performance (chapter 3). Performers are able to perceive intrinsic feedback more or less directly, without special assistance from other sources (e.g., instructors or mechanical devices). When

It Depends . . .

Can You Differentiate Possible Sources of Intrinsic and Extrinsic Feedback?

Depending on the nature of the skill and the goal of learning, people may be able to improve their performance through intrinsic feedback alone. However, sometimes improvements are difficult or impossible without extrinsic feedback. For each of the following skills or movement goals, list some of the sources of intrinsic and extrinsic feedback performers would need for learning to occur: riding a bicycle, roller-skating, snow skiing, three-ball juggling, throwing a Frisbee, pitching horseshoes.

the patient lifts a cup of tea to her mouth, she hears the sound of the cup leaving the saucer, feels the weight of the object, sees ripples in the liquid, and feels the warmth of the tea against her lips and tongue. When a beginner drops the bean bags he is juggling, he feels them glancing off his hands, hears them hitting the floor, and sees where they are located relative to his feet.

Extrinsic Feedback

Now we finalize the conceptual model by adding the other category of information that follows movement completion (see the highlighted section in figure 10.2). **Extrinsic feedback,** sometimes called enhanced feedback or **augmented feedback,** consists of information that is provided to the learner by some outside source, such as the comments of an instructor or therapist, the digital display of a stopwatch, the displayed score of a gymnastics judge, the film of a game, or the videotape replay of a movement. Ideally, but not always, extrinsic feedback conveys information about the outcome of the movement that performers sometimes are unable to obtain on their own and that supplements the intrinsic information they have available.

extrinsic feedback—Sensory information provided by an outside source in addition to that which normally occurs when performers produce their movements (i.e., intrinsic feedback); sometimes referred to as augmented feedback.

augmented feedback—Another name for extrinsic feedback.

Most important, extrinsic feedback is under the control of the instructor or therapist; thus, it can be provided at different times, in different forms, or not at all. When scientists in motor learning refer to feedback, they are usually talking about augmented, or extrinsic, feedback as defined here, and that's the way we will refer to feedback as well. Some scientists also differentiate two categories of extrinsic feedback: knowledge of results and knowledge of performance.

Knowledge of Results (KR)

Knowledge of results (KR) refers to extrinsic information that tells learners something about the success of their actions with respect to the intended environmental goal. For example, the therapist might tell a patient, "You buttoned that button in less than five seconds." In many real-world tasks, KR is redundant, because it contains the same information as intrinsic feedback. An example of KR redundancy is when the parent says to the child, "Oh, no, you let the cat out!" Similar redundancies may also occur during movement instruction. A music teacher might tell a student, "That note was flat." KR that is redundant with the intrinsic feedback learners can pick up and interpret on their own is of little value and can even be irritating to them.

knowledge of results (KR)—Augmented information usually provided in verbal form after the action is completed; indicates something about the degree to which the performer achieved the desired movement outcome or environmental goal.

It is, of course, possible that beginners don't know what the desired response is. When this is the case they are unable to interpret their own intrinsic feedback because they don't know with what it is to be compared. Figure 10.2 shows that the actual state (consisting of intrinsic and extrinsic feedback) enters the comparator and is compared with the desired state. To determine whether there is a mismatch between the two states, performers must know the characteristics of the desired state and be able to interpret intrinsic feedback arising from their movements. If they can't do that, they will need instructional assistance and extrinsic feedback until they can.

Some types of KR are not, however, redundant. Gymnasts, divers, and dancers must wait for the judges' scores to know exactly how their performance was evaluated. Golfers sometimes hit shots that travel to targets they can't see (e.g., approach shots to elevated

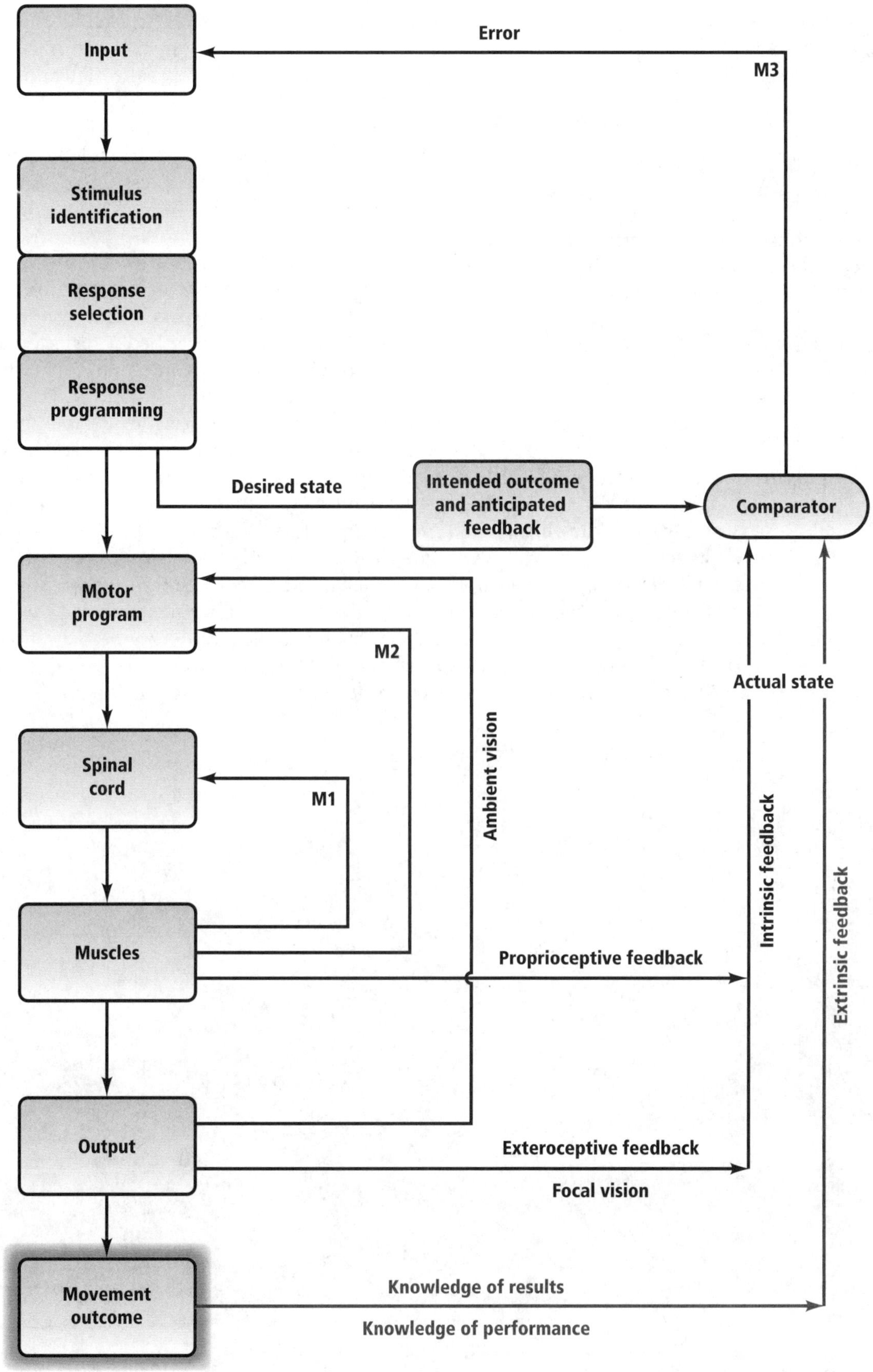

Figure 10.2 The conceptual model of motor performance, highlighting the sources of extrinsic information that follow movement production and provide additional information about the actual state of the system.

It Depends . . .

Can You Identify Redundant KR?

Sometimes KR can be redundant, duplicating the intrinsic feedback that learners are able to pick up on their own. For each of the following tasks, list several examples of KR that might be redundant considering the intrinsic feedback available to performers: playing miniature golf, bowling, digging a posthole, mowing a lawn, feeding an infant.

greens), so they need (extrinsic) KR (figure 10.3) if they want immediate information about the outcome (e.g., the ball stopped 8 ft [2.4 m] to the left of the pin). Therapy patients learning to sort objects into categories may need KR that indicates how many objects they sorted successfully during a given practice period. In cases such as these, KR is more important for performance and learning because the available intrinsic feedback is insufficient. Extrinsic feedback is also essential when a person's intrinsic feedback sources are diminished or distorted, as in the case of blind people, or patients who have neurological impairments.

The effect of KR on motor performance and learning has received considerable attention in the research literature. In most of these studies, the experimenter determines the type and frequency of feedback available to participants. Much of the early research involved very simple tasks in which participants were prevented from detecting their own errors, such as drawing a 3 in. (7.6 cm) line while blindfolded. Not surprisingly, the results generally showed that without KR, there was little or no learning (e.g., Trowbridge & Cason, 1932). On the other hand, when KR was provided following movement attempts, rapid improvement occurred over practice, and the gains persisted during retention tests when KR was no longer furnished (Bilodeau, Bilodeau, & Schumsky, 1959). These findings suggested that when people do not have sufficient intrinsic feedback to detect their own performance errors, they are unable to learn without KR.

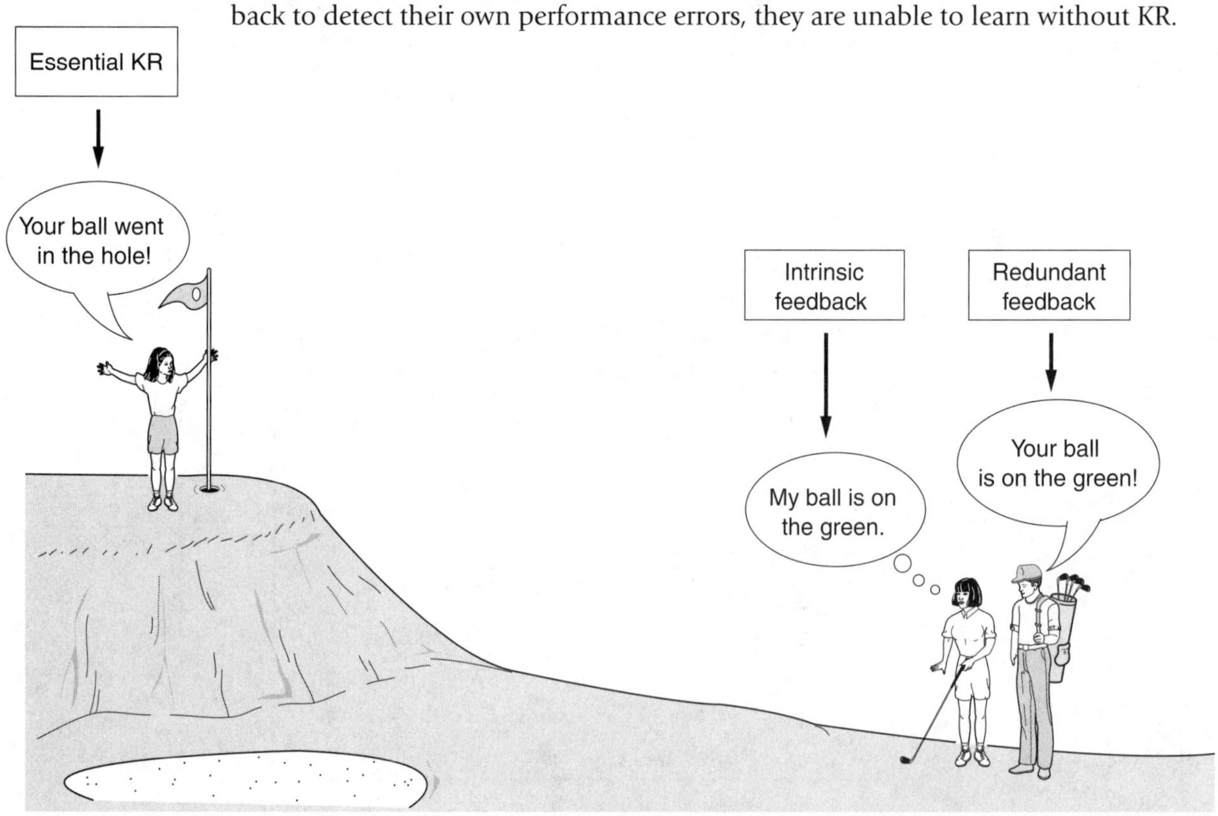

Figure 10.3 Knowledge of results is helpful mainly when it provides information performers are not able to obtain from their own intrinsic feedback.

Clearly, this is not to say that people can't learn any skills in the absence of KR. During your own lifetime, you have learned many skills without (extrinsic) KR from an instructor (e.g., throwing darts, brushing your teeth, pouring water into a glass). For each of these skills, you received goal achievement information (i.e., where the dart hit the target, whether your teeth felt clean, a glass that was full) through intrinsic feedback, and this feedback served as the basis of your learning. Thus the experimental evidence and our own experience tell us that for learning to occur, people must receive some type of feedback information, from either intrinsic or extrinsic sources. This is one of the most important principles of learning.

knowledge of performance (KP)—Augmented feedback that provides information about the quality of the movement (e.g., rhythmic, smooth, mechanically efficient, beautiful, etc.).

Knowledge of Performance

Another type of extrinsic, or augmented, feedback helps performers interpret the quality of their actual movements. **Knowledge of performance (KP)**, sometimes referred to as **kinematic feedback**, is a type of information that instructors and therapists provide frequently in real-world settings. Coaches might use KP statements such as "That approach was a little too slow," "Your tuck was not tight enough," or "Your backswing was too long." Therapists might provide KP statements such as "Your step was too short" or "You did not lift your knees high enough." Each of these examples of KP contains information about the kinematics (the pattern in space or time) either of the movement or of the implement the learner is moving (e.g., a golf club). Notice that KP information, unlike the information provided by KR, does not necessarily indicate anything about the level of goal achievement. Rather, KP informs learners about the quality of their movements. Some of the important similarities and differences between KR and KP are summarized in table 10.1.

kinematic feedback—Feedback about the displacement, velocity, acceleration, or other aspects of the movement itself or of the object being moved; a subcategory of knowledge of performance (KP).

Table 10.1 Comparison of Knowledge of Results and Knowledge of Performance

Knowledge of results	Knowledge of performance
Similarities	
Usually verbal	
Extrinsic	
Provided after the movement	
Differences	
Information about outcome in terms of environmental goal	Information about movement quality or patterning (kinematics)
Often redundant with intrinsic feedback	Usually distinct from intrinsic feedback
More useful in the laboratory	More useful in real-world tasks

It Depends . . .

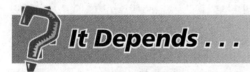

Can You Identify Some Examples of Helpful KP?

Although KR is an important source of feedback for learners, people can often obtain KR without the assistance of the practitioner. This is less so for KP because beginners usually are not capable of interpreting the kinematic properties of their own movements. For each of the following tasks, suggest some examples of KP that an instructor might provide for a learner: kicking a soccer ball, playing shuffleboard, shooting arrows at a target, and performing a back handspring.

PROPERTIES OF EXTRINSIC FEEDBACK

In many learning situations, extrinsic feedback is under the direct control of the instructor or therapist who can provide it in a spoken, visual, or sometimes written, form. The messages conveyed by practitioners' feedback statements can influence the learning process in different ways. Consider these feedback examples:

- Halfway through a long and frustrating session with the typewriter keyboard, the instructor says to her student, "Keep it up—you're doing fine."
- After a daring but successful pass to an open teammate under the basket, a basketball player hears "Good work!" from her coach.
- When one of her violin students finally performs a piece correctly, the high school music teacher stops criticizing him (i.e., says nothing).
- After a beginning tennis player completes a forehand ground stroke, her instructor says, "You need to lengthen your backswing and take the racket back sooner."
- After each rehearsal attempt, the ballet instructor informs a student about the height of her leap.

operant learning—The process of acquiring the capability to behave in ways that produce desirable outcomes.

Each of these feedback examples illustrates a unique property, or function of feedback, that can influence performance and learning. On the positive side, instructional feedback can serve as motivation, reinforcement, and information. Conversely, it can sometimes create a dependency, which diminishes learning. In this section, we examine the motivational, reinforcing, informational, and dependency-producing properties of extrinsic feedback. All of this comes under the heading of **operant learning**, or the type of learning that leads people to behave in such a way as to generate desirable outcomes (Kassin, 2004).

Motivational Properties

Motivation is strongly linked to goal achievement. When people are making progress toward the goals they set for themselves, their motivation is enhanced (Duda & Treasure, 2006). Certainly, one important function of extrinsic feedback is to provide learners with information about their progress so that they will continue to strive to achieve their goals. Early research revealed that for boring, repetitive tasks of long duration, the addition of feedback produced an immediate increase in performance proficiency, as if the feedback served as a kind of stimulant that energized people again. Learners who are given feedback during task practice say that they enjoy what they are doing more, they try harder, and they are willing to practice longer. Unless practitioners overdo the provision of feedback, learners seem to like it. Even when instructors have other reasons for giving feedback (e.g., to help people correct their errors), the motivational properties of feedback information often provide added benefits.

Instructors and therapists can capitalize on the motivational aspects of feedback during practice sessions by providing information that challenges learners to continue pursuing their goals. Generally speaking, it seems best if practitioners do not allow performers to go too long without providing feedback, especially during the early stages of learning. Learners like to know how they are doing. Without the practitioner's feedback, learners' motivation can sag and their practice can become inefficient or even cease altogether. Keeping learners informed of their progress usually translates into greater effort during task practice. And, as most practitioners know, performers who give greater effort during practice generally acquire benefits that are seen later on.

Extrinsic feedback can also be a helpful source of motivation when learners are making minimal progress toward achieving their goals. Let's suppose a patient is having a difficult time and is feeling frustrated. The therapist sees that the patient is making progress and says, "Keep it up—you're doing fine." Sometimes, performers are doing the right things in practice, but they fail to see much improvement in the results. A javelin thrower, for instance, may be doing a better job keeping his shoulders back before release—even though the javelin is traveling no farther than it did before. Or perhaps a patient is increasing the consistency of her aiming movements, even though her accuracy is not yet improving. In situations such as these, instructors and therapists can motivate learners with the feedback they provide about the process characteristics of their movements. Hearing the verbal praise of an instructor or therapist for such things can motivate performers to try even harder.

Coaches can reinforce athletes' actions by giving them positive feedback when they do something well.

Reinforcing Properties

Consider the example of the basketball coach who shouts, "Good work!" when a player completes a daring pass. This coach's exclamation illustrates a second major function of feedback—**reinforcement.** When instructors provide positive reinforcement following a performance, it increases the probability that the performance will be repeated again under similar circumstances. **Negative reinforcement** occurs when instructors remove an aversive condition following performance and thus increase the likelihood that the action will be produced again (see Kassin, 2004). An example is the off-set of

reinforcement— An event following a response that increases the likelihood that the performer will repeat the response under similar circumstances.

negative reinforcement— An event following a response that removes an aversive condition and increases the likelihood that the performer will repeat the response again under similar circumstances.

Functions of Extrinsic Feedback

When practitioners provide extrinsic feedback for learners, the feedback can serve at least four possible functions. These functions, which are often produced simultaneously and are therefore difficult to separate, include the following:

1. Motivation, which energizes learners to increase their efforts to achieve the goals they have set for themselves
2. Reinforcement, which causes learners to repeat the actions they have produced, or, in the case of punishment, to avoid repeating the actions
3. Information that indicates, either directly or indirectly, the kinds of things learners can do to refine their movement patterns and correct their errors
4. Dependence, which causes learners to rely too heavily on instructional feedback, resulting in diminished performance when the feedback is later withdrawn

punishment—An event following a response that decreases the likelihood that the response will be produced again under similar circumstances.

positive reinforcement—An event following a response that increases the likelihood that the performer will repeat the response again under similar circumstances; similar to a reward.

the warning buzzer or light in your car when you (finally) buckle your seat belt; this event increases the likelihood that you will buckle your seat belt next time. Finally, the notion of **punishment** is exactly the opposite of reinforcement—to decrease the chances of a response being repeated again. Although punishment does not always influence behavior in a predictable fashion (see Adams, 1978, for a discussion of the uncertain effects of punishment), **positive reinforcement** produces rather consistent and beneficial changes in performance.

Practitioners can provide reinforcement in both verbal (i.e., spoken words) and nonverbal (i.e., facial expressions or body language) forms. In fact, a smile or a frown on the face of a practitioner sometimes conveys clearer feedback to a learner than does the spoken word. To increase the effectiveness of reinforcement, some instructors often provide verbal (e.g., "Nice job") *and* nonverbal (e.g., a smile) messages that convey the same meaning (i.e., approval) to learners.

A common misconception is that punishment and **negative reinforcement** are synonymous. However, negative reinforcement and punishment are designed to achieve opposite purposes. Like positive reinforcement, negative reinforcement increases the probability that a response will be repeated again in the future. However, negative reinforcement operates in a slightly different way than positive reinforcement. Assume that a factory worker has a bad day and makes a number of technical errors, each of which has prompted the supervisor to comment, "That's terrible!" Now suppose the worker performs a task correctly. At that moment, the supervisor can provide negative reinforcement by simply remaining silent. By withdrawing his critical (negative) comments, the supervisor would be reinforcing the worker for the correct action he has performed.

It Depends . . .

When Might Feedback Not Be Motivating?

Instructional feedback is more motivating for learners when it informs them about the progress they are making in achieving their goals. An expert is teaching a beginner how to kayak and, after several practice sessions, the instructor notices that the learner is not responding as enthusiastically to his feedback as she had previously. What are some things the expert might be omitting in his feedback that would possibly motivate the learner?

The available research indicates that positive reinforcement produces greater improvements in learning than do negative reinforcement and punishment (see Smith, 2006, for a discussion). Perhaps the reason that negative reinforcement and punishment are not as effective is that they provide learners with feedback that is more difficult to interpret. Punishing feedback tells learners that the action they produced is not acceptable, but it doesn't tell them what is acceptable or, better yet, desirable. The withdrawal of unpleasant (negative) feedback tells the worker that his most recent action is not as bad as earlier ones, but it doesn't tell him what about the performance made it better. It is also possible that the supervisor was silent after an errant action only because he was not watching the worker when the action was produced, so the wrong message would be sent. Positive reinforcement, on the other hand, clearly conveys the message that performance was acceptable and encourages the performer to repeat it in the future.

intermittent reinforcement—A feedback schedule in which reinforcement is provided only occasionally.

One principle of operant learning (see "Law of Effect" on page 312) is that feedback that is given only occasionally (i.e., **intermittent reinforcement**) is generally more effective for learning than feedback that is given after every performance attempt. The effects of reinforcement are best seen when the reinforcing agent is removed. The results of studies examining the effects of various schedules of reinforcement show that participants who receive intermittent reinforcement during practice continue to perform at higher levels when the reinforcement is withdrawn in a retention test than participants who receive reinforcement after every attempt in practice. Apparently, when it is given too often, feedback loses some of its reinforcing power, at least in terms of performance when the feedback is removed.

One effective way practitioners can provide intermittent reinforcement is by using a *fading procedure,* in which they gradually reduce the frequency with which they provide reinforcing feedback as they see learners becoming more adept at performing the task. In addition, for skilled performers, the timing of reinforcement can be important. Less frequent reinforcement for these performers is usually more effective when it follows performances they believe are particularly exceptional compared with performances that they feel are less impressive (Cervone, 1992).

Informational Properties

In most motor-learning situations, the learner's problem is not performing a correct action more frequently than an incorrect action but rather performing a particular action more effectively. It is frequently clear what the learner is supposed to do (assemble a part on a production line faster), but it is not clear to the learner how to do it. The learner is trying to create a pattern of movement that accomplishes a single, clearly defined goal. In a therapy situation, there is no question that the stroke patient wants to recover the skill of feeding herself, but the challenge is to make the necessary limb movements that will enable her to transfer food from the plate to her mouth accurately.

It might be argued that the most important function of feedback during motor-skill instruction is to provide learners with information about their patterns of action. Wulf, McConnel, Gärtner, & Schwarz (2002) have shown that feedback can be used to focus learners' attention on the desired outcome (e.g., "Serve the volleyball as if using a whip, like a horseman driving horses") (see figure 10.4). Sometimes, this information is referred to as prescriptive feedback, because it provides direction about how to change the action next time.

Figure 10.4 Extrinsic feedback can provide learners with helpful information for modifying their subsequent movement attempts. Depicted here is a learner who has just been told to serve the volleyball as if using a whip, like a horseman driving horses.

information feedback—Feedback that provides performers with error-correction information; this feedback can be either descriptive or prescriptive.

The capability to provide feedback is one of the most important reasons why instructors and therapists are so vital to the learning process. Skilled instructors know the proper patterns of action; therefore, they are able to provide learners with the type of feedback information needed for effective learning.

Consider again the example of feedback we listed at the beginning of this section, in which the instructor tells the beginning tennis player that she should try to lengthen her backswing and take the racket back sooner. This example of **information feedback** tells the player something about the desired characteristics of her movement (i.e., knowledge of performance) and clearly defines two things that she is doing incorrectly. It also becomes the basis for the player to make corrections on the next movement, thus helping her improve the quality and effectiveness of her backswing. By providing information feedback, practitioners can help learners minimize their errors, correct them more quickly, and bring their movement patterns closer to the goal pattern.

The fact that extrinsic feedback is mainly informational in nature raises many interesting and important questions for instructors and therapists. These questions deal with the kinds of information that skilled practitioners can provide as feedback (e.g., information about limb position, movement timing, coordination, forces, any objects being moved), the amount and precision of feedback that are most effective, and the frequency of feedback presentation (i.e., how often it should be given). Because each of these questions involves a number of important issues, we discuss them in more detail in the next section of this chapter, which contains practical considerations for providing information feedback.

It Depends . . .

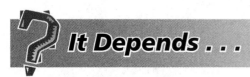

How Might Learners Interpret a Practitioner's Silence Following a Performance Bout?

An instructor is helping a piano student practice her finger positioning. During one particular lesson, the student makes many mistakes, and the instructor spends a lot of time saying, "That's wrong." Finally, the student produces an effective movement sequence and immediately looks at the instructor. She sees him silently sitting there with a smile on his face. What are some ways the student might interpret the instructor's silence and smile?

Use of Negative Reinforcement to Correct a Swimmer's Stroke

An interesting case study illustrating how a practitioner might use negative reinforcement to alter the movement pattern of a performer was reported by Rushall (1967). Working in collaboration with a competitive swimmer and his coach, Rushall determined that at least seven components of the swimmer's stroke were inefficient. Because the swimmer said that he was reinforced intrinsically by correct performance, Rushall decided that providing positive reinforcement for correct performance would be an ineffective method. Therefore, he used a negative-reinforcement technique that involved shining a flashlight in the swimmer's face until he made the required change in the designated stroke component. Once the coach determined that the swimmer was executing the component in a consistently acceptable fashion, the flashlight was turned off. This process of negative reinforcement was repeated until the swimmer had altered all seven components satisfactorily.

Dependency-Producing Properties

Recently, scientists have realized that feedback containing error-correction information can have a dependency-producing function. In the ballet example at the beginning of this section, the instructor provides the dancer with error-correction information following each of her leaps. When instructors give feedback frequently, it tends to guide the learner's actions very strongly in the direction of the goal movement, analogous to the way physical guidance does (as discussed in chapter 8). Just as with physical guidance, augmented information feedback allows learners to maintain their movements near the intended goal, allowing the correction of errors quickly and preserving the desired form or outcome. Again, as with physical guidance, people can become dependent on the feedback if the practitioner provides it too often. As a result, learners may tend to rely on the feedback to generate their movements and keep them on target rather than rely on intrinsic feedback processes. Unless learners develop the capability to produce the movement on their own, their performance suffers markedly when extrinsic feedback is removed, as is usually the case when the instructor is no longer present. Fortunately, practitioners can structure feedback in a number of ways to minimize its dependency-producing effects, and we discuss several of these techniques in the next section.

PRACTICAL CONSIDERATIONS WHEN PROVIDING INFORMATION FEEDBACK

For people to achieve their learning goals, they often need feedback from movement practitioners. However, eventually learners must be able to perform movements in the desired target context without the teacher's assistance. Good instructors and therapists know how to provide feedback in a way that prepares learners for unassisted performance (Cole, 1991). In this section, we discuss several issues to consider when providing information feedback.

Determining Whether to Give Feedback

When it comes to providing feedback, the first question practitioners must ask is whether it's needed. After all, there are many sources of sensory information that learners can pick up for themselves (i.e., intrinsic feedback). We also know that feedback dependency can become a problem if learners receive extrinsic information too often. In addition, studies have shown that instructional feedback is more effective when learners request it than when it is given more frequently (Janelle et al., 1997).

Two factors practitioners probably need to consider before providing feedback are the complexity of the task and the experience of the learner. The more complex the skill to be learned and the less experienced the learner, the more likely extrinsic feedback will be necessary. The results of one study with fourth-grade children revealed that instructor feedback was beneficial during the learning of a difficult perceptual–motor task but not for one that was simple (Fredenburg, Lee, & Solomon, 2001). Apparently, participants were able to rely on their own feedback to learn the simpler task.

How, then, do we characterize the practitioner's purpose in providing extrinsic feedback? Flach, Lintern, and Larish (1990) suggested an answer to this question that is consistent with our view of motor learning (see chapter 7). They proposed that for every task, there is a hierarchy of relevant intrinsic information of which performers must be aware if they want to produce effective movements. One purpose of instructional feedback, then, is to channel the learner's search for this information. Once learners are able to identify the relevant intrinsic information and produce effective movements

Providing Feedback When the Learner Requests It

In most skill learning, people are able to see and feel something about their own movements using intrinsic feedback. If learners are throwing a ball, they can see where it lands and feel the temporary sensation in the arm and shoulder. If they are jumping, they can judge roughly how high or far they jumped and feel the sensation in the legs and feet. If they are playing a musical instrument, they can hear the pleasant- and not-so-pleasant-sounding notes they produce and feel the sensation in the fingers. Because some amount of intrinsic feedback is always available during task performance, practitioners must consider carefully whether additional extrinsic feedback is necessary.

In a study by Janelle and colleagues (1997), participants attempted to learn a task that involved throwing a tennis ball with their nondominant hand a distance of 9 m to a target. The learners could always see where the ball struck the target. During the practice phase of the study (200 throws), some participants received additional extrinsic feedback (videotape replay of the throw and verbal comments or suggestions from an expert) about certain aspects of their movement form, whereas others did not. Of those participants who received additional information, some received it following each group of five throws, but others received it only when they requested it. Later on, all participants were given a retention test in which they attempted 20 more throws in the absence of any extrinsic feedback; this was the test indicating the relative amount learned under the various practice conditions.

During the practice phase, participants who received additional information demonstrated better throwing form relative to participants who received no additional feedback. However, on the retention test, participants who had received additional information *only* when they asked for it during practice demonstrated better throwing form and accuracy than participants in the other groups. These results suggest that skill retention may be enhanced if instructors provide feedback only when learners request it during practice sessions.

on their own, they should have little need for additional feedback. An example of a flowchart practitioners might use to channel learners' search for this information is shown in figure 10.5.

Whiting and Vereijken (1993) recommended that practitioners consider what must be learned before deciding whether to provide extrinsic feedback during skill practice. In several experiments using a ski-training apparatus, these researchers determined that participants needed to learn how to delay applying force to the platform until it passed the center point of the apparatus. They found that a discovery-learning group (receiving no feedback) improved their performance over 4 days of practice to the same extent as (and in some cases more than) groups that received feedback. Because experimental participants were not tested later under no-feedback conditions, unfortunately, the effect of the various feedback conditions on more permanent learning of the skill was not determined. Nevertheless, the results suggest that in some cases, practitioners might allow learners time to discover the person–task–environment relationship before providing extrinsic feedback. Once learners have a general idea of task requirements, they might benefit more from such feedback.

When practitioners are convinced that extrinsic feedback is necessary, they can consider the appropriate content, amount, precision, and frequency of feedback. In the following sections, we address each of these questions in greater detail.

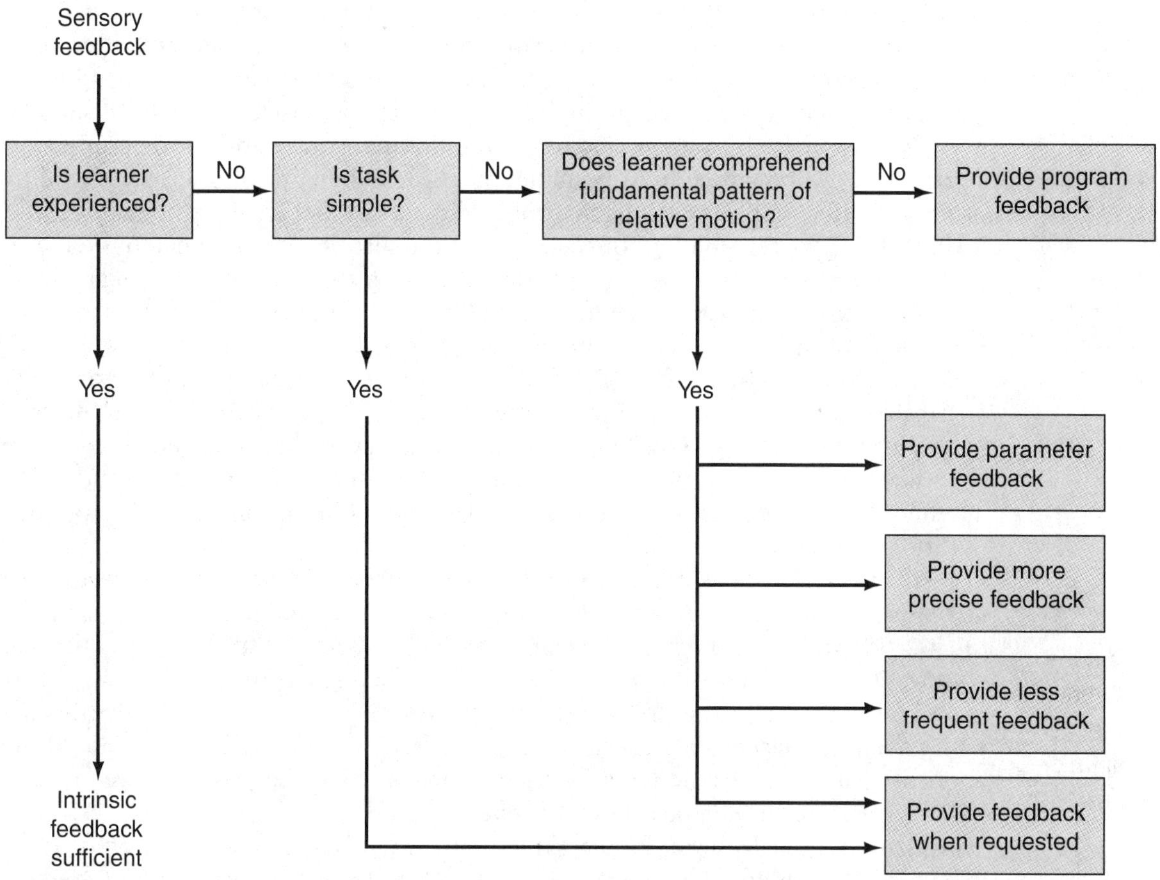

Figure 10.5 A flowchart for determining the provision of instructional feedback.

Determining What Information to Give

One of the first questions practitioners might ask themselves before giving feedback is "For which features of the learner's movements should I provide information?" It is important that feedback address features that are under the learner's control, so it is helpful for instructors and therapists to understand how people control their movements. This is one of the reasons that the motor-performance sections precede the motor-learning sections in this book. Knowing how people control their movements allows practitioners to provide more effective feedback for learners.

Program Feedback and Parameter Feedback

People who are trying to learn generalized motor programs sometimes struggle because they are unable to adjust the program in the most effective ways. For example, a soccer player may be producing a heading movement characterized by trunk movement that begins too early relative to the beginning of neck flexion. We know it is much more difficult for people to adjust the relative timing (or temporal structure) of their movements than it is for them to change parameter values, such as overall movement speed, which influences the speed of the entire action.

The processes involved in altering temporal structure are not well understood, but practitioners can keep a few guidelines in mind when providing **program feedback** about this dimension of movements. As we mentioned earlier, instructional feedback

program feedback—Feedback that provides error information about the fundamental pattern of a movement (i.e., the generalized motor program).

is more helpful when it addresses movement features that people can control. In the soccer example, the player is able to control the moment of movement initiation (e.g., when to begin the trunk movement). On the other hand, she may have more difficulty generating a particular relative timing pattern among the muscles of the trunk and the neck, because these movements occur almost simultaneously and are determined to some extent by nonconscious (automatic) processes. When practitioners are providing program feedback about the relative-timing structure of movements, they can remind learners that progress can be quite slow. They can also inform learners that relative-timing patterns sometimes take a long time to acquire, that ineffective timing patterns are difficult to eliminate, and that they should try to be patient when their performance is not as smooth or consistent as they would like.

Once learners achieve a rough idea of the desired generalized motor program (regardless of how well the timing structure is developed), they can begin to practice specifying the parameters (such as duration, direction, and amplitude) that define the superficial features of the movement. Performers can usually do this quickly and easily, as when the soccer player heads the ball with various amounts of force and projects it in different directions.

parameter feedback—Feedback that provides error information about the changeable surface features (e.g., amplitude, speed, force) of movements.

Instructional feedback that leads to parameter adjustments is almost always useful as long as the learner's overall movement pattern is essentially correct. For example, the practitioner might provide **parameter feedback** statements such as "Head the ball with less force" or "Head the ball to the left" to assist learners in selecting parameters more effectively. An important part of motor learning is discovering the rules dealing with parameter selection. Therefore, parameter feedback that tells learners about the appropriateness of the parameter values they are selecting (i.e., faster, slower, longer, shorter, earlier, later) can be extremely beneficial.

Initially, it is usually better for practitioners to give feedback directed at the correction of errors in the fundamental movement pattern (i.e., the generalized motor program) before giving parameter feedback. For example, the patient who is learning to walk with a cane might be given program feedback first about the coordination of his arm and leg movements and then about the function of the cane as a stabilizing device. If people are allowed to practice ineffective movement patterns, they will have a difficult time changing them later on.

It Depends . . .

Can You Think of Examples of Program and Parameter Feedback?

The practitioner's feedback statements are most effective initially if they emphasize characteristics of the basic movement pattern. Presumably, as soon as learners have demonstrated that they can produce the desired relative timing, they are receptive to feedback about parameter selection (see Newell, 1985, for more on this). For each of the following tasks, suggest one example of program feedback and one example of parameter feedback that a practitioner might give to a learner: skipping rope, dealing a deck of cards, rowing a boat.

Program feedback promotes the development of the correct pattern of relative motion.

Once learners have achieved an approximation of the correct movement pattern, they can be given feedback about parameter selection. For example, the patient could be given parameter feedback about the speed with which he is moving, the amplitude of his steps, or other parameters (e.g., walk faster, take longer steps, veer to the right and then back to the left).

Videotape Feedback

Although most feedback is presented in a verbal (or, perhaps, written) form, there are a few other nonverbal forms of feedback—most of them visual—that can assist learners in program development and parameter selection. One of the most common forms of visual feedback is videotape replay. Soon after video recorders became commercially available in the 1960s, gymnastics coaches began using them to provide nearly immediate feedback to athletes during practice sessions and also to record athletes' performances during competition. Video technology solved many of the problems associated with using film: Performers could view feedback about the entire performance after only a few seconds, and they could see the patterns of their movements in relatively good detail and, eventually, in color and with sound. And, it was motivating: Nearly everyone wants to see themselves on TV.

Whereas early video technology was not particularly portable, recent systems, including portable camcorders and computer software, allow practitioners to record performance in field settings. With these systems, the camcorder serves as the recording and video input device, and a computer monitor feeds back visual information about the efficiency and form of the performer's actions, allowing on-the-spot analysis ("Digital Video Gives Athletes an Edge," 2004; Seat & Wrisberg, 1996).

Video replay is a common form of visual feedback that allows athletes to evaluate their practice sessions and competitive performances in detail.

It Depends . . .

What Information Might Be Contained in Verbal and Visual Feedback?

Instructors usually present augmented feedback in a verbal form, although in some cases they are able to provide visual feedback. If a practitioner has the luxury of giving feedback in either form, how might he or she provide verbal and visual feedback for someone who is trying to learn each of the following tasks?

A social dance routine

Driving a stick-shift car

Making a pizza

Which of your feedback examples would assist the learner in program development? Which would promote more effective parameter selection? Which would facilitate the learning of procedural information?

There are several factors to keep in mind when using video feedback (Rothstein & Arnold, 1976). Perhaps most important is that there are literally thousands of things that one could examine in a video, and beginners can attend to only a limited amount of information at a time. In addition, they are able to change only one or two movement features on their next attempt. Therefore, initially, pointing out specific cues contained in a video display is effective; in this way, learners can process and use the feedback more readily—this is called attentional cueing. For example, a physical therapist might direct the patient's attention to the position of her chin relative to her neck during locomotion. As learners become more skilled at producing their actions and recognizing the key movement components they need to address, their attention can be directed to increasingly more subtle aspects of the performance.

Concurrent Feedback Can Sometimes Help and Sometimes Impair Learning

In certain kinds of tasks, it is often tempting to provide feedback of the action while the performer is producing the action. This can be done via mirrors in dance, by video camera and monitor adjacent to a cyclist on a stationary bicycle, or by special computer techniques in industrial or military simulators. This kind of feedback—called *concurrent feedback*—is different from the feedback we have discussed in the chapter so far because it is provided during the action, not after it as are KR and KP.

Such information provides a basis for the learner to correct errors, adjust movement tempo, and alter the coordination patterns during the attempt, particularly if the movement is of relatively long duration. As you might expect, such information is almost always strongly beneficial for performance. But what does this kind of feedback do for learning when it is taken away in a retention test, such as with a dance performance without the mirror? Note the results from the following research studies.

Research on concurrent visual feedback suggests that it is detrimental for learning, as measured on a no-feedback retention test. That is, practicing with concurrent feedback is far less effective for learning than practicing with feedback provided following the movement (see Wulf & Schmidt, 1997). In fact, recent research has shown that completely different neural pathways are used when individuals practice a two-hand coordination task with concurrent visual feedback than without such feedback (Debaere, Wenderoth, Sunaert, Van Hecke, & Swinnen, 2003). If so, then concurrent feedback has changed the task.

Research with concurrent auditory feedback suggests that it may facilitate skill learning. Konttinnen, Mononen, Viitasalo, and Mets (2004) found that the learning of Finnish military conscripts was enhanced if they received concurrent audio feedback on 50% of their training trials (i.e., a tone that increased in frequency as the rifle became increasingly stabile and pointed in the direction of the bull's-eye) than if they didn't. Although no difference was noted in the performance accuracy of audio-trained plus KR and KR-only conscripts during practice, the audio-trained soldiers demonstrated significantly superior accuracy on retention tests given (with feedback removed) 48 hr, 10 days, and 40 days later. These findings are consistent with those of earlier studies examining concurrent auditory feedback with golfers (Jagacinski, Greenberg, & Liao, 1997), rowers (Gauthier, 1985), and tennis players (Takeuchi, 1993).

The results of these studies suggest that concurrent visual feedback provides guidance (chapter 8) that enhances practice performance but degrades learning when the feedback is removed, yet concurrent auditory feedback enhances learning. Could this be attributable to the differences between the way visual and auditory feedback work (we doubt this), or is something else going on to produce these different effects? More research might give us the answers.

Split-Screen Visual Feedback

Occasionally, instructors can display video feedback of a learner's movements alongside a visual model of the correct action. This is called a split-screen display. One advantage of this feedback is that it provides learners with an image of the desired movement as well as their own movement. That way they can have increased awareness of the desired state (see figure 10.2) as they attempt to reduce the discrepancy between the goal movement and the movements they are producing (i.e., actual state).

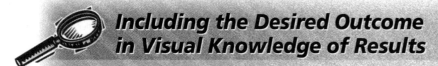

Including the Desired Outcome in Visual Knowledge of Results

Research by Newell, Carlton, and Antoniou (1990) suggests that learners' previous experience and the complexity of the task to be learned are relevant when an instructor is deciding what type of visual KR to provide. In this study, participants attempted to draw shapes that were either familiar (i.e., a circle) or unfamiliar (i.e., an irregular form). After each practice attempt, participants received one of three types of visual KR: a number representing the difference in the area of the shape they drew and that of the correct shape (termed *absolute integrated error,* AIE), AIE plus a computer-generated representation of the shape they drew, and AIE plus a computer-generated representation of the shape they drew superimposed on a representation of the correct shape. After 70 practice attempts with KR, participants in each group attempted to draw the shapes 30 more times without feedback. KR that included the participant's drawing superimposed on a representation of the correct shape was beneficial only when learners were drawing figures that were unfamiliar to them (i.e., the irregular patterns, not the circles). Early in the practice of unfamiliar movements, learners might benefit from visual KR that includes a portrayal of the desired outcome along with the outcome of their own movement.

Table 10.2 Types of Instructional Feedback

Type	Function or consideration	Example
Program	Assists learners in developing fundamental relative motion pattern More useful for beginners or inexperienced learners	"Make the hands move faster than the arms" to convey importance of a rapid wrist action in a bat swing
Parameter	Assists learners in adjusting fundamental relative motion pattern More useful for more experienced learners	"Swing faster" to convey need to increase the amount of force applied
Visual	Provides learners with a visual depiction of their action More useful for more experienced learners Beginners may need additional verbal cueing	Videotape replay of a bat swing to convey image of action from several different viewing perspectives
Descriptive	Directs learners' attention to a particular aspect of the action More useful for more experienced learners	"Your swing is too stiff" to convey observable characteristic or action
Prescriptive	Suggests a specific alteration or correction for the action More useful for beginners or inexperienced learners	"Relax the hands and move them faster" to convey adjustment that might correct observed error

descriptive feedback—Feedback that describes the errors made during the performance of a skill.

Descriptive and Prescriptive Feedback

Feedback can be descriptive, prescriptive, or sometimes both. **Descriptive feedback** merely restates something the learner did, as when a therapist says, "You performed 4 out of 10 sit to stands correctly," which conveys relatively little useful information, or "Your hand position was better," which is somewhat more precise but still presumes that the patient knows how to achieve the correct hand position on the next attempt.

Prescriptive feedback provides learners with information they can use to make more effective corrections in their subsequent movements (Newell & McGinnis, 1985). Such feedback prescribes a solution that the learner can try on the next attempt, in much the same way as the physician prescribes medicine to remedy a patient's illness. For example, the physical therapist might say, "In the next series of attempts remember to place your hands in line with your hips before standing up." Research suggests that prescriptive feedback is more useful to learners than descriptive feedback, at least until they are able to interpret the descriptive feedback. The primary function and a practical example of each type of feedback discussed in this section are provided in table 10.2.

prescriptive feedback— Feedback that describes the errors made during the performance of a skill and some things the learner might do to correct the errors.

Providing Prescriptive Feedback

Janelle and colleagues (1997) developed an *attentional cueing* protocol (referred to as transitional information) that they used to provide prescriptive feedback to participants who were trying to learn a throwing task with the nondominant hand. Their cueing protocol is shown in figure 10.6, and samples of the transitional feedback statements they used are presented in figure 10.7.

1. Focus on the initial position of the body.
2. Focus on the initial movement of the trunk.
3. Focus on the left arm during the preparatory phase of the left arm swing.
4. Focus on the right foot during the throwing phase.
5. Focus on the hips during the throwing phase.
6. Focus on the shoulders during the throwing phase.
7. Focus on the upper arm and elbow during the throwing phase.
8. Focus on the left hand and the ball during the throwing phase.
9. Focus on the left arm at the point of ball release.
10. Focus on the left arm during the final phase of the throw.

Good throw (correct form).

Figure 10.6 Attentional cueing feedback protocol used to promote the learning of a nondominant-hand throwing task. (Adapted from Janelle et al., 1997).

attentional cueing— Prescriptive feedback that directs learners' attention to the most pertinent information for correcting a particular performance error.

1. (a) Align your body so that the right shoulder faces the target area. (b) Place your feet close together, parallel to each other, and at a 90-degree angle to the target area.
2. Rotate the hips 15–20 degrees from right to left during the initial phase of the throw.
3. Begin the arm backswing with initiation of the right food stride. (a) Keep the left arm relatively straight during the backswing. (b) During the backswing, raise the left arm until it is even with the shoulder. (c) At the end of the backswing, flex the elbow and allow the hand and ball to drop down behind the back.
4. Stride forward with the right foot toward the target area.
5. Rotate the hips from left to right during the throwing phase.
6. Rotate the shoulders left to right during the throwing phase.
7. Lag the movement of the upper arm and elbow behind the rotation of the shoulders during the throwing phase.
9. Extend the arm at ball release.
10. (a) Release the ball earlier in the movement. (b) Release the ball later in the movement. (c) Keep the left arm extended as you follow through down and across to the right side of the body.

Good throw (correct form).

Figure 10.7 Transitional feedback information used to promote the learning of a nondominant-hand throwing task. (Adapted from Janelle et al., 1997).

Figure 10.8 Feedback should be clear, direct, and limited to avoid information overload.

Determining How Much Information to Give

Because practitioners sometimes find themselves in a position to give feedback about countless features of a learner's movements, they have the potential to overload learners with too much information. As we know, this can be a problem because the information-processing and memory capabilities of humans—particularly those who are young or mentally challenged—are limited (see chapter 2). Feedback messages such as those given by the tennis instructor in figure 10.8 are probably too difficult for most learners to translate into an effective correction.

When providing feedback for program development, an instructor might consider the one feature of the learner's movement that is most fundamental for task improvement and restrict his or her feedback to that feature. For example, a logger who is teaching his son how to use an axe might provide feedback that promotes development of the fundamental pattern of the arm swing. Once his son has mastered that feature, the father could provide transitional information about the next most important feature (e.g., accelerating the wrists during the downswing), and so on, until the learner is producing the entire movement pattern effectively. On the other hand, when giving feedback for parameter selection, instructors occasionally can provide information about more than one parameter at a time because parameters can be modified more easily. For example, a track-and-field athlete who has already developed an effective generalized motor program for the javelin throw might be told, "Try moving your left leg faster and farther next time."

summary feedback—Feedback provided after a series of performance attempts that informs learners about each of the attempts in the series.

Summary Feedback

Practitioners can maximize the effectiveness of feedback they give, while minimizing the dependency-producing effects of feedback, by providing learners with **summary feedback**. Instructors do this by withholding feedback for a particular number of

Prescriptive Feedback Is Sometimes More Helpful Than Descriptive Feedback

A study by Kernodle and Carlton (1992) suggested that prescriptive feedback that focuses performers' attention on important movement cues or on movement transitions produces greater learning than descriptive feedback that only informs participants about the outcome of an action or that consists of a simple videotape replay of the movement.

In this experiment, participants attempted to learn to throw a foam ball as far as possible with their nondominant hand. An opaque partition prevented them from seeing their actual throwing distance. During practice, participants received one of four types of extrinsic feedback after each throw. Two groups received descriptive feedback only: the distance thrown in feet and inches (KR) or a videotape replay of the movement (KP). The other two groups received a videotape replay plus a prescriptive statement: One received attentional cueing that indicated what to look at in the video (e.g., "Focus on your hips during the throwing phase"), whereas the other received transitional information that told participants what to do on the next trial (e.g., "Rotate your hips from left to right during the throwing phase").

Participants in all conditions improved their distance thrown and their movement form. However, those who received prescriptive and transitional information learned considerably more than those who only received descriptive feedback. These findings suggest that prescriptive feedback can be beneficial during motor-program development and that simple video replays might not be optimal. The challenge for practitioners is to identify the important focus cues, or transitional information, to convey as prescriptive feedback.

practice attempts—say, from 5 to 20—and then providing it in summary form. For example, a tennis teacher who is helping a player learn to hit serves closer to the service line might ask her to hit 15 serves. If the teacher records the location where the ball lands for each of the 15 serves, the graph might look something like the one shown in figure 10.9. After the player's last practice attempt, the instructor shows her the graph. In this way, the learner receives feedback about each of her attempts but not until she completes them all.

The potential benefits of summary feedback were first discovered by Lavery (1962) in a series of experiments investigating the learning of simple laboratory tasks (see the research highlight "Lavery's Experiment on Summary Feedback" on page 306). Lavery found that, as compared with feedback that was given after every practice attempt, summary feedback produced poorer performance during practice but more effective retention performance later on when the extrinsic feedback was withdrawn.

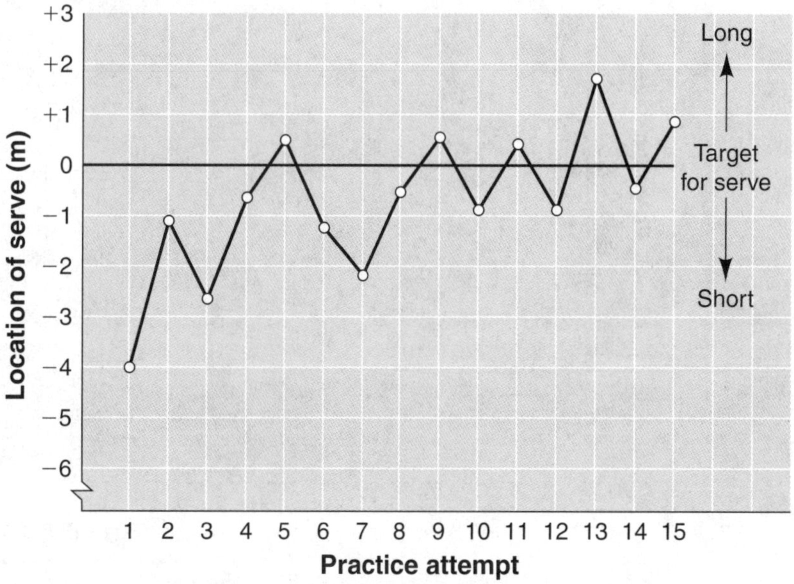

Figure 10.9 Summary feedback in learning a tennis serve. Scores are plotted on a graph, which is shown to the learner only after the last attempt is completed.

Lavery's Experiment on Summary Feedback

The Canadian scientist J.J. Lavery (1962; Lavery & Suddon, 1962) examined several kinds of feedback schedules during the learning of simple motor tasks in the laboratory, such as striking a small ball with a special hammer to propel it up a ramp to a target. All participants performed the skill the first day without any feedback; then for the next 5 days, they received different schedules of feedback. One group received immediate feedback (KR) after each practice attempt. A second group received summary feedback after 20 attempts in a manner similar to that shown in figure 10.9. A third group received both kinds of feedback, that is, feedback after each attempt and summary feedback after each set of 20 attempts. Following the 5 days of practice, all groups were tested without any feedback on each of the next 4 days, as well as 1 month later and again 3 months later.

The results can be seen in figure 10.10. During the practice (or acquisition) stage, the summary group performed much less accurately than did either of the other groups. However, during the no-feedback tests, the summary group performed more accurately than the other groups on all but the 3-month test. Lavery concluded that, although summary feedback may produce ineffective performance during practice relative to KR, it leads to more effective learning.

You might ask, "Why is summary feedback so good for learning?" But, is this the real question? Notice that two of the groups (summary and both) received summary feedback, but only one of them (summary) experienced the enhanced learning. Notice also that the two groups that produced the least learning (KR and both) both had immediate KR. So, maybe the question at the start of this paragraph should be "Why is every-trial KR so bad for learning?" How would you answer his question?

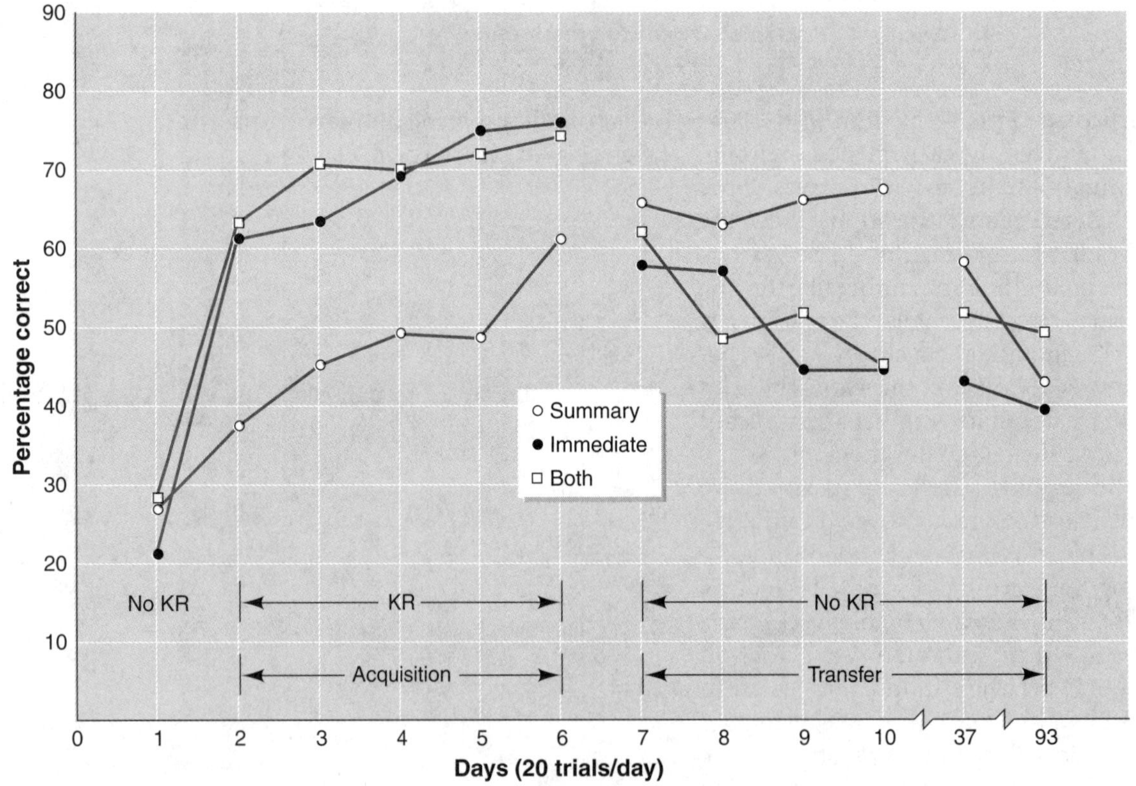

Figure 10.10 Percentage correct trials for various conditions of feedback during practice and for no-feedback retention tests. Those in the "Immediate" group had KR after each trial; those in the "Summary" group had KR about every trial presented only after each block of 20 trials; and those in the "Both" group had both kinds of feedback. (Reprinted from Lavery, 1962.)

How many performance attempts can be included in the summary feedback statement? Here again, it depends. Research evidence suggests that there is an optimal number; including either too few or too many attempts in the summary statement diminishes learning. If instructors give feedback after only two or three attempts, learners are guided strongly to the movement goal, but they also become more dependent on the feedback. On the other hand, if instructors summarize too many attempts (say, 100), learners become less dependent on the feedback, but they are also less strongly guided toward the goal.

Schmidt, Lange, and Young (1990) explored the effects of different lengths of summary feedback statements on the learning of a timing skill. In this study, participants practiced a laboratory task that resembled baseball batting. During practice, participants received summary feedback about their timing accuracy after 1, 5, 10, or 15 attempts. As you can see in figure 10.11, the group that received summary feedback for five attempts demonstrated the most learning, as measured by their performance on a no-feedback retention test. The five-trial summary was apparently somewhere near the optimum for this task.

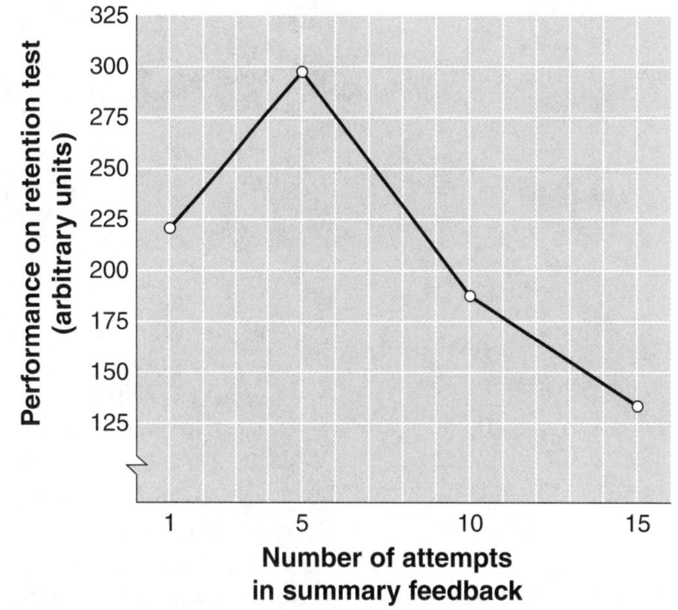

Figure 10.11 Performance on a retention test as a function of the number of attempts used for summary feedback in acquisition. In this particular case, the five-attempt summary length was the most effective for learning. (Reprinted from Schmidt, Lange, and Young, 1990.)

The number of performance attempts practitioners summarize in their feedback statements probably depends on the complexity of the skill. For very simple tasks, such as those used in Lavery's experiment, a relatively large number of attempts (e.g., 20 or more) might be included in the summary feedback statement. However, for more complex tasks, like the one used in the study by Schmidt, Lange, and Young (1990), fewer attempts (e.g., five) might be summarized. For extremely complex tasks, the optimal number of attempts might be no more than one or two, at least until learners master the essential movement elements. Generally, for maximal learning, it appears that as the complexity of the task increases, the shorter the number of summarized attempts needs to be. We depict this general trend in figure 10.12.

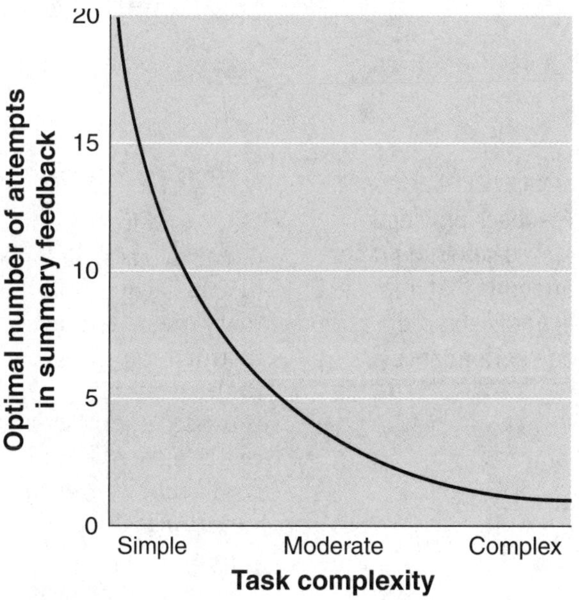

Figure 10.12 The probable relationship between task complexity and the optimal number of movement attempts to include in summary feedback.

Lavery's experiment produced another interesting result. Specifically, the group that received both immediate feedback and summary feedback during practice performed as poorly when feedback was withdrawn as the group that received immediate feedback only. Why did this happen if summary feedback is supposed to be so beneficial? The most likely reason is that the participants in the combined group ignored the summary feedback in favor of the more immediate, dependency-producing, every-trial feedback, so that they did not develop the capability to perform without feedback during the retention test. The every-trial KR was acting as a kind of "crutch."

How Does Summary Feedback Work?

How might the benefits of summary feedback be explained? Any or all of the following reasons appear to be viable explanations:

1. Learners must perform independently for a number of practice attempts before they finally receive feedback. When they receive summary feedback, learners use this information to make corrections in their general movement pattern on the next series of attempts. For example, the tennis player looking at the graph of his serves shown in figure 10.9 would see that he tended to hit his serves short of the service line, at least initially; therefore, he might try to increase the force of his shots during the next series of attempts.
2. Summary feedback produces more stable movements. Because learners perform a number of attempts before receiving summary feedback, they have no reason to change their movements very much from one attempt to the next. This reduces the amount of variability from trial to trial—perhaps caused by minor adjustments following every-trial KR; this perhaps decreases what Bjork (1994; Schmidt & Bjork, 1992; Wulf, 2007) termed "maladaptive short-term corrections." According to this idea, frequent feedback signals even the smallest errors—errors so small that they are a part of the natural movement variability and thus cannot ever be corrected. Yet, this KR encourages the learner to change the action on the next trial, preventing repetition of a stable action. These corrections might be beneficial for performance in the short term, but they are not beneficial for learning (i.e., when the feedback is removed later).
3. Summary feedback encourages learners to analyze their own movement-produced (kinesthetic, visual) feedback. Because they receive summary feedback less often, learners are encouraged to pay more attention to intrinsic feedback and to develop their own error-detection skills.

average feedback—Feedback provided after a series of practice attempts that informs learners about their average performance.

Average Feedback

One variation of summary feedback is called **average feedback**. With this method, practitioners again provide feedback information after a series of performance attempts, but the feedback in this case represents an average of all the actions rather than a summary of performance of each of them. In the tennis example shown in figure 10.9, the instructor might say to the student, "Your serves were (on the average) about 1 m short of the service line." Young and Schmidt (1992) found that average kinematic feedback provided after a series of five performance attempts was more effective for the learning of a simulated batting task than feedback given following each attempt. In addition, we could modify this method of providing feedback to give the range of individual trial variations (the difference between the longest and the shortest), the median of these values, or any other of a wide variety of ways of describing the collection of scores.

Average feedback and summary feedback likely function in a similar fashion—by blocking the detrimental, dependency-producing effects of feedback that is given after each performance attempt. When giving average feedback, practitioners are able to form a better idea of the learner's general movement pattern and can filter out the occasional extreme errors or other variations. In this way, they can provide learners with more reliable information about the prominent features of their movements generally, and the aspects they need to change during the next series of performance attempts.

"Put your hand in the basket" is an example of a concise feedback statement conveying information about a particular component of the motor program, that is, the follow-through.

Determining How Precise to Make Feedback

The issue of feedback precision concerns the degree to which the instructor's feedback approximates actual performance. For example, a carpenter teaching a trainee how to use a handsaw might provide only a rough estimate of a movement feature (e.g., movement length) by saying, "Your stroke was a little too short." A more precise feedback statement would be "Your stroke was 5.2 cm too short." Feedback information generally does not have to be very precise to be effective. Early in practice, learners' errors are so large that precise information about their exact size simply does not matter (Magill & Wood, 1986). At a high level of skill, however, performers may benefit from somewhat more detailed feedback because they are trying to make more precise adjustments in their movements.

Sometimes practitioners provide learners with information about directional errors in their movements (e.g., early or late, high or low, left or right) in addition to the magnitude of their errors. For example, an archery instructor might say, "The arrow landed two centimeters to the left of center," or a therapist might say, "Your first step was six inches shorter than it should be." You may recall from chapter 7 that **constant error** for a given trial is the directional deviation of a person's movement relative to some target value (e.g., a golf putt that stops 3 in. [7.6 cm] past the hole; a baseball swing that delivers the bat through the hitting zone 200 ms before the ball arrives). Average constant error

constant error (CE)—The deviation, with respect to amount and direction, of the result of a performer's movement relative to some target value. Average constant error is the average value of several movement attempts.

Maximal Information With Minimal Words

One way to maximize the information in a feedback statement is to develop a list of words and phrases that characterize the essence of what learners are trying to do. Using this list, practitioners can provide feedback statements that are brief and to the point and that enable the learners to make the necessary corrections in their movements. An example from the sport of basketball is "Put your hand in the basket," which is intended to convey to the shooter an image of the position of her hand after she releases the ball. Can you think of a similar phrase for some other motor skill with which you are familiar? What information or image would this phrase convey to the performer?

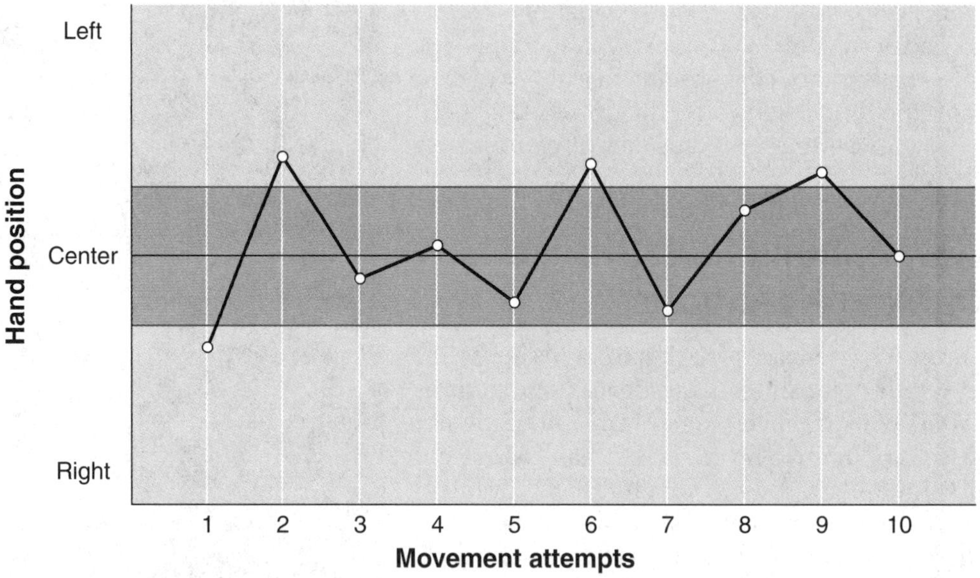

Figure 10.13 Bandwidth feedback is effective for learning. Feedback is given only if performance falls outside the band of correctness.

bandwidth feedback—Feedback provided only when errors exceed a certain tolerance level.

is the average directional deviation of the results of several movement attempts (e.g., three putts that stop an average of 2.8 cm past the hole). Of the two aspects of constant error, directional information alone is more important than magnitude information alone. In fact, feedback about magnitude is of little use to learners unless they are also informed about the direction of their errors.

One type of feedback information that speaks to the issue of precision is **bandwidth feedback** (Sherwood, 1988). Instructors who use this method give feedback only when a person's movements fall outside some acceptable level of correctness, or bandwidth. For example, let's say a therapist is working with a patient who is practicing moving from a wheelchair to a bed by placing her hands first in certain positions on the armrests of the wheelchair. The therapist would not give feedback unless the patient's hand placement was outside some predefined bandwidth (e.g., more than 2 cm from the center position). In figure 10.13 we present a graph showing the location of the patient's hand positions during 10 hypothetical attempts to stand up from the wheelchair. The bandwidth is represented by the shaded area in the figure and spans the center of acceptable hand positions. In the example here, the therapist would give feedback about the direction and extent of hand placement errors only after the first, second, sixth, and ninth attempts.

It Depends . . .

How Would You Estimate the Bandwidth for Providing Feedback?

When providing bandwidth feedback, movement practitioners must decide the level of a learner's performance that will be considered outside the bandwidth of acceptability. What factors might an instructor consider when determining the feedback bandwidth for a child learning to swim? A therapy patient learning to use crutches? A middle school student learning a new dance?

The bandwidth feedback method has several advantages. First, it decreases learners' dependency on extrinsic feedback as they become more skilled. When learners are just beginning to practice, their movements tend to fall outside the acceptable bandwidth of correctness, requiring more frequent feedback from the instructor. However, as their

Providing Transitional Prescriptive Feedback in a Bandwidth Schedule

A study by Smith, Taylor, and Withers (1997) illustrates how practitioners might use several feedback methods simultaneously when assisting learners with their skill development. In this study, beginning students attempted to learn the golf chip shot. The distance the ball landed from a designated target represented participants' error on each attempt. During the practice phase (50 attempts), learners received feedback according to one of three bandwidth schedules (0%, 5%, 10%). The wider the error bandwidth, the more error was tolerated and the less frequently feedback was provided. Participants received no feedback whenever their shots landed within the bandwidth. The other factor of interest was the type of feedback provided. Half of the participants received descriptive KR regarding the distance the ball landed from the target line. The other half received transitional (prescriptive) KP about some aspect of their movement form they needed to improve. For example, a participant who failed to perform a correct backswing might be told to focus on bringing the club back to the correct position. Once participants in this group demonstrated proficiency on one form component, they received feedback about another. In this way, participants in the transitional prescriptive KP group received information that guided them toward the correct form.

Following the practice phase, all participants performed 10 additional shots with no feedback as a test of the relative amount learned in the earlier practice with different kinds of feedback. The transitional prescriptive KP group with the largest bandwidth demonstrated greater consistency than all the other groups during practice, and this advantage persisted during the retention test without feedback. These results suggest that a feedback schedule that allows learners to perform more attempts without feedback (i.e., 10% bandwidth), and that offers them information dealing with progressively more advanced aspects of movement form, produces the most effective learning.

skill improves, learners' movements fall within the bandwidth more often. Therefore, the practitioner gives extrinsic feedback less frequently, and intrinsic feedback becomes more important. Second, learners receive information when error feedback is not given, indicating that the movement was acceptable that time. However, research (Badets & Blandin, 2005) indicates that for this to occur, learners need to know the meaning of no feedback (i.e., that performance is good or at least acceptable). Finally, the absence of extrinsic feedback information during advanced performance fosters the production of more consistent actions, because performers are not receiving information that suggests they should change anything. This allows them to strengthen their permanent memory of the action.

Determining How Often to Give Feedback

The frequency of providing feedback is related to the amount and precision of feedback. Early in the 20th century, the understanding of how feedback operated for skill learning was largely based on Thorndike's law of effect for operant learning. Because Thorndike believed that learning involved the strengthening of the bond between a stimulus and a response, and that extrinsic feedback increased the strength of that bond, he assumed that feedback should be presented as often as possible. Furthermore, Thorndike

UNIVERSITY OF WINCHESTER
LIBRARY

Law of Effect

Psychologists who study instrumental (or operant) learning are interested in the effects of reinforcing stimuli on the learning of actions. More specifically, they are concerned about how reinforcement produces correct actions more frequently and incorrect actions less frequently. Scientists have long realized that the nature and timing of feedback have a marked influence on the instrumental learning of a goal response. This influence is best summarized in Thorndike's (1927) empirical *law of effect,* which holds that an action elicited by a stimulus and followed by pleasant, or rewarding, consequences tends to be repeated when that stimulus appears again; an action followed by unpleasant or punishing consequences tends not to be repeated.

proposed that if feedback was not presented after a movement attempt and learners could not determine the outcome based on their own intrinsic feedback, the bond would not be strengthened at all on that attempt.

Over the next few decades, scientists discovered little that contradicted Thorndike's viewpoint. Therefore, a notion emerged that more feedback is better, and it was assumed that feedback information that was more immediate, more precise, more frequent, more detailed, or more useful in general would be most beneficial for learning. "More is better" seemed to make such good sense—giving more information to the learner had to benefit learning.

In time, though, scientists began to discover that more is not always better. Researchers began to realize that feedback frequency could be viewed in two ways. One way is in terms of **absolute feedback frequency,** which refers to the total number of times feedback is presented during a practice session. If a performer attempts 300 repetitions of a movement and the instructor gives feedback on 100 of them, the absolute feedback frequency is 100. **Relative feedback frequency,** on the other hand, refers to the total number of times feedback is presented divided by the number of movement attempts (multiplied by 100 to arrive at a percentage). In this example, 100 feedback presentations divided by 300 attempts and then multiplied by 100 yields a relative feedback frequency of 33%; that is, the instructor would deliver feedback after 33% of a person's performance attempts.

absolute feedback frequency— The total number of times feedback is given for a series of performance attempts.

relative feedback frequency— The percentage of performance attempts for which feedback is given; equal to absolute feedback frequency divided by the number of performance attempts and multiplied by 100.

What principles describe the roles of absolute and relative feedback frequency for learning? In general, increasing the absolute frequency of feedback enhances learning. This is especially true for learners who cannot detect their own errors without feedback

It Depends . . .

Guidance Effects of Feedback

A person wants to learn to play golf. Her instructor decides that she should start by going to the practice range and hitting a bucket of balls. The instructor shows the learner how to hold the club and then demonstrates the swing for her. The learner begins hitting balls; after each shot she receives feedback from the instructor about her swing (e.g., too slow, too fast, too stiff, too jerky). The learner repeatedly adjusts the swing according to the instructor's feedback until, by the end of the lesson, she is producing swings that are close to the correct pattern and timing. The next night, teacher and student return to the range, but unfortunately the instructor has developed laryngitis (from all the talking he did the night before). The learner tries her best to produce the correct swing, but she has little success. The learner worries that she has let her instructor down. What is another interpretation of the learner's diminished performance?

HERMAN® by Jim Unger

"Up and left."

(HERMAN® is reprinted with permission from LaughingStock Licensing Inc., Ottawa, Canada. All rights reserved. © David Waisglass and Gordon Coulthart, COMIC PROPERTY.)

because they can't see or feel the outcome (e.g., the location of misses in shooting a rifle at targets 200 m away) or determine the outcome on their own (e.g., the distance from the hole of a miniature golf attempted by a blind person). There are, however, limitations to this rule.

Consider the following situation: A group of learners practices a skill for which errors are difficult to detect without extrinsic feedback (e.g., archery, welding, knitting, adjusting brakes on a car). Because the instructor is busy rotating among them, the learners do not receive feedback information very often. That is, the relative feedback frequency is quite low. Does infrequent instructor feedback impair their learning?

Research has shown that practice attempts followed by no feedback can actually be beneficial for learning, even when participants cannot detect their own errors. In one study, Winstein and Schmidt (1990) found that participants who received extrinsic feedback after 50% of their practice attempts performed (during practice) as accurately as those who received feedback following every attempt (100% relative frequency). Moreover, immediate retention of the skill (10 min after practice ended) performed in the absence of extrinsic feedback was about the same for both groups. Results such as these challenge Thorndike's assumption that movements followed by no extrinsic feedback produce no learning.

But it gets better. When Winstein and Schmidt tested participants again 2 days later, the group that had received less frequent feedback (50% relative frequency) during practice performed more accurately than the group that had received feedback after every attempt (100% relative frequency). Even more impressive are the results of studies examining the learning of correct movement form. Weeks and Kordus (1998) found that 12-year-old children who received KP following 33% of their practice attempts of the soccer throw-in movement demonstrated significantly better movement form (based on eight biomechanical characteristics) than children receiving KP 100% of the time.

How could less feedback during practice produce more learning? One answer may be that when people don't receive feedback, they engage in various kinds of information-processing activities they do not engage in when they receive feedback. In addition, when learners are given feedback less frequently, they are less likely to

faded feedback—A schedule for providing extrinsic feedback in which relative frequency of feedback presentation is high during early practice and diminishes during later practice.

become dependent on the feedback. The result is more effective learning and better retention of the skill.

One way practitioners can reduce the dependency-producing effects of feedback is to reduce the relative frequency of the feedback they provide gradually. A **faded feedback** approach begins with the instructor providing feedback after most of the learner's initial practice attempts (essentially 100% of the time). With this information, the learner can achieve the goal pattern quickly and can experience the sensations associated with it. However, once the learner reaches a satisfactory level of proficiency, the instructor can reduce or "fade" the feedback frequency gradually. After considerable practice, the instructor can withdraw feedback entirely without diminishing the learner's performance. If for some reason performance proficiency should drop off, the instructor can reintroduce feedback for one or two attempts to bring the learner's performance back to the target level. Once this is accomplished, the instructor can withdraw feedback again.

With faded feedback, instructors can adjust feedback scheduling so that it matches each learner's proficiency level and improvement rate. The ultimate goal of this approach is to develop learners' capabilities to produce the required action on their own, without requiring extrinsic feedback. Although effective instructors enhance learning by providing feedback while learners are developing and ingraining the goal movement pattern, they gradually remove it to enhance permanent skill learning.

It Depends . . .

When Might Feedback Frequency Be Reduced?

A person is helping his friend learn to bowl. What might the person look for in his friend's performance that would help him determine when to begin reducing the relative frequency of his feedback?

Two types of learning situations that do not appear to be negatively affected by more frequent feedback are when learners are instructed to estimate their own errors before receiving instructor feedback or when they are told to focus on the intended result of the action. In chapter 8 we mentioned the concepts of error-detection practice and directing learners' attentional focus. Research suggests that, when learners receive 100% KR during error-detection practice, their retention is greater than when they receive 100% KR without estimating their errors (Guadagnoli & Kohl, 2001). Apparently, extrinsic KR can help learners evaluate the accuracy of their error estimates without creating a feedback dependency. This suggests that the tendency for KR to block the learner's analysis of his or her own response-produced feedback can be reduced or eliminated by having the learners attend to feedback in the course of generating estimates of their own errors.

With respect to the focusing of learners' attention, one study revealed that the acquisition and retention performance of university students instructed to adopt an external focus during the learning of the lofted soccer pass were superior to those of students told to adopt an internal focus (Wulf et al., 2002). Moreover, the performance of participants in the external-focus condition (who received feedback following every practice attempt—100% frequency) was just as proficient as that of their external-focus counterparts who received feedback 33% of the time. These findings suggest that more frequent feedback does not diminish learning as long as participants focus on the desired outcome of their actions rather than on movement mechanics.

More Frequent Feedback May Be Needed for Complex Skill Learning

In a series of experiments by Wulf, Shea, and Matschiner (1998), three groups of participants practiced on a slalom-type ski simulator (see figure 8.4 in chapter 8). Two of the groups received different frequencies of continuous KP about the foot forces they exerted on the platform. One group received this feedback on 100% of their practice attempts, whereas the other group received it on 50% of their attempts. A third group received no KP during practice. After the practice phase, a retention test was administered without feedback. On the retention test, the group that had received feedback on 100% of their practice attempts outperformed the groups that had received feedback on 50% of their attempts or no feedback at all. For complex skills like the slalom-type ski simulator, a higher relative frequency of continuous knowledge of performance may be more effective for skill learning than a reduced frequency, at least until learners reach an acceptable level of proficiency. Thus, the type of feedback given and the relative difficulty of the task (i.e., the learner's capability relative to the complexity of the task) are both important in determining the optimal feedback frequency for skill learning.

One other issue related to feedback presentation concerns the timing of feedback delivery. Regardless of how frequently they give feedback, effective instructors are sensitive to the timing of their feedback. As we mentioned earlier, the interval immediately following movement completion is a good time for learners to process their own feedback and estimate their own errors. In a study by Swinnen and colleagues (1990), participants attempted to learn a simulated batting task. One group received **instantaneous feedback** (literally, with no delay at all) after each movement, whereas another group received **delayed feedback** a few seconds after movement completion. The instantaneous group performed more poorly than the delayed group on the second day of practice and on several retention tests administered over a 4-month period. Instantaneous feedback actually degraded learning (compared with delayed feedback), contrary to the common view that feedback must be immediate to be effective.

instantaneous feedback—Feedback provided immediately following movement completion.

delayed feedback—Feedback provided several seconds or more following movement completion.

One reason instantaneous feedback may have been detrimental to learning here is that it might have prevented learners from processing their own intrinsic feedback (i.e., how the movement felt, sounded, looked) and from estimating their own errors. Research (Anderson, Magill, Sekiya, & Ryan, 2005) has indicated that learners pay closer attention to feedback, and explore the available intrinsic feedback more, when KR is delayed than when it is given immediately after a movement. As one participant in the delayed-feedback condition in this study noted, "I would experiment with different (feedback) sources now and then" (p. 236). Moreover, as we mentioned in chapter 8, asking participants to critique their movements before providing extrinsic feedback can enhance learning. A recent study revealed that competitive swimmers who were questioned by the coach before receiving feedback during practice improved their short-course (25 m) times over the course of a season more than swimmers who were not questioned (Chambers & Vickers, 2006). Successful practitioners allow enough time for both feedback processing and error evaluation before providing extrinsic feedback.

How Would You Analyze This Golf Practice?

One of Dick Schmidt's neighbors can be seen in the early morning walking his dog and practicing golf at the same time. An experienced golfer, this individual carries a different club each day, but not a ball. He chooses a target for each shot, addresses the imaginary ball as if were real, and swings his club the way he would on the golf course. He hits about 50 of these shots on his walk.

Using this method, the golfer selects a program and a parameter for each shot, executes the swing, and obtains response-produced feedback from the swing. However, at no time does he receive feedback about where the ball goes. Do you think he can learn without outcome feedback? Does this practice method make sense to you, given what you know about feedback frequency and learning? Or is this just a waste of time? Why?

SUMMARY

A learner can receive various kinds of sensory information during skill practice, but extrinsic feedback about errors that is provided by the instructor is one of the more important sources of information. Practitioners can present feedback verbally (i.e., telling learners what they did correctly and incorrectly), but they can also present feedback in other forms, primarily visually (e.g., video replays). Instructional feedback is best when it is simple and refers to only one or two movement features, particularly when those features deal with something over which the learner has control.

Extrinsic feedback can serve the following simultaneous functions:

- Energize learners and increase their motivation to pursue their goals
- Reinforce learners for correct performance
- Provide learners with information about the nature and direction of their errors and suggest ways of correcting them
- Allow learners to become dependent on the feedback, causing their performance to suffer when the feedback is withdrawn

When considering various forms of feedback for practice, good practitioners attend to these questions:

- What information will the feedback contain?
- How much information will the feedback contain?
- How precise will the feedback information be?
- How often will the feedback information be presented?

When considering the type of information to give in feedback, skilled practitioners remember the following:

- Feedback about the timing or sequencing of a movement pattern leads to changes in the fundamental structure of the generalized motor program.
- Feedback about program features (e.g., the relative timing of arm and leg movements) is sometimes difficult for learners to use, but it is crucial for modifying faulty features.

- Feedback about parameters (e.g., movement speed, force) leaves the program's structure intact, and learners can easily use this information to match their movements to the current environmental demands.
- Prescriptive feedback, which informs about specific changes to make in movements, is more effective than descriptive feedback that simply tells about the errors made.

When considering the amount of information to include in feedback, effective practitioners remember these points:

- The optimal amount of information to include in feedback decreases as the complexity of the task increases.
- Summary feedback and average feedback are particularly effective ways of providing learners with an optimal amount of information without creating a feedback dependency.

Some important principles dealing with the precision of feedback information include these:

- Increasing the precision of feedback enhances learning only to a point (e.g., saying that a person's follow-through was slightly left of center is better than saying that the follow-through was not very good); beyond that point, further increases in feedback precision result in little additional learning.
- Feedback about the direction of learners' errors alone is more useful than feedback about the magnitude of their errors alone.
- Bandwidth feedback is an effective way of manipulating feedback precision and reducing learners' dependence on feedback information.

Generalizations dealing with the frequency and timing of feedback presentation include the following:

- Feedback can be presented more frequently early in learning but then reduced (or faded) as learners become more skilled in task performance.
- Instantaneous feedback degrades learning, probably because it interferes with learners' intrinsic feedback processing and the development of error-detection capabilities.

FROM PRINCIPLES TO PRACTICE

Check your comprehension of the concepts and terms discussed in this chapter by responding to each of the exercises in the following sections. The first section contains several exercises designed to test your working knowledge of key terms. The second section poses a variety of problems designed to check your understanding of key concepts. In the third section you are challenged to apply your knowledge by discussing a defensible solution for two scenarios.

Know Your Key Terms

Matching: Feedback Considerations

Match the following terms with their respective categories or definitions by placing the most appropriate letter on each of the blanks below.

Feedback Considerations—Terms

a. program feedback
b. prescriptive feedback
c. knowledge of results
d. summary feedback
e. negative reinforcement
f. knowledge of performance
g. parameter feedback

Feedback Considerations—Category or Definition

_____1. Conveys information about the degree of goal achievement

_____2. Informs learners of ways to adapt the generalized motor program to meet environmental demands

_____3. Given after a series of performance attempts; provides learners with information about each of the attempts

_____4. Conveys information about the quality of the action

_____5. Informs learners of ways to produce the fundamental relative timing pattern

_____6. Suggests something learners might do to correct errors in their movements

_____7. Designed to encourage the repetition of an action by withdrawing unpleasant feedback

Consider: Feedback Properties

List the feedback property that is most likely operating for each of the following feedback statements. Provide rationales for your answers.

1. "Try to lengthen your backswing more." _______

   ____

2. "Great forward dive!" ____________________

   ____

3. "Your time was two seconds faster than your previous best." ________________________________

   ____

4. "Keep your head down." "Keep your left arm straight." "Point your knee at the ball." "Rotate your hips more." "Square up your stance." "Relax."

   ____

   ____

Fill in the Blank: Feedback Timing

Complete the following sentences:

Effective movement practitioners know how and when to reduce the frequency of extrinsic feedback. One way instructors might do this is to provide _______________ feedback that conveys information about each of a series of movement attempts once the learner completes them. Instructors might also provide _______________ feedback that gives learners a general idea of the dominant features of a series of movement attempts. By reducing the frequency of extrinsic feedback, instructors encourage learners to become familiar with their own ____________________ feedback and develop their own ____________________ ____________________ skills. By receiving extrinsic feedback less frequently, learners are also able to produce movements that are more _______________. However, learners who are ________________________ may need more frequent extrinsic feedback during initial practice sessions, particularly if the target skill is _______________.

Check Your Understanding

1. Explain the difference between intrinsic feedback and extrinsic feedback and between knowledge of results and knowledge of performance. Give an example of each type of feedback that an experienced chef might give to a beginner learning to make a pizza.
2. Describe three ways that extrinsic feedback can modify a learner's behavior, and then discuss how a diving coach might use each in teaching a child how to do a back dive.
3. Discuss three advantages and three disadvantages of instructor feedback for a person who is learning to play the piano.
4. Explain the difference between descriptive feedback and prescriptive feedback and give two examples of each that a driving instructor might give to a student driver.
5. Discuss two procedures a therapist might use to reduce the dependency-producing properties of feedback when teaching a person recovering from knee surgery how to correctly perform a leg-strengthening exercise.

Apply Your Knowledge

Exercise 1

A college gymnastics coach is trying to teach an athlete a new routine on the still rings. The gymnast has competed for 10 years and is among the best performers in his conference. The routine contains some highly practiced components and one or two that have received nearly no practice. Discuss some factors the coach might consider when deciding whether to provide extrinsic feedback or to allow the athlete to process his own intrinsic feedback. Explain how the coach might provide feedback in a way that promotes the gymnast's learning of the routine and successful transfer to the target context (i.e., a competitive gymnastics meet). Please provide rationales for your answers and furnish two supporting references.

Exercise 2

A man has recently lost his sight in both eyes as a result of an industrial accident. To maintain his aerobic fitness level, he needs to learn how to swim using the freestyle stroke. Discuss three types of extrinsic feedback an instructor might provide that would help the man learn to swim. Explain how, if at all, the amount, precision, and frequency of feedback provided by the instructor would be different for this learner than for a sighted learner with a similar background (i.e., assume the two learners are theoretically the same except for their present visual condition). Please provide rationales for your answers and furnish two supporting references.

PART FOUR

INTEGRATION AND APPLICATIONS

chapter 11

Facilitating Learning and Performance

▷ Chapter Outline

▷ Chapter Objectives

When you have completed this chapter, you should be able to

- integrate the conceptual model of motor performance and the various principles presented in the book and be able to apply them when teaching skills in applied settings;
- appreciate how various kinds of learners, skills, and environments influence the design of effective learning experiences; and
- determine appropriate instructional strategies for a variety of learning experiences.

PREVIEW

How many classes have you taken in school for which you diligently copied lecture notes, memorized them along with other facts from the textbook, regurgitated as much of the information as you could on exams (perhaps even earning an A in the course), but used (not to mention, remembered) little of the material once the class ended? We hope this will not be the case with the concepts you have learned in this book. Moreover, the situation-based approach to motor learning and performance is one that could prove useful in the future.

One day you may find yourself in a therapeutic setting where you are expected to help people recover skills they have lost as a result of an accident or stroke, skills those individuals once produced with ease but that now require their best effort to achieve at the crudest level. Perhaps you will have the opportunity to teach or coach people to play the violin, tune the engine of a car, swim the freestyle, or throw darts. When your time comes to help others learn or relearn skills, what kind of approach will you take? What will you do to make each person's learning experience efficient, interesting, and productive? How will you organize practice sessions? How and when will you provide feedback? How will you assess the quality of each learning experience and the improvements of learners?

OVERVIEW

To design an effective plan of instruction, practitioners must know something about the background, abilities, and experiences of learners (see chapter 6); the underlying mechanisms of human performance (see chapters 2-5); the learning goal and target context (see chapter 7); and the principles of practice organization (see chapter 8), structure (see chapter 9), and feedback (see chapter 10). In this book, we present scientific literature addressing all of these issues. Many times, the research provides clear direction for practitioners. Sometimes the evidence still is either inconsistent or nonexistent.

Regardless of the amount of supporting evidence at their disposal, effective practitioners want to design learning experiences that optimize learners' chances to achieve their goals. For those situations in which relevant research is partial or incomplete, practitioners need to be more cautious and prepared to adjust the instructional plan if necessary.

In this chapter, we pull together the key themes we have discussed throughout the book. Our purpose is to suggest and demonstrate how you can use the material you have learned to solve a variety of instructional challenges you are apt to face in the future. First, we propose a strategy that combines the conceptual model of motor performance with many of the principles of skill learning. Then, we present four case studies that illustrate how practitioners can use the strategy to design helpful learning experiences for various types of learners.

WORKING STRATEGY FOR PROVIDING INSTRUCTIONAL ASSISTANCE

Sometimes, the most difficult and, frequently, the most important part of life's major undertakings (e.g., earning a degree, teaching a class, or writing this book) is preparing a plan of action. However, once an effective plan is devised, even if it is not perfect, we are often able to accomplish the main task rather easily, leaving us wondering why we had so much difficulty preparing the plan in the first place.

The plan of action, or working strategy, presented in this chapter begins with the conceptual model we have developed throughout this book (shown in finalized form in figure 11.1). Regardless of the types of instructional challenges you might face as a practitioner, you can always rely on the fundamental mechanisms of motor performance that form the basis of skill learning. Knowledge of these mechanisms will allow you to determine things such as the possible effects of task demands on the three information-processing stages, the extent to which performers can make feedback-based adjustments in their movements, and the types of intrinsic and extrinsic feedback learners need to improve their skills and develop their error detection capabilities.

The remainder of the working strategy consists of the various concepts and principles presented in chapters 1 through 10. Many of these concepts and principles are

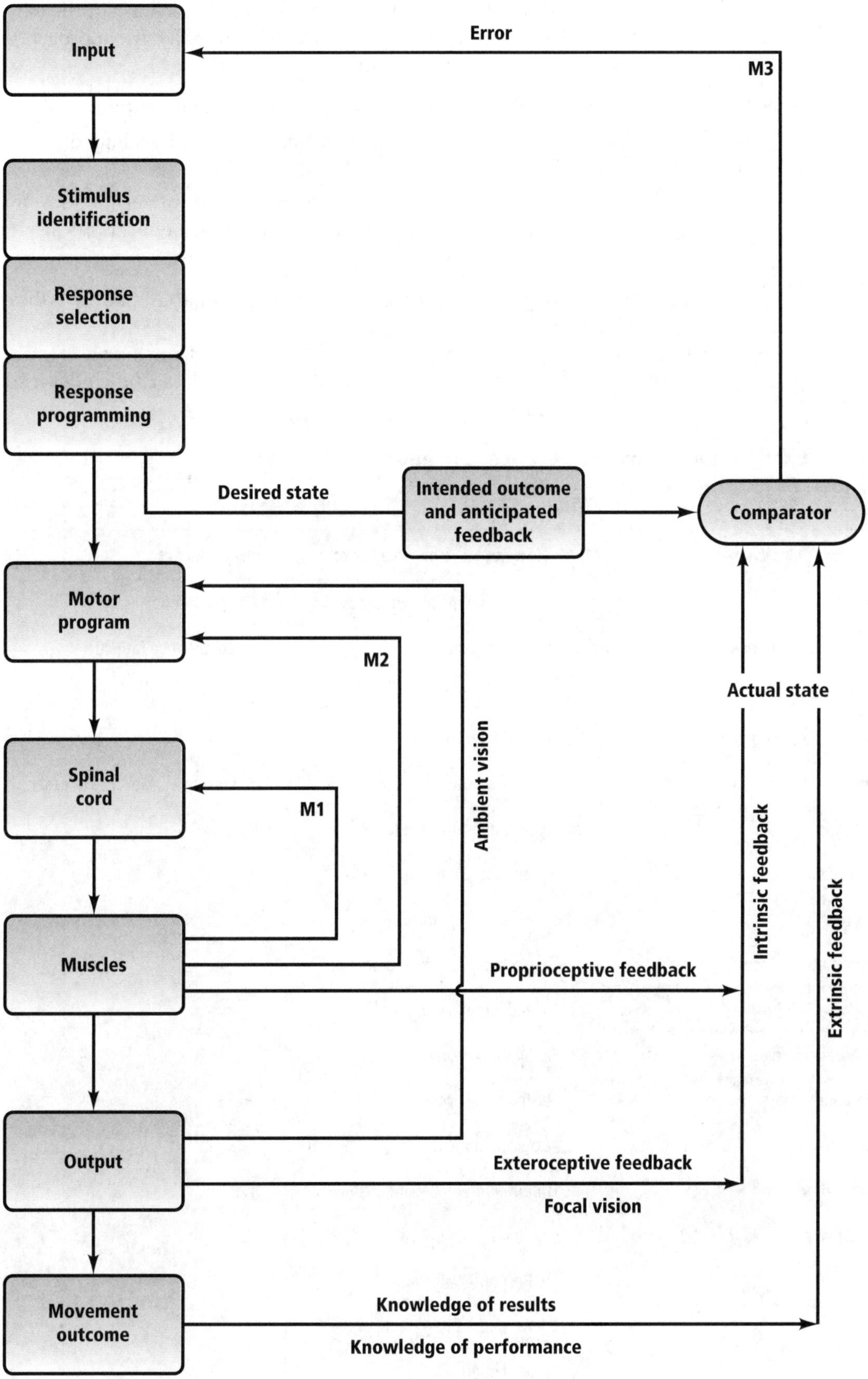

Figure 11.1 The completed model of motor performance, which is used here as a basis for the organization of effective practice.

not hard-and-fast rules. Rather, they include qualifying phrases such as "in the early stages of learning" or "when dealing with a complex task." An effective approach to skill instruction depends on answers to such questions as these:

- Who is the learner (a child, an athlete, a rehab patient, a senior citizen)?
- What is the target skill (handwriting, using a wheelchair, hitting a ball, driving a car)?
- Where is the target context within which the person must ultimately perform the skill (at home, during a sport tournament, during a physical education class, at a musical recital)?

An effective working strategy provides practitioners with reasonable answers to these and other relevant questions.

In table 11.1 is a checklist of items you can refer to when diagnosing a learning situation. As you review this table, you might think of other items to include. If so,

Table 11.1 Checklist for Diagnosing a Learning Situation

Who?	What?	Where?
Learner characteristics	**Task (target skill) characteristics**	**Target context**
☐ Age	☐ Discrete, serial, or continuous	☐ Recreational
☐ Previous experience	☐ Motor or cognitive	☐ Competitive (athletic)
☐ Motivation	☐ Closed or open	☐ Clinical
☐ Stage of learning	☐ Closed-loop control	☐ Home
☐ Abilities	a. Exteroceptive feedback	☐ Presence or absence of others
☐ Attention	b. Proprioceptive feedback	
☐ Arousal	☐ Open-loop control	
☐ Memory	a. Motor programs	
☐ Information-processing capability	b. Generalized motor programs	
Goal(s) of learning	☐ Speed–accuracy trade-offs	
☐ Program learning	a. Spatial accuracy	
☐ Parameter learning	b. Temporal accuracy	
☐ Error detection and correction	☐ Object manipulation	
☐ Skill refinement	☐ Information-processing demands	
☐ Generalization	a. Stimulus identification	
	b. Response selection	
	c. Response programming	
	☐ Risk of injury	

From R.A. Schmidt and C.A. Wrisberg, 2008, *Motor Learning and Performance, 4th ed.* (Champaign, IL: Human Kinetics).

we encourage you to add them. You should, however, be able to provide supporting rationale and, wherever possible, research evidence for any additions you make.

Once you complete the checklist in table 11.1, you can decide what types of instructional assistance to provide. Table 11.2 is a checklist for designing a particular learning experience. Here again, you might think of other items to add to this list, and if so, we encourage you to do so.

The conceptual model of motor performance, along with the checklists of factors for diagnosing a learning situation and designing a learning experience, provides a working strategy you can use for just about any instructional setting. In the remainder of this chapter, we present four hypothetical case studies to illustrate how this might be accomplished. These case studies are not just detailed explanations of how instruction might be offered; rather they are intended to illustrate how the concepts and principles presented in this book can provide a foundation for providing effective instructional assistance.

Table 11.2 Checklist for Designing the Learning Experience

Practice preparation	Practice presentation	Practice feedback
☐ Goal setting	☐ Clarifying expectations	☐ Intrinsic feedback
a. Outcome goals	☐ Managing arousal	☐ Extrinsic feedback
b. Performance goals	☐ Focusing attention	a. Knowledge of results
c. Process goals	☐ Providing instructions	b. Knowledge of performance
☐ Stage of learning	☐ Providing demonstrations	☐ Instructional decisions
☐ Transfer of learning	☐ Offering guidance	☐ Type of feedback
☐ Target skills	☐ Providing physical practice	a. Program or parameter
☐ Target behaviors	a. Simulations	b. Visual, verbal, or manual
☐ Target context	b. Part practice	c. Descriptive or prescriptive
☐ Performance measures	c. Slow-motion practice	☐ Amount of feedback
a. Outcome	d. Error detection practice	a. Average feedback
b. Process	☐ Providing mental practice	b. Summary feedback
Practice structure	a. Procedures	☐ Precision of feedback
☐ Schema development	b. Imagery	☐ Frequency of feedback
a. Constant practice		
b. Varied practice		
☐ Facilitating transfer		
a. Blocked practice		
b. Random practice		
c. Consistent and varied mapping		

From R.A. Schmidt and C.A. Wrisberg, 2008, *Motor Learning and Performance, 4th ed.* (Champaign, IL: Human Kinetics).

UNIVERSITY OF WINCHESTER LIBRARY

FOUR CASE STUDIES

For each of the following hypothetical case studies, we present a diagnosis of the learning situation, a possible design for the learning experience, and two modifications of the learning situation with relevant instructional adaptations. At the end of each case study we include a list of supporting references from the research literature in motor learning and performance.

Case Study 1: Teaching the Backhand Ground Stroke in Tennis

Maria is a 50-year-old woman who has played tennis recreationally for many years but has never developed a satisfactory backhand ground stroke. Maria's strategy during matches has been to avoid hitting backhands whenever possible. Recently, however, Maria has decided she's tired of that strategy and wants to learn how to hit the backhand correctly so that she can produce the shot with confidence during competition. Maria asks her friend Liz, an experienced player, to teach her. How might Liz approach this task?

Diagnosing the Learning Situation

Using the checklist for diagnosing the learning situation (see table 11.1), Liz identifies some of the factors to consider in assisting Maria. In the following paragraphs we provide a narrative description of the items this practitioner might select (with specific checklist items shown in italics):

Learner Characteristics

Maria is a 50-year-old woman with 25 years of tennis experience. Maria appears to have average to better-than-average levels of the important *abilities* for playing tennis (i.e., multilimb coordination, motor timing, perceptual timing, and force control). She is sufficiently fit physically and has no obvious handicapping conditions. She is highly motivated to improve her backhand ground stroke. Maria is in the *stage of learning* where *skill refinement* is the primary goal (i.e., the motor stage). However, she may need to do some of the things associated with the verbal–cognitive stage of learning if she intends to revamp her stroke completely.

Goal of Learning

Because Maria's backhand requires serious adjustment and possibly a complete overhaul, *program learning* is a primary goal. Maria also needs to be able to produce a variety of backhand shots *(parameter learning)* and to generalize her performance from practice settings to competition situations *(generalization)*. A final goal is the development of *error-detection* and *error-correction* capability, which Maria needs in order to adjust her backhand on her own.

Characteristics of the Target Skill

The tennis backhand is a *discrete, open skill* involving both large and small muscles. The task also requires *object manipulation:* Maria must control the racket to produce specific angles and spins with her shots. *Speed–accuracy trade-offs* are a consideration, in that Maria must hit the ball with pace while at the same time keeping it within the boundaries of the court. An abundance of *intrinsic feedback* is available, including vision of the ball's trajectory, angle, and speed; *proprioceptive feedback* from limb movements and racket–ball impact; and auditory feedback from the sound of racket–ball impact. This skill involves all of the following *information-processing* demands: *stimulus identification, response selection*, and *response programming*. There seems to be little *risk of injury* unless Maria uses incorrect mechanics.

Nature of the Target Context

Because Maria's goal is to hit the backhand ground stroke within the *context* of competitive tennis matches, an evaluative audience *(presence of others)*, including other players and perhaps spectators, is part of the *target context*. Time pressure is also a part of the target context, because occasionally Maria must produce the backhand shot with very little time for preparation. Possible distractions include her fear of failure as well as an overemphasis on the importance of the match, the score, and others' evaluations of her. Also, she must perform the various shots without having the opportunity to repeat a just-previously-made shot; thus, the target context resembles *random practice*. The primary strategy demands include selecting and producing a variety of backhand shots in different situations.

Once Liz has summarized all relevant information from table 11.1, she uses the conceptual model of motor performance (figure 11.1) and the checklist for designing the learning experience (see table 11.2) to devise a working strategy for providing instructional assistance. In the following section we provide a narrative summary of how Liz designs Maria's learning experience (with actual checklist items from tables 11.1 and 11.2 shown in italics).

Designing the Learning Experience

Liz decides that Maria's biggest challenge is changing the ineffective motor program she has developed over the years. Liz makes *program learning* the major emphasis of her initial instruction. She decides to introduce the backhand ground stroke in the same way she would for a beginner who has never played tennis before. Liz begins by explaining verbally (with *instructions)* and showing visually (with *demonstrations)* the proper grip, stance, and swing.

When Liz is sure that Maria understands this preliminary information, she describes and demonstrates the most important rhythmic component of the swing (i.e., one flowing motion of the arm, wrist, and racket in a straight path). Then Liz asks Maria to produce the component in isolation *(part practice)*. Maria performs repetitions of the component, and Liz provides *verbal feedback* and a *visual demonstration* whenever Maria requests it. When Maria asks for feedback, Liz offers *prescriptive feedback* that alerts Maria to possible changes to make in the swing component (e.g., the head of the racket should lead the wrist and arm). If Maria does not request feedback, Liz lets Maria perform repetitions of the action without interruption. Occasionally, Liz encourages Maria to rehearse the swing component with her eyes closed so that she gets a better feel of the movement *(intrinsic proprioceptive feedback)*. Once Liz notices that Maria is producing the component consistently, she introduces the next most important component (i.e., keeping the shoulders level with the court throughout the entire stroke) and asks Maria to practice it in combination with the previous component *(progressive part practice)*. Liz repeats this process until Maria demonstrates that she can produce the fundamental pattern of the entire swing consistently.

Then Liz decides to create a situation in which Maria has to produce the newly learned pattern while hitting a tennis ball. Because Liz knows that automation of the pattern requires many more repetitions, she is careful to minimize *stimulus-identification* and *response-selection* demands. Liz does this by suspending the ball from a string with a Velcro band and asking Maria to focus only on the swing and on ball contact *(focusing attention)*. She tells Maria not to be concerned with the accuracy of ball placement *(speed–accuracy trade-off)* but to focus on hitting her strokes at full speed.

Maria's practice sessions continue this way for several days until she demonstrates that she can produce the new backhand pattern consistently and can strike the ball firmly. At this point, Liz decides to increase *stimulus-identification* demands by using a ball machine to project the balls at a constant speed to Maria's backhand side *(simulation)*. This requires Maria to identify the speed, trajectory, and direction of the approaching ball *(open skill)*. Again, Liz tells Maria to focus only on producing the correct pattern and making solid contact with the ball. Liz provides occasional *prescriptive feedback* for program adjustment (e.g., keeping the shoulders level) but reduces the *frequency of feedback* as Maria continues to progress.

Once Liz sees that Maria is striking the ball consistently with the correct pattern, she shifts her instructional emphasis to *parameter learning* by asking Maria to hit backhands to several targets located at different distances and locations on the court. The targets are numbered, and Liz calls out a different sequence of numbers as Maria hits shots in a *varied-practice* format (e.g., Maria attempts to hit a variety of returns for each of a variety of shots hit to her). With practice, Maria becomes more adept at producing variations of the backhand pattern, resulting in shots that travel at various angles and speeds to various locations. Occasionally, Liz asks Maria to create her own sequence of shots and challenges her to see how many ways she can produce the fundamental pattern. When Maria performs an incorrect shot, Liz asks her to describe what she thinks went wrong (e.g., backswing preparation was too late) and what she believes is needed on the next shot to correct the error *(error-detection practice)*.

Once Liz sees that Maria is able to produce a variety of backhand shots using the ball machine (*simulation*), she encourages her to begin rallying with a partner. Liz instructs Maria to focus on the approaching ball while continuing to hit variations of the backhand shot. In time, Maria hits her backhand so consistently that Liz has her combine practice of the backhand with practice of her forehand and volley in a *random-practice* format. In this way, Maria has to select the most appropriate shot *(response selection)* and produce it *(response programming* and *parameter learning)* in a way that maximizes her chances of winning each point.

At some point, Liz believes that Maria is ready to test her new backhand ground stroke in competition *(target context)*. Before doing so, Liz encourages Maria to set goals *(goal setting)* for each game that include hitting a certain percentage of backhands that travel over the net and inside the boundaries, focusing on the process of hitting effective backhands (e.g., watch the ball and make solid contact), and hitting a variety of backhand shots *(outcome and process goals)*. To help Maria deal with distractions, Liz creates additional practice opportunities that are more matchlike in nature *(random practice)*, using a variety of opponents and tennis court locations that include other players and spectators. In this way, Maria can practice her shots under real-world competitive conditions *(generalization)*.

Two Modifications of the Learning Situation

Relearning the Backhand and the Volley. What if Maria had asked Liz to help her relearn both the backhand ground stroke and the volley? Liz might still emphasize program learning initially but might block Maria's practice *(blocked practice)* of each stroke until she demonstrates that she can produce both strokes consistently. At that point, Liz shifts Maria to a *random-practice* format and perhaps provides *average feedback* and *summary feedback* so that Maria understands the types of adjustments she needs to make in the general pattern of each movement. For example, after Maria hits a sequence of backhands and volleys, Liz says, "Your weight was generally too far forward on your volleys" *(average feedback)* and "Your backswing preparation was a bit late for the first few backhands but better timed for the rest of them" *(summary feedback)*. As Maria's performance continues to improve, Liz fades the *frequency of feedback*.

Resisting Old Habits When Competing. When performers confront stressful situations, they sometimes revert to older, more familiar habits. For Maria, this might happen if she is playing a close tennis match and begins thinking about winning and losing. In the excitement of the moment, she might begin hitting her old backhand ground stroke again. If so, an effective instructor like Liz would not be surprised because she knows that Maria has produced many more repetitions of her ineffective backhand during her lifetime than she has of her new backhand pattern. But how might Liz help Maria resist reverting to her earlier backhand style?

One thing Liz might do is provide Maria with a focus cue (e.g., telling her to lead with the racket head) that would redirect Maria's attention *(focusing attention)* to the new movement pattern *(prescriptive feedback)*. Liz might also encourage Maria to rehearse a key component of the correct movement pattern in isolation *(part practice)* with her eyes closed to reinforce the feel and timing of the correct pattern *(intrinsic proprioceptive feedback)*. Liz might also ask Maria to explain what caused the old backhand to reoccur and what might be done to keep it from happening in the future *(error-detection practice)*. When Maria returns to competition, Liz encourages her to set a goal of focusing more on correct execution of her new backhand pattern *(process goal)* and less on winning the point *(outcome goal)*. This type of process focus *(focusing attention)* might reduce Maria's competitive anxiety *(managing arousal)* and enhance her game performance *(generalization)*. As Maria becomes more adept at producing the new pattern in practice and in competition, her relapses will likely become less frequent and, when they do occur, she will be able to recognize them and correct them on her own.

Supporting References

Chambers, K.L., & Vickers, J.N. (2006). Effects of bandwidth feedback and questioning on the performance of competitive swimmers. *The Sport Psychologist, 20*, 184–197.

Filby, W.C.D., Maynard, I.W., & Graydon, J.K. (1999). The effect of multiple-goal strategies on performance outcomes in training and competition. *Journal of Applied Sport Psychology, 11*, 230–246.

Fleishman, E.A. (1964). The *structure and measurement of physical fitness*. Englewood Cliffs, NJ: Prentice-Hall.

Fleishman, E.A. (1965). The description and prediction of perceptual motor skill learning. In R. Glaser (Ed.), *Training research and education* (pp. 137–175). New York: Wiley.

Hagemann, N., Strauss, B., & Cañal-Bruland, R. (2006). Training perceptual skill by orienting visual attention. *Journal of Sport and Exercise Psychology, 28*, 143–158.

Janelle, C.M., Barba, D.A., Frehlich, S.G., Tennant, L.K., & Cauraugh, J.H. (1997). Maximizing performance feedback effectiveness through videotape replay and a self-controlled learning environment. *Research Quarterly for Exercise and Sport, 68,* 269–279.

Keele, S.W., Ivry, R.I., & Pokorny, R.A. (1987). Force control and its relation to timing. *Journal of Motor Behavior, 19,* 96–114.

Landin, D. (1994). The role of verbal cues in skill learning. *Quest, 46,* 299–313.

Liu, J., & Wrisberg, C.A. (1997). The effect of knowledge of results delay and the subjective estimation of movement form on the acquisition and retention of a motor skill. *Research Quarterly for Exercise and Sport, 68,* 145–151.

Schmidt, R.A., & Lee, T.D. (2005). *Motor control and learning* (4th ed.). Champaign, IL: Human Kinetics.

Southard, D. (2006). Changing throwing pattern: Instruction and control parameter. *Research Quarterly for Exercise and Sport, 77,* 316–325.

Wightman, D.C., & Lintern, G. (1985). Part-task training strategies for tracking and manual control. *Human Factors, 27,* 267–283.

Williams, A.M., Ward, P., Smeeton, N.J., & Allen, D. (2004). Developing anticipation skills in tennis using on-court instruction: Perception vs. perception and action. *Journal of Applied Sport Psychology, 16,* 350–360.

Woods, J.B. (1967). The effect of varied instructional emphasis upon the development of a motor skill. *Research Quarterly, 38,* 132–142.

Case Study 2: Preparing a Collegiate Springboard Diver for Competition

Tracy is a 17-year-old female collegiate athlete who aspires to win the conference championship in 3 m springboard diving. Tracy's event requires her to perform a sequence of 10 dives of various levels of complexity. Before entering the sport of diving, Tracy was a successful competitive gymnast. However, a shoulder injury forced her to give up that sport when she was 14. Tracy's diving coach, Dave, believes that she has the physical abilities to compete for the championship. During training sessions, Tracy produces each of her dives in an effective fashion. However, during competition Tracy's performance is less consistent, particularly when she receives a low score on one of the first two or three dives in her program. Tracy also seems to struggle with two particular dives: the reverse two-and-one-half in the pike position and the reverse two-and-one-half in the tuck position. Dave's challenge is to provide Tracy with the kind of instructional assistance that will allow her to produce all of her dives as effectively in competition as she does in practice.

Diagnosing the Learning Situation

Using the checklist for diagnosing the learning situation (see table 11.1), Dave would be able to identify some of the factors to consider in assisting Tracy. In the following paragraphs we provide a narrative description of the items that this practitioner might have selected (with specific checklist items shown in italics):

Learner Characteristics

Tracy is a 17-year-old female with 3 years of *previous experience* in competitive diving at the junior national level. Before that Tracy competed in gymnastics for 7 years. Tracy appears to have high levels of the relevant *abilities* for diving (i.e., gross body coordination, explosive strength, and dynamic flexibility). Tracy's prior shoulder injury has healed sufficiently for her to experience success in diving. Tracy is highly motivated to win the conference championship *(motivation)*. Tracy's *stage of learning* varies from the motor stage to the autonomous stage, depending on the particular dive.

Goal of Learning

Tracy's primary goal is to execute all of her dives in competition with championship quality and perform them in competition the same way she performs them in practice.

Characteristics of the Target Skill

All of the dives in Tracy's routine are classified as *discrete closed skills,* primarily requiring the activity of large muscles. Relevant *intrinsic feedback* consists of kinesthetic and *proprioceptive feedback* about body and limb movements. *Response programming* is the only real *information-processing demand.* There is always the *risk of injury* in competitive diving (which may be a significant issue for Tracy, given her previous experience of injury).

Nature of the Target Context

Tracy must perform her dives in the *presence of others* (i.e., other divers, swimmers, officials, spectators, media). Possible distractions include the importance of the score, the success of other competitors, a noisy environment, and an unfamiliar diving board. In the midst of all this, Tracy must execute each of her 10 dives effectively to achieve the highest possible score. Also, she must perform the various dives sequentially, never having the opportunity to repeat a given dive; thus, the *target context* resembles *random practice.*

Once Dave has summarized all relevant information from table 11.1, he uses the conceptual model of motor performance (figure 11.1) and the checklist for designing the learning experience (see table 11.2) to devise a working strategy for providing instructional assistance. In the following section we provide a narrative summary of how Dave designs Tracy's learning experience (with actual checklist items from tables 11.1 and 11.2 shown in italics).

Designing the Learning Experience

Dave and Tracy decide that, up to now, there have been two primary differences between Tracy's training and competition experiences: the *frequency of feedback* that Dave provides and the repetition and sequencing of Tracy's dives. During training, Dave usually provides Tracy with *verbal prescriptive feedback* after each of her dives. In addition, in this initial practice, he has her perform each of her dives in a *blocked practice* format (i.e., five consecutive attempts for the first dive, five consecutive attempts for the second dive), realizing that he must shift her to a *random-practice schedule* relatively quickly because, in the target context, she is allowed only one attempt at each of the dives. During competition, the rules prevent Dave from providing Tracy with any feedback, so Dave tries to limit her dependence on feedback from him.

To *facilitate transfer* of Tracy's training experiences to the competition setting, Dave changes Tracy's practice to a *random-practice* format and gives her less-frequent feedback *(frequency of feedback).* After each sequence of 10 dives, Dave provides Tracy with *summary feedback* (i.e., one feedback statement for each dive), which she then uses to make necessary adjustments during her next sequence of dives. Dave also asks her to evaluate briefly the kinesthetic and *proprioceptive feedback* she receives following each dive *(error detection practice).* After each sequence of dives, Dave asks Tracy to report the feedback she remembers about each dive and estimate the score she thinks the judges would have given her.

Dave also decides that Tracy needs to assume more responsibility for her performance preparation during competition. He refers Tracy to the team's sport psychology consultant, who helps her develop a mental plan for competition. A key component of Tracy's mental plan might be a predive mental routine that includes a breathing technique for adjusting her arousal level *(managing arousal)*, *mental imagery* of each dive performed correctly, and the repetition of a simple verbal cue that reminds her of the appropriate attentional focus for successful execution *(focusing attention)*. For example, the verbal cue "kick tight" reminds Tracy to come out of the tuck position quickly on the reverse two-and-one-half dive.

Once Tracy incorporates her predive routine into her training sessions, she notices that the quality of her performance seems to be related to her *arousal* level. She realizes that she performs her simpler dives better at higher levels of arousal but performs her more complex dives better at lower arousal levels. Tracy shares this perception with Dave, and he encourages her to pay more attention to her arousal levels during training and in competition to see if she detects any differences *(focusing attention)*. Dave also asks Tracy to rate her arousal level for each dive on a scale of 1 to 3, where 1 means low arousal, 2 means intermediate arousal, and 3 means high arousal. By doing this, Tracy begins to notice that her arousal levels are higher during competition than they are during training, particularly if she competes against highly skilled opponents or performs in front of large audiences *(presence of others)*.

She also notices that the two dives she has the most difficulty producing in competition are the two most difficult dives in her routine. During training sessions, when Tracy's arousal levels are lower, she performs those dives quite well. However, during competition, when her arousal levels are higher, Tracy produces the two dives less consistently. Dave suggests that Tracy explore ways of adjusting her arousal levels *(managing arousal)* so that, during competition, she can adjust arousal as needed for each of the dives.

After several more sessions with the sport psychology consultant, Tracy acquires a simple breathing technique for raising and lowering her arousal level. During training, Dave then begins to incorporate distractions (e.g., noisy conditions) and competition stressors (e.g., reminders of the scores of highly regarded opponents), which usually elevate Tracy's arousal level during competition. Then Tracy practices using her pre-dive mental routine and breathing technique to focus her attention and adjust her arousal level in the appropriate direction for each dive.

As the season progresses, Dave creates more challenges for Tracy by having her perform her dives in a different order each time *(random practice)* and by introducing a greater variety of possible distractions (e.g., warm and cool air temperature, unexpected performance delays, an occasional unfair judge's rating, varying noise conditions).

Two Modifications of the Learning Situation

Adjusting to Unfamiliar Diving Boards. Let's say that Tracy dives well in practice in large part because she is familiar with the diving board in her "home" pool. She likes the level of spring in the board and knows exactly how it would respond during each of her dives. As a result, she is relaxed before each dive and is able to focus all of her attention on correct execution. However, when she travels to competitions in other locations, Tracy is anxious *(arousal level)*, because she knows that the boards always feel different than the one at her home pool. How might Dave handle this situation?

One way would be to create opportunities for Tracy to practice making the necessary adjustments in board tension (diving boards have an adjustment). Before each practice, Dave alters the tension of the board (to a low, medium, or high level) and then challenges Tracy to adjust the tension until she achieves the level that feels comfortable to her *(closed-loop control)*. Initially, Dave provides *knowledge of results* (regarding the tension level Tracy set and whether it was less than, equal to, or greater than the preferred level). After a few days of practice, however, Dave begins to fade *feedback frequency* and provides *summary feedback* after each sequence of Tracy's adjustments. This exercise directs Tracy's attention *(focusing attention)* to the *intrinsic proprioceptive feedback* associated with the feel of different levels of board tension and helps her make the appropriate adjustments before hearing Dave's feedback *(error detection practice)*.

Dave then develops a *random-practice* format that requires Tracy to adjust the board to the appropriate tension level before each of her dives. In this way, Tracy achieves a more sophisticated understanding of the level of board tension that is optimal for each of her dives. Once Tracy becomes adept at adjusting the board in her home pool, Dave takes her to other pools in town so that she can transfer what she has learned to unfamiliar boards *(generalization)*. As Tracy's proficiency increases, Dave introduces other potential deterrents to Tracy's ability to adjust the board (e.g., fatigue, crowd noise, air temperature, and telling Tracy that she has to produce a high score to win the competition). With increased experience in a *varied-* and *random-practice* format of dives and distractions, Tracy learns how to adjust any board to an optimal level for all of her dives, regardless of the environmental circumstances. As a result of these types of practice experiences, Tracy develops a more sophisticated understanding of the relationship between springboard tension and her performance under a variety of environmental conditions. It makes her more confident during competition because she is able to make the appropriate adjustments in board tension at any time and any place *(generalization)*.

Learning Synchronized Diving. Synchronized diving is a fairly new event in competitive diving. In this event, two divers attempt to execute the same dive on adjacent boards, simultaneously and synchronized with each other. The pair's performance is evaluated with respect to both the quality of the dives and the extent to which the two divers execute their dives synchronously. Let's say Tracy and one of her teammates, Kathy, ask Dave to help them learn synchronized diving. Dave knows that although both young women are accomplished divers, each executes her dives in a unique way.

Dave begins by asking Tracy and Kathy to attempt each of their dives in synchrony on adjacent boards. He video-records all of their dives and then replays them side by side in a split-screen format *(visual feedback)*. In this way, Dave and the divers are able to identify the elements of each dive that are not synchronous. After several replays of each dive, Dave, Tracy, and Kathy agree on the adjustments in form and timing that each diver needs to make to produce two simultaneous dives synchronously. Because Tracy is taller than Kathy, Tracy needs to make adjustments *(parameter learning)* that compress her form and reduce the total time of her dives. For Kathy, the challenge is just the opposite—she needs to elongate her form and increase the total time of her dives.

Dave assists Tracy and Kathy with verbal cues that direct their attention to respective aspects of the dives that each of them needs to modify *(focusing attention)*. Dave also provides *verbal and visual prescriptive feedback* that suggests changes the divers might make in their movements. With the assistance of the team's sport psychology consultant, Tracy and Kathy develop individual preperformance routines for each dive that include arousal adjustment *(managing arousal)*, *imagery* of the dive, and a simple focus cue (e.g., "stay in line in the press" or "throw over the top" might be appropriate cues for executing the inward two-and-one-half dive in the tuck position). After some discussion, the divers agree that Tracy should verbalize the spoken commands they use to initiate each dive in a synchronized fashion.

Because synchrony is the primary goal of learning, Dave conducts practices that involve only synchronous rehearsal. Initially, he uses a *blocked-practice format* and provides split-screen *visual feedback* and *verbal prescriptive feedback* (e.g., "throw over the top") after each dive. As the level of synchrony begins to improve, Dave fades the *frequency of feedback* and provides *summary feedback* at the end of each block of five attempts. In addition, Dave asks Tracy and Kathy to estimate their own errors before showing them the video replay of their dives *(error-detection practice)*.

Once Tracy and Kathy demonstrate that they can perform each dive with a satisfactory level of synchrony, Dave shifts the structure of practice sessions to a *random practice* format. Initially, he provides *visual and verbal feedback* after each dive but gradually reduces the *frequency of feedback* until he presents it only at the end of each sequence of dives. Following each sequence, Tracy and Kathy evaluate their performance before Dave shows them the *visual feedback*. Working together, Tracy and Kathy continue to detect and correct their errors and determine the types of adjustments each needs to make to maximize their collective performance.

The final stage of learning involves practicing under varied environmental conditions *(generalization)*. Tracy and Kathy do this by rehearsing their entire sequence of dives at different pools, on different boards, under a variety of conditions of noise and other distractions and by asking Dave to simulate some of the pressures of competition (e.g., telling them that their closest competitors have just achieved a high score).

Supporting References

Edmonds, W.A., Mann, D.T.Y., Tenenbaum, G., & Janelle, C.M. (2006). Analysis of affect-related performance zones: An idiographic method using physiological and introspective data. *The Sport Psychologist, 20,* 40–57.

Landin, D. (1994). The role of verbal cues in skill learning. *Quest, 46,* 299–313.

Lavery, J.J. (1962). Retention of simple motor skills as a function of type of knowledge of results. *Canadian Journal of Psychology, 16,* 300–311.

Liu, J., & Wrisberg, C.A. (1997). The effect of knowledge of results delay and the subjective estimation of movement form on the acquisition and retention of a motor skill. *Research Quarterly for Exercise and Sport, 68,* 145–151.

Magill, R.A., & Hall, K.G. (1990). A review of the contextual interference effect in motor skill acquisition. *Human Movement Science, 9,* 241–289.

Newell, K.M., & McGinnis, P.M. (1985). Kinematic information feedback for skilled performance. *Human Learning, 4,* 39–56.

Orlick, T. (1986). *Psyching for sport: Mental training for athletes.* Champaign, IL: Leisure Press.

Overduin, S.A., Richardson, A.G., Lane, C.E., Bizzi, E., & Press, D.Z. (2006). Intermittent practice facilitates stable motor memories. *Journal of Neuroscience, 26*(46), 11888–11892.

Schmidt, R.A., & Lee, T.D. (2005). *Motor control and learning: A behavioral emphasis* (4th ed.). Champaign, IL: Human Kinetics.

Seat, J.E., & Wrisberg, C.A. (1996). The visual instruction system. *Research Quarterly for Exercise and Sport, 67,* 106–108.

Vealey, R.S., & Greenleaf, C.A. (2006). Seeing is believing: Understanding and using imagery in sport. In J.M. Williams (Ed.), *Applied sport psychology: Personal growth to peak performance* (pp. 306–348). New York: McGraw-Hill.

Wrisberg, C.A. (1994). The arousal-performance relationship. *Quest, 46,* 60–77.

Case Study 3: Teaching a Child With Cerebral Palsy to Walk Up and Down Stairs

Joe is an 8-year-old boy with cerebral palsy (spastic diplegia). Joe can ambulate independently with modified ankle and foot orthoses and bilateral straight canes, but he doesn't do so spontaneously. When he is at home, Joe prefers to crawl. If he does try to walk, Joe is able to come to a standing position without assistance but must place his hands on the floor to do so. Once Joe achieves a vertical posture, he prefers to place his hands on furniture and other objects to maintain balance during locomotion. Joe can stand independently to perform routine tasks such as washing his face or throwing a ball.

Lisa is a physical therapist who has been assisting Joe with independent walking. Now Joe's mother asks Lisa to help Joe learn how to walk up and down stairs using a railing. Lisa knows that Joe prefers crawling to independent walking, even when it comes to climbing stairs. Joe loves candy, so Lisa uses Joe's favorite sweets to reinforce his attempts at independent walking. However, Lisa realizes that for Joe to choose independent walking when ambulating at home or in a variety of nonclinical settings, his intrinsic motivation must increase. One potentially influential factor that might motivate Joe to choose walking over crawling is time-efficiency—if Joe is able to get from one place to another more quickly by walking than by crawling, he is more likely to try walking.

Diagnosing the Learning Situation

Using the checklist for diagnosing the learning situation (see table 11.1), Lisa identifies some of the factors to consider in assisting Joe. In the following paragraphs we provide a narrative description of the items this practitioner selects (with specific checklist items shown in italics):

Learner Characteristics

Joe is an 8-year-old boy with spastic diplegia. His lower extremities are often in a state of extreme flexion or extreme extension, and he demonstrates scapulohumeral association (i.e., the tendency to hold extremities close to the midline of the body). Joe's *previous movement experiences* include crawling, independent standing, and occasional independent walking with ankle and foot orthoses and bilateral straight canes. Joe possesses average to below-average levels of the *abilities* relevant to stair walking (i.e., an active range of motion in the lower extremities; range of motion in the upper extremities; scapulohumeral dissociation; trunk strength and control; dynamic balance; and strength in the lower extremities, especially the quadriceps, hip extensors, and pelvic stabilizers). Joe has only low-level *motivation* to learn stair walking. He prefers crawling to independent walking, unless she knows she will receive candy for attempting to walk independently. Because stair walking is a new activity for Joe, he is assumed to be in the verbal–cognitive *stage of learning*.

Goal of Learning

Joe's goals include *program learning, parameter learning,* and *generalization.* He is still in the process of developing a consistent and effective program for locomotion; he needs to be able to adapt his locomotion when walking up and down stairs using a railing, and he needs to be able to climb stairs of various heights or textures and at various locations (e.g., at the clinic, at home, in the homes of family and friends).

Characteristics of the Target Skill

The task of stair walking is a *closed, serial skill* that primarily requires the activity of large muscle groups. There is no object manipulation, although Joe must use straight canes and a stair railing to assist locomotion. *Intrinsic visual and proprioceptive feedback* is available but is sometimes unreliable because of Joe's inability to inhibit inappropriate reflex activity. The primary *information-processing demands* are those dealing with *response programming.* There is a *risk of injury,* and Joe is extremely afraid of falling.

Nature of the Target Context

An evaluative audience *(presence of others)* is often present at the clinic and in the home (e.g., parents, therapists, staff, and other patients at the clinic; parents, siblings, and occasionally friends and other family members at home). There is no time pressure to perform the task unless Joe perceives pressure from others (e.g., parents, siblings). Possible distractions include Joe's fear of failure, fear of injury, impatience, and short attention span.

Once Lisa has summarized all relevant information from table 11.1, she uses the conceptual model of motor performance (figure 11.1) and the checklist for designing the learning experience (see table 11.2) to devise a working strategy for providing instructional assistance. In the following section we provide a narrative summary of how Lisa designs Joe's learning experience (with actual checklist items from tables 11.1 and 11.2 shown in italics).

Designing the Learning Experience

As a result of extensive physical therapy, Joe likely has achieved sufficient levels of lower-extremity active range of motion, upper-extremity range of motion, and lower-extremity strength (quadriceps, hip extensors, pelvic stabilizers). Knowing that Joe has a short *attention* span and low intrinsic *motivation* to use independent walking, Lisa limits the length of each instructional session to no more than 5 or 10 min.

At some point Lisa decides to introduce Joe to the stair-stepping task by asking him if he would like to try something different. When Joe says, "Maybe. . . What is it?" Lisa shows him a special staircase built for the therapy setting (consisting of five steps, each 6 in. [15 cm] high, and a hand railing) and asks Joe if he thinks he can walk up the first step *(simulation).* In this way, Lisa assists Joe in setting a goal that is realistic for him *(goal setting).* If Lisa sees that Joe is apprehensive about the height of the step, she creates a modified stepping task *(part practice)* that is less threatening for him (e.g., stepping onto a curb in the parking lot).

Initially, Lisa uses manual assistance *(guidance)* by placing her hands on Joe's legs to help him get an idea of the stepping motion and to alleviate his fear of falling. As Joe lifts his right foot onto the step, Lisa says, "Up right." Then as Joe lifts his left foot, shifting his entire weight onto the step, Lisa says, "Up left" *(focusing attention).* If Joe completes a step successfully, Lisa says, "That's great" to provide reinforcing *verbal feedback.* Then Lisa asks Joe if he thinks he could step down. If Joe says yes, Lisa assists him manually in stepping down one foot at a time and provides verbal focus cues ("Down right, down left"). Lisa then praises Joe's effort *(feedback)* and tells him that they can play the stepping game again the next time Joe comes to the clinic.

If Joe forgets to ask Lisa for candy as a reward for his performance, Lisa assumes that Joe's intrinsic motivation is improving. If Joe asks to play the stepping game the next time he comes for therapy, Lisa provides less manual guidance by diminishing the pressure she places on Joe's legs. Lisa also begins to use *prescriptive feedback* to help Joe understand what he should try to do to play the stepping game better. For example, if Lisa wants Joe to stand more erectly, she says, "Higher, higher, pants on fire." If Joe's weight is too far up on his toes, Lisa says, "Flea, fly, flat feet" to get her to come down. As Joe's performance gradually improves, Lisa asks him if he thinks she can walk up and down two steps, then three, then four, and eventually five *(goal setting)*. With each level of progression, Lisa provides appropriate *prescriptive feedback* to help Joe preserve his balance, shift his weight, and use the handrail (e.g., "reach and lift"). As Joe's errors diminish, Lisa gradually reduces the *frequency of feedback* she provides. However, she decides to continue praising Joe for his effort (e.g., "You look just like a mountain climber!") and gives him a hug before he leaves each day *(reinforcing and motivating feedback)*.

Lisa assists Joe in improving his functional efficiency by asking him to set movement time *outcome goals* (e.g., "How fast can you walk up and down one step? Two steps?"). Each time Joe sets a movement time goal, Lisa times his performance and provides him with *knowledge of results* (e.g., "You climbed that step in only eight seconds!"). After several months, if Joe is able to walk up and down all of the steps at the clinic consistently, Lisa asks him if he'd like to play the stepping game somewhere else *(generalization)*. If Joe seems interested, Lisa introduces him to other staircases at the clinic that vary in the number of steps, step height, surface material, and location of the handrail *(varied practice)*. Lisa also reminds Joe that he can play the stepping game at home any time he feels like it.

Eventually Lisa decides to combine Joe's practice of stair climbing and other independent walking activities with the practice of other functional tasks, such as brushing teeth and putting on shoes *(random practice)*. To reinforce independent walking even further, Lisa asks Joe to set movement-time goals for walking various distances and for climbing up and down different sets of stairs *(goal setting)*. Occasionally, Lisa creates opportunities for Joe to practice independent walking and stair climbing in a variety of other situations (e.g., at his grandparents' home, at the local Little League baseball stadium). As Joe's sense of accomplishment increases, he eventually decides that crawling is no longer an attractive option for moving from place to place.

Two Modifications of the Learning Situation

Overcoming the Reluctance to Abandon Crawling as the Preferred Mode of Locomotion. Although Joe's independent walking and stair-climbing performance continue to improve with practice, he still chooses to crawl when moving about in his home environment. Lisa asks Joe's mother why she thinks this is happening. One explanation is that Joe's brothers tease him about being slow when he tries to walk from one place to another. Because Joe is still able to crawl faster than he can walk independently, he decides to crawl when he is at home because he doesn't want to be teased. Lisa also notices that Joe's mother offers little praise when Joe tells her about his accomplishments at the clinic. For example, his mother either minimizes them ("That's all you did today?") or reminds her son of what he still has not accomplished ("I still haven't seen you walk up the stairs at home"). Lisa decides that something more has to be done to create practice experiences for Joe that reinforce independent walking and discourage crawling in the home environment *(generalization)*.

Lisa decides to meet with Joe's mother and brothers and request their assistance in helping Joe. She encourages them to reinforce Joe's independent walking by providing positive *feedback* whenever he attempts it. Lisa also asks them to come up with some games Joe can play at home that encourage his use of independent walking (varied practice). Lisa also reminds Joe's mother that Joe responds better to short periods of activity than he does to longer practice sessions. Finally, Lisa stresses the importance of randomizing Joe's activities *(random practice)*, perhaps by mixing stair walking, playing with puzzles, and tossing and catching a Nerf ball. If Joe still tends to revert to crawling in the home environment, Lisa suggests that Joe's mom set short-term *outcome goals* that encourage Joe to climb progressively more steps using independent walking before reverting to crawling. With continued practice and positive *feedback* for effort, eventually Joe chooses to walk up more and more steps before switching to crawling.

Lisa then encourages Joe's family to think of ways he can practice independent walking in other functional contexts, such as walking from the kitchen table to the living room sofa or walking from the house to the family car *(varied practice and generalization)*. Lisa also suggests that family members allow Joe to attempt tasks with less supervision and *feedback*—for example, when Joe walks all the way from the downstairs living room to his upstairs bedroom without crawling.

Independent Walking in Other Functional Environments. If Joe achieves a satisfactory level of independent walking at the clinic and at home, he can then begin to attempt independent walking in a wider variety of functional *target contexts (varied practice* and *generalization)*. Variations of independent walking include moving up and down various types of stairs and handicapped-accessible ramps, walking alone and in the midst of other walkers, walking around obstacles, and walking on various types of surfaces (e.g., carpet, vinyl, gravel, asphalt, hardwood, ceramic tile, brick, and stone). Also, Joe can attempt to walk in various types of inclement weather (e.g., windy or rainy conditions) with appropriate *guidance*. Initially, Lisa exposes Joe to some of these contexts in the clinical setting (e.g., walking on carpet and vinyl floor surfaces, walking up and down stairs, walking around obstacles) and takes Joe outside the clinic to experience other situations (e.g., walking on a rainy sidewalk).

Two functional contexts that could be particularly difficult for Joe are walking up and down open stairs and walking in the midst of other pedestrians. With open stairs, Joe perceives that he is higher off the ground than he really is, which might feed his fear of falling. This in turn alters Joe's perception of the height of each step and causes him to overshoot or undershoot the step with his leg movements. In the presence of other pedestrians, Joe perceives that they don't see him and is afraid they will bump into him.

To assist Joe in generalizing independent walking to these two situations, Lisa uses a combination of techniques. First, she alerts Joe to the nature of the situation (open stairs or an approaching pedestrian) beforehand *(instructions)* and reminds him that he can count on his instructor to be there if he has any problems *(guidance* and *managing arousal)*. Next, Lisa focuses Joe's attention on relevant environmental cues *(focusing attention)* specific to each situation (e.g., the top of each successive step or the eyes of the approaching pedestrian).

Like most children, Joe has a vivid imagination, so Lisa capitalizes on this by instructing Joe to picture himself walking exactly the way he intends to walk in each situation *(imagery)*. Initially, Lisa supervises Joe's imagery practice by asking him to close his eyes and try to see and feel himself walking up the open stairs or walking past an approaching pedestrian. To enhance the vividness of Joe's imagery, occasionally Lisa asks Joe to describe what type of shirt he is wearing in his mental picture or how his imaginary steps look and feel.

Initially, Lisa uses a *blocked practice* schedule to allow Joe to experience several repetitions of each task by itself. However, as Joe becomes more skilled and confident in performing the tasks, Lisa shifts to a *varied-* and *random-practice* format (e.g., walking in the midst of other pedestrians, climbing open stairs, walking alongside a single person, climbing open stairs while another person is descending the stairs). Eventually, Lisa is able to help Joe adapt his independent walking to a variety of functional contexts consisting of both open and closed environments *(generalization)* and requiring subtle alterations of the *generalized motor program (parameter learning)*, for example, climbing steps of different heights at different speeds.

Supporting References

Adams, J.A. (1978). Theoretical issues for knowledge of results. In G.E. Stelmach (Ed.), *Information processing in motor control and learning* (pp. 229–240). New York: Academic Press.

Guadagnoli, M.A., & Lee, T.D. (2004). Challenge point: A framework for conceptualizing the effects of various practice conditions in motor learning. *Journal of Motor Behavior, 36,* 212–224.

Hagemann, N., Strauss, B., & Cañal-Bruland, R. (2006). Training perceptual skill by orienting visual attention. *Journal of Sport and Exercise Psychology, 28,* 143–158.

Janelle, C.M., Barba, D.A., Frehlich, S.G., Tennant, L.K., & Cauraugh, J.H. (1997). Maximizing performance feedback effectiveness through videotape replay and a self-controlled learning environment. *Research Quarterly for Exercise and Sport, 68,* 269–279.

Kernodle, M.W., & Carlton, L.G. (1992). Information feedback and the learning of multiple-degree-of-freedom activities. *Journal of Motor Behavior, 24,* 187–196.

Kerr, R., & Booth, B. (1978). Specific and varied practice of motor skill. *Perceptual and Motor Skills, 46,* 395–401.

Landin, D. (1994). The role of verbal cues in skill learning. *Quest, 46,* 299–313.

Schmidt, R.A., & Lee, T.D. (2005). *Motor control and learning: A behavioral emphasis* (4th ed.). Champaign, IL: Human Kinetics.

Shea, C.H., Kohl, R., & Indermill, C. (1990). Contextual interference: Contributions of practice. *Acta Psychologica, 73,* 145–157.

Wrisberg, C.A., & Mead, B.J. (1983). Developing coincident-timing skill in children: A comparison of training methods. *Research Quarterly for Exercise and Sport, 54,* 67–74.

Case Study 4: Training a Level I Firefighter

Lin is a 27-year-old volunteer firefighter who is training to meet the fire-related performance objectives of the National Fire Protection Association. For the past 5 years, Lin has been a fitness instructor at a local health club. Before that, he was a competitive collegiate athlete in soccer. Lin's goal is to achieve the level of Firefighter I, that is, a person "who is minimally trained to function safely and effectively as a member of a fire-fighting team under direct supervision" (Wieder, Smith, & Brackage, 1996, p. 1). During the past 2 years, Lin has achieved minimum performance requirements for most of the basic firefighting tasks (e.g., donning a self-contained breathing apparatus, handling ladders, rescuing and extricating victims, loading and coupling hoses). However, Lin has not yet learned how to advance hose lines.

Advancing a hose line is typically the last task firefighters perform before applying water to a fire. Once firefighters have moved hose lines from the truck and laid them out, they advance the hose into the final position. In addition to learning the basic technique for advancing hose lines, firefighters also must know how to adapt this technique when advancing the hose to a variety of destinations (e.g., up stairways, down inside and outside stairways, up ladders, from a standpipe). It is easier for firefighters to advance a hose line before it is charged with water (because it is lighter and more flexible); however, sometimes they must advance hose line that is already charged.

Firefighters must also be aware of a variety of potential dangers when advancing a hose line (e.g., backdraft, flashover, structural collapse).

Jerry is a veteran firefighter who is responsible for supervising the training experiences of firefighter candidates. Jerry knows the essential tasks of firefighting and the performance-based objectives required of Level I firefighters. Jerry is also aware of the varied demands of firefighting situations and has supervised Lin during his other training experiences. How might Jerry use the working strategy for skill instruction presented in this chapter to assist Lin in achieving his learning goal?

Diagnosing the Learning Situation

Using the checklist for diagnosing the learning situation (see table 11.1), Jerry identifies some of the factors to consider in assisting Lin. In the following paragraphs we provide a narrative description of the items this practitioner might select (with specific checklist items shown in italics).

Learner Characteristics

Lin is a 27-year-old man with considerable *previous movement experience,* including participation as a collegiate athlete in soccer, employment as a fitness instructor, personal involvement in a variety of strength and endurance activities, 2 years of service as a volunteer firefighter, and demonstrated competence in performing most Level I firefighting tasks. Lin appears to have above-average levels of the *abilities* relevant to the performance of advancing hose line (i.e., manual dexterity, static strength, dynamic strength, and stamina). He is highly motivated to learn the tasks necessary for him to achieve the status of a Level I firefighter *(motivation).* Lin is physically, mentally, and emotionally fit. Because he has had previous experience loading and coupling hose lines,

Lin's *stage of learning* for advancing hose lines is late-verbal–cognitive to early-motor.

Goal of Learning

Lin's first goal is to learn the general procedures for advancing hose lines. His second goal is to learn how to adapt these procedures so that he can advance hose lines in a variety of ways (e.g., up stairways, down inside and outside stairways, up ladders, from a standpipe). A third goal is *error detection and correction;* Lin must be able to recognize errors in his movements and make the appropriate corrections, sometimes under extreme time pressure or danger. And Lin must demonstrate that he can advance hose lines under a wide variety of environmental conditions *(generalization)*.

Characteristics of the Target Skill

Advancing a hose line is classified as a *closed skill* that can be either *serial or continuous.* It involves the use of the large muscles primarily, although small-muscle activity is sometimes needed to untangle a hose line. Object manipulation is an important component of the task; Lin wants to be able to achieve an optimal final position each time he advances a hose. To some extent, *speed–accuracy trade-offs* are part of the task; however, the weight of the hose naturally limits the speed with which the firefighter can move it. The amount of available *intrinsic feedback* varies (e.g., both vision of the problem situation and approach route can sometimes be reduced by extensive smoke; both audition and proprioception can be distorted by firefighting apparel). *Information-processing demands* include *stimulus identification* (particularly when visibility is poor), *response selection* (i.e., determining the best possible route), and *response programming* (i.e., modifying the general actions to meet the demands of each situation). The *risk of injury* is high and performance mistakes can be fatal.

Nature of the Target Context

There is almost always an evaluative audience *(presence of others)* at a firefighting scene (e.g., other firefighters, police and other emergency personnel, fire inspectors, and occasionally media personnel and spectators). Firefighters usually operate under extreme time pressure. Other possible distractions include failure anxiety and equipment breakdown. Because every firefighting situation is unique, firefighters must be able to devise innovative solutions for advancing hose line at a moment's notice.

Once Jerry has summarized all relevant information from table 11.1, he uses the conceptual model of motor performance (figure 11.1) and the checklist for designing the learning experience (see table 11.2) to devise a working strategy for providing instructional assistance. In the following section we provide a narrative summary of how Jerry designs Lin's learning experience (with actual checklist items from tables 11.1 and 11.2 shown in italics).

Designing the Learning Experience

At first, Jerry introduces Lin to the various techniques for advancing preconnected and unconnected hose lines. After describing *(instructions)* and demonstrating each technique *(demonstration)*, Jerry lets Lin practice the technique in a *blocked practice* format. Because Lin has had previous firefighting experience, he is able to produce each technique with only limited instructional assistance. He and Jerry decide that Lin should receive *extrinsic feedback* only when he requests it. On those occasions, Jerry offers *prescriptive feedback* and occasionally provides an additional visual *demonstration*.

Once Jerry sees that Lin is producing each of the techniques for carrying a hose line satisfactorily, he shifts Lin to a *varied practice* format. During each session, Lin performs the various hose-carrying techniques in a random order. Following each attempt, Jerry asks Lin to tell him what he thinks of his performance *(error-detection practice)* and then, if necessary, provides feedback. If Jerry observes no errors in Lin's performance, he provides positive feedback (reinforcement). If Jerry detects an error, he offers *prescriptive feedback* (e.g., "Stay low and lock the arms") and perhaps provides a visual *demonstration* to indicate how Lin might try to adjust his performance on the next attempt of that movement.

After several rounds of this type of *varied and random practice*, Jerry reduces the *frequency of feedback* and begins to provide *summary feedback*. Once Jerry is satisfied that Lin can produce all of the hose-line–carrying techniques effectively on command, he introduces Lin to the various situations that require firefighters to advance a hose line *(varied practice)*. These include advancing a hose up a stairway, advancing a hose down inside and outside stairways, advancing a hose up a ladder, and advancing a hose from a standpipe. All these situations require knowledge of both procedural guidelines and effective movement patterns. Realizing this, Jerry decides to combine Lin's rehearsal of guidelines and of the movement patterns for each type of situation. For example, when Lin practices advancing a hose line up a stairway, he needs to perform the three most appropriate hose-carrying techniques (shoulder carry, underarm carry, minuteman load and carry) and adhere to the following guidelines: Carry rather than drag the hose if it is uncharged, clamp the hose off before carrying it if it is charged, lay the hose against the outside wall around stairways to avoid sharp bends in the line, and toss sections of the excess hose up the stairs to make it easier to advance into the fire floor *(random practice)*.

Initially, Jerry combines *blocked practice* of the situation (e.g., advancing a hose line up a stairway) and *random practice* of each of the possible hose-carrying techniques. Lin's challenge is to produce any of the techniques effectively on command while following the appropriate guidelines. Following each block of practice attempts, Lin is asked to evaluate his own performance *(error-detection practice)*. Then, if needed, Jerry provides Lin with *summary feedback* about either the effectiveness of his movements, the degree of adherence to the appropriate guidelines, or both.

Jerry repeats this procedure for each of the various hose-advance situations. When he sees that Lin is able to produce the proper hose-carrying techniques and follow the recommended guidelines for each situation, Jerry shifts him to a *random-practice* and *varied-practice* format. During practice sessions, Lin tries to advance hose lines in all four situations in a random order. Before each attempt, Jerry tells Lin to which situation he should respond and which hose-carrying technique to use. After each series of attempts, Jerry asks Lin for a self-evaluation (*error-detection practice)* and, if errors are detected, for a proposed correction. Then Jerry provides Lin with *summary feedback* about both the effectiveness of his movements and the degree of adherence to proper guidelines for all of the situations in the series.

Two Modifications of the Learning Situation

Integrating Firefighting Skills. Once Lin meets the fire-related performance objectives for all of the skills required of level I firefighters, he needs to be able to integrate and automate those skills. During intermittent lulls in firefighting activity, Jerry structures *random-practice* sessions that require Lin to perform a variety of firefighting skills (e.g., performing cardiopulmonary resuscitation, donning and doffing protective breathing apparatus, changing cylinders, coiling a rope for service, performing lone rescuer lift and carry, carrying out a one-firefighter ladder raise, advancing a hose line up a stairway). Sometimes Jerry asks Lin to perform two or three skills in a *random practice* format; at other times Jerry asks him to produce several variations *(varied practice)* of the same skill (e.g., proper lifting and lowering of a hose line). Occasionally, Jerry asks Lin to attempt a single skill chosen at random.

By practicing this way, Lin becomes more adept at producing all the essential firefighting skills on command at any time. In addition, Lin and Jerry set goals *(goal setting)* that challenge Lin to achieve a performance standard that minimizes both performance errors *(process measures)* and movement time *(outcome measure)*. Now *extrinsic feedback* begins to function as motivation and reinforcement as well as for error correction. Lin continues to improve his *error detection and correction* capability by providing Jerry with a self-evaluation following each of his practice sessions.

Adapting to Firefighting Situations. The ultimate test of the firefighter's skill comes at the scene of the fire. Regardless of the situation, firefighters are expected to assess the conditions accurately and to perform the most appropriate sequence of skills in a smooth, deliberate fashion. This can be a challenge for firefighters when they encounter situations that are extremely dangerous or that include the physical and psychological burden of extricating victims from the structure.

Like any good firefighter, Lin wants to perform his duties effectively at the scene of a fire, regardless of the type of situation he encounters. Jerry uses his knowledge of the essentials of firefighting, the conceptual model of motor performance, and the working strategy of skill instruction to design several learning experiences for Lin.

One of the first factors Jerry addresses is the arousal–performance relationship. He knows that high arousal and anxiety are problems for many novice firefighters and that they must be able to *manage arousal* so that they don't place themselves and others at risk. For one thing, high arousal increases the rate of respiration, which causes a more rapid depletion of the available air supply in a protective-breathing apparatus. In addition, high anxiety creates a narrowing of focus *(attention)*, which can lead to serious errors in judgment. One thing Jerry does to help Lin manage his arousal and maintain an effective focus is to create practice situations that approximate those of actual fires as closely as possible *(simulation)*.

Because Jerry has access to local facilities that allow him to simulate firefighting situations, he creates different sets of conditions and provides Lin with opportunities to perform a variety of firefighting skills in situations similar to those found at actual fires. As a result of *random* and *varied* exposure to a number of simulated situations (e.g., high and low visibility, advancing charged and uncharged hose lines), Lin learns which techniques are more appropriate under various circumstances *(generalization)*.

Because firefighting consists of both *consistent* and *varied mapping* conditions, Jerry also exposes Lin to challenges that require him to produce the same response to some stimuli (e.g., before entering any fire area, always bleed the air out of the hose line) and to different responses to other stimuli (e.g., when advancing a hose line down a flight of stairs, charge the hose first if there is the chance of intense heat—but don't charge the hose first if there is not, because advancing a hose line is easier if the hose is uncharged). With repeated exposure to a variety of simulated situations, Lin develops the capability to be innovative when the conditions are less predictable and to be deliberate, smooth, and systematic when they are more predictable.

Each time Jerry provides Lin with a simulated experience, Jerry asks him for a self-evaluation *(error-detection practice)* before giving him *summary feedback*. Jerry's feedback also includes several performance characteristics, such as the quality of Lin's motor performance *(process measures)*, the appropriateness of his decisions, and the level of composure he demonstrates under stress. Jerry also teaches Lin a *mental practice* technique that combines relaxation *(managing arousal)* and *imagery*. With repeated mental practice, Lin is able to create vivid mental images of specific firefighting situations quickly and can "see" himself producing appropriate responses for each.

Supporting References

Bjork, R.A. (1994). Memory and metamemory considerations in the training of human beings. In J. Metcalfe and A. Shimamura (Eds.), *Metacognition: Knowing about knowing* (pp.185–205). Cambridge, MA: MIT Press.

Easterbrook, J.A. (1959). The effect of emotion on cue utilization and the organization of behavior. *Psychological Review, 66,* 183–201.

Fleishman, E.A. (1964). *The structure and measurement of physical fitness.* Englewood Cliffs, NJ: Prentice-Hall.

Landers, D.M., & Arent, S.M. (2006). Arousal-performance relationships. In J.M. Williams (Ed.), *Applied sport psychology: Personal growth to peak performance* (pp. 260–284). New York: McGraw-Hill.

Landin, D., & Hebert, E.P. (1997). A comparison of three practice schedules along the contextual interference continuum. *Research Quarterly for Exercise and Sport, 68,* 357–361.

Lee, T.D., Wulf, G., & Schmidt, R.A. (1992). Contextual interference in motor learning: Dissociated effects due to the nature of task variations. *Quarterly Journal of Experimental Psychology, 44A,* 627–644.

Liu, J., & Wrisberg, C.A. (1997). The effect of knowledge of results delay and the subjective estimation of movement form on the acquisition and retention of a motor skill. *Research Quarterly for Exercise and Sport, 68,* 145–151.

Newell, K.M., & McGinnis, P.M. (1985). Kinematic information feedback for skilled performance. *Human Learning, 4,* 39–56.

Orlick, T. (1986). *Psyching for sport: Mental training for athletes.* Champaign, IL: Leisure Press

Roediger, H.L., & Karpicke, J.D. (2006) The power of testing memory: Basic research and implications for educational practice. *Perspectives on Psychological Science, 1,* 181-210.

Schmidt, R.A., Lange, C.A., & Young, D.E. (1990). Optimizing summary knowledge of results for skill learning. *Human Movement Science, 9,* 325–348.

Schmidt, R.A., & Lee, T.D. (2005). *Motor control and learning: A behavioral emphasis* (4th ed.). Champaign, IL: Human Kinetics.

Schoenfelder-Zohdi, B.G. (1992). *Investigating the informational nature* of a *modeled visual demonstration.* Unpublished doctoral dissertation, Louisiana State University, Baton Rouge.

Shiffrin, R.M., & Schneider, W. (1977). Controlled and automatic human information processing: II. Perceptual learning, automatic attending, and a general theory. *PsychologicalReview, 84,* 127–190.

Tubbs, M.E. (1986). Goal setting: A meta-analysis examination of the empirical evidence. *Journal of Applied Psychology, 71,* 474–483.

ASSESSMENT OF LEARNER PROGRESS

In each of the case studies presented in this chapter, the hypothetical practitioner had to decide how he or she would assess the learner's progress. In several places, we mentioned specific measures the practitioner might have used (e.g., in case study 4, the practitioner measured the time it took the volunteer firefighter to perform various tasks). In other places, we said only that the practitioner made instructional decisions based on the progress he or she observed in the learner's performance. Obviously, those observations had to be based on something the practitioner observed and that reflected performance improvements.

As we discussed in chapter 7, assessment is an important component of any learning situation. Practitioners must measure learners' performance to determine the extent to which they are making progress toward goal achievement and to assess the effectiveness of instructional strategies. And, the very process of testing learners also strengthens memory for skills (Roediger & Karpicke, 2006). However, determining how and when to assess learner progress is not a simple matter.

How might instructors and therapists—not to mention the learners themselves—assess the quality of learning experiences? What measures might they obtain? How often might formal assessments take place, and where would they occur? To a large extent, the answers to these questions depend on the goals of the learner and on the outcomes and behaviors that most clearly reflect goal achievement. For a tennis player learning a new serve, a valid outcome measure might be the percentage of successful first serves performed in one set of tennis. For an aspiring carpenter, it might be the number of hammer blows needed to drive a dozen nails. Valid process measures might include form ratings of the serving and nail-striking actions, respectively. Regardless of the instructional situation, the skilled practitioner knows which outcomes and processes (i.e., behaviors) to look for and how to assess them accurately and reliably.

Determining how often to perform skill assessments is another challenging decision for the practitioner. Learners want to know whether they are making progress, but they are not always excited about formal evaluations. At what points during skill learning might a person's performance be assessed most meaningfully? Sometimes practitioners are required to perform assessments at predefined intervals (e.g., skills testing in school physical education classes). In other cases, the frequency of assessment is the result of a joint decision by the practitioner and the learner. As is the case with other types of instructional feedback, formal assessments are probably more helpful for learners who ask, "How am I doing?" Practitioners who maintain good communication with learners and who are sensitive to the needs of each individual are usually more adept at determining the optimal timing and frequency of assessments. To ensure the most valid and accurate assessments, instructors also need to be aware of temporary factors (e.g., fatigue) that can affect performance scores (e.g., time in the 110 m high hurdles). In some cases, learners might want to know how well they are performing under various circumstances (e.g., competitive situations), whereas at other times they might be more interested in the quality of their performance uninfluenced by temporary factors.

Ultimately, the most important assessments of skill learning are those that take place in the desired target context. In sports, the context might be the game, match, meet, or race. In rehabilitation settings, the context might be the home or work environment. In industrial environments, the context might be the work site. In recreational pursuits, the context may be at the lake, in the mountains, or on a bike trail.

In the final chapter, you will learn how to test your own understanding of the principles and concepts in this book and to apply what you have learned to a hypothetical learning situation that is relevant and interesting to you. We hope you enjoy the experience.

SUMMARY

Instructors and therapists are faced constantly with the challenge of providing learners and patients with interesting and beneficial practice experiences that are consistent with research-based principles of motor learning and performance. In this chapter, we proposed a working strategy for skill instruction based on the conceptual model of motor performance and the principles of motor performance and learning discussed throughout the book. Using the conceptual model as a backdrop along with two checklists for diagnosing the learning situation and designing the learning experience, respectively, we presented four cases studies illustrating how practitioners might provide appropriate and effective instructional assistance.

Effective practitioners consider the following factors when diagnosing learning situations:

- Characteristics of the learner (e.g., age, previous experiences, stage of learning, handicapping conditions)
- The goals of learning (e.g., program learning, parameter learning, generalization, error detection and correction)
- Characteristics of the target skill (e.g., types of information-processing demands, level of environmental stability, speed–accuracy trade-offs, risk of injury)
- Nature of the target context (e.g., time pressure, evaluative audience, possible distractions, strategy demands)

Practitioners might provide any of the following types of instructional assistance:

- Prepractice assistance in the form of goal setting, instructions, and demonstrations
- Early practice assistance, such as physical guidance and attention focusing
- Special types of physical practice experiences, such as simulator practice, part–whole practice, slow-motion practice, and error detection practice
- Appropriate practice structure (i.e., constant practice, varied practice, blocked practice, random practice)
- Development of additional skills, such as arousal control and mental practice or imagery
- Augmented feedback (i.e., type, amount, precision, and frequency)

The scenarios presented in the chapter differed with respect to factors such as the age and experience of the learner, the goal of learning, characteristics of the target skill, and the nature of the target context. For each case study, we offered a working strategy and then illustrated how the practitioner might change the strategy if the scenario was altered in two ways. We also included references at the end of each scenario that provided samples of possible research documentation for instructional decisions.

To assess the progress of learners and determine the effectiveness of instructional strategies, practitioners must decide how and when to measure performance. We suggest that when measuring learners' progress, practitioners consider the following issues:

- The goal of learning, the target skill, and the target context
- The outcome and process characteristics that are the most valid indicators of skill improvement
- The gains in learning provided by the testing process itself
- The optimal timing and frequency of formal assessments
- The fact that formal assessment represents a type of augmented feedback and therefore should conform to the same principles used when providing instructional feedback (i.e., choosing the type, amount, precision, and frequency of feedback that is optimal for each learner, task, and situation)
- The recognition that evaluations of learning can be influenced by temporary factors (e.g., fatigue) and that such factors need to be controlled or eliminated as much as possible to obtain the most valid estimates of learning

chapter 12

Applying the Principles of Skill Learning

▷ Chapter Outline

▶ Chapter Objectives

When you have completed this chapter, you should be able to

- demonstrate your ability to integrate the conceptual model of motor performance and the various principles presented in this book to assist an individual who is trying to learn or relearn a motor skill,
- describe a hypothetical or real instructional situation and then diagnose the problem and design and assess the learning experience, and
- provide supporting research documentation for your decisions.

PREVIEW

We hope that by now you have developed a solid understanding of the principles and processes underlying skill learning and of the factors successful practitioners consider when diagnosing, designing, and assessing a person's learning experience. However, the best way to evaluate your comprehension of this information is to see how well you can apply it in providing instructional assistance for an actual learner. For some of you, that opportunity might arise when you try to help a surgery or stroke patient relearn movements in a therapy setting. For others, it might come when you are given the opportunity to coach athletes or provide instruction for people trying to learn a variety of recreational or job-related skills. For still others of you, the moment might come if you are asked to provide assistance for aspiring musicians or dancers who want to refine their skills. Only when your knowledge of the conceptual model and the important concepts and principles in this book are tested under fire can you really appreciate how much you have learned.

How do you think you might respond to the challenge? How well can you diagnose a learning situation? How well can you design a learning experience? How effectively can you assess that experience? What types of rationale and research documentation might you offer in support of your decisions?

OVERVIEW

Throughout this book we have challenged you to demonstrate your comprehension of concepts and principles of motor performance and learning by relating them in meaningful ways to skill-learning situations with which you are familiar. In this final chapter we provide some guidelines for you to use in diagnosing a learning situation you might encounter at some future time, and in designing a learning experience for an individual pursuing a particular learning goal. We hope that this experience will reinforce your confidence in the situation-based approach to providing instructional assistance and your ability to apply what you have learned in this book to a real-world situation.

NOW IT'S YOUR TURN

In chapter 11 we presented four hypothetical case studies describing various types of instructional situations. Each situation involved a specific learner and learning goal, unique skill requirements, and particular situational demands. Possible diagnoses of each situation and possible ways of designing each learning experience were based primarily on the concepts and principles presented in the book and were supported by a sample of the research evidence presented in the first 10 chapters. Following this same working strategy, you can now create your own instructional situation, provide a systematic diagnosis of the situation, and then present the concepts and principles you might use to design and assess the learning experience effectively. In addition, you can provide samples of supporting literature and compile a list of references to document your decisions. In the following sections are several guidelines for you to follow as you complete this task along with an example showing how a student in one of our classes approached the assignment.

Creating the Learning Situation

Each case study in chapter 11 is an example of a particular learning situation that might occur in a real-world setting. In much the same way, the situation you create (real or hypothetical) can involve a common skill-learning situation, such as teaching physical education, coaching, assisting performing artists, providing physical therapy, or offering instruction in industrial operations (e.g., job skills, equipment operation).

When creating your instructional situation, you might want to choose one with which you are familiar or have had personal experience. That way you will have some sense of the challenges people typically face when they try to learn or perform the skills necessary for that situation. The situation might involve a person who wants to learn a new skill or refine an existing one. Your learner might need assistance in recovering a skill lost because of injury or partial paralysis. If you would like to discover more about the essential aspects of a particular learning situation, you might interview an experienced movement practitioner. This is what we did when we were putting together the third and fourth case studies in chapter 11.

For the third learning situation, we interviewed a physical therapist and asked her to tell us about some of the patients with whom she was currently working and the skills she was trying to teach them. After several rounds of discussion with the therapist, we decided that the problem of teaching a young patient with cerebral palsy to climb stairs would be an interesting and novel learning situation to include in the chapter. For the fourth case study, we asked a local fire chief to tell us about some of the skills required of the average firefighter. In addition to sharing his experiential knowledge with us, the chief sent us a copy of the book *Essentials of Fire Fighting* (Wieder, Smith, & Brackage, 1996), which contains useful information about the skills firefighters are required to learn, and pictures showing the correct ways to perform those skills.

Diagnosing the Learning Situation

Once you have chosen a possible learning situation, you can begin diagnosing it. In chapter 11 we introduced a working strategy for providing instructional assistance that begins with a diagnosis of the learning situation. As you attempt to diagnose the situation you have chosen, refer again to the components of the conceptual model of motor performance (figure 11.1 on p. 325) to identify those that might be relevant for skill learning. They might include the stages of information processing, the forms of intrinsic (exteroceptive and proprioceptive) feedback available to the learner, and the extrinsic feedback (which could convey knowledge of results and knowledge of performance) you might provide during instruction.

Experienced movement practitioners are excellent resources for information about the demands and challenges of teaching, coaching, or physical therapy.

Your diagnosis might also include items from table 11.1 that address questions about the learner, the learner's goal (i.e., what types of skill learning are required), and the target context (i.e., under what conditions the learner wants to be able to perform the skills).

Designing the Learning Experience

Once you have identified the factors that are relevant to your chosen situation (you need to include only those factors that are relevant, not everything in the list), decide how you might design the learning experience—or, in other words, determine the instructional options listed in table 11.2 that might promote the most effective goal achievement for your learner. You might want to make several photocopies of this table on which to make notes as you proceed with this task. The following are questions you might consider in designing the learning experience:

- How will I establish communication with the learner?
- What types of outcome, performance, and process goals do we need to set?
- Will I need to assist the learner in managing arousal? If so, how?
- Will attentional focus be an issue? If so, how might I promote an optimal focus?
- What types of practice do I need to provide?
- How might I go about structuring practice?
- How might I go about providing feedback?

To check the appropriateness of the items you select from table 11.2, refer to the information that you selected from table 11.1 when diagnosing the learning situation. If you can see a clear connection between your diagnosis and your selections from table 11.2, you are on the right track. By this we mean that the type of instruction you have decided to provide (even if only hypothetical) is appropriate for the learning situation you have created and diagnosed. For example, if your learner is a beginner (verbal–cognitive stage), it would be appropriate to design a learning experience that includes rather frequent demonstrations and feedback, as well as an initial practice structure that is blocked.

Assessing the Learning Experience

The final piece of the working strategy pertains to assessment. If you can evaluate improvements in skill learning accurately, you will be able to provide the learner with helpful information about goal achievement as well as feedback about possible adjustments to make performance even better.

Before deciding how to assess progress, review again the learner's goals. What level of skill does the learner hope to acquire, and under what conditions (target context) does the learner want to be able to perform the skills? For example, if your learner is a beginning tennis player who wants to keep the ball in play when rallying with a friend, your assessment would likely focus more on movement characteristics and performance outcomes than if the learner were more advanced and wanted to compete for the singles tennis championship at her local country club. Always remember that the purpose of assessments is to provide learners with feedback about the extent to which they are making progress toward their goals.

When deciding how to assess your learner's performance, refer to the practice preparation and practice feedback sections of table 11.2, which contain the types of measures to use to assess learning and the types of feedback to provide. When measuring learning, do not forget the concepts of performance curves and retention and transfer tests (see pages 204 and 205).

To assess performance effectively, you must be able to identify movement components and movement outcomes that indicate skilled actions. Once you do this, you must be able to measure each component or outcome reliably and accurately. To determine which aspects of performance to assess, you could consult instructional manuals or books containing information about pertinent components of the target skills. The components you select can include both process characteristics (e.g., movement form or quality) and outcome scores (e.g., distance from the target, movement time). If you attempt to rate the quality of the learner's movement form, you must know which movement criteria to look for and be able to assess those criteria reliably (see Knudson & Morrison, 2002, for some helpful guidelines). If you have access to video recording equipment, you can videotape the learner's movements and check the reliability of your ratings by evaluating the same movement on separate occasions.

Consider how you will share assessment information with the learner. Relevant issues here include the most effective type (e.g., program or parameter; verbal, visual, or manual; descriptive or prescriptive), amount (e.g., summary feedback, average feedback), precision level, and frequency of information. By maintaining open communication with the learner, you can determine how to provide helpful assessments at times when the learner appreciates them the most.

Documenting the Instructional Strategy

Effective practitioners base their instructional decisions on the best supporting evidence available. As a prospective practitioner, you want to provide answers for people who might ask, "Why are you doing what you are doing?" or "Why do you think your approach produces effective learning?" Many instructional decisions are the result of conclusions based on a pattern of consistent findings from a series of controlled studies. For example, motor skills theorists are reasonably certain (a) that a random-practice structure facilitates the retention and transfer of skills to a greater extent than does a blocked-practice format (Bjork, 1975; Hanlon, 1996; Lee & Magill, 1985; Magill & Hall, 1990; Shea & Zimny, 1983; Wrisberg & Liu, 1991); (b) that, compared with a constant-practice format, a varied-practice format promotes parameter selection when performers are using a generalized motor program (Catalano & Kleiner, 1984; Kerr & Booth, 1978; Lee, Magill, & Weeks, 1985; Lee, Wulf, & Schmidt, 1992; Schmidt, 1975); and (c) that a reduced frequency of augmented feedback produces retention that is superior to that produced by a more frequent feedback schedule (Janelle et al., 1997; Winstein & Schmidt, 1990).

In the scenarios we presented in chapter 11, we provided supporting references that each practitioner might have selected to document the principles and concepts used to provide instructional assistance. For the learning situation you select, you should do the same thing. For example, if you create a situation involving a college football player who wants to learn how to identify and respond rapidly to the movements of opposing players, you could use a visual reaction-time procedure similar to the one used by Christina, Barresi, and Shaffner (1990) in their study with a college football linebacker. If so, cite that study as supporting documentation for your decision.

By providing supporting rationale and documentation for as many of your instructional decisions as possible, you will demonstrate that you are aware of the relevant available evidence and of the importance of citing it. Whenever possible, find primary source evidence (i.e., references to actual experiments) to support your decisions. However, secondary sources (e.g., textbooks, professional articles, review articles) are also acceptable. For any decisions lacking research support or secondary-source documentation, offer the best rationale possible but also acknowledge that the decision is based on informed logic rather than empirical evidence.

EXAMPLE

To give you an idea of how to create and diagnose your own instructional situation and then design an effective learning experience, we offer the following example from one of Craig Wrisberg's former students. This student was an exercise science major and an experienced soccer player. He had begun playing organized soccer when he was 7 years old and had continued participating in the sport during high school and college. The following sections provide a brief narrative description of the learning situation that this student created and the information from tables 11.1 and 11.2 that he used to diagnose the situation and design the learning experience. You will also see a brief description of the outcome and process measures that the student proposed to use in assessing the learning experience along with a list of supporting references he selected to document his instructional decisions.

Creating the Learning Situation: The Student's Narrative Description

"Mario is a 12-year-old boy who has just moved into my neighborhood. In his original hometown, Mario played many sports, including baseball, basketball, soccer, and roller hockey. His favorite sport is roller hockey. However, he wants to improve his soccer skills because soccer is the big sport at his new school. Since Mario lives just a few houses away, he occasionally sees me playing soccer with my friends. Once we got to know each other better, Mario asked me if I'd help him improve his kicking technique to improve his chances of making the seventh-grade team at his school. He thinks that being on the team would be a good way for him to meet other kids in town and make some new friends. I can see that Mario is very motivated to learn, but his current kicking skills are limited to making good contact with the ball in the same way every time. He seems to possess some of the abilities that are important for successful kicking, and he has a pretty good knowledge of the concept of field position (gained from his previous roller hockey and basketball experience). However, Mario knows he will need to handle the ball much better than he currently does to make the team. In particular, Mario would like to be able to pass the ball on the ground with speed and accuracy, cross the ball in the air to various targets, and strike (shoot) the ball with power and control."

Diagnosing the Learning Situation: Using Table 12.1

Table 12.1 shows the important categories the student identified in diagnosing Mario's learning situation. Although he might have checked other categories, the ones the student checked are those that he believed contained the most relevant information for Mario's situation. In much the same way, you would select those categories you

Table 12.1 Categories the Student Checked in Diagnosing His Instructional Scenario

Who?	What?	Where?
Learner characteristics	**Task (target skill) characteristics**	**Target context**
☑ Age	☑ Discrete, serial, continuous	☑ Recreational
☑ Previous experience	☑ Motor or cognitive	☐ Competitive (athletic)
☑ Motivation	☑ Closed or open	☐ Clinical
☐ Stage of learning	☐ Closed-loop control	☐ Home
☐ Abilities	a. Exteroceptive feedback	☐ Presence or absence of others
☐ Attention	b. Proprioceptive feedback	
☐ Arousal	☑ Open-loop control	
☐ Memory	a. Motor programs	
☐ Information-processing capability	b. Generalized motor programs	
Goals of learning	☑ Speed–accuracy trade-offs	
☑ Program learning	a. Spatial accuracy	
☑ Parameter learning	b. Temporal accuracy	
☐ Error detection and correction	☑ Object manipulation	
☐ Skill refinement	☑ Information-processing demands	
☐ Generalization	a. Stimulus identification	
	b. Response selection	
	c. Response programming	
	☐ Risk of injury	

believe contain the information of greatest relevance to any learning situation you might create.

Designing the Learning Experience: Using Table 12.2

Table 12.2 shows the categories the student checked in designing Mario's learning experience. Once again, the student didn't check all of the categories but only the ones he believed would contribute the most to Mario's learning experience.

Table 12.2 Categories the Student Checked in Designing His Instructional Scenario

Practice preparation	Practice presentation	Practice feedback
☑ Goal setting	☑ Clarifying expectations	☑ Intrinsic feedback
a. Outcome goals	☐ Managing arousal	☑ Extrinsic feedback
b. Performance goals	☐ Focusing attention	a. Knowledge of results
c. Process goals	☑ Providing instructions	b. Knowledge of performance
☐ Stage of learning	☑ Providing demonstrations	☑ Instructional decisions
☐ Transfer of learning	☐ Offering guidance	☑ Type of feedback
☑ Target skills	☑ Providing physical practice	a. Program or parameter
☐ Target behaviors	a. Simulations	b. Visual, verbal, or manual
☑ Target context	b. Part practice	c. Descriptive or prescriptive
☑ Performance measures	c. Slow-motion practice	☐ Amount of feedback
a. Outcome	d. Error detection practice	a. Average feedback
b. Process	☐ Providing mental practice	b. Summary feedback
Practice structure	a. Procedures	☐ Precision of feedback
☑ Schema development	b. Imagery	☑ Frequency of feedback
a. Constant practice		
b. Varied practice		
☐ Facilitating transfer		
a. Blocked practice		
b. Random practice		
c. Consistent and varied mapping		

Assessing the Learning Experience

Because Mario's goal was to be able to produce a variety of soccer kicks with good pace and control, the student selected several outcome and process measures for assessing improvements in each of the three target skills. Notice that the student proposed outcome measures as well as a process measure for each skill. To assess the learner's form, the student selected process measures taken from standard soccer instruction books (Pronk & Gorman, 1991; Rees, 1995) and from a volume containing discussion of the qualitative analysis of human movement (Knudson & Morrison, 1997).

Target skill: Passing ball on the ground

Outcome measures

1. The task is to pass the ball a distance of 20 m to a target defined by two cones spaced 5 m apart. For variety, learner could attempt passes with the right foot only, the left foot only, and with alternating feet. The score is the number of passes that go between the cones out of 20 attempts.
2. Here, while dribbling, learner passes the ball to designated target zones (defined by pairs of cones spaced 5 m apart and separated by a distance of 10 m) located to the left and right of the learner. For cones on the right, passes should be made with the left foot. For cones on the left, passes should be made with the right foot. For variety, a series of cones could be randomly placed to the left and right along the path the learner is dribbling. The score is the number of passes that go between the cones out of 20 attempts.
3. As the learner's passing skill improves, one or two receivers could be added to the previous test to assess the learner's timing of the pass off the dribble. In this test, the receivers run parallel to the learner (on the right, left, or both) and outside of the series of cones. The learner then dribbles the ball up field and attempts to pass it between the cones so that it is easily received by the moving partner. The score is the number of passes (out of 20 attempts) that (a) go between the cones and (b) are easily received by the moving partner.

Process measure: Successful execution of each of the following form components. Score is total number of components performed correctly for 20 attempts with either the right or left foot.

1. Foot planted close to ball and pointed toward target.
2. Opposite arm held out for balance.
3. Head kept over ball at moment of contact.
4. Eyes kept on ball at moment of contact.
5. Contact made with instep of kicking foot.
6. Kicking foot follows imaginary line from center of ball to center of target zone.

Target skill: Crossing ball in the air to targets

Outcome measures

1. The task is crossing the ball a distance of 20, 25, 30, and 35 m to target zones that are 4, 6, 8, and 12 m square, respectively. For variety, the learner could attempt crosses with the right foot only, the left foot only, and alternating feet. The score is number of crosses that land in the four target zones (five kicks each) out of 20 attempts.
2. Here, the goal is to cross the ball from corner into a target zone 8 m square. The target is located in the scoring area directly in front of the goal. Half of kicks are made with right foot and half with left foot. The score is the number of kicks landing in the target zone out of 20 attempts.
3. As the learner's skill level improves, crossing could be assessed by having the learner receive a pass while running down the right or left side of the field toward

the goal and then attempting a crossing pass into the 8 m square target zone located in the scoring area. Half of the crosses could be attempted from the left side of the goal and half from the right side. The score is number of crosses landing in the target zone out of 20 attempts.

Process measure: The measure is based on the successful execution of each of the following components. The score is total number of components performed correctly for 20 attempts with either or both feet.

1. Shoulders kept back.
2. Foot planted close to ball and pointed toward target.
3. Opposite held arm out for balance.
4. Eyes kept on ball at contact.
5. Contact made with laces, not inside of foot.
6. Kicking leg follows through in direction of the target.

Target skill: Shooting with power and control

Outcome measures

1. The task is shooting to targets from a distance 16.5 m to the goal line (penalty area). Targets are defined by cones placed 1 to 1.5 m inside both goalposts. The ball is placed on the ground and the learner attempts to kick it between the cone and the post, with half of the kicks to the left scoring zone and half to the right. The score is number of successful kicks out of 20 attempts.
2. The goal is to shoot to targets from a distance of 16.5 m to the goal line (penalty area). Targets are defined by cones placed 1 m inside both goalposts and by a piece of striped tape (2.54 cm wide) placed horizontally and halfway up each post. The ball is placed on the ground and the learner attempts to kick it into one of the four scoring zones (upper left, lower left, upper right, lower right). Five attempts at each zone. Kicks can be made with either foot, and the instructor calls out the designated scoring zone before each kick. The score is number of successful kicks out of 20 attempts.
3. In this case, the learner stands 10 m outside penalty area while the instructor rolls the ball toward the learner from a location near the right or left goalpost. The learner approaches the ball, controls it, and then shoots it into one of the four scoring zones. Five attempts at each zone. Kicks can be made with either foot, and the instructor calls out the designated scoring zone before each kick. The score is number of successful kicks out of 20 attempts.
4. In this task, the learner stands 10 m outside penalty area while the instructor rolls the ball toward learner from a location near the right or left goalpost. The learner approaches the ball and shoots it (without controlling it) into one of the four scoring zones. Five attempts at each zone. Kicks can be made with either foot, and the instructor calls out the designated scoring zone prior to each kick. The score is number of successful kicks out of 20 attempts.

Process measure: The measure is based on the successful execution of each of the following components. The score is total number of components performed correctly for 20 attempts with either or both feet.

1. Foot planted close to ball and pointed toward target.
2. Opposite arm held out for balance.
3. Eyes kept on ball at contact.

4. Contact made with laces, not inside of foot.
5. Kicking leg follows through in direction of the target.
6. For moving kicks, ball (coming from left or right side) allowed to cross midplane of body before controlling or striking it.
7. For moving kicks, the step in and foot plant accurately timed.
8. For kicks to lower target zones, head kept over ball.
9. For kicks to upper target zones, shoulders kept back.

Documenting the Instructional Decisions

To provide supporting literature and research for his instructional decisions, the student compiled a list of references (see figure 12.1). Note that the list includes the third edition of this textbook as well as other primary and secondary sources.

References

Fleishman, E.A. (1964). *The structure and measurement of physical fitness.* Englewood Cliffs, NJ: Prentice-Hall.

Gentile, A.M. (1972). A working model of skill acquisition with application to teaching. *Quest Monograph,* XVII, 3–23.

Gould, D. (2001). Goal setting for peak performance. In J.M. Williams (Ed.), *Applied sport psychology: Personal growth to peak performance* (pp. 190–205). Mountain View, CA: Mayfield.

Guadagnoli, M.A., Holcomb, W.R., & Weber, T.J. (1999). The relationship between contextual interference effects and performer expertise on the learning of a putting task. *Journal of Human Movement Studies,* 37, 19–36.

Knudson, D.V., & Morrison, C.S. (1997). *Qualitative analysis of human movement.* Champaign, IL: Human Kinetics.

Lee, D.N. (1980). Visuo-motor coordination in space-time. In G.E. Stelmach & J. Requin (Eds.), *Tutorials in motor behavior* (pp. 281–285). Amsterdam: North-Holland.

Mielke, D. (2003). *Soccer fundamentals.* Champaign, IL: Human Kinetics.

Newell, K.M., & McGinnis, P.M.(1985). Kinematic information feedback for skilled performance. *Human Learning,* 4, 39–56.

Pronk, N., & Gorman, B. (1991). *Soccer everyone.* Winston-Salem, NC: Hunter Textbooks, Inc.

Rees, R. (1995). *The manual of soccer coaching* (2nd ed.). Collingswood, NJ: Port City Press.

Schmidt, R.A. (1975). A schema theory of discrete motor skill learning. *Psychological Review,* 82, 225–260.

Schmidt, R.A., & Wrisberg, C.A. (2004). *Motor learning and performance* (3rd ed.). Champaign, IL: Human Kinetics.

Schmidt, R.A., & Young, D.E. (1987). Transfer of motor control in motor skill learning. In S.M. Cormier & J.D. Hagman (Eds.), *Transfer of learning* (pp. 47–79). Orlando, FL: Academic Press.

Seat, J.E., & Wrisberg, C.A. (1996). The visual instruction system. *Research Quarterly for Exercise and Sport,* 67, 106–108.

Wrisberg, C.A., & Pein, R.L. (2002). Note on learners' control of the frequency of model presentation during skill acquisition. *Perceptual and Motor Skills,* 94, 792–794.

Figure 12.1 List of supporting references cited in student's paper.

Once he had compiled all of the previous information, the student was able to write a paper describing the approach he would take to providing instructional assistance. The student's example might be a helpful template for you to use when creating, diagnosing, and designing your own instructional scenario.

FINAL COMMENT

We hope you find the material in this book beneficial in your personal and professional pursuits, particularly when you are learning skills or helping others achieve their learning goals. The conceptual model of motor performance and the situation-based approach we have presented can be useful for diagnosing learning situations in a systematic fashion and then designing and assessing learning experiences effectively. Whether it's your own skill learning or that of others you have the opportunity to assist, we wish you the best and hope you enjoy the experience.

UNIVERSITY OF WINCHESTER
LIBRARY

Appendix

Following are the answers to the matching and fill-in-the-blank items for each chapter. Note: For the other From Principles to Practice questions, you should expect students to provide rationale and, where possible, supporting documentation for their answers.

CHAPTER 1

Matching

1. d, 2. f, 3. c, 4. g, 5. b, 6. e, 7. a

Fill in the Blank

Motor performance is observable movement behavior that is sometimes susceptible to temporary factors, such as *(two of the following four)*: **physical condition**, **fatigue**, **arousal**, **or motivation.** A person's level of motor learning can be estimated only by observing the person's **motor performance.**

CHAPTER 2

Matching

1. g, 2. e, 3. c, 4. b, 5. a, 6. d, 7. f

Fill in the Blank

An interesting aspect of many types of **bimanual or two-hand** movements is that the hands seem to be **linked** to each other. Research and our own experience suggest that the motor system prefers to produce simultaneous two-hand movements that have a common underlying **time or temporal structure.** A classic example of the difficulty people have in attempting to produce two different actions simultaneously is **patting** the head and **rubbing** the belly.

CHAPTER 3

Matching

1. e, 2. d, 3. b, 4. a, 5. c, 6. g, 7. f

Fill in the Blank

Performers use **focal** vision to identify objects in the center of their visual field and **ambient** vision to detect the orientation of their body in the environment. **Optical flow** refers to the movement of light patterns over the retina that allows people to perceive **motion**, **position**, and **timing**. **Visual proprioception** is a type of sensory information arising from the visual system that also provides performers with information about their movements.

CHAPTER 4

Matching

1. e, 2. g, 3. a, 4. f, 5. c, 6. d, 7. b

Fill in the Blank

A particular strength of generalized motor programs is that they allow performers to produce fundamental patterns of action. Three aspects of the generalized program that performers can adjust to meet changing environmental demands are movement time, movement amplitude, and limb and muscles used. However, regardless of the adjustments made, the fundamental temporal structure of the movement remains essentially the same.

CHAPTER 5

Matching

1. d, 2. f, 3. e, 4. c, 5. b, 6. a

Fill in the Blank

Fitts' law illustrates an important point about performers when they are required to make movements that are both fast and accurate. To examine the speed-accuracy trade-off, Fitts devised a task that required participants to hold a stylus and tap back and forth between two targets as quickly and accurately as possible. The two variables Fitts manipulated to make the task more or less difficult were movement distance and target width. Fitts found that for many different combinations of these two variables, increases in movement difficulty were linearly related to increases in the time per movement.

CHAPTER 6

Matching

1. f, 2. d, 3. a, 4. b, 5. c, 6. g, 7. e

Fill in the Blank

Practitioners can classify motor tasks or motor skills by analyzing the various components or demands of the task and then considering the types of abilities that underlie performance. Different tasks or skills rely on different combinations of underlying abilities.

CHAPTER 7

Matching

1. f, 2. e, 3. g, 4. a, 5. c, 6. b, 7. d

Fill in the Blank

The stages of learning are relatively distinct, because some overlap usually exists between them. In the verbal–cognitive stage, gains in performance tend to be somewhat large. According to Gentile (1972), the primary goal of learners in this stage is to get a **general idea** of the movement. The motor stage of learning is primarily devoted to the task of **skill refinement** and to meeting the particular demands of the performance environment. After extensive practice, some learners enter the **autonomous** stage of learning, where they are able enjoy the advantage of diminished **attention demands** for movement production.

CHAPTER 8

Matching

1. f, 2. e, 3. b, 4. g, 5. a, 6. d, 7. c

Fill in the Blank

Before providing instructional assistance, practitioners should familiarize learners with the learning environment and encourage an open line of **two-way** communication. Because the attentional capacity of people is limited, practitioners need to assist learners in identifying **focus cues** that are relevant for performance at different moments. Those who experience anxiety during performance or learning sessions should be encouraged to focus on **process** goals rather than on **outcome** goals. **Massed** practice sessions are helpful for learners who are rehearsing discrete skills for which minimal rest has little or no influence on learning. However, **distributed** practice sessions are sometimes necessary when fatigue leads to sloppy performance or places learners at risk of injury.

CHAPTER 9

Matching

1. b, 2. f, 3. e, 4. g, 5. a, 6. d, 7. c

Fill in the Blank

Open skills are those that require performers to produce often rapid responses to changing environmental events. If performers know which responses are more effective for particular stimuli, they can speed up the **processing** of **information** in the **response selection** and **response programming** stages. An effective way for practitioners to increase learners' response speed is to provide them with **consistent** stimulus-response mapping practice opportunities. The development of response speed is more difficult, however, for **varied mapping** situations in which a given stimulus may require different responses at different times or in different situations.

CHAPTER 10

Matching

1. c, 2. g, 3. d, 4. f, 5. a, 6. b, 7. e

Fill in the Blank

Effective movement practitioners know how and when to reduce the frequency of extrinsic feedback. One way instructors might do this is to provide **summary** feedback that conveys information about each of a series of movement attempts once the learner completes them. Instructors might also provide **average** feedback that gives learners a general idea of the dominant features of a series of movement attempts. By reducing the frequency of extrinsic feedback, instructors encourage learners to become familiar with their own **intrinsic** feedback and develop their own **error detection** skills. By receiving extrinsic feedback less frequently, learners are also able to produce movements that are more **consistent**. However, learners who are **beginners** may need more frequent extrinsic feedback during initial practice sessions, particularly if the target skill is **complex**.

References

Abbs, J.H., Gracco, V.L., & Cole, K.J. (1984). Control of multi-joint movement coordination: Sensorimotor mechanisms in speech motor programming. *Journal of Motor Behavior,* 16, 195–231.

Abernethy, B. (1993). Attention. In R.N. Singer, M. Murphey, & L.K. Tennant (Eds.), *Handbook of research on sport psychology* (pp. 127–170). New York: Macmillan.

Adams, J.A. (1971). A closed-loop theory of motor learning. *Journal of Motor Behavior,* 3, 111–150.

Adams, J.A. (1978). Theoretical issues for knowledge of results. In G.E. Stelmach (Ed.), *Information processing in motor control and learning* (pp. 229–240). New York: Academic Press.

Ainsworth, J., & Fox, C. (1989, September-October). Learning to learn: A cognitive processes approach to movement skill acquisition. *Strategies,* 2(1), 20–22.

Allard, F., & Burnett, N. (1985). Skill in sport. *Canadian Journal of Psychology,* 39, 294–312.

Amato, I. (1989). The finishing touch: Robots may lend a hand in the making of Steinway pianos. *Science News,* 135, 108–109.

Ames, C. (1992). Achievement goals, motivational climate, and motivational processes. In G.C. Roberts (Ed.), *Motivation in sport and exercise* (pp. 161–176). Champaign, IL: Human Kinetics.

Annett, J. (1959). *Feedback and human behavior.* Middlesex, England: Penguin Books.

Anderson, D.I., Magill, R.A., Sekiya, H., & Ryan, G. (2005). Support for an explanation of the guidance effect in motor skill learning. *Journal of Motor Behavior*, 37, 231–238.

Anshel, M.H. (1990). An information processing approach to teaching motor skills, *Journal of Physical Education, Recreation, and Dance,* May/June, 70–75.

Armstrong, T.R. (1970). *Training for the production of memorized movement patterns* (Tech. Rep. No. 26). Ann Arbor: University of Michigan, Human Performance Center.

Baddeley, A.D., & Longman, D.J.A. (1978). The influence of length and frequency of training session on the rate of learning to type. *Ergonomics,* 21, 627–635.

Badets, A., & Blandin, Y. (2005). Observational learning: Effects of bandwidth KR. *Journal of Motor Behavior*, 37, 211–216.

Bahill, A.T., & LaRitz, T. (1984). Why can't batters keep their eyes on the ball? *American Scientist,* 72, 249–253.

Baker, J., Côté, J., & Abernethy, B. (2003). Sport-specific practice and the development of expert decision-making in team ball sports. *Journal of Applied Sport Psychology,* 15, 12–25.

Barrett, D.D., & Burton, A.W. (2002). Throwing patterns used by collegiate baseball players in actual games. *Research Quarterly for Exercise and Sport,* 73, 19–27.

Bartlett, F.C. (1932). *Remembering: A study in experimental and social psychology.* Cambridge, England: Cambridge University Press.

Battig, W.F. (1966). Facilitation and interference. In E.A. Bilodeau (Ed.), *Acquisition of skill* (pp. 215–244). New York: Academic Press.

Beals, R.P., Mayyasi, A.M., Templeton, A.E., & Johnston, W.L. (1971). The relationship between basketball-shooting performance and certain visual attributes. *American Journal of Optometry and Archives of American Academy of Optometry,* 48, 585–590.

Beek, P.J., & van Santvoord, A.A.M. (1992). Learning the cascade juggle: A dynamical systems analysis. *Journal of Motor Behavior,* 24, 85–94.

Behrman, A.L., Teitelbaum, P., & Cauraugh, J.H. (1998). Verbal instructional sets to normalize the temporal and spatial gait variables in Parkinson's disease. *Journal of Neurology, Neurosurgery, and Psychiatry,* 65, 580–582.

Beilock, S.L. (in press). Choking under pressure. In R. Baumeister and K. Vohs (Eds.), *Encyclopedia of social psychology*. Thousand Oaks, CA: Sage.

Beilock, S.L., & Carr, T.H. (2005). When high-powered people fail: Working memory and "choking under pressure" in math. *Psychological Science, 16,* 101–105.

Beilock, S. L. & Carr, T. H. (2004). From novice to expert performance: Attention, memory, and control of complex sensorimotor skills. In A.M. Williams, N.J. Hodges, M.A. Scott, & M.L.J. Court (Eds.), *Skill acquisition in sport: Research, theory, and practice* (pp. 309–328). London: Routledge.

Beilock, S. L. & Carr, T. H. (2001). On the fragility of skilled performance: What governs choking under pressure? *Journal of Experimental Psychology: General, 130,* 701–725.

Belen'kii, V.Y., Gurfinkel, V.S., & Pal'tsev, Y.I. (1967). Elements of control of voluntary movements. *Biofizika,* 12, 135–141.

Bennett, S., Button, C., Kingsbury, D., & Davids, K. (1999). Manipulating visual information constraints during practice enhances the acquisition of catching skill in children. *Research Quarterly for Exercise and Sport,* 70, 220–232.

Bernstein, N.I. (1967). *The co-ordination and regulation of movements.* Oxford, England: Pergamon Press.

Bilodeau, E.A., Bilodeau, I.M., & Schumsky, D.A. (1959). Some effects of introducing and withdrawing knowledge of results early and late in practice. *Journal of Experimental Psychology,* 58, 142–144.

Bjork, R.A. (1975). Retrieval as a memory modifier. In R. Solso (Ed.), *Information processing and cognition:* The Loyola Symposium (pp. 123–144). Hillsdale, NJ: Erlbaum.

Bjork, R.A. (1979). *Retrieval practice.* Unpublished manuscript, University of California, Los Angeles.

Bjork, R.A. (1994). Memory and metamemory considerations in the training of human beings. In J. Metcalfe and A. Shimamura (Eds.), *Metacognition: Knowing about knowing* (pp.185–205). Cambridge, MA: MIT Press.

Bjork, R. A. (1999). Assessing our own competence: Heuristics and illusions. In D. Gopher and A. Koriat (Eds.*), Attention and peformance XVII. Cognitive regulation of performance: Interaction of theory and application* (pp. 435–459). Cambridge, MA: MIT Press.

Blakemore, S.J., Wolpert, D., & Frith, C. (2000). Why can't you tickle yourself? *NeuroReport,* 11, R11–R16.

Blandin, Y., & Proteau, L. (2000). On the cognitive basis of observational learning: Development of mechanisms for the detection and correction of errors. *Quarterly Journal of Experimental Psychology: Human Experimental Psychology,* 53A, 846–867.

Blandin, Y., Lhuisset, L., & Proteau, L. (1999). Cognitive processes underlying observational learning of motor skills. *Quarterly Journal of Experimental Psychology: Human Experimental Psychology,* 52A, 957–979.

Bliss, C.B. (1892–1893). Investigations in reaction time and attention. *Studies from the Yale Psychological Laboratory,* 1, 1–55.

Boder, D.P. (1935). The influence of concomitant activity and fatigue upon certain forms of reciprocal hand movement and its fundamental components. *Comparative Psychology Monographs,* 11 (article 54).

Boschker, M.S.J., Bakker, F.C., & Michaels, C.F. (2002). Memory for the functional characteristics of climbing walls: Perceiving affordances. *Journal of Motor Behavior,* 34, 25–36.

Bogacz, S. (2005). Understanding how speed affects performance of polyrhythms: Transferring control as speed increases. *Journal of Motor Behavior,* 37, 21–34.

Boyce, B.A., & Del Rey, P. (1990). Designing applied research in a naturalistic setting using a contextual interference paradigm. *Journal of Human Movement Studies,* 18, 189–200.

Brace, D.K. (1927). *Measuring motor ability.* New York: A.S. Barnes.

Bransford, J.D., Franks, J.J., Morris, C.D., & Stein, B.S. (1979). Some general constraints on learning and memory research. In L.S. Cermack & F.I.M. Craik (Eds.), *Levels of processing in human memory* (pp. 332–354). Hillsdale, NY: Erlbaum.

Bridgeman, B., Kirch, M., & Sperling, A. (1981). Segregation of cognitive and motor aspects of visual information using induced motion. *Perception and Psychophysics,* 29, 336–342.

Buchanan, P.A., & Ulrich, B.D. (2001). The Feldenkrais Method: A dynamic approach to changing motor behavior. *Research Quarterly for Exercise and Sport,* 74, 315–323.

Button, C., MacLeod, M., Sanders, R., & Coleman, S. (2003). Examining movement variability in the basketball free throw action at different skill levels. *Research Quarterly for Exercise and Sport,* 74, 257–269.

Calmels, C., Berthoumieux, C., & d'Arripe-Lpngueville, F. (2004). Effects of an imagery training program on selective attention of national softball players. *The Sport Psychologist*, 18, 272–296.

Carril, P., & White, D. (1997). *The smart take from the strong*. New York: Simon & Schuster.

Carroll, L. (1994). *Alice in wonderland and through the looking glass*. New York: Grosset & Dunlap. (Original work published 1865.)

Carr, G. (2004). Sport mechanics for coaches (2nd ed.). Champaign, IL: Human Kinetics.

Carron, A.V (1967). Performance and learning in a discrete motor task under massed versus distributed conditions. Unpublished doctoral dissertation, University of California, Berkeley.

Carson, L.M., & Wiegand, R.L. (1979). Motor schema formation and retention in young children: A test of Schmidt's schema theory. *Journal of Motor Behavior*, 11, 247–252.

Catalano, J.F., & Kleiner, B.M. (1984). Distant transfer and practice variability. *Perceptual and Motor Skills*, 58, 851–856.

Cervone, D. (1992). The role of self-referent cognitions in goal setting, motivation, and performance. In M. Rabinowitz (Ed.), *Applied cognition* (pp. 79–96). New York: Ablex.

Chambers, K.L., & Vickers, J.N. (2006). Effects of bandwidth feedback and questioning on the performance of competitive swimmers. *The Sport Psychologist*, 20, 184–197.

Christina, R.W., & Alpenfels, E. (2002). Why does traditional training fail to optimize playing performance? In E. Thain (Ed.), *Science and Golf IV: Proceedings of the World Scientific Congress of Golf* (pp. 1–15). New York: Routledge.

Christina, R.W., Barresi, J.V., & Shaffner, P. (1990). The development of response selection accuracy in a football linebacker using video training. *The Sport Psychologist*, 4, 11–17.

Christina, R.W., & Corcos, D.M. (1988). *Coaches guide to teaching sport skills*. Champaign, IL: Human Kinetics.

Churchland, M.M., Afshar, A., & Shenoy, K.V. (2006). A central source of movement variability. *Neuron*, 52, 1085–1096.

Clark, S.E., & Ste-Marie, D.M. (in press). Investigating the impact of self-as-a-model interventions on chldren's self-regulation of learning and swimming performance. Journal of Sport Sciences.

Clark, S.E., Ste-Marie, D.M., & Martini, R. (2006). The thought processes underlying self-as-a-model interventions: An exploratory study. *Psychology of Sport and Exercise*, *7*, 381–386.

Cole, J. (1991, January). Feedback: A one to one strategy. *Strategies*, 4(3), 5–7.

Cole, J. (2004). On the relation between sensory input and action. *Journal of Motor Behavior*, 36, 243–244.

Colley, A.M., & Beech, J.R. (1988). Grounds for reconciliation: Some preliminary thoughts on cognition and action. In A.M. Colley & J.R. Beech (Eds.), *Cognition and action in skilled behavior* (pp. 1–11). Amsterdam: North-Holland.

Combs, A.W. (1981). What the future demands of education. *Phi Delta Kappan*, 62, 369–372.

Connolly, C.T., & Janelle, C.M. (2003). Attentional strategies in rowing: Performance, perceived exertion, and gender considerations. *Journal of Applied Sport Psychology*, 15, 195–212.

Contractor wins Toolcat challenge contest (2005). http://www.bobcat.com/worksaver/05sp/contest.html.

Crossman, E.R.F.W. (1959). A theory of the acquisition of speed skill. *Ergonomics*, 2, 153–166.

Cuddy, L.J., & Jacoby, L.L. (1982). When forgetting helps memory. Analysis of repetition effects. *Journal of Verbal Learning and Verbal Behavior*, 21, 451–467.

Cumming, J., Nordin, S.M., Horton, R., & Reynolds, S. (2006). Examining the direction of imagery and self-talk on dart-throwing performance and self-efficacy. *The Sport Psychologist*, 20, 257–274.

D'Arripe-Longueville, F., Saury, J., Fournier, J., & Durand, M. (2001). Coach-athlete interaction during elite archery competitions: An application of methodological frameworks used in ergonomics research to sport psychology. *Journal of Applied Sport Psychology*, 13, 275–299.

Day, M.C., Thatcher, J., Greenlees, I., & Woods, B. (2006). The causes of and psychological responses to lost move syndrome in national level trampolinists. *Journal of Applied Sport Psychology*, 18, 151–166.

Debaere, F., Wenderoth, N., Sunaert, S., Van Hecke, P., & Swinnen, S.P. (2003). Internal vs. external generation of movements: Differential neural pathways involved in bimanual coordination performed in the presence of/absence of augmented visual feedback. *NeuroImage*, 19, 764–776.

Deci, E.L., & Ryan, R.M. (1985). *Intrinsic motivation and self-determination in human behavior*. New York: Plenum.

UNIVERSITY OF WINCHESTER
LIBRARY

Deshaies, P., Pargman, D., & Thiffault, C. (1979). A psychobiological profile of individual performance in junior hockey players. In G.C. Roberts & K.M. Newell (Eds.), *Psychology of motor behavior and sport—1978* (pp. 36–50). Champaign, IL: Human Kinetics.

Dewhurst, D.J. (1967). Neuromuscular control system. *IEEE Transactions on Bio-Medical Engineering,* 14, 167–171.

Digital video gives athletes an edge. (2004, July 26). *Knoxville (TN) News Sentinel,* p. C1-2.

Drowatzky, J.N., & Zuccato, F.C. (1967). Interrelationships between selected measures of static and dynamic balance. *Research Quarterly,* 38, 509–510.

Druckman, D., & Bjork, R.A. (1991). *In the mind's eye: Enhancing human performance.* Washington, DC: National Academy Press.

Duda, J.L. (1993). Goals: A social-cognitive approach to the study of achievement motivation in sport. In R.N. Singer, M. Murphey, & L.K. Tennant (Eds.), *Handbook of research on sport psychology* (pp. 421–436). New York: Macmillan.

Duda, J.L., & Treasure, D.C. (2006). Motivational processes and the facilitation of performance, persistence, and well-being in sport. In J.M. Williams (Ed.), *Applied sport psychology: Personal growth to peak performance* (pp. 57–81). New York: McGraw-Hill.

Easterbrook, J.A. (1959). The effect of emotion on cue utilization and the organization of behavior. *Psychological Review,* 66, 183–201.

Edmonds, W.A., Mann, D.T.Y., Tenenbaum, G., & Janelle, C.M. (2006). Analysis of affect-related performance zones: An idiographic method using physiological and introspective data. *The Sport Psychologist,* 20, 40–57.

Ericsson, K.A. (1996). The acquisition of expert performance: An introduction and some issues. In K.A. Ericsson (Ed.), The road to excellence: *The acquisition of expert performance in the arts and sciences, sports, and games* (pp. 1–50). Mahwah, NJ: Erlbaum.

Etnier, J., & Landers, D.M. (1996). The influence of procedural variables on the efficacy of mental practice. *The Sport Psychologist,* 10, 48–57.

Feldenkrais, M. (1972). *Awareness through movement: Health exercises for personal growth.* New York: Harper and Row.

Feltz, D.L., & Landers, D.M. (1983). The effects of mental practice on motor skill learning and performance: A meta analysis. *Journal of Sport Psychology,* 5, 1–8.

Filby, W.C.D., Maynard, I.W., & Graydon, J.K. (1999). The effect of multiple-goal strategies on performance outcomes in training and competition. *Journal of Applied Sport Psychology,* 11, 230–246.

Fitts, P.M. (1954). The information capacity of the human motor system in controlling the amplitude of movement. *Journal of Experimental Psychology,* 47, 381–391.

Fitts, P.M., & Peterson, J.R. (1964). Information capacity of discrete motor responses. *Journal of Experimental Psychology,* 67, 103–112.

Fitts, P.M., & Posner, M.I. (1967). *Human performance.* Belmont, CA: Brooks/Cole.

Flach, J.M., Lintern, G., & Larish, J.F. (1990). Perceptual motor skill: A theoretical framework. In R. Warren & A.H. Wertheim (Eds.), *The perception and control of self motion* (pp. 327–355). Hillsdale, NJ: Erlbaum.

Fleishman, E.A. (1956). Psychomotor selection tests: Research and application in the United States Air Force. *Personnel Psychology,* 9, 449–467.

Fleishman, E.A. (1964). *The structure and measurement of physical fitness.* Englewood Cliffs, NJ: Prentice-Hall.

Fleishman, E.A. (1965). The description and prediction of perceptual motor skill learning. In R. Glaser (Ed.), *Training research and education* (pp. 137–175). New York: Wiley.

Fleishman, E.A. (1972). Structure and measurement of psychomotor abilities. In R.N. Singer (Ed.), *The psychomotor domain: Movement behavior* (pp. 78–106). Philadelphia, PA: Lea & Febiger.

Fleishman, E.A., & Bartlett, C.J. (1969). Human abilities. *Annual Review of Psychology,* 20, 349–380.

Fleishman, E.A., & Hempel, W.E. (1955). The relationship between abilities and improvement with practice in a visual discrimination reaction task. Journal of Experimental Psychology, 49, 301–312.

Fleishman, E.A., & Parker, J.F. (1962). Factors in the retention and relearning of perceptual motor skill. *Journal of Experimental Psychology,* 64, 215–226.

Fleishman, E.A., & Stephenson, R.W. (1970). *Development of a taxonomy of human performance: A review of the third year's progress* (Tech. Rep. No. 726-TPR3). Silver Spring, MD: American Institutes for Research.

Forssberg, H., Grillner, S., & Rossignol, S. (1975). Phase dependent reflex reversal during walking in the chronic spinal cat. *Brain Research,* 85, 103–107.

Franz, E.A., Zelaznik, H.N., & Smith, A. (1992). Evidence of common timing processes in the control of manual, orofacial, and speech movements. *Journal of Motor Behavior,* 24, 281–287.

Franz, E.A., Zelaznik, H.N., Swinnen, S., & Walter, C. (2001). Spatial conceptual influences on the coordination of bimanual actions: When a dual task becomes a single task. *Journal of Motor Behavior,* 33, 103–112.

Fredenburg, K.B., Lee, A.M., & Solomon, M. (2001). The effects of augmented feedback on students' perceptions and performances. *Research Quarterly for Exercise and Sport,* 72, 232–242.

Gabriele, T., Hall, C.R., & Lee, T.D. (1989). Cognition in motor learning: Imagery effects on contextual interference. *Human Movement Science,* 8, 227–245.

Gaina, B., & Sparrow, W.A. (2006). Energetics of bimanual coordination. *Journal of Motor Behavior,* 38, 411–422.

Gallwey, T. (1974). *The inner game of tennis.* New York: Random House.

Gardner, H. (1975). *The shattered mind.* New York: Knopf.

Gauthier, G.M. (1985). Visually and acoustically augmented performance feedback as an aid in motor control learning: A study of selected components of the rowing action. *Journal of Sport Sciences,* 3, 3–25.

Gentile, A.M. (1972). *A working model of skill acquisition with application to teaching.* Quest Monograph XVII, 3–23.

Gentile, A.M. (1987). Skill acquisition: Action, movement, and the neuromotor processes. In J.H. Carr, R.B. Shepherd, J. Gordon, A.M. Gentile, & J.M. Hinds (Eds.), *Movement science: Foundations for physical therapy in rehabilitation* (pp. 93–154). Rockville, MD: Aspen.

Gentner, D.R. (1987). Timing of skilled motor performance: Tests of the proportional duration model. *Psychological Review,* 94, 255–276.

Gibson, J.J. (1966). *The senses considered as perceptual systems.* Boston: Houghton Mifflin.

Gibson, J.J. (1979). *The ecological approach to visual perception.* Boston: Houghton Mifflin.

Gladwell, M. (2000). The art of failure. *The New Yorker,* August 21 & 28, pp. 84–88.

Goode, S., & Magill, R.A. (1986). The contextual interference effects in learning three badminton serves. *Research Quarterly for Exercise and Sport,* 57, 308–314.

Goslow, G.E., Reinking, R.M., & Stuart, D.G. (1973). The cat step cycle: Hind limb joint angles and muscle lengths during unrestrained locomotion. *Journal of Morphology,* 141, 1–42.

Gould, D. (2006). Goal setting for peak performance. In J.M. Williams (Ed.), *Applied sport psychology: Personal growth to peak performance* (pp. 240–259). New York: McGraw-Hill.

Graw, H.M.A. (1968). *The most efficient usage of a fixed work plus rest practice period in motor learning.* Unpublished doctoral dissertation, University of California, Berkeley.

Gregg, M., & Hall, C. (2006). The relationship of skill level and age to the use of imagery by golfers. *Journal of Applied Sport Psychology,* 18, 363–375.

Grillner, S. (1975). Locomotion in vertebrates: Central mechanisms and reflex interaction. *Physiological Reviews,* 55, 247–304.

Guadagnoli, M.A., Holcomb, W.R., & Weber, T.J. (1999). The relationship between contextual interference effects and performer expertise on the learning of a putting task. *Journal of Human Movement Studies,* 37, 19–36.

Guadagnoli, M.A., & Kohl, R.M. (2001). Knowledge of results for motor learning: Relationship between error estimation and knowledge of results frequency. *Journal of Motor Behavior,* 33, 217–224.

Guadagnoli, M.A., & Lee, T.D. (2004). Challenge point: A framework for conceptualizing the effects of various practice conditions in motor learning. *Journal of Motor Behavior,* 36, 212–224.

Guadagnoli, M., McNevin, N., & Wulf, G. (2002). Cognitive influences to balance and posture. *Orthopaedic Physical Therapy Clinics of North America,* 11, 131–141.

Guthrie, E.R. (1952). *The psychology of learning.* New York: Harper & Row.

Hagemann, N., Strauss, B., & Cañal-Bruland, R. (2006). Training perceptual skill by orienting visual attention. *Journal of Sport and Exercise Psychology,* 28, 143–158.

Hall, K.G., Domingues, D.A., & Cavazos, R. (1994). Contextual interference effects with skilled baseball players. *Perceptual and Motor Skills, 78*, 835–841.

Hanin, Y.L. (1980). A study of anxiety in sports. In W.F. Straub (Ed.), *Sport psychology: An analysis of athlete behavior* (pp. 236–249). Ithaca, NY: Mouvement.

Hanlon, R.E. (1996). Motor learning following unilateral stroke. *Archives of Physical Medicine and Rehabilitation, 77*, 811–815.

Hardy, L. (1997). The Coleman Robert Griffith Address: Three myths about sport psychology consultancy work. *Journal of Applied Sport Psychology, 9*, 277–294.

Hardy, L., & Callow, N. (1999). Efficacy of external and internal visual imagery perspectives for the enhancement of performance on tasks in which form is important. *Journal of Sport and Exercise Psychology, 21*, 95–112.

Harle, S.K., & Vickers, J.N. (2001). Training quiet eye improves accuracy in the basketball free throw shot. *The Sport Psychologist, 15*, 289–305.

Hatfield, J., & Murphy, S. (2007). The effects of mobile phone use on pedestrian crossing behaviour at signalised and unsignalised intersections. *Accident Analysis and Prevention, 39*, 197–205.

Hausdorff, J.M., & Durfee, W.K. (1991). Open-loop position control of the knee joint using electrical stimulation of the quadriceps and hamstrings. *Medical Biological Engineering and Computing, 29*, 269–280.

Hay, J.G. (1993). *The biomechanics of sports techniques* (4th ed.). Englewood Cliffs, NJ: Prentice-Hall.

Hayne, H., Boniface, J., & Barr, R. (2000). The development of declarative memory in human infants: Age-related changes in deferred imitation. *Behavioral Neuroscience, 114*, 77–83.

Haywood, K.M. (1993). *Life span motor development.* Champaign, IL: Human Kinetics.

Heavy hat credited with best golfing. (1998, January 9). *Knoxville (TN) News Sentinel*, p. A2.

Henry, F.M. (1961). Reaction time-movement time correlations. *Perceptual and Motor Skills, 12*, 63–66.

Henry, F.M. (1968). Specificity vs. generality in learning motor skill. In R.C. Brown & G.S. Kenyon (Eds.), *Classical studies on physical activity* (pp. 331–340). Englewood Cliffs, NJ: Prentice-Hall. (Original work published 1958.)

Henry, F.M., & Rogers, D.E. (1960). Increased response latency for complicated movements and a "memory drum" theory of neuromotor reaction. *Research Quarterly, 31*, 448–458.

Hick, W.E. (1952). On the rate of gain of information. *Quarterly Journal of Experimental Psychology, 4*, 11–26.

Hird, J.S., Landers, D.M., Thomas, J.R., & Horan, J.J. (1991). Physical practice is superior to mental practice in enhancing cognitive and motor task performance. *Journal of Sport and Exercise Psychology, 8*, 281–293.

Hogan, J., & Yanowitz, B. (1978). The role of verbal estimates of movement error in ballistic skill acquisition. *Journal of Motor Behavior, 10*, 133–138.

Hollerbach, J.M. (1978). *A study of human motor control through analysis and synthesis of handwriting.* Unpublished doctoral dissertation, Massachusetts Institute of Technology, Cambridge.

Horn, R.R., Williams, A.M., Scott, M.A., & Hodges, N.J. (2005). Visual search and coordination changes in response to video and point-light demonstrations without KR. *Journal of Motor Behavior, 37*, 265–274.

Housner, L.D. (1981). Expert-novice knowledge structure and cognitive processing differences in badminton [Abstract]. Psychology of motor behavior and sport, 1981, (p. 1). *Proceedings of the annual meeting of the North American Society for the Psychology of Sport and Physical Activity*, Asilomar, CA.

Howley, E.T., & Franks, B.D. (2003). *Health fitness instructor's handbook (4th ed.)*. Champaign, IL: Human Kinetics.

Hoyt, D.F., & Taylor, C.R. (1981). Gait and the energetics of locomotion in horses. *Science, 292*, 239–240.

Hubbard, A.W., & Seng, C.N. (1954). Visual movements of batters. *Research Quarterly, 25*, 42–57.

Hyman, R. (1953). Stimulus information as a determinant of reaction time. *Journal of Experimental Psychology, 45*, 188–196.

Illinois mason wins third annual SPEC MIX Bricklayer 500 (2005, January/February). *Trowel Tales, 14*, 1–2.

Ivry, R., & Hazeltine, R.E. (1995). Perception and production of temporal intervals across a range of durations: Evidence for a common timing mechanism. *Journal of Experimental Psychology: Human Perception and Performance, 21*, 3–18.

Jacobson, E. (1930). Electrical measurement of neuromuscular states during mental activities. *American Journal of Physiology,* 94, 22–34.

Jacoby, L.L., Bjork, R.A., & Kelley, C.M. (1994). Illusions of comprehensions and competence. In D. Druckman & R.A. Bjork (Eds.), *Learning, remembering, believing: Enhancing human performance* (pp. 57–80). Washington, DC: National Academy Press.

Jagacinski, R.J., Greenberg, N., & Liao, M-J. (1997). Tempo, rhythm, and aging in golf. *Journal of Motor Behavior,* 29, 159–173.

Jagacinski, R.J., Repperger, D.W., Moran, M.S., Ward, S.L., & Glass, B. (1980). Fitts' Law and the microstructure of rapid discrete movements. *Journal of Experimental Psychology: Human Perception and Performance,* 6, 309–320.

James, W. (1890). *The principles of psychology* (Vol. 1). New York: Holt, Reinhart & Winston.

Janelle, C.M., Barba, D.A., Frehlich, S.G., Tennant, L.K., & Cauraugh, J.H. (1997). Maximizing performance feedback effectiveness through videotape replay and a self-controlled learning environment. *Research Quarterly for Exercise and Sport,* 68, 269–279.

Janelle, C.M., Hillman, C.H., Apparies, R.J., Murray, N.P., Meili, L., Fallon, E.A., & Hatfield, B.D. (2000). Expertise differences in cortical activation and gaze behavior during rifle shooting. *Journal of Sport and Exercise Psychology,* 22, 167–182.

Janelle, C.M., Singer, R.N., & Williams, A.M. (1999). External distraction and attentional narrowing: Visual search evidence. *Journal of Sport and Exercise Psychology,* 21, 70–91.

Johansson, R.S., & Westling, G. (1984). Roles of glabrous skin receptors and sensorimotor memory in automatic control of precision grip when lifting rougher or more slippery objects. *Experimental Brain Research,* 56, 560–564.

Johnson, H.W. (1961). Skill = speed 3 accuracy 3 form 3 adaptability. *Perceptual and Motor Skills,* 13, 163–170.

Jordan, T.C. (1972). Characteristics of visual and proprioceptive response times in the learning of a motor skill. *Journal of Experimental Psychology,* 24, 536–543.

Kahneman, D. (1973). *Attention and effort.* Englewood Cliffs, NJ: Prentice-Hall.

Kassin, S. (2004). *Psychology* (4th ed.). Upper Saddle River, NJ: Pearson Education, IncKato, T., & Fukuda, T. (2002). Visual search strategies of baseball batters: Eye movements during the preparatory phase of batting. *Perceptual and Motor Skills,* 94, 380–386.

Keele, S.W., & Hawkins, H.L. (1982). Explorations of individual differences relevant to high level skill. *Journal of Motor Behavior,* 14, 3–23.

Keele, S.W., & Ivry, R. (1987). Modular analysis of timing in motor skill. In G.H. Bower (Ed.), *The psychology of learning and motivation* (Vol. 21, pp. 183–228). San Diego: Academic Press.

Keele, S.W., Ivry, R.I., & Pokorny, R.A. (1987). Force control and its relation to timing. *Journal of Motor Behavior,* 19, 96–114.

Keele, S.W., Pokorny, R.A., Corcos, D.M., & Ivry, R. (1985). Do perception and motor production share common timing mechanisms: A correlational analysis. *Acta Psychologica,* 60, 173–191.

Keele, S.W., & Posner, M.I. (1968). Processing of visual feedback in rapid movements. *Journal of Experimental Psychology,* 77, 155–158.

Keetch, K.M., Schmidt, R.A., Lee, T.D., & Young, D.E. (2005). Especial skills: Their emergence with massive amounts of practice. *Journal of Experimental Psychology: Human Perception and Performance,* 31, 970–978.

Kelso, J.A.S. (Ed.) (1995). *Dynamic patterns: The self-organization of brain and behavior.* Cambridge, MA: MIT Press.

Kelso, J.A.S., & Schöner, G. (1988). Self-organization of coordinative movement patterns. *Human Movement Science,* 7, 27–46.

Kelso, J.A.S., Tuller, B., Vatikoitis-Bateson, E., & Fowler, C.A. (1984). Functionally specific articulatory cooperation following jaw perturbations during speech: Evidence for coordinative structures. *Journal of Experimental Psychology: Human Perception and Performance,* 10, 812–832.

Kernodle, M.W., & Carlton, L.G. (1992). Information feedback and the learning of multiple-degree-of-freedom activities. *Journal of Motor Behavior,* 24, 187–196.

Kerr, R., & Booth, B. (1978). Specific and varied practice of motor skill. *Perceptual and Motor Skills,* 46, 395–401.

Klapp, S.T., Hill, M.D., Tyler, J.G., Martin, Z.E., Jagacinski, R.J., & Jones, M.R. (1985). On marching to two different drummers: Perceptual aspects of the difficulties. *Journal of Experimental Psychology: Human Perception and Performance,* 11, 814–827.

Knudson, D.V., & Morrison, C.S. (1997). *Qualitative analysis of human movement.* Champaign, IL: Human Kinetics.

Knudson, D.V., & Morrison, C.S. (2002). *Qualitative analysis of human movement.* Champaign, IL: Human Kinetics.

Konttinen, N., Mononen, K., Viitasalo, J., & Mets, T. (2004). The effects of augmented auditory feedback on psychomotor skill learning in precision shooting. *Journal of Sport and Exercise Psychology,* 26, 306–316.

Konzem, P.B. (1987). *Extended practice and patterns of bimanual interference.* Unpublished doctoral dissertation, University of Southern California, Los Angeles.

Kottke, F.J., Halpern, D., Easton, J.K., Ozel, A.T., & Burrill, B.S. (1978). The training of coordination. *Archives of Physical Medicine and Rehabilitation Medicine,* 59, 567–572.

Lambert, S.M., Moore, D.W., & Dixon, R.S. (1999). Gymnasts in training: The differential effects of self- and coach-set goals as a function of locus of control. *Journal of Applied Sport Psychology,* 11, 72–82.

Landauer, T.K., & Bjork, R.A. (1978). Optimum rehearsal patterns and name learning. In M.M. Gruenberg, P.E. Morris, & R.N. Sykes (Eds.), *Practical aspects of memory* (pp. 625–632). London: Academic Press.

Landers, D.M., & Arent, S.M. (2006). Arousal-performance relationships. In J.M. Williams (Ed.), *Applied sport psychology: Personal growth to peak performance* (pp. 260–284). New York: McGraw-Hill.

Landers, D.M., Boutcher, S.H., & Wang, M.Q. (1986). A psychobiological study of archery performance. *Research Quarterly for Exercise and Sport,* 57, 236–244.

Landers, D.M., Han, M.W., Salazar, W., Petruzello, S.J., Kubitz, K.A., & Gannon, T.L. (1995). Effect of learning on electroencephalographic and electrocardiographic patterns in novice archers. *International Journal of Sport Psychology,* 25, 313–320.

Landin, D. (1994). The role of verbal cues in skill learning. *Quest,* 46, 299–313.

Landin, D., & Hebert, E.P. (1997). A comparison of three practice schedules along the contextual interference continuum. *Research Quarterly for Exercise and Sport,* 68, 357–361.

Lavery, J.J. (1962). Retention of simple motor skills as a function of type of knowledge of results. *Canadian Journal of Psychology,* 16, 300–311.

Lavery, J.J., & Suddon, F.H. (1962). Retention of simple motor skills as a function of the number of trials by which KR is delayed. *Perceptual and Motor Skills,* 15, 231–237.

Leavitt, J.L. (1979). Cognitive demands of skating and stickhandling in ice hockey. *Canadian Journal of Applied Sport Sciences,* 4, 46–55.

Lee, D.N. (1980). Visuo-motor coordination in space-time. In G.E. Stelmach & J. Requin (Eds.), *Tutorials in motor behavior* (pp. 281–285). Amsterdam: North-Holland.

Lee, D.N., and Aronson, E. (1974). Visual proprioceptive control of standing in human infants. *Perception and Psychophysics,* 15: 529–532.

Lee, D.N., & Young, D.S. (1985). Visual timing of interceptive action. In D. Ingle, M. Jeannerod, & D.N. Lee (Eds.), *Brain mechanisms and spatial vision* (pp. 1–30). Dordrecht, Netherlands: Martinus Nijhoff.

Lee, D.N., Young, D.S., & Rewt, D. (1992). How do somersaulters land on their feet? *Journal of Experimental Psychology: Human Perception and Performance,* 18, 1195–1202.

Lee, T.D. (1998). On the dynamics of motor learning research. *Research Quarterly for Exercise and Sport,* 69, 334–337.

Lee, T.D., & Genovese, E.D. (1988). Distribution of practice in motor skill acquisition: Learning and performance effects reconsidered. *Research Quarterly for Exercise and Sport,* 59, 277–287.

Lee, T.D., & Magill, R.A. (1983). The locus of contextual interference in motor-skill acquisition. *Journal of Experimental Psychology: Learning, Memory, and Cognition,* 9, 730–746.

Lee, T.D., & Magill, R.A. (1985). Can forgetting facilitate skill acquisition? In D. Goodman, R.B. Wilberg, & I.M. Franks (Eds.), *Differing perspectives in motor learning, memory and control* (pp. 3–22). Amsterdam: North-Holland.

Lee, T.D., Magill, R.A., & Weeks, D.J. (1985). Influence of practice schedule on testing schema theory predictions in adults. *Journal of Motor Behavior,* 17, 283–299.

Lee, T.D., & Wishart, L.R. (2005). Motor learning conundrums (and possible solutions). *Quest,* 57, 67–78.

Lee, T.D., Wulf, G., & Schmidt, R.A. (1992). Contextual interference in motor learning: Dissociated effects due to the nature of task variations. *Quarterly Journal of Experimental Psychology,* 44A, 627–644.

Lee, W.A. (1980). Anticipatory control of postural and task muscles during rapid arm flexion. *Journal of Motor Behavior,* 12, 185–196.

Lersten, K.C. (1968). Transfer of movement components in a motor learning task. *Research Quarterly,* 39, 575–581.

Lidor, R., & Mayan, Z. (2005). Can beginning learners benefit from preperformance routines when serving in volleyball? *The Sport Psychologist,* 19, 343–363.

Linden, C.A., Uhley, J.E., Smith, D., & Bush, M.A. (1989). The effects of mental practice on walking balance in an elderly population. *Occupational Therapy Journal of Research,* 9, 155–169.

Liu, J., & Wrisberg, C.A. (1997). The effect of knowledge of results delay and the subjective estimation of movement form on the acquisition and retention of a motor skill. *Research Quarterly for Exercise and Sport,* 68, 145–151.

Liu, Y-T., Mayer-Kress, G., & Newell, K.M. (2004). Beyond curve fitting to inferences about learning. *Journal of Motor Behavior,* 36, 233–238.

Locke, E.A., & Latham, G.P. (1985). The application of goal setting to sports. *Sport Psychology Today,* 7, 205–222.

Lotter, W.S. (1960). Interrelationships among reaction times and speeds of movement in different limbs. *Research Quarterly,* 31, 147–155.

MacKay, D.G. (1981). The problem of rehearsal or mental practice. *Journal of Motor Behavior,* 13, 274–285.

Magill, R.A. (1998a). *Motor learning: Concepts and applications* (5th ed.). Dubuque, IA: Brown.

Magill, R.A. (1998b). Knowledge is more than we can talk about: Implicit learning in motor skill acquisition. *Research Quarterly for Exercise and Sport,* 69, 104–110.

Magill, R.A., & Hall, K.G. (1990). A review of the contextual interference effect in motor skill acquisition. *Human Movement Science,* 9, 241–289.

Magill, R.A., & Wood, C.A. (1986). Knowledge of results precision as a learning variable in motor skill acquisition. *Research Quarterly for Exercise and Sport,* 57, 170–173.

Martell, S. G., & Vickers, J. N. (2004). Gaze characteristics of elite and near-elite athletes in ice hockey defensive tactics. *Human Movement Science* 22: 689–712.

Maxwell, J.P., Masters, R.S.W., Kerr, E., & Weedon, E. (2001). The implicit benefit of learning without errors. *Quarterly Journal of Experimental Psychology: Human Experimental Psychology,* 54A, 1049–1068.

McBride, E., & Rothstein, A. (1979). Mental and physical practice and the learning and retention of open and closed skills. *Perceptual and Motor Skills,* 49, 359–365.

McClements, J. (1982). Goal setting and planning for mental preparations. In L. Wankel & R.B. Wilberg (Eds.), Psychology of sport and motor behavior: Research and practice. *Proceedings of the Annual Conference of the Canadian Society for Psychomotor Learning and Sport Psychology* (pp. 16 5–172). Edmonton: University of Alberta.

McCloy, C.H. (1934). The measurement of general motor capacity and general motor ability. *Research Quarterly,* 5(Suppl. 5), 45–61.

McCullagh, P. (1986). Model status as a determinant of attention in observational learning and performance. *Journal of Sport Psychology,* 8, 319–331.

McCullagh, P. (1987). Model similarity effects on motor performance. *Journal of Sport Psychology,* 9, 249–260.

McDavid, R.F. (1977). Predicting potential in football players. *Research Quarterly,* 48, 98–104.

McLeod, P., McLaughlin, C., & Nimmo-Smith, I. (1985). Information encapsulation and automaticity: Evidence from the visual control of finely tuned actions. In M.I. Posner & O.S.M. Marin (Eds.), *Attention and performance XI* (pp. 391–406). Hillsdale, NJ: Erlbaum.

McLeod, P., & Dienes, Z. (1996). Do fielders know where to go to catch the ball or only how to get there? *Journal of Experimental Psychology: Human Perception and Performance,* 22, 531–543.

McMahon, T.A. (1984). *Muscles, reflexes, and locomotion.* Princeton, NJ: Princeton University Press.

McPherson, S.L. (1999). Tactical differences in problem representations and solutions to collegiate varsity and beginning female tennis players. *Research Quarterly for Exercise and Sport*, 70, 369–384.

Memory study. (1997, October 29). Knoxville (TN) *News Sentinel*, p. A8.

Merkel, J. (1885). Die zeitlichen Verhaltnisse der Willen-statigkeit. *Philosophische Studien*, 2, 73–127. (Cited in Woodworth, 1938)

Merton, P.A. (1972). How we control the contraction of our muscles. *Scientific American*, 226, 30–37.

Meyer, D.E., Abrams, R.A., Kornblum, S., Wright, C.E., & Smith, J.E.K. (1988). Optimality in human motor performance: Ideal control of rapid aimed movements. *Psychological Review*, 95, 340–370.

Miller, G.A. (1956). The magical number seven, plus or minus two: Some limits on our capacity for processing information. *Psychological Review*, 63, 81–97.

Miller, J.O., & Franz, E.A. (2005). Dissociation of bimanual responses with the Simon Effect: On the nonunitization of bimanual responses. *Journal of Motor Behavior*, 37, 146–156.Miller, L., Stanney, K., Guckenberger, D., & Guckenberger, E., (1997, July). Above real-time training. *Ergonomics in Design*, 21–24.

Milner, B., Corkin, S., & Teuber, H.L. (1968). Further analysis of the hippocampal amnesic syndrome: 14-year follow-up study of H.M. *Neuropsychologia*, 6, 215–234.

Moen, S. (1989, June). Visual skills: Watch the ball? *Strategies*, 2(10), 20–22.

Moore, S.P., & Marteniuk, R.G. (1986). Kinematic and electromyographic changes that occur as a function of learning a time-constrained aiming task. *Journal of Motor Behavior*, 18, 397–426.

Morgan, W.P. (1979). Prediction of performance in athletics. In P. Klavora & J.V. Daniel (Eds.), *Coach, athlete, and the sport psychologist* (pp. 173–186). Toronto: University of Toronto.

Nashner, L., & Berthoz, A. (1978). Visual contribution to rapid motor responses during postural control. *Brain Research*, 150, 403–407.

Neumann, O. (1987). Beyond capacity: A functional view of attention. In H. Heuer & A.F. Sanders (Eds.), *Perspectives on perception and action* (pp. 361–394). Hillsdale, NJ: Erlbaum.

Newell, K.M. (1985). Coordination, control, and skill. In D. Goodman, R.B. Wilberg, & I.M. Franks (Eds.), *Differing perspectives in motor learning, memory, and control* (pp. 295–317). Amsterdam: North-Holland.

Newell, K.M. (2003). Schema theory (1975): Retrospectives and prospectives. *Research Quarterly for Exercise and Sport*, 74, 383–388.

Newell, K.M., Carlton, L.G., & Antoniou, A. (1990). The interaction of criterion and feedback information in learning a drawing task. *Journal of Motor Behavior*, 22, 536–552.

Newell, K.M., Carlton, L.G., Carlton, M.J., & Halbert, J.A. (1980). Velocity as a factor in movement timing accuracy. *Journal of Motor Behavior*, 12, 47–56.

Newell, K.M., & McGinnis, P.M. (1985). Kinematic information feedback for skilled performance. *Human Learning*, 4, 39–56.

Nicholls, J.G. (1989). *The competitive ethos and democratic education*. Cambridge, MA: Harvard University Press.

Nideffer, R.M. (1995). *Focus for success*. San Diego: Enhanced Performance Services.

Nordin, S.M., & Cumming, J. (2005). More than meets the eye: Investigating imagery type, direction, and outcome. *The Sport Psychologist*, 19, 1–17.

Nordin, S.M., Cumming, J., Vincent, J., & McGrory, S. (2006). Mental practice or spontaneous play? Examining which types of imagery constitute deliberate practice in sport. *Journal of Applied Sport Psychology*, 18, 345–362.

Nourrit, D., Delignières, D., Caillou, N., Deschamps, T., & Lauriot, B. (2003). On discontinuities in motor learning: A longitudinal study of complex skill acquisition on a ski simulator. *Journal of Motor Behavior*, 35, 151–170.

Oudejans, R.R.D., Koedijker, J.M., Bleijendaal, I., & Bakker, F.C. (2005). The education of attention in aiming at a far target: Training visual control in basketball jump shooting. *International Journal of Sport and Exercise Psychology*, 3, 197–221.

Orlick, T. (1986). *Psyching for sport: Mental training for athletes*. Champaign, IL: Leisure Press.

Orlick, T. (2000). *In pursuit of excellence* (3rd ed.). Champaign, IL: Leisure Press.

Orlick, T., & Partington, J. (1986). *Psyched: Inner views of winning.* Ottawa, Ontario: Coaching Association of Canada.

Otsuji, T., Abe, M., & Kinoshita, H. (2002). After-effects of using a weighted bat on subsequent swing velocity and batters' perceptions of swing velocity and heaviness. *Perceptual and Motor Skills, 94,* 119–126.

Overduin, S.A., Richardson, A.G., Lane, C.E., Bizzi, E., & Press, D.Z. (2006). Intermittent practice facilitates stable motor memories. *The Journal of Neuroscience,* 26(46), 11888–11892.

Panchuk, D. & Vickers, J.N. (2006). Gaze behaviours of goaltenders under spatial-temporal constraints. *Human Movement Science.* In press.

Parson, M.L. (1998, January–February). Focus student attention with verbal cues. *Strategies,* 11(3), 30–33.

Pashler, H. (1993, January–February). Doing two things at the same time. *American Scientist,* 81(1), 48–49.

Pashler, H. (1994). Dual-task interference in simple tasks: Data and theory. *Psychological Bulletin,* 116, 220–244.

Pew, R.W. (1974). Levels of analysis in motor control. *Brain Research,* 71, 393–400.

Pigott, R.E., & Shapiro, D.C. (1984). Motor schema: The structure of the variability session. *Research Quarterly for Exercise and Sport,* 55, 41–45.

Polanyi, M. (1958). *Personal knowledge: Towards a post-critical philosophy.* London: Routledge & Kegan Paul.

Polit, A., & Bizzi, E. (1978). Processes controlling arm movements in monkeys. *Science,* 201, 1235–1237.

Polit, A., & Bizzi, E. (1979). Characteristics of motor programs underlying arm movements in monkeys. *Journal of Neurophysiology,* 42, 183–194.

Poon, P.P.L., & Rodgers, W.M. (2000). Learning and remembering strategies of novice and advanced jazz dancers for skill level appropriate routines. *Research Quarterly for Exercise and Sport,* 71, 135–144.

Posner, M.I., & Keele, S.W. (1968). Attentional demands of movement. *Proceedings of the 16th congress of applied psychology.* Amsterdam: Swets and Zeitlinger.

Prezuhy, A.M., & Etnier, J.L. (2001). Attentional patterns of horseshoe pitchers at two levels of task difficulty. *Research Quarterly for Exercise and Sport,* 72, 293–298.

Prinz, W. (1997). Perception and action planning. *European Journal of Cognitive Psychology,* 9, 129–154.

Pronk, N., & Gorman, B. (1991). *Soccer everyone.* Winston-Salem, NC: Hunter Textbooks, Inc.

Quesada, D.C., & Schmidt, R.A. (1970). A test of the Adams-Creamer decay hypothesis for the timing of motor responses. *Journal of Motor Behavior,* 2, 273–283.

Raab, M. & Haug, U. (2000). Effectiveness of distal and proximal instructions with the spike in volleyball. In P. Kuhn & K. Langolf (Eds.), *Vision in volleyball 2000* (pp. 99–110). Hamburg: Czwalina.

Radlo, S.J., Janelle, C.M., Barba, D.A., & Frehlich, S.G. (2001). Perceptual decision making for baseball pitch recognition: Using P300 latency and amplitude to index attentional processing. *Research Quarterly for Exercise and Sport,* 72, 22–31.

Radwin, R.G., Vanderheiden, G.C., & Lin, M.L. (1990). A method for evaluating head-controlled computer input devices using Fitts' law. *Human Factors,* 32, 423–438.

Raibert, M.H. (1977). *Motor control and learning by the state-space model* (Tech. Rep. No. AI-TR-439). Cambridge: Massachusetts Institute of Technology, Artificial Intelligence Laboratory.

Rees, R. (1995). *The manual of soccer coaching (*2nd *ed.).* Collingswood, NJ: Port City Press.

Roberton, M.A. (1982). Changing motor patterns during childhood. In J.R. Thomas (Ed.), *Motor development during childhood and adolescence* (pp. 48–90). Minneapolis: Burgess.

Robertson, S., Lantero, D., & Zelaznik, H. (1997). Individual differences in timing ability. *Journal of Sport and Exercise Psychology,* 19 (Supplement), S99.

Robertson, S.D., Zelaznik, H.N., Lantero, D.A., Gadacz, K.E., Spencer, R.M., Doffin, J.G., & Schneidt, T. (1999). Correlations for timing consistency among tapping and drawing tasks: Evidence against a single timing process for motor control. *Journal of Experimental Psychology: Human Perception and Performance,* 25, 1316–1330.

Rodionov, A.V. (1978). *Psikhologiia Sportivnoi Deiatel'nosti* [The psychology of sport activity]. Moscow.

Roediger, H.L., & Karpicke, J.D. (2006) The power of testing memory. Basic research and implications for educational practice. *Perspectives on Psychological Science,* 1, 181–210.

Rosenbaum, D.A. (1980). Human movement initiation: Specification of arm, direction, and extent. *Journal of Experimental Psychology: General,* 109, 444–474.

Rosenbaum, D.A. (1989). *On the selection of physical actions. Five College Cognitive Science Papers,* #89–4.

Rothstein, A.L., & Arnold, R.K. (1976). Bridging the gap: Application of research on videotape feedback and bowling. *Motor Skills: Theory Into Practice,* 1, 35–62.

Rotter, J.B. (1954). *Social learning and clinical psychology.* Englewood Cliffs: Prentice Hall.

Rushall, B.S. (1967). *An evaluation of the effect of various reinforcers used as motivators in swimming.* Unpublished manuscript, Indiana University, Bloomington.

Sackett, R.S. (1934). The influences of symbolic rehearsal upon the retention of a maze task. *Journal of General Psychology,* 10, 376–395.

Sacks, O. (1985). *The man who mistook his wife for a hat and other clinical tales.* New York: Harper and Row.

Schmidt, R.A. (1969). Movement time as a determiner of timing accuracy. *Journal of Experimental Psychology,* 79, 43–47.

Schmidt, R.A. (1975). A schema theory of discrete motor skill learning. *Psychological Review,* 82, 225–260.

Schmidt, R.A. (1985). The search for invariance in skilled movement behavior. *Research Quarterly for Exercise and Sport,* 56, 188–200.

Schmidt, R.A. (1988). Motor and action perspective on motor behavior. In O.G. Meijer & K. Roth (Eds.), *Complex movement behaviour: "The" motor-action controversy* (pp. 3–44). Amsterdam: North-Holland.

Schmidt, R.A. (2003). Motor schema theory after 27 years: Reflections and implications for a new theory. *Research Quarterly for Exercise and Sport,* 74, 366–375.

Schmidt, R.A., & Bjork, R.A. (1992). New conceptualizations of practice: Common principles in three paradigms suggest new concepts for training. *Psychological Science,* 3, 207–217.

Schmidt, R.A., & Gordon, E.B. (1977). Errors in motor responding, "rapid" corrections, and false anticipations. *Journal of Motor Behavior,* 9, 101–111.

Schmidt, R.A., & White, J.L. (1972). Evidence for an error detection mechanism in motor skills: A test of Adams' closed-loop theory. *Journal of Motor Behavior,* 4, 143–154.

Schmidt, R.A., Heuer, H., Ghodsian, D., & Young, D.E. (1998). Generalized motor programs and units of action in bimanual coordination. In M. Latash (Ed.), *Bernstein's traditions in motor control* (pp. 329–360). Champaign, IL: Human Kinetics.

Schmidt, R.A., Lange, C.A., & Young, D.E. (1990). Optimizing summary knowledge of results for skill learning. *Human Movement Science,* 9, 325–348.

Schmidt, R.A., & Lee, T.D. (1998). *Motor control and learning: A behavioral emphasis* (3rd Ed.). Champaign, IL: Human Kinetics.

Schmidt, R.A., & Pew, R.W. (1974). *Predicting motor-manipulative performances in the manufacture of dental appliances* (Tech. Rep. to Heritage Laboratories, Romulus, Michigan). Ann Arbor: University of Michigan.

Schmidt, R.A., & Sherwood, D.E. (1982). An inverted-U relation between spatial error and force requirements in rapid limb movements: Further evidence for the impulse-variability model. *Journal of Experimental Psychology: Human Perception and Performance,* 8, 158–170.

Schmidt, R.A., & Wulf, G. (1997). Continuous concurrent feedback degrades skill learning: Implications for training and simulation. *Human Factors,* 39, 509–525.

Schmidt, R.A., & Young, D.E. (1987). Transfer of motor control in motor skill learning. In S.M. Cormier & J.D. Hagman (Eds.), *Transfer of learning* (pp. 47–79). Orlando, FL: Academic Press.

Schmidt, R.A., Young, D.E., Swinnen, S., & Shapiro, D.C. (1989). Summary knowledge of results for skill acquisition: Support for the guidance hypothesis. *Journal of Experimental Psychology: Learning, Memory, and Cognition,* 15, 352–359.

Schmidt, R.A., Zelaznik, H.N., Hawkins, B., Frank, J.S., & Quinn, J.T. (1979). Motor-output variability: A theory for the accuracy of rapid motor acts. *Psychological Review,* 86, 415–451.

Schoenfelder-Zohdi, B.G. (1992). *Investigating the informational nature of a modeled visual demonstration.* Unpublished doctoral dissertation, Louisiana State University, Baton Rouge.

Scripture, C.W. (1905). *The new psychology.* New York: Scott.

Seat, J.E., & Wrisberg, C.A. (1996). The visual instruction system. *Research Quarterly for Exercise and Sport,* 67, 106–108.

Shapiro, D.C., Zernicke, R.F., Gregor, R.J., & Diestel, J.D. (1981). Evidence for generalized motor programs using gait-pattern analysis. *Journal of Motor Behavior,* 13, 33–47.

Shea, C.H., Kohl, R., & Indermill, C. (1990). Contextual interference: Contributions of practice. *Acta Psychologica,* 73, 145–157.

Shea, C.H., Wright, D.L., Wulf, G., & Whitacre, C. (2000). Physical and observational practice afford unique learning opportunities. *Journal of Motor Behavior,* 32, 27–36.

Shea, C.H., & Wulf, G. (2005). Schema theory: A critical appraisal and reevaluation. *Journal of Motor Behavior,* 37, 85–101.

Shea, C.H., Wulf, G., Park, J., & Gaunt, B. (2001). Effects of an auditory model on the learning of relative and absolute timing. *Journal of Motor Behavior,* 33, 127–138.

Shea, C.H., Wulf, G., Whitacre, C.A., & Park, J.H. (2001). Surfing the implicit wave. *Quarterly Journal of Experimental Psychology: Human Experimental Psychology,* 54A, 841–862.

Shea, J.B., & Morgan, R.L. (1979). Contextual interference effects on the acquisition, retention, and transfer of a motor skill. *Journal of Experimental Psychology: Human Learning and Memory,* 5, 179–187.

Shea, J.B., & Zimny, S.T. (1983). Context effects in memory and learning movement information. In R.A. Magill (Ed.), *Memory and control of action* (pp. 345–366). Amsterdam: North-Holland.

Sherrington, C.S. (1906). *The integrative action of the nervous system.* New Haven, CT: Yale University Press.

Sherwood, D.E. (1988). Effect of bandwidth knowledge of results on movement consistency. *Perceptual and Motor Skills,* 66, 535–542.

Sherwood, D.E., & Lee, T.D. (2003). Schema theory: Critical review and implications for the role of cognition in a new theory of motor learning. *Research Quarterly for Exercise and Sport,* 74, 376–382.

Sherwood, D.E., Schmidt, R.A., & Walter, C.B. (1988). The force/force-variability relationship under controlled temporal conditions. *Journal of Motor Behavior,* 20, 106–116.

Shiffrin, R.M., & Schneider, W. (1977). Controlled and automatic human information processing: II. Perceptual learning, automatic attending, and a general theory. *Psychological Review,* 84, 127–190.

Shim, J., Carlton, L.G., & Kwon, Y-H. (2006). Perception of kinematic characteristics of tennis strokes for anticipating stroke type and direction. *Research Quarterly for Exercise and Sport,* 77, 326–339.

Simon, D.A., & Bjork, R.A. (2001). Metacognition in motor learning. *Journal of Experimental Psychology: Learning, Memory, and Cognition,* 27, 907–912.

Singer, R.N., Lidor, R., & Cauraugh, J.H. (1993). To be aware or not aware? What to think about while learning and performing a motor skill. *The Sport Psychologist,* 7, 19–30.

Slater-Hammel, A.T. (1960). Reliability, accuracy, and refractoriness of a transit reaction. *Research Quarterly,* 31, 217–228.

Smith, R.E. (2006). Positive reinforcement, performance feedback, and performance enhancement. In J.M. Williams (Ed.), *Applied sport psychology: Personal growth to peak performance* (5th ed., pp. 40–56). Dubuque, IA: McGraw-Hill.

Smith, D., & Collins, D. (2004). Mental practice, motor performance, and the late CNV. *Journal of Sport and Exercise Psychology,* 26, 412–426.

Smith, P.J.K., Taylor, S.J., & Withers, K. (1997). Applying bandwidth feedback scheduling to a golf shot. *Research Quarterly for Exercise and Sport,* 68, 215–221.

Southard, D. (1989). Changes in limb striking pattern: Effects of speed and accuracy. *Research Quarterly for Exercise and Sport,* 60, 348–356.

Southard, D. (2006). Changing throwing pattern: Instruction and control parameter. *Research Quarterly for Exercise and Sport, 77*, 316–325.

Southard, D., & Groomer, L. (2003). Warm-up with baseball bats of varying moments of inertia: Effect on bat velocity and swing pattern. *Research Quarterly for Exercise and Sport, 74*, 270–276.

Southard, D., & Higgins, T. (1987). Changing movement patterns: Effects of demonstration and practice. *Research Quarterly for Exercise and Sport, 58*, 77–80.

Sparrow, W.A., & Irizarry-Lopez, V.M. (1987). Mechanical efficiency and metabolic cost as measures of learning a novel gross motor task. *Journal of Motor Behavior, 19*, 240–264.

Spencer, R.M.C., & Zelaznik, H. (2003). Weber (slope) analyses of timing variability in tapping and drawing tasks. *Journal of Motor Behavior, 35*, 371–381.

Spencer, R.M.C., Zelaznik, H.N., Diedrichsen, J., & Ivry, R.B. (2003). Disrupted timing of discontinuous but not continuous movements by cerebellar lesions. *Science, 300*, 1437–1439.

Ste-Marie, D.M., Clark, S.E., Findlay, L.C., & Latimer, A.E. (2004). High levels of contextual interference enhance handwriting skill acquisition. *Journal of Motor Behavior, 36*, 115–126.

Steenbergen, B., Marteniuk, R.G., & Kalbfleisch, L.E. (1995). Achieving coordination in prehension: Joint freezing and postural contributions. *Journal of Motor Behavior, 27*, 333–348.

Sternad, D. (1998). A dynamic systems perspective to perception and action. *Research Quarterly for Exercise and Sport, 69*, 319–325.

Stroop, J.R. (1935). Studies of interference in serial verbal reactions. *Journal of Experimental Psychology, 18*, 643–662.

Summers, J.J. (1975). The role of timing in motor program representation. *Journal of Motor Behavior, 7*, 229–241.

Summers, J.J., Rosenbaum, D.A., Burns, B.D., & Ford, S.K. (1993). Production of polyrhythms. *Journal of Experimental Psychology: Human Perception and Performance, 19*, 416–428.

Swinnen, S., Schmidt, R.A., Nicholson, D.E., & Shapiro, D.C. (1990). Information feedback for skill acquisition: Instantaneous knowledge of results degrades learning. *Journal of Experimental Psychology: Learning, Memory, and Cognition, 16*, 706–716.

Takeuchi, T. (1993). Auditory information in playing tennis. *Perceptual and Motor Skills, 76*, 1323–1328.

Taub, E. (1976). Movements in nonhuman primates deprived of somatosensory feedback. *Exercise and Sport Sciences Reviews, 4*, 335–374.

Taub, E., & Berman, A.J. (1968). Movement and learning in the absence of sensory feedback. In S.J. Freedman (Ed.), *The neuropsychology of spatially oriented behavior* (pp. 173–192). Homewood, IL: Dorsey Press.

Thorndike, E.L. (1914). *Educational psychology: Briefer course.* New York: Columbia University Press.

Thorndike, E.L. (1927). The law of effect. *American Journal of Psychology, 39*, 212–222.

Trevarthen, C.B. (1968). Two mechanisms of vision in primates. *Psychologische Forschung, 31*, 299–337.

Trowbridge, M.H., & Cason, H. (1932). An experimental study of Thorndike's theory of learning. *Journal of General Psychology, 7*, 245–260.

Tsutsui, S., Lee, T.D., & Hodges, N.J. (1998). Contextual interference in learning new patterns of bimanual coordination. *Journal of Motor Behavior, 30*, 151–157.

Tubbs, M.E. (1986). Goal setting: A meta-analysis examination of the empirical evidence. *Journal of Applied Psychology, 71*, 474–483.

Ulrich, B.D., Ulrich, D.A., Coffer, D.H., & Cole, E.L. (1995). Developmental shifts in the ability of infants with Down syndrome to produce treadmill steps. *Physical Therapy, 75*, 14–23.

Vealey, R.S., & Greenleaf, C.A. (2006). Seeing is believing: Understanding and using imagery in sport. In J.M. Williams (Ed.), *Applied sport psychology: Personal growth to peak performance* (pp. 306–348). New York: McGraw-Hill.

Vickers, J.N. (1992). Gaze control in putting. *Perception, 21*, 117–132.

Vickers, J.N. (1996). Visual control when aiming at a far target. *Journal of Experimental Psychology: Human Perception and Performance, 22*, 342–354.

Vickers, J.N. (1997). Control of visual attention during the basketball free throw. *American Journal of Sports Medicine, 24*, 93–97.

Wadman, W.J., Denier van der Gon, J.J., Geuze, R.H., & Mol, C.R. (1979). Control of fast goal-directed arm movements. *Journal of Human Movement Studies, 5*, 3–17.

Walter, C.B. (1998). An alternative view of dynamical systems concepts in motor control and learning. *Research Quarterly for Exercise and Sport, 69*, 326–333.

Ward, P., & Williams, M. (2003). Perceptual and cognitive skill development in soccer: The multidimensional nature of expert performance. *Journal of Sport and Exercise Psychology, 25*, 93–111.

Ward, P., Williams, A.M., & Bennett, S.J. (2002). Visual search and biological motion perception in tennis. *Research Quarterly for Exercise and Sport, 73*, 107–112.

Warner, L., & McNeill, M.E. (1988). Mental imagery and its potential for physical therapy. *Physical Therapy, 68*, 516–521.

Weeks, D.L., Hall, A.K., & Anderson, L.P. (1996). A comparison of imitation strategies in observational learning of action patterns. *Journal of Motor Behavior, 28*, 348–358.

Weeks, D.L., & Kordus, R.W. (1998). Relative frequency of knowledge of performance and motor skill learning. *Research Quarterly for Exercise and Sport, 69*, 224–230.

Wegner, D.M. (2002). *The illusion of conscious will*. Cambridge, MA: The MIT Press.

Weinberg, R.S., & Hunt, V.V. (1976). The interrelationships between anxiety, motor performance, and electromyography. *Journal of Motor Behavior, 8*, 219–224.

Weiss, P., Stelmach, G.E., & Hefter, H. (1997). Programming of a movement sequence in Parkinson's disease. *Brain, 120*, 91–102.

Weltman, G., & Egstrom, G.H. (1966). Perceptual narrowing in novice divers. *Human Factors, 8*, 499–505.

Wenderoth, N., Puttemans, V., Vangheluwe, S., & Swinnen, S. (2003). Bimanual training reduces spatial interference. *Journal of Motor Behavior, 35*, 296–308.

Whiting, H.T.A., & Vereijken, B. (1993). The acquisition of coordination in skill learning. *International Journal of Sport Psychology, 24*, 343–357.

Wieder, M.A., Smith, C., & Brackage, C. (1996). *Essentials of fire fighting* (3rd ed.). Stillwater, OK: Fire Protection Publications.

Wiener, N. (1948). *Cybernetics: or control and communication in the animal and the machine*. New York: Wiley.

Wightman, D.C., & Lintern, G. (1985). Part-task training strategies for tracking and manual control. *Human Factors, 27*, 267–283.

Wilkerson, J.D. (1988, January). Volleyball: Optimal striking force in volleyball spiking. *Strategies, 1*(5), 9–10.

Williams, A.M., & Davids, K. (1998). Visual search strategy, selective attention, and expertise in soccer. *Research Quarterly for Exercise and Sport, 69*, 111–128.

Williams, A.M., Davids, K., Burwitz, L., & Williams, J.G. (1992). Perception and action in sport. *Journal of Human Movement Studies, 22*, 147–205.

Williams, A.M., Singer, R.N., & Frehlich, S.G. (2002). Quiet eye duration, expertise, and task complexity in near and far aiming tasks. *Journal of Motor Behavior, 34*, 197–207.

Williams, A.M., Ward, P., Smeeton, N.J., & Allen, D. (2004). Developing anticipation skills in tennis using on-court instruction: Perception vs. perception and action. *Journal of Applied Sport Psychology, 16*, 350–360.

Williams, H.G., Woollacott, M.H., & Ivry, R. (1992). Timing and motor control in clumsy children. *Journal of Motor Behavior, 24*, 165–172.

Williams, J.M., & Harris, D.V. (2006). Relaxation and energizing techniques for regulation of arousal. In J.M. Williams (Ed.), *Applied sport psychology: Personal growth to peak performance* (5th ed., pp. 285–305). Dubuque, IA: McGraw-Hill.

Williams, T., & Underwood, J. (1988). *My turn at bat*. New York: Fireside.

Winstein, C.J., & Schmidt, R.A. (1990). Reduced frequency of knowledge of results enhances motor skill learning. *Journal of Experimental Psychology: Learning, Memory, and Cognition, 16*, 677–691.

Woman is fitted with "bionic" arm. (2006, September 15). www.bbc.co.uk.

Woods, J.B. (1967). The effect of varied instructional emphasis upon the development of a motor skill. *Research Quarterly, 38*, 132–142.

Woodworth, R.S. (1899). The accuracy of voluntary movement. *Psychological Review,* 3 (Suppl. 2), 1–114.

Woodworth, R.S. (1938). *Experimental psychology.* New York: Holt.

Wrisberg, C.A. (1994). The arousal-performance relationship. *Quest,* 46, 60–77.

Wrisberg, C.A., & Liu, Z. (1991). The effect of contextual variety on the practice, retention, and transfer of an applied motor skill. *Research Quarterly for Exercise and Sport,* 62, 406–412.

Wrisberg, C.A., & Mead, B.J. (1983). Developing coincident-timing skill in children: A comparison of training methods. *Research Quarterly for Exercise and Sport,* 54, 67–74.

Wrisberg, C.A., & Pein, R.L. (2002). Note on learners' control of the frequency of model presentation during skill acquisition. *Perceptual and Motor Skills,* 94, 792–794.

Wulf, G. (2007). *Attention and motor skill learning.* Champaign, IL: Human Kinetics.

Wulf, G., Höß, M., & Prinz, W. (1998). Instructions for motor learning: Differential effects of internal versus external focus of attention. *Journal of Motor Behavior,* 30, 169–179.

Wulf, G., Lauterbach, B., & Toole, T. (1999). The learning advantages of an external focus of attention in golf. *Research Quarterly for Exercise and Sport,* 70, 120–126.

Wulf, G., McConnel, N., Gärtner, M., & Schwarz, A. (2002). Enhancing the learning of sport skills through external-focus feedback. *Journal of Motor Behavior,* 34, 171–182.

Wulf, G., McNevin, N.H., Fuchs, T., Ritter, F., & Toole, T. (2000). Attentional focus in complex skill learning. *Research Quarterly for Exercise and Sport,* 71, 229–239.

Wulf, G., Mercer, J., McNevin, N., & Guadagnoli, M. (2004). Reciprocal influences of attentional focus on postural and suprapostural task performance. *Journal of Motor Behavior,* 36, 189–199.

Wulf, G., & Schmidt, R.A. (1988). Variability in practice: Facilitation in retention and transfer through schema formation or context effects? *Journal of Motor Behavior,* 20, 133–149.

Wulf, G., & Schmidt, R.A. (1997). Variability of practice and implicit motor learning. *Journal of Experimental Psychology: Learning, Memory, and Cognition,* 23, 987–1006.

Wulf, G., Shea, C.H., & Matschiner, S. (1998). Frequent feedback enhances complex motor skill learning. *Journal of Motor Behavior,* 30, 180–192.

Wulf, G., Shea, C.H., & Whitacre, C. (1998). Physical guidance benefits in learning a complex motor skill. *Journal of Motor Behavior,* 30, 367–380.

Wulf, G., & Toole, T. (1999). Physical assistance devices in complex motor skill learning: Benefits of a self-controlled practice schedule. *Research Quarterly for Exercise and Sport,* 70, 265–272.

Wulf, G., & Weigelt, C. (1997). Instructions about physical principles in learning a complex motor skill: To tell or not to tell. *Research Quarterly for Exercise and Sport,* 68, 362–367.

Young, D.E., & Schmidt, R.A. (1992). Augmented kinematic feedback for motor learning. *Journal of Motor Behavior,* 24, 261–273.

Zebas, C.J., & Johnson, H.M. (1989, June). Transfer of learning: From the overhand throw to the tennis serve. *Strategies,* 2(10),17–27.

Index

Note: The italicized *f* and *t* following page numbers refer to figures and tables, respectively.

UNIVERSITY OF WINCHESTER
LIBRARY

About the Authors

Richard A. Schmidt, PhD, heads his own consulting firm, Human Performance Research, in Marina del Rey, California, where he researches issues in human performance, human factors, and ergonomics. He is also a professor emeritus of psychology at the University of California at Los Angeles. Known as one of the research leaders in motor behavior, Dr. Schmidt has 35 years of experience and has published widely in his field.

The originator of schema theory, Dr. Schmidt founded the *Journal of Motor Behavior* and was its editor for 11 years. He authored the first edition of *Motor Control and Learning* in 1982 and *Motor Learning and Performance* in 1991, and he has since followed up with new editions of both books.

Dr. Schmidt is a member of the North American Society for the Psychology of Sport and Physical Activity (NASPSPA), the Human Factors and Ergonomics Society, and the Psychonomic Society. He has received honorary doctorates from the Katholieke Universiteit Leuven in Belgium and Université Joseph Fourier in France for contributions to his research field. Dr. Schmidt has served as president of NASPSPA, and he received the C.H. McCloy Research Lectureship from the American Alliance for Health, Physical Education, Recreation and Dance.

Dr. Schmidt's leisure-time activities include sailboat racing, swimming, and automobile racing.

Craig A. Wrisberg, PhD, is a professor of sport psychology at the University of Tennessee at Knoxville, where he has taught since 1977. During the past 30 years Wrisberg has published more than 90 refereed research articles and book chapters on the topics of anticipation and timing in performance, knowledge of results and motor learning, and the role of cognitive strategies in sport performance. His book *Skill Instruction for Coaches* is one of the volumes included in the American Sport Education Program (ASEP) Silver Level sport science curriculum. He earned his PhD with a specialization in motor learning from the University of Michigan and has focused his teaching, research, mentoring, and consulting in the field of applied motor learning and sport psychology.

A former president of both the Association for Applied Sport Psychology (AASP) and the North American Society for the Psychology of Sport and Physical Activity, Wrisberg is a fellow of AASP as well as the American Academy of Kinesiology and Physical Education. In 1982 he received the Brady Award for Excellence in Teaching, and in 1994 the Chancellor's Award for Research and Creative Achievement, both from the University of Tennessee at Knoxville.

In addition to his teaching and research, Wrisberg provides performance consulting for college and professional athletes in a variety of sports. In his work with athletes, he applies many of the concepts and principles covered in this edition of *Motor Learning and Performance* using the situation-based learning approach on a consistent basis.

Wrisberg enjoys several outdoor activities, including tennis, canoeing, and hiking in the Great Smoky Mountains. He and his wife, Sue, live in Knoxville, Tennessee.

You'll find other outstanding motor behavior resources at

www.HumanKinetics.com

In the U.S. call

1-800-747-4457

Australia..08 8372 0999
Canada 1-800-465-7301
Europe..+44 (0) 113 255 5665
New Zealand......................................0064 9 448 1207

HUMAN KINETICS
The Information Leader in Physical Activity
P.O. Box 5076 • Champaign, IL 61825-5076 USA